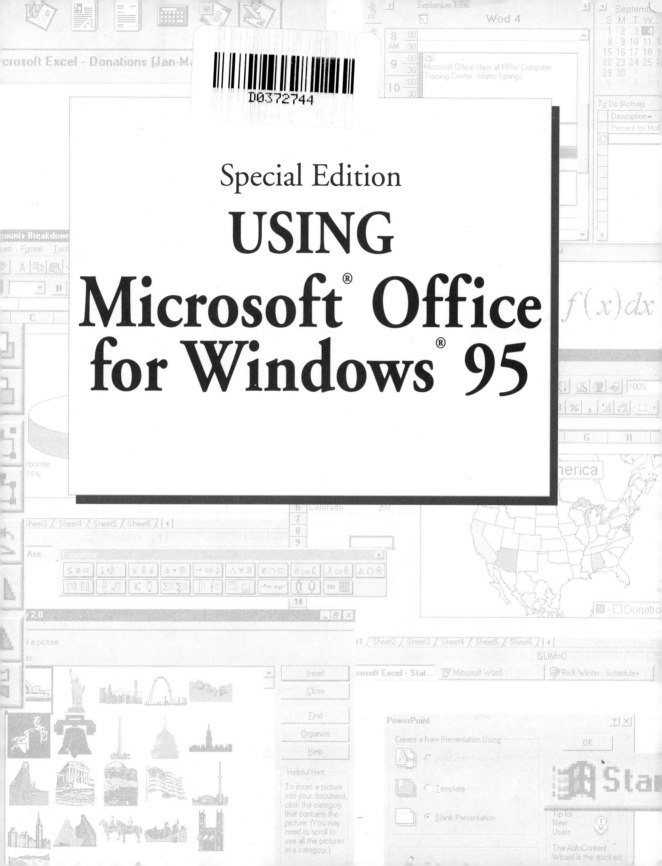

Special Edition

USING
Microsoft® Office
for Windows® 95

Special Edition

USING
Microsoft® Office
for Windows® 95

Written by

Rick Winter and Patty Winter

with

Jeff Bankston	*Donna Minarik*
Robert Garrison	*Patrice-Anne Rutledge*
Carman Minarik	*Diane Tinney*

que®

Special Edition Using Microsoft Office for Windows 95

Copyright© 1995 by Que® Corporation

Library of Congress Catalog No.: 95-070645

ISBN: 0-7897-0146-4

97 96 95   6 5 4 3 2 1

Interpretation of the printing code: the rightmost double-digit number is the year of the book's printing; the rightmost single-digit number, the number of the book's printing. For example, a printing code of 95-1 shows that the first printing of the book occurred in 1995.

Screen reproductions in this book were created with Collage Plus from Inner Media, Inc., Hollis, NH.

Que Corporation has made every effort to supply trademark information about company names, products, and services mentioned in this book. Trademarks indicated below were derived from various sources. Que Corporation cannot attest to the accuracy of this information.

Credits

President
Roland Elgey

**Vice President
and Publisher**
Marie Butler-Knight

Associate Publisher
Don Roche, Jr.

**Editorial Services
Director**
Elizabeth Keaffaber

Managing Editor
Michael Cunningham

Director of Marketing
Lynn E. Zingraf

Senior Series Editor
Chris Nelson

Acquisitions Editor
Deborah Abshier

Product Director
Kathi-Jo Arnoff

**Product Development
Specialist**
Lisa D. Wagner

Production Editor
Lori A. Lyons

Technical Specialist
Cari Skaggs

Editors
Lisa M. Gebken, Julie McNamee,
Geneil Breeze, Tom Hayes,
Alice Martina-Smith, Christy Prakel

**Assistant Product
Marketing Manager**
Kim Margolius

Technical Editors
Bruce Wynn, Microsoft Certified Professional
Jeff Bankston
Greg Dew

**Acquisitions
Coordinator**
Tracy M. Williams

Operations Coordinator
Patricia J. Brooks

Editorial Assistants
Carmen Phelps, Jill Byus

Book Designer
Ruth Harvey

Cover Designer
Dan Armstrong

Production Team
Steve Adams, Anne Dickerson, Maxine
Dillingham, Chad Dressler, Joan Evan,
Karen Gregor-York, John Hulse, Damon
Jordan, Barry Jorden, Daryl Kessler,
Kaylene Riemen, Brenda Sims, Jody York

Indexer
Carol Sheehan

Composed in *Stone Serif* and *MCPdigital* by Que Corporation

Dedications

To my husband Michael Leonard—Love can survive! Thank you for the courage to ask me to marry you, and the help you gave me to follow through while I was in the process of working on a book.

Patty

To Ann and Lee Hansen. I couldn't have asked for greater in-laws. Thank you for producing my wonderful wife, Karen, and putting up with her long enough until I could marry her.

Rick

About the Authors

Patty Winter is a Senior Partner at PRW Computer Training and Services. She has worked with computers since 1982, training adults, testing programs, developing course material, and creating solutions for user productivity. Her emphasis has been on peopleware. She is the author of *Excel 5 for Windows Essentials,* contributing author of *Special Edition Using Microsoft Office for Windows 95, and* co-author of *Excel for Windows Sure Steps, Look Your Best with Excel,* and *Q&A QueCards.*

Rick Winter is a Senior Partner at PRW Computer Training and Services. He has trained over 3,000 adults on personal computers. He is the co-author of Que's *Excel for Windows SureSteps, Look Your Best with Excel,* and *Q&A QueCards*. He is also the revision author for Que's *1-2-3 QuickStart Release 3.4* and *1-2-3 QuickStart Release 2.4, MicroRef Quick Reference Guide to Lotus 1-2-3 Release 3.0,* and *MicroRef Quick Reference Guide to Lotus 1-2-3, Release 2.2.* Rick is a contributing author for Que's *Special Edition Using Microsoft Office for Windows, Using Excel 5 for Windows, Using WordPerfect 6 for Windows,* and *Using PC Tools 8.* He is the revision script writer for *Video Professor Lotus 1-2-3 Version 2.2 and 3.0 Level I* and *Lotus 1-2-3 Version 2.2 and 3.0 Level II* and script writer for *Video Professor Lotus 1-2-3 Version 2.2 and 3.0 Level III.* In 1994, Rick was president and is currently a director of Information Systems Trainers, a professional training organization based in Denver, Colorado. In 1959, Rick acquired a sister Patty (see above), and has been bossed around since.

PRW Computer Training and Services, based in Idaho Springs, Colorado, is a recognized leader in training, training materials, and consulting. PRW won the prestigious Rocky Mountain Chapter Society for Technical Communication's Distinguished Award for their work on Que's *Excel for Windows SureSteps* in 1994. If your company needs training on any of the Microsoft Office applications, you should contact PRW regarding on-site courses.

For information on course content, on-site corporate classes, or consulting, contact PRW at the following address:

PRW Computer Training and Services
720 Skyline Drive
Idaho Springs, CO 80452

(303) 567-4943 or (303) 567-2987 Voice (8-5 MST)
CompuServe: 71702,1462
Internet: 71702.1462@compuserve.com

Jeff Bankston is a Systems and Network Integration specialist in sunny Panama City, Florida. He has been involved in nearly every aspect of computing life since 1980. He has extensive background in hardware systems and advanced integration of data processing equipment. He enjoys database programming, client/server networking, and all aspects of the Internet and the on-line community. He has published several technical and white papers on hardware integration and Systems Analysis. He is a Category Manager of the new Microsoft Network where he is working closely with Microsoft in development and administration of MSN. He is married with 2 children ages 8 and 10. He loves to fish and enjoys the outdoors, but he can't find a laptop with a small enough communications satellite dish to fit into a backpack to connect with the Internet.

Robert Garrison has worked with computers since 1973 and has owned and operated a computer store for 10 years, beginning in 1981. He is currently one of the Network Administrators for a NYSE company. Robert has designed network systems for small to large companies and has trained many computer users on network applications. He has a B.S. in Computer Science from Texas A&M and an MBA from the University of Wyoming.

Carman Minarik manages the computer services and training department for an Intelligent Electronics reseller in Midland, MI whose clients range from Fortune 100 companies to small businesses to individual users. He has written and presented training materials for most major operating systems and software packages for more than seven years and is a member of the American Society for Training and Development. Helping computer users become more productive is a commitment Carman takes very seriously. His motto is "They're smart enough if I'm good enough."

Carman lives is Midland with his wife, his son, and his cat. His off-line time is spent enjoying his family, camping (where there are no computers), and listening to music.

Donna Minarik is an independent consultant with more than six years of consulting, training, and technical writing experience. Past Que projects include *Using the Macintosh and Using Microsoft Office 4.2* for Macintosh. Donna lives in a renovated 100-year-old farmhouse in Midland, Michigan, with her husband Carman, their son Warren, and her cat and administrative assistant, Bailey.

Patrice-Anne Rutledge is a computer trainer and database developer and systems analyst who works for an international high-tech company in the San Francisco Bay area. She writes frequently on a variety of topics, including technology, business, and travel and is a co-author of *Using Paradox 5 for Windows* and *Using PerfectOffice*, both published by Que. Patrice discovered computers while pursuing her original career as a translator and was quickly hooked. She holds a degree from the University of California and has been using FoxPro for the past four years.

Diane Tinney in the past 15 years has created over 50 complex, spreadsheet-based end-user applications. As a system architect at KPMG Peat Marwick, Diane created several complex spreadsheet-based tax applications, including a Multistate Tax Planning system and a Foreign Tax Credit compliance and planning system. Since then, Diane has founded her own business, *The Software Professional,* which specializes in Windows-based spreadsheet and database applications. Diane's clients include large organizations such as Exxon, ALCOA, City of New York, and KPMG Peat Marwick as well as smaller companies that need the same quality software solutions. In her spare time, Diane is a freelance writer who writes for Que and creates programming and operating system courseware for Productivity Point International.

Acknowledgments

We'd like to thank Don Roche, Associate Publisher, for always being available to discuss ideas and make suggestions for publishing the best book possible. Thanks also to Kathie-Jo Arnoff, Senior Product Development Specialist, for her ideas, suggestions, and gentle prompting that helped make this book as complete and understandable as possible.

Thanks to Debbie Abshier, Acquisitions Editor, who provided much needed moral support and extraordinary assistance in getting answers quickly. Her amazing ability to pull all the authors together and keep us running as a team was outstanding. Who knows where this project would have ended up without her hard work and dedication.

We appreciate the kind prodding and awareness of the authors' fragile egos by the editing team headed by Lori Lyons, Production Editor. Thanks for the attention to details and many changes that occurred while pulling this book together. The friendly and even humorous reminders from Lisa Gebken, Christine Prakel, Alice Martina-Smith, Geneil Breeze, and Julie McNamee, that some things were not so clear or did not make sense helped keep us on the straight and narrow. Thanks also go to the Production team, who had to endure through last-minute changes.

We would also like to thank Jan Snyder and Sue Plumley for jumping in at the last minute to provide author review for the "Using PowerPoint" and "Using Multimedia" sections. Their ability to review someone else's work and make the necessary changes is greatly appreciated.

Thanks to the contributing authors for using their expertise and knowledge to help us provide the most comprehensive work possible. We appreciate everyone's willingness to give up time with family, miss weekends and work long nights, to help write and edit *Special Edition Using Microsoft Office for Windows 95*.

Patty Winter and Rick Winter

Contents at a Glance

Contents

VIII Using Microsoft Office in a Group   807

36 Using Microsoft Exchange   809

Introduction

Special Edition Using Microsoft Office for Windows 95 pools the talents of a diverse collection of software experts. Que chose the members of this team for their proven ability to write clear, instructional text as well as their expertise with Microsoft Office and the individual applications that make up the suite: Word, Excel, PowerPoint, and Schedule+.

This collaborative approach gives you the best information about the individual suite applications as well as expert advice on how to get the most out of integrating them. For the integration part of this book, we chose an authoring team with much experience using Word, Excel, PowerPoint, and Schedule+ together. The information they present shows you how to combine information in ways nearly impossible or extremely difficult before Microsoft Office.

Microsoft designed the Office applications to work extremely well together. You can create documents that rely on information from multiple applications and accomplish this feat nearly seamlessly. Microsoft designed the applications to act and look alike to reduce your "learning curve." Office includes all the tools to help you get your work done so that you can concentrate on the task without worrying about the application. Office includes shared programs, such as ClipArt Gallery, Microsoft Graph, Organization Chart, and Data Map. These programs and the many common interface features point the way beyond what columnist Jeff Raskin has called the "walled cities" of traditional applications.

Corporate America is witnessing an increasing emphasis on Windows integration, especially in settings where support and productivity are critical. *Special Edition Using Microsoft Office for Windows 95* helps you take advantage of this new way of working with software. Many of the authors in this book have corporate experience and their expertise will show you how to use Microsoft Office to increase your productivity.

Who Should Use This Book?

Special Edition Using Microsoft Office for Windows 95 is the right choice for home-office workers, corporate personnel, workers in small business and nonprofit organizations, students, instructors, consultants, computer support staff—anyone using any of the Office suite applications and wanting to get up to speed quickly on the Office applications.

This book assumes that you are familiar with Microsoft Windows but not familiar with all the applications in the Office suite.

If you want to integrate two or more of the Office applications and exchange information, Que designed *Special Edition Using Microsoft Office for Windows 95* to meet your needs. If you are sharing data across a workgroup, this book shows you how Office helps you and others collaborate effectively on a project.

Special Edition Using Microsoft Office for Windows 95 is the ideal companion volume to *Special Edition Using Windows 95, Special Edition Using Word for Windows 95, Special Edition Using Excel for Windows 95,* and *Special Edition Using PowerPoint for Windows 95*—all from Que.

How This Book Is Organized

The authors designed *Special Edition Using Microsoft Office for Windows 95* to complement the documentation that comes with Microsoft Office. Less experienced users will find the step-by-step information in this book helpful; experienced users will appreciate the comprehensive coverage and expert advice. After you become proficient with one or more of the applications within Office, you can use this book as a desktop reference.

Special Edition Using Microsoft Office for Windows 95 is divided into nine parts:

> Part I: Discovering Common Features
>
> Part II: Using Word
>
> Part III: Using Excel
>
> Part IV: Using Multimedia in Microsoft Office
>
> Part V: Using PowerPoint
>
> Part VI: Working Together with Microsoft Applications
>
> Part VII: Customizing Microsoft Office

Part VIII: Using Microsoft Office in a Group

Part IX: Techniques from the Pros

Part I introduces you to Microsoft Office and creates the foundation you need for working with all the Office applications. In Chapters 1-3, you learn about the features shared by the Office applications that enable you to move from program to program without starting over every time you begin learning a new application. Chapter 4 deals with managing files and work areas across applications. Chapter 5 shows you how to use the on-line help feature that is similar for all the Office applications. Part I helps prepare you for Part VI, which deals with using the Office applications together to create a range of documents. If you are unfamiliar with Office and need to work with one or more of the applications, you should read Part I.

Parts II, III, and V cover the essentials of Word 7, Excel 7, and PowerPoint 7. Chapters 6-11 cover the essentials of Word, Chapters 12-18 cover the essentials of Excel, and Chapters 24-29 cover the essentials of PowerPoint. If you know one of the Office applications and need to get up to speed quickly on one or more of the other suite applications, you should work through these focused presentations. Even if you haven't used any of the Office applications, you can get up to speed quickly by working through this part of the book.

Part IV covers the appealing opportunities multimedia presents for your Microsoft Office documents. In all the applications, you can visually enhance your documents and even include sound and motion pictures. Chapters 19 and 20 show you how to create charts from your data by using Microsoft Graph or Excel and place them in any Microsoft Office application. Chapter 21 shows you how to add pictures and clip art to your documents. Chapter 22 shows you how to add voice, sound, movie, and video clips to your documents. Chapter 23 shows you how to manipulate pictures by adding shapes, curves, and lines.

Part VI presents one of the strongest reasons for using Microsoft Office— dealing with how these suite applications work in concert. Chapter 30 shows you how to cut, copy, and paste to bring information from various sources into a letter and memo. Chapter 31 allows you to link information between different applications, which means that when you change information in the source document, the target document will change. The target document in this chapter is a business report.

In Chapter 32, you learn how to create a presentation, switch between windows; look up information, cut, copy, and paste text and data; and link and embed information. You create an outline in Word, grab data and create charts from Excel, and pull all this together into a PowerPoint and Word presentation. Chapter 33 shows you how to use Microsoft Binder to combine files from different programs into a single file for editing, storage, and printing.

Part VII deals with customizing Microsoft Office. Chapter 34 shows you how to customize the desktop, toolbars, and menus in the Office applications. In Chapter 35, you learn how to create macros and use Visual Basic for Applications (VBA) to automate tasks across applications in the suite.

Part VIII shows you how you can work with Microsoft Office in a group and across a network. Chapter 36 shows you how to communicate with people in your office and the outside world with Microsoft Exchange. Chapter 37 shows you how use Schedule+ to manage your time and schedule meetings. Chapter 38 gives you special notes for using Office on a network, including sharing files, protecting documents, and scheduling meetings.

In Part IX, expert users of Microsoft Office provide you with lots of tips, tricks, and advice on how to design and develop successful, professional Microsoft Office applications.

In Chapter 39 you learn how to use Microsoft Word to create forms and dialog boxes with edit boxes, check boxes, and pull-down lists. The form feature allows you to print a form on demand, which can be a huge cost savings over pre-printing large volumes of forms.

Chapter 40 shows you the tricks to create a mass mailing using Word, Excel, or Address Book sources for names and addresses. This chapter discusses customized letters, mailing labels, and envelopes. This chapter also shows you how to edit, sort, and select data for a more systematic mailing.

Chapter 41 teaches you about advanced Excel functions that allow you to use formulas to manipulate text, make decisions, test input, use lookup tables, analyze data, and show trends.

Chapter 42 shows you how to use VBA—Visual Basic for Applications—to automate tasks in Excel. The tasks include manipulating files, finding values in large worksheets, using color for labels, creating automatic procedures, and performing commands based on certain events or conditions in your worksheets.

Chapter 43 culminates the techniques from the professionals section with advice on how to use Microsoft Office to your advantage in business. Included are special notes for sales reports, customer letters, and presentations.

The "Index of Common Problems" cross-references the troubleshooting techniques you find throughout the book. The general index gives you a comprehensive listing of topics you may want to look up. At the end of the book is a tear-out card that you can use for quick reference for what's new, keyboard shortcuts, and Microsoft support phone numbers.

Conventions Used in This Book

Office enables you to use both the keyboard and the mouse to select menu and dialog items: you can press a letter or you can select an item by clicking it with the mouse. Underlined letters such as File, Open identify letters you press or click to activate menus, choose commands in menus, and select options in dialog boxes.

This book assumes that your mouse is set for right-handed operation. You use the left mouse button for clicking on toolbar buttons, menus, and dialog box choices. You use the right mouse button for bringing up shortcut menus. Unless otherwise indicated, a mouse click means clicking the left mouse button. If you switch the mouse to left-handed operation through the Control Panel in Windows, you will use the right button for choosing toolbars, menus, and dialog box choices and the left button for shortcut menus.

Your screen may appear slightly different from the examples in this book because of your installation and hardware setup. The screen items may change due to which applications and portions of applications are installed as well as your hardware and network options. You may see slight changes for menus, dialog box options, and toolbars. If you installed Microsoft Office through the default installation choices, the Microsoft Office Shortcut Bar will be placed in your Taskbar's Programs Startup location. This means that every time you turn on Microsoft Office, the Shortcut Bar will appear in the top right corner of your screen. Most of the figures in the book do not include the Shortcut Bar. You can turn off the Shortcut Bar by clicking the Control menu button and choosing Exit on the menu. Chapter 34 shows you how you can customize the Microsoft Office Shortcut Bar.

Names of dialog boxes (such as Open) and dialog box options (such as File Name) have initial capital letters. Messages that appear on-screen display in a special font: Document1. New terms are introduced with *italic* type. Text that you type appears in **boldface**.

The book uses uppercase letters to distinguish file and folder names.

The following example shows typical command sequences:

Choose File, Open, or press Ctrl+O.

The programs included with Office provide toolbars for your convenience. By clicking a button in the toolbar, you can execute a command or access a dialog box. Chapters in this book often contain button icons in the margins, indicating which button you can click to perform a task.

So you can quickly see the new items added since Microsoft Office 4, there is a new icon in the margin.

Note

This paragraph format indicates additional information that may help you avoid problems or that you should consider when you use the described features.

Caution

This paragraph format warns the reader of hazardous procedures (for example, activities that delete files).

Tip
This paragraph format suggests easier or alternative methods of executing a procedure.

▶ See "Later Section title," p. xx

◀ See "Earlier section title," p. xx

Troubleshooting

Troubleshooting sections anticipate common problems...

...and then provide you with practical suggestions for solving those problems.

Special Edition Using Microsoft Office for Windows 95 uses margin cross-references to help you access related information in other parts of the book. Right-facing triangles point you to related information in later chapters. Left facing triangles point you to information in earlier chapters.

Part I

Discovering Common Features

Chapter 1

New Ways of Working

by Rick Winter and Patty Winter

Combining a vendor's software products to sell them as one unit is not new. Software bundles have been around for years. However, what is new is the full integration of these software products. Integration no longer means just switching between applications or one application that attempts but fails to do the work of four applications.

In what is termed the *office suite*, leading software vendors provide core office applications such as word processing, spreadsheet, database, and presentation graphics. The core products are the award-winning applications in their categories. Vendors add to this core some auxiliary applications such as electronic mail, graphing, personal information management, and organization charting, offering the entire suite of products for as much as 50 percent less than the sum of the individual product purchase prices.

Microsoft Office 95 leads the way with key applications that work together and offer a common user interface. The applications look alike and work alike—thus reducing the learning curve and improving productivity. Office 95 makes it easier for users to share data, documents, and graphics across applications.

In this chapter, you learn

- What's included in Office 95

- What's new with Office 95

- The design goals of Office 95

- How to determine which application to use

What's Included in Office 95

The standard edition of Microsoft Office 95 includes the following applications:

- Microsoft Word for Windows, Version 7.0

- Microsoft Excel, Version 7.0

- Microsoft PowerPoint, Version 7.0

- Microsoft Schedule+, Version 7.0

- Microsoft Office Binder

- Microsoft Office Shortcut Bar

The professional edition of Office 95 adds to the basic suite a powerful database, Microsoft Access, Version 7.0.

What's New with Office 95

Microsoft Schedule+ and Microsoft Office Binder are two new applications that are bundled with Office 95. Additionally, you get a number of new features in all the products, as well as in the interoperability between products.

Windows 95

Tip
To find an on-line summary of new features, choose Help, Microsoft Help Topics, click on the Find tab, and type **What's New** in the first text box.

Windows 95 is not part of Office 95. In fact, you first need to install Windows 95 to run Office 95. However, there are many features in Windows 95 that integrate well with Office 95.

Screen
The new Windows taskbar (see fig. 1.1) allows you to start applications as well as open minimized applications with a single click. The new close button (x) in the upper-right corner of a window makes closing documents and applications much easier. When you minimize an application by using the redesigned minimize underscore button, the application appears minimized as a rectangle on the taskbar.

File Names and Properties
Windows 95 now allows you to use file names of up to 255 characters including spaces. This greatly increases flexibility, finding, and understanding of what you have saved. Windows 95 also has added a number of file properties

that Office 95 expands. Now you can quickly look up statistics on your document such as creation date, number of words, and save author and document information with your file. Now built in directly to standard file dialog boxes are enhanced search capabilities to help you find your file based on the contents, time, or other properties of your file (see fig. 1.2).

Minimize button   Restore button

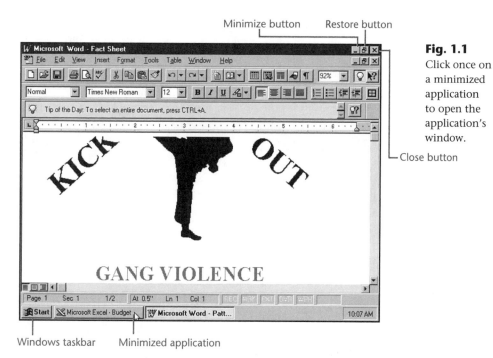

Fig. 1.1
Click once on
a minimized
application
to open the
application's
window.

Close button

Windows taskbar   Minimized application

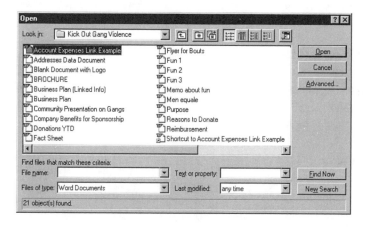

Fig. 1.2
Long file names
help you remember and find your
documents.

Microsoft Exchange and Microsoft Network

In Microsoft Office Version 4, a license for using Microsoft Mail was included with the product. The administrator still had to set up the program for each user. In Windows 95, Microsoft Exchange ships with the product, including Microsoft Mail and Microsoft Fax. Together with another new product, Microsoft Network, you have many opportunities to send your Word document, Excel spreadsheet, or PowerPoint presentation to people inside and outside your office. Microsoft Mail is even combined with Word to allow you to compose and access messages with all of Word's powerful tools (see fig. 1.3).

Fig. 1.3
You can use WordMail to compose e-mail messages within Word.

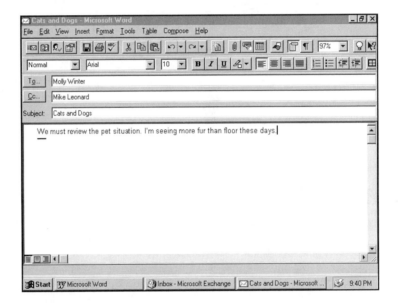

New Products

In addition to the new features of Windows 95, you will see new programs in Office 95. Schedule+ is an existing application that has been improved and added to Office 95. Binder is a new feature that allows you to combine documents from different applications.

Schedule+

Microsoft Schedule+ (see fig. 1.4) has been added to Office 95. The previous product was sold separately and debuted in 1992. The version for Office 95 is the first upgrade to Schedule+ 1.0. Schedule+ allows you to create appointments, write to-do lists, and set meetings with colleagues using the new Meeting Wizard. Schedule+ now has a feature to help you set and manage your life goals. Look for the Seven Habits of Highly Effective People wizard based on the popular seminar and book from Steven Covey. For more information on working with Schedule+, see Chapter 37, "Using Schedule+."

Fig. 1.4
Schedule+ automates your life by making appointments and tasks easier to manage.

Microsoft Binder

Use Microsoft Binder to add Word, Excel, and PowerPoint documents to create a single document for printing, editing, storing, and distribution. Figure 1.5 shows a binder document with two Word documents, an Excel worksheet, and a PowerPoint presentation. The left side of the screen shows the documents that make up the binder file. You add, delete, and rename documents through the Section menu. You open, save, create, and print binder documents through the File menu. The other menus and toolbars change depending on the source documents (Word, Excel, and PowerPoint). For more information on Binder, see Chapter 33, "Using Binder."

Fig. 1.5
The left side of the screen shows the source documents. Since a Word document (Introduction) is highlighted, the toolbars are those from Microsoft Word.

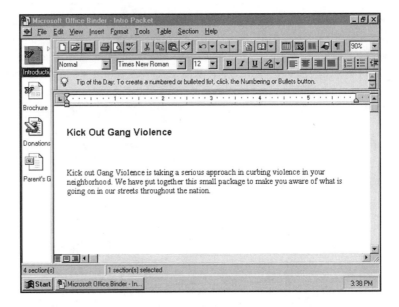

Improvements in All Office Products

In Office 95, there are improved consistencies between applications as well as new features. The following table lists major changes, new features, and what you need to do to get started with the feature.

Feature	Get Started
AutoCorrect is now available in Word, Excel, and PowerPoint and can correct misspellings as soon as you type them.	Tools, Auto-Correct or, click the Spelling button, p. 95
Help is now the same in all Office applications. A new Find feature allows you to search for text not just in the titles of help pages (as the old search did) but throughout the entire help file or multiple help files in some cases.	Help, Topics or F1, p. 141
Answer Wizard (see fig. 1.5) is another new help feature that allows you to type a help request in your own words.	Help, Answer Wizard, p. 152
TipWizard in Word and Excel watches what you do. When TipWizard has a suggestion to make a task easier, the TipWizard button lights up. Click the button for a quick tip.	Click the *TipWizard* button, p. 160

I

Feature	Get Started	
The Microsoft Office Shortcut Bar (see fig. 1.6) allows you to start new files. Choose from an organized series of tabs showing the general types of documents, such as brochures, letters, memos, business planners, awards, reports, and time cards. The Office Shortcut Bar will also launch an application that creates a document. You don't have to remember which application you used. The Shortcut Bar also allows you to make appointments, add tasks, and add contacts in Schedule+ and start the Answer Wizard for all applications.	Windows taskbar Start, Programs, Microsoft Office Shortcut Bar, p. 34	
Getting Results Book (fig 1.5) is on the CD-ROM that comes with Microsoft Office. When you click the Shortcut Bar button and have the Microsoft Office CD-ROM in the CD-ROM reader, you can read and search for detailed instructions and explanations of tasks you need to perform.	Click the Getting Results Book button	
Office Compatible (fig. 1.5) also launches information on the CD-ROM. This feature shows other products that work well with Microsoft Office.	Click the Office Compatible button	

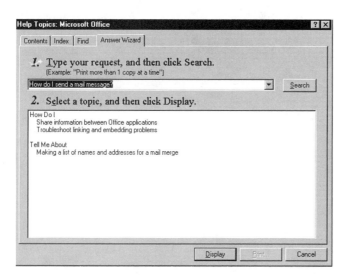

Fig. 1.6
The Answer Wizard allows you to type questions the way you want to ask them.

Individual Software Improvements

In addition to the general improvements throughout Office 95, each of the products in the suite has enhancements.

Microsoft Word for Windows 95

The following table shows some of the enhancements to Microsoft Word and how to get started with the feature.

Feature	Get Started	
Spell It, a new feature, identifies misspelled words as soon as you type them with a wavy red line and offers suggestions with a click of the right mouse button or Shift+Backspace.	Tools, Options, Spelling, Automatic Spell Checking, p. 210	
Enhanced AutoFormat applies borders, headings, fractions, and list formatting as you type.	Tools, Options, Auto-Format tab, p. 264	
Address Book (see fig. 1.7) manages your contacts for envelopes, labels, mail merges and can connect to your Schedule+ contact information.	Click Address Book button, p. 925	
Highlighter accentuates important parts of the document with a color background.	Click the Highlighter button, p. 194	

Fig. 1.7
The address book manages names and addresses for you.

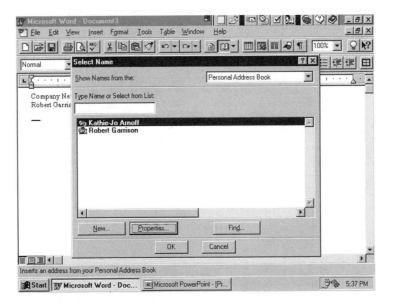

Microsoft Excel for Windows 95

The following table shows some of the enhancements to Microsoft Excel and how to get started with the feature.

Feature	Get Started
Data Map (see fig. 1.8) will geographically represent your data.	Click the Map button, p. 499 
Template Wizard with Data Tracking will allow you to turn your existing spreadsheets into forms and capture the fill-ins into a separate database.	Data, Template Wizard, p. 423
AutoComplete and Pick-Lists will allow you to automatically complete an entry. You can create an entry based on previous entries as the first few letters are typed in a cell. You can also right-click the mouse, choose Pick from List, and choose from a list of previous entries.	p. 313
Cell Tips appear when you pause a mouse over the cell with a note.	Insert, Note, p. 458
AutoFilter with Top 10 allows you to see the highest or lowest items in a list.	Data, Filter, AutoFilter then Top 10, p. 428
AutoCalculate your highlighted data by selecting a range and viewing the sum in the status bar or the average or count with a right click.	See status bar, p. 309
Protection settings are improved for more thorough and flexible protection of custom work.	Tools, Protection, p. 453

I

Common Features

Fig. 1.8

You can now map your data geographically with Data Map.

Map button

Microsoft PowerPoint for Windows 95

The following table shows some of the enhancements to Microsoft PowerPoint and how to get started with the feature.

Feature	Get Started
AutoClip Art suggests appropriate images for your message.	Tools, AutoClipArt, p. 515
The Pack and Go Wizard allows you to save your presentation to a disk for display on other computers.	File, Pack and Go, p. 657
Enhanced AutoContent Wizard changes your message according to the size and type of your audience and how long you have for your presentation.	p. 578
Title Animation allows you to create special effects for Animation titles.	View, Toolbars, Animation Effects or Tools Effects p. 657
Presentation Conferencing allows a workgroup to simultaneously review a presentation over the network while you can check your notes, timing, and next slide.	Tools, Presentation Conference, p. 870
Meeting Minder (see fig. 1.9) allows you to take and save notes during your presentation or export to Word to create minutes. You can also record action items and show them on a slide at the end of your presentation.	Tools, Meeting Minder, p. 650

Fig. 1.9
Use the Meeting Minder to type your action items so they can appear on the last slide.

Design Goals of Microsoft Office

The goal of Microsoft Office is to provide users with the following:

■ A common user interface (standardized operation of menus, toolbars, and dialog boxes)

■ Quick access from one office suite application to another

■ Data shared across applications

■ Resources shared across applications

■ Information shared across workgroups

■ In the future, a common task automation language

Microsoft strives to meet these goals. Many of the core applications underwent (and continue to undergo) revisions to meet these goals. To some long-time users of a core product, the resulting menu or toolbar changes may be annoying. In the long run, however, a common user interface across applications increases efficient and effective use of all applications.

Providing a Common User Interface

A clear benefit of a common user interface across applications is that by learning one application in the suite, you know the operational basics of the other applications. Figure 1.10 illustrates the similarity between Excel and Word menu bars and toolbars. Notice that Word has a Table menu option, but Excel has a Data menu option. Although the goal is to provide one common user interface, some degree of uniqueness will remain in each application. However, key common features such as the File, Open and Edit, Find commands can be found in exactly the same place in each application.

Microsoft Office applications provide consistency in more than just similar toolbars and menus. Dialog boxes, customizable features, and operational features are similar too. On-line help is available in several forms in Office 95 applications:

■ Help Application

■ Answer Wizards

■ The use of Wizards

■ Tip Wizards and Tip of the Day

▶ See "On-Line Help," p. 143

▶ See "Using Wizards," p. 162

▶ See "Viewing Tips," p. 160

Word menu bar and toolbars   Word document window

Fig. 1.10
Menus and
toolbars are
consistent across
applications.

Excel menu bar
and toolbars

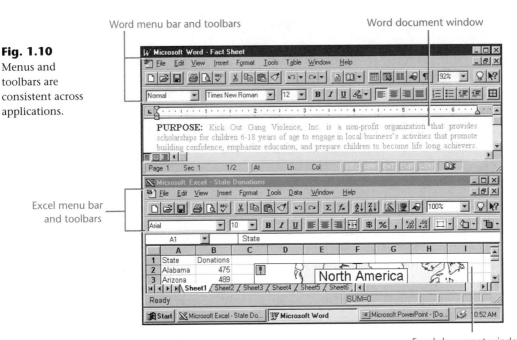

Excel document window

Quick Access to Other Applications

Microsoft Office provides the Microsoft Office Shortcut Bar. By default, this toolbar appears in the upper-right corner of the Windows 95 desktop (see fig. 1.11). You can use the Shortcut Bar to do the following:

- Start new files based on templates and wizards.

- Open existing files and automatically launch the related application.

- Add tasks, make appointments, and add contacts.

- Use Office features such as Setup and Answer Wizards.

- Add other applications to the Office Shortcut Bar.

- Switch between Microsoft Office applications.

- Launch Microsoft Office applications.

The Shortcut Bar is just one way that Microsoft Office provides quick access to applications. In each Microsoft Office application, the application toolbar provides direct access to pertinent features of other applications. For example, in Word you can insert an Excel Worksheet into a document by simply clicking a toolbar button. Doing so launches Excel and provides the full features of Excel for that embedded worksheet (see fig. 1.12). Note that, without having to leave Word, the menus and toolbars change to Excel's when you edit the worksheet.

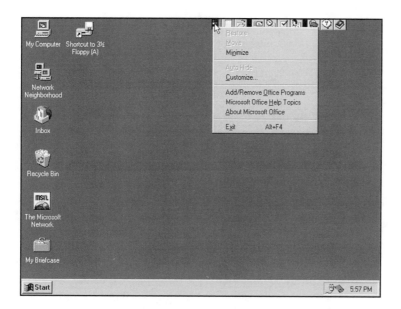

Fig. 1.11
The Microsoft Office Shortcut Bar provides easy access to opening and creating documents and Office Manager features.

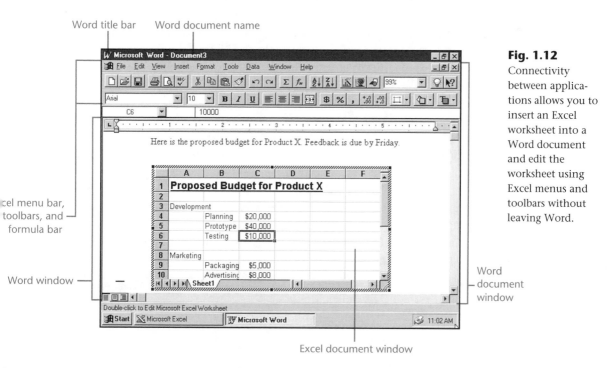

Word title bar   Word document name

cel menu bar, toolbars, and formula bar

Word window

Word document window

Excel document window

Fig. 1.12
Connectivity between applications allows you to insert an Excel worksheet into a Word document and edit the worksheet using Excel menus and toolbars without leaving Word.

Sharing Data across Applications

▶ See "Switching Between Documents," p. 138

Microsoft Office products provide several methods of sharing data between applications:

Method	Description
Copying	Copies the data from the source application to the target application using the Clipboard.
Linking	Links a copy of the data from the source document to the target document (and saves data with the source document).
Embedding	Embeds data from the source document into the target document (saves data with the target document).

▶ See "Copying Spreadsheet Information," p. 675

The Microsoft Office applications share data effortlessly. When you copy a table from Excel to Word, for example, you get a Word table that retains all the fonts and formats from Excel. You do not need to reformat your table, as you might with some other products.

▶ See "Using Common Steps to Link Documents," p. 689

Linking and embedding features take advantage of Microsoft Windows OLE specifications. Linked documents automatically update when a source document changes. Embedded documents provide access to the source application while storing the data in the target application. Each feature has its pros and cons and serves a specific purpose.

Microsoft Office extends the data sharing beyond application integration by providing workgroup integration with Microsoft Exchange. Users can mail documents, spreadsheets, and data files from within the source application. Routing slips can be attached to files that Exchange then broadcasts to the group—or routes to each person, in sequence, one at a time.

Sharing Resources across Applications

▶ See "Using Microsoft ClipArt Gallery," p. 515

A key element in Microsoft Office is the recognition that certain resources are needed by more than one application. Clip art is needed to perform word processing tasks, spreadsheet tasks, and presentation graphic tasks, for example. Rather than duplicating program overhead, Microsoft Office provides an auxiliary application, Microsoft ClipArt Gallery, for use with all applications. The same is true of the need for a query engine (to ask questions of your data), a graphing tool (see fig. 1.13), and an organization chart drawing tool.

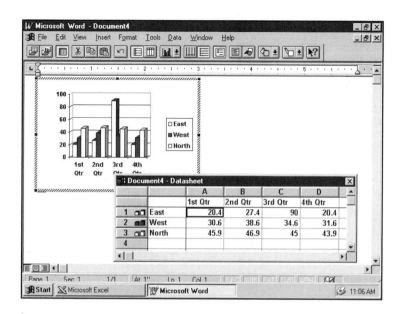

Fig. 1.13
Microsoft Graph, one of the auxiliary applications that ships with Microsoft Office, is used by all applications to draw graphs.

Providing a Common Language

Providing a common language across applications is the most challenging goal of Microsoft Office. In the past, each product had a different programming and/or macro language. Excel Version 5.0 is the first Microsoft Office suite product to provide what will be the common language of the Office products: Visual Basic, for Applications (VBA). VBA uses OLE and can send keystrokes to other applications (making it possible for VBA to run a cross-application process).

▶ See "Understanding Visual Basic for Applications," p. 767

Until VBA is added to the other suite products, users will have to learn WordBasic and VBA to automate common office tasks.

Determining Which Application To Use

The following table lists some common office tasks and suggested application tools to accomplish each task:

Tip
Use the shortcut bar's Start a New Document button, and let Office decide which application you need to use.

Task	Application	Comments
Create letters, memos, reports, term papers	Word	Use Word for projects that are word intensive.

(continues)

Task	Application	Comments
Create budgets, invoices, income tracking, statistics	Excel	Use Excel for projects that are heavy on numbers with lots of calculations.
Create slides, overheads, presentations	PowerPoint	Use PowerPoint for presentations when you want to produce 35mm slides, transparencies, audience handouts, or computer-run presentations.
Maintain mailing lists	Word, Excel, or Schedule+	Maintain data in Word, Excel, or Schedule+.
Create mailouts or personalized documents	Word	Merge mailing list data into Word to print personalized cover letters, brochures, and labels.
Create a table of financial data to be used in a presentation	Excel	Create a table in Excel.
	Power Point	Embed a table into a PowerPoint slide.
Send a document to a group of people for feedback, and receive a response	Word, Excel	Create the document, spreadsheet, or presentation in the desired application(s).
	Exchange	Send the file(s) using the Exchange routing feature.
Provide audit trail between supporting spreadsheet data and annual report document	Excel	Create the supporting schedules needed in Excel.
	Word	Create the annual report document in Word. Use OLE to link the data from Excel to the Word document. Whenever the spreadsheet data changes, the annual report document is updated automatically.
Create, print, and distribute a department newsletter	Word	Create a newsletter in Word.
	Exchange	Distribute a newsletter electronically using Exchange's Send feature.

With four or five new software applications so tightly integrated, deciding on which product to use for which task could be difficult. Experience with each application is the best guide on how to combine the powers of each application to meet your needs.

The rest of this book is dedicated to helping you in this endeavor. The next few chapters in Part I review the common features found in all Microsoft suite applications and point out any digressions.

Parts II, III, and V guide you through the features and capabilities of each product. Part IV shows you how to use multimedia objects such as charts, pictures, sound, and motion pictures. Part VI provides business scenarios to illustrate how Microsoft Office products work together. Part VII teaches you how to customize Microsoft Office with your own toolbars, menus, and automation (macros and VBA). Part VIII shows you how to use Microsoft Office in a Group. Part IX is written by five experts in their fields showing you powerful user techniques.

Sit back and enjoy the new way of working that Microsoft Office provides.❖

Chapter 2

Getting Started and Identifying Screen Parts

by Patty and Rick Winter

One of the benefits of Microsoft Office applications is that after you know one application, each new application is easier to learn than the previous program. Microsoft has redesigned each of the programs to use the Windows 95 structure and also maintain consistency with the other applications in the suite. Microsoft reorganized menus, toolbars, and dialog boxes so that the products are now even more similar.

For experienced users, these changes may be a little disconcerting. For example, if you're a former Windows 3.1 or 3.11 user, you may be familiar with using the Restore/Maximize button in the top right corner of a window. In Windows 95, this button is the Close button, so you may accidentally close windows when you don't intend to. Until you become comfortable with the new features of Windows 95 and Microsoft Office, some of the changes may be frustrating. Hang in there; Microsoft does have your best interest at heart. The benefit of using this version of Microsoft Office is worth the original bother.

In this chapter, you learn to

- Start and exit programs and files

- Move between programs

- Move around the screen

- Use menus and dialog boxes

- Manipulate parts of the screen

- Compare work areas of different applications

Launching Programs

Windows applications are designed to accommodate users coming from different platforms and possessing different skills. Just as with other Windows procedures, you can launch an application in several different ways. You can use the keyboard, the mouse, or both devices together. You can use the Windows taskbar, the Microsoft Office Shortcut Bar, or Explorer. Windows also enables you to launch Windows programs by typing their name at the command prompt or using Run from the taskbar.

> **Note**
>
> You can create a shortcut to a program or document on your desktop by clicking on the file name (in Explorer for example) and choosing File, Create Shortcut. You can then drag the shortcut to the desktop or click the right mouse button on the shortcut, choose Properties, click the Shortcut tab, click in Shortcut key and press the key combination you want to use to launch the program or document.

Tip

You can change which programs and program groups appear on the taskbar program submenu by using Start, Settings, Taskbar and options on the Start Menu Programs tab. See Chapter 34.

Starting a Program from the Taskbar

With Windows 3.1, the standard way to begin any application was to double-click the group icon where the application was located and then double-click the program icon. With Windows 95, launching an application has become even easier.

To start a program in Windows 95, you begin by clicking the Start button on the bottom left corner of the desktop (screen). A menu list appears. Simply point to the Programs folder, and a submenu appears listing the program groups or programs not in groups. (When you move the mouse, Windows tracks the position of the mouse pointer so you don't need to click the commands that display submenus.) Move the mouse to a program or first to a program group and then to a program on the program group submenu. Once you find the program you want, such as Microsoft Word, click the left mouse button to open the program. See figure 2.1 to see how easily you can open a program using the taskbar at the bottom of the desktop. This method enables you to open a program with two single clicks.

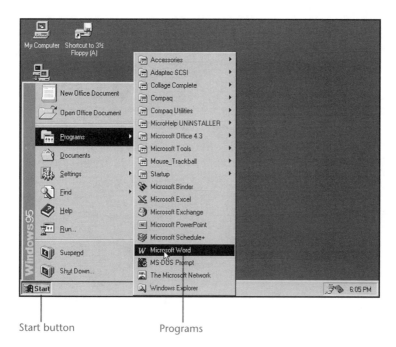

Start button   Programs

Fig. 2.1
Use the Start
button on the
taskbar to launch
any program.

I

Common Features

Caution

If the program is already open, you may launch another session of the same program, which causes unnecessary use of memory and may create difficulty in finding a
document. Use the taskbar at the bottom of the desktop to see all the programs that
are currently open. If you cannot decipher the buttons on the taskbar, you can press
Alt+Tab to display a list of icons for each program that is running. See more about
Alt+Tab later in the section "Switching between Programs" later in this chapter.

Opening a Document from the Taskbar

Opening a document from the desktop using the taskbar is as easy as starting
a program from the taskbar—maybe even easier. You perform the same actions as you do when you launch programs. Click the Start button, point
to the Documents folder (rather than the Programs folder), point to the
document you want to open, and click the left mouse button. The document
submenu stores the last 15 files you opened regardless of what program
created them. This technique makes it easy to find documents you use over
and over again, even if you use more than one program to create them (see
fig. 2.2).

Fig. 2.2
Use the taskbar to
open existing
documents from
any program you
have been using.

Documents folder—

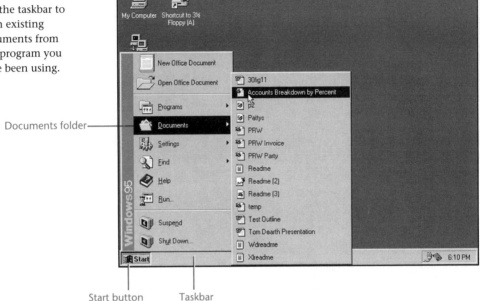

Start button   Taskbar

When you use the taskbar to open documents, Windows first looks to see whether
the associated program is currently running. If it is, Windows switches to the current
session of the associated program and then opens the document you requested.
Windows does not start a new session of the program for each document you open.

Tip
You can also click
your right mouse
button on the My
Computer or any
folder icon on
your desktop and
choose Explore
from the shortcut
menu to launch
Explorer.

Opening a Document from Windows Explorer

If you prefer using a tree structure to access your files, you can use Windows
Explorer to open specific documents from folders. You launch Windows Explorer the same way you launch any program. Click the Start button on the
taskbar, point to the Programs folder, point to Windows Explorer at the bottom of the Programs submenu, and click your left mouse button. After you
have opened Windows Explorer you can use the tree to move to the subfolder
or folder that stores the document file you want to open (see fig. 2.3).

The left side of the Explorer window shows a list of folders. If there is a + next to the yellow folder icon, the folder has subfolders. Click the + to see subfolders under the folder. After you expand the folder a – appears next to the subfolder indicating you can collapse this branch of folders. Click the minus sign to shrink the list back without the subfolders. When you reach the folder you want, click on the folder to show the contents in the right side of the window.

Find the document you want to open in the right side of the Explorer window and double-click the file name to switch to or open the program and open the document at the same time.

Common Features

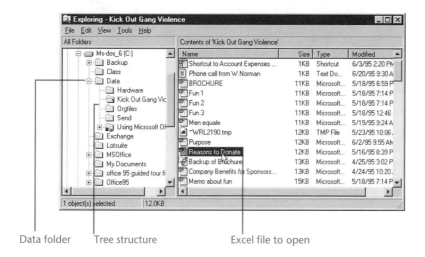

Data folder   Tree structure   Excel file to open

Fig. 2.3
Use Windows Explorer to launch files from subfolders or folders in a tree structure.

Opening a Document from the Shortcut Bar

If you were used to using the Microsoft Office Manager toolbar in Microsoft Office Version 4.0, you may want to use the Microsoft Office Shortcut Bar to start a document in Microsoft Office 95. If the Shortcut Bar is not displayed, you can turn it on the same way you launch programs. Click the Start button on the taskbar, point to the Programs folder, point to the Startup folder, point to and click the Microsoft Office Shortcut Bar icon. The Shortcut Bar is displayed on the top right corner of the desktop, as shown in figure 2.4.

Note

You can also start a new document or open an existing document from the Windows taskbar. When you click the Start button, you see New Office Document and Open Office Document at the top of the menu.

Fig. 2.4
The Microsoft
Office Shortcut Bar
allows you to
quickly launch
programs.

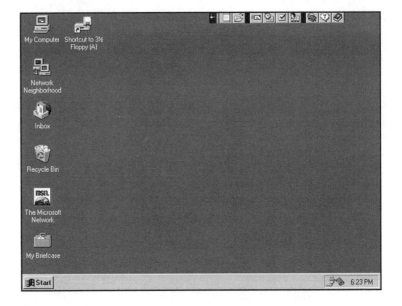

 After you have the Shortcut Bar displayed, you can use any of the tools to perform common actions. The first tool is Start a New Document; click this tool to start a new document. Microsoft Office displays the New dialog box as shown in figure 2.5. From this dialog box you first determine what type of document you want to create and click the appropriate tab to display the built-in templates and wizards.

To start a new document using the Microsoft Office Shortcut Bar, follow these steps:

1. If necessary, display the shortcut bar by choosing Start on the taskbar and choosing Programs, Microsoft Office, Microsoft Office Shortcut Bar.

2. Click the Start a New Document button on the Microsoft Office Short-cut Bar. The New dialog box appears.

3. Select the appropriate tab for the type of document you want. Figure 2.5 shows the Letters & Faxes tab selected.

4. Select the appropriate icon on the tab you wish to use. Figure 2.5 shows the Professional Letter icon selected.

5. Click OK or press Enter.

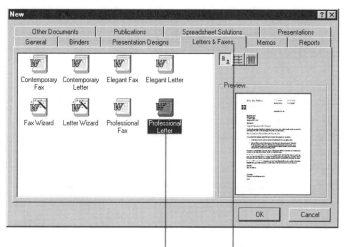

Fig. 2.5
Choose the type of document you want to create from the New dialog box.

Icons for document types   Tabs for groups of document types

Common Features

You don't even need to know which program to use; you just determine the type of document you need to create, and Microsoft Office starts the program. The wizard or template you choose is also opened. Figure 2.6 shows the Microsoft Word program with the Professional Letter template open for you to type a letter. You follow the prompts to type information into the letter.

▶ See "Typing and Editing," p. 68

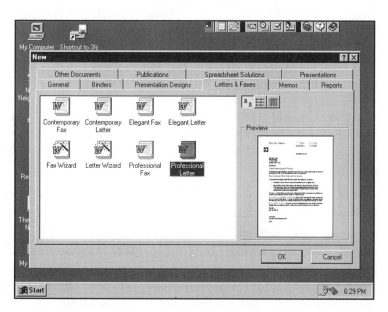

Fig. 2.6
The Professional Letter template is open and ready for you to type a letter.

> **Troubleshooting**
>
> *When I double-click a file name in the Explorer, the file does not open and I get a box around the file name.*
>
> If you do not double-click quick enough, Windows interprets your action as two single clicks. The first click selects the file name and the second click puts you into edit mode, allowing you to edit the file name. You can rename the file when you have this rectangle surrounding the file name (just type in a new file name). If you want to open the file, double-click faster or make sure you position the mouse pointer on the icon to the left of the file name when you double-click. You can also click your right mouse button once and choose Open on the pop-up menu.

Looking at the Microsoft Office Shortcut Bar

▶ See "Searching for Topics with the Answer Wizard," p. 152

Microsoft Office for Windows 95 has changed what was the Microsoft Office Manager toolbar not only in name but in design. The name is now the Microsoft Office Shortcut Bar, and it enables you not only to start a program, but to start a new document, open an existing document, make an appointment, add a task, add a contact, or launch the Answer Wizard. You can even choose to customize the Microsoft Office Shortcut Bar by adding your own buttons. You can even use multiple toolbars.

Using the Microsoft Office Shortcut Bar

After you have the Shortcut Bar displayed (using the Start button on the taskbar and choosing Programs), just click the button that represents the task you want to accomplish, and Microsoft takes you to the program associated with that task. For example, if you choose Add a Contact, Microsoft opens your Schedule+ file in the Schedule+ program and takes you to the Contacts dialog box for you to add your contact (see fig. 2.7).

There are 10 default buttons on the Shortcut Bar (you can change, add, and remove the buttons). The default buttons on the Shortcut Bar are as follows:

> **Note**
>
> The first time you go into Schedule+, the program may prompt you if you want to work in group enabled mode or to work alone. If you are on a network with other people who use Schedule+, choose Yes, Work in Group-Enabled Mode, otherwise choose No, Work Alone.

Use this	To do this
	The Control-menu box brings up a menu that gives choices on modifying the Shortcut Bar, bringing up Help, and Exiting (removing the Shortcut from the screen).
	Display the New dialog box and choose the type of document you want to create.
	Display the Open dialog box and choose the location and existing file you want to edit.
	Launch Microsoft Exchange to send an e-mail message.
	Launch Schedule+ and go to the Appointment dialog box, allowing you to create a new appointment.
	Launch Schedule+ and go to the Task dialog box, allowing you to create a new task.
	Launch Schedule+ and go to the Contact dialog box, allowing you to add a new person.
	Opens the CD-ROM version of the Getting Results Book with instructions and explanations on how to use Microsoft Office applications.
	Opens the CD-ROM demonstrations of products that work well with Microsoft Office applications.
	Opens the help program which allows you to search for help based on text you type.

▶ See "Starting Schedule+," p. 829

Common Features

I

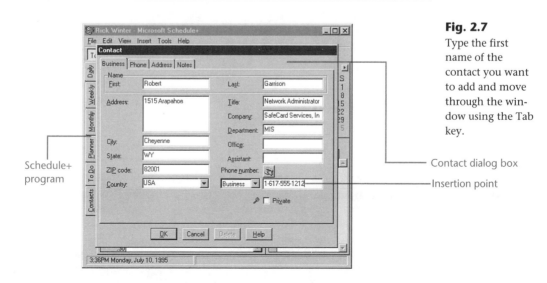

Schedule+ program

Contact dialog box

Insertion point

Fig. 2.7
Type the first name of the contact you want to add and move through the window using the Tab key.

Moving between Programs

You can use the Microsoft Office Shortcut Bar to move between programs in two different ways. You can also use the taskbar to move between programs (see "Switching between Programs" later). You can click a button on the Office Shortcut Bar to start or switch to a program and open a specific document window. If you have more than one toolbar selected under the Customize Toolbars tab, you can click one of the toolbar buttons at the end of the Shortcut bar to display different Shortcut Bars:

1. If you need to show more than one toolbar, click the first button on the toolbar (the Control-menu icon), choose Customize, click on the Toolbars tab and select the toolbars in the Show These Folders as Toolbars box (see fig. 2.8) and choose OK. The Microsoft Office Shortcut Bar will show additional buttons for each of the toolbars you selected.

Fig. 2.8
The Toolbars tab allows you to display one or more different toolbars.

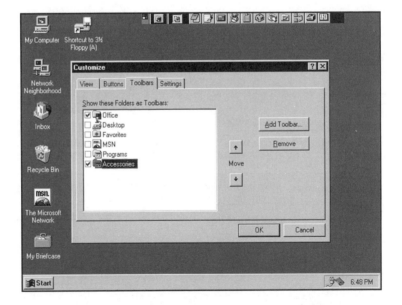

2. On the Shortcut Bar, click one of the toolbar buttons (in figure 2.8, this is the last button on the toolbar).

3. Choose one of the new buttons on the Shortcut Bar (see fig. 2.9).

▶ See "Customizing the Office Shortcut Bar," p. 753

4. To return to the Office toolbar, click the toolbar button. In figure 2.9, this is the first button after the Control-menu box (the Microsoft logo).

Office tools button   Accessories tools button   Accessories program buttons

I

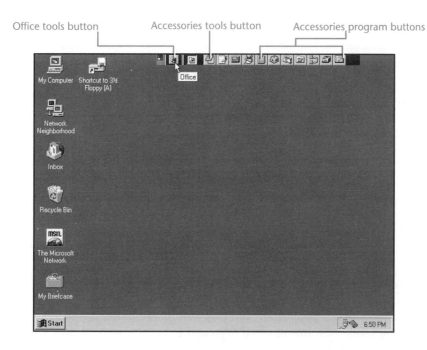

Fig. 2.9
The Microsoft
Office Shortcut
Bar shows the Office
ToolTip and the
Accessories toolbar
and program
icons.

Common Features

Closing the Microsoft Office Shortcut Bar

If you no longer want to see the Shortcut Bar, double-click the Control-menu box (the Microsoft logo) on the left side of the Shortcut Bar. This method is the fastest way to close the Shortcut Bar. You also can choose the Exit command from the Control pull-down menu (see fig. 2.10).

Control-
menu box

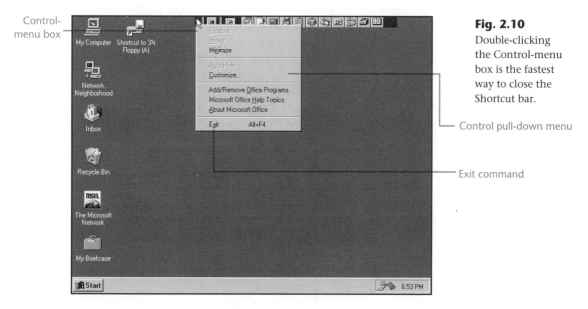

Fig. 2.10
Double-clicking
the Control-menu
box is the fastest
way to close the
Shortcut bar.

Control pull-down menu

Exit command

Troubleshooting

I can't find the Shortcut Bar to launch it.

Depending on your setup and how the programs may be customized, the program may be in different locations. Popular places to look for the Microsoft Office Shortcut Bar after you choose the Start button on the task bar is on the Programs submenu or the Microsoft Office submenu (off of the Programs submenu).

I would like to add Microsoft Office programs to the Microsoft Office Shortcut Bar.

From the Microsoft Office Shortcut Bar, click the Control-menu box and choose Customize. Click on the Button tab and select the applications you want to add and choose OK.

Switching between Programs

After you open one application you may want to close the application or keep the application running and open another application. The following section deals with closing programs. If you want to open another application that is currently not running, use the Start button on the taskbar or one of the other procedures mentioned earlier in the "Launching Programs" section.

If the application is already running, you will see the button on the taskbar. Depending on the number of applications you have running, the button may be large so you can see the entire name of the application, or small so you can see only the application icon and a portion of the program name. If you don't know what the name of the program is, you can pause your mouse pointer over the button on the taskbar and see a ToolTip that tells you the name of the program and an open document (if available).

You can also use the Alt+Tab feature to switch between applications. Hold down your Alt key and press Tab and you will see a number of icons representing open applications as shown in figure 2.11. One of the icons will have a square box surrounding the icon; the name of the application and an open document (if available) will appear below the icons. While you continue to hold Alt down, press Tab until the application you want is selected. Then release the Tab and Alt keys to go to that application.

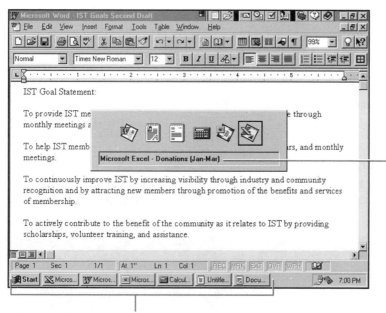

Fig. 2.11
Choose between
running programs
with Alt+Tab.

The name of the program
and document shows
below the selected icon

Alt+Tab is helpful when you can't read the program
names because so many applications are open

Troubleshooting

I can't see ToolTips for the buttons on the Microsoft Office Shortcut Bar.

Make sure you pause your mouse pointer over the button. You may need to turn
ToolTips on by choosing the Control-menu box, Customize, choosing the View tab
and checking Show Tooltips.

I see a different toolbar than the one shown in the book.

You can have a number of different toolbars for the Microsoft Office Shortcut Bar or
change the tools on the bar. Click the Control-menu box, choose Customize, choose
the Toolbars tab, and check which toolbars you want to use. To return to the toolbar
shown in this book, deselect all options except the Office toolbar.

Closing Programs

After you have finished working in an application, you probably want to
close it—especially if you have limited memory. All Windows programs,
whether they are Microsoft Office applications or not, close the same way.
Do one of the following:

Tip
You can close a maximized or minimized appli-cation by clicking the right mouse button on the application icon on the taskbar and choosing Close.

▶ See "Saving, Opening, and Closing Files," p. 106

▶ See "Using the Word Screen," p. 168

■ Click the Close button (the X) in the upper right corner of the applica-tion window.

■ Double-click the program Control-menu icon in the upper left corner of the application window.

■ On the menu bar, choose File, Exit.

■ Press Alt+F4.

If you have not saved changes to your documents, you will see a dialog box asking whether you want to save changes to each of your open documents. You probably want to save your documents. If prompted, type the name of the file and the location in the File Save As dialog box.

Note

If you run non-Windows applications, you need to exit through the procedure for exiting the specific application you are running. For example, you need to press F7 in WordPerfect for DOS or press /Q in Lotus 1-2-3 for DOS.

Viewing Parts of the Window

▶ See "Using the Word Screen," p. 168

▶ See "Defining Excel Terms," p. 301

▶ See "Getting Familiar with the PowerPoint Window," p. 562

One of the best parts of learning Windows and Microsoft Office is the similar-ity between different applications. After you learn one program, the next and subsequent programs are easier to learn. This point is especially true because parts of the window are similar.

Understanding Common Window Elements

Figure 2.12 shows a review of the elements on a screen. Each application usually displays the application window itself and at least one document window. Table 2.1 describes the common elements on the application win-dow and the document window.

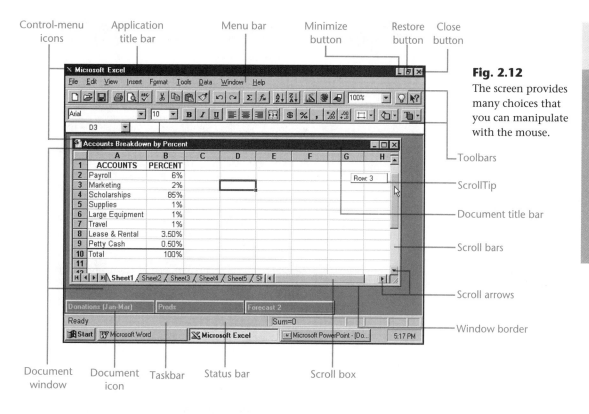

Fig. 2.12
The screen provides many choices that you can manipulate with the mouse.

Control-menu icons — Application title bar — Menu bar — Minimize button — Restore button — Close button

Toolbars

ScrollTip

Document title bar

Scroll bars

Scroll arrows

Window border

Document window — Document icon — Taskbar — Status bar — Scroll box

Common Features

Table 2.1   Window Features Common to Application and Document Windows

Feature	Description/Use
Control-menu icon	Microsoft Program icon in upper left corner of window. If the document window is maximized, the document icon is located directly below the program Control-menu icon. If the document window is not maximized, the document Control-menu icon is in the upper left corner of the document window.
	Double-click to close the application or the document. Single-click to open the Control menu and choose the Restore, Minimize, Maximize, or Close commands.
Title bar	On top of window. Title bar is dark if window is active, grayed if other window is active. The color may be different if you have changed colors in the Display Properties of the Control Panel.)

(continues)

Table 2.1	Continued
Feature	**Description/Use**
Title bar (continued)	Shows name of program or document. If document window is maximized, the program title bar shows the name of the application and of the document. Double-click to toggle between maximize and restore. If a window is restored (not full screen), drag the title bar to move the window.
Minimize button	First button in group of three buttons in upper right corner of document or program window.
	Click to shrink window to icon. Program minimize button shrinks program to icon on the taskbar. Document minimize button shrinks document to icon in work area above status bar (and probably behind another document).
Maximize button	Second button in group of three buttons in upper right corner of document or program window. Looks like full-screen window (rectangle with thick black line on top).
	When window is restored (not full screen), click button to change window to largest possible size. This action causes button to change to Restore button.
Restore button	Second button in group of three buttons in upper right corner of document or program window. Looks like two windows cascaded.
	When window is maximized, click this button to change window to last smaller size window. This action causes button to change to Maximize button.
Close button	Third button in group of three buttons in upper right corner of document or program window. An X appears on this button.
	Click this button to close the window. If you have not saved your work, you are prompted to save and continue or close without saving.
Menu bar	Line below title bar starting with File.
	Click one of the words to select a menu or press Alt and then type underlined letter on menus.
Window border	Thin gray line surrounding a window that is not maximized.
	Move mouse pointer until double arrow appears and drag to change size of window.
Window corner	Textured box in bottom right corner of window.
	Move mouse pointer until double arrow appears and drag to change both the width and height of window.

Tip

You can minimize all open programs by clicking the right mouse button in an empty spot on the taskbar and choosing Minimize All Windows.

Some items generally occur just on application windows (and not document windows) but are common to most applications. Table 2.2 discusses these items. Microsoft Word, Excel, PowerPoint, and Exchange call the pictorial strip of buttons toolbars.

Table 2.2 Window Features Common to Application Windows	
Feature	**Description/Use**
Toolbar(s)	Picture buttons below menu bar or other places on-screen.
	When you move mouse pointer to a button, a ToolTip description appears on the button and the status bar describes the button in more detail. Click button for the most frequently used commands. Sometimes the button gives you only one feature for a command. Use the menu for more options on a feature.
Status bar	Bottom line of application window.
	The status bar may tell information about insertion point location on document and status of some toggle keys on the keyboard such as the Insert/Overwrite or Num Lock key. In some programs, the status bar describes a menu or toolbar choice in more detail. In some programs, you can double-click status bar to accomplish tasks.
Document window	Area between toolbars and status bar.
	Shows open document, scroll bars, and possible title of document in title bar.
Document icon	Icon on bottom of screen above status bar, visible if document window is not maximized.
	Document is minimized. Double-click to open into a document window.

Most document windows also have features common to each other. Table 2.3 shows some of the features common to document windows across applications.

Common Features

Table 2.3 Window Features Common to Document Windows	
Feature	**Description/Use**
Scroll bar	Gray area between scroll arrows on right and bottom of the document window.
	Click above or below scroll box on vertical scroll bar or to the left or right of scroll box on horizontal scroll bar to move view of document a full screen up, down, left, or right.
Scroll box	Gray square or rectangle box inside scroll bars.
	Drag scroll box to position view of document.
Scroll arrows	Arrow on either side of scroll bar.
	Click arrow to move view one line in the direction of the arrow. Hold down mouse pointer on arrow to scroll quickly.
ScrollTip	Description that appears when you drag a vertical scroll box.
	In Excel this shows the row number, in Word the page number, and in PowerPoint the slide number when you drag the vertical scroll box.
Document window	Area inside the window.
	Location where document resides and where editing takes place.

Using Toolbars in Microsoft Office Applications

One of the improvements Microsoft made with the last upgrades of Word, Excel, and PowerPoint was to reorganize and improve the toolbars so that the tools are more consistent across the Microsoft Office applications. Although some buttons are unique to each application, many buttons are common to all or some of the applications. You now can choose from more than one toolbar in all the applications. You also can customize the toolbars by adding or removing buttons.

▶ See "Customizing Application Toolbars," p. 759

To turn a toolbar on or off, follow these steps:

1. Click the right mouse button on an active toolbar.

A pop-up menu shows a list of the potential toolbars. Microsoft displays those toolbars with a checkmark to the left of the name. Figure 2.13 shows a list of the toolbars for each application described later in this chapter.

2. Click the toolbar you want to turn on or off. If the toolbar is floating, you can also click the toolbar's Control-menu icon to close the toolbar.

> **Note**
>
> If the program does not show any toolbars, choose <u>V</u>iew, <u>T</u>oolbars and select the toolbar(s) you want to display.

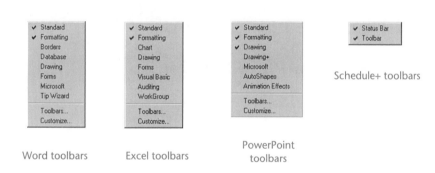

Word toolbars   Excel toolbars   PowerPoint toolbars

Fig. 2.13
When you click the right mouse button on a toolbar, a menu appears, showing the active and available toolbars.

Some buttons change on toolbars when you change the view. For example, Word adds an Outline toolbar when you change to Outline view. Excel adds a Charting toolbar when you use the Chart Wizard.

Standard Toolbars

Figure 2.14 shows the Standard toolbar for each Microsoft Office application. Notice how many of the buttons are the same. Table 2.4 shows the common buttons and their purpose.

Word Standard toolbar

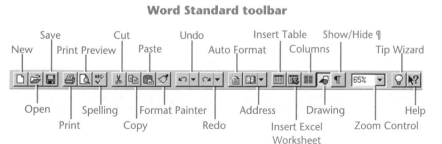

Fig. 2.14
The Standard toolbars for Word, Excel, PowerPoint, and Schedule+ show many similarities.

Fig. 2.14

The Standard toolbars for Word, Excel, PowerPoint, and Schedule+ show many similarities.

Excel Standard toolbar

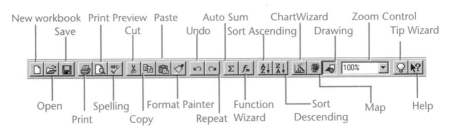

PowerPoint Standard toolbar

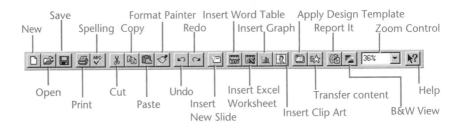

Schedule+ toolbar

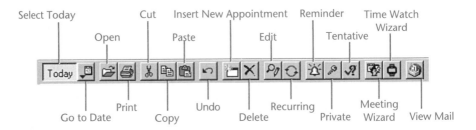

Table 2.4	Common Buttons on the Standard Toolbars				
Button	**W***	**E***	**P***	**S**	**Use**
New	X	X	X		Create a new, blank document.
Open	X	X	X	X	Open an existing document.
Save	X	X	X		Save the active document on screen.
Print	X	X	X	X	Print the document.
Print Preview	X	X			Preview what the printed document will look like.

Button	W*	E*	P*	S	Use
Spelling	X	X	X		Check the spelling of the document.
Cut	X	X	X	X	Remove the selection from the document and place a copy into the Clipboard.
Copy	X	X	X	X	Copy the selection from the document and place a copy into the Clipboard.
Paste	X	X	X	X	Copy the contents of the Clipboard into the document at the location of the insertion point.
Format Painter	X	X	X		Copy the formatting from the selected items to the next selection.
Undo	X	X	X	X	Reverse your last action.
Redo	X		X		Redo the last action or actions that were undone.
Repeat		X			Repeat the last action or redoes last undone action.
Insert Microsoft Excel Worksheet	X		X		Insert a Microsoft Excel worksheet into the document.
Zoom Control	X	X	X		Change the size of your display (does not affect printing).
TipWizard	X	X			Show or hide the TipWizard toolbar which lists tips of the day and help for your procedures.
Help	X	X	X		Click toolbar button or menu option for help on that choice. Double-click to search for help on a topic you type.

W, E, P, S columns are for the Word, Excel, and PowerPoint Standard toolbars and the Schedule+ toolbar.

Formatting Toolbars

Just as Standard toolbars have common buttons, Formatting toolbars also have many similar buttons. Figure 2.15 shows the formatting toolbars for Word, Excel, and PowerPoint. Table 2.5 lists the common buttons and their purpose.

Fig. 2.15

The formatting toolbars for Word, Excel, and PowerPoint show many similarities.

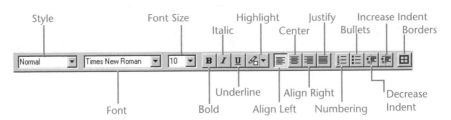

Word Formatting Toolbar

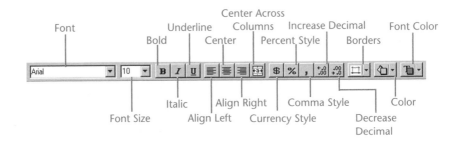

Excel Formatting toolbar

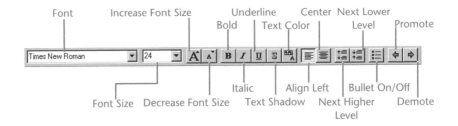

PowerPoint Formatting toolbar

Table 2.5	**Common Buttons on the Formatting Toolbars**			
Button	**W***	**E***	**P***	**Use**
Font	X	X	X	Click arrow to right of font name to display a list of typefaces. Click the desired font.
Font Size	X	X	X	Click arrow to display and choose desired size for text.
Bold	X	X	X	Bold the selected text.
Italic	X	X	X	Italicize the selected text.
Underline	X	X	X	Underline the selected text.

Button	W*	E*	P*	Use
Align Left	X	X	X	Align the items so the left side of each is lined up.
Center	X	X	X	Align the items so each is centered.
Align Right	X	X		Align the items so the right side of each is lined up.
Bullet	X		X	Place a bullet before each line of the selected text.

W, E, P columns are for the Word, Excel, and PowerPoint formatting toolbars.

Drawing Toolbars

The Drawing toolbars for Word, Excel, and PowerPoint also have common buttons, as shown in figure 2.16. Table 2.6 lists the common buttons and their purpose.

Word Drawing toolbar

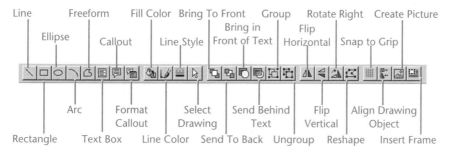

Excel Drawing toolbar

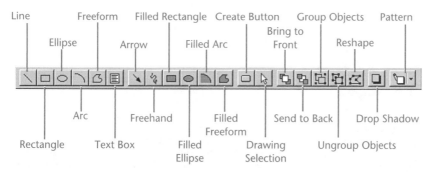

Fig. 2.16
The Drawing toolbars for Word, Excel, and PowerPoint show many similarities.

(continues)

PowerPoint Drawing and Drawing+ toolbar

Fig. 2.16
Continued

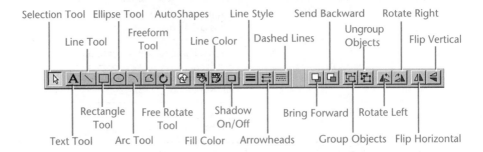

Table 2.6			Common Buttons on the Drawing Toolbars	
Button	**W***	**E***	**P***	**Use**
Line	X	X	X	Click and drag to start and draw the line. Release the mouse button to end the line. Use the Shift key to draw lines at 30, 45, and 60 degree angles.
Rectangle	X	X	X	Click and drag from one corner to the opposite corner. Release the mouse button to complete the rectangle. Use the Shift key to draw a square.
Ellipse	X	X	X	Click and drag from one corner to the opposite corner. Release the mouse button to complete the ellipse. Use the Shift key to draw a circle.
Arc	X	X	X	Click and drag to start and draw the arc. Release the mouse button to end the arc.
Freeform	X	X	X	Drag the mouse to draw. Double-click to end the drawing.
Selection Tool	X	X	X	To select multiple objects, drag mouse from upper left corner to bottom right and release mouse. Black boxes (selection handles) tell you the object is selected.
Bring to Front /Bring Forward	X	X	X	With two objects stacked on each other, bring the selected object to the top (or front).
Send to Back /Send Backward	X	X	X	With two objects stacked on each other, send the selected object to the bottom (or back).

Button	W*	E*	P*	Use
Group Objects	X	X	X	Combine more than one drawn object into a single object for editing and moving.
Ungroup Objects	X	X	X	Uncombine grouped objects back into their original drawings.
Flip Horizontal	X		X	Flip object from top to bottom.
Flip Vertical	X		X	Flip object from right to left.
Reshape	X	X		Drag black selection handles to reshape freeform object.
Drop Shadow		X	X	Apply a shadow to the bottom and right of the object.

W, E, P columns are for the Word, Excel, and PowerPoint drawing toolbars.

Using Menus

In addition to common toolbars, Microsoft also has reworked the menus in the Microsoft Office applications to come up with similar placement for commands.

Directly below the title bar in all applications is the *menu bar*. In all Microsoft Office applications and most Windows applications, the menu bar begins with the File, Edit, and View menus and ends with the Window and Help menus. When the mouse pointer is on a menu, the pointer changes to a white arrow. To pull down a menu, click the menu name. If you want to use the keyboard, press Alt and the underlined letter on the menu. When you open a menu, a list of commands appears. Click the command or type the letter of the underlined character. As you point to menu choices, the status bar on the bottom of the screen shows a description of the menu or command.

If you accidentally go into the wrong menu, you can take one of these steps:

- Click another menu.

- Click in the document to turn off the menu.

- Press Alt or click the menu again to get out of the menu.

- Press Esc to keep the menu word highlighted and see the description of the menu on the status bar. Press Esc a second time to get out of the menu.

Common Features

Common Menu Symbols

Menus throughout Windows applications have common symbols that help you know what will happen when you select the command. The symbols include ellipses, arrows, checkmarks, and option bullets.

Tip

Look for shortcuts to your most used commands on the right side of any menu.

Some menus also give you keyboard shortcuts to do the commands. Each menu is divided into sections by horizontal lines. The sections generally group similar commands together (such as Save, Save As, and Save All) or group commands that are mutually exclusive. The following list describes common menu symbols:

- Three dots, or an *ellipsis*, after a command indicates that a dialog box appears after you choose the command. For example, the command File, Print occurs in all four applications, and an ellipsis indicates that the Print dialog box follows the selection of this command. For more information on dialog boxes, see "Using Dialog Boxes" later in this chapter.

- Some Microsoft Office applications (all except Word) have *arrows* on the right side of some menus indicating that another drop-down menu will appear. After you point to the command with an arrow, you choose another command on the resulting menu. Figure 2.17 shows that in Excel if you choose Format, Row, you get another menu that begins with Height.

Fig. 2.17
An arrow on the right side of a command indicates another menu follows.

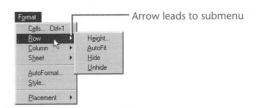

- Another character on some menus is a *checkmark* to the left of the menu choice. A checkmark indicates that this choice is selected and that the choice can be on or off. For example, the Window menu of all Microsoft Office applications shows a list of open documents on the bottom of each menu. The active open document is indicated by a checkmark.

■ Another on or off indicator on some applications (Word and PowerPoint) is an *option bullet* to the left of a menu item. The bullet indicates that only one item in a menu section (the area between two horizontal lines) can be selected at a time. If you choose any other command in the same section, the bullet moves to the selected item. For example, the View menu of Word in figure 2.18 indicates that you can choose only Normal, Outline, Page Layout, or Master Document at one time and that Normal is currently selected.

Fig. 2.18
Normal is the exclusive choice in this menu section.

■ To the right of some commands are *keyboard shortcuts*. Instead of using the menu, you can press the shortcut key or key combination to choose the command. Most shortcuts begin with holding the Ctrl key down in combination with a letter. For example, to undo your latest action, press Ctrl+Z in all applications. Shortcut keys also include function keys (for example, F7 for Spelling) and editing keys (for example, Delete to erase the selection).

Menu Similarities in Microsoft Office

In addition to maintaining common symbols on menus, Microsoft has repositioned menu commands to appear on the same menus within each application as much as possible. Figure 2.19 shows a diagram with the menu bars for each application. You can see the menu bar similarities between the different applications. Table 2.7 lists the menus and their general functions.

Common Features

Fig. 2.19
The Microsoft
Office applications
have similar menu
names on their
menu bars.

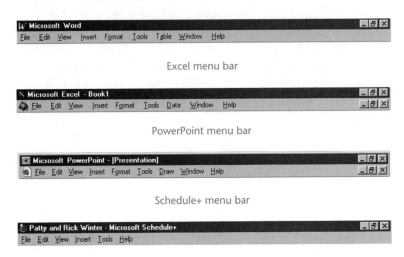

Word menu bar

Excel menu bar

PowerPoint menu bar

Schedule+ menu bar

Table 2.7 Common Menus on the Microsoft Office Applications					
Menu	**W***	**E**	**P**	**S**	**Similar Command Functions**
File	X	X	X	X	Open, create new, save, close, print files, and exit program.
Edit	X	X	X	X	Copy, move, paste from other applications, delete selections; undo last command, search and replace text.
View	X	X	X	X	Change the way the document and screen items such as toolbars display on-screen.
Insert	X	X	X	X	Insert objects into the document.
Format	X	X	X		Change font, line spacing or row height, add lines, have program pick out a "look" for your document with pre-determined formatting.
Tools	X	X	X	X	Check spelling, create macros, customize the way the keyboard, menus, and toolbars look.

Menu	W*	E	P	S	Similar Command Functions
Window	X	X	X		Arrange document windows on the screen; switch between documents.
Help	X	X	X	X	Show step-by-step procedures, definitions, and examples. Do on-screen tutorials, list Microsoft technical support phone numbers and procedures.

W, E, P, S, columns are for the Word, Excel, PowerPoint, and Schedule+ menu bars.

Shortcut Menus

Microsoft has shortcut menus for Word, Excel, PowerPoint, and Schedule+. To access a shortcut menu, select the item you want to change and click the *right* mouse button in the selected area. The menu that appears gives you options for only the selection. You don't have to wade through the menu bar to figure out what menu items go with what you are doing.

In addition to shortcut menus for toolbars, Microsoft has shortcut menus for selected text, drawing and graphics objects, rows, columns, and others depending on your application. Figure 2.20 shows an example of the shortcut menus for selected text in each of the applications. Notice that each of the shortcut menus has Cut, Copy, and Paste, but each menu also has items specific to the application.

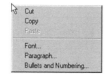  

Word shortcut menu

Excel shortcut menu

PowerPoint shortcut menu

Schedule+ shortcut menu

Fig. 2.20
The shortcut menus for selected text contain similar and different menu items for each application.

Using Dialog Boxes

When you choose a command with an ellipsis, a dialog box appears. The dialog box can be very simple with only one button (such as OK), or the dialog box can have many choices. Just as the menus have common symbols, so do the dialog boxes. Figure 2.21 shows examples of two dialog boxes.

Fig 2.21

The Print dialog box of Word and Format Cells dialog box of Excel show Features of all dialog boxes.

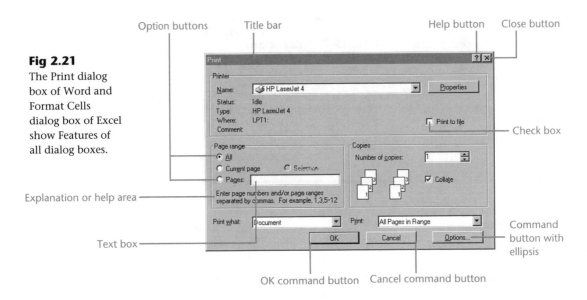

Option buttons   Title bar   Help button   Close button

Check box

Explanation or help area

Text box

OK command button   Cancel command button

Command button with ellipsis

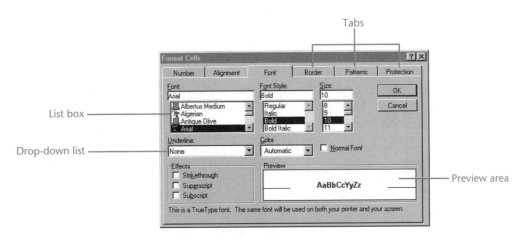

Tabs

List box

Drop-down list

Preview area

Dialog boxes enable you to see all the current settings for a command as well as change them. On the newer applications, Microsoft added tabs (the Font tab shows in the Format Cells dialog box shown in fig. 2.21). Click a tab to go to that area of the dialog box. Sometimes, you may need to see your underlying document to make a choice in the dialog box. Drag the title bar of the dialog box to move the dialog box out of the way. Within a dialog box you click an object to select or change the value. For example, in the Font Style list box, click Italic to select italic. Within a dialog box you generally click an object, type a value, or select from a list. For more detail, see figure 2.21.

Microsoft also removed the Help command button and replaced it with the ? button on the top right corner of the dialog box window. If you need help on a specific part of the dialog box, you can click the ? button and then point to the part of the dialog box where you need help and click again. Microsoft displays a pop-up help window for that area of the dialog box. This method is called *context-sensitive help*.

In addition to using the mouse to make selections in a dialog box, you also can use several keyboard methods:

- Press Tab to move to each section of a dialog box.

- Press Shift+Tab to move backward through the dialog box.

- Press Alt+ any underlined letter on a choice in the dialog box to move to that choice.

- Press the up or down arrow to make a selection in a list.

- Press the space bar to select or deselect a choice in a check box.

To get out of a dialog box without selecting any of the settings, choose Cancel or press Esc. To use the settings, choose OK or the Close button (top right corner). In some cases, click the Close button to finish your selections. Notice that some command buttons have ellipses (Options button in fig. 2.21). An ellipsis indicates that another dialog box will appear when you choose this button.

Troubleshooting

I accidentally chose a menu or a toolbar.

If you are still in a menu, click on another menu or press Alt to turn off the menu. If you are in a dialog box, click the Close (X) button or press Esc. If you changed the text or a graphic, click Undo or press Ctrl+Z. If you launched another program, click the Close (X) button.

A menu or dialog box choice doesn't work or it is dimmed.

The choice may not be available depending on what you're doing. One of the most common things you need to do is to select your item first before you can change it. For example, you can't choose Edit, Copy unless something is selected.

Manipulating Parts of the Screen

Tip

To see what an item is on-screen (if help is available), click the Help button on a Standard toolbar and then click the screen item. A pop-up explanation appears.

When you're working in an application with all the new features of Microsoft Office for Windows 95, you may find that your screen gets cluttered. When this happens you can choose to hide elements in the program window, the Microsoft Office Shortcut Bar, or even the taskbar on the desktop.

Hiding Screen Elements

Most applications that come with the Microsoft Office suite have a View and Tools menu. You begin with these menus if you want to change the way the screen looks.

Using the View, Toolbars Command

If you decide you want to change the view of your screen, the best place to start is with the View menu. For instance, in any of the programs that display toolbars, you can choose to turn the toolbars off or display other toolbars. You simply choose View, Toolbar(s). Depending on the application, you turn the toolbar off as in the case of Schedule+, or a dialog box appears enabling you to choose which toolbars to have on or off (see fig. 2.22). Word, Excel, and PowerPoint display the dialog box (as indicated by the ellipses points after the menu command).

Fig. 2.22
The View menu for the applications in the Microsoft Office suite turns on or off toolbars.

Tip

You can also use View, Full Screen to temporarily conceal all toolbars, status bars, and other screen items for maximum editing space. To return to normal view click the Full Screen button on the small remaining toolbar.

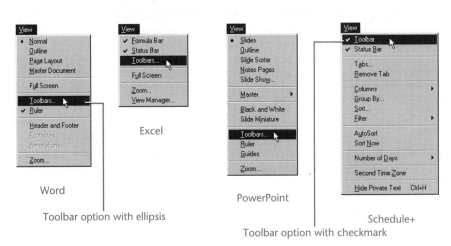

Using the Tools, Options Command

You can choose Tools, Options (generally the View tab) to change the view of window elements such as the status bar, scroll bars, and in Excel the formula bar, row and column headings, and sheet tabs as well as others. When you choose Tools, Options, the Options dialog box opens. You then turn on or off specific options by clicking the option you want to change. Figure 2.23 shows the View tabs of the Word and Excel Options dialog boxes.

Word

View tab ——

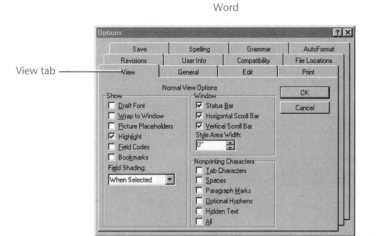

Fig. 2.23
Change options by turning them on or off with a click of the mouse.

Excel

View tab ——

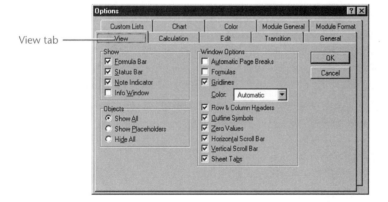

Magnifying the View

You may determine that you need to change the view of your document for editing purposes. With most Microsoft Office applications, you have an option on the Standard toolbar called Zoom Control. You also can use the Zoom command on the View menu. If your document doesn't fit on the screen, you may need to make it smaller to see how it lays out on the page. In some instances you may want to make the document bigger to see detail better. In either case, you can change the view using the Zoom Control or the Zoom command on the View menu. Figure 2.24 shows a brochure in Word after the Page Width zoom control was selected.

Tip
In Excel you can select a row (or range) of columns and then click the Zoom button and choose Selection to force the zoom to display all columns from your selection.

Fig. 2.24
Zoom in to see
more of the page
at a time.

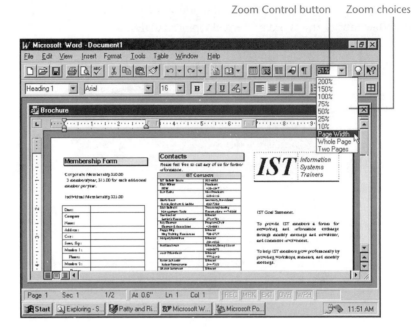

Zoom Control button   Zoom choices

Using Auto Hide on the Shortcut Bar

You may turn on the Microsoft Office Shortcut Bar and become frustrated
with all the clutter Microsoft adds to the screen. Using the Shortcut Bar is
nice, but being able to see more of your workspace may take priority. One of
the added features with the Shortcut Bar is the Auto Hide command. If you
want the Shortcut Bar visible when you are working in another part of the
screen, but hidden while you are working in an application, you need to turn
on Auto Hide. To turn on the Auto Hide command for the Shortcut Bar, follow these steps:

1. Point to an open spot on the Shortcut Bar (where a button is not) and
   click your right mouse button.

2. Point to and click the Auto Hide command.

To see how this method works, move into your workspace and click to make
the application window active. Move the pointer back over the Shortcut Bar
and back into the workspace. When you get into the workspace the Shortcut
Bar disappears. If you move the pointer to the edge of the screen where the
Shortcut Bar is located, it reappears. See figures 2.25 and 2.26 to compare the
screens.

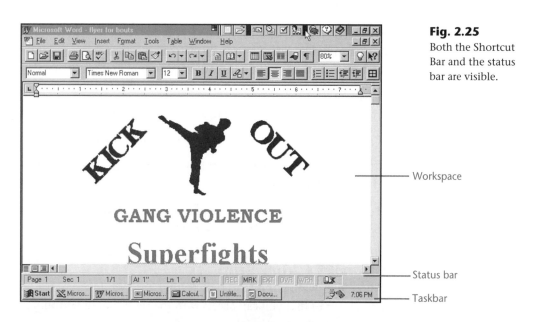

Fig. 2.25
Both the Shortcut
Bar and the status
bar are visible.

Workspace

Status bar

Taskbar

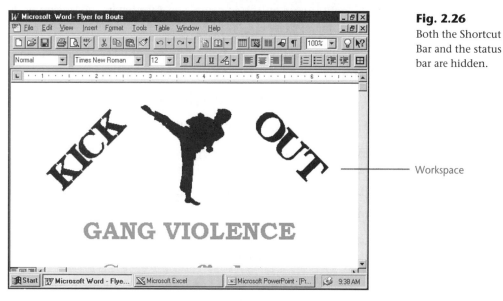

Fig. 2.26
Both the Shortcut
Bar and the status
bar are hidden.

Workspace

Common Features

Using Auto Hide on the Taskbar

Just as you can hide the Shortcut Bar in Microsoft Office, you can use Auto Hide on the taskbar. To turn on the Auto Hide command for the taskbar, follow these steps:

1. Point to an open spot on the taskbar and click the right mouse button.

2. Choose Properties. The Taskbar Properties sheet appears.

3. Click the Auto Hide option to turn it on. Then click OK for your changes to take effect.

4. Test the use of this option the same way you did for the Shortcut Bar. See figures 2.25 and 2.26 for a comparison of the screens.

Additional Taskbar Features

In addition to providing the Auto Hide feature, the Windows taskbar has additional features that you can access with the right mouse button.

Click the right mouse button in a gray area (not on an application button) and choose one of these options:

- Cascade stacks the applications, with the title bar of each window showing.

- Tile Horizontally displays the applications in horizontal rows.

- Tile Vertically displays the applications in vertical columns.

- Minimize All Windows reduces all applications to the Windows taskbar only.

- Properties changes which applications appear on the Start menu and other taskbar options.

- Click the right mouse button on an application icon on the Windows taskbar and choose Close to exit that application.

- Click the right mouse button on the clock on the right of the Windows taskbar and choose Adjust Date/Time to change the date or time.

Tip

A fast way to exit Windows is to click the Start button on the Windows taskbar and choose Shut Down. If you made changes in any documents, you are prompted to save the files.

I

Troubleshooting

I lost my toolbars.

You could have accidentally clicked a right mouse button on a toolbar and unmarked the toolbar on the shortcut menu. To bring back toolbars, use the View, Toolbars command and choose the toolbars you want.

If you accidentally clicked View, Full Screen in Word or Excel, you lost all toolbars and the status bar. Click on the Full Screen button, or press Esc to return the screen to normal. You can also type Alt+V to bring up the View menu (hidden in Word) and type U to choose the Full Screen command.

I can't find other parts of the screen.

Use the following table to get your screen back to normal.

Screen Item	How To Get It back
Typing	Check the scroll bars to see if you moved outside the typing area. You may also have selected typing and pressed a key replacing the typing. Click on the Undo button to see if you deleted the text.
The whole document	Check the Window menu and choose the document name. If you haven't saved the document yet, you may need to choose each of the generic document names (Document3, Book1, Presentation).
The whole application	Check taskbar to see if the program is minimized. Otherwise, you will need to open the application again by choosing Start on the taskbar and choosing Programs and the application name.
Any edge or edge item (title bar, maximize button, restore button, minimize button) of document window.	Drag title bar or choose Window Arrange.
Any specific button on a toolbar	View, Toolbars, select the toolbar and choose Reset.
Status Bar	Tools, Options, View Tab, Status Bar check box
Scroll Bars	Tools, Options, View Tab, Horizontal Scroll Bar and Vertical Scroll Bar check boxes

(continues)

Screen Item	How To Get It back
Ruler (Word)	View, Ruler
Formula Bar (Excel)	View, Formula Bar
Gridlines (Excel)	For on screen view—Tools, Options, View tab, Gridlines (and make sure Color doesn't match worksheet back ground). If you want to turn on or off printing of gridlines, choose File, Page Setup, Sheet tab and use Gridlines.
Gridlines (Word Table)	To turn on and off view, choose Table, Gridlines. To print gridlines, select the table, click the Borders button on the formatting toolbar and choose both the Inside Border and Outside Border buttons.
Row and Column Headers (Excel)	Tools, Options, View tab, Row & Column Headers. To turn on or off row and column headers, choose File, Page Setup, Sheet tab and use Row and Column Headings.
Sheet Tabs (Excel)	Tools, Options, View tab, Sheet Tabs
Paragraph and tab symbols (Word)	To turn on or off, click the Show/hide ¶ button on the Standard toolbar.
Pictures (Word)	Uncheck Tools, Options, View tab, Picture Placeholders.

Looking at the Work Areas of Office Applications

The Microsoft Office applications have many similarities; for example, all applications have at least one document window, a menu bar, toolbars, and status bars. However, each Microsoft Office application has a different focus and a different kind of work area.

Word Document

The work area of Word is the document (see fig. 2.27). The document window is like a blank sheet of paper on which you can type. When your typing reaches the margin, the text automatically wraps to the next line. The focus of Word is text. Although you can place numbers and data in Word documents, the strength of Word is its capability to format text documents, such as letters, memos, and reports. The length of your document is virtually unlimited.

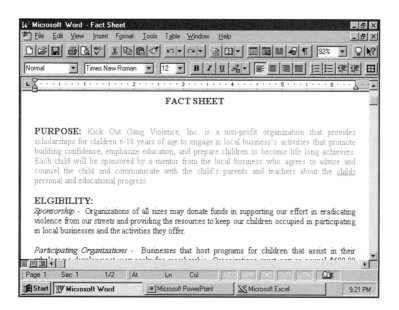

Fig. 2.27
Text automatically
wraps in a Word
document.

Excel Worksheet

The work area of Excel is a grid of columns and rows called a worksheet and is similar to a table (see fig. 2.28). The Excel document is called a *workbook* and is a collection of worksheets and/or charts. The focus of Excel is a *cell*, which is the intersection of a row and column. All data must go into cells. Although you can place text boxes across a range of cells, long sections of text are better left to Word. Excel's strength is its capability to summarize and analyze numbers. Excel also has significant charting capabilities that enable you to create many types of pie, bar, column, and line charts.

An Excel worksheet has 256 columns (indicated by letters A to IV) and 16,384 numbered rows. Each cell is indicated by the column letter and the row number. E6, for example, is the cell in the fifth column and sixth row. An Excel workbook can have several sheets. Each sheet has 256 columns and 16,384 rows.

PowerPoint Slide

The focus of PowerPoint is the slide (see fig. 2.29). PowerPoint is used primarily to make presentations. You can create slides for uses such as overhead transparencies, 35mm slides, or on-screen presentations.

Fig. 2.28
One of Excel's strengths is the ability to work with numbers and create formulas.

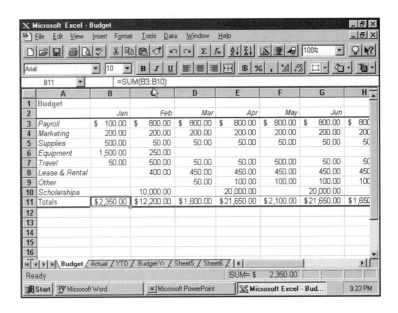

Each slide has attached objects, which may include a title, bulleted items, other text, and graphics. To edit an object, you first need to select the object.

You can view PowerPoint slides in different ways. Outline view shows the titles of all slides in list format with their attached bulleted items. Slide view (the normal view) shows one slide at a time. Slide Sorter view shows more than one slide at a time. Notes Pages view enables you to type notes for each slide.

Fig. 2.29
PowerPoint is strong on creating bulleted slides to support your ideas.

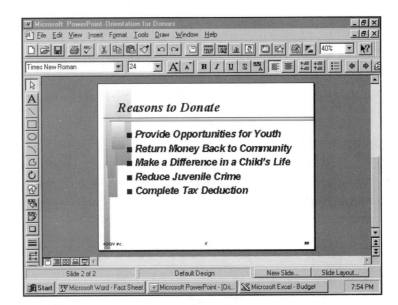

Chapter 3
Typing and Formatting Basics

by Patty Winter and Rick Winter

With the new versions of applications in the Microsoft Office suite, typing and formatting information is even easier than it was before. Not only do the screens look and act similar in the Microsoft Office suite of programs, but the basics for typing and formatting information across the applications also are similar. After you learn one application, learning the next one is easier. So many of the functions work the same way throughout the applications that your learning curve should be small. For example, if you want to enhance text with bold, italic, or underline characteristics, you choose the same command using the menu, the buttons on the toolbars, or the keyboard shortcuts regardless of which application you are using.

In this chapter, you learn to

- Type, edit, and select text

- Undo mistakes

- Move around the document

- Format documents using the toolbars, keyboard shortcuts, and menus

- Check spelling and use AutoCorrect

- Find and replace text

Typing and Editing

Typing and editing within different Windows applications is similar. When you're working in an application, you are in one of three modes: text, cell, or object. In text mode, a vertical blinking line called the insertion point is visible. As you type, the insertion point moves to the right; when you come to the end of the line, and text automatically wraps to the next line. In cell mode, the cell is selected, and when you type whatever was in the cell is replaced. In object mode, you first need to select the object and then single- or double-click to edit the object. Each of the Microsoft Office applications can include any of these modes. The way you edit items differs depending on the mode. The following sections explain these three different modes in greater detail.

Working in Text Mode

▶ See "Editing Text in a Word Document," p. 176

▶ See "Editing Worksheet Data," p. 321

The normal Word screen is an example of *text mode*. When you come to the right margin, text automatically wraps to the next line. As you type, a blinking vertical line called the *cursor* or *insertion point* moves. When you move the mouse across an area in text mode, the mouse pointer becomes an I-beam as shown in figure 3.1. Click the I-beam mouse pointer to position the insertion point. As you type, the insertion point pushes existing text after the insertion point to the right. If you want to replace text, drag the I-beam mouse pointer to select the text to replace. When you begin typing, the new text replaces any selected text.

Fig. 3.1
To replace existing text, first select what you want to replace, and then type the new text.

I-beam

Selected text

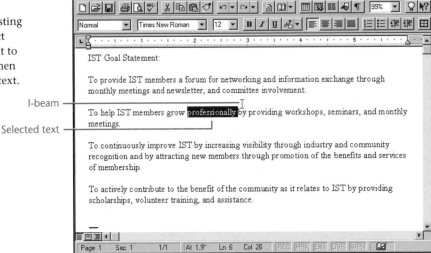

When you move the mouse pointer into a text box in a dialog box, the I-beam replaces the arrow, as shown in the File Name text box in the Save As dialog box (see fig. 3.2). Drag the mouse pointer across text in the text box to select the text, and then type the new entry. In this example, text was selected and the letters **IST Goal St** were typed. IST Goal St replaced the selected text.

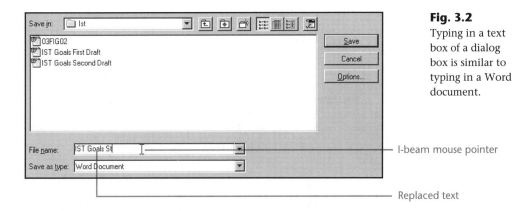

I-beam mouse pointer

Replaced text

Fig. 3.2
Typing in a text box of a dialog box is similar to typing in a Word document.

In Excel, the mouse pointer is normally a thick white plus sign as you move the mouse pointer across the screen. When the mouse pointer is on a menu or on a toolbar for any application, the pointer is an arrow. When your cursor enters the formula bar at the top of the screen, however, the mouse pointer changes to an I-beam and you can drag across to select text or click to position the insertion point (see fig. 3.3). You also can accomplish in-cell editing if you move the thick white plus sign to the cell and double-click. The mouse pointer changes to an I-beam while you are in the cell, and the blinking insertion point appears. This mode is called *edit mode* in Excel.

▶ See "Selecting Cells and Ranges," p. 309

In PowerPoint, when you move the mouse pointer across most text items, the mouse pointer is an I-beam. While you are in Outline view, you can click and drag on any text to select the text as if you were in a Word document. However, editing a slide works slightly differently. You cannot drag to select text within a text object (title, bullet item, or added text) until you click the object. When you click, you position the insertion point within the text and select the text object at the same time. When the text object is selected, a hatched outline appears around the object (see fig. 3.4). After this outline and insertion point appear, you can drag to select text and edit as necessary. If you use text boxes in other applications, you also need to first select the text object (the text box) and then edit the text as you do for PowerPoint.

▶ See "Entering and Editing Text," p. 593

I

Common Features

Fig. 3.3
When the mouse pointer is in the formula bar it changes to an I-beam mouse pointer.

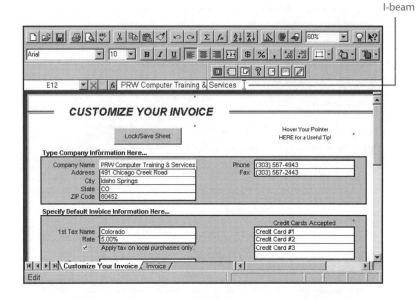

Fig. 3.4
You can edit text within a selected text object in PowerPoint.

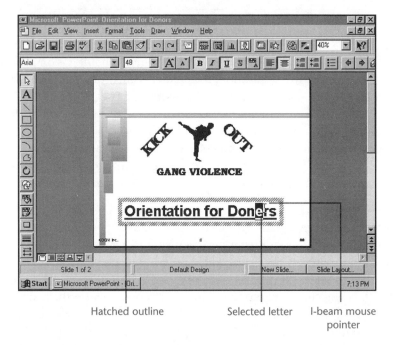

Hatched outline   Selected letter   I-beam mouse pointer

Working with Cells, Text Boxes, and Fields

▶ See "Defining Excel Terms," p. 301

Excel worksheets and Word tables are organized in rows and columns (see fig. 3.5 and fig. 3.6). The intersection of a row and column is called a *cell*. When you press Tab, you move to the next cell. If you press Shift+Tab, you move to the previous cell. When you move to a cell with Tab or Shift+Tab in Word, the text within the cell is selected as in figure 3.5. When you type, new text replaces the existing text. In Excel, when you press Tab or Shift+Tab, the text is not selected in a cell as in figure 3.6. Type the new entry for the cell and press Enter or Tab to replace the entry.

▶ See "Moving around in a Worksheet," p. 302

I

Common Features

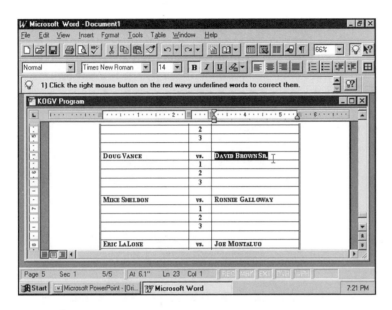

Fig. 3.5
Tables in Word use rows, columns, and cells.

▶ See "Working with Tables," p. 286

▶ See "Inserting a Word Table or Excel Worksheet," p. 599

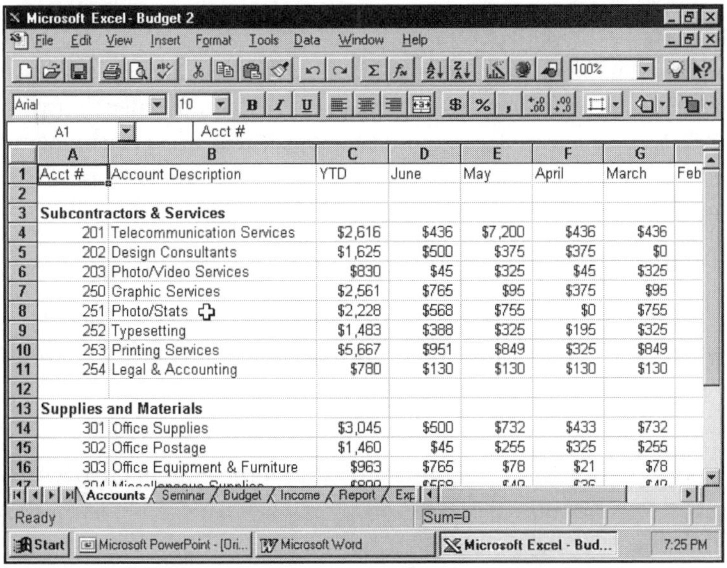

Fig. 3.6
Excel worksheets use rows, columns and cells.

Forms and dialog boxes work similarly to tables. In a dialog box, if you press Tab or Shift+Tab until you come to a text box, the current item in the text box is selected. As soon as you type the first character, the old entry is erased. Word data-entry forms, Excel data forms, and the upper part of a Mail message contain fields for entering or editing information (see fig. 3.7). Fields are hidden codes you insert into a document to perform a function. In Word, fields are related to word functions for document information and mail merge functions. In Excel, fields are oriented towards number functions. In both Word and Excel, a field can contain data and not a function or formula. When you press Tab or Shift+Tab to move to a field, the entry within a field is selected. When you type, the old entry is replaced with the new entry. If you want to edit an entry rather than replace it, click the I-beam mouse pointer to position the insertion point.

Fig. 3.7
The Excel data-entry form (shown here) and the Word data-entry form have fields for data input. Simply move to the field you want to edit, and type the new information.

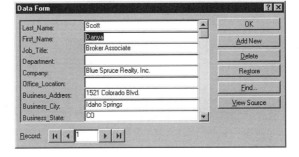

Working with Objects

In some cases, you may have objects attached to your document. Objects can include charts, pictures, clip art, WordArt, and other documents. If you click an object, an outline appears around the object with small square handles at each corner and in the middle of each line. You can perform any of the following actions on an object:

▶ See "Creating and Printing Excel Charts," p. 481

■ To delete the object, press Delete.

▶ See "Inserting Microsoft Visual Objects," p. 511

■ To move the object, move the mouse pointer onto the object (or on the border surrounding the object) until the pointer changes to a white arrow. Drag the object to the new position on the document.

▶ See "Selecting and Grouping Objects," p. 608

■ To change the size, stretch, or flatten the object, move the mouse pointer on top of one of the handles until the pointer changes to a small, black double arrow (see fig. 3.8). Drag the double arrow to make the object smaller or larger.

■ To edit the object, you can double-click the object. One of two things happens: you enter the program that created the object, or the menu and toolbar of your current program change to the menu and toolbar of the source object. Figure 3.9 shows an example of an Excel worksheet object within a Word document.

▶ See "Editing an Embedded Object," p. 714

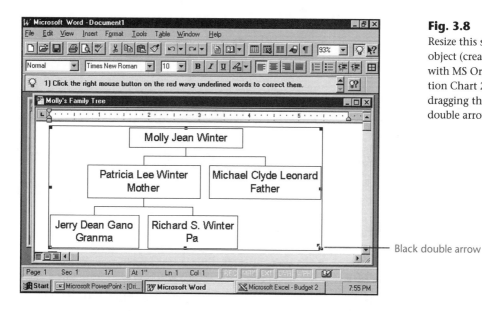

Black double arrow

Fig. 3.8
Resize this selected object (created with MS Organiza- tion Chart 2.0) by dragging the black double arrow.

Common Features

Note

MS Organization Chart 2.0 (shown in fig. 3.8) is provided as an applet (small pro- gram) with PowerPoint. Even if you don't use PowerPoint, you can use MS Organiza- tion Chart to create organization charts within your documents. If you don't have MS Organization Chart 2.0 available, you may not have performed a complete installa- tion of Microsoft Office.

Most products work by clicking the object once to display the binding box. In PowerPoint, if you click a text object once, you get a cross-hatched outline around the text that enables you to select text within the box. Move the mouse pointer to the cross-hatched outline and click a second time to display the binding box.

Fig. 3.9
When you insert an Excel work-sheet into Word, you can select the object and then double-click to edit the worksheet in Excel.

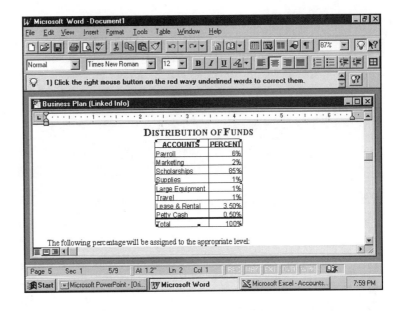

Selecting Text

▶ See "Selecting Text," p. 256

▶ See "Selecting Cells and Ranges," p. 309

▶ See "Selecting Cells, Rows, and Columns," p. 470

As mentioned in the preceding section, you select an object by clicking it. However, you have much more flexibility when you select text rather than the object. You can edit, change the appearance, copy, or move text by first selecting the text and then performing the procedure to make the change. Some text selection techniques are similar in all applications. For example, you can always drag across a text area with the I-beam mouse pointer to se-lect text. You also can hold down the Shift key and use your direction keys to expand the selection or click the mouse at the end of the selection. Some applications have different text selection techniques, as shown in table 3.1. For example, to select a row in Word and Excel, position the mouse pointer before the row and click. In Word, the mouse pointer changes to a right-pointing arrow; in Excel the pointer is a white plus sign.

Table 3.1	**Text Selection Techniques Using the Mouse**		
Application	**Selection Area**	**Mouse Pointer Appearance**	**Perform This Function**
All	Text	I-beam	Drag
All	Word	I-beam	Double-click word

Application	Selection Area	Mouse Pointer Appearance	Perform This Function
Word	Line(s)	White arrow	Click or drag before text in left margin
Excel	Row(s)	White plus sign	Click or drag on row selector(s) before text
Word	Table column(s)	Black down arrow	Click or drag above first row of table
Excel	Column(s)	White plus sign	Click or drag on column letter(s) in worksheet frame
Word	Entire document	White arrow	Hold down Ctrl and click in left margin
Excel	Entire worksheet	White plus sign	Click Select All button above row numbers and to the left of column letters

Common Features

Using Undo

Keep in mind that after you select text, anything you type will replace the selected text. If you replace text by mistake, you can undo your last action by immediately choosing Edit, Undo or pressing Ctrl+Z.

Word has a multiple-level undo feature that enables you to undo more than just the last procedure. To use Word's undo feature, click the Undo button to undo the last procedure. Click the drop-down arrow portion of the button to show a list of procedures, and select the procedure you want to undo, as shown in figure 3.10.

Word also has a Redo button that enables you to redo any of the actions you have undone. The Redo button reverses an undo. If you want to undo your undo, use redo. The Redo button also has a drop-down arrow that shows a list of procedures you can redo.

Moving around the Document

To move throughout the document, you can use the mouse and the keyboard. Moving around a document is similar in each application. To position the insertion point or cell pointer, click a visible area on-screen.

▶ See "Moving around in a Worksheet," p. 302

Fig. 3.10

You can reverse typing and formatting mistakes in Word using the Undo and Redo buttons.

Drop-down arrows

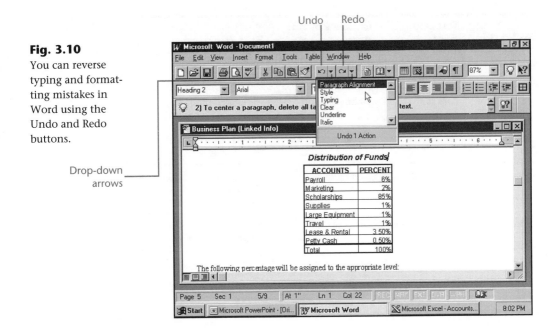

Using Scroll Bars

▶ See "Moving through a Presentation," p. 581

Scroll bars enable you to scroll the view of the document. They are located on the right side and the bottom of the workspace. To use the scroll bars, you can point to a scroll arrow or the scroll bar and then click the left mouse button. Or you can drag the scroll box. Be careful when using the scroll bar, however; the cursor remains in the location before the scroll took place and may not be visible on-screen. You may start typing in the wrong place. To avoid typing in the wrong place, make sure that the cursor is visible by clicking where you want to begin typing.

The scroll bars are divided into three parts: the scroll arrows, the scroll box, and the scroll bar (see fig. 3.11). Use each part as follows:

- *Down or up scroll arrow.* Click an arrow to move one line at a time. This technique is true except in PowerPoint. Although clicking an arrow moves just one line in Outline view, clicking a scroll arrow in slide view moves one slide at a time.

- *Vertical scroll box.* Drag the scroll box in the scroll bar. When you drag the box all the way to the bottom, you are at the bottom of the document, no matter how many pages the document has.

- *Vertical scroll bar.* Click between the scroll box and a scroll arrow to move one full screen at a time.

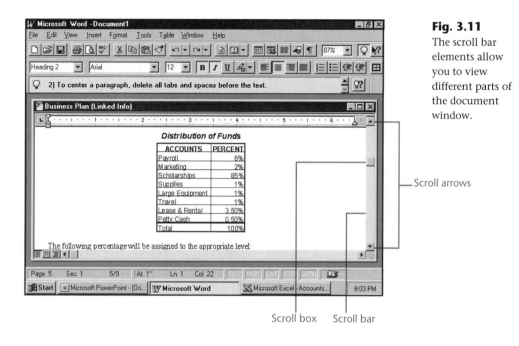

Fig. 3.11
The scroll bar
elements allow
you to view
different parts of
the document
window.

Scroll arrows

Scroll box   Scroll bar

- *Horizontal scroll bar.* Drag the box in the scroll bar, click an arrow, or click in the scroll bar to move left and right on wide documents.

- *Double arrows.* In Word Page Layout view and PowerPoint Slide view, you have two double arrows at the bottom of the vertical scroll bar. Click the double arrows to move down or up a page or slide at a time.

Using Direction Keys

The direction keys on the keyboard work similarly in all Office applications, but the result may be different depending on the mode you are in. Direction keys do the following:

- Left- and right-arrow keys move the insertion point one character to the left or right in text mode, or one column to the left or right in cell mode.

- Up- and down-arrow keys move the insertion point one line or row up or down.

- Page Up and Page Down keys move the insertion point one full screen up or down.

- Ctrl+Home moves the insertion point to the top of the document.

- Ctrl+End moves the insertion point to the bottom of the document. In Excel, this key combination moves to the last cell containing data.

- Home moves the insertion point to the beginning of the line in Word. In Excel, Home moves the active cell pointer to the first column in cell mode or the insertion point to the beginning of an entry in text mode.

- End moves the insertion point to the end of the line in Word or end of an entry in Excel text mode. End also works differently in Excel. You press End followed by an arrow key on the keyboard to move to the end of a continuous range of cells.

- Ctrl+↑ and Ctrl+↓ in text mode move the insertion point one paragraph at a time.

- Ctrl+→ and Ctrl+ ← in text mode move the insertion point one word at a time.

- Ctrl+G is the Go To key. Press Ctrl+G in Word and then type the page number to go to. Press Ctrl+G in Excel and type the cell reference.

Copying and Moving Data

▶ See "Copying Worksheet Data," p. 324

▶ See "Moving and Copying Objects," p. 611

The procedure for copying and moving is generally the same for all Office applications. The procedure works for copying information from one area of a document to a different place on the document, or for copying information from one document to a different document. This same procedure also works for copying information from a document in one application (such as Excel) to a document in another application (such as Word). The item that you are copying can be text, numbers, a chart, a picture, or any other Windows object.

Using the Clipboard

▶ See "Copying Text between Word Documents," p. 670

The Clipboard is a Windows accessory that you use for copying and moving information in all Office applications. The Clipboard is a temporary storage area that holds a copy of the item when you cut or copy. When you cut, the item is removed from the source application and placed into the Clipboard. When you copy, the item remains in the source application and a copy is placed into the Clipboard. When you paste, a copy of the item you cut or copied goes from the Clipboard into the active application. Because all Windows applications share the Clipboard, you can easily copy information between applications.

Using Cut, Copy, and Paste

The procedure for copying or moving is as follows:

1. Select the item you want to copy or move. If the item is text, drag the I-beam mouse pointer or use some other shortcut. If the item is a picture, chart, or object created in another application, click the object to show the binding box.

2. Do one of the following:

   ■ To move the selected item, choose <u>E</u>dit, Cu<u>t</u>, or press Ctrl+X.

   ■ To copy the selected item, choose <u>E</u>dit, <u>C</u>opy, or press Ctrl+C.

3. Use the scroll bars and direction keys to position the cursor in the document.

4. Choose <u>E</u>dit, <u>P</u>aste, or press Crtl+V.

All Office applications have the <u>E</u>dit menu from which you can choose Cu<u>t</u>, <u>C</u>opy, or <u>P</u>aste. In some minor cases, you may not be able to use the menu (as in editing within a field such as To or Cc in Mail). In these cases, you can use the keyboard shortcuts.

◀ See "Moving between Programs," p. 36

Troubleshooting

I thought I used the Copy command, but when I tried to paste, something else appeared.

Click the Undo button immediately or choose <u>E</u>dit, <u>U</u>ndo to remove any unwanted copy. Select whatever you want to copy again and use <u>E</u>dit, <u>C</u>opy. Then try pasting again.

Moving with Drag-and-Drop

Microsoft Word, Excel, and PowerPoint have a capability that makes moving easier than using the Cut and Paste commands. This feature is called *drag-and-drop*. You first select the text or cells to move and then drag the selection to the new location. This new location may be in the same document, in a different document, or in a different application.

Note

To go to another open application to drag-and-drop the selection, click the application's button on the taskbar. To go to another open document, choose <u>W</u>indow from the menu bar and select the open document.

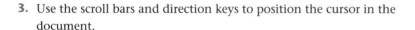

The drag-and-drop mouse pointer changes to a left-pointing arrow when you position the mouse pointer in the selected text (the normal mouse pointer is right-pointing). In Word and PowerPoint, you position the mouse pointer anywhere within the selected area. In Excel, you point to the outline surrounding the selected cells. When you click and drag the mouse in Word and PowerPoint, two additional shapes are added to the left-pointing mouse pointer. A small rectangle appears under the mouse pointer, and a dashed vertical line (*ghost cursor*) appears where the new text will be inserted when you release the mouse button. In Excel, a gray outline appears where the new text will appear when you release the mouse button.

Note

Right-click in the selected area to open the shortcut menu to cut or copy. To use the shortcut menu to paste, right-click in the document where you want to paste. Most Office applications have these commands on the shortcut menu.

The drag-and-drop feature is limited in PowerPoint. You can move text only from one area of the current text object to another area of the same text object on the slide. In Excel, you can drag-and-drop items from one area of a worksheet to another area of the same worksheet. You can even drag the selection into a document in an open Word or PowerPoint window. However, you cannot drag the selection between two open documents in the same Excel program window.

Figure 3.12 shows the drag-and-drop feature between Excel and Word. Excel and Word were tiled using the shortcut menu on the taskbar. In Word, you can drag the selection to another place on the same document, to another open document window within the Word program window, or to an Excel worksheet or PowerPoint slide.

Note

If you want to copy rather than move the selected item, hold down the Ctrl key, then begin to drag. The mouse pointer adds a small plus sign. To complete the copy, first release the mouse button and then release the Ctrl key.

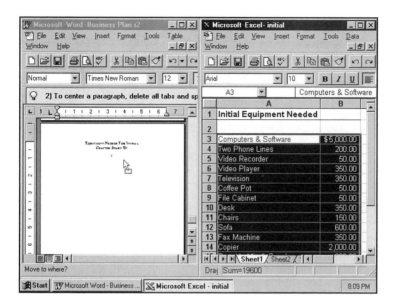

Fig. 3.12
The status bar in
each application
provides help
about the task you
are performing.
This is an example
of moving infor-
mation from Excel
to Word.

Common Features

Troubleshooting

*I forgot to hold down the Ctrl key when I tried to copy an object. Now my original object
is out of place.*

◀ See "Shortcut
Menus," p. 55

The operation of the Ctrl key is essential. If you need to restore the source application, return to the source application and click the Undo button or choose Edit,
Undo.

*When I try to drag from an Excel window to a Word window, I keep deselecting my range
in Excel.*

When you want to drag a range from Excel, make sure you point to the edge of the
selected range until the mouse pointer changes to a white arrow, then click and
drag.

Formatting Documents

Formatting text involves changing the font (typeface), font size, font characteristics (such as bold, italic, and underline), and alignment of text. The general procedure to format text is the same in the different Office applications.
First you select the text to format and then you do the formatting. As with

▶ See "Format-
ting Text,"
p. 190

other procedures, you can use buttons on toolbars, menu items, shortcut menus, and keyboard shortcuts.

Using Toolbars and Keyboard Shortcuts To Format

▶ See "Changing Fonts in Word," p. 191

▶ See "Enhancing Text," p. 627

Formatting is usually quicker when you use buttons on the toolbar or keyboard shortcuts than it is when you use the menu. To format text, select the text you want to format, or position the insertion point where you want to begin typing formatted text. Then choose a toolbar button or press a keyboard combination (see table 3.2).

Table 3.2   Formatting Buttons and Keyboard Shortcuts

Command	Button	Program*	Keyboard	Program*
Bold	**B**	W, E, P	Ctrl+B	W, E, P
Italic	*I*	W, E, P	Ctrl+I	W, E, P
Underline	U	W, E, P	Ctrl+U	W, E, P
Align Left		W, E, P	Ctrl+L	W, P
Center		W, E, P	Ctrl+E	W, P
Align Right		W, E	Ctrl+R	W, P
Justify		W	Ctrl+J	W, P
Font		W, E, P		
Font Size		W, E, P		

In the Program columns, W, E, and P represent Word, Excel, and PowerPoint.

Format Painter allows you to copy the formatting of one section to one or more sections in your document. To use Format Painter, see the section "Copying the Format" later in this chapter.

▶ See "Using AutoFormat," p. 264

Using Menus To Format

The formatting toolbars give you the most-used choices for formatting. If you want more complete choices, use the menu bar. Word, Excel, and PowerPoint have Format menus. Word and PowerPoint display different formatting categories on the Format menu itself. Excel displays the formatting categories on tabs of the Format Cells dialog box, as shown in figure 3.13. Table 3.3 summarizes some of the formatting possible on the Format menus of Word and PowerPoint, and the Format Cells dialog box of Excel. As with the toolbar and shortcut keys, you first need to select the text to format. When you finish with a dialog box, choose OK.

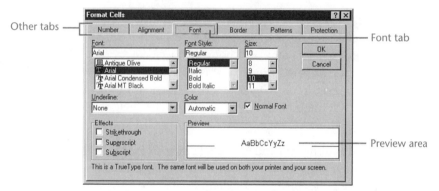

Fig. 3.13
This Excel dialog box enables you to change many characteristics of the font.

Table 3.3   Formatting Commands

Format	Word	PowerPoint	Excel
Font, Font size, Font color, Underline	Font	Font	Font
Border (lines)	Borders and Shading	Colors and Lines	Border
Shading (patterns)	Borders and Shading	Colors and Lines	Patterns
Alignment	Paragraph	Alignment	Alignment
Line spacing	Paragraph	Line Spacing	Format, Rows, Height

◀ See "Format-
ting Toolbars,"
p. 47

Tip
When you are
formatting docu-
ments in Word,
you may see the
results of your
changes more
easily if you view
the document in
Page Layout view.

Troubleshooting

I was changing formatting and accidentally used the wrong format.

Immediately choose Undo. If Undo doesn't work (meaning you have performed another procedure since your accidental formatting), you can sometimes click the same button to undo the format or another button to change the format. For example, click the Bold button to bold or unbold. You also can click Align Left to change from any other alignment.

I just formatted some text with the Format, Font command, and I want to use the same formatting for text on the next page of my document.

Select the text to be formatted, and then choose Edit, Repeat or press Ctrl+Y. Word, Excel, and PowerPoint repeat the last formatting command you used.

Changing Fonts

Font is the typeface of the text. For example, a typeface can be Times New Roman or Helvetica. The font you choose helps create an impression or set the mood for the document. Suppose that you want to create an informal flyer for a sale. You can use a light italic font, such as Brush, Cooper, or Univers italic. A formal, sophisticated font could be Shelley, Old English, or Caslon Openface.

First select the existing text you want to change, or move the insertion point to the position you want the new font to begin. Then select the font you want to use from the formatting toolbar's Font drop-down list, shown in figure 3.14.

Changing Font Size

▶ See "Using
Wizards,"
p. 162

Font size is measured in *points*. Points and *picas* are typesetting measurements used for measuring spacing, line thickness, and so on. There are 12 points to a pica and 6 picas to an inch; therefore, there are 72 points to an inch.

Font Size drop-down list

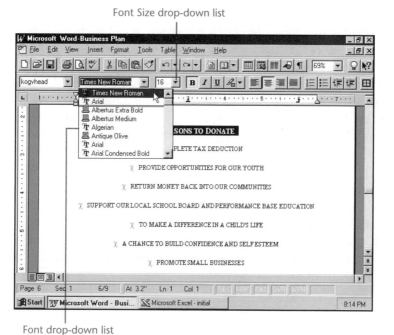

Fig. 3.14
Word lists the
most recently used
fonts at the top of
the list so you can
find them quickly.
The rest of the
available fonts are
listed in alphabeti-
cal order.

Common Features

Font drop-down list

If you have not changed the default font in Word, all text you enter in a new
document is 10-point Times New Roman. In an Excel worksheet the default
font is 10-point Arial. In a PowerPoint presentation the default font is 24-
point Times New Roman. You can, of course, change the type size. Use the
drop-down Font Size list in the formatting toolbar to select the size you want
(refer to fig. 3.14).

The font sizes available in the Font Size drop-down list depend on your
printer. If you know that your printer can print a size not listed in the box—
126-point, for example—type the number in the Font Size text box and press
Enter.

Troubleshooting

*I have changed the font, font size, font style, and alignment of the selected text, and now
I want to change the text back to its original formatting.*

Undo the formatting using the Undo drop-down list in the standard toolbar.

Changing Column Width

► See "Formatting with Styles," p. 259

Changing the column width of tables in Word, spreadsheets in Excel, or columns in Schedule+ is essentially the same. You move above the workspace to the column marker until the mouse pointer changes to a double black arrow and then drag the mouse to the width you want. In Word, the area you change is called the ruler, and the insertion point must be inside the table. In Excel, the area you change is called the column headings, and the mouse pointer is between the column letters. In Schedule+, this area is also called the column headings.

Setting Margins

► See "Changing Column Width and Row Height," p. 349

You can change the margins of your document from the default settings to any margin you want. Word and Excel both use 1-inch top and bottom margins. Word uses 1 1/4-inch left and right margins, and Excel uses 3/4-inch left and right margins. You can set the margins using the Page Setup dialog box, shown in figure 3.15.

Margins tab

Fig. 3.15
You can change margins using the Page Setup dialog box in Word and Excel.

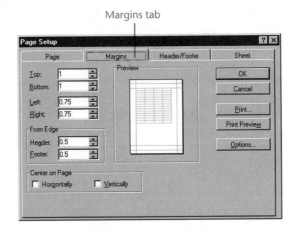

► See "Working with Large Documents," p. 251

To change the margins of your document, follow these steps:

1. Choose File, Page Setup. The Page Setup dialog box appears.

2. Select the Margins tab.

3. Enter measurements in the Top, Bottom, Left, and Right boxes.

4. Choose OK to close the dialog box.

> **Note**
>
> When you set margins in Word, those measurements apply to all pages in the document, unless you divide your document into sections.

Copying the Format with Format Painter

Microsoft Office makes formatting text easy with the Format Painter feature, which enables you to format an entire document quickly.

When you format text such as a heading, complicated tabs, or columns, and you need to format other text in the document the same way, you can save time and energy by copying the formatting of the original text. Suppose that you formatted a heading as 18-point Univers, bold and italic, center-aligned, with five points spacing below the head. Rather than select and format each head in your document separately, you can use the Format Painter to copy the format to another head.

First, select the formatted text—the text with the format you want to copy— then click the Format Painter button in the standard toolbar. The pointer changes to a paintbrush and I-beam (see fig. 3.16). Select the text to be formatted, and that text automatically changes to the copied text format.

Tip
To copy the format to more than one location in your document, double-click the Format Painter button. Format Painter keeps the format for you to copy over and over. Click Format Painter once to turn it off.

Format Painter button

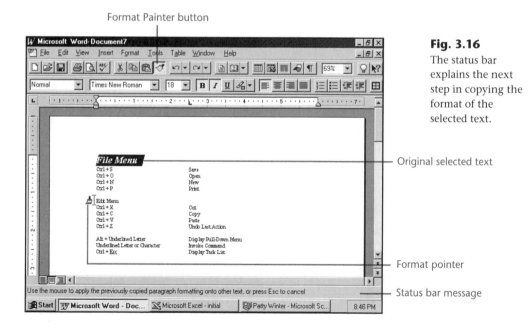

Fig. 3.16
The status bar explains the next step in copying the format of the selected text.

Original selected text

Format pointer

Status bar message

> **Troubleshooting**
>
> *How do I get the columns on all the sheets in my Excel workbook to look like the columns on my first sheet?*
>
> Select the column headings, click the Format Painter button, switch to the sheet you want to apply your formatting to, and click and drag across the column headings to copy the format.

Using Automatic Formatting

▶ See "Using Wizards," p. 162

Formatting can be fun, but you can spend a lot of time and still not get a professional look for your effort. The Microsoft Office suite of applications can give you choices of a series of styles that automatically format the document for you. These formats automatically add fonts, shading, colors, and borders for you. If you want to maintain a consistent image with your documents, using the pre-defined formats is worth your while.

▶ See "Creating a Presentation Using a Wizard," p. 578

To apply automatic formatting to your document, do the following:

- For a Word document, choose F<u>o</u>rmat, AutoFormat. In the AutoFormat dialog box, choose OK. After Word formats the document, you can accept or reject the changes or choose the <u>S</u>tyle Gallery command button and select from styles in the <u>T</u>emplates list box. An example of the format is shown in the <u>P</u>review area (see fig. 3.17).

- For Excel, position the cell pointer within the area to format and choose F<u>o</u>rmat, AutoFormat. Choose from a list of examples in the <u>T</u>able Format list box (see fig. 3.18).

- For PowerPoint, choose F<u>o</u>rmat, Apply Design Te<u>m</u>plate and select from the Look <u>I</u>n list box of file templates in one of the template folders (see fig. 3.19).

You also can use professionally designed formats through Wizards. Refer to Chapter 5, "Using Help."

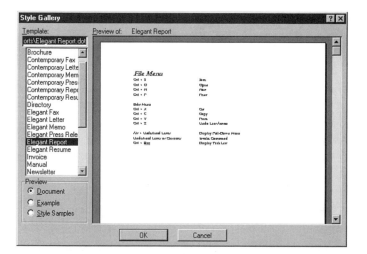

Fig. 3.17
Click the Style Gallery button to change the automatic formatting that Word created for you.

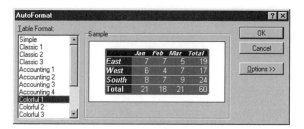

Fig. 3.18
Choose from a list of table formats provided by Excel in the AutoFormat dialog box.

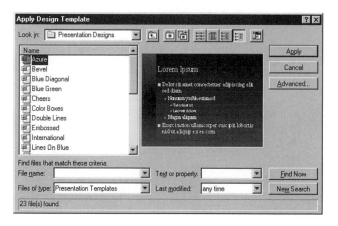

Fig. 3.19
On PowerPoint's Apply Design Template, choose the template that has the formatting features you want to apply to your presentation.

Checking Spelling

Microsoft offers the Spelling command in Word, Excel, and PowerPoint. Most often you think to check spelling in a word processing document, but now you can check spelling in documents that are worksheets and presentations. The Tools, Spelling command looks for words that are not in the dictionary. In addition, the Spelling command alerts you to punctuation and capitalization problems as well as to repeated words. You can choose to change the spelling or ignore the problem; you even can add the word to the dictionary for later use.

Using the Spelling Command

The Spelling command reads text and notifies you when it finds a word that is not in its main dictionary or your custom dictionary. The Spelling dialog box shows you the word in question, suggests a replacement word, and displays a list of other words that are similar in spelling as possible replacements.

To solve a spelling problem, you can use a variety of options. You can change the word, ignore the word, add the word to the dictionary, and so on. This section describes each of these options.

To use the Spelling command in Word, Excel, or PowerPoint, choose Tools, Spelling. The Spelling dialog box appears (see fig. 3.20).

Fig. 3.20
Select a word in the Suggestions box or type the correct word in the Change To text box to correct the mistake in the text.

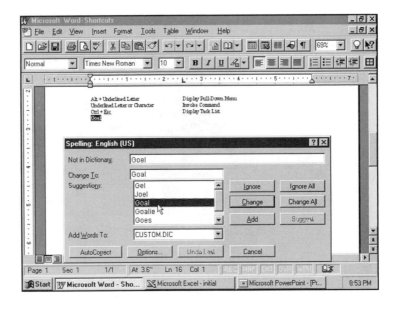

Table 3.4 describes each option in the Spelling dialog box and which application supports the options.

Table 3.4	Spelling Options			
Option	**W**	**E**	**P**	**Description**
Not in Dictionary	X	X	X	Displays the word in question.
Change To	X	X	X	Suggests an alternative spelling; you can enter your own new spelling in this text box.
Delete	X	X	X	If the Change To text box is empty, the Change button becomes Delete, which deletes the word.
Delete All	X	X	X	If the Change To text box is empty, the Change All button becomes Delete All, which deletes all occurrences of the word in the document.
Suggestions	X	X	X	Select a word in the Suggestions list box to replace the misspelled word.
Ignore	X	X	X	Skips this occurrence of this word.
Resume/Start	X		X	The Ignore button changes to Resume or Start when you click outside the Spelling dialog box to edit your document. The dialog box remains on-screen; choose the Resume or Start button to resume the spelling check.
Ignore All	X	X	X	Skips all occurrences of this word in the document.
Change	X	X	X	Substitutes the selected or entered word for the misspelled word.
Change All	X	X	X	Substitutes the selected or entered word for all occurrences of this word in the document.
Add	X	X	X	Updates the dictionary to include a word that you often type. The added word must appear in the Not in Dictionary text box.
Suggest	X	X	X	If the Always Suggest option in the Options dialog box is deactivated, choose Suggest to list suggestions for correcting the misspelled word.

Tip

You also can start the Spelling Checker by clicking the Spelling button in the standard toolbar or by pressing F7.

Common Features

(continues)

Table 3.4 Continued				
Option	**W**	**E**	**P**	**Description**
Add Words To	X	X	X	If you installed more than one dictionary, select the dictionary to which you want to add from the drop-down list.
AutoCorrect	X	X		Adds frequently misspelled words to the AutoCorrect list. See the "Letting AutoCorrect Do Your Spelling for You" section later in this chapter for more information.
Options	X	X		Enables you to choose default settings or customize the Spelling Checker.
Undo Last	X	X		Choose Undo Last to change your mind about the last spelling change.
Close/Cancel	X	X	X	Cancel ends the spelling check and cancels any changes; Close ends the spelling check and saves any changes. The Cancel button changes to Close after you make a change in the document.
Help (? in top right corner of dialog box)	X	X	X	Choose this button for detailed help on the Spelling dialog box options.

Editing the Document without Leaving Spelling

If you find you need to edit your document after you have started the spelling check, follow these steps:

1. Click in your document to make the document window active.

   Notice the Ignore button in the Spelling dialog box changes to Resume in Word and Start in PowerPoint.

2. Make the changes needed in the document.

3. Click the Resume or Start button to continue the spell check procedure.

Using Dictionaries

When you use the Spelling command, all three applications look in a default dictionary named CUSTOM.DIC. However, you can create your own custom dictionaries.

Adding Words to a Dictionary

The CUSTOM.DIC dictionary, as well as any other dictionary you create, is stored in either the Program Files\Common Files\Proof folder or the WINDOWS\MSAPPS\PROOF folder normally on your hard drive. If you click the Add button in the Spelling dialog box, any new words you add will automatically become part of the CUSTOM.DIC file. If you add a word in Excel or Word, both of those programs will recognize the added word. PowerPoint, on the other hand, will not recognize the added word until you close Word or Excel and PowerPoint and then open PowerPoint again.

Creating Additional Dictionaries

If you have specific jargon associated with your work, you may choose to create a separate dictionary. You then could share this dictionary with your co-workers.

When you are in Word you can create the new dictionary file while you are using Spelling. When the Spelling command stops at a word that is spelled correctly and you want to add it to a new custom dictionary, do the following:

1. Click the Options command button.

2. Click the Custom Dictionaries command button.

3. Click the New command button.

4. Type the name of the new dictionary and choose the Save command button.

5. Click OK twice to get back to the Spelling dialog box.

6. Select the new dictionary in the Add Words To list box.

7. Click the Add command button to add the word to the new dictionary.

In Excel you can also create the new dictionary file while you are using Spelling. Before you add any words, change the name of the file in the Add Words To text box in the Spelling dialog box. If the dictionary file does not exist, you are prompted to create it. Choose Yes to create the new dictionary (see fig. 3.21).

Fig. 3.21
Excel's Spelling command enables you to create new dictionaries that Word can access.

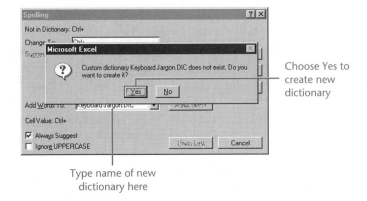

Choose Yes to create new dictionary

Type name of new dictionary here

When you use the Spelling command, both Word and Excel check all the dictionaries available. You may be checking spelling in your Word or Excel document and come across a word that you need to add to one of the custom dictionaries. To select a custom dictionary, click the arrow in the Add Words To list box and then click the dictionary you want to use.

Turning Dictionaries On and Off

You may need to use a dictionary you have already created for specific company-wide or industry-wide jargon. If you are in Word and the dictionary you want to use is not listed, follow these steps:

1. Click the Options button in the Spelling dialog box.

2. Click the Custom Dictionaries button in the Options dialog box.

3. Select the dictionary file name in the Custom Dictionaries list box. (A check mark means the dictionary is on.)

4. Choose OK in the Custom Dictionaries dialog box.

5. Choose OK in the Options dialog box.

6. Click the arrow in the Add Words To list box and select the dictionary you want to use from the list.

Letting AutoCorrect Do Your Spelling for You

Using AutoCorrect, you can instruct Word, Excel, or PowerPoint to correct spelling mistakes as you make them. If, for example, you often type *teh* rather than *the*, AutoCorrect can fix the error immediately after you make it.

The AutoCorrect feature automatically corrects spelling mistakes and formatting errors, or replaces characters you enter with specific words or phrases. Using this feature saves you time. Suppose that you consistently need to type *Kick Out Gang Violence, Inc.;* rather than typing it out each time, you can add a shortcut *kogv* to your AutoCorrect list and have Word, Excel, or PowerPoint type the name for you. You can enter common mistakes or shortcuts into AutoCorrect, and the next time you make the mistake or type the shortcut, Word, Excel, or PowerPoint corrects it automatically.

Caution

If PowerPoint does not pick up your new AutoCorrect entries, exit out of PowerPoint and Word or Excel, and then open PowerPoint again.

Adding Words as You Check Spelling

To add words to AutoCorrect while you are checking spelling in Word or Excel, make sure the incorrect word is listed in the Not in Dictionary box and the correct word is listed in the Change To box. Then choose the AutoCorrect button rather than the Change or Change All button in the Spelling dialog box.

Adding Words through the Tools Menu

To set options and make entries for AutoCorrect, choose the Tools, AutoCorrect command. Figure 3.22 shows the AutoCorrect dialog box with a new entry for Word and Excel.

The AutoCorrect dialog box in Word lists five options including converting quote marks and correcting capitalization problems. You can choose to turn these options on or off. The Excel dialog box does not give you the Quotes or Sentence options. The Replace and With text boxes enable you to enter your own items, and the list at the bottom of the AutoCorrect dialog box displays Word and Excel's default list plus any items you add. You can add or delete items at any time.

Fig. 3.22
You can add shortcuts to the AutoCorrect entry list. For example, enter two or three letters to represent a name or company name that you often type.

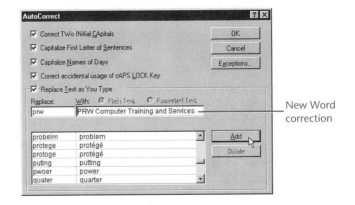

New Word correction

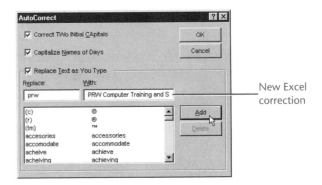

New Excel correction

To use the AutoCorrect feature, follow these steps:

1. Choose Tools, AutoCorrect. The AutoCorrect dialog box appears.

2. Select the options you want to use.

3. If you enter items in the Replace and With text boxes, click Add to add items to the list. To remove an entry from the list, select the item in the list box and then click Delete.

4. Choose OK to close the dialog box.

Troubleshooting

I have a lot of words that contain numbers, such as measurements, in my document, and I want Word to ignore those words.

Choose Tools, Options, and select the Spelling tab. In the Ignore area, choose Words with Numbers. Choose OK to close the dialog box.

I want to edit some of the words in a custom dictionary.

Choose Tools, Options, and select the Spelling tab. In the Custom Dictionaries area, select the dictionary you want to modify and then click the Edit button.

Finding and Replacing Text

Microsoft provides the capability to find and (optionally) replace specific text in your documents, worksheets, or presentations. For example, you can search for all occurrences of the value 1995 and replace it with **1996**.

Using the Find Command

You can search the entire document, workbook, or presentation, or you can search only a selected area. To search the entire document or presentation, move the insertion point to the top. To search the entire workbook, select a single cell. To search a specified area or range, select the area or range you want to search. Then follow these steps:

1. Choose Edit, Find; or press Ctrl+F. The Find dialog box appears (see fig. 3.23).

Fig. 3.23

The Find command enables you to locate specific text in your documents, worksheets, or presentations.

2. In the Find What text box, type the data you want to find. Then specify the search options, described in table 3.5.

3. Click Find Next to begin the search. When the application locates the characters, click Find Next to find the next occurrence, or click Replace to access the Replace dialog box (this option is discussed in the next section).

4. Choose Close to end the search and close the dialog box.

Note

In Excel, if you're not sure of the specific string you are looking for, you can specify wild-card characters in the search string to locate data that contains some or all of the characters. You can use an asterisk (*) to search for any group of characters and a question mark (?) to search for any single character. In Word you can use the same technique if you also select the Use Pattern <u>M</u>atching option on the dialog box.

Table 3.5   Find and Replace Options

Options	W*	E*	P*	Action
Search	X	X	X	Word and PowerPoint— specify whether to search the entire document from the insertion point or only up or down. Excel—specify whether to search across rows or down columns.
Look In		X		Select the location of the data: cell formulas, cell values, or cell notes.
Find Entire Cells Only		X		Searches for an exact match of the characters you specified. This option does not find partial occurrences.
Match Case	X	X	X	Finds only characters that match the case of the characters you specified.
Find Whole Words Only	X		X	Finds whole words, not words that are part of another word.
Use Pattern Matching	X			Select to use special search operators such as ? or * in a string.
Sounds Like	X			Finds words that sound like the specified word but are spelled differently.
Find Next	X	X	X	Finds the next occurrence of the search string.
Close or Cancel	X	X	X	Ends the search and returns to the document.

Options	W*	E*	P*	Action
Replace	X	X	X	If the Replace dialog box is not open, this changes the Find dialog box to the Replace dialog box. Then this command replaces this specific occurrence of the Find What characters with the characters in the Replace With text box.
Replace All	X	X	X	Replaces all occurrences of the characters with those specified in the Replace With text box.

W, E, P columns are for the Word, Excel, and PowerPoint applications.

Using the Replace Command

The Replace command (Ctrl+H) is similar to the Find command in that it enables you to locate specific characters in your document (Word, Excel, or PowerPoint). The Replace command then enables you to replace the characters with new data.

To replace data, follow these steps:

1. To search the entire document, move the insertion point anywhere in the document or select a single cell. To search a specified area or range, select the area or range you want to search.

2. Choose Edit, Replace. The Replace dialog box appears (see fig. 3.24).

3. In the Find What text box, type the data you want to replace. In the Replace With text box, type the data with which you want to replace the current data.

4. Specify the replace options, described previously in table 3.5.

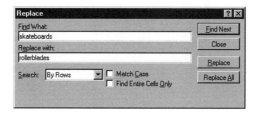

Fig. 3.24
You can choose Edit, Replace to replace formulas, text, or values.

> **Caution**
>
> Make sure that you activate Find Entire Cells <u>O</u>nly if you are replacing values or
> formulas. If this option is not selected, Excel replaces characters even if they
> are inside other strings. For example, replacing 20 with 30 also makes 2000
> become 3000.

Tip

If you make a
mistake when
replacing data,
close the dialog
box and choose
<u>E</u>dit, <u>U</u>ndo
(Ctrl+Z) immedi-
ately to reverse the
replacement.

5. Click <u>F</u>ind Next to begin the search. When the application locates the first occurrence of the characters, choose the appropriate replace option (refer to table 3.5).

6. Choose Close to close the dialog box.

> **Caution**
>
> When replacing data in your worksheet, use Replace <u>A</u>ll with care, because the results
> may not be what you expect. Whenever you use the <u>R</u>eplace command, it's a good
> idea to first locate the data you want to replace to make sure that the data is correct.

Chapter 4

Managing Files and Work Areas

by Rick Winter and Patty Winter

One of the most noticeable areas for change in Microsoft Office for Windows 95 is in file management—particularly when you save, open, and search for files. When you work with files, you have more flexibility, more features, and more options. As with anything new, these changes can be overwhelming at first. However, if you spend the time learning these file management features you will be rewarded with worthwhile improvements.

File management improvements include expanded file names, many changes in file dialog boxes, and the expansion of Summary Info to file properties. The Save and Open dialog boxes now have their own toolbars that provide viewing and other options. Instead of the old File Find option in the previous version of Microsoft Office, find features are now built directly into the file dialog boxes.

In this chapter, you learn to

- Open, save, and close documents

- Choose a location to save your file to

- Find a file by name, contents, or properties

- Attach identification information to a file and view other file properties

- Print documents

- Switch to different documents

Working with Files

◀ See "Opening a Document from Windows Explorer," p. 30

◀ See "Opening a Document from the Taskbar," p. 29

For most applications, the work you do on-screen is only in the computer's memory. If the power fails or some other accident happens, you may lose all or part of your work. The process of *saving* a file copies the information from memory to a file on disk (floppy disk or hard disk). You can manually save the file or set up the program to save the file automatically. When you *close* a file, you are removing the information from the computer's memory or from your screen. The program prompts you to save the file if you have made any changes since the last save or if you have not yet saved the file. *Opening* a file involves copying the information from a disk into memory. When you create a *new* file, a new document window opens.

Using File Dialog Boxes

In addition to using the Windows Explorer and the Desktop folders, you can manage files through Microsoft Office programs. When you open, save, or insert a file, a standard file dialog box appears. Table 4.1 shows commands that display a file dialog box. Many of the features on the file dialog box are the same whether you use Word, Excel, or PowerPoint, or whether you are opening, saving, or inserting. Figure 4.1 shows a standard Open dialog box with many of the common features. The toolbar helps you organize your files. The bottom section and Advanced command button help you find your files.

Table 4.2 shows a list of dialog box features and summarizes their use. The other sections of this chapter discuss these features in more detail.

Fig. 4.1
The Excel Open dialog box has many features common to all standard file dialog boxes.

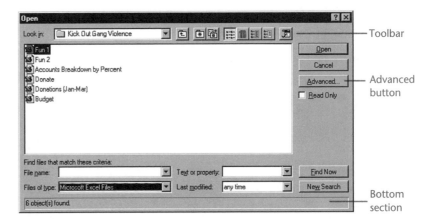

Table 4.1   Commands That Display a File Dialog Box

Command	Description	Application*
File, Open	Looks for and opens a document that has already been created.	W, E, P
File, Save	Saves your work.	W, E, P
File, Save As	Saves your work and enables you to see or make an additional file with a new name.	W, E, P
File, Save Workspace	Saves all open Excel documents into a container that enables you to open multiple documents at one time.	E
Insert, File	Places an existing document inside the current document.	W
Insert, Picture	Inserts a graphics file into the document.	W, E, P
Insert, Database, Get Data	Inserts a database table into the document.	W
Insert, Object, Create from File, Browse	Inserts a file into your document so you can later edit the object with the application that created it.	W, E, P
Insert, Slides from File	Inserts slides from another PowerPoint file.	P
Insert, Slides from Outline	Makes slides from a Word or Excel outline.	P
Insert, Movie	Inserts a moving video into the presentation.	P
Insert, Sound	Inserts sound into the presentation.	P
Tools, Mail Merge,	Uses a database or Get Data spreadsheet file for the merge data.	W

*W = Word, E = Excel, P = PowerPoint

Common Features

Table 4.2 Common Features on File Dialog Boxes

Button/Element	Description	Use
	? help button	After you click the question mark, click the part of the dialog box you want explained.
	Close button	Closes the dialog box without performing any actions. You also can press Esc.
Drop-down list	Save In/Look In drop-down list	Changes location for your files.
List box	Contents List box	Shows the names and optionally other information about the files.
	Up One Level button	Goes to next higher level in hierarchy of file containers.
	Look in Favorites button	Goes to the locations you designate as your "favorites" with the Add Favorites button.
	Add to Favorites button	Adds the file or folder to the location where you have your most-used documents.
	Create New Folder button	Creates a new folder in the location shown in the Look In/Save In drop-down list box.
	List button	Shows names of files only in contents list box.
	Details button	Shows name, size, date of files.
	Properties button	Shows user-entered information about the file.
	Preview button	Shows the first part of the file.
	Commands and Settings button	Shows menu of options for printing, editing properties, sorting, subfolders, saving searches.

Button/Element	Description	Use
Open	Save/Open/Insert OK buttons	Performs actions requested with all settings from dialog box.
Cancel	Cancel button	Don't do anything. Return to document.
Options...	Options button	Displays save options dialog boxes.
Advanced...	Advanced button	Prompts for advanced search capabilities for finding files.
Text box	File Name	Types the name of the file or uses wild cards to display a shortened list of files.
Text box	Files of Type/ Save as Type	Changes the display to show files created by different programs or saves the file so a different program can open the file.
Text box	Text or Property	Searches for text within the document or in property settings.
Text box	Last Modified	Searches for a file based on the date it was last saved.
Check box	Read Only checkbox	Opens file so you can't overwrite the existing file.
Find Now	Find Now button	Applies the find criteria and looks for the file.
New Search	New Search button	Clears any search criteria.
Check box	Link To File checkbox	When inserting a file, attaches instructions to read file on disk but do not insert actual file into document.
Check box	Save with Document checkbox	When linking a file, includes the entire file in the document.

Common Features

Saving, Opening, and Closing Files

▶ See "Saving, Closing, and Opening Word Documents," p. 180

▶ See "Saving Workbooks," p. 318

▶ See "Saving a Presentation," p. 590

The procedures for saving, opening, and closing files are similar to each other. You choose the necessary commands by using a button, menu item, or shortcut key. In most cases, a standard file dialog box opens, requesting information about the file name, location (drive and folder), and type of file you are using. Sometimes a dialog box does not open. For example, when you save a file after naming it, the program assumes you want to use the default choices in the file dialog box for the name, location, and file type. You can rename the file with the Save As command.

Table 4.3 shows the different methods of saving, opening, and closing files.

Table 4.3 Methods to Save, Open, and Close Files			
Action	**Button**	**Menu Command**	**Shortcut Key**
Save	💾	File, Save	Ctrl+S
Save As	No shortcut key	File, Save As	
Open	📂	File, Open	Ctrl+O
New	📄	File, New	Ctrl+N
Close	✖ or Double-click document's Control menu icon	File, Close	Ctrl+F4

Tip

Before you leave your computer, always press Ctrl+S if you have a document on-screen. Ctrl+S also wouldn't hurt before you spell-check or start printing.

Saving a Document

If you want to reuse a document or keep a copy, you need to save the document. If creating a document takes you a while (say, more than 15 minutes), you also want to save your document to protect against power outages, nasty computer gremlins (problems), and hitting the wrong button.

You can save a document in a number of ways. You can click the Save button on the Standard toolbar, press Ctrl+S, or choose File, Save. When you attempt to close an unsaved document or exit a program with an unsaved document, you can answer Yes to the prompt to save changes. No matter which method you use, the first time you save a document you enter the Save As dialog box as shown in figure 4.2.

Choose file location

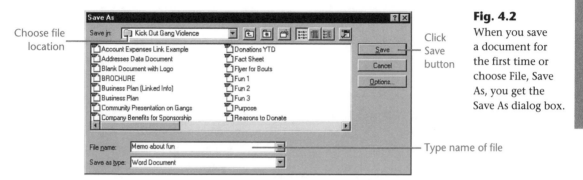

Click Save button

Fig. 4.2

When you save a document for the first time or choose File, Save As, you get the Save As dialog box.

Type name of file

To save the file, type the name in the File Name text box, choose a location in the Save In drop-down list, and choose the Save button.

Naming a Document

The old rules for naming a file with a maximum of eight characters, a period, and three more characters was very confining. These rules produced cryptic file names such as BUSPLN.DOC, ACCPER.XLS, and GANGPON.PPT. You are free at last of such restrictive rules. You can now have names such as *Business Plan, Accounts Breakdown by Percent, and Community Gang Presentation.* One of the most useful additions is the ability to use a space in naming files.

Valid file names may now contain the following:

- Spaces

- Up to 255 characters

- All characters except \ / ? : ; [" < > and |

Uppercase and lowercase characters are usually displayed as you type them, but you cannot give a document the same name in different cases (you cannot have one file called *PLAN* and another one called *plan* in the same folder).

> **Note**
>
> Windows 95 doesn't really alter DOS's 8+3 file-naming system. Windows 95 converts the file name you type to an acceptable name which is usually the first six non-space characters, a tilde, and a 1 for the first occurrence of the name (2 for second occurrence, etc.). For example, the Word file name *Business Plan* becomes BUSINE~1.DOC. When you copy or use this file on a DOS computer, the file name is the shortened version. On Windows 95 systems, the long file name is stored with a cross reference to the short file name. To see the short DOS file name when you are in a file dialog box, click the right mouse button, choose Properties, and look on the General Properties tab.

Saving Changes to a Named Document

 After you save a document one time, the name of the document appears in the title bar as shown in figure 4.3. When you want to save a document a second time and continue to use the same name, use any of the procedures mentioned earlier (the Save button, Ctrl+S, File, Save, or exiting the document or program and choosing Yes to save changes).

Fig. 4.3
The title bar shows the name of the document: Donations (Jan-Mar).

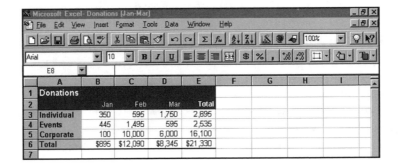

If you want to give the document another name, choose File, Save As. The Save As dialog box appears with the existing name in the File Name text box. Edit the name of the document or change the location in the Save In drop-down list.

Saving All Open Documents

If you continue to open documents or create new documents without closing your document, you get more and more documents in memory for the current application. To see a list of documents in memory, choose the Window menu. The open documents appear on the bottom of the menu as shown in figure 4.4.

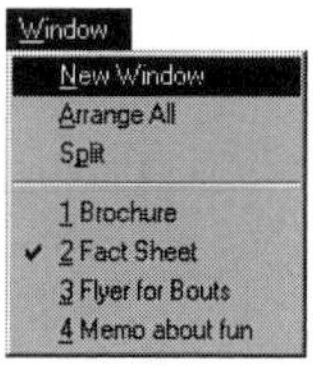

Common Features

Fig. 4.4
Four documents are open. To move to an open document, click the document name.

In Word you can save all open documents with File, Save All. If you have not named one or more of the documents, the Save dialog box appears, prompting you for the file name and location.

Choosing a Location To Save Your File

When you save a file, the file goes to a disk somewhere. In the simplest case, a computer may have a hard disk inside the computer (drive C:) and one floppy disk drive (drive A:). However, your personal computer may have additional floppy and hard drives, removable disk cartridges and optical drives, and a CD-ROM. Your computer also may be connected to a network, giving you access to computer drives that are not directly attached to your personal computer.

When you first enter a standard file dialog box, you see a drop-down list box. In the Save dialog box you see the Save In list. In the Open dialog box you see the Look In list. A prompt in the list box represents the current location or container where you can save or open files. Underneath the drop-down list is a large open area (the contents list box) showing you the contents of the current container. The contents can be other containers or files.

When you select the drop-down list as shown in figure 4.5 you get an overview of the containers available to you for saving or opening files. A cascading list of locations displays. This list represents the hierarchy of locations where you can find or store files. This hierarchy may have many different levels; each level is represented by an indent. Whenever you choose a level through the drop-down list, the new level's contents are shown in the contents list box. If the list has more items than can fit, you see a vertical scroll bar on the right side of the list box. If you want to go back up a level you can choose the Save In or Look In drop-down list box or click the Up One Level button.

Fig. 4.5
Locate the place
where you want to
work with files in
the Look In drop-
down list.

Look In drop-down list

Icon for floppy drives

Icon for hard drives

The hierarchy is diagrammed in figure 4.6. At the top level is the Desktop
indicating that all potential locations branch from this location. The two
main branches from the Desktop are My Computer and Network Neighborhood, indicating that you work with a file that is physically part of your computer system or other computers that are connected to your computer
through a network.

Fig. 4.6
The hierarchy for
storing files
contains many
different levels.

If you select Network Neighborhood from the drop-down list, you see a list of
computers on your network in the contents list box as shown in figure 4.7.
You then can double-click any computer besides your own, and a list of
shared folders appears in the contents list box. If you double-click a folder
you may see subfolders and files in the contents list box.

Fig. 4.7
Two computers
are listed in this
computer network.

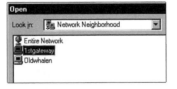

Under My Computer in the drop-down list are the different storage devices
attached to the computer, such as a 3 1/2" floppy drive (A:) and a 5 1/4"
floppy drive (B:), shown earlier in figure 4.5. When you click one of the
floppy drives, you are working with files on a floppy disk. If you are saving a
file, you can optionally type A: or B: before the name of the file in the File
Name text box.

The icon for a hard drive (usually fixed inside your computer) is slightly different in figure 4.5 and usually is indicated by a C:. Because the hard drive has so much more space, files are usually placed inside folders. In figure 4.5, the highlight is on the folder *Kick Out Gang Violence* which is a subfolder of *Data*.

To navigate through the hierarchy of computers, drives, and folders, you can do any of the following:

- Use the Save In or Look In drop-down list box.

- Double-click a folder in the contents list box to view the contents of the folder.

- Click the folder one time with the right mouse button and click Open to view the contents of the folder.

- Click the Up One Level button to return to a previous level in the hierarchy.

- Click the Create New Folder button to create a folder underneath the container or folder identified in the Save In drop-down list box.

- If you know the location of the file you want to open or save, you can type the hierarchy of drive and folders in the File Name text box such as this example: C:\Office95\Excel\95Revenue.

Opening a Document

You have even more options for opening a document than you do for saving a document. Some of these options were discussed in Chapter 2, "Getting Started and Identifying Screen Parts." This section contains a summary of your options to open a document.

► See "Opening a Word Document," p. 182

Outside a program, take one of the following steps:

- From the Microsoft Office Shortcut Bar, click the Open a Document button, select the location, and choose the file. You also can customize the Shortcut Bar to contain files and folders. See Chapter 34, "Customizing the Desktop, Toolbars, and Menus." After you click the Open a Document button, you enter an Open dialog box.

◄ See "Launching Programs," p. 28

► See "Opening an Existing Presentation," p. 590

- From the Windows taskbar, choose Start, then Documents, then click one of your last 15 documents.

- From the Windows taskbar choose Start, then Programs, then find the file through the Windows Explorer.

■ Minimize or close all open programs and double-click a desktop icon such as My Computer, Network Neighborhood, or shortcut folders and navigate through the windows to find your file.

■ From the Windows Taskbar, choose Start, and then Open Office Document.

■ Press any shortcut keys you attached to a file using the Shortcut tab on the Properties dialog box of a shortcut icon. (See the "Using Advanced File Find Capabilities" section below.)

From within a program, take one of the following steps:

■ Click the Open button.

■ Press Ctrl+O.

■ Choose File, Open.

If you choose any of the preceding steps, you enter the Open dialog box. Type the file name in the File Name text box and choose the location from the Look In drop-down list.

You can also easily find one of the last files you worked with. At the bottom of the File menu is a list of your most recently used files (see fig. 4.8). If no drive and folder displays with the file name, the file is from the active folder. Choose the file name to open the file.

Fig. 4.8
The last few files you opened appear at the bottom of the File menu.

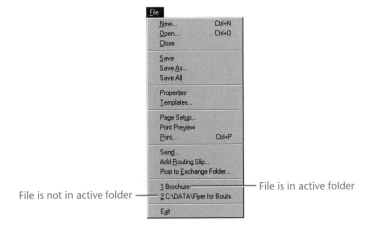

File is not in active folder

File is in active folder

Troubleshooting

When I look for a file, the file name does not appear in the contents list box.

The file name may not appear in a contents list box for several reasons. First, you may need to use the scroll bars to display more files in the list. Second, the file may not be the correct type. In the Files of _T_ype list box, select All Files, and see if your file is listed. Third, you may need to change the drive and folder. Finally, if all else fails, search for the file using features discussed in the next section, "Finding Files."

I can't access a file on someone else's computer on the network.

On the Windows Desktop choose Network Neighborhood then choose the other person's computer name. The other computer needs to have shared folders to enable you to access its files.

I can't read a file from the CD-ROM.

Make sure you set up the CD-ROM correctly. If you haven't done so, set up the CD-ROM by choosing Start on the Windows taskbar. Then choose Settings, Control Panel, Add New Hardware, and follow the Hardware Wizard. Additionally, make sure you have the CD-ROM player turned on and the proper CD in the CD drive.

Finding Files

You can use the Open a Document button on the Microsoft Office Shortcut Bar to open a document and launch the program that created the document at the same time. After you click the Open a Document button, the Open dialog box appears. This dialog box is the same one that appears when you are in a program and use _F_ile, _O_pen.

When you get to the Open dialog box, you have many options to narrow or expand your search. You can change the display and order of the files, use wild cards in file names, choose a file type, or identify a file by its contents, date, or other properties. These options in the Open dialog box replace the Find File feature from the previous version of Microsoft Office.

Displaying File Lists

After you have selected a computer, drive, and folder through the Look _I_n drop-down list, you see a list of files (and possibly other folders) in the contents list box. You have four options for viewing this file list. Figures 4.9 through 4.12 show the different views of the files. Click one of the following buttons:

Button	Name	Purpose
	List	Shows file names with a file type icon only.
	Details	Shows file names, file type icon, size of file, file type, and modified date and time.
	Properties	Shows user-added summary information such as title, author, keywords, and others.
	Preview	Shows what the first part of the file looks like.

Fig. 4.9

Click the List button to display file names.

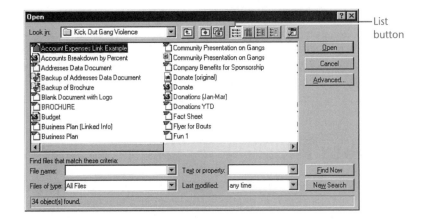

—List button

Fig. 4.10

Click the Details button to display file names, size, type, and date.

Click to sort by file name   Click to sort by file type   Details button

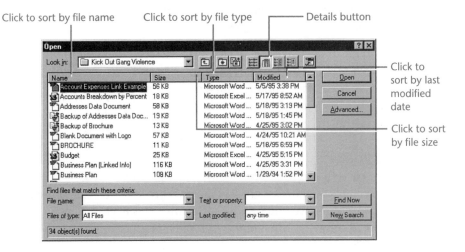

Click to sort by last modified date

Click to sort by file size

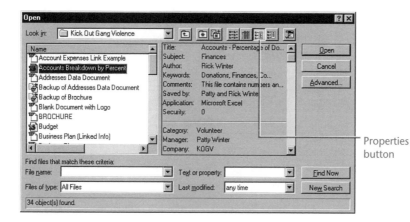

Fig. 4.11
Click the Properties button to display file names and user-supplied information about the file.

Properties button

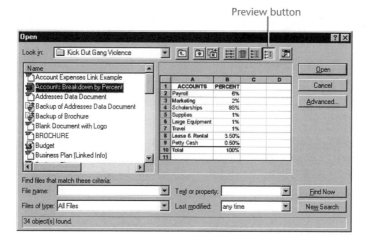

Preview button

Fig. 4.12
Click the Preview button to see a picture of the file.

Sorting the File List

When you choose the Details button, the list of files displays with the file name, size, type, and modified date and time. The top of the contents list box shows column headers Name, Size, Type, and Modified as shown in figure 4.10. Click any of these column headers to sort the list ascending by that category. Click the column header again to sort the list descending by that category. For example, to sort the files by date, click the Modified header. Click again to sort the files with the latest date on top of the list.

Using Wild Cards To Shorten the File List

If your file list is particularly long, you may want to limit the list by the file name. Two wild cards can help you limit the list by characters in the name of

Tip
Unlike the DOS wild card, you can use multiple asterisks within file names.

the file: * (asterisk) and ? (question mark). The asterisk means replace any number of characters. The question mark means replace one character. In the File Name text box of the Open dialog box, you can type the text with wild cards and then choose the Find Now command button. The following list shows some examples.

Type	To Display
B*	All files that begin with B
Rev??	Rev95, Rev96, Rev97
Don	Reasons to Donate, Donations YTD, Orientation to Donors, Don Campbell's Resume

To remove the wild card and all restrictions on the file list, choose the New Search command button.

Finding a File by Date

When your list is long and you do not remember the exact file name but you do remember the approximate time you last worked on the file, you can limit the file list to just those files modified at a certain time. Use the Last Modified drop-down list and click the Find Now command button to limit the file list by time. Figure 4.13 shows the choices from Last modified include today, yesterday, last week, this week, last month, and this month. To return the file list to show all dates, select any time.

Fig. 4.13
To display only files meeting date criteria, choose the Last Modified drop-down list.

Finding a File by Contents

You may remember where you put a file but don't have any clue what you called it. You can look for a file by the contents inside the file or by the summary information you added to the file. In the Text or Property text box, type some text that you put in the file such as who you addressed the file to, the subject, or maybe an expense category. Figure 4.14 shows all the files containing *Rick*, which means that *Rick* can be typed in the file, an author of the file, or part of any other file property. After you fill in the Text or Property text box, choose the Find Now button.

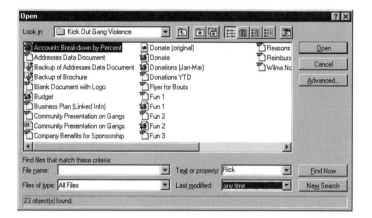

Fig. 4.14
All files that have Rick as part of the document or a property are shown here.

To reset the Open dialog box, choose the New Search command button.

Expanding the Search To Include Subfolders

If the search text isn't found in the current folder, you can expand your search to other folders on the hard drive. Choose the highest level you want to search (for example, the C: drive) in the Look In drop-down list. Then choose the Commands and Settings button. From the drop-down menu choose Search Subfolders as shown in figure 4.15. Now when you do any of the search procedures such as using the File Name, Text or Property, Last Modified, Files of Type, or Advanced Searches, subfolders display as well as the files. To group files by their subfolders, check the Group Files by Folder option on the Commands and Settings button. To return to display only the contents of the Look In choice, uncheck the Search Subfolders option.

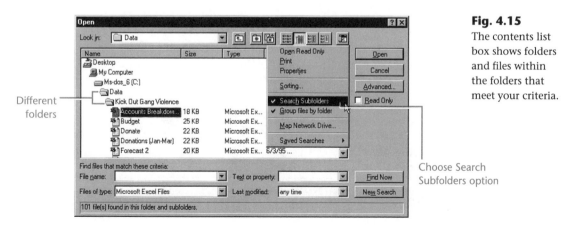

Different folders

Choose Search Subfolders option

Fig. 4.15
The contents list box shows folders and files within the folders that meet your criteria.

Displaying Types of Files

If you enter the Open dialog box through the Open a Document button on the Microsoft Office Shortcut Bar, the dialog box shows files of all types. If you enter the Open or Save dialog boxes through a specific program such as Word, Excel, or PowerPoint, the default is to show only those files created by that program. If you want to see a list of all files, choose the File of Type drop-down list and choose All Files. You also can display files from different word processors such as WordPerfect or spreadsheets such as Lotus 1-2-3. This capability is helpful if you want to open a file created by a different program, or if you want to save a file in a different format for use in a different program. Figure 4.16 shows some of the Files of Type choices for the Excel Open dialog box. These types include text files, different spreadsheet formats, older versions of Excel, and database file formats.

> **Note**
>
> If the Files of Type list has more choices than you can see, a vertical scroll bar appears, enabling you to scroll to other items in the list and select the file type you want.

Fig. 4.16
Use Files of Type to open or save files that are not the default type for your application.

You usually change the file type when you want to convert a file from one kind of worksheet (Lotus 1-2-3 to Excel), word processing document (WordPerfect to Word), or database (dBASE to Access) to another. In some cases, however, you may want to open a different kind of file. For example, you can open an Excel worksheet file in a Word document. Table 4.4 shows some possibilities for opening different kinds of files.

Table 4.4   File Types You Can Open in a Different Application

Application Opening File	File Type	Result
Word	Excel worksheet	Word table (can be a merge data document)

Application Opening File	File Type	Result
PowerPoint	Word (outline)	Heading 1 = slide title, Heading 2, 3 = points and subpoints
PowerPoint	Excel worksheet	Each row becomes the title of the slide

When you try to open a file of a different type, if your application can't convert the file type, an error message appears, stating that the file format is not valid.

Using Advanced File Find Capabilities

Although the Text or Property option searches for the contents of the file or any property, you may want to limit your search to one property or use many properties at one time. Do the following steps:

1. Click the Open button on your program's standard toolbar or click the Open a Document button of the Microsoft Office Shortcut Bar.

2. If you want, fill out the File Name, Text or Property, Files of Type, and Last Modified options as described earlier.

3. Choose the Advanced button. The Advanced Find dialog box appears with any choices you made in the Open dialog box.

4. Choose the Property drop-down list and select the property you want as shown in figure 4.17.

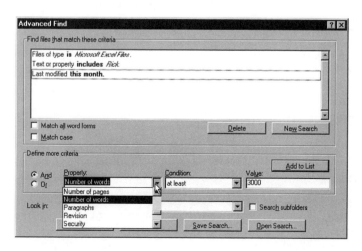

Fig. 4.17
Choose one of many properties to search in the Property drop-down list.

5. In the Value text box, type the text you are looking for.

6. Choose the Add to List button.

7. If you want to add another condition, choose the And option button (both conditions must be true) or the Or option button (either condition must be true) and complete steps 2-6.

8. When you finish filling in the Advanced Find dialog box, choose the Find Now button on the bottom left of the Advanced Find dialog box.

You return to the Open dialog box with the list of files that meet your criteria in the contents list box.

Some of the other options in the Advanced Find dialog box are listed in table 4.5.

Table 4.5 Other Options in Advanced Find Dialog Box	
Option	**Description**
Match All Word Forms checkbox	For contents, comments, and other item searches, you can find files that match different forms of the word. For example, if the Value is *to be*, the search looks for *to be, are, is, am*.
Match Case checkbox	For contents, comments, and other items in the Property choice, you find only those items that match capitalization (uppercase and lowercase) the way you typed the options in the Value text box.
Delete button	Click one of the items in the Find Files That Match These Criteria, and then choose the Delete button to remove that criteria.
New Search button	Clear all search criteria and start over.
Condition drop-down list	This list changes depending on the Property selected and enables you to find matches that contain the entire Value choice, a portion of it, one of the items in the Value choice, items greater or less than a date, and others.
Look In drop-down list	The same as the Look In on the Open dialog box; it enables you to change the location of your search.
Search Subfolders checkbox	Same as the menu choice on the Commands and Settings menu in the Open dialog box; it enables you to include files from the current folder and any subfolders you want.
Save Search button	Save any search criteria with a name for later retrieval.

Option	Description
<u>O</u>pen Search button	Choose one of the named searches you created with the <u>S</u>ave Search command.
Cancel button	Don't do any of the Advanced Find options and return to the Open dialog box the way you left it.

Saving and Using Saved Search Criteria

If you continually search for the same kinds of files, you may want to save your search settings. After you identify the file name, location, property information, text, or date search criteria, you can save these settings. Follow these steps:

1. If you are in an Open dialog box, choose <u>A</u>dvanced to open the Advanced Find dialog box.

2. Choose the <u>S</u>ave Search button.

3. Type the name of the search and choose the OK button.

When you want to use a named search, select the search from the <u>O</u>pen Search button. To delete the search, choose the Delete button. Figure 4.18 shows a list of saved searches.

Fig. 4.18
Select saved searches in the Saved Searches list box.

Saving Your Favorite Files and Folders

If you use the same files or folders over and over, you may want to save them in a special folder called Favorites. In an Open dialog box, move to your favorite file or folder and click the Add to Favorites button.

When you want to see the Favorites files and folders, click the Look in Favorites button in any file dialog box.

Copying and Moving Files, Printing, and Other Hidden Features

When you are in an Open or Save dialog box, you have other options that are "hidden" and do not display as a choice in the dialog box. Access these options by selecting a file or files and then clicking your right mouse button (see fig. 4.19).

You can select files in one of several ways:

■ Click one file name.

■ Hold down the Ctrl key and click any files to select more than one file.

■ Click the first file, hold down the Shift key and then click the last file to select a group of adjacent files.

Fig. 4.19
Clicking the right mouse button on a file gives you more file management options.

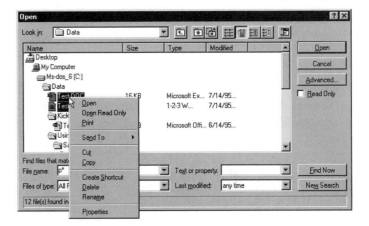

After you have selected your file(s), click the right mouse button in part of the selection and choose one of the following:

■ Choose Open to open all the selected files.

■ Choose Open Read Only to open the files, but you need to give a new name if you want to save the files.

■ Choose Print to print the files.

■ Choose Send To, then choose a floppy drive to copy the file, Fax Recipient to fax the file, Mail Recipient to send a mail version of the file, or My Briefcase.

> **Note**
>
> The Briefcase is a new Windows 95 feature that allows you to keep your documents up-to-date between your desktop computer and a laptop computer.

■ Choose Cut to move the files to the Clipboard (and remove the original files).

■ Choose Copy to copy the files to the Clipboard (and keep the original files in place).

■ Choose Create Shortcut to create another icon in the directory which is a shortcut to the file (click the right mouse button on the shortcut name and choose Properties to give the shortcut a keyboard shortcut. The shortcut name starts with "Shortcut to.")

■ Choose Delete to remove the files to the Recycle Bin.

■ Choose Rename to give the file a new name.

■ Choose Properties to give a keyboard shortcut to a shortcut file or see file information such as DOS filename, date created, file attributes, summary information, and statistics.

> **Note**
>
> If you accidentally delete files, you can get them back if you haven't emptied the Recycle Bin. With all programs minimized, choose Recycle Bin on the Windows Desktop. Choose the file name and choose File, Restore.

If you choose Cut or Copy, choose the location where you want the file to go and then click the right mouse button and choose Paste from the shortcut menu.

Closing a Document

You can close a document in one of several ways:

◀ See "Closing Programs," p. 39

■ Double-click the Control menu icon in the upper left corner of the document window as shown in figure 4.20.

■ Click one time on the Control menu icon and choose Close from the pull-down menu.

■ Choose File, Close.

■ Press Ctrl+W.

■ Click the document Close button (X).

> **Caution**
>
> Make sure you click the document close button rather than the program close button. If the document is maximized, the document close button is on the same row as the menu bar. If the document is not maximized, the close button is on the right side of the document title bar.

Fig. 4.20
Click once on the Close button to close a document.

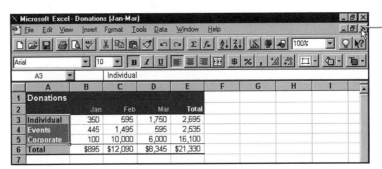

Document Close button

If you saved your last changes to the document, the document closes. If you made changes since your last save or you haven't yet saved, you are prompted to save the document as shown in figure 4.21.

Fig. 4.21
When you try to close an unsaved document, a dialog box asks if you want to save changes.

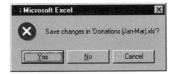

Choose one of the following buttons:

■ Choose Yes to save changes. If you have already given the document a name, the document closes. If you haven't given the document a name, the Save As dialog box appears.

■ Choose No to not save changes. You lose any changes you have made since your last save, or you lose the entire document if you haven't saved it at all.

■ Choose Cancel to return to the document without saving or exiting the document.

If you have not saved the latest changes to your file and you close a file using any normal method, including exiting the application, the prompt shown in figure 4.21 asks whether you want to save your changes. If you choose Yes, the Save As dialog box appears if you haven't named the file.

> **Note**
>
> Obviously, you won't get a prompt to save your document if you or mother nature powers off the computer.

Starting a New Document

In Excel and Word, when you click the New button or press Ctrl+N, a new blank file window opens. In PowerPoint, a new presentation starts by asking you what kind of slide you want. If you use the menu command File, New in a program or click the Start a New Document button on the Microsoft Office Shortcut Bar, the New dialog box appears with a series of tabs on the top as shown in figure 4.22. The tabs show general categories of files you can create. On each tab are files that are templates or wizards. *Templates* are files that may have stored formatting, macros, styles, text, and different menus and toolbars. After you open a template with the File, New command, you still need to give the document a name to save it. *Wizards* are a series of dialog boxes that lead you through the steps of creating a document or performing a function.

◄ See "Starting a Document from the Shortcut Bar," p. 31

► See "Using Template Wizards," p. 269

► See "Understanding Masters and Templates," p. 571

► See "Creating a Presentation Using a Wizard," p. 578

Troubleshooting

When I choose subfolders with the Commands and Settings button I don't see any subfolders.

You do not see subfolders with the list choice selected. You need to click the Details, Properties, or Preview buttons. Another possibility is that you don't have any files in other areas that meet your search criteria.

I know that a file is in the folder but I don't see it.

You may need to use the scroll bar on the bottom or right side of the contents list box. Another possibility is that you have search criteria that excludes your file. Click the New Search button in a file dialog box. Make sure that your file type is correct in the Files of Type drop-down list.

Common Features

Fig. 4.22

The Start a New Document button displays New dialog box with templates and wizards for Microsoft Office applications.

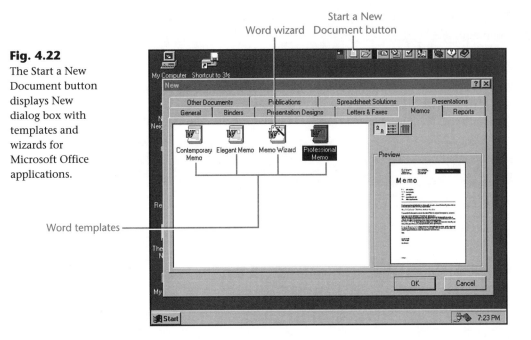

Using Save Options

Although most applications require that you save files, Word and Excel enable you to create backup files and set up automatic saving. You still should use the Save button, the menu command, or the shortcut key to save often, especially after you spend a significant amount of effort to make the document look the way you want or before you perform a major procedure on your file (such as spell checking, sorting, replacing, automatic formatting, or importing). You may want to use the Save As feature to save different revisions of the same file until your project is complete.

A backup file has a different icon, and the name begins with *Backup of* (see fig. 4.23). You create a backup file after you have saved the file at least once. When you save a file the second time and all subsequent times, the backup procedure renames the old file on disk with the same file name, but with a *Backup of* prefix. The document on-screen saves with the original file name. If you need to use your backup file, change the file type to All Files or type **backup*** in the File Name text box. To start the backup procedure, choose the File, Save As command and then choose the Options command button, then check the Always Create Backup checkbox.

Backup Word icon

Normal Word icon

Fig. 4.23
The file type icon
changes to show a
backup file.

In Word and Excel, you can set up the automatic-save feature so the program
saves your work at time intervals you specify. In Word, set up the automatic-
save feature this way:

1. Choose Tools, Options.

2. Click the Save tab.

3. Check the Automatic Save Every checkbox and fill in the setting for
   Minutes by typing or using the increment buttons.

If desired, to change the location where files are saved, continue as follows,
otherwise skip to step 7:

4. Click the File Locations tab.

5. In the File Types list box, click AutoSave Files and choose the Modify
   button.

6. In the Modify Location dialog box, type the name of the location where
   you want to save AutoSave files in the Folder Name text box as shown
   in figure 4.24 and choose OK.

7. Choose the Close button in the Options dialog box.

Fig. 4.24
Type the name of
the backup folder
in the Folder Name
text box.

Set up the AutoSave feature in Excel this way:

1. Choose Tools, Add-Ins. The Add-ins dialog box appears, as shown in figure 4.25.

Fig. 4.25
Check the AutoSave option in the Add-Ins dialog box to activate automatic save.

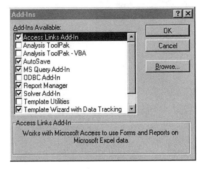

> **Note**
>
> The Add-Ins dialog box may look different on your screen because of your installation.

2. Check the AutoSave checkbox and choose OK.

3. To activate AutoSave, choose Tools, AutoSave. The AutoSave dialog box appears.

4. Check the Automatic Save Every checkbox and fill in the setting for Minutes.

5. Choose OK to return to the document.

When you restart Word after a crash or power problem, the file may automatically appear on-screen due to the automatic-save feature. In Excel, the program prompts you for a file name if you have not already saved the file.

Using File Properties

In the old version of Windows your file name was limited to 8 characters plus a three character extension. Windows 95 and Microsoft Office have greatly expanded the capacity to 255 characters. If you need more than your file name to identify a document, however, you now have many properties you can fill out in the new properties feature.

Viewing and Editing File Properties

You can enter or view properties for a file in many ways. The following lists
describe some ways to use file properties.

To view and change file properties:

■ With the file displayed in Word, Excel, or PowerPoint, choose File,
Properties.

■ In a file dialog box, select the file and click the Commands and Settings
button. Then choose Properties on the menu.

To view properties only:

■ In a file dialog box, select the file and click the Properties button. The
properties of the highlighted file show in a small area you can scroll
with a vertical scroll bar as shown in figure 4.26.

Properties button

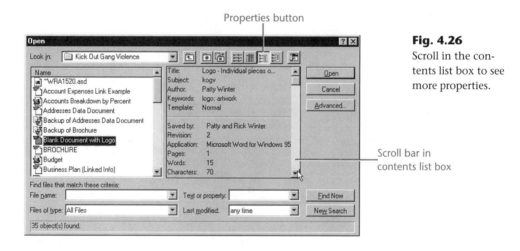

Fig. 4.26
Scroll in the con-
tents list box to see
more properties.

Scroll bar in
contents list box

You can print your properties for Word files only. Choose File, Print and from
the Print What drop-down list choose Summary Info.

Reviewing the File Properties

Depending on how you entered the file properties, you see a dialog box similar to the one shown in figure 4.27. Up to five tabs appear in the Properties
dialog box. The tabs are described in the following sections.

Fig. 4.27
The General page
in the Properties
sheet shows infor-
mation about the
file.

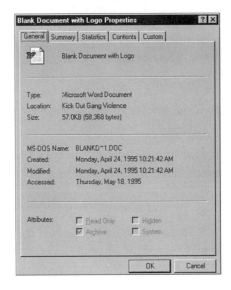

General Tab

Figure 4.27 shows the General page for a Word document. The program has
entered the information on this tab for you. The information includes the
following:

Item	Description
Name of file	In the top section of the tab, the name also shows an icon representing the program type.
Type:	Type of file. This example shows Microsoft Word Document.
Location:	Name of folder that contains the file.
Size:	The file size shows both in KB (kilobytes) and bytes.
MS-DOS Name:	The converted name based on the first six characters of the file name, a period, and the file type extension. You use this name if you copy to a DOS system.
Created:	The date you first created (or copied) the file.
Modified:	The last time you saved the file.
Accessed:	If you are currently looking at the file, today's date.
Attributes:	You cannot change these attributes from the program's File, Properties command, but you can change them if you enter properties through the Explorer.

Item	Description
Read Only attribute	You can read the file but not save it with the same name.
Archive attribute	The file has been changed since the last backup.
Hidden attribute	The file is normally hidden from file lists.
System attribute	The file is a system file required to run the operating system and should not be modified.

Summary Tab

Figure 4.28 shows the Summary page, where you can enter information about the file to help you organize and later search for the file. Choose any of the text boxes (Title, Subject, Author, Manager, Company, Category, Keywords, or Comments) and enter the text you like. Although you can enter more characters, you can view about 42 characters in each of the fields except Comments. The Comments field has a large view area and you can use the vertical scroll bar to see more text than fits in the text box.

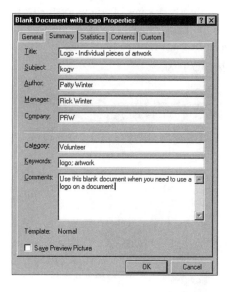

Fig. 4.28
Fill in the Summary page of the Properties sheet to help you find or manage your file.

Statistics Tab

Figure 4.29 shows the Statistics page. This information tells when your file was created, modified, accessed, and printed; who last saved the file; how many times the file has been revised; and what the total editing time is. Also, Word documents include how long the document is in pages, paragraphs, lines, words, characters, and bytes.

Common Features

Fig. 4.29
The Statistics page shows information about dates, times, editing, and document length.

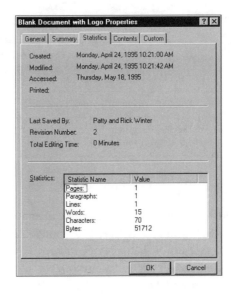

Contents Tab

The information on the Contents page depends on the type of file you have. If the file is an Excel file, the names of the worksheet or module tabs appear. If the file is a PowerPoint file, the names of each of the slides appear as well as information about formatting (see fig. 4.30). A Word file shows only the Title from the Summary page.

Fig. 4.30
The Contents page shows each slide title for Power-Point files.

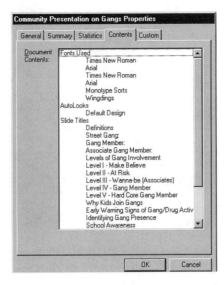

Custom Tab

If you want to create your own properties, you have plenty of flexibility with the Custom page. You can add your own field names and values for whatever properties you want (see fig. 4.31).

To add your own properties, follow these steps:

1. Choose File, Properties.

2. Click the Custom tab.

3. Type the name of your field in the Name text box or choose from one of over 20 field names in the drop-down list box. Included in the drop-down list are items such as Checked By, Department, Source, and Typist.

4. Choose the data type from the Type drop-down list. Types include Text, Date, Number, and Yes or No.

5. Type a Value in the Value area or choose Yes or No (if data type is Yes or No, you see Yes, No options only). The value has to match the data type.

> **Note**
>
> If you check the Link to Content check box on the Custom page, the Value box will have a drop-down list where you can choose items within the document to link to, such as a bookmark in Word or a named range in Excel.

6. Choose the Add command button.

7. Repeat steps 3-6 for any additional fields.

> **Troubleshooting**
>
> *I don't see five tabs on my Properties sheet.*
>
> Make sure you are using the original file, not a shortcut name when you look at file properties.
>
> *I need to associate my documents with account numbers.*
>
> Open the file and choose File Properties and click on the Custom tab. Click in the Name text box and type **Account Number**. Choose a Type and type the number in the Value field.

Fig. 4.31
A completed Word
custom set of
properties may
include the
additional
information you
need to manage
your documents.

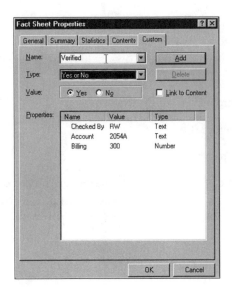

Printing Documents

To print or preview the current document, you can use menu commands,
toolbar buttons, or shortcut keys. As mentioned in an earlier section, you can
print one or more files by clicking the right mouse button on a file name in
an Open dialog box, then choosing the Print command.

Printing All or Part of the Document

To print the current document, choose the File, Print command, press Ctrl+P,
or click the Print button on the Standard toolbar.

When you use the Print button or shortcut key, the entire document prints.
If you use the menu command, a dialog box similar to figure 4.32 appears,
displaying more choices.

Options in the Print dialog box enable you to print the entire document, the
current page, specific pages, or selected text. You also can specify the number of copies to print. In the Pages text box in Word or Slides text box in
PowerPoint, you can skip pages (you can type **1-2**, **4-7**, or just **13-** to print
page 13 to end of document).

Changing Printing Options

If you want to make additional printing choices, use the Page Setup dialog
box, shown in figure 4.33. The options in this dialog box enable you to set
margins, print headers and footers, specify the print orientation, and change
the printer settings.

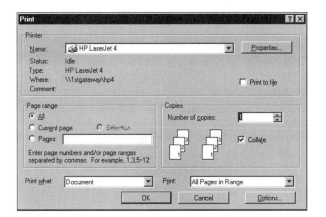

Fig. 4.32
The Print dialog box enables you to specify what you want to print in more detail.

To change margins, paper size, and other features, use the following command:

Application	Menu Command
Word	File, Page Setup
Excel	File, Page Setup
PowerPoint	File, Slide Setup

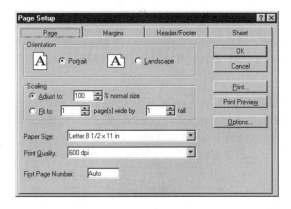

Fig. 4.33
You can specify additional printing options in the Excel Page Setup dialog box.

To change the printer, choose the printer from the drop-down list in the Printer section of the Print dialog box.

Using Print Preview

Although your screen shows what you will see on the printed page, Word and Excel have a Print Preview option that enables you to see the entire page (or more than one page), including headers and footers, page numbers, and margins. You enter the preview by choosing the File, Print Preview command. Table 4.5 shows the features available while you are in preview mode.

Table 4.5	Print Preview Options		
Option		**Word**	**Excel**
Change margins			X
View Ruler (to change margins, indents, and tabs)		X	
Magnify/Zoom		X	X
Zoom to different sizes		X	
Multiple pages		X	
Shrink to fit		X	X
Print		X	X
Edit		X	
Next (go to next page)			X
Previous (go to previous page)		X	
Setup (go to setup dialog box)		X	

Figure 4.34 shows Print Preview for Word, and figure 4.35 shows Print Preview for Excel.

To change margins, click the Margins or View Ruler button, move the mouse pointer to the top or side until the pointer changes to a double-headed black arrow, and drag the margin. To magnify, click the Magnifier (Word) or Zoom (Excel) button and click the document where you want magnification. To turn magnification off, click the document again. In Word, to edit the document, click the Magnifier button to turn magnification off and editing on. In Excel, to use shrink to fit, choose the Setup button, click the Page tab, and choose Fit To and fill in the Page(s) Wide by Tall text boxes.

Zoom Control

Multiple Pages

Magnifier

View Ruler

Shrink to Fit

Full Screen

Print

One Page

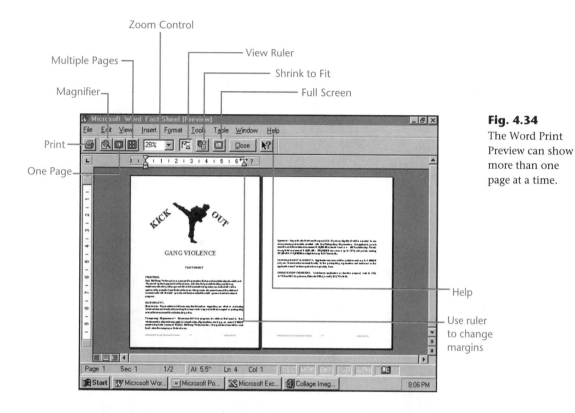

Fig. 4.34
The Word Print
Preview can show
more than one
page at a time.

Help

Use ruler
to change
margins

Drag
double-
headed
arrow to
change
margins

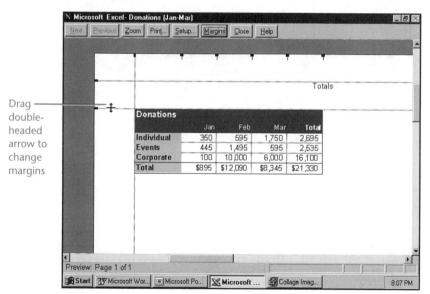

Fig. 4.35
You can change
margins and view
a document in
Excel's Print
Preview.

Switching between Documents

◀ See "Switching between Programs," p. 38

When you open more than one file at a time, you have a window for each file. You can switch between open documents using one of the following ways:

■ Choose the open document from the bottom of the <u>W</u>indow menu.

■ Press Ctrl+F6 to cycle through the open documents.

■ If parts of documents are visible on-screen, click the one you want to see. If a document is minimized, as shown in figure 4.36, double-click its icon.

Fig. 4.36

In Word or any other application, click the Minimize button to shrink the document to an icon; double-click the icon to open the document.

Click to minimize document to an icon

Double-click to open document

If you want to copy information between documents, you may want to display two or more windows. In Word, Excel, and PowerPoint, you can use the drag-and-drop feature to move or copy items between document windows. To move, just click and drag the item to another window; to copy, hold down the Ctrl key while you drag.

■ In Word, choose the <u>W</u>indow, Arrange <u>A</u>ll command to display the documents as shown in figure 4.37.

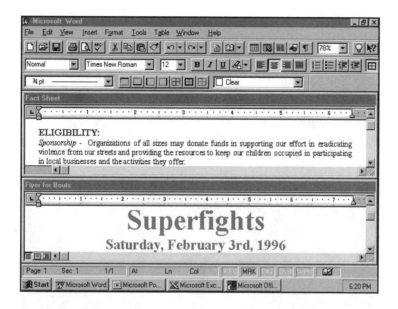

Fig. 4.37
In Word, choose
Window, Arrange
All to arrange the
document win-
dows horizontally.

■ In Excel, choose the Window, Arrange command. A dialog box appears, asking how you want to arrange the windows. The Tiled option displays the windows in small rectangles (see fig. 4.38). Horizontal displays the windows in rows (like Word). Vertical displays the windows in columns. Cascade stacks the windows, with the title bar of each window showing.

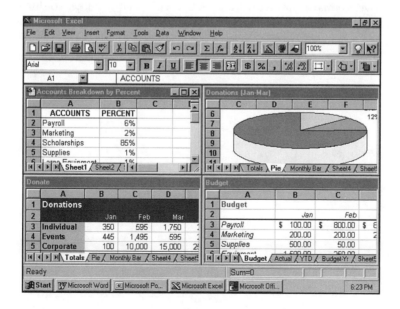

Fig. 4.38
In Excel, choose
Window, Arrange,
Tiled to display the
document win-
dows in equal-size
squares.

■ In PowerPoint, choose the <u>W</u>indow, <u>A</u>rrange All command to show the documents in tiled form. You also can choose the <u>W</u>indow, <u>C</u>ascade command to stack the windows, with the title bar of each window showing (see fig. 4.39).

Fig. 4.39
In PowerPoint, choose <u>W</u>indow, <u>C</u>ascade to stack the document windows.

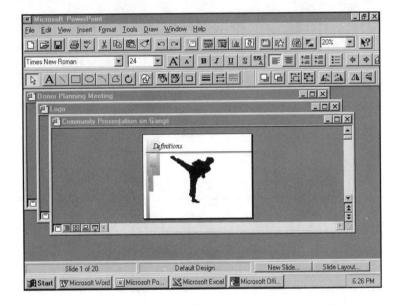

When several documents are visible, a dark title bar indicates which window is active. To make another window active, click that window. To show one of the windows full-screen, click the Maximize button or double-click the title bar.❖

Chapter 5

Using Help

by Rick Winter and Patty Winter

In addition to the screen elements such as toolbars, ToolTips, and rulers mentioned in Chapter 2, "Getting Started and Identifying Screen Parts," Microsoft has many additional tools to help you become more productive.

In this chapter, you learn to

- Use online help

- Review screen elements you use for help

- View tips related to the procedures you're performing

- Use Wizards to help you create documents and perform other tasks

Using the Variety of Help Features

Help is available in many different forms. Help includes the traditional online help to many other features that identify parts of the screen or help you accomplish your tasks. Table 5.1 shows a list of help features you can use.

▶ See "Using Template Wizards," p. 269

Table 5.1	Help Features Available for Office Applications	
Feature	**Description**	**Applications**
Online help	Allows you to look up help on a topic by searching through a table of contents or index, or searching for a specific topic.	W, E, P
Answer Wizard	Allows you to type a request in plain English and select from a list of possible responses.	W, E, P

(continues)

Table 5.1 Continued

Feature	Description	Applications
Getting Results Book	Rather than having a book in your library, you can use the book on the CD-ROM for information about Microsoft Office products.	W, E, P
Transition Help	Help for users of a competing product (WordPerfect or Lotus 1-2-3), which allows you to change the settings so keys are similar to the old product and help you look up equivalent procedures in the new product.	W, E
System Info	A window that shows information about your computer operating system, memory, storage, printing, and so on.	W, E, P
Technical Support Contacts	A window that allows you to find phone numbers and procedures for support, downloading files, and asking questions.	
Help Pointer	Allows you to point to an item on-screen for a description of the item.	W, E, P
Tip of the Day	When you first start the program, a helpful hint appears.	W, E, P
TipWizard Toolbar	Shows you Tip of the Day or tips related to the actions you perform.	W, E
Wizards	Provides dialog boxes that take you step-by-step through a process. You are prompted for choices throughout the process to build your document.	W, E, P

W = Word, E = Excel, P = PowerPoint

Note

To get information about your computer such as processor type, operating system, memory, hard drive space, and information about printing, fonts, and files, choose Help, About and click the System Info button.

To find telephone numbers for contacting Microsoft, choose Help, About and click the Tech Support button. You will also find information you need to log on to the Internet, CompuServe, and other communication services. This information will help you to download files and join Microsoft forums to talk to Microsoft support personnel and other users of the product.

Using Online Help

You can find help on a topic in a number of ways. Table 5.2 describes some of the ways to enter a help topic.

Table 5.2 Finding Help on a Topic	
To Do This...	**Do This...**
To find help on options in a dialog box	Press F1 while you're in the dialog box, click the dialog box's ? help button, or right-click on the dialog box item.
To find help on a button on a toolbar	Place the cursor on the button to view its ToolTip and status bar; or click the Help button on the Standard toolbar and then click the button.
To find help on a menu item	Highlight the item on the menu, and look at status bar or press F1; or click the Help button on the Standard toolbar and then click the menu item.
To search for help	From the Help menu, choose Microsoft Excel Help Topics or double-click the Help button on the Standard toolbar. From the Help Topics window, choose the Find or Index tab; see the "Searching for a Help Topic with Index or Find" section later in this chapter for how to use the Find window.
To display a list of Help topics	From the Help menu, choose Microsoft Excel Help Topics or double-click the Help button on the Standard toolbar. From the Help Topics window, choose the Contents tab.
To type in your question	From the Help menu, choose Answer Wizard or double-click the Help button on the Standard toolbar, and choose the Answer Wizard tab. Alternatively, click the Answer Wizard button on the Microsoft Office Shortcut Bar.

Using the Help Topics Window

In the previous choices that lead you to a help file, you can bring up a Help Topics window (see fig. 5.1). The different ways to bring up the Help Topics window are as follows:

- Choose Help, Help Topic.

- Double-click the Help button on a Standard toolbar.

- From a specific topic window, click the Help Topics button.

Fig. 5.1
The Help Topics
window allows
you to search for a
topic in different
ways.

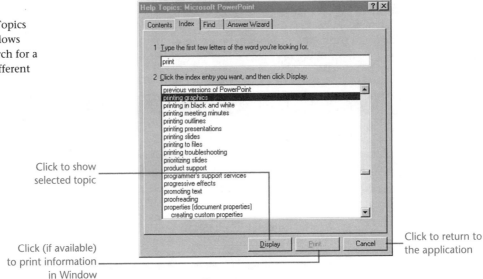

Click to show
selected topic

Click (if available)
to print information
in Window

Click to return to
the application

The Help Topics window shown in figure 5.1 has four tabs: Contents, Index, Find, and Answer Wizard.

- *Contents tab.* Allows you to browse topics, similar to a table of contents in a book.

- *Index tab.* Allows you to search for text based on the title of each page in help.

- *Find tab.* Allows you to search for any text on a help page.

- *Answer Wizard tab.* Allows you to type a question and choose from possible responses.

These tabs are described in more detail in the sections that follow. The following sections also describe additional buttons that are specific to each of the tabs in the Help Topics window.

Finding Help by Looking at Contents

When you aren't sure what the term is you're looking for, you can use the Contents tab of the Help Topics window to scan through possible areas of interest. The Contents tab for Microsoft Word is shown in figure 5.2.

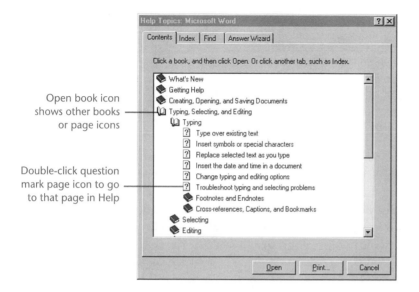

Open book icon shows other books or page icons

Double-click question mark page icon to go to that page in Help

Fig. 5.2
The Contents tab allows you to scan through a list of general topics.

Common Features

When you first go to the Contents tab, each general area is called a book and is indicated by a book icon and the "title" of the book. To open a book, double-click the book icon, or click the topic once and then click the Open button at the bottom of the window. The book icon changes to show an open book, and a list of topics appears under the book icon with question mark icons or more book icons, as shown in figure 5.2. If the selection is still on the open book, the Open button changes to Close. You can close an open book by double-clicking the book again or choosing Close.

To go to any topic, double-click the question mark page icon title, or click the topic once and click the Display button. A Help Topic window opens, containing information about the topic. For more information about the Help Topic windows, see the section "Using Help Topic Pages" later in this chapter.

Tip

Generally, one of the first books on the Contents tab for an application is What's New. Look at the sub-topics to see changes from the previous release.

Note

The first command button on the bottom of the Contents tab has three different possibilities:

■ When a closed book is selected, click Open to expand the book to show available topics.

(continues)

(continued)

- When an open book is selected, click Close to compress the book and not show the outline of topics.

- When a subtopic is selected, click Display to go to the topic.

Looking at Related Information

After you double-click the question mark page icon, the window opens to show you help on that topic. If related references exist, you may see one of two types of screen items. When you move your mouse to a double-arrow button, as shown in figure 5.3, the mouse pointer changes to a pointing finger. Click the topic to move to a different page.

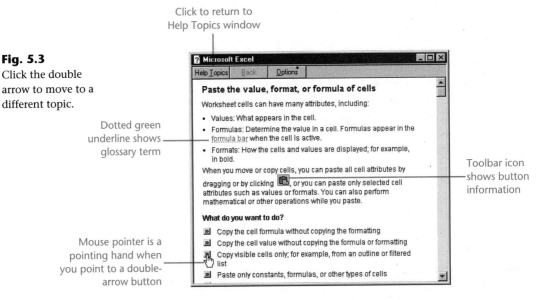

Fig. 5.3
Click the double arrow to move to a different topic.

Click to return to Help Topics window

Dotted green underline shows glossary term

Toolbar icon shows button information

Mouse pointer is a pointing hand when you point to a double-arrow button

If you want to return to the Help Topics window with the Contents, Index, Find, and Answer Wizard tabs, click the Help Topics button.

The second set of related information shows you a partial pop-up window, but keeps the original help topic visible. Within this set are dotted green underlines for glossary terms shown in figure 5.4, pictures of toolbar buttons shown in figure 5.5, and pop-up illustrations, as shown in figure 5.6.

Click the dotted
green underline to
turn the definition
on or off

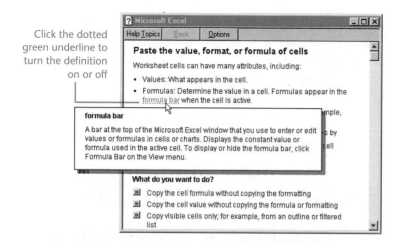

Fig. 5.4
Click a dotted
green underline
to show the
definition of
a term.

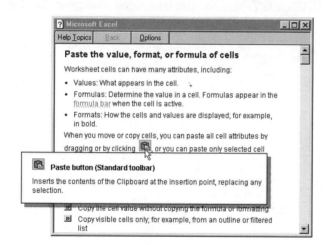

Fig. 5.5
Click the picture
of the toolbar
button to show
how the button
is used.

If more information is available than will fit in the Help window, you see a
scroll bar as shown in figure 5.7. You can either use the scroll bar to view
other parts of the help topic or move the mouse pointer to the edge of the
Help window until it is a double-headed arrow and drag to increase the size
of the window.

Fig. 5.6
Each of the different options has a separate pop-up that provides instructions for how to accomplish the task.

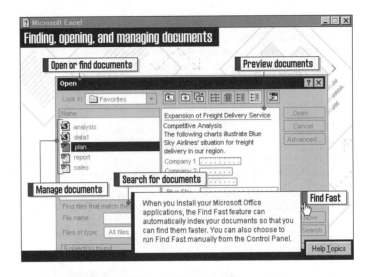

Fig. 5.7
Use the scroll bar to see more of the topic.

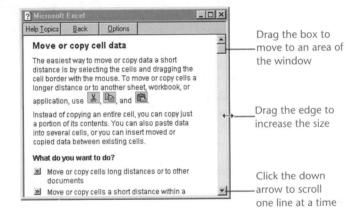

Drag the box to move to an area of the window

Drag the edge to increase the size

Click the down arrow to scroll one line at a time

Using Help Options

In addition to the Help Topics button, most topic windows have two other buttons, Back and Options. If you've used buttons to see related topics, you can click the Back button to retrace your steps. The other button, Options, gives you a number of choices described in table 5.3.

I

Table 5.3   Options Choices on a Help Window

Choose This...	To Do This...
Annotate	Add your own notes to this page in the Help reference. Choose Annotate and then type your note. When finished typing, choose Save. Your note is indicated on the page with a paper clip in the upper left-hand corner of the topic window. To delete the note, choose Annotate and Delete.
Copy	Place a copy of the entire Help window on the Clipboard. Move to the location where you want the text to go (for example, a Word, Notepad, or WordPad document) and choose Edit, Paste to place the Help text in the document. You can also select a portion of the text to copy with the I-beam mouse pointer before you choose Options and then Copy.
Print Topic	Print the displayed topic.
Font	Change the size of fonts in the Help window. You can choose from Small, Normal (the default), and Large.
Keep Help on Top	Some Help windows will automatically remain visible when you click back in the document. To change the default, choose On Top to force the Help window to remain visible when you click back to the application. You can also choose Not On Top or Default.
Use System Colors	Change the Help window to the colors defined in the Control Panel.

Searching for a Help Topic with Index or Find

The Contents tab of the Help Topics window takes you to the topics displayed in the figures mentioned so far in this chapter. Three other tabs enable you to search for a topic based on text within the topic. The Index tab allows you to search for text in the title of the help topic. The Find tab allows you to search for text anywhere on the help topic. The procedure to search through Index and Find is essentially the same. Find has more options, though, so it is discussed here. The third tab allowing you to search for help, Answer Wizard, is discussed in the next section.

Note

The first time you try to search using Find, the help file requires you to build a help database file. This database is a list of all the words from the application's help file. You get a dialog box with a bookshelf, as shown in figure 5.8. Follow the prompts to create the file. The Minimize Database Size option is recommended.

Fig. 5.8
If you get the dialog box to build a Help index, select <u>M</u>inimize Database Size; click the Next button and then click Finish in the next dialog box.

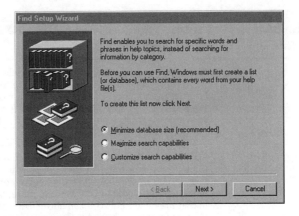

> **Note**
>
> If you select Maximize Search Capabilities when you build the index, you will need to wait much longer while the database is built with its options. You will have more choices (such as marking topics you've already looked at and finding similar topics to a marked topic) when you choose this option. The Maximize Search Capabilities option also takes up more space on the hard drive and has check boxes before each topic in the step 3 area of the Find tab.

To search for text within help, follow these steps:

1. From a document, choose <u>H</u>elp and the application <u>H</u>elp Topics item on the <u>H</u>elp menu.

   Or from a Help window, choose Help <u>T</u>opics.

2. Choose the Find tab in the Help Topics window.

3. In the first step of the Find window, type the word or phrase you want to find, as shown in figure 5.9.

4. In the second step of the window, matching words appear. Select matching words if necessary to limit the search. You can choose multiple matchings by pressing Ctrl and clicking the matchings.

5. In the third step of the window, topics that contain the match appear. Double-click a topic, or click the topic and click <u>D</u>isplay.

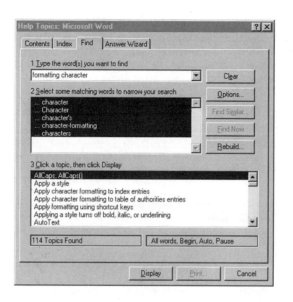

Fig. 5.9
After you type, matching words appear in the second area, and a list of related topics appears in the third area.

A window appears (refer to fig. 5.3). If you want to return to the Help Topics window to choose other topics, choose Help Topics.

A number of additional choices are available from the Find tab to enhance your search. Table 5.4 describes the choices.

Table 5.4   Choices in the Find Tab

To Do This...	Do This...
Use more than one word in the search	Type each word followed by a space in step 1.
To highlight more than one matching word in step 2 on the Find tab	Select first matching word. Hold down Shift while you click the last item to highlight a series of adjacent items, or hold down Ctrl and click non-adjacent items.
Delete text in step 1 on the Find Tab and undo any choices in steps 2 and 3	Click the Clear button.
Look up related topics to step 3 in the dialog box	Click the check box for the topic(s) and then click the Find Similar button. This option is only available if you use the Maximize Search Capabilities when you build your Find Help database file.
Change the Help database to include more (or fewer) items	Click the Rebuild button and follow the steps to create the index database.

(continues)

Table 5.4 Continued	
To Do This...	**Do This...**
Change how help finds the words in step 1	Choose the Options button and in the Search for Topics section, select whether you want help to look for all words in step 1, at least one of the words in step 1, or the exact order of the words you typed in step 1. On the Show Words That option of the Find Options dialog box, you can also choose whether you want the entire word(s) or a portion of the word(s) typed in step 1 to be used for matching.
Change whether you need to click the Find Now button	Choose the Options button and choose an option in the Begin Searching section to determine whether you need to click Find Now or just type a word.
Change which help files you search when using Help	Choose Options, Files and then select which files you want to search.

Note

In most of Microsoft Office, you see the Find and Index tabs on the Help Topics window. However, you may encounter the old Windows 3.1 Help window once in a while (in Microsoft Graph, for example). This Help window does not have tabs and includes a menu bar which includes File, Edit, Bookmark, Options, and Help. Instead of book icons and double arrows, there is a solid green underline; click the underlined word to go to a "book" of topics or a page in the book. Pop-up definitions are indicated by a dotted green underline. To look for help, choose Help, Search for Help On from the application or click the Search button in a Help window.

Searching for Topics with the Answer Wizard

A new feature to Microsoft Office 95 is the Answer Wizard. This feature is on the fourth tab of the Help Topics window. To use the feature, choose Help from the menu bar of an application and then choose Answer Wizard. You will go to the fourth tab on the Help Topics window, as shown in figure 5.10. If you already are in the Help Topics window (on another tab), click the Answer Wizard tab.

Type text here

Click here to
display topics

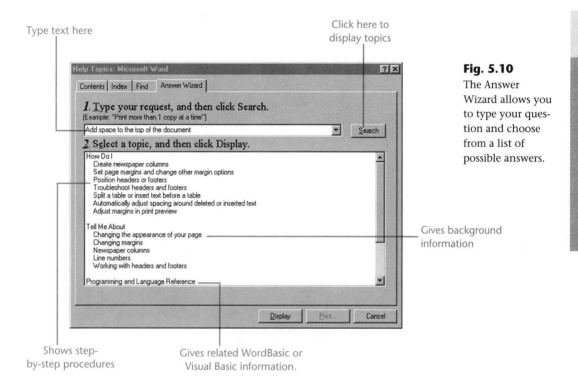

Fig. 5.10
The Answer
Wizard allows you
to type your ques-
tion and choose
from a list of
possible answers.

Gives background
information

Shows step-
by-step procedures

Gives related WordBasic or
Visual Basic information.

Type a question in step 1 of the Answer Wizard tab and then click the Search
button. The Answer Wizard will interpret your request and give you a list of
possible topics in the step 2 area of the Answer Wizard tab. These topics are
generally organized under three separate categories:

- How Do I

- Tell Me About

- Programming and Language Reference

Double-click any topic in the step 2 area of the Answer Wizard tab, or choose
the topic and click Display.

When you choose an item in the How Do I section, you get step-by-step instructions on how to accomplish a task, as shown in figure 5.11. The Tell
Me About section gives you background information about the topics and
usually leads you to a graphical example document with labels you can use
to explain the document, as shown in figure 5.12. The Programming and
Language Reference section gives you WordBasic, Visual Basic, or other
programming notes, as shown in figure 5.13.

Fig. 5.11
If you select
Create Newspaper
Columns from the
How Do I section
in figure 5.10,
these step-by-step
instructions
appear.

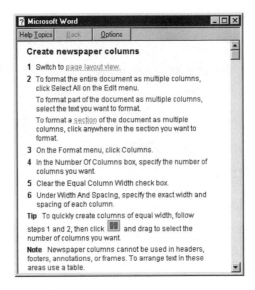

Fig. 5.12
If you choose
Changing the
Appearance of
Your Page from
the Tell Me About
section in figure
5.10, this picture
of the document
appears with pop-
up explanations.

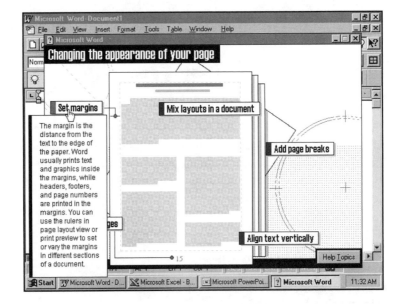

Note

You can get to the same Help Topic window through the Contents, Index, Find, or
Answer Wizard tabs. Your method for searching depends on the terms you know,
your objective (browsing for general information versus finding help on a specific
topic), and your personal preference.

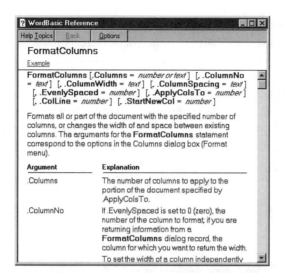

Common Features

Fig. 5.13
If you choose FormatColumns under Programming and Language Reference, the Help window shows how you use the FormatColumns command in WordBasic.

When you choose a topic from the Contents, Index, or Find tabs, the Answer Wizard may also automatically launch to help you with the selected topic.

Troubleshooting

After I type a word in the first step of the Find tab of the Help Topics window, nothing happens.

You may need to click the Find Now button to activate the choice. You can also click Options and select the Immediately after Each Keystroke check box.

I know that a Help topic should exist for the text that I type, but I can't find it.

You may be looking in the wrong file for the help you need. On the Find tab of the Help Topics window, choose Options, Files and then pick the files you need. If you want to see information from all files, choose Select All. You may also need to rebuild the help index database. On the Find tab, choose the Rebuild option and follow the prompts to create your index database.

Reviewing Screen Elements

In addition to the online help, there are many help features built into Microsoft Office products. The most visible are the toolbars, but other screen features included to help you are ToolTips, the status bar, view buttons, and special areas on dialog boxes.

◄ See "Using Toolbars in Microsoft Office Applications," p. 44

◄ See "Formatting Documents," p. 81

Using Toolbars

◀ See "Using Toolbars in Microsoft Office Applications," p. 44

Usually one or more toolbars are visible on-screen, as shown in figure 5.14. The buttons on the toolbars allow you to quickly make a choice. For example, after you highlight a word, you can choose the Bold and Italic buttons to change the font style. You could also choose F̲ormat, F̲ont and make choices in the dialog box. The toolbar buttons are quicker, but the menu choices offer more thorough choices. If a toolbar is not visible, choose V̲iew, T̲oolbars to bring it up. For diagrams of all the toolbars, see Chapter 2, "Getting Started and Identifying Screen Parts." If you want to add or remove buttons to or from your toolbars, see Chapter 34, "Customizing the Desktop, Toolbars, and Menus."

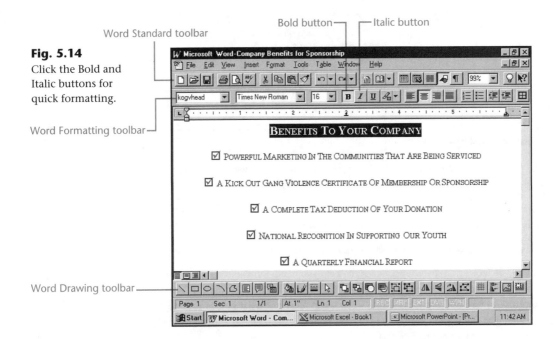

Fig. 5.14
Click the Bold and Italic buttons for quick formatting.

Word Standard toolbar

Bold button ── ┌─ Italic button

Word Formatting toolbar ─

Word Drawing toolbar ──

Displaying ToolTips

ToolTips assist you in your use of toolbars. When ToolTips are on, you can leave your mouse pointer on a button momentarily, and a short description appears at the mouse pointer, as shown in figure 5.15. If ToolTips are not visible, choose V̲iew, T̲oolbars and select the S̲how ToolTips check box.

Microsoft Word has an added feature with ToolTips that enables you to see whether a shortcut key exists that duplicates the function of the button. In the Toolbars dialog box, select With Shortcut K̲eys. When you place your mouse pointer on a toolbar button, the ToolTip displays the shortcut key if it is available, as shown in figure 5.16.

Open button with ToolTip

Fig. 5.15
When you leave
your mouse
pointer on a
button, the
ToolTip appears.

Longer description on
the status bar

Fig. 5.16
The Open button
ToolTip shows
Ctrl+O as the
shortcut for
opening a file.

Looking at the Status Bar

Regardless of whether you have ToolTips turned on, the status bar at the
bottom of the screen shows a longer description of what the button does
(refer to fig. 5.15). If the status bar is not visible, choose <u>T</u>ools, <u>O</u>ptions and
select Status Bar on the View tab. The status bar may also show information
about your location in the document, the status of on/off keys (such as Caps
Lock, Num Lock, Insert), and program status (such as Macro Record or
WordPerfect Help Keys on). Figure 5.17 shows the status bar for Microsoft
Word.

◄ See "Viewing
Parts of the
Window,"
p. 40

► See "Modifying
Viewing Op-
tions," p. 233

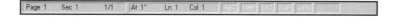

Fig. 5.17
Word's status
bar shows the
location on the
document and
program status
options.

Using View Buttons

At the bottom of the screen, Word and PowerPoint also have view buttons to
help you with your work. The view buttons are similar to toolbar buttons
because they also can display ToolTips. They can change the size of the

document that you can see at one time or show additional features for editing and formatting. Figure 5.18 shows the view buttons for Microsoft Word.

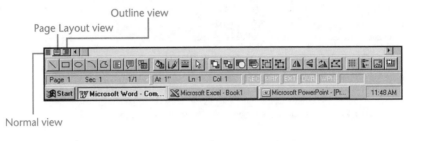

Outline view
Page Layout view

Fig. 5.18
The view buttons change the amount of the document displayed and add other features.

Normal view

Using Help Features in Dialog Boxes

In Microsoft Office 95, toolbar buttons are now included on more dialog boxes. Figure 5.19 shows an Open dialog box for Microsoft Excel with the buttons. ToolTips are also available so that you can see the functions of the buttons.

? Help button

Fig. 5.19
Microsoft Office 95 adds more toolbar buttons and the ? button to dialog boxes.

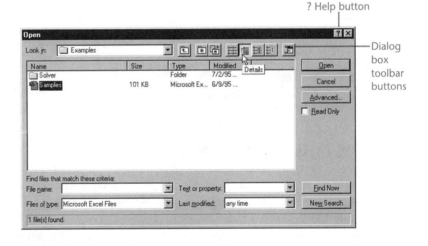

Dialog box toolbar buttons

◀ See "Using Dialog Boxes," p. 55

In addition to more toolbar buttons in dialog boxes, Microsoft Office 95 dialog boxes also have a new feature. The question mark in the upper right-hand corner of most dialog boxes enables you to explore the items in a dialog box. When you click on the question mark, the mouse pointer changes to a question mark. You can then click an item in the dialog box to get a pop-up description of the feature, as shown in figure 5.20. Instead of using the question mark, you can also click the right mouse button on many features of dialog boxes to see descriptions of those features.

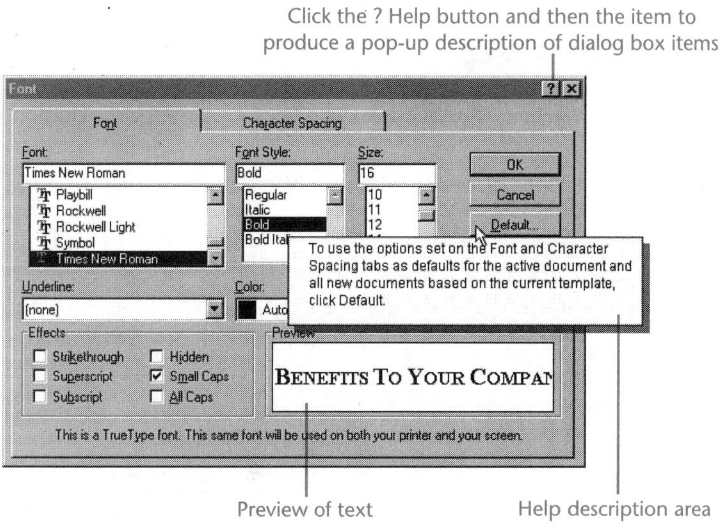

Click the ? Help button and then the item to
produce a pop-up description of dialog box items

Fig. 5.20
Dialog boxes
allow help with
the ? Help button,
description areas,
and preview areas.

Preview of text   Help description area

Also shown in figure 5.20, some dialog boxes have additional help through a
description area that gives tips, explains potential problems, or tells about the
command. A dialog box may also include a preview area that shows the result
of the dialog box settings before you choose OK.

Troubleshooting

The Toolbar button is not visible.

The toolbar may not be turned on. Choose View, Toolbars; select the toolbars you
want to see; then choose OK. Another possibility is that the toolbars have been
changed. In the Toolbars dialog box, choose the toolbar where the button should be
and choose Reset.

The ToolTip does not display for a button.

Leave the mouse pointer stationary on a button. If you move the mouse, the ToolTip
does not appear. You may also need to turn ToolTips on by choosing View, Toolbars,
Show ToolTips.

The status bar or view buttons are not visible on my screen.

Choose Tools, Options, and on the View tab check the Status Bar or Horizontal Scroll
Bar check boxes.

Viewing Tips

The Microsoft Office applications will also suggest tips to help you become more proficient with the products. These tips appear at two different times— when you start the application and while you are performing procedures.

PowerPoint displays a dialog box with a helpful tip when you start the program (see fig. 5.21). To skip the tips, deselect the Show Tips at Startup check box. To see additional tips, choose Next Tip or the More Tips button and choose one of the topics in the Help window. You can also display the Tip of the Day dialog box by choosing Help, Tip of the Day.

Fig. 5.21
The Tip of the Day shows when you start the program or when you choose the Help menu item.

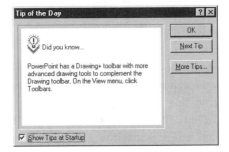

Tip
Keep the TipWizard toolbar displayed as you work to see how you can increase your productivity.

Microsoft Word and Excel also show a tip of the day when you start the application. However, you need to select the TipWizard button on the standard toolbar to display the TipWizard box, which is on a separate toolbar appearing beneath the Standard and Formatting toolbars, as shown in figure 5.22. You can turn the TipWizard toolbar on or off with the TipWizard button on the Standard toolbar; or, like other toolbars, choose View, Toolbars and turn the TipWizard on or off.

TipWizard button turns the
TipWizard toolbar on and off

TipWizard toolbar

Fig. 5.22
The TipWizard toolbar displays suggestions to help you improve your productivity.

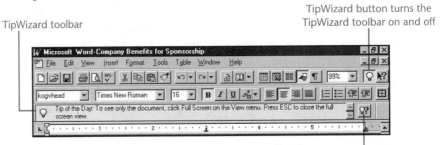

Show Me button gives more information on the tip

The TipWizard toolbar may also include a light bulb with a question mark which will give you additional information about the tip, as shown in figure 5.22.

If you keep the TipWizard toolbar open as you perform procedures, the application will occasionally make suggestions based on the steps that you perform. For example, if you change the column width in Excel by choosing Format, Column, Width, the TipWizard displays a tip suggesting that you drag the right boundary of the column heading, as shown in figure 5.23. Regardless of whether you display the TipWizard box, the TipWizard button changes to yellow when it has a new tip for you to read.

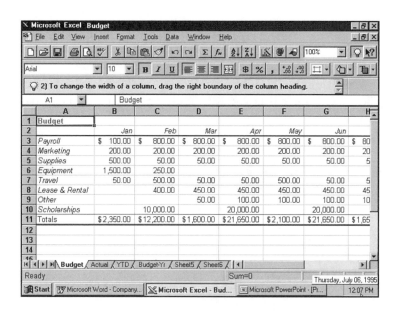

Fig. 5.23
The TipWizard toolbar shows a simpler way of doing the same task you just completed.

Troubleshooting

Tip of the Day does not appear for PowerPoint.

Choose Help, Tip of the Day and select the Show Tip at Startup check box.

I want to use TipWizards and have the TipWizard toolbar displayed, but no tips seem to appear.

In Word, choose Tools, Options, and on the General tab make sure that you have selected the TipWizard Active check box. It is also possible that you are doing procedures in the most efficient way possible.

Using Wizards

▶ See "Using
Template
Wizards,"
p. 269

▶ See "Creating a
Presentation
Using a
Wizard,"
p. 578

One of the greatest help features in the Microsoft Office applications is not really a help feature at all. Wizards do not appear on the Help menu (except for the Answer Wizard), but appear throughout the applications. *Wizards* are special dialog boxes that ask you questions about the document you want to create and then use your answers to lay out and format the document.

When you start a wizard (see fig. 5.24), the wizard asks you to enter text in text boxes or choose from a list of options. When you finish filling in one step of the wizard, click the Next button to go to the next step. You can skip to the last step if you know the default settings for your wizard by clicking Finish. If you want to cancel the wizard, click Cancel or press Esc. On some dialog boxes, you also have the capability to return to a previous step by clicking Back.

Fig. 5.24
Word's Award
Wizard prompts
you for a name
and a title, as well
as other options.

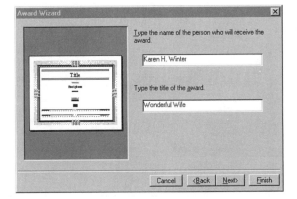

You activate a wizard by different means in the programs. Table 5.5 lists some of the wizards.

Note

You can also start a majority of the wizards by clicking the Microsoft Office Shortcut Bar Start a Document button. The tabs on the dialog box match the names in the File New dialog box, shown in the How To Start column of table 5.5.

Note

If any of these wizards don't appear, they may have not been installed during the setup procedure. You can install them by going through setup again and clicking the Add/Remove button.

Table 5.5 Wizards Available To Make Your Work Easier

Program and Wizard	How To Start	What It Does
Word Newsletter	File, New, Publications tab, Newsletter Wizard	Creates a newsletter with wizard formatting and table of contents.
Word Resume Wizard	File, New, Other Documents tab, Resume Wizard	Creates a résumé.
Word Memo Wizard	File, New, Memos tab, Memo Wizard	Creates a memo.
Word Letter Wizard	File, New, Letters & Faxes tab, Letter Wizard	Creates a business or personal letter.
Word Fax Wizard	File, New, Letter & Faxes tab, Fax Wizard	Creates a fax cover sheet.
Word Agenda Wizard	File, New, Other Documents tab, Agenda Wizard	Creates a meeting agenda.
Word Award Wizard	File, New, Other Documents tab, Award Wizard	Creates an award certificate.
Word Calendar Wizard	File, New, Other Documents tab, Calendar Wizard	Creates a monthly calendar.
Word Pleading Wizard	File, New, Other Documents tab, Pleading Wizard	Creates a pleading format used for legal documents.
Word Table Wizard	File, New, Other Documents tab, Table Wizard, or Table, Insert Table, Wizard	Creates or inserts a formatted table.
Excel Chart Wizard	Click Chart Wizard button and drag mouse area where chart will appear.	Creates a chart.
Excel Pivot Table Wizard	Data, PivotTable	Analyzes and summarizes a list of data.
Excel Text Import Wizard	File, Open and in Files of type, choose Text Files and click Open	Separates data into columns.
Excel Convert Text	Data, Text to Columns to Columns Wizard	Separates (parses) data from a long line of text into columns.

Note

Although they are not technically wizards, many of PowerPoint's templates work similarly and are very helpful for starting a presentation. Instead of answering questions through a wizard dialog box, you replace text on existing slides. These templates are on the Presentations tab when you choose File, New from PowerPoint or click the Start a New Document button on the Microsoft Office Shortcut Bar. Presentations included are:

- Business Plan
- Communicating Bad News
- Company Meeting
- Creativity Session
- Employee Orientation
- Financial Report
- General

- Marketing Plan
- Recommending a Strategy
- Reporting Progress
- Selling a Product, Service, or Idea
- Top Ten List
- Training

Some of these presentations have both short and long versions.

Part II

Using Word

Chapter 6

Creating and Editing Documents

by Patty Winter and Rick Winter

Of all the applications included with Microsoft Office, Word may be the one you use most. You probably need a word processor to produce at least letters and envelopes in your everyday work. Using Word, you also can create memos, fax cover sheets, reports, newsletters, mailing labels, brochures, tables, and many other business and personal documents.

In this chapter, you learn to

- Identify the parts of the Word screen and the toolbar buttons

- Enter text

- Select text

- Edit text

- Reverse the last editing action

- Save a document

- Close and open documents

- Start a new document

Word offers many commands and features that help you complete your work quickly and easily. Word provides easy graphics handling, outlining, calculations of data in tables, the capability to create a mailing list, list sorting, and efficient file management. In addition, you can perform many desktop publishing tasks, such as formatting fonts, creating display type, aligning text, adding graphic borders, and adding shading.

Microsoft Office offers another advantage for using Word as your day-to-day word processor. When you use Word, you have the flexibility to share data and tools with Excel, PowerPoint, Mail, and other Windows applications.

Understanding Word Basics

◀ See "Using
Help," p. 141

Word offers many excellent features that help you perform your word processing tasks efficiently. If you are familiar with Windows 3.1 or Windows 95 applications, you probably already know quite a bit about operating Word. You should know, for example, how to use such features as the Control menu icon, the Window menu, and Help. Additionally, you understand the use of the mouse, scroll bars, dialog boxes, and other features of a Windows application. For more information about Word for Windows, refer to Que's book *Special Edition Using Word for Windows 95*.

This section shows you how to use some features and screen elements particular to the Word program, including the toolbars, scroll bars, and the status bar.

Using the Word Screen

◀ See "Viewing
Parts of the
Window,"
p. 40
◀ See "Using
Menus," p. 51

When you start the program, Word displays specific screen elements as defaults, including the title bar, menu bar, two toolbars, a ruler, and scroll bars. You can, of course, hide these elements or show different components, at any time, by choosing a command from the View menu or the Tools menu. Suppose that you want to hide the ruler. Choose View, Ruler to hide it; choose View, Ruler again to display the ruler. Suppose that you want to turn off the scroll bars. Choose Tools, Option, click the View tab and click the option you want to turn off in the Windowbox, then click the OK command button; do the same thing to turn the option back on. A checkmark indicates that the option is currently "on" or enabled; a blank checkbox indicates that the option is off.

Figure 6.1 shows the default Word screen and indicates the components of the screen.

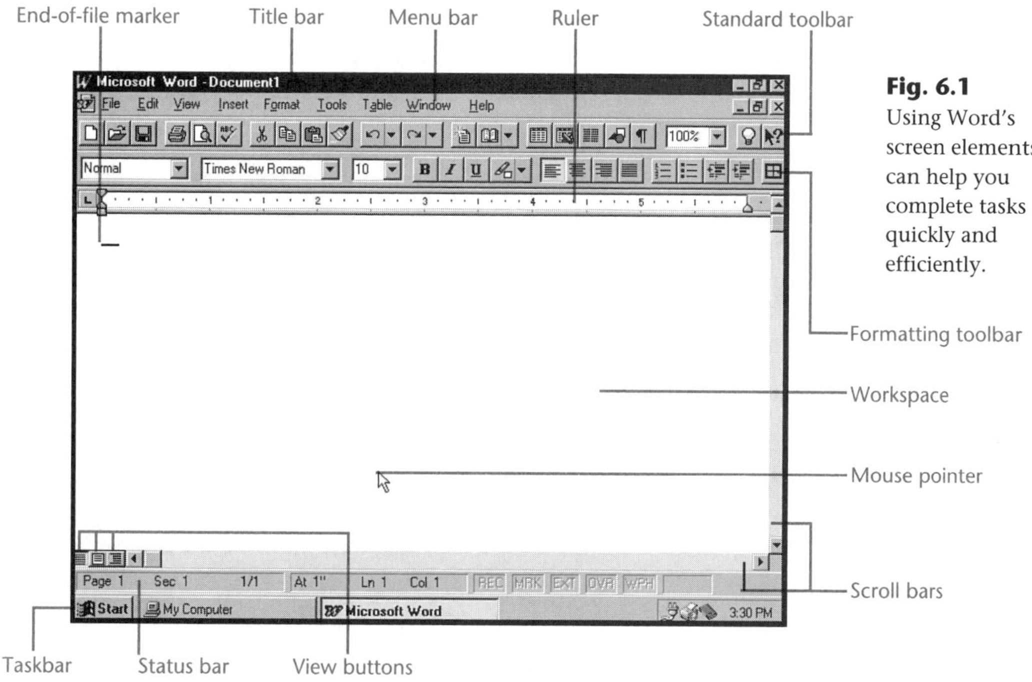

End-of-file marker
Title bar
Menu bar
Ruler
Standard toolbar
Formatting toolbar
Workspace
Mouse pointer
Scroll bars
Taskbar
Status bar
View buttons
Microsoft Word - Document1
File Edit View Insert Format Tools Table Window Help
Normal
Times New Roman
10
100%
Page 1 Sec 1 1/1 At 1" Ln 1 Col 1 REC MRK EXT OVR WPH
Start
My Computer
Microsoft Word
3:30 PM

Fig. 6.1
Using Word's screen elements can help you complete tasks quickly and efficiently.

The following list describes the screen elements. The toolbars are covered in more detail in the next chapter.

- *Title bar.* The title bar contains the name of the program and the name of the document, the Control-menu icon, and the Minimize, Maximize, Restore, and Close buttons. Additionally, the title bar contains the Microsoft Office toolbar.

- *Menu bar.* The menu bar contains specialized menus containing related commands. Choose commands from the Format menu, for example, to change fonts, set tabs, add a border, and so on.

- *Standard toolbar.* This toolbar contains buttons you click to perform common tasks, such as starting a new document, saving a document, checking spelling, and undoing an action. The buttons in the Standard toolbar provide shortcuts for common menu commands.

▶ See "Customizing Predefined Toolbars," p. 759

  When you leave the mouse pointer on a button, a ToolTip appears with the mouse pointer, giving the name of the button. With the View, Toolbars command you can turn these ToolTips on or off as well as show the ToolTips shortcut keys (Ctrl+O for Open, and so on).

- *Formatting toolbar.* The buttons in the Formatting toolbar provide shortcuts for choosing character or paragraph formatting such as changing fonts, font sizes, styles, alignments, and so on. Use this toolbar to format text quickly as you work.

▶ See "Formatting Paragraphs," p. 194

- *Ruler.* The ruler provides a quick and easy method of setting tabs and indents in your text. For more information about the ruler, see Chapter 7, "Formatting Documents."

- *Workspace.* The workspace consists of a blank "page" in which you enter or edit text, place pictures and graphics, and work with your document.

◀ See "Moving around the Document," p. 75

- *Scroll bars.* Use the scroll bars to move quickly to another area of the document.

◀ See "Viewing Parts of the Window," p. 40

- *Status bar.* The status bar lists information and displays messages as you work in Word. When you position the mouse pointer on a toolbar button, for example, a description of that button's function appears in the status bar.

◀ See "Launching Programs," p. 28

- *Taskbar.* The taskbar is part of Windows 95 and allows you to start applications through the Start button and to switch between applications that have been launched.

- *End-of-file marker.* The short horizontal line indicates the end of the document. You cannot move past this marker.

- *Mouse pointer.* As you move your mouse, the mouse pointer moves on-screen. The mouse pointer may change shape depending on the screen location (I-beam, left-pointing white arrow, right-pointing white arrow, etc.), indicating that you can accomplish different tasks.

▶ See "Understanding Views," p. 186

- *View buttons.* To the bottom left of the horizontal scroll bar are three View buttons (Normal View, Page Layout View, Outline View). These buttons allow you to change your view to include margins, headers and footers, or show additional organizing tools.

Entering Text in a Word Document

When you start the Word program, Word supplies you with a new, blank document (named Document1 in the title bar). You can begin to type at the blinking insertion point. When you enter text, that text appears at the insertion point.

This section describes the basic techniques of entering text, moving around in a document, and selecting text for editing.

Typing Text

When entering text, you type as you would in any word processor. Word automatically wraps the text at the end of a line—you do not have to press Enter to begin a new line. Press Enter only when you want to start a new paragraph or create a blank line. Word defines a paragraph as any number of letters, words, or sentences ending with a paragraph mark.

A *paragraph mark* is a nonprinting character inserted whenever you press Enter. You can view paragraph marks by clicking the Show/Hide ¶ button in the Standard toolbar. To hide paragraph marks, click the Show/Hide ¶ button again. Figure 6.2 shows paragraph marks and the Show/Hide ¶ button in the Standard toolbar. In addition, the right indent marker in the figure is set at 4 1/2 inches so that you can see the automatic word wrap.

Paragraph marks

Show/Hide ¶ button

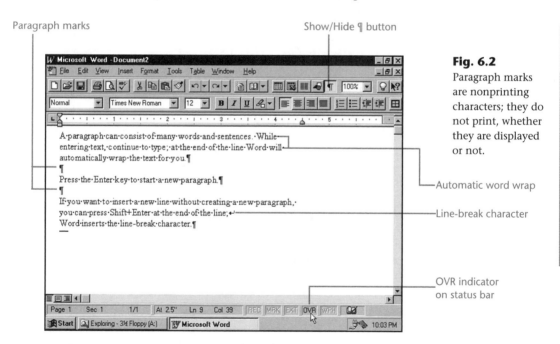

Fig. 6.2
Paragraph marks are nonprinting characters; they do not print, whether they are displayed or not.

Automatic word wrap

Line-break character

OVR indicator on status bar

II

Using Word

The following list contains some useful shortcuts and features you can use when entering text in Word:

- If you make a mistake while typing, press the Backspace key to erase a character to the left of the insertion point.

- Press the Delete key to remove characters to the right of the insertion point.

- To repeat the text you just typed, choose <u>E</u>dit, <u>R</u>epeat Typing; or press Ctrl+Y.

- To erase the text you just typed, choose <u>E</u>dit, <u>U</u>ndo Typing; or press Ctrl+Z. You also can click the Undo button in the Standard toolbar.

- To start a new line without inserting a paragraph mark, press Shift+Enter. Word inserts a line-break character.

- Double-click the OVR indicator in the status bar to use Overtype mode, in which the text you enter replaces existing text. Double-click the indicator again to turn off Overtype mode.

Positioning the Insertion Point

To move the insertion point, move the I-beam mouse pointer to the new location and click the left mouse button. You can position the insertion point anywhere in the text area except below the *end marker* (the short horizontal line displayed in the text area). You can move the end marker by inserting paragraph returns (pressing Enter) before the marker.

If you want to move the insertion point to a location that doesn't appear in the current window, you can use the horizontal or vertical scroll bar to move to the new location. When the new location appears in the window, place the I-beam pointer where you want to position the insertion point and click the left mouse button.

> **Note**
>
> The insertion point always stays within the text area. If you click outside the margin boundary, Word places the insertion point in the nearest text.

Additionally, you can press certain keys on the keyboard to move the insertion point quickly to a new location. Using the keyboard to move around in a document is sometimes faster and easier than using the mouse. The following table lists common keys you can use to move around in your documents:

Key	Moves Insertion Point
Arrow keys	One character up, down, left, or right
Page Up/Page Down	One screen up or down
Ctrl+ ←/→	One word to the left or right
Home/End	Beginning or end of a line

Key	Moves Insertion Point
Ctrl+Home/End	Beginning or end of the document
Ctrl+Page Up/Page Down	Top or bottom of screen
Alt+Ctrl+Page Up/Page Down	Top of the previous or next page

Selecting Text

After entering text, you may want to delete or move a word, sentence, or paragraph. In addition, you may want to format the text by changing the font or font size, indenting text, and so on. Before you can perform one of these actions on the text in your document, you must select the text. *Selecting* the text shows Word where to perform the action. After you select text, the selected text temporarily changes to white text on a black background. Selected text allows you to perform one or more actions on the selected text.

You can select text by using the mouse, the keyboard, or a combination of methods, depending on how much text you want to select. The following list describes the methods of text selection:

- To select one word, position the I-beam pointer anywhere in a word and double-click. The word and the space following the word are selected.

- To select a sentence, hold down the Ctrl key while clicking anywhere in the sentence. Word selects all words in the sentence to the ending punctuation mark, plus the blank spaces following the punctuation mark.

- To select a paragraph, triple-click the paragraph, or place the mouse pointer in the selection bar, and double-click. The *selection bar* is a vertical band to the left of the workspace. When you point the mouse in the selection bar, the I-beam pointer changes to an arrow (see fig. 6.3).

- To select specific text, click and drag the I-beam pointer over one character, one word, or the entire screen.

- To select one line of text, place the mouse pointer in the selection bar to the left of the line and click once.

- To select the entire document, hold down the Ctrl key while clicking the selection bar. Alternatively, press Ctrl+A to select the entire document.

II

Using Word

■ To select a vertical block of text—the first letters of words in a list, for example—hold down the Alt key while you click and drag the mouse pointer across the text. Figure 6.4 shows a vertical block of selected text.

■ To select text with the keyboard arrow keys, position the insertion point where you want to start selecting, press and hold down the Shift key, and then press the appropriate arrow key to move up, down, left, or right.

■ To select to the end of a line of text with the keyboard, position the insertion point where you want to start selecting and then press Shift+End. Alternatively, select to the beginning of the line of text by pressing Shift+Home.

■ To select a block of text, position the insertion point where you want to start selecting, move the mouse pointer to the end of the text you want to select, hold down the Shift key, and click the left mouse button.

■ To deselect text, click once anywhere in the workspace of a document or press an arrow key.

Mouse pointer   Selected line of text

Fig. 6.3
Use the selection bar to select one line quickly; select more than one line by dragging the mouse pointer in the selection bar.

Selection bar

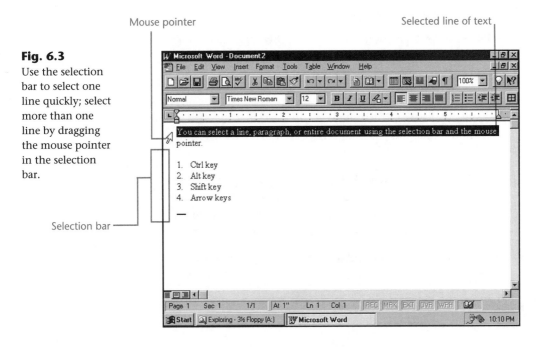

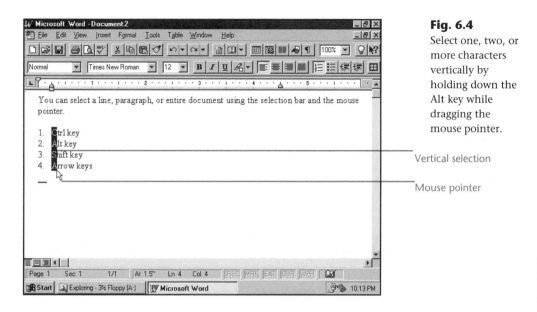

Fig. 6.4
Select one, two, or
more characters
vertically by
holding down the
Alt key while
dragging the
mouse pointer.

Vertical selection

Mouse pointer

To deselect text, click the mouse anywhere in the document or workspace, or
press any of the arrow keys.

Caution

If you have text selected and press the space bar or any character key, the selected
text is deleted and is replaced by the characters you typed.

Troubleshooting

*I began typing the text, and I messed up my document in a completely different area of
the document from where I was looking.*

You must click the mouse to position the insertion point before you begin typing the
text. A blinking vertical line indicates the insertion point.

I tried to select text with the mouse, but I had trouble controlling the selection.

It takes practice to control the mouse when you select text. Try one of the alternative
methods of selecting text described in this section. For example, try positioning the
insertion point at the beginning of the selection, holding down the Shift key, and
then clicking the mouse at the end of the selection. Another option is to change the
mouse properties (choose the Start button on the taskbar, choose Settings Control
Panel, and select the Mouse program).

II

Using Word

Editing Text in a Word Document

◀ See "Typing and Editing," p. 68

With Word, changes and corrections are easy to make. You can select any text in your document and delete it, copy it, or move it. You also can make other changes easily. How many times have you typed text, only to discover that the Caps Lock feature was on? Don't type the text again; use Word's Change Case command. This section shows you how to edit your document quickly and easily. You can use the Backspace and Delete keys to edit one character at a time, or you can select text first and then edit it. Table 6.1 summarizes the editing commands, buttons, and shortcuts that you can use to edit selected text.

Table 6.1   Procedures for editing selected text

	Delete	Copy	Move	Undo	Redo
Keyboard	Delete or Backspace	Ctrl+C then Ctrl+V	Ctrl+X then Ctrl+V	Ctrl+Z or Alt Backspace	Ctrl+Y
Toolbar buttons	[scissors icon]	[copy icon] then [paste icon]	[cut icon] then [paste icon]	[undo icon]	[redo icon]
Commands	Edit Clear	Edit Copy then Edit Paste	Edit Cut then Edit Paste	Edit Undo	Edit Redo
Right mouse button	Cut	Copy then Paste	Cut then Paste		
Drag mouse		Drag selection	Ctrl+Drag selection		

Tip
If you make a mistake while typing text, pressing Backspace or Delete to delete the mistake may be easier than using Undo.

Undoing a Mistake

You can reverse many mistakes by using the Undo command. Suppose that you type a sentence and decide you don't like the way it reads. You can delete the sentence by choosing Edit, Undo or by pressing either of the shortcut keys: Ctrl+Z or Alt+Backspace. If you make a correction and change your mind, you can use the Undo command to reverse the action.

Word also provides a Redo command (also on the Edit menu) you can use to reverse the last Undo. The keyboard shortcut for the Redo command is Ctrl+Y or Alt+Shift+Backspace. Both the Undo and Redo commands describe the action you just performed, like Undo Typing, Redo Clear, and so on.

The Edit, Undo, or Redo command works only on the last task you performed. If, for instance, you delete a sentence and decide that you want it back, you must choose the Undo command before carrying out another task. However, Word supplies Undo and Redo buttons in the Standard toolbar that enable you to undo or redo other recent actions. Figure 6.5 shows the Undo drop-down list displaying six of the most recent actions.

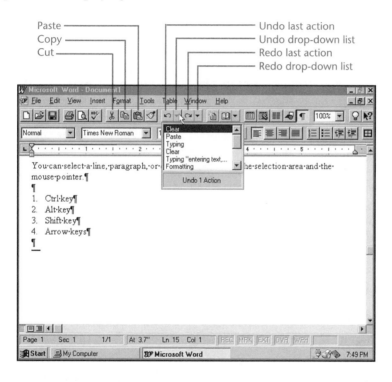

Fig. 6.5
Use the Undo and Redo drop-down lists to reverse any of the last several actions performed. The Cut, Copy, and Paste buttons allow you to cut, copy and move text.

II

Using Word

Deleting and Moving Text

To delete any amount of text, select the text and press the Delete key. When you press Delete, the text is erased; the only way to recall the text is to choose the Undo command. Alternatively, you can delete text by selecting it and then choosing Edit, Clear. The Edit, Clear command deletes the text just as the Delete key does. You can also delete the previous word by pressing Ctrl+Backspace.

You also can choose Edit, Cut, or press Ctrl+X to remove the text. Edit, Cut moves the selected text from the document to the Windows Clipboard. The text remains on the Clipboard until you use the Edit, Cut or Edit, Copy command again. Figure 6.5 shows the Cut, Copy, and Paste buttons on the Standard toolbar.

Tip
You can also click
the right mouse
button on a selec-
tion to cut, copy
and paste.

Tip
Use the Cut button
to remove text
instead of the
Delete key. You
can bring back the
last deletion with-
out undoing any
other work by
positioning the
insertion point
and clicking the
Paste button.

Tip
To copy the text or
graphic instead of
moving it, hold
down the Ctrl key
as you point to the
selected text or
graphic, and drag
the dotted inser-
tion point to a
new location.

To move text that you cut to another location in the same document or to another document, position the insertion point where you want the text to appear and choose Edit, Paste; or press Ctrl+V. The cut text reappears at the insertion point. You can paste this text again and again until you cut or copy new text.

Copying Text

To copy text, select the text and then choose Edit, Copy; or press the shortcut key Ctrl+C. Word copies the text to the Clipboard. You then can paste the copied text in a new location or document by positioning the insertion point and then choosing Edit, Paste or pressing Ctrl+V. You can also use the Copy and Paste buttons shown earlier in figure 6.5.

Copying text or other elements in your documents, such as pictures and charts, is one way to share data between applications. The Windows Clipboard is used by all the Microsoft Office applications. You can, for example, create text in Word, copy it, and paste it in PowerPoint. You also can copy a worksheet from Excel and paste it to a table in Word.

Drag-and-Drop Editing

An additional method you can use to move or copy text is called *drag-and-drop editing*. Word supplies this shortcut for moving or copying selected text. You also can use drag-and-drop editing to copy or move graphics or other objects.

To use drag-and-drop editing to move text or graphics, follow these steps:

1. Select the text or graphics you want to move.

2. Point to the selected text or graphic and hold down the left mouse button. The drag-and-drop pointer appears (see fig. 6.6).

3. Drag the pointer and the dotted insertion point that appears to the new location and release the mouse button.

> **Note**
>
> The drag-and-drop editing option is activated by default. If you do not want to use drag-and-drop editing, you can turn the feature off by choosing Tools, Options. In the Edit tab, select Drag-and-Drop Text Editing to turn off the option.

Insertion point   Drag-and-drop pointer   Selected text

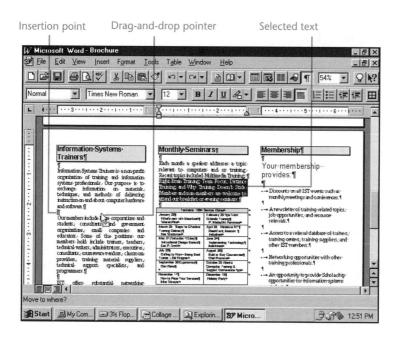

Fig. 6.6
Using the drag-and-drop pointer, drag the selected text or graphic to a new location.

Converting Case

Word includes a handy command you can use to convert the case of text you entered earlier. Suppose that you decide you do not want a heading to appear in all caps. You can select the text you want to change and choose Format, Change Case. The Change Case dialog box appears. Select one of the following options:

- *Sentence Case.* Capitalizes only the first letter in selected sentences.

- *Lowercase.* Changes all selected text to lowercase.

- *Uppercase.* Converts all selected text to all capital letters.

- *Title Case.* Capitalizes the first letter of each word of selected text.

- *Toggle Case.* Changes uppercase to lowercase and lowercase to uppercase in all selected text.

Note

You also can use the shortcut key to change case. Select the text and press Shift+F3. Each time you press the shortcut key, Word cycles through lowercase, uppercase, and initial caps. If a sentence or multiple sentences is selected, initial caps changes the first word of the sentence. If a phrase is selected, initial caps will capitalize the first letter of every word as in book titles.

Troubleshooting

I accidentally deleted or cleared text that I did not mean to delete.

Click the Undo button in the Standard toolbar or use the Ctrl+Z shortcut key to undo the last action.

I pasted selected text in the wrong place.

Press Ctrl+Z to undo the paste. Then position the insertion point in the correct location and choose Edit, Paste again.

I accidentally get the drag-and-drop editing pointer when I do not want it.

Be careful not to drag a text block after selecting it. If you do drag the mouse and you get the drag-and-drop pointer, press Esc before you release the mouse button. If you do not use the drag-and-drop pointer, consider turning the option off by choosing Tools, Options, selecting the Edit tab, and deselecting the Drag and Drop Text Editing checkbox.

Saving, Closing, and Opening Word Documents

◀ See "Working with Files," p. 102

This section shows you how to save and close a document, open an existing document, and start a new one. The following discussion is specific to the Word program; for information about basic file management, refer to Chapter 4, "Managing Files and Work Areas."

Saving a Word Document

As in other Microsoft Office programs, you save a Word document by assigning it a name and a location in your drive and folder list. After naming the file, you can save changes made in that document without renaming the file by pressing a shortcut key or clicking a button in the Standard toolbar.

Caution

Save your documents early in their creation and save often as you work on them. If a power failure occurs while you are working on your document and you have not saved it as a file, you lose the document.

Naming a Word Document

The first time you save a document, choose File, Save. Word displays the Save As dialog box, shown in figure 6.7.

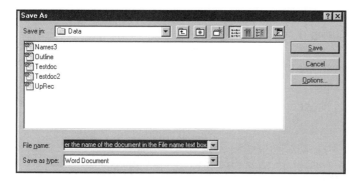

Fig. 6.7
Use the Save As dialog box to identify the document name in the File Name text box or accept Word's default name.

When you save a document, Word places the file in the WINWORD folder on your hard drive, unless you specified a different folder for Word when you installed Microsoft Office. In addition, Word's default file type is Word Document. Word also suggests a file name for the document; you can accept the suggested name or rename the document to suit yourself by typing a new name in the File Name text box.

Word suggests a name depending on the text in your document. If you have short lines at the top of the document, Word uses the first phrase of text up to a punctuation mark, new line character, or paragraph mark and then adds a . (period) and suggests Word Document for the file type.

You can choose to save a file to a hard drive, floppy drive, network drive, and so on; available drives are in the Save In list. Next, select a folder. Finally, in the Save as Type box, you can select a format other than Word in case you want to use the file in another application, such as DOS Text, WordPerfect 5.1, Word 2.x for Windows, or Word for Macintosh.

To save a new document, follow these steps:

1. Choose File, Save. The Save As dialog box appears.

2. Type the name of the file in the File Name text box or accept Word's suggested file name. You have up to 255 characters and can include spaces in your file name.

II

Using Word

3. Select and change the drive, folder, and file type if you do not want to save with Word's defaults.

4. Choose OK to save the document.

Saving Changes to a Named Document

After you save your document by assigning it a name and location on the disk, you can continue to work on it. The changes you make are not saved, however, unless you tell Word to save them. You do not need to rename the document file to save changes; you can simply use File, Save or click the Save button.

After modifying or editing an already-named document, choose File, Save; or press Ctrl+S. Word quickly saves the changes, and you are ready to proceed.

Saving All

The File, Save All command saves all open documents. Additionally, this command saves any open templates, macros, and AutoText entries. When you use the Save All command, Word displays a message box, asking you to confirm that you want to save each open document. If you have not named a document, Word displays the Save As dialog box so that you can name the document.

Opening a Word Document

To open a saved document in Word, click the Open button, choose File, Open, or press Ctrl+O. Word displays the Open dialog box (see fig. 6.8).

Fig. 6.8
Select the file from the list of files and choose OK to open the document.

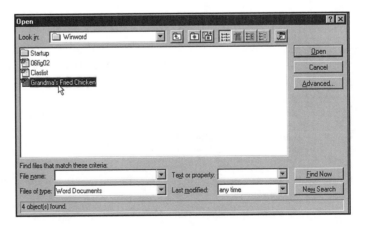

In the Open dialog box, select the file name from the list of files, if you saved it in Word's default folder. Otherwise, you can change the drive and folder, or even the file type, to access the file you want. You can sort, view, and do many options with the Open dialog box. For more information, refer to Chapter 4, "Managing Files and Work Areas.

◄ See "Opening a Document," p. 111

Starting a New Word Document

You can start a new document at any time by clicking the New button, choosing File, New, or by pressing Ctrl+N. When you use the New button or Ctrl+N, a blank document appears using default fonts and other settings from Word's Normal template. When you choose File, New, the New dialog box appears (see fig. 6.9).

Dialog box tabs   Templates

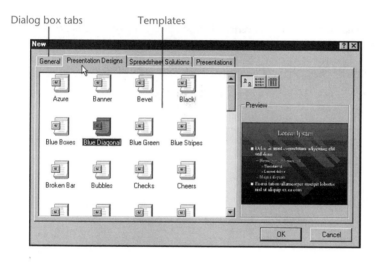

Fig. 6.9
In the New dialog box, select the tab for the templates you want to use and then select the template on which you want to base the new document.

► See "Using Template Wizards," p. 269

The New dialog box lists several tabs that are categories for the different templates. A *template* is a basic document design that can include page size and orientation, font sizes, fonts, tab settings, page margins, boilerplate text, tables, and columns. For more information about templates, see Chapter 10, "Working with Large Documents."

The Normal template is Word's default. The Normal template has the following characteristics:

- Uses an 8 1/2-by-11-inch portrait-oriented page

- Includes 1-inch top and bottom margins and 1 1/4-inch left and right margins

Tip
Using the shortcut Ctrl+N or the New button in the Standard toolbar skips the New dialog box and bases the new document on the Normal template.

II

Using Word

- Uses Times New Roman 10-point body text

- Supplies three heading styles: Arial 14-point bold, Arial 12-point bold italic, and Arial 12-point. All three heading styles are left-aligned and use single line spacing. They all also add a 12-point space above the heading and a 3-point space below the heading.

To accept the Normal template, choose OK. Word displays a new, blank document.

Troubleshooting

I wanted to save a file in a different file format, but that format is not listed in the file types.

You did not install that file converter when you installed Word. See Appendix A, "Installing Microsoft Office," for more information about installing the file converters.

I opened a document that was created in another file format, and now I want to save it.

Choose <u>F</u>ile, Save <u>A</u>s. In the Save As dialog box, select the format from the Save as <u>T</u>ype drop-down list.

Chapter 7

Formatting Documents

by Rick Winter and Patty Winter

Many of Word's distinctive features and commands pertain to formatting documents. Formatting a document includes assigning fonts and font sizes, adjusting the spacing between lines and paragraphs, aligning text, dividing text into columns, and setting page margins. You may consider many of these tasks to be part of *desktop publishing*—designing and formatting a document so that it is attractive and professional looking. Word provides many desktop publishing features and commands you can use to enhance your business documents.

In this chapter, you learn to

- View the document in the way that best fits the task

- Change font, font size, and format styles

- Adjust line and paragraph spacing

- Set tabs and indents

- Left-align, right-align, center, or justify text

- Use bullet and numbered lists

- Change page size and orientation

- Set page margins and create columns

Word not only supplies methods for improving the look of your documents but also makes formatting quick and easy. You can use menu commands and toolbar buttons to transform an ordinary business document into an eye-catching piece.

This chapter shows you how to format text, paragraphs, and pages using the easiest and fastest methods.

Understanding Views

Word enables you to view your document in a variety of ways. Each view—Normal, Outline, Page Layout, Master Document, and Print Preview—offers advantages for text editing, formatting, organizing, and similar tasks. You may prefer one view, but you also may want to use other views while formatting documents. This section covers the two most commonly used views: Normal and Page Layout.

Tip
No matter what view or magnification you use, the insertion point remains where it was in the preceding view.

In addition to views, Word provides magnification options for viewing a document. You can magnify the view to 200 percent, for example, or reduce it to fit the entire page (or even the entire document) on-screen. Finally, you can remove or display the various screen elements to produce a better view. This section describes the views and their advantages and disadvantages.

Viewing the Document

▶ See "Previewing a Document," p. 220

▶ See "Outlining a Document," p. 252

The two most common views are Normal and Page Layout. Normal view is mainly for entering and editing text; Page Layout view is perfect for formatting the text and page.

Two other views are more specialized:

■ Outline view allows you to collapse documents to heading levels so you can move or copy text easily to reorganize long documents. Outline view is covered in detail in Chapter 10, "Working with Large Documents."

■ Master Document view is a method of viewing and organizing several documents at one time; this view is not discussed in this book.

Finally, Print Preview shows how the document is formatted and allows you to make changes from this view without having to go back to an Edit mode. Print Preview is discussed in detail in Chapter 8, "Proofreading and Printing Documents."

Normal View

Normal view—the default view in Word—shows the basic document and text. Although you can view various fonts and font sizes, tabs, indents, alignments, and so on, you cannot view formatted columns, page margins, or headers or footers (see fig. 7.1).

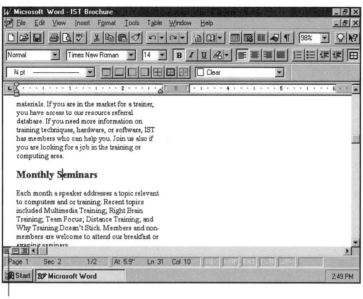

Fig. 7.1
The text in columns appears one column per page in Normal view.

Normal View button

Use Normal view for entering and editing text or for formatting text. Figure 7.1 shows the Normal View button. You learn about the other view buttons in the following sections. You can use the view buttons in the horizontal scroll bar to switch between views quickly.

Page Layout View

Page Layout view shows how the text, columns, margins, graphics, and other elements look on the page. Page Layout view provides the *WYSIWYG* (what-you-see-is-what-you-get) view of your document.

Editing and formatting may be slower in Page Layout view, but you can get a better idea of how your document looks as you format and when you finish formatting. Figure 7.2 shows the same document as in figure 7.1, but in Page Layout view. In Page Layout view, the vertical scroll bar adds two extra buttons to move up or down a page at a time.

To change views by using the View menu, use one of these options:

- ■ Choose <u>V</u>iew, <u>N</u>ormal for text editing and entering.

- ■ Choose <u>V</u>iew, <u>P</u>age Layout to format the text and page.

II

Using Word

Fig. 7.2

You can view columns and page margins in Page Layout view.

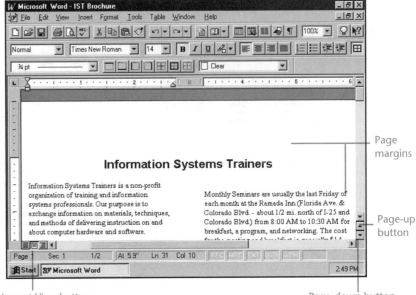

Page margins

Page-up button

Page Layout View button

Page-down button

Hiding Screen Elements

◄ See "Manipulating Parts of the Screen," p. 58

► See "Modifying Viewing Options," p. 233

In addition to changing views, you can display or hide the screen elements so that you can see the document design better. Use the View menu to remove the rulers and toolbars. You also can choose View, Full Screen to view a document with nothing but the Full Screen button on-screen with the document. The view in Full Screen will still be in Normal or Page Layout view, depending on what view is active when you choose Full Screen.

Figure 7.3 shows the Full Screen view. You can enter and edit text in this view as well as move pictures and objects. To return to your previous view, press the Esc key or click the Full Screen button.

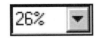

Tip

To set magnification, click the down arrow next to the Zoom Control button, then select a percentage or enter any number between 10 and 200.

Magnifying the View

You can change the magnification of the view to better control how much of your document you see on-screen at any time. Word provides two methods of changing views: choosing View, Zoom or clicking the Zoom Control button in the Standard toolbar. Figure 7.4 shows a document at 115% of magnification. The document also is in Page Layout view.

To change magnifications by using the Zoom dialog box, follow these steps:

1. Choose View, Zoom. The Zoom dialog box appears, as shown in figure 7.5.

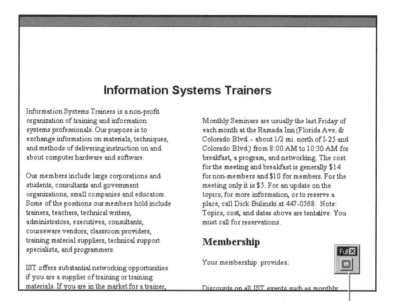

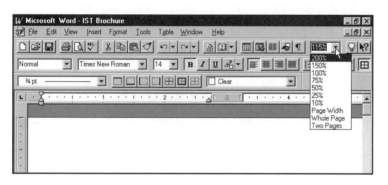

Full Screen button

II

Using Word

Fig. 7.3
Full Screen view enables you to see and work with your document with no screen elements or obstructions.

Fig. 7.4
You can format the text and document at any view magnification.

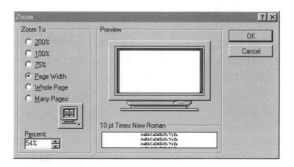

Fig. 7.5
Choose Page Width in the Zoom dialog box to see an entire line of text.

Tip
The Zoom dialog box enables you to view more than two pages at a time in Page Layout view.

2. In the Zoom To area, select the magnification you want, enter a percentage in the P̲ercent box, or click the monitor button and choose the number of pages you want.

> **Note**
>
> The Zoom dialog box and Zoom Control button may appear differently depending on which view (Normal or Page Layout) you are in when you choose the Zoom command. For example, in Page Layout view you have the Whole Page option available in the Zoom dialog box. This option is dimmed if you enter the dialog box while in Normal view.

3. Choose OK to close the dialog box.

Troubleshooting

My document is in landscape orientation, but I cannot see enough of it to edit the text.

Use the Zoom Control button in the Standard toolbar to change the view to page width or whole page.

I formatted two columns, but I see only one column on the page.

You are in Normal view. Choose V̲iew, P̲age Layout.

My page is formatted with many fonts, font sizes, and graphics; screen redraw is slow.

Choose V̲iew, N̲ormal to view the less-formatted version of the document and speed screen redraw.

Formatting Text

Tip
To display the Formatting toolbar when it's hidden, choose V̲iew, T̲oolbars, select Formatting, and then choose OK.

Word, like the other programs in Microsoft Office, provides many options for formatting text. You can select a variety of fonts, sizes, and styles to enhance your documents. In addition, Word provides a Formatting toolbar that makes text formatting easy. Alternatively, you can use the Font dialog box, described later in this section.

You can format text by first selecting the text and then making the formatting changes. Alternatively, you can position the insertion point, make the formatting changes, and then enter the text. All text entered from that point on is formatted according to your specifications until you change the formatting again or move the insertion point to another part of the document.

Changing Fonts in Word

Font is the typeface of the text. A typeface can, for example, be Times New Roman or Helvetica. The font you choose helps create an impression or set the mood for the document. Suppose that you want to create an informal flyer for a sale. You can use a light Italic font, such as Book Antiqua, Century Schoolbook, or Arial Italic. Formal, sophisticated fonts are those like Brush Script MT, Matura MT Script Capitals, or Britannic Bold.

◀ See "Changing Fonts," p. 84

Select the font you want to use from the Formatting toolbar's Font drop-down list, shown in figure 7.6.

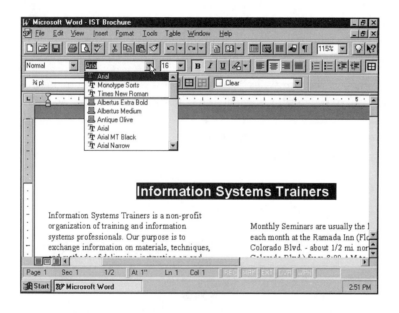

Fig. 7.6
Word lists the most recently used fonts at the top of the list so that you can find them quickly. The rest of the available fonts are listed in alphabetical order.

When you are looking at the list of available fonts, Microsoft tries to show you where the fonts are coming from. The TT symbol stands for TrueType; this means the font is a scalable font and will print just like it appears. The printer icon next to the font name means the font is generated by the printer definition you have installed. Some fonts don't have anything next to them; those are screen fonts and may or may not print correctly on your printer.

Tip
When selecting fonts, choose those with a TT next to the name, indicating TrueType. These fonts look the same on-screen as they do on paper and can be printed on most printers.

Changing Font Size

Font size is measured in *points*. Points and *picas* are typesetting measurements used for measuring spacing, line thickness, and so on. There are 12 points to a pica and six picas to an inch; therefore, there are 72 points to an inch.

◀ See "Using
Toolbars and
Keyboard
Shortcuts To
Format," p. 82

All text you enter in a new, Normal template document is 10-point Times New Roman by default. You can, of course, change the type size. Use the Font Size drop-down list in the Formatting toolbar to select the size you want.

The font sizes available in the Font Size drop-down list depend on your printer and the selected font. If you know that your printer can print a size that is not listed in the box—15 point, for example—type the number in the Font Size text box and press Enter.

Choosing Font Styles

Character formats, also called font *styles*, change the appearance of text. The Formatting toolbar supplies buttons for three font styles: bold, italic, and underline. To apply any of these attributes, simply click the B, I, or U button. You can apply one, two, or all three attributes at the same time.

Tip
The keyboard shortcuts for bold, italic, and underline are Ctrl+B, Ctrl+I, and Ctrl+U.

Besides these three font styles, Word supplies several effects—including strikethrough, superscript, subscript, and all caps—in the Font dialog box.

Using the Font Dialog Box

You can choose Format, Font to display the Font dialog box. Use this dialog box to format the text all at once; for example, you can use the dialog box options to change the font, size, and font style of the selected text. Figure 7.7 shows the Font tab of the Font dialog box.

Fig. 7.7
Use the Font dialog box to perform many changes at one time on the selected text.

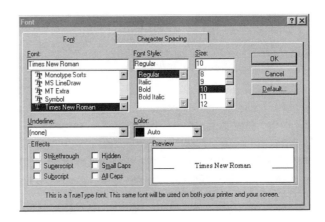

Tip
You can also format text by using Word's paragraph and character styles and your own to format the text the same way over and over. For more information, see Chapter 10.

Using the Font tab of the Font dialog box, you can select a font and style; look at the results in the Preview box. You also can choose from more attributes than are available in the Formatting toolbar, including single, double, or dotted underlines and colors. After you select the options you want, choose OK to close the dialog box.

Copying Formats

Word makes formatting text easy with the Format Painter, which enables you to format an entire document quickly and easily.

When you format text—such as a heading, complicated tabs, or indents—and you need to format other text in the document the same way, you can save time and energy by copying the formatting of the original text. Suppose that you formatted a heading as 18-point Univers, bold and italic, center-aligned, and with five points spacing below the heading. Rather than select and format each heading in your document separately, you can use the Format Painter to copy the format to another heading:

> **Note**
>
> You can copy formatting to multiple locations using the Format Painter. Select the formatted text you like, and double-click the Format Painter button to copy the format. For each location you want to apply the format to, select the text. Click the Format Painter button again or press Esc when you're finished.

1. Select the formatted text—the text with the format you want to copy.

2. Click the Format Painter button in the Standard toolbar. The pointer changes to a paintbrush and I-beam (see fig. 7.8).

3. Select the text to be formatted, and that text automatically changes to the copied text format.

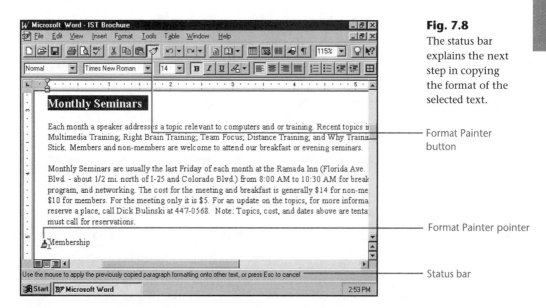

Fig. 7.8
The status bar explains the next step in copying the format of the selected text.

Format Painter button

Format Painter pointer

Status bar

Adding Highlighting to a Document

Microsoft Word 7 has added a new feature for making text stand out in a document. This new feature is called *highlighting* and is accomplished similar to how you make text bold, italic, or underlined. First select the text you want to change, and then click the Highlight button on the Formatting toolbar. The background behind the text will change to a different color. If you want to change the highlight color, click the drop-down arrow to the right of the Highlight button and choose a different color. To turn off all highlighting, choose Tools, Options, and on the View tab, deselect Highlight.

▶ See "Modifying Viewing Options," p. 233

Troubleshooting

I have changed the font, font size, font style, and alignment of the selected text, and now I want to change the text back to its original formatting.

Undo the formatting using the Undo drop-down list in the Standard toolbar. To remove formatting, you also can select the text first and then press Ctrl+Shift+Z.

I just formatted some text by choosing Format, Font, and I want to use the same formatting for text on the next page of my document.

Select the new text to format and then choose Edit, Repeat, or press Ctrl+Y. Word repeats the last formatting command you used. You could also choose to use the Format Painter. Select the text you just formatted, click the Format Painter icon, and select the text you want to change.

Formatting Paragraphs

A large part of formatting a page of text occurs when you format the paragraphs of body text, headings, lists, and so on. When producing an attractive, professional-looking document, you want to present a unified arrangement of the text elements. You can accomplish this by specifying line, word, and paragraph spacing; aligning the text; setting tabs and indents; and specifying how the text flows on the page.

> **Note**
>
> Word's definition of a paragraph is any amount of text—one character or 10 sentences—ending with a paragraph mark.

Tip
You can enter text, select it, and then format it, or you can specify the formatting before you enter text.

Word enables you to select a paragraph of text and change its arrangement by choosing commands or clicking buttons in the Formatting toolbar. This section shows you how to format paragraphs of text.

Adjusting Spacing

You can use spacing to change the design and readability of your text. For the most part, Word's default spacing works quite well for most documents, but you may sometimes want to apply specific spacing. This section shows you how to change line and paragraph spacing, and gives you a few tips on when to adjust spacing.

Line Spacing

Line spacing, also called *leading* (pronounced LED-ing), is the space that separates a line of text from the text above and below it. Without line spacing, uppercase letters, ascenders (the top strokes of t, b, d, and so on), and descenders (the bottom strokes of g, j, y, and so on) in one line would touch those in the next line.

Word's default line spacing is single. Word measures spacing in points or in lines. Text typed in 10-point uses approximately 12-point spacing, or one line (single). Text typed in 12-point uses 14-point spacing, which still is one line. The "line" spacing depends on the size of the type. The larger the type size, the greater the line spacing: 24-point text, for example, uses about 27-point line spacing. Typesetting guidelines generally call for leading to be about 120 percent of the point size of the text.

> **Caution**
>
> In most cases, don't use different line spacings in one document (see fig. 7.9). Different spacings confuse the reader and make the text hard to read.

Word enables you to change the line spacing in your text. You can set spacing to single, double, or one and a half lines, or you can set a specific measurement in points. Figure 7.9 shows four paragraphs of text with different line spacings. The top and bottom paragraphs have Word's default: single spacing, or 12-point text on 14-point spacing. The second paragraph is 12 on 16, and the third paragraph is 12 on 20.

To set line spacing, follow these steps:

1. Place the insertion point in the paragraph you want to format or select multiple paragraphs.

2. Choose F<u>o</u>rmat, <u>P</u>aragraph. The Paragraph dialog box appears, as shown in figure 7.10.

Tip
Keyboard shortcuts for line spacing are Ctrl+2 for double spacing, Ctrl+1 for single spacing, and Ctrl+5 for 1.5 spacing.

II

Using Word

Fig. 7.9
Line spacing
affects readability
and page design.

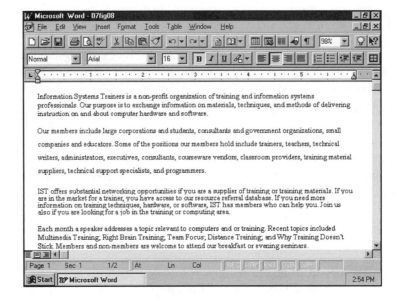

Fig. 7.10
This Paragraph
dialog box shows
the Indents and
Spacing tab
displayed. Use the
Spacing area to
control line
spacing.

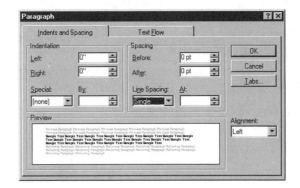

3. Select the Indents and Spacing tab.

4. In the Line Spacing drop-down list, select the option you want; enter a value in the At box, if necessary. These options are described in table 7.1.

5. Choose OK to close the dialog box.

Table 7.1 Line-Spacing Options	
Option	**Result**
Single	Default line spacing (two to five points larger than text size).
1.5 Lines	Spacing that is one and a half times the size of the normal spacing. For 12-point spacing, the spacing is 18 points.
Double	Spacing that is twice the size of the normal spacing. For 12-point spacing, the spacing is 24 points.
At Least	Accommodates larger font sizes within a line of text. In the At box, enter a specific line spacing amount that Word can use as minimum spacing. To allow for a larger font—for example, 12-point text that includes some 18-point characters—the spacing is 20; if you enter **20** in the At box, spacing is adjusted to 20 points.
Exactly	Limits Word to a certain amount of spacing, which you enter in the At box.
Multiple	Decreases or increases line spacing by the percentage you enter in the At box. To increase spacing by 20 percent, for example, enter **1.2**; to decrease spacing by 20 percent, enter **.8**.

Paragraph Spacing

You can add extra space between paragraphs to improve readability in your documents and to add valuable white space. *White space*, or areas of a page that contain no text or graphics, provides rest for the reader's eyes and prevents the page from being too crowded. Readability often is improved when you add space between paragraphs.

Use extra paragraph spacing instead of a first-line indent when you use left-aligned body text, as shown in figure 7.11. The reader's eyes can find the beginning of a paragraph easily without the indent. You also can add more spacing after headings or subheadings, between items in a list, within tables, and in outlines.

To add extra paragraph spacing, follow these steps:

1. Place the insertion point in the paragraph you want to format or select multiple paragraphs.

2. Choose Format, Paragraph. The Paragraph dialog box appears (refer back to fig. 7.10).

3. Select the Indents and Spacing tab.

Fig. 7.11

Extra spacing makes the beginning of each paragraph easy to find and provides valuable white space.

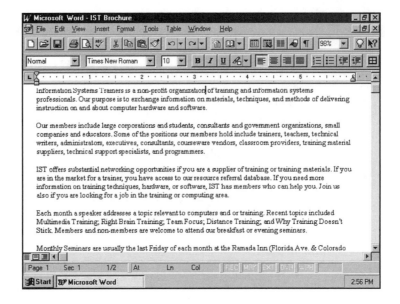

4. In the Spacing area, enter a value in the Before box, the After box, or in both boxes. You can enter the measurement in lines (li) or points (pt). (Note that Word converts lines into a points measurement.)

5. Choose OK to close the dialog box.

Troubleshooting

I set the line and paragraph spacing in the Paragraph dialog box, and I don't like the results. I want to change the line spacing back to the way it was, but I don't want to change the paragraph spacing.

Choose Format, Paragraph, and then select the Indents and Spacing tab. In the Line Spacing drop-down list, select Single. Then choose OK to close the dialog box.

Tip

If you want to use leaders with tabs, first choose Format, Tabs; then select tab position, alignment, and leader options in the Tabs dialog box.

Setting Tabs

You can set tabs in a document by using either the Tabs dialog box or the ruler. This section describes using the ruler to set tabs because it is a quick and easy method for the task. The ruler also is handy for other kinds of paragraph formatting, such as indenting text and changing margins.

Note

Whether you use the ruler or the Tabs dialog box, you can select the text and then set the tabs, or set the tabs and then enter the text.

To use the ruler to set tab stops in your text, first position the insertion point in the paragraph you want to format or select multiple paragraphs. Click the tab alignment button on the horizontal ruler (as shown in fig. 7.12) until the type of tab you want appears. Then click the place in the bottom half of the ruler where you want to set the tab stop.

You can reposition any tab stop in the ruler by clicking and dragging the tab marker to a new location. To remove a tab stop, drag the tab marker off the ruler.

Tip
When you position the insertion point in any paragraph of text, tab and indent settings for that paragraph appear in the ruler.

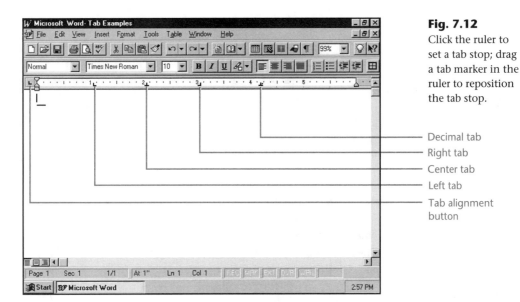

Fig. 7.12
Click the ruler to set a tab stop; drag a tab marker in the ruler to reposition the tab stop.

- Decimal tab
- Right tab
- Center tab
- Left tab
- Tab alignment button

II

Using Word

Indenting Text

You can use the ruler or the Paragraph dialog box to set indents for text. Using the ruler, you can indent the left side, the right side, or only the first line of a paragraph. Figure 7.13 shows indents for selected text.

Word also supplies Increase Indent and Decrease Indent buttons, shown in the Formatting toolbar in figure 7.13. Each time you click one of these buttons, you indent the selected text to the next tab stop or to the preceding tab stop.

Left indent   First-line   Right indent   Decrease indent   Increase indent
marker   indent marker   marker   button   button

Fig. 7.13
Word supplies a
dotted guideline
to help you align
indents and tab
stops when using
the ruler.

Guideline

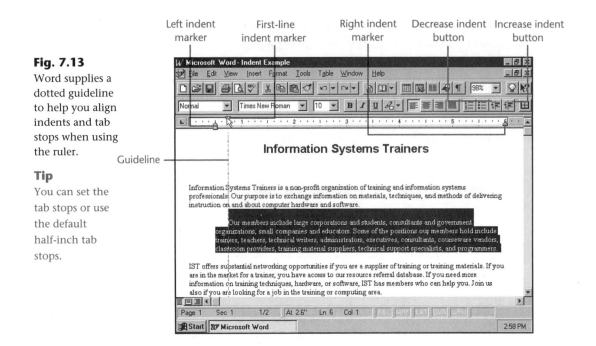

Tip
You can set the
tab stops or use
the default
half-inch tab
stops.

A *hanging indent* is another type of indent you can create (see fig. 7.14). To create a hanging indent, position the insertion point anywhere in the paragraph and drag the left indent marker (the rectangle and up-pointing triangle on the bottom of the ruler) to the position where you want to indent the paragraph beginning with the second line. Then drag the first-line indent marker (the down-pointing triangle on the top of the ruler) to the position where you want the overhanging line to start.

Adjusting Alignment

Alignment is a way of organizing your text. The way you align the text in a document makes the text easy to read, decorative, eye-catching, formal and sophisticated, or casual and flexible. Word enables you to left-align, right-align, center, or justify the text in your documents.

Figure 7.15 shows the four alignments and the corresponding toolbar buttons.

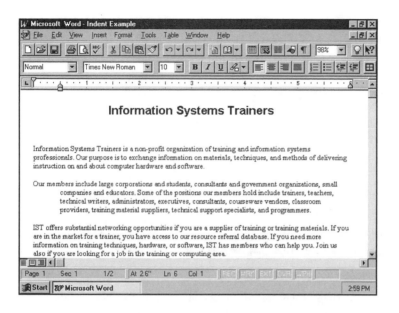

Fig. 7.14
Create a hanging indent by first dragging the left indent marker and then dragging the first-line marker into position.

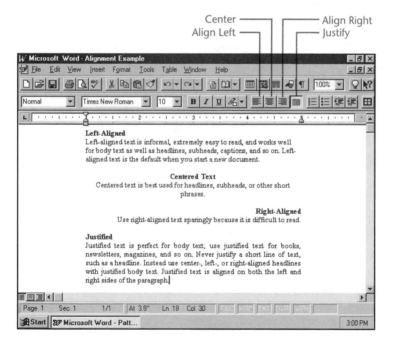

Fig. 7.15
Align your text so that the reader can easily follow the message and so that the page is attractive.

Note

When you use justified text, be sure that you turn on the hyphenation feature. To do so, choose Tools, Hyphenation. In the Hyphenation dialog box, select Automatically Hyphenate Document, and then choose OK. The standard installation does not include the hyphenation feature; you may have to add this feature by going through the custom installation process described in Appendix A.

Troubleshooting

I want to see how the tabs or indents are set in a specific paragraph of text.

Position the insertion point in the paragraph and view the indent and tab markers in the horizontal ruler. (To display the ruler, choose View, Ruler.)

I justified the text in a paragraph, and now there are large gaps between the words.

Turn on the hyphenation feature by choosing Tools, Hyphenation and then selecting Automatically Hyphenate Document. Choose OK to close the dialog box.

When I try to change the indent, my left margin appears too far in the middle of the screen and the right margin is off the screen.

Drag the left indent marker by the box on the bottom back to the correct position. Then click the mouse to the right of the horizontal scroll box and then to the left of the scroll box to reset the screen view.

I want to align the first part of a line of text on the left side of the screen and the second part of the same line of text on the right side of the screen.

Use tabs rather than the align buttons. Create a right tab at the right margin for the right justification.

Adding Bullets and Numbering

Bullets and Numbering allow you to pull out information in your documents by making lists easier to read. You can bring emphasis to text by applying either bullets or numbering to lists.

To create a bulleted list, you simply type the list, select the list after it is typed, and click the Bullet button on the Formatting toolbar. You could also choose to turn the bullets on before you type the list. In this case you would click the Bullet button on the Formatting toolbar, type the list, and click the Bullet button again, when you are finished, to turn bullets off (see fig. 7.16).

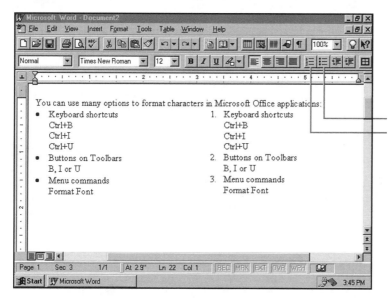

Fig. 7.16
A Word document with both a bulleted list and a numbered list.

To create a numbered list, you simply type the list, select the list after it is typed, and click the Numbering button on the Formatting toolbar. You could also choose to turn numbering on before you type the list. In this case you would click the Numbering button on the Formatting toolbar, type the list, and click the Numbering button again, when you are finished, to turn numbering off (see fig. 7.16).

Note

If you want to insert a blank line or lines without bullets in your list, use Shift+Enter to create manual line breaks. The line following the manual line break does not have a bullet. To add more lines with bullets, press Enter (see fig. 7.17).

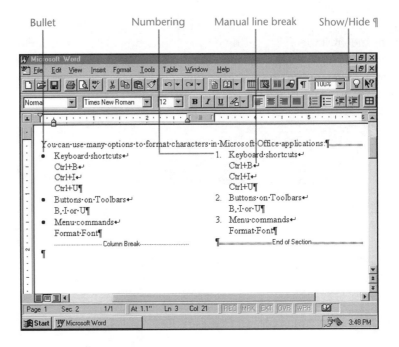

Fig. 7.17
Bullet and numbered lists with Show/Hide on to see manual line breaks.

Formatting the Page

Formatting the page includes changing page size and orientation, setting margins, and creating columns. The way you format the page depends on the amount of text, the size and orientation of graphics, the type of document, and so on. Keep in mind that you want to create an attractive, eye-catching page of easy-to-read text.

Suppose that you have several drawings of cars to go into an advertisement with very little text. You can create the ad in *landscape* (wide) orientation with one-inch margins. On the other hand, if your text contains two long lists of items and no graphics, you can use *portrait* (tall) orientation with two columns and half-inch margins.

Word's page-formatting commands are flexible and easy to use. You can change the page to fit your text so that you present the most professional-looking document possible. This section describes page formatting.

Changing Size and Page Orientation for Word Documents

The size and orientation of the paper you use depends mostly on your printer. Some printers take 8 1/2-by-11-inch sheets only; others can print sheets ranging from small envelopes to legal-size paper. Most laser and inkjet printers can print in either orientation. Check your printer manual before changing paper size and orientation.

To change page size and orientation, use the Page Setup dialog box. Figure 7.18 shows the Paper Size tab in the Page Setup dialog box.

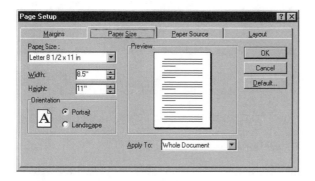

Fig. 7.18
Choose paper size and orientation, and then view the change in the Preview box.

To change paper size and orientation, follow these steps:

1. Choose File, Page Setup. The Page Setup dialog box appears.

2. Select the Paper Size tab.

3. Select a size from the Paper Size drop-down list or use the Width and Height text boxes to specify a custom size.

4. In the Orientation area, select Portrait or Landscape.

5. Choose OK to close the dialog box.

Setting Margins

You can change the margins of your document from the default settings to any margin you want. Word's Normal template uses 1-inch top and bottom margins and 1.25-inch left and right margins. You can set the margins by using the Page Setup dialog box, shown in figure 7.19. Keep in mind that your printer may limit the page margins you can select.

◄ See "Setting Margins," p. 86

> **Note**
>
> When you set margins, Word applies those measurements to all pages in a document, unless you have selected text or divided your document into sections.

II

Using Word

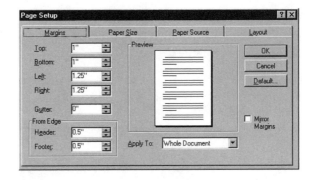

To change the margins of your document, follow these steps:

1. Choose File, Page Setup. The Page Setup dialog box appears.

2. Select the Margins tab.

3. Enter measurements in the Top, Bottom, Left, and Right boxes.

4. Select what portion of the document you want to apply the new margins to in the Apply to drop-down list,

5. Choose OK to close the dialog box.

Creating Columns

You can divide the page into one, two, three, or more columns to make the text well organized and easy to read. Documents such as books, magazines, catalogs, newsletters, brochures, and even advertisements often are divided into columns. Word makes dividing your documents into columns easy. To see your text formatted in columns, you must be in Page Layout view or Print Preview.

Note

Normally, divide an 8 1/2-by-11-inch portrait-oriented page into no more than three columns; divide the same-size landscape-oriented page into no more than five columns. When you use too many columns on a page, the lines of text become too short and are hard to read.

Tip
You can create equal-sized columns by holding down the mouse pointer on the Columns button of the Standard toolbar and dragging down and across to choose the number of columns.

You divide a document into columns by using the Columns dialog box (see fig. 7.20). You can select a preset number of columns and designs or enter a number of columns and each column width, if you prefer. When you enter your own column width, you must specify spacing, called *gutter space*, between the columns.

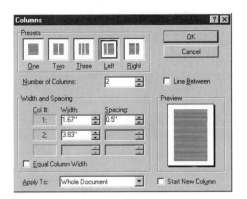

Fig. 7.20
You can make one
column wider than
the other for an
interesting effect.
View the result in
the Preview box
before choosing OK.

If you like, you can add a line, or rule, between the columns by selecting the
Line Between option. Word even enables you to start a new column at the
insertion point by selecting the Start New Column option. Preview your column choices in the Preview box before accepting or rejecting the changes in
the dialog box.

To format the columns in your document, follow these steps:

1. If you have different numbers of columns throughout your document
   or if only a portion of your document is to have columns, select the
   text for which you want to change columns.

2. Choose Format, Columns. The Columns dialog box appears.

3. In the Presets area, select the number or type of columns you want.
   One, Two or Three will create that number of equal columns. Left or
   Right will create two unequal columns with the left or right column
   smaller than the other. You can add additional columns through the
   Number Of Columns increment box.

4. Use the other options in the dialog box to customize columns. You can
   adjust the width of the columns in the Width and Spacing section or
   select Equal Column Width to automatically adjust width and spacing.

5. Choose OK to accept the changes and close the dialog box.

II

Using Word

Troubleshooting

I created an 8 1/2-by-14-inch document, and now I can't print it.

Check your printer manual. You may have changed the page to a size larger than your printer can print.

I made my margins narrower than 1/4 inch, and now some of the edges of the text will not print.

Most printers have a required margin—usually 1/4 or 3/8 inch—because they cannot print to the edge of the page. Check your printer manual. Make a habit of allowing at least 3/8-inch margins in all your documents.

Chapter 8

Proofreading and Printing Documents

by Rick Winter and Patty Winter

After you finish entering and editing text, you want to proofread and then print your documents. Word supplies three tools that make proofreading easy. You can use Word's Spelling, Thesaurus, and Grammar commands to proofread your documents and supply suggestions for improvement. You can also use the Find and Replace commands to help you review or change text.

No matter how long or short a document is, using the Spelling command is well worth the time it takes. Word quickly reviews the text and alerts you if it finds a misspelled word. Additionally, you can use Word's Thesaurus to find alternative words so that your text is not monotonous and repetitive. Finally, Word supplies a Grammar Checker that critiques your writing and offers suggestions for improvement.

After your document is complete, you can print it. Word has a special Print Preview mode in which you can view the document and make last-minute changes in the design before printing. Finally, you can print your document by using Windows defaults or by setting options in Word.

In this chapter, you learn to

- Use the Spelling command
- Use the Thesaurus
- Use the Grammar Checker
- Use AutoText

- Use the Find and Replace commands

- Preview a document before you print it

- Print a document

Spelling, Correcting, and Automating Document Entries

The Spelling command reads text and notifies you when it finds a word that is not in its main dictionary or any custom dictionaries you may have added; Word also notifies you when you have repeated words. The Spelling dialog box shows you the word in question, suggests a replacement word, and displays a list of possible replacement words that are similar in spelling.

> **Note**
>
> You can check the spelling of the entire document, or you can select text and check spelling in only the selected text.

This section briefly reviews the steps to get started with Word's Spelling command. You also learn about AutoCorrect, a Word feature that automatically corrects words as you type them, and AutoText, a feature that allows you to insert text and/or graphics that you use repeatedly.

Using Automatic Spell Checking

One of the new features in Word is Automatic Spell Checking; This feature, if turned on, will check your spelling for you as you type. When Word encounters a misspelled word, the word will be underlined with a wavy line. To check the word, point to it and click the right mouse button. The shortcut menu is displayed, with the suggested words in bold at the top of the menu, an Ignore All command, an Add command, and finally the Spelling command (see fig. 8.1). You can choose any of the commands by clicking the left mouse button.

> **Note**
>
> Notice the book icon in the status bar. A check mark on the book icon indicates no spelling errors detected by Automatic Spell checking. An X indicates errors. To jump through the errors, double-click indicator. Word will move to a line with a wavy line under it and open the shortcut menu for you.

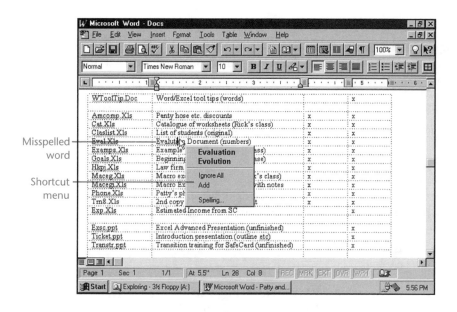

Misspelled word

Shortcut menu

Fig. 8.1
The wavy underline indicates a misspelled word.

Using the Spelling Command in Word

To check the spelling in a document, click the Spelling button in the Standard toolbar. The Spelling dialog box appears (see fig. 8.2).

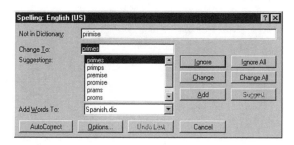

Fig. 8.2
Select a word in the Suggestions box or enter the correct word in the Change To text box to correct the mistake in the text.

Tip
You can also check spelling in a document by choosing Tools, Spelling, or by pressing F7.

▶ See "Changing Spelling Options," p. 244

Word highlights a questionable word, displays the word in the Not in Dictionary text box, and suggests a change in the Change To text box. If you want, you can choose another word from the Suggestions list box or edit the word in the Change To box. After you select the proper word, you can click the Change button to change this one occurrence or click Change All to change all occurrences of the misspelling throughout your document. If you want the program to automatically correct the misspelling after this spelling session, click the AutoCorrect button.

II

Using Word

If the word is correct and not in the dictionary (such as a person or company's name), you can choose to Ignore this one occurrence, Ignore All occurrences in the document, or Add the word to the dictionary so that the Spelling command will not stop at the word again.

When you have a repeated word, you can choose to Delete the second occurrence of the word or Ignore the repetition.

Using AutoCorrect

The AutoCorrect feature automatically corrects spelling mistakes and formatting errors, or replaces characters you enter with specific words or phrases. Using this feature saves you time. Suppose that you consistently type **anohter** instead of *another* or **WHen** instead of *When*. You can enter these common mistakes into AutoCorrect, and the next time you make the mistake, Word corrects it automatically.

To set options and make entries for AutoCorrect, choose Tools, AutoCorrect. Figure 8.3 shows the AutoCorrect dialog box with a new entry.

Fig. 8.3
In the AutoCorrect entry list, type a word that you normally spell incorrectly in the Replace text box and type the correct spelling in the With text box.

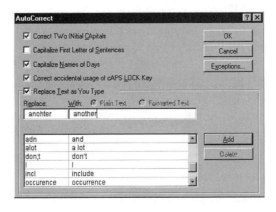

Tip
You can use AutoCorrect to expand an abbreviation every time you write one. For example, you could have **adr** automatically replaced with your address.

The AutoCorrect dialog box lists options you can turn on or off. The Replace and With text boxes enable you to enter your own items, and the list at the bottom of the AutoCorrect dialog box displays Word's default list plus any items you add. You can add or delete items at any time. To change options related to AutoCorrect, see "Changing AutoFormat Options" in Chapter 9. For more details on AutoCorrect, see "Letting AutoCorrect Do Your Spelling for You" in Chapter 3.

> **Caution**
>
> Don't include words or abbreviations that you ever use intentionally in the Replace text box; if you do, every time you type the word, it will change! In this case, you probably want to use the AutoText feature.

To add an incorrect and correct spelling to AutoCorrect, you can click the AutoCorrect button in the Spelling dialog box as mentioned earlier in this section. Or you can choose Tools, AutoCorrect and add the incorrect word in the Replace text box and the correct word in the With text box. Then click Add to add them to the list. Choose OK to close the dialog box.

Using AutoText

The AutoText command allows you to automate entering information that you use frequently. You can create an AutoText entry that includes text only, formatted text, or graphics. The difference between AutoText and AutoCorrect is AutoText entries use abbreviations to insert your entries when you need them. AutoCorrect automatically changes misspellings when you press the space bar. See figure 8.4 to create an AutoText entry.

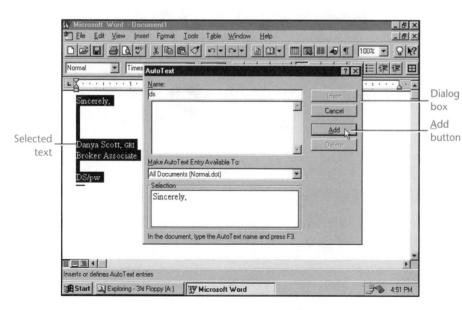

Fig. 8.4
Type the name for your AutoText entry. The shorter the names, the easier they are to use later.

To create AutoText entries, follow these steps:

1. Create the text and/or graphics you repeatedly use.

2. Select the text and/or graphics you just created.

3. Choose Edit, AutoText. The AutoText dialog box appears.

4. Type a name for the AutoText entry in the Name box.

5. Click the Add button to create the entry.

After you define the entry, you can use it in your documents by simply typing the AutoText name and then pressing F3.

Using Find and Replace

◄ See "Finding and Replacing Text," p. 97

You may find in reviewing a document that it would be easier to locate specific text or formatting so you can move to different sections of the document quickly. The Find command allows you to search for specifics in your document. If you use the Replace command instead, you not only find what you are looking for, but can then replace what you found with something else. For instance, you could find a word and replace it with a different word (see fig. 8.5).

Fig. 8.5
Click the Replace button to replace the text in the Find What text box with something new.

To use the Find command, follow these steps:

1. Choose Edit, Find. The Find dialog box appears.

2. In the Find What text box, type the text you need to find. You can choose one or more options in the Find dialog box to enhance your search.

3. Click the Find Next button to find the text.

4. When you get to the first occurrence of the Find What text box, you can either click Find Next again, Cancel, or Replace.

5. To replace the found text with new text, click the Replace button (see fig. 8.6).

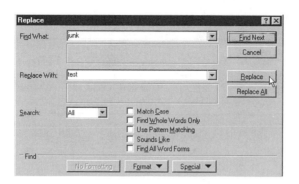

Fig. 8.6
The Find dialog box changes to the Replace dialog box when you click the Replace button.

6. In the Replace With text box, type the text you want to use. You can choose one or more options in the Replace dialog box to enhance your search.

7. Click the Replace button again to replace and look for the next occurrence of the Find What text box.

While you are finding or replacing text, you have a number of options for your search. The following table describes additional options on the Find and Replace dialog boxes.

Tip
The keyboard shortcut for Find is Ctrl+F and for Replace is Ctrl+H.

II

Using Word

Option	Description
Search drop-down list	Searches forward (Down), backward (Up), or through the entire document (All).
Match Case check box	Matches capitalization (uppercase or lowercase) when searching for text.
Find Whole Words Only check box	Finds a match that is an entire word only (if looking for *the* will not find o*the*r or *the*ir).
Use Pattern Matching check box	Use with special character (? is a wild card for any one character, * is a wild card for any number of characters). *S?t* will find *Sat, Sit, Set*. *S*t* will find all the previous items as well as *Soot, Sachet, Saddest* and others.
Sounds Like check box	Looks up different spellings of words that sound the same. *There* will find *their, there,* and *they're*.
Find All Word Forms check box	Looks for all the different grammatical forms of a word. If you type *is* in the Find What text box, will find *is, are, be, am*.
No Formatting command button	Removes formatting if any formatting is added with the Formatting button.

(continues)

Option	Description
Format drop-down button	Looks for item in the Find What text box that includes fonts, styles, and other formatting.
Special drop-down button	Looks for special characters such as paragraph marks, tabs, line breaks, and others.

For more detailed information on using Find and Replace, see Chapter 3.

Using the Thesaurus

The Thesaurus supplies a variety of synonyms you can use to replace the word you are looking up. To use the Thesaurus, position the insertion point in the word you want to look up and choose Tools, Thesaurus. Word automatically highlights the word, and the Thesaurus dialog box appears.

Tip
You also can use Shift+F7 to start the Thesaurus.

Suppose that you want to find a synonym for the word *second*. Using the words in the Meanings list box, you can look up either *next* or *moment* (see fig. 8.7). Selecting a word in the Meanings list on the left displays several synonyms in the Replace with Synonym list on the right. Additionally, you can look up new words—related or unrelated to the original word—or go back to a word you looked up earlier. If you want to look up a word that is different from the original word, position the insertion point in the Replace with Synonym text box, type a new word, and then click Look Up.

Fig. 8.7
Replace the selected word with any of the displayed synonyms, or continue to look up words until you find the meaning you want.

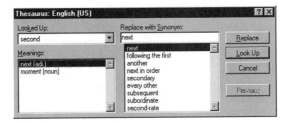

The following table describes the options in the Thesaurus dialog box:

Option	Description
Looked Up/Not Found	A drop-down list of all the words you have looked up since you opened the Thesaurus dialog box; the list disappears when you close the dialog box. The text-box name changes to Not Found if the word is not in the Thesaurus.
Meanings/Alphabetical List	Definition and part of speech of the selected word; selecting a different meaning results in a new list of synonyms. Alphabetical List appears if the selected word is not in the Thesaurus.
Replace with Synonym	The word in the text box is the selected word you can Look Up or Replace when you choose either of those command buttons. The list of words below the text box is a list of synonyms from which you can select.
Replace with Antonym	If Antonyms is available in the Meanings list box, you can highlight it and then select an antonym from this list box.
Replace	Click this button to substitute the selected word (in the Replace with Synonym text box) for the original word in the text.
Look Up	Displays meanings and synonyms for the selected word (in the Replace with Synonym text box).
Cancel	Closes the dialog box.
Previous	Displays the last word you looked up. Works only in the current Thesaurus dialog box.

To use the Thesaurus, follow these steps:

1. Position the insertion point in the word you want to look up.

2. Choose Tools, Thesaurus. Word automatically highlights the word, and the Thesaurus dialog box appears.

3. In the Meanings list, select the meaning you want.

4. In the Replace with Synonym list, select the word you want to use as a replacement.

5. Click Replace to close the dialog box and substitute the new word (the one in the Replace with Synonym text box) for the old one, or choose Cancel to close the dialog box without replacing the word.

Tip
Double-click a synonym or meaning to display more synonyms.

Using Word

Troubleshooting

I looked up several meanings, and now I want to go back to the original word I looked up in the Thesaurus.

Click Looked Up, or click the down arrow to the right of that option. A drop-down list of the words you looked up during this session appears. Select the original word.

I want to go back to the last word I looked up.

Click the Previous button.

Checking Grammar

▶ See "Customizing Grammar Options," p. 247

If you have problems with your writing, Word may be able to help you. Word's Grammar Checker reviews text in your document and reports possible problems, such as passive verbs, pronoun errors, punctuation errors, jargon, and double negatives. You can review the error and suggestion, and then decide whether or not to change the text. You even can ask for a further explanation of the grammar rule.

Tip
You can set grammar rules and styles by using the Customize Grammar Settings dialog box.

Note

The Grammar Checker is not automatically installed when you use the typical installation of Microsoft Office. If you need to install the Grammar Checker, choose Add/Remove Programs in the Control Panel, select Microsoft Office from the list and click the Add/Remove button. (You will need your MS OFFICE Setup disks or CD-ROM!) In the Microsoft Word section, choose Proofing Tools and select the Grammar option. For more information on installing the Grammar Checker, see Appendix A.

To check the grammar in a document, choose Tools, Grammar. The Grammar dialog box appears (see fig. 8.8).

Fig. 8.8
You can choose to ignore or change the problem, ignore the rule for this document, or ask for an explanation of the problem.

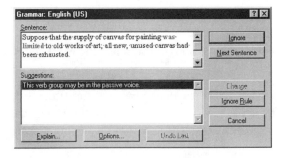

> **Note**
>
> You must read the suggestions carefully. You may find that the suggestion is not valid and that the problem, as the Grammar Checker sees it, is not really a problem.

The following table describes the options in the Grammar dialog box:

Option	Explanation
Sentence	The sentence in question appears in this text box, where you can edit the sentence.
Suggestions	Word defines the problem and may suggest alternative solutions.
Ignore	Click this command button if you want to ignore the problem and move to the next grammar problem, which can be in the current sentence.
Next Sentence	Click this button to look for potential problems in the next sentence, ignoring any other problems that may be in the current sentence.
Change	Click this button to change the sentence if an alternative suggestion was made in the Suggestions box.
Ignore Rule	Click this button if you want to ignore a specific rule for the rest of the document.
Cancel/Close	Cancel closes the dialog box without making a change; after you make a change, the Cancel button changes to Close. Choose Close to return to your document.
Explain	This button displays a message box that further explains the rule and often offers examples (see fig. 8.9).
Options	This button enables you to customize rules and style for the Grammar Checker. For more information, see Chapter 9, "Customizing Word."
Undo Last	Click this button if you change your mind about the last grammar change you made.
Start	Appears in place of the Ignore button when you click the document. The Grammar dialog box remains on-screen while you edit your document; choose Start to continue the grammar check.

II

Using Word

Fig. 8.9
Click Explain to
learn more about
the grammar rule
in question.

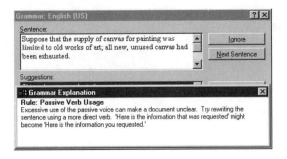

Troubleshooting

I don't want to check the spelling at the same time I check the grammar.

Choose Tools, Options, and select the Grammar tab. Click the Check Spelling option
to deactivate it. Then choose OK.

I changed my mind about the last change I applied in the Grammar dialog box.

Click the Undo Last button in the dialog box.

Previewing a Document

◀ See "Printing
Documents,"
p. 134

After you enter, edit, format, and proofread your text, you are ready to print
your document. Sometimes when you format a page of text in Normal view,
problems are revealed when you print the document. The margins may be
too wide, a headline may break in an odd place, a paragraph may be indented
by mistake, and so on. You can save time, effort, and paper if you view your
document in Print Preview before you print it. You can click the Print Preview
button on the Standard toolbar, choose File, Print Preview, or press CTRL+F2.

Note

You do not have to use Print Preview before you print a document. If you want to
print without first previewing a document, choose File, Print; or click the Print button
on the Standard toolbar. For more information, see "Printing Word Documents,"
later in this chapter.

Tip
You can edit and
format your docu-
ment in Print
Preview just as you
can in Page Layout
or Normal view.
Use the menus
and commands, or
display any of the
toolbars to use as
shortcuts.

Figure 8.10, which shows a document in Print Preview, reveals a problem
with a graphic line that is too short to extend from the left edge of the body
text to the right edge. You can quickly fix the problem in this view before
you print: drag the indent marker in the ruler to set a new right indent for
the line.

Left indent   Right indent   Right margin
marker   marker   marker

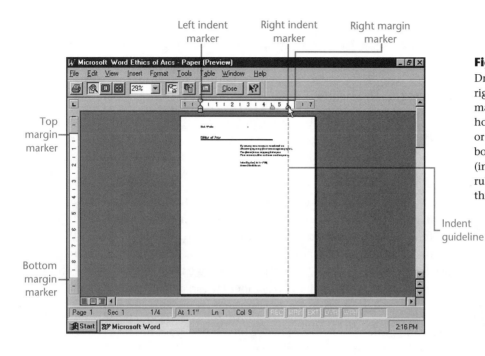

Top margin marker

Bottom margin marker

Fig. 8.10
Drag the left and right margin markers (in the horizontal ruler) or the top and bottom margins (in the vertical ruler) to change the margins.

Indent guideline

II

Using the Rulers

By default, Word does not display the rulers in Print Preview. You can, however, choose View, Ruler to display both the horizontal and vertical rulers. Use the rulers as you would in any other view: to set tabs, adjust indents, and change the margins.

To adjust the margins by using the ruler, position the insertion point at the point in the text you want to change. Any margin changes affect the current section.

◄ See "Setting Tabs," p. 199

◄ See "Indenting Text," p. 200

Move the mouse pointer over the margin marker on the ruler (the point where the white ruler meets the gray area) until the mouse pointer changes to a double-headed arrow. Click and drag the arrow left or right (in the horizontal ruler) or up or down (in the vertical ruler) to change the margin. A dotted guideline appears (shown in fig. 8.10) across the page as you drag the margin; use the guideline to align elements on the page.

Tip
The default view in Print Preview is Whole Page view, which is best for adjusting margins.

Using the Preview Toolbar

Print Preview includes a special toolbar you can use to edit your document. The Preview toolbar works in much the same way as the other toolbars. You can place the mouse pointer on a toolbar button to view the ToolTip and the description of the button in the status bar.

Using Word

You can use a toolbar button to print your document, view one page or multiple pages, display or hide the ruler, view the full screen (without screen
elements such as the title bar, scroll bars, and so on), exit Print Preview, and
get help on a specific topic. Two toolbar buttons are particularly useful:
Shrink to Fit and Magnifier.

The Shrink to Fit button adjusts the font size in a document, so that you can
fit a little bit more on the page. Suppose that your document fills one page,
and one or two sentences overflow to a second page. Try clicking the Shrink
to Fit button to squeeze all the text onto the first page.

The Magnifier enables you to toggle between the normal mouse pointer and
the magnifier pointer. When the magnifier pointer contains a plus sign (+) as
shown in figure 8.11, you can magnify the document to 100 percent. When
the magnifier pointer contains a minus sign (–), clicking the page reduces the
view to Whole Page view (32 percent). To change the magnifier pointer back
to the normal pointer, click the Magnifier button again.

Clicking the Print button on the Preview toolbar prints the document using
the default options in the Print dialog box. If you want to make changes to
any printing options, see the following section, "Printing Word Documents."

Fig. 8.11
Enlarge a specific
area of the
document by
clicking the
magnifier pointer
on that area.

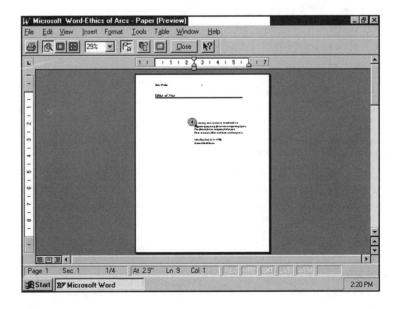

Troubleshooting

I have several lines of text that overflow to the second page of my document, but I would like them to be on the first page.

Click the Shrink to Fit button in the Preview toolbar. Magnify the document and look carefully at the changes in the text spacing and sizing. You may prefer to undo the change if the text appears to be too crowded on one page.

I have trouble setting the margins for the document with the ruler in Print Preview.

Choose File, Page Setup, and choose the Margins tab. You can type a measurement in the dialog box for the margins you want to change.

Printing Word Documents

When you print from Word, you generally use the defaults set up in Windows. You can, however, change these defaults in the Print dialog box. Most often, however, you will print with the default options in the Print dialog box (see fig. 8.12). The default options print one copy of all the pages in the document.

◄ See "Printing Documents," p. 134

► See "Customizing Printing," p. 237

II

Using Word

Fig. 8.12
To print using the default options in the Print dialog box, choose OK.

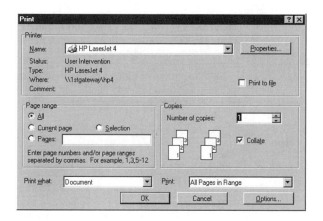

The following table describes the options in the Print dialog box:

Option	Description
Printer Section	
<u>N</u>ame	Click this drop-down button to select another printer on which to print this document.
<u>P</u>roperties	Click this button to change the properties of the selected printer (including paper size, paper orientation, and graphics resolution). The properties are in effect for all documents printed with the printer (not just this document).
Print to Fi<u>l</u>e	Choosing this option prints the document to a file on disk so that you can transport the file to another computer or service bureau.
Page Range Section	
<u>A</u>ll	Prints all pages in the document.
Curr<u>e</u>nt Page	Prints only the page in which the insertion point is located.
Pa<u>g</u>es	Prints the specified pages. Enter a page range in the text box. Separate individual pages with commas (**1,4,5**); indicate a page range with a hyphen (**1-5**); indicate pages in a section with P and S (p1s2).
<u>S</u>election	Select text in the document before choosing to print; choose <u>S</u>election to print only the selected text.
Copies Section	
Number of <u>C</u>opies	Prints specified number of copies. Enter the number of copies to be printed.
Colla<u>t</u>e	Select this option to print copies in order. If you want two copies of a five-page document, the first copy of pages 1 to 5 will print and then the second copy will print.
Other Options	
Print <u>W</u>hat	Specify what to print: the document, summary information, a list of styles, key assignments, annotations, or AutoText assignments associated with the document.
P<u>r</u>int	Specify which pages to print: all pages, even pages, or odd pages in the page range.

Other Options	
OK	Click this button to send the selected pages to the printer.
Cancel	Click this button to cancel all changes and close the dialog box without printing the document.
Options	Click this button to customize printing options. For more information, see Chapter 9, "Customizing Word."

Troubleshooting

I tried to print a document and I didn't get an error message, but I don't see my document in my printer.

Verify that the correct printer is selected in the Name drop-down list box of the Print dialog box. Make sure that your printer is turned on and plugged in, and that you have paper in the printer.

I want to change to a different printer before printing a document.

Choose the Name drop-down list in the Print dialog box. Select a printer from the list of Printers and choose OK.

Printing Envelopes

You can print envelopes in Word quickly and easily by choosing Tools, Envelopes and Labels. Word makes it easy to enter the delivery and return addresses, choose an envelope size and method of feed, and then print an envelope. Figure 8.13 shows the Envelopes and Labels dialog box.

▶ See "Modifying User Info," p. 240

▶ See "Creating Envelopes Using Mail Merge," p. 931

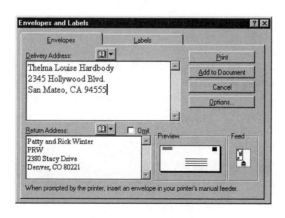

Fig. 8.13
Enter the delivery and return addresses, and then choose OK to print the envelope.

Tip
You can merge
many addresses
at one time
with the mail
merge feature
(see Chapter
40).

The following table describes the options in the Envelopes and Labels dialog box:

Option	Description
Delivery Address	Enter the name and address to which the envelope will be mailed.
Return Address	Enter your name and address.
Omit	Select this option to exclude the return address.
Preview	Click the envelope in the Preview box to display the Envelope Options dialog box and the Envelope Options tab. Select the size, bar code, placement, and font for the addresses in this dialog box.
Feed	Click the Feed box to display the Envelope Options dialog box and the Printing Options tab. Select the method of feeding envelopes that best fits your printer.
Options	Displays the Envelope Options dialog box.
Add to Document	Adds the envelope style and contents to the document so that you can save it for later use.
Print	Click this button to send the envelope to the printer.
Cancel	Click this button to cancel your choices and close the dialog box without printing the envelope.

To print an envelope in Word, follow these steps:

1. Insert an envelope into the printer.

2. Choose Tools, Envelopes and Labels. The Envelopes and Labels dialog box appears.

3. Choose the Envelopes tab.

4. Enter a Delivery Address and Return Address. If you have an address on the document, Word may find the address and place it in the Delivery Address area. You can also click the Insert Address button for either address and choose an address from your Personal Address Book.

5. Select envelope and feed options, if necessary.

6. Choose OK.

Troubleshooting

I'm trying to print an envelope but I get too much margin for the return address.

While you are typing the name and address of the recipient, click the Envelopes dialog box Options button. Choose the Envelope Options tab and change the From Left text box in the Return Address section. You can also position the delivery address as well as change the font for both addresses on this dialog box.

I have a problem formatting the text in the Delivery Address area—I frequently get a double-spaced address that doesn't fit on the envelope. How do I adjust formatting?

If the Envelope Options tab does not give you enough flexibility to change what you need to on an envelope, return to the Envelopes and Labels dialog box and click the Add to Document option button. Word will place a new page at the beginning of your document that contains the information and formatting for your envelope. Change this page as you would any other document. For spacing, select the text you want to change and press Ctrl+1 for single spacing, or choose Format, Paragraph and change the Spacing section of the Paragraph dialog box.

II

Using Word

Chapter 9

Customizing Word

by Rick Winter and Patty Winter

As you work in Word, you discover many ways to speed up your work. Word not only provides shortcuts for commands and procedures, but it also offers ways to customize the program to your working habits and preferences. You can change many of Word's default settings to make the program more suitable for you.

Ways of customizing Word include changing measurement units, selecting various grammar and style rules for the Grammar Checker, instructing Word to create backup copies automatically, and prompting for document properties. In addition, you can change the default file locations, such as the location of documents, clip art, and templates.

In this chapter, you learn to

- Change the default location to a folder you create for document files

- Modify User Info to place your company's name and address automatically in the return address area of envelopes

- Set save options

- Establish spelling and grammar-checking options

- Select printing options

- Establish editing options

Customizing Options

Word provides various methods for customizing the program to meet your needs. By choosing Tools, Options, you can modify Word's default view, save, spelling, user information, and other settings when you install the program. When you install Word, for example, the program automatically displays the status bar and the scroll bars on-screen. You can change this default setting. When you change any option in the Options dialog box, that option then applies to all documents until you change the option again.

You can change Word's default settings in two ways. One way is to choose Tools, Options, which displays 12 tabs containing options for customizing. Figure 9.1 shows the Options dialog box.

Fig. 9.1
The Options dialog box enables you to modify several options at one time.

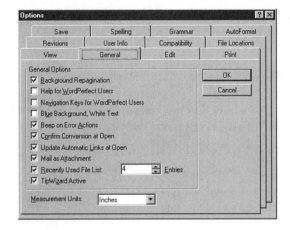

Alternatively, you can customize specific options in certain dialog boxes. The Save As dialog box, for example, includes the Options command button, shown in figure 9.2. When you click Options in any dialog box, the Options dialog box appears; all tabs except the applicable one are dimmed and thus unavailable.

Fig. 9.2
You can modify options in a dialog box before you complete the command.

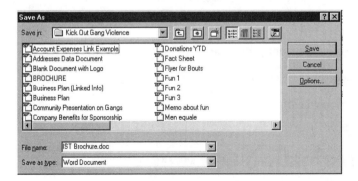

To customize various options in Word, follow these steps:

1. Choose Tools, Options. The Options dialog box appears.

2. Select the tab representing the options you want to modify.

3. Make your changes.

4. When you finish, choose another tab and make more changes or choose OK to close the dialog box.

To customize relevant options from a specific dialog box, follow these steps:

1. Choose Options in the dialog box. The Options dialog box appears, with only one tab available.

2. Make your changes.

3. When you finish, choose OK to close the Options dialog box and return to the preceding dialog box.

> **Note**
>
> Options that show a checkmark in the check box are activated. If you select an option with a checkmark in the check box, you deactivate that option. Selecting an option with no checkmark in the check box activates that option and places a checkmark in the box.

The following sections briefly describe options on each of the Option dialog box tabs.

Changing General Settings

The General tab in the Options dialog box includes options that affect the common operations of Word. You can select one, several, or all the options in the General Options area. The following list describes these options:

- *Background Repagination.* Background Repagination governs how Word deals with page breaks as you enter or edit text. When the option is on, Word automatically adjusts the text on each page as you type. Background Repagination is on all the time in Page Layout view and Print Preview; you cannot turn it off in either view. You can turn this option off in Normal and Outline views, however.

Tip
Other dialog boxes that feature the Options button include Print, Spelling, and Grammar.

II

Using Word

Tip
When you turn off Background Repagination, you may notice a slight increase in the program's speed and efficiency.

■ *Help for Word_Perfect Users.* When you select this option, Word helps you make the shift from WordPerfect for DOS to Word for Windows. Each time you press a WordPerfect key combination, Word displays information or demonstrates a command. Figure 9.3 shows a Help dialog box that appears when you press Shift+F7, for example.

Fig. 9.3
In WordPerfect, Shift+F7 prints a document. This Help dialog box describes how to print in Word, and offers options, more help, and a demonstration.

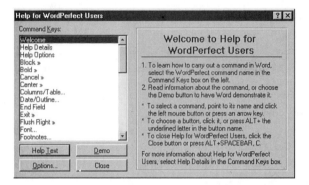

■ *Navigation Keys for WordPerfect Users.* If you select this option, Word acts like WordPerfect when you press Page Up, Page Down, Home, End, and Esc.

■ *Blue Background, White Text.* If you're used to the old WordPerfect 5.1 screen, you can use this option to change the Word screen's background to blue and the text to white.

■ *Beep On Error Actions.* By default, Word beeps when you make an error or perform a wrong action, such as clicking outside a dialog box. This option governs whether the program beeps to warn you of an error.

■ *Confirm Conversion at Open.* By default, Word does not display a dialog box when you open a document in a file format other than Word. If you want to display a dialog box to confirm opening a different file format, check this box.

► See "Using Common Steps to Link Documents," p. 689

■ *Update Automatic Links at Open.* If you have included links to other files in your document using object linking and embedding (OLE), this option automatically updates data added to other files when you open your document in Word. It's a good idea to keep the Update Automatic Links at Open option activated if you use Microsoft Office to its full capacity.

■ *Mail as Attachment.* This option attaches a document to a message that is to be sent with an e-mail program, such as Microsoft Mail. This option works only if an e-mail program is installed.

▶ See "Starting Exchange and Addressing the Message," p. 810

■ *Recently Used File List.* This option enables Word to display the most recently used files at the end of the File menu. You must enter the number of files (0 to 9) to be displayed in the Entries text box. Figure 9.4 shows the File menu listing the last four files opened.

◀ See "Opening a Document," p. 111

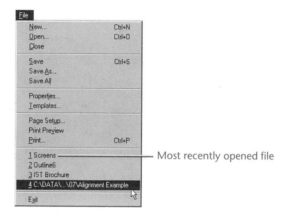
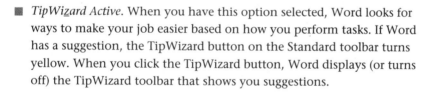

Fig. 9.4
You can open one of these files quickly by clicking the file name instead of choosing File, Open.

II

Using Word

■ *TipWizard Active.* When you have this option selected, Word looks for ways to make your job easier based on how you perform tasks. If Word has a suggestion, the TipWizard button on the Standard toolbar turns yellow. When you click the TipWizard button, Word displays (or turns off) the TipWizard toolbar that shows you suggestions.

■ *Measurement Units.* This option governs the default unit of measurement in Word. The unit you specify—inches, picas, points, or centimeters—is the unit of measurement that appears in dialog boxes and in the rulers.

◀ See "Viewing Tips," p. 160

Modifying Viewing Options

View options represent another tab in the Options dialog box. Using the View tab, you can specify whether to show or hide Window elements, nonprinting characters, and various other components of Word.

The options you can customize vary slightly from view to view. For example, you can hide or show the vertical ruler in Page Layout view but, because there is no vertical ruler in Normal view, that option is not available in Normal view. To set the options for a certain view, change to that view before opening the Options dialog box. Figure 9.5 shows the View tab for Page Layout view.

Fig. 9.5
Use the View tab of the Options dialog box to select the screen and window elements you want to view.

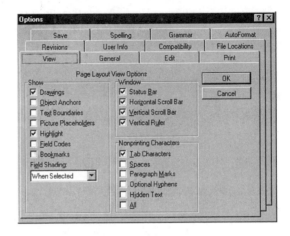

▶ See "Creating a New Object," p. 514

The following list describes the options in the View tab for Page Layout view. The options are divided into three categories: Show, Window, and Non - printing Characters.

The Show area contains several elements you can choose to hide (no checkmark in the check box) or show (checkmark in the check box). Following is a brief description of each option:

- *Drawings* (Page Layout view only). Drawings include clip art, imported art, or pictures you create in Word.

- *Object Anchors* (Page Layout view only). This option show or hides anchors for all objects, including spreadsheets, charts, and graphs.

- *Text Boundaries* (Page Layout view only). Select this option to show or hide column guides and section marks that help you format pages.

- *Picture Placeholders*. If selected, this option displays empty frames that show picture placement to save memory and speed scrolling through the document.

- *Highlight*. Word has added the highlight feature, which allows you to change the background color of a selected area of text. When you

Tip
Use the Picture Placeholders option to quickly print a proof without pictures or to speed up screen redraw.

deselect this option, you turn off all highlights you added to text with the Highlight button on the Formatting toolbar. You can turn the highlights back on by selecting this option. The highlight is also turned back on the next time you apply highlighting to text in the document.

◀ See "Adding Highlighting to a Document," p. 194

- *Field Codes.* This option shows or hides the field code names when a field is inserted into the document.

▶ See "Entering the Fields in Your Data Source," p. 916

- *Bookmarks.* Bookmarks allow you to create placeholders in your document so you can refer back to them through the Go To dialog box or for cross references. Select the Bookmarks option to view bookmarks in the document. It's especially useful to show bookmarks when you want to edit them.

▶ See "Using Bookmarks and Cross References," p. 282

- *Field Shading.* Select this option to indicate the location of merge, date, and other fields. Shading \makes fields easier to find in a large document. You have the options to Never or Always display field shading, or to display field shading when the field is selected.

- *Draft Font* (Outline and Normal views). This option speeds up your video display. Draft font shows all text, no matter what size, as the same size as your Normal font. Draft font also indicates larger fonts with an underline and will show graphics as empty boxes.

- *Wrap To Windows* (Outline and Normal views). This option wraps the text from one line to the next within the document window for easier viewing.

- *Style Area Width* (Outline and Normal views). This option shows or hides the area at the left side of the document that lists the applied styles.

The Window area of the View tab enables you to specify which window elements appear on-screen and which elements are hidden. You can hide or show the following elements: Status Bar, Horizontal Scroll Bar, Vertical Scroll Bar, and Vertical Ruler (in Page Layout view).

◀ See "Viewing Parts of the Window," p. 40

The Nonprinting Characters area enables you to show or hide any of the following nonprinting characters: Tab Characters, Spaces, Paragraph Marks, Optional Hyphens, Hidden Text, or All. This gives you more control over which characters you display compared to the Show/Hide ¶ button on the Standard toolbar. With the Show/Hide ¶ button, you have only the option of showing all nonprinting characters or none.

Changing Editing Options

The Edit tab of the Options dialog box enables you to change such options as how the Insert key works, how Overtype mode works, and whether typing replaces selected text. Figure 9.6 shows the Edit tab in the Options dialog box.

Fig. 9.6
You can modify the editing settings, such as whether to use drag-and-drop editing and whether to remove spaces during a cut-and-paste procedure.

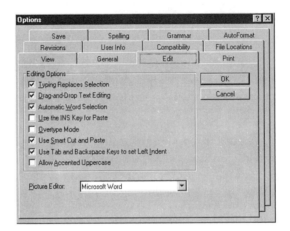

◄ See "Editing Text in a Word Document," p. 176

The following list describes the Edit tab's options:

■ *Typing Replaces Selection.* If this option is selected, selected text is deleted when you type new text. If the option is unchecked, text is inserted at the beginning of the selection and the selection is turned off.

■ *Drag-and-Drop Text Editing.* Drag-and-drop is a method of editing text without cutting, copying, or pasting. When this option is activated, you can select the text and then drag the selection to another location in the document.

■ *Automatic Word Selection.* This option selects the entire word when you select part of it. If this option is activated, Word automatically selects the whole word any time you drag the I-beam across part of a word and past the beginning or end of the word.

■ *Use the INS Key for Paste.* This option enables you to paste items from the Clipboard by pressing the Insert key.

■ *Overtype Mode.* When selected, this option replaces existing text as you type, one character at a time. Pressing the Insert key gives you the same option. The Insert key turns Overtype on and off.

- *Use Smart Cut and Paste.* This option removes unneeded spaces when you delete text and adds spaces when you add text.

- *Use Tab and Backspace Keys to set Left Indent.* If you select this option and press Tab at the beginning of a paragraph, the first line indent of the paragraph changes. If you press Tab at the beginning of any other line of the paragraph or when the entire paragraph is selected, the entire paragraph is indented. If this option is not selected, pressing Tab will place a tab character in the document.

- *Allow Accented Uppercase.* This option suggests that Word add an accent mark to uppercase letters formatted as French.

- *Picture Editor.* Use the drop-down list to specify the program Word displays when you edit a picture. If, for example, you double-click an imported clip-art graphic, Word's default Picture Editor selection is the Word drawing program. If you prefer, select a different program in the drop-down list, such as PowerPoint Presentation or PowerPoint Slide. The list depends on what other programs you have installed. For more information about PowerPoint, see Chapter 24, "Getting Acquainted with PowerPoint."

Customizing Printing

The Print tab in the Options dialog box offers various options for printing documents, including how the documents print and what elements print. Figure 9.7 shows the Print tab of the Options dialog box. As with any option in the Options dialog box, your choices apply to all documents. If you select Draft Output as a printing option, for example, all documents printed from this point on print in draft form.

II

- *Draft Output.* Prints a copy of your document for proofreading. Depending on your printer, graphics and pictures may not print.

- *Reverse Print Order.* Changes the page-printing order—3, 2, 1 instead of 1, 2, 3, for example. This may be helpful if your copier requires a different order or if you punch and bind documents from the bottom toward the top.

- *Update Fields.* Revises fields (codes that instruct Word to insert elements into the document automatically) in the document before printing.

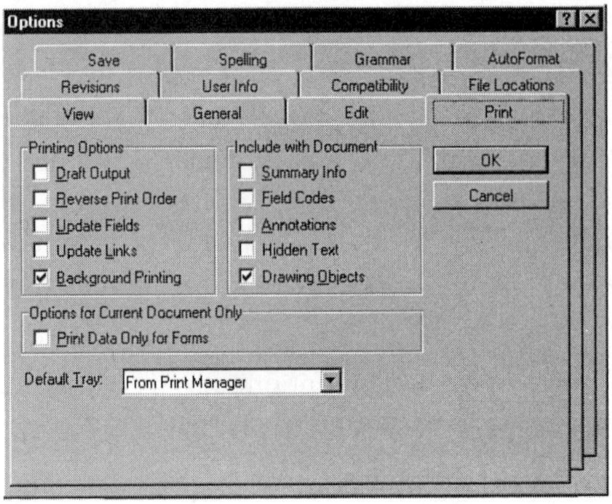

Fig. 9.7
In the Print tab of
the Options dialog
box, select options
that affect all
documents
you print.

▶ See "Embed-
ding Informa-
tion in Your
Documents,"
p. 711

■ *Update Links.* Brings links (information created in another document and connected with the Word document) up to date before printing.

■ *Background Printing.* Documents print in the background so that you can continue your work.

The Include with Document section prints additional information with your document: Summary Info, Field Codes (in place of field results), Annotations (on a separate page), Hidden Text, and Drawing Objects.

The Options for Current Document Only section contains only one option: Print Data Only for Forms. This option applies only to the active document and pertains only to an online or preprinted form. If you select Print Data Only for Forms, Word prints only the input for a form instead of the input and the actual form lines and text.

The Default Tray drop-down list box is found at the bottom of the Print tab. This choice allows you to identify where the paper is coming from, such as upper tray, lower tray, manual feed, or if the Print Manager will specify the paper source.

Tip
You usually use
revision marks
when more
than one per-
son works on a
document and
you want to see
what has been
added, deleted,
and modified.

Changing Revisions Options

The Revisions tab of the Options dialog box governs the display of revision marks. You can select different options for inserted text, deleted text, and revised lines. *Inserted text* is text that has been added to the original text; *deleted text* has been erased from the original; *revised lines* describes how Word marks all lines of text that have been modified in any way.

Each area on the Revisions tab offers similar options (but with different hot keys) and shows the results in the Preview box. Figure 9.8 shows the Revisions tab of the Option dialog box.

► See "Working with Revisions," p. 284

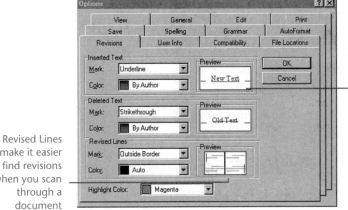

Fig. 9.8
Select different marks for each area so that you can tell inserted text from deleted or revised text.

If you use underlining in your document, select another mark or color for Inserted Text to prevent confusion

Revised Lines make it easier to find revisions when you scan through a document

The following list describes the Revisions options:

- *Inserted Text.* This area enables you to specify the Mark Word uses to identify added text: no mark, underline, bold, italic, or double underline. Additionally, you can specify a Color to help identify the added text. The default choice in the color drop-down options are By Author for all three types of revisions. This means that when more than one person is working on a document, the revisions that each author makes will be in a different color.

- *Deleted Text.* You can Mark text that has been deleted from the document with either the Strikethrough or Hidden Text format. Additionally, you can choose a Color to mark the text.

- *Revised Lines.* You can Mark lines of text that have been altered with a vertical border at the left margin, right margin, or (for odd and even pages) outside margin. You also can specify a Color for the border.

- *Preview.* A Preview box appears next to each area so that you can see the results of your choices before closing the dialog box.

- *Highlight Color.* Highlight color allows you to change the background color behind text. You can choose the default color for the Highlight button on the Formatting toolbar. Although the Highlight button drop-down list on the toolbar allows you to choose a color, that method does not offer as many choices as this option.

Tip
If you choose to mark deleted text as hidden text, use the View tab of the Options dialog box to show the hidden text.

◄ See "Adding Highlighting to a Document," p. 194

II

Using Word

Modifying User Info

◀ See "Printing Envelopes," p. 225

The User Info tab of the Options dialog box lists the name that was entered when Word or Microsoft Office was installed. The name may be yours, the person who installed the program, or your company's name. The name entered when Word was installed also is the name that appears in the Mailing Address text box. The information in the Mailing Address text box is inserted automatically into the Return Address text box in the Envelopes tab of the Envelopes and Labels dialog box.

Other information in the User Info tab is used elsewhere in Word. The Name information is used as the author on the Summary tab of the Properties dialog box, and Initials are used to identify the person who entered annotation marks.

You easily can change the Name, Initials, and Mailing Address text boxes in the User Info tab. Figure 9.9 shows the User Info tab.

Fig. 9.9
If you enter a name and address in the Mailing Address text box, that same address appears in the Return Address text box when you use the Envelopes and Labels dialog box in Word.

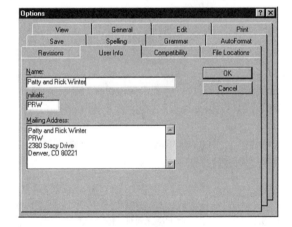

◀ See "Saving, Opening, and Closing Files," p. 106

◀ See "Saving, Closing, and Opening Word Documents," p. 180

Changing File Locations

To change the location of document files, clip-art files, templates, and so on, use the File Locations tab of the Options dialog box. Suppose that you want to create a DOCUMENT folder within the WINWORD folder so that you can save specific documents in one place. Use this tab to direct saved documents to the new folder automatically. Figure 9.10 shows the File Locations tab.

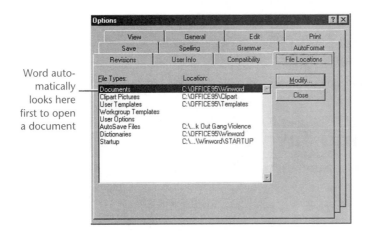

Word auto-
matically
looks here
first to open
a document

Fig. 9.10
Specify the file
type and location
you want to
change and then
click Modify.

To change the location for specific files, follow these steps:

1. In the File Locations tab, select the File Type you want to relocate.

2. Choose the Modify button. The Modify Location dialog box appears
    (see fig. 9.11).

Look In
drop-down
list shows
overview of
computer
storage
areas

Up One Level button   Create New Folder button

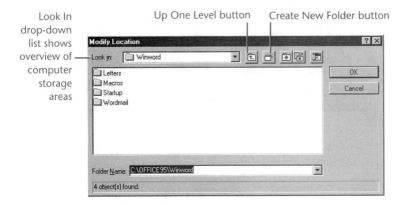

Fig. 9.11
Enter a new
location for the
documents in the
Folder Name text
box or select a new
location from the
list of folders; you
can even add a
new folder, if
needed.

3. To select a new folder, you can do any of the following: select the new
    folder from the Look In drop-down list, double-click a subfolder in the
    list box, click the Up One Level button, enter the path of the new folder
    in the Folder Name text box, or click the Create New Folder button to
    create a new folder.

II

Using Word

4. Choose OK to close the Modify Location dialog box and return to the File Locations tab of the Options dialog box.

5. Choose OK from the File Locations tab to close the Options dialog box and save your settings.

Changing Save Options

◀ See "Saving, Opening, and Closing Files," p. 106

The options available in the Save tab of the Options dialog box affect how and when Word saves your document. In addition, you can add a protection device, such as a password, to specific documents. Figure 9.12 shows the Save tab of the Options dialog box.

Fig. 9.12
In the Save tab, specify whether Word automatically creates backups and how often it automatically saves your documents.

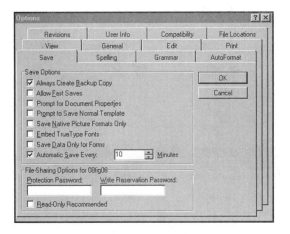

◀ See "Saving, Opening, and Closing Word Documents," p. 180

There are two sections of the Save tab. The first, Save Options, provides options for saving your documents and certain elements of those documents:

■ *Always Create Backup Copy.* Select this option to tell Word to create a copy of each document you create. Backup file names begin with `Backup of` and have the name of your original file.

■ *Allow Fast Saves.* Activate this option to save only the changes you've made to your document since the last save. Otherwise, Word will save the complete revised document.

Note

Although they take less time, fast saves take up more disk space than a full save. You also can not fast-save over a network; you should deselect this option if you are saving a file on the network.

■ *Prompt for Document Properties*. Select this option to display the Properties dialog box each time you save a new document.

■ *Prompt to Save Normal Template*. When activated, this option warns you when you have changed the Normal template by displaying a message to save changes. You may want to save the changes to the template; if you do not, however, selecting this option allows you to choose whether you want to save the changes or not.

◀ See "Using File Properties," p. 128

■ *Save Native Picture Formats Only*. This option saves imported graphics in the Windows format only. If you import a graphic from a Macintosh program, for example, you can save disk space by saving the graphic only in the native picture format (Windows version) instead of in the Macintosh format.

■ *Embed TrueType Fonts*. This option embeds TrueType fonts used in the document so that the fonts display correctly, even if the document is used on a computer that does not have those fonts installed.

◀ See "Changing Fonts," p. 84
◀ See "Changing Fonts in Word," p. 191

■ *Save Data Only for Forms*. This option saves the data in a form as a single record for use in a database.

■ *Automatic Save Every*. Select this option to tell Word to save your document automatically; set the interval in the Minutes text box.

Note

The maximum time allotment for the Automatic Save option is two hours, while the minimum time is 0 (don't save the document). If you have very important documents or lots of power problems, you'll want to set this time to something very short like 10 minutes. If you have long documents, however, you may have to wait each time a document is saved, so you'll want to set to a longer time such as 30 minutes.

II

Using Word

> **Note**
>
> Use the Automatic Save Every option all the time so that if a power failure occurs, Word recovers the document when you restart the program. Word then prompts you to save, delete, or continue to work on the saved version of your document. The amount of time you set for automatic save depends on how critical the document is and on personal preference.

The second section, File-Sharing Options for *current filename*, of the Save tab only has to do with the current document. The prompt will change to include the name of the document you are working on (or a generic name like Document 1). Select the following protection options for the current document:

- *Protection Password*. Enter a password (up to 15 characters) to keep other users from opening the document. Word displays an asterisk for each character you enter.

> **Caution**
>
> You must remember your password; you cannot open a password-protected file without the password.

- *Write Reservation Password*. This option permits anyone to open the document, but only users who know the password can modify or edit the document and save the document with the same name. Enter a password and then choose OK. Word prompts you for confirmation; enter the password and choose OK again.

- *Read-Only Recommended*. This option means that when the document is opened, Word suggests that the document be opened as read-only. The reader can open the document either way. If the document is opened as read-only, no changes can be made in the document with the original name; the original document is available only for reading, not for alteration.

◀ See "Using Automatic Spell Checking," p. 210

Changing Spelling Options

Although Word's spelling dictionary is sufficient for most documents, you may have a special need for a medical, legal, or foreign-language dictionary

(which you must purchase separately). You can add a third-party dictionary
for use with Word by using the Spelling tab in the Options dialog box. Additionally, you can customize other options that handle the Spelling Checker.

Figure 9.13 shows the Spelling tab with the Custom Dictionaries button.

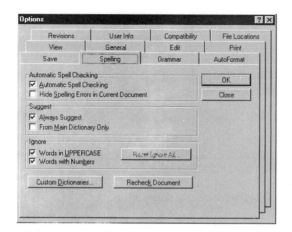

Fig. 9.13
You can add a
custom dictio-
nary—even a
foreign-language
dictionary—in the
Spelling tab.

The first area of the Spelling tab is Automatic Spell Checking:

- *Automatic Spell Checking.* This new feature in Word shows you incorrect
  spellings with wavy red underlines as you type.

- *Hide Spelling Errors in Current Document.* This option turns off all incorrect spelling markers.

The second area of the Spelling tab is Suggest. This area lets you choose how
Word will prompt you with suggestions in the Spell dialog box. You can select either or both options:

- *Always Suggest.* If this option is selected, Word displays a list of likely
  candidates to replace the misspelled word.

- *From Main Dictionary Only.* This option limits Word's suggestions to the
  main dictionary. If you have another dictionary in which the word may
  appear, such as a legal dictionary, do not select this option.

The third section of the Spelling tab is Ignore:

- *Words in UPPERCASE.* Check this box to ignore uppercase words.

- *Words with Numbers.* Check this option to ignore words with numbers.

II

Using Word

■ *Reset Ignore All*. During a spell check, you may have told Word to ignore too many words and you may want to clear the list. You can enter this Spelling tab directly from the Spell dialog box and empty the Ignore list. Thereafter, Word again questions any words for which you used the Ignore All command earlier in the session.

Other options in the Spelling tab include the following:

■ *Custom Dictionaries*. This button displays another dialog box with all the installed dictionaries; you can select up to 10 dictionaries for use during any session. Within this area are several more options:

New. This option creates a new custom dictionary. You can create an empty new file name which you can edit in the next option, Edit.

Edit. This option opens the selected dictionary so that you can edit it. When you use this option, your list of words in the dictionary appears in a normal Word document. Search for the words you need to change and edit them or add more words in the list. When you finish editing the dictionary, save and close the file (which will have a DIC extension).

Add. This option adds a third-party dictionary that you purchased separately. Choose the folder and drive location where you installed the dictionary.

Remove. If your spell check is too slow or you want to update an added dictionary with a new file, you may want to remove an existing dictionary. This option deletes a dictionary from the list, but not from your disk.

Language. When you are using a custom dictionary, select the language in the drop-down list to apply special formatting for that language. Make sure that the correct custom dictionary is selected in the list.

Customizing Grammar Options

> **Note**
>
> The Grammar Checker is not automatically installed when you use the typical install of Microsoft Office. If you need to install the Grammar Checker, use the Setup program. In the Microsoft Word section, choose Proofing Tools and select the Grammar option.

Word enables you to select various grammar rules and styles of writing for checking the grammar in your documents. The default style is business writing. There are two other styles included with Word. The second style is more strict and includes all grammar rules, while the third style is for more casual writing and has fewer rules than business writing. You can also create your own custom styles. Additionally, you can review the grammar rules used with a specific style and even deactivate some of those rules.

◄ See "Checking Grammar," p. 218

Figure 9.14 shows the Grammar tab of the Options dialog box.

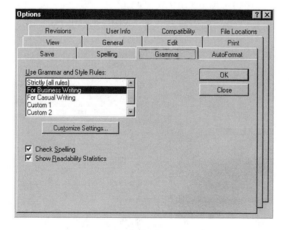

Fig. 9.14
Select the style you want the Grammar Checker to use when checking your documents, or customize the settings by selecting your own rules.

II

Using Word

> **Note**
>
> To view all grammar and style rules attached to the highlighted item in the Use Grammar and Style Rules list box, click the Customize Settings button. In the Customize Grammar Settings dialog box, click either the Grammar button or the Style button, and scroll through the list of rules. You can click the Explain button for further information about any rule. Choose OK to exit the dialog box.

When you specify grammar and style rules, you can select options from the following categories in the Use Grammar and Style Rules list box:

- *Strictly (All Rules).* This option applies all grammar and style rules, including checking for clichés and quoted text, homonyms, jargon expressions, pretentious words, redundant expressions, vague quantifiers, weak modifiers, and some wordy expressions.

- *For Business Writing.* This option includes all grammar rules, but leaves out the style rules mentioned for Strictly (All Rules).

- *For Casual Writing.* This option, which is informal in both grammar and style rules, leaves out three grammar rules: format errors, informal usage, and jargon words. In addition, this option leaves out about half the style rules.

- *Custom 1, Custom 2*, or *Custom 3*. You can create your own set of rules by selecting one of these options and then clicking the Customize Settings button. The Customize Grammar Settings dialog box appears (see fig. 9.15). All the check boxes are marked when this dialog box opens; deselect the rules you do not want to use. When you finish, choose OK to close the dialog box and return to the Grammar tab.

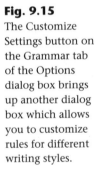

Fig. 9.15
The Customize Settings button on the Grammar tab of the Options dialog box brings up another dialog box which allows you to customize rules for different writing styles.

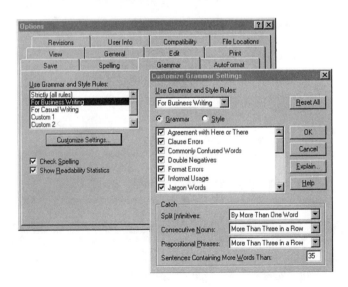

Each set of rules has two options, Grammar and Style. While a phrase may be grammatically correct, the style may not be appropriate for your audience. Incorrect style can include sexist expressions, stock phrases, jargon, and overused phrases.

Additionally, the Catch area of the Customize Grammar Settings dialog box enables you to specify when Word should catch (or alert you to) split infinitives, consecutive nouns, prepositional phrases, and long sentences. You can select options for each of these settings; for example, you can catch split infinitives always; when they are split by more than one word, two words, or three words; or never. Also, you can limit the number of words a sentence can contain—15, 30, or 40, for example.

In addition to choosing grammar and style rules, you can specify whether you want Word to Check Spelling while checking grammar and whether to Show Readability Statistics. The Readability Statistics dialog box displays the number of words, characters, paragraphs, and sentences in the document and the average number of sentences per paragraph, words per sentence, and characters per word. In addition, the dialog box shows readability indexes based on the average number of syllables per word and the average number of words per sentence. These readability indexes are Reading Ease and Grade Level values.

Changing AutoFormat Options

AutoFormat is a formatting tool within Word that automatically applies built-in styles and a template to your document. You can select various options for AutoFormat to apply. Figure 9.16 shows the AutoFormat tab of the Options dialog box.

◀ See "Formatting Documents," p. 81

▶ See "Formatting with Styles," p. 259

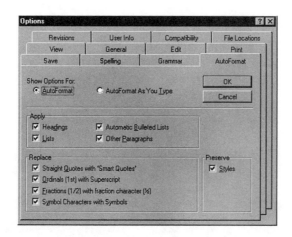

Fig. 9.16
Select the options you want AutoFormat to apply when formatting your documents.

II

Using Word

Tip
To use
AutoFormat,
choose Format,
AutoFormat. For
more information,
see Chapter 10,
"Working with
Large Documents."

The following list describes the options in the AutoFormat tab:

■ *AutoFormat and AutoFormat as You Type*. The top area of the dialog box has two options. Depending on which option you choose, the other parts of the dialog box will change. The AutoFormat option applies when you choose Format, AutoFormat to format your document. The other option on the Options dialog box, AutoFormat as You Type, applies to formatting that changes as you type characters in a document.

■ *Preserve*. This option appears only if you click the AutoFormat button and has only one option: Styles. Select this option to keep any styles you have already assigned within your document.

■ *Apply As You Type (or Apply)*. Depending on the option button you click for Show Options For, select the types of text to which you want to assign the styles: Headings, Borders, Lists, Automatic Bulleted Lists, Automatic Numbered Lists, and Other Paragraphs (such as subheads, tabs, and indented text).

■ *Replace As You Type (or Replace)*. Select the elements you want to substitute: Straight Quotes with 'Smart Quotes' (also called *open and closed quotes*), Ordinals (1st) with Superscript formatting, Fractions (1/2) with Fraction Character ($^1/_2$), and Symbol Characters with Symbols (for example, replaces TM with ™).❖

Chapter 10

Working with Large Documents

by Rick Winter and Patty Winter

When you are producing a document that contains many pages—from ten or fifteen to hundreds—you need special organizational and managerial techniques. Word provides several features that help you manage long documents. (You can use these features for short documents as well.)

In this chapter, you learn to

- Create an outline by using Word's Outline view and Outline toolbar

- Edit an outline by rearranging text and headings

- Use Word's built-in styles to format the text in a document

- Use AutoFormat and Style Gallery to have Word format a document for you

- Create and edit your own styles

- Use templates and wizards to format your documents

- Add headers and footers to each page of your document

- Create a table of contents based on the heading styles you use in your document

- Create endnotes, footnotes, and annotations for document notations

- Add bookmarks and cross-references to your document

- Use the Revision feature to mark additions, deletions, and revisions

One organizational feature you can use in a large document is *outlining*. Word provides special outlining features, including an outline view that helps you order your text. You can arrange headings and text, move headings to new positions in the outline, and print the outline as you work on it.

Word also provides document-formatting methods that make your work easier. You can use *styles*—preformatted fonts and paragraph attributes—to format your documents quickly and to guarantee consistency within the document.

Word offers a variety of techniques and processes to help you work with large documents. This chapter introduces many of those techniques.

Outlining a Document

Tip

Create an outline first in Word and then use the outline as the basis for a PowerPoint presentation (see Chapter 32).

When creating a large document, use an outline and Outline view to get an overview of how the document is put together. You can also easily rearrange headings and text to better suit the flow of information. Finally, use outlining in long documents to quickly move to a specific location and then view the text.

To outline a document, you assign headings to the text to signify different levels of topic development. You can create up to nine different levels of text, including body text. Word formats and indents each level so that you can organize the text quickly. The headings remain formatted in other views as well, although the indents shown in outline view disappear in Normal and Page Layout views.

Figure 10.1 shows an initial outline for a document. This sample outline contains four levels of headings: *Ethics of Arcs* is Heading 1, *Suppose no more canvas for painting* is Heading 2, *Have to use existing art to create new art* is Heading 3, and *A. Carr - Travels of a Naturalist* is Heading 4. As you enter more headings and body text, you can format the text, arrange the headings, and move text around to better organize the document.

Word provides an outline view in which you can organize your documents. Outline view provides an Outline toolbar (see fig. 10.1) that enables you to assign headings to your text, hide body text or headings, and rearrange your outline. You can outline an existing document or create a new document in Outline view.

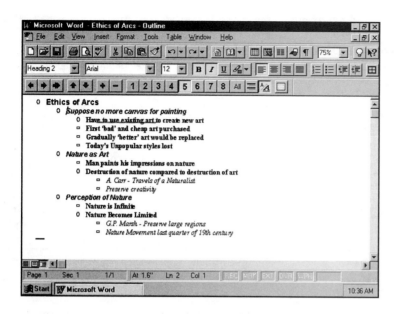

Fig. 10.1
You can plan a document from scratch in Outline view, assigning levels of importance to headings as you write.

The following table gives a brief description of each tool in the Outline toolbar:

Button	Button Name	Description
	Promote	Elevates a heading to a higher level
	Demote	Reduces a heading to a lower level
	Demote to Body Text	Reduces the heading to body text
	Move Up	Repositions the selected heading(s) up one heading in the outline
	Move Down	Repositions the selected heading(s) down one heading in the outline
	Expand	Shows subheadings and body text under selected heading

(continues)

Button	Button Name	Description
–	Collapse	Hides subheadings and body text under selected heading
1 through **8**	Show Headings 1 through 8	Expands or collapses the outline to a specific level
All	All	Expands or collapses the entire outline or hides all body text
≡	Show First Line Only	Shows all body text or only the first line of the body text
ᴬ𝐴	Show Formatting	Shows or hides character formatting
▤	Master Document view	Changes to Master Document view or back to simple outline view. If Master Document view is selected, the Master Document toolbar appears to the right of the Outline toolbar.

Creating an Outline

You create an outline by entering, formatting, and assigning headings in Word's Outline view. The view provides helpful features you can use to organize your document. After creating your outline, you easily can change heading levels, add text, and otherwise edit your document by using the Outline toolbar and other features of outline view.

Viewing the Outline

Tip
To change to Outline view, simply click the third view button in the horizontal scroll bar.

To start creating an outline, choose View, Outline. In Outline view, use the Outline toolbar to specify various levels of headings and body text (see fig. 10.2). Word indents each heading and its text, and formats the text for you.

> **Note**
>
> You can reformat any text formats easily by using styles. For more information, see "Formatting with Styles," later in this chapter.

Outline toolbar

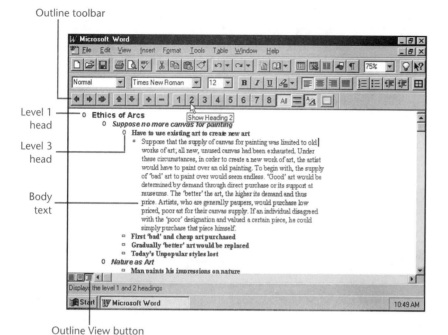

Level 1 head

Level 3 head

Body text

Outline View button

Fig. 10.2
Place the mouse pointer on a button to view the ToolTip and a description of the button in the status bar.

Entering Text

You can enter text as you normally do by typing paragraphs, heading text, and so on in Normal, Page Layout, or Outline view. You can assign heading styles to existing text by using the Formatting toolbar.

The Formatting toolbar includes a drop-down list of styles (see fig. 10.3). In the Normal template—the default template for documents—Heading 1 style is used for the broadest topics; Heading 2 is used for the subdivisions of Heading 1 topics; and so on. To view or change the style, click the I-beam mouse pointer anywhere in the paragraph and use the Formatting toolbar.

Alternatively, you can designate outline levels as you enter text. Simply select a heading style from the drop-down list in the Formatting toolbar and type the heading. Then change the style, if necessary, and type the next heading or body text (the Normal style is the same as body text style; see the section "Formatting with Styles," later in this chapter).

◄ See "Viewing the Document," p. 186

◄ See "Entering Text in a Word Document," p. 170

◄ See "Formatting Text," p. 190

Using Word

Fig. 10.3

You can assign heading styles by using the Formatting toolbar.

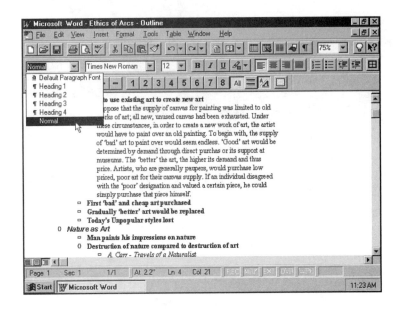

Selecting Text

Outline view provides a slightly different method of selecting text than do the other views. Each paragraph of text, whether that text is a heading or body text, is preceded by a hollow plus sign (+) or a hollow minus sign (–). If you position the mouse pointer on one of these symbols, the pointer changes to a four-headed arrow. When the pointer changes shape, simply click the plus sign or minus sign to select the associated paragraph and any lower-level headings and body text below it.

Note

The plus and minus signs also indicate whether more text has been entered under that level of the outline. A hollow plus sign before a Heading 1 entry, for example, means that other headings and/or body text have been entered under that heading. A hollow minus sign appears when there are no headings or body text associated with this level. A small, hollow box precedes body text.

Suppose that you click the hollow plus sign preceding the *Ethics of Arcs* heading (refer back to fig. 10.2). By doing so, you select all text from that point to the next Level 1 heading. (In this case, all the text is selected.) Similarly, if you click the plus sign preceding the Level 2 head, *Suppose no more canvas for painting*, you select all text from that point to the next Level 2 heading, *Nature as Art*. You also can select text by clicking the selection bar (to the left of the text area) or by dragging the I-beam pointer across specific text. After you select the text, you can then choose the level of the heading you want to assign.

Promoting and Demoting Headings

After assigning various heading levels to your text, you may decide to change those levels. You can do so by using the Promote and Demote buttons in the Outline toolbar. Simply select the text and then click the Promote or Demote button.

The Promote button—the first button from the left in the Outline toolbar— looks like an arrow pointing left. Each time you click the button, the selected text moves up one level (until it reaches Level 1) and displays with less indentation. Similarly, the Demote button—an arrow pointing right—bumps the selected text down one heading level at a time (until it reaches Level 8) and displays with further indentation toward the right. Remember, when you select a heading, you select all text and subheadings within that heading. When you promote or demote the heading, all subheadings follow suit.

To change a selected heading to body text in a single step, click the Demote to Body Text button—a double arrow pointing right.

Editing an Outline

You can edit an outline by adding, deleting, or rearranging body text and headings. In Outline view, you can add or delete text as you do in any view. But Outline view also provides two features that make it easier for you to rearrange your text: viewing and moving outline levels.

You can use the Outline toolbar to view specific levels of the outline. In addition, you can rearrange topics easily without cutting and pasting text.

Collapsing and Expanding Outlines

You can view various levels of an outline by using the Show Heading buttons—the buttons numbered 1 through 8 in the Outline toolbar. If you click the Show Heading 1 button, for example, only Heading 1 text appears on-screen. If you click the Show Heading 2 button, you see only Heading 1 and Heading 2 text.

If you show only headings with no body text, you are *collapsing* the outline. *Expanding* the outline means just the opposite. If only Heading 2 text is showing, for example, click the Show Heading 3, Show Heading 4, or All button to expand the outline.

Tip
Double-click the plus sign that precedes a heading to display all the text below that heading. Double-click again to hide all the text.

Figure 10.4 shows a collapsed outline. The hollow plus sign next to each heading indicates that more text levels exist within that heading. If a hollow minus sign appears next to a heading, the heading contains no further text levels.

Fig. 10.4

Use the Expand and Collapse buttons to reveal text below the selected head.

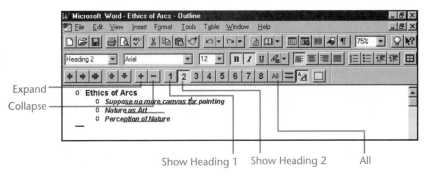

Expand

Collapse

Show Heading 1   Show Heading 2   All

Rearranging Headings and Text

◀ See "Drag-and-Drop Editing," p. 178

You can rearrange topics in your document by selecting and moving headings in Outline view. The easiest method is to collapse the outline to the level to be moved, select the heading you want to move, and drag the heading to its new position. Subheads and body text move with the selected heading.

> **Caution**
>
> If you do not collapse the outline before moving the text, you may leave some body text behind. Be sure to select *all* text to be moved.

Tip

To print the outline at any level, choose File, Print, or click the Print button.

Figure 10.5 shows how the screen looks when you move a heading (and its subheadings and body text) to a new position. The mouse pointer changes to a double-headed arrow, and a guideline moves with the mouse to help you position the heading.

Fig. 10.5

For the most efficient and easiest rearranging of topics, collapse the outline to the heading level to be moved.

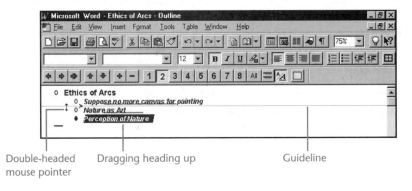

Double-headed   Dragging heading up   Guideline
mouse pointer

Troubleshooting

I collapsed the outline so that I could focus on the headings while scrolling through the document, but I want to remind myself about the contents of the body text below each heading.

 Click the Show First Line Only button in the Outline toolbar to display the first line of body text below each heading.

I want to print only the headings and first lines of body text.

Word prints only what is displayed on-screen in Outline view. Display the level of headings you want to print, and then click the Show First Line Only button in the Outline toolbar.

I want to copy only the headings from my document but I get all the subordinate text below the headings.

You cannot copy just the headings unless you do it one heading at a time. Instead, create a Table of Contents from the headings (as described in the "Creating a Table of Contents" section later in the chapter). After you create the table of contents, press Ctrl+Shift+F9 to convert the table of contents to regular text.

Formatting with Styles

A *style* is a collection of formats you can assign to selected text in a document. Each style includes attributes such as font, type size and style, spacing, leading, alignment, indents, and tabs. Styles enable you to format your documents quickly and consistently. Word provides a large number of ready-to-use styles; you also can create your own styles as you work.

◀ See "Formatting Text," p. 190

There are two types of styles in Word: *paragraph styles* and *character styles*. If you position the insertion point or select any portion of a paragraph and apply a paragraph style, the entire text of the paragraph changes to reflect the new style. Character styles only change text that is selected. In the Style pull-down box on the Formatting toolbar (shown earlier in figure 10.3), the paragraph symbols before the style name indicate paragraph styles; the *a* with an underscore indicates a character style.

◀ See "Formatting Paragraphs," p. 194

▶ See "Changing Fonts, Sizes, and Styles," p. 357

One of Word's paragraph styles, for example, is the Heading 1 style used to outline a document. Using the Normal template, heading 1 text initially appears in 14-point Arial, bold, and left-aligned. You can assign this style, or any other style, as often as necessary in your documents.

Tip
Click the New button on the Standard toolbar to start a new document using the settings from the Normal template.

Word's styles are associated with its *templates*, which are a preset collection of page, paragraph, and character formatting styles you can use to develop a particular type of document. Each time you start a new document, the New dialog box lists many different templates. The Normal template (Word's default) offers three heading formats and a body-text format. Other templates, such as the Invoice, Letter, and Memo templates, provide different styles for your use.

Styles are particularly useful when you are working on a large document. Rather than moving from page to page and formatting each heading, list, tab setting, and so on, separately, you can format a style one time and then assign the style to each portion of text you want to format with the style's formats. After you assign styles, you may decide you want to change all occurrences of text formatted with a particular style. Rather than reformatting each occurrence separately, you only need to edit the style.

> **Note**
>
> ◀ See "Starting a New Word Document," p. 183
>
> Examine some of Word's templates by working with the Style Gallery (see "Using Style Gallery" later in this chapter). From the menu bar choose Format Style Gallery. Choose the template you want to review in the Template list box. In the Preview section choose Style Samples. The styles for the template will display with the style name and the formatting associated with the style.

This section shows you how to use Word's styles and how to create and assign your own styles.

Using Word's Styles

To apply a style, first select the text you want to format. Then open the Style drop-down list in the Formatting toolbar and select the style you want to apply (see fig. 10.6).

Tip
To see the style names in the left margin, choose Tools, Options and change the Style Area Width on the View tab to .5.

> **Note**
>
> The formatting for Heading 2 (and other headings) shown in figure 10.6 are specific to the Normal Template. If the styles have been edited on the Normal Template or if you are using a different template, the formatting may be different for each style. If you want to convert styles in your document to take on the formatting characteristics of styles with the same name from another template, you can use the File Templates command.

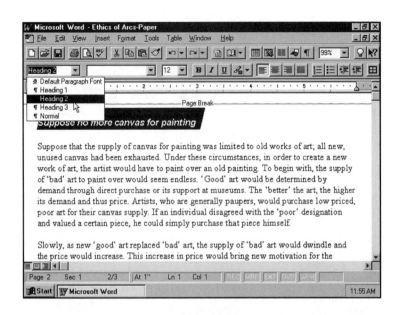

Fig. 10.6
The Normal Template's Heading 2 style is 12-point Arial, bold italic, left-aligned, with spacing set at 12 points before and 3 points after the paragraph.

You can change the format of text after applying a style. You can, for example, change the *Suppose no more canvas for painting* heading in figure 10.6 to 14 point or center aligned. Changing the format of a particular heading, however, does not change the style itself or other headings to which you apply that style. For more information about changing the attributes of styles, see "Editing a Style," later in this chapter.

Creating a Style

Creating your own styles in Word is easy. Suppose that you want to create a heading style for use throughout your document; you want the style to be 18-point Times New Roman, bold, and center aligned. You can create this style, add it to the Style drop-down list, and use it as you would any other Word style.

To create your own style, follow these steps:

1. Select the text on which you want to base your style, and apply the desired formatting.

2. With the text still selected, click in the Style box in the Formatting toolbar to select the current style name. Which style name you choose does not matter.

3. Type your own name for the style (see fig. 10.7).

4. Press Enter to add the name to the Styles list.

Type the style name in the Style box

Fig. 10.7
When you enter a
new name in the
Style box, you do
not actually delete
the original style;
you are just
adding a new style
to the list.

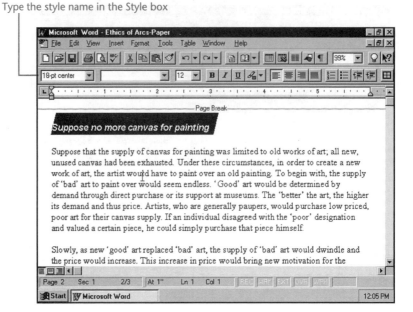

Editing a Style

You can edit any style by changing font, size, alignment, tab stops, and so
on, whether it is a preset style provided with Word or a style you created. To
edit a style, follow these steps:

1. Choose F_ormat, _Style. The Style dialog box appears (see fig. 10.8).

Fig. 10.8
You can view the
attributes of a style
in the Description
area at the bottom
of the dialog box.

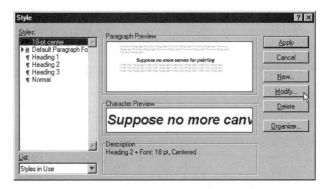

2. In the S_tyles list box, select the style you want to modify. Samples of
the text as it is now formatted appear in the Paragraph Preview and
Character Preview boxes.

3. Choose the <u>M</u>odify button to edit the style. The Modify Style dialog box appears (see fig. 10.9).

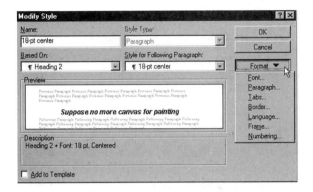

Fig. 10.9
Modify a style by selecting an option in the F<u>o</u>rmat drop-down list.

4. Click F<u>o</u>rmat to display a drop-down list of the style attributes you can edit.

5. Select an attribute—<u>F</u>ont, <u>P</u>aragraph, <u>T</u>abs, and so on—from the list; make the desired changes in the dialog box that appears. (The dialog box that appears is exactly like the one that appears when you choose the corresponding command from the F<u>o</u>rmat menu.) Choose OK to return to the Modify Style dialog box.

6. Repeat step 5 as often as necessary to modify additional style attributes.

7. After making all desired changes, choose OK in the Modify Style dialog box. You return to the Style dialog box.

8. Choose Close to exit the Style dialog box. All text that has been formatted with your style will be changed throughout your document.

Tip
To save the styles you create or edit in a document, save the document so that the styles are always available with that document.

Caution

After you choose OK from the Modify Style dialog box, the formatting of the style changes throughout your document. If you choose <u>A</u>pply in the Style dialog box, the selected text or text where the insertion point is will now have the changed style, even if this text originally was not formatted with that style. Make sure you choose Close in the Style dialog box at step 8.

II

Using Word

Troubleshooting

I try to create a style for a few words within a paragraph but after I finish creating the style, the whole paragraph takes on the characteristics of the style.

You need to create a character style instead of a paragraph style. To do this, you cannot use the Style pull-down in the Formatting toolbar. Choose Format Style and choose the New command button. In the Style Type pull-down list of the New Style dialog box, choose Character.

I've applied the same style throughout my document, but it looks different at different places in the document.

After you apply a style, you can override the style by manually applying font and paragraph formatting. If you want to remove any manual formatting, select the paragraph—including the paragraph symbol—and press Ctrl+space bar to remove character formatting and Ctrl+Q to remove paragraph formatting.

Using AutoFormat

Tip
Use Auto-Format to remove unnecessary spacing and change asterisk bullets to round bullets and headings to styles.

◀ See "Changing AutoFormat Options," p. 249

AutoFormat is a feature of Word that analyzes your document and automatically applies styles (such as headings, subheadings, bulleted lists, and tabs) to your document when you use the AutoFormat command or as you type. When you use the AutoFormat command, you can review AutoFormat's choices and accept or reject them. Using AutoFormat can save you time because Word assigns styles for you. The formatting may not be exactly what you want, but you can still change fonts, styles, sizes, and so on after using AutoFormat.

You can use AutoFormat with unformatted text, or you can begin formatting (by creating and applying a few styles) and then let AutoFormat complete the process. AutoFormat finds similar text and assigns the same styles. If you choose the latter method, you have more control over which styles AutoFormat uses. Experiment with both methods and see which you prefer.

Formatting Text as You Type

If you want to use the AutoFormat feature as you type text, choose Tools, Options and select the AutoFormat as You Type option button. You can check as many of the following dialog box options as you want:

Option	How To Make It Work
Headings	Type a line of text and press Enter twice for Heading 1 style. The Start with Tab applies Heading 2.
Borders	Type three or more hyphens (-) and press Enter for a thin border or equal signs (=) for a double border.
Automatic Bulleted Lists	Start a list with a number. When you press Enter, each new item will be numbered.
Automatic Numbered Lists	Start a list with an asterisk. When you press Enter, each new item will be bulleted.
Straight Quotes with Quotes	When you type 'single' or "double" quotes, Word Smart automatically changes them to 'smart quotes' or "smart quotes."
Ordinals (1st) with Superscript	Type **1st** or **2nd** to get 1st, 2nd, and so on.
Fractions (1/2) with fraction character ($\frac{1}{2}$)	Type 1/2, 3/4 to get $\frac{1}{2}$ and $\frac{3}{4}$.
Symbol Characters with Symbols	Type **(c)** for ", **(r)** for ®, **(tm)** for '. Type **:),** :l, and :(for faces; <-, -> for thin arrows; <=, => for thick arrows.

Formatting Text Automatically

To start AutoFormat, choose F̲ormat, A̲utoFormat. A message box—the first AutoFormat dialog box—appears, announcing that formatting is about to begin (see fig. 10.10). Choose OK to begin formatting. You can also use the AutoFormat button on the Standard toolbar to apply all formatting without being prompted.

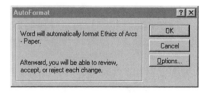

Fig. 10.10
Choose OK to begin formatting, Cancel to cancel the command, or O̲ptions to customize formatting.

Accepting or Rejecting Changes

After AutoFormat completes the formatting, another dialog box appears (see fig. 10.11). Choose A̲ccept to accept all changes. If you choose A̲ccept too hastily, you can reverse your decision by clicking the Undo button in the

Standard toolbar. If you do not like the changes you see behind the AutoFormat dialog box, choose Reject All. Alternatively, choose Review Changes or Style Gallery.

Fig. 10.11

You can choose to review changes, reject changes, or accept changes.

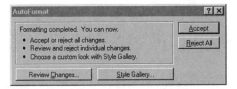

If you choose to Review Changes, Word shows you each change to the formatting by highlighting the change and displaying a dialog box with a description of the change. You can choose to accept or reject individual changes. If you choose the Style Gallery button, you can apply different templates and styles to the document to see what they look like.

Reviewing Changes

If you choose to review the changes, Word takes you through the document step-by-step, enabling you to examine each change that AutoFormat made. Figure 10.12 shows the Review AutoFormat Changes dialog box.

The Review AutoFormat Changes dialog box enables you to accept or reject changes. To accept a change, choose one of the Find buttons. Find with a left arrow moves to the previous change; Find with a right arrow moves to the next change. If you do not like the formatting, choose the Reject button. Word changes the current selection back to its original formatting.

If you don't reject any changes, you'll have a Cancel button that allows you to return to the AutoFormat dialog box. If you reject any changes, the Cancel button changes to Close. Choose Close after reviewing the changes, or at any time, and Word displays the initial AutoFormat dialog box again. You can choose to accept or reject all changes.

As you go through reviewing changes, AutoFormat will show items that have been deleted in red (such as paragraph marks) as well as items that have been added in blue. If you don't want to see the marks where changes have been made, choose the Hide Marks button. If you want Word to automatically go to the next change after you choose the Reject button, check the Find Next after Reject checkbox. If you make a mistake and don't want to reject a change after you choose the Reject button, choose the Undo Last button.

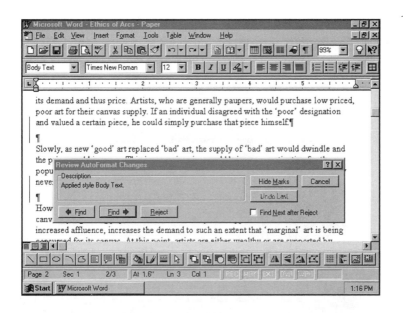

Fig. 10.12
Use this dialog box to examine each change and decide whether to keep or reject the change.

> **Note**
>
> You can click the mouse outside the Review AutoFormat Changes dialog box to work in your document. The dialog box remains on-screen. This way, you can scroll through the document to compare changes, format text, and add or edit text.

Using Style Gallery

Style Gallery is a special dialog box that contains Word's various templates. Each template contains preset page formatting and preset styles. You can use Style Gallery to apply various templates and styles to your document, and view an example in the dialog box before choosing to accept the style.

You can use the Style Gallery with or without AutoFormat. When you use AutoFormat, Word automatically applies a template and style sheet. If you do not like Word's choice, you can choose the Style Gallery command button and choose a different template and style for your document. On the other hand, you can format your document yourself by applying styles to text and paragraphs, and then decide to look at the document with various templates applied. Style Gallery gives a formatted document a different look using various styles of fonts, indents, type sizes, and so on.

Tip
You can choose Style Gallery in the AutoFormat dialog box to choose a different template and style for the document.

II

Using Word

◀ See "Changing
AutoFormat
Options,"
p. 249

To open the Style Gallery from the menu, choose Format, Style Gallery. To open Style Gallery from the AutoFormat dialog box, choose Style Gallery. Figure 10.13 shows the Style Gallery dialog box with the Professional Report template displayed.

Fig. 10.13
Apply any of the templates and styles to your document or choose to preview examples of the template.

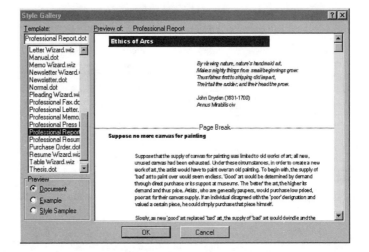

To use the Style Gallery, follow these steps:

1. From the second AutoFormat dialog box, choose Style Gallery. To use Style Gallery directly, choose Format, Style Gallery. The Style Gallery dialog box appears.

2. Select a template from the Template list.

3. To change what displays in the Preview Of box, choose one of the options in the Preview section. The default choice, Document, shows your document with styles applied from the selected template. To see an example document with many of the styles for the template, choose Example. To see a list of styles in the template and how they are formatted, choose Style Samples in the Preview section.

4. If you find a template and style you like, choose OK. If you do not find a template you like, choose Cancel. Word returns to the AutoFormat dialog box or to your document.

5. If you started from AutoFormat, choose to Accept or Reject All changes. The dialog box closes, and you return to the document.

Troubleshooting

I want to use the styles with a particular template, but I can't find the style names.

Choose View, Toolbars and select the Formatting toolbar; then choose OK. The Style box is the first box at the left end of the toolbar. In addition, change the view from normal or outline to page layout (use the View menu to change the view) to display all formatting in the document.

AutoFormat does not seem to change the formatting of my document.

By default, AutoFormat assigns styles only to paragraphs formatted in Normal or Body Text style. If you have selected some text and applied a style, or if you used commands in the Format menu to format some text, AutoFormat does not change any of those styles.

I want to format only a section of a document.

Select the text you want to format, and then choose Format AutoFormat.

Using Template Wizards

A *template wizard* is a special template that asks questions and uses your answers to format a document automatically. The available template wizards include Newsletter, Resume, Memo, Letter, Fax, Agenda, Calendar, Pleading, and Table.

◀ See "Using Wizards," p. 162

If you use a template wizard, you must use it before you actually enter text in a document. Choose File, New to display Word's list of templates. Select the type of template wizard you want to use, and then answer the questions as they appear on-screen. This section describes the questions, answers, and formatting associated with the Memo Wizard.

Choosing a Wizard

To begin a wizard document, choose File, New. The New dialog box appears (see fig. 10.14) with tabs for each type of templates and wizards. Select the tab you want and then the template wizard you want to use (for this example, select the Memo tab and then select the Memo Wizard); choose OK.

II

Using Word

Fig. 10.14
Template wizard icons include a wand to distinguish them from template icons.

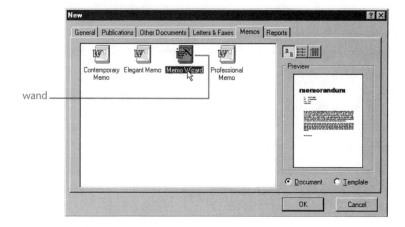

wand

Choosing Text Options

Word displays the Memo Wizard dialog box (see fig. 10.15). The dialog box shows you an example of the memo the wizard will format for you. Each dialog box that appears asks you questions about the text and formatting of the document. You choose general text, such as the headings *Interoffice Memo*, *To*, *From*, and so on, from these dialog boxes; Word applies them to the final memo. You fill in specific text—such as the name, date, and subject—after the memo is created. Additionally, Word asks about other formatting concerns, such as the addition of page numbers, graphics lines, and so on.

Fig. 10.15
Answer the questions and choose Next to continue creating the memo with the Memo Wizard template.

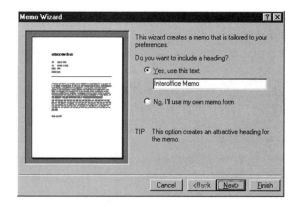

The first dialog box asks whether you want to use a heading and what text you want to use as a heading. After making your decision, choose Next to continue formatting the memo.

Word displays a second dialog box, asking whether you want a separate page for your distribution list. Choose Yes if you are sending the memo to several people; choose No if you are sending the memo to only one or two people. Choose Next to move to the next dialog box.

In this dialog box (see fig. 10.16), select the options you want to use: Date, To, CC, From, Subject, and Priority. Enter text in the Date and From text boxes, replacing the date if it is incorrect. If you want to get names from your address book, choose the Address Book command button. For more information about the Address Book, see Chapter 3.

▶ See "Using the Address Book for Merging," p. 925

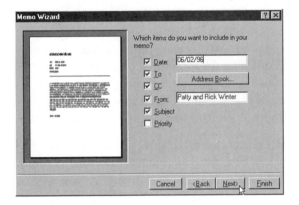

Fig. 10.16
Select the options you want to include, and enter text in the appropriate text boxes.

II

Using Word

After you select options, choose Back to return to the preceding dialog box or Next to continue. The next dialog box asks whether you want to include the Writer's and Typist's Initials, Enclosures, and/or Attachments. Select the options you want and then choose Next.

The next dialog box lets you select a *header*, or title that appears on all pages after the first page of your memo. The header can contain a Topic, Date, and/or Page Number; select one, two, or all three to include in the header. Additionally, you can select a footer, which can include the Date, the Page Number, or the word *Confidential*. Select any of the options for your footer, and then choose Next.

Formatting the Memo

The Memo Wizard dialog box that appears after you select header and footer options governs the formatting of the document. Figure 10.17 shows the wizard's prompt for the style of memo to be used. The style Word assigns to the document includes margins, text formatting, tab settings, graphics lines, and so on.

Fig. 10.17

Select a style that best suits your needs; you can modify the style later, if you want.

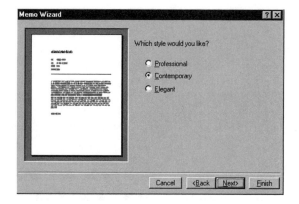

You can select Professional, Contemporary, or Elegant style. Most wizards ask this style question about the formatting of documents. Professional usually is plain, formal-looking, and straightforward. Contemporary, which often contains various fonts and graphics lines, is more modern in design. Elegant looks as though the document had been typed on a typewriter.

When you select one of the styles, an example displays in the dialog box. Select the style that best suits your memo or document. After selecting the style, choose the Next button and decide whether you want to use help with the memo you've created. Make your choice about displaying help and choose Finish to close the wizard.

> **Note**
>
> If you know what the settings are on Wizard dialog boxes (from repeated use), you can choose the Finish button at any time to go to the document and skip intermediate dialog boxes. The last dialog box displays a Finish flag and the Next button is dimmed because there are no more steps. You can also choose the Back button to go to a previous step.

Word then creates the memo document for you, adding text and formatting the document with the choices you made. Word displays the memo, as shown in figure 10.18. This memo was created in the Contemporary style. Fill in the specific text and your memo is complete.

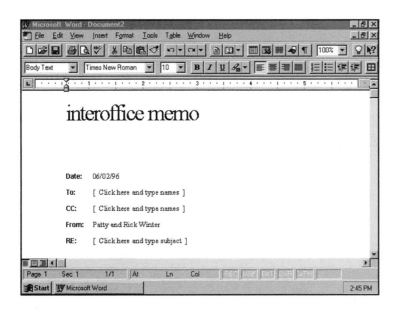

interoffice memo

Date:	06/02/96
To:	[Click here and type names]
CC:	[Click here and type names]
From:	Patty and Rick Winter
RE:	[Click here and type subject]

Fig. 10.18
Fill in the text to complete your memo. You can select and format the text, just as you can in any other Word document.

Creating a Template

As mentioned above, Word comes with many built-in templates. You may have instances where you would like to modify an existing template for your office use or start completely from scratch and create a template that you can use over and over. Creating a template is almost as easy as saving a document. However, templates can also be extremely complex because of all the items you can include on them, such as text and formatting, AutoText entries, macros, styles.

◄ See "Saving, Opening, and Closing Files," p. 106

Based on Template from the File New Menu

You can modify an existing template and save it is a new template. To create your own template by modifying an existing template, follow these steps:

1. Choose File, New.

2. In the New dialog box, choose the template you want to base your new template on by choosing a Tab and template.

3. On the bottom right of the New dialog box, choose the Template option button.

4. Choose OK to go to the document.

II

Using Word

5. Make any changes to the document, including adding styles, adding text, changing formatting, adding macros.

6. Choose File, Save or click the Save button.

7. In the Save As dialog box, the Templates folder will show in the Save in pull-down list and the Save as Type drop-down will show Document Template. If you want to change the location of the template on the File New dialog box, choose a different folder.

8. Type the name of the template in the File Name text box and choose the Save button.

To use your template, choose File, New and pick your template from the File New dialog box.

If you want to create your own template, use the template closest to what you need. In the bottom right of the New dialog box, choose Template and then click the OK button. Make any changes you want to the template. When you save the template, the Save as Type option indicates Document Template.

Saving as a Template File

You can create a template from "scratch" or use an existing Word document and convert it to a template. To save a file as a template, follow these steps:

1. Open your existing document or start with a blank document.

2. Make any changes to the document, including adding styles, adding text, changing formatting, adding macros.

3. Choose File, Save As.

4. In the Save As dialog box, change the Save as Type drop-down to Document Template.

5. Change the location in the Save In pull-down to the location where Word templates are located (it is probably in the Templates subfolder of the MSOFFICE folder). If you want to change the location of the template on the File New dialog box, choose a different folder.

6. Type the name of the template in the File Name text box and choose the Save button.

Troubleshooting

I want to use a wizard that is not listed in the New dialog box.

Make sure that you are in the Template folder in the Word program folder. If you installed the templates in another folder, change to that folder. Alternatively, you may have to run Word Setup and install the templates, if you did not install them with the original program.

Adding Headers and Footers

Headers and *footers* contain repeated information at the top and bottom of documents. Headers and footers are typically used in long documents and may include one or more of the following: page number, date, company name, author name, or chapter title. You can edit and format headers and footers like any other part of a Word document.

▶ See "Creating Headers and Footers," p. 410

Inserting a Header or Footer

When you add a header or footer, Word switches to Page Layout view, opens up the Header pane, and displays a Header and Footer toolbar. To add a header or footer, choose <u>V</u>iew, <u>H</u>eader and Footer. The Header and Footer toolbar appears along with a dotted area surrounding the header area (see fig. 10.19). Type in the header pane or use the Switch Between Header and Footer button to go to the footer.

In the header or footer pane, you can do any of the following:

- Type and format text as you can in a normal document.

- Press Tab to get to the center tab; press Tab again to get to the right-alignment tab. You can also change the tab settings if you want.

- Click the Page Numbers button to add a page number for each page.

- Click the Date button to add a field that will show today's date. To have this field updated when printing, make sure that <u>T</u>ools, <u>O</u>ptions, Print Tab shows <u>U</u>pdate Fields is checked.

- Click the Time button to add a field that will show the current time.

■ If you want headers and footers for the first page to appear differently than on other pages, or different headers and footers on odd and even pages, click the Page Setup button. In the Headers and Footers section of the Layout tab, you can check the Different Odd and Even checkbox to have headers and footers change on facing pages. You can check the Different First Page option to have headers and footers that are different for the first page (this is usually done for report title pages). If you have different sections in your document, you can choose This Section or Whole Document in the Apply To pull-down list. When finished with the Page Setup dialog box, choose OK to return to the Header and Footer pane.

When you are finished entering information for the headers and footers, click the Close button to return to the document.

Fig. 10.19
A special area appears to write headers and footers.

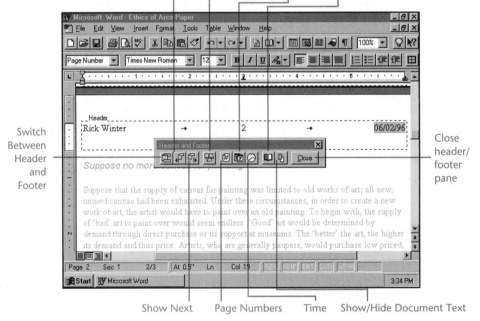

Inserting Fields in the Header or Footer

You can add field codes to the document or in the header or footer—the procedure is the same. To add a code to the header or footer while you are in the header or footer pane, choose Insert, Field. You can choose any of the field codes from the Field dialog box shown in figure 10.20.

Choose an item in the Field Names list

Choose one
of the
Categories

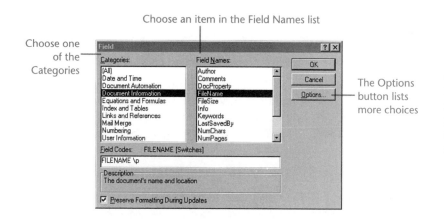

Fig. 10.20
The FileName
code with the \p
switch adds a file
name with the file
location, includ-
ing the drive and
folder.

The Options
button lists
more choices

The following table shows some useful fields for headers and footers:

Result	Categories	Field Names
Document name (include the \p switch for the path name)	Document Information	FileName \p
Total number of pages	Document Information	NumPages
Author or User Information	Document Information UserName	Author
Section numbering	Numbering	Section

II

Using Word

Editing or Deleting a Header or Footer

To edit the header or footer, you can double-click the header or footer in page
layout view or choose View, Header and Footer. Edit the header or footer as
you would regular document text. If you want to delete the header or footer,
select the text (press Ctrl+A to select the entire header or footer) and press
Delete. Click the Close button on the Header and Footer toolbar to return to
the document.

Tip
Double-click a
header or
footer in Page
Layout view to
open the pane
for editing.

Troubleshooting

When I edit a header or footer, it appears in only part of my document.

You could have multiple sections in your document or have another option on the page layout dialog box checked. Choose View, Header and Footer and click the Page Setup button on the Header and Footer toolbar. Make sure that both checkboxes in the Header and Footer section are deselected. In the Apply To pull-down, make sure that Whole Document is selected.

When I look at my document, the wrong date shows in the header or footer.

If you use the Insert Date and Time choice to insert a date, you need to make sure that you choose the Update Automatically (Insert as Field) check box on the Date and Time dialog box. If you use the Header and Footer toolbar, a field code is inserted in your document. The field code generally will not update until you print or open the document. You can manually update the code if you click in the field and press F9.

Creating a Table of Contents

If you use the Heading 1, Heading 2, and Heading 3 styles, you can quickly create a table of contents for your document. To create the table of contents, follow these steps:

1. Press Ctrl+Home to move to the top of the document (or move the insertion point to the location where you want the table of contents to go).

2. If necessary, press Ctrl+Enter to add a page break and press Page Up to move back to the new first page.

3. Choose Insert, Index and Tables. The Index and Tables dialog box appears.

4. Select the Table of Contents tab, as shown in figure 10.21.

5. Click the Show Levels increment buttons to indicate how many heading levels you want to include.

6. Pick the style for the table of contents from the Formats list box.

7. Choose OK to generate the table of contents.

Table of Contents tab

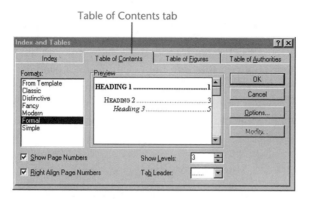

Fig. 10.21
The Index and
Tables dialog box
allows you to
choose from
different styles
for your table
of contents.

If you later edit the document, choose Insert, Index and Tables again; when you see the confirm dialog box, indicate that you want to replace the old table of contents.

Troubleshooting

I was able to get some of my heading levels to appear in the table of contents, but not all.

After you choose Insert, Index and Tables and choose the Table of Contents tab, change the Show Levels increment box to show the number of headings you want.

I don't really want to see page numbers but would like to see the table of contents to have an outline of my work.

Choose the Outline View button on the horizontal scroll bar and select the number of levels you want to view. Alternatively, on the Table of Contents tab of the Index and Tables dialog box, deselect the Show Page Numbers check box.

I would like to have something else beside dots leading up to the page numbers.

On the Table of Contents tab of the Index and Tables dialog box, you have Tab Leader choices of none, solid line, and dashes in addition to dots leading up to the page numbers. You can also deselect the Right Align Page numbers checkbox to have the numbers appear directly after the text.

Note

If you use captions on your figures (through Insert, Caption), you can generate a table of figures by choosing Insert, Index and Tables and making choices on the Table of Figures tab. If you need an index or table of authorities, you first need to mark the text (select the text and then make the appropriate Mark choice on the Index and Tables dialog box). When you want to generate the index or table, choose Insert, Index and Tables, choose the tab on the dialog box you want, and then choose OK.

II

Using Word

Using Footnotes and Endnotes

When you write a report or want to identify the source of your text, you can use *footnotes* (which go on the bottom of each page) or *endnotes* (which appear at the end of the document). To create an endnote or footnote, first position the insertion point at your reference in the document and then choose Insert, Footnote. The Footnote and Endnote dialog box appears, as shown in figure 10.22.

Fig. 10.22
Choose Insert, Footnote to add notes at the bottom of the current page. Choose Insert, Endnote to add notes at the end of the document.

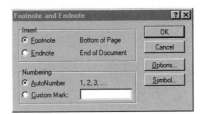

In the Insert section of the dialog box, select Footnote or Endnote; then choose OK. The bottom portion of the screen opens up to allow you to type the reference (see fig. 10.23). When finished, click the Close button. A superscript number appears next to your text in the document referring to the footnote numbers at the bottom of your page or the endnote numbers at the end of your document. To delete a footnote or endnote, highlight the superscript number and press Delete.

Fig. 10.23
A new pane opens up to allow you to add a footnote or endnote. Choose Close to get out of the pane or click in your document to continue working.

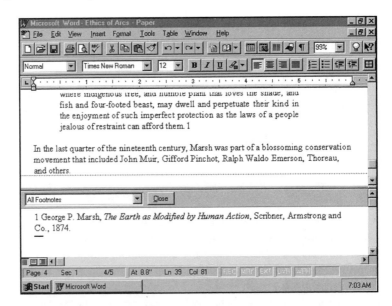

Note

When creating footnotes or endnotes, you have options on how you want them displayed. After you choose Insert, Footnote to go to the Footnote and Endnote dialog box, AutoNumber is the default choice, which means that each new note will be incremented by one. You can change the mark to appear as a letter, a number, or another character by choosing the Custom Mark option and typing in your choice. The Symbol command button allows you to choose symbols for your custom mark from the Symbol dialog box. The Options command button leads to another dialog box, which allows you to change the location of the footnotes and endnotes, the number format (numbers, letters, symbols), which number to start with, and when to restart numbering.

Annotating Your Work

Annotations are similar to endnotes except that they are usually used when more than one person works on a document (annotations help identify the reviewer). To create an annotation, choose Insert, Annotation. A window opens on the lower part of the document for your annotation (see fig. 10.24). When finished writing your comment, click the Close button. The reviewer's initials appear in superscript in the document, followed by a number. This number references the annotations at the end of the document.

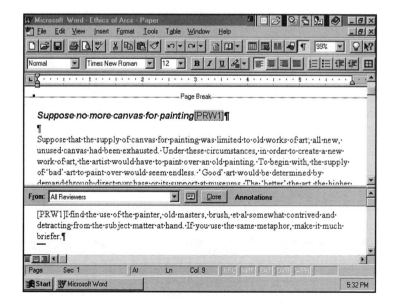

Fig. 10.24
A pane is also created for annotations.

II

Using Word

> **Note**
>
> The reviewer's initials are based on the user information from the reviewer's computer. To view or change the initials, choose Tools, Options, select the User Info tab, view or change the Initials text box, and choose OK.

To edit an annotation, double-click the annotation reference. To delete the annotation, select the superscript reference and press Delete. To print annotations, choose File, Print and choose Annotations from the Print What pull-down list.

Troubleshooting

I want to edit my annotation but can't seem to get to it.

 Click the Show/Hide button on the Standard toolbar. Your annotation codes will appear on-screen. Double-click a code to edit it.

Using Bookmarks and Cross-References

You can use bookmarks to create easy jump-to sections in your document or for cross-references. To create a bookmark, move to or select the text you want to mark as the bookmark. Choose Edit, Bookmark, type the name of the bookmark in the Bookmark dialog box (see fig. 10.25), and choose Add.

Tip
Instead of using a bookmark, you can use Shift+F5 to move to your last three revisions.

Once you have a bookmark, you can press F5 to display the Go To dialog box (see fig. 10.26). Choose Bookmark from the Go to What list and type or choose the bookmark name from the Enter Bookmark Name section.

To add a cross-reference to the bookmark in your document (for example, *see page 25* where *25* is the page on which the bookmark appears), first position your insertion point where you want the cross-reference to go, and then choose Insert, Cross-Reference. The Cross-Reference dialog box appears, as shown in figure 10.27. Choose Bookmark from the Reference Type list. From the Insert Reference To list, choose Page Number; then choose the appropriate bookmark in the For Which Bookmark list box. The reference goes into the document as a field.

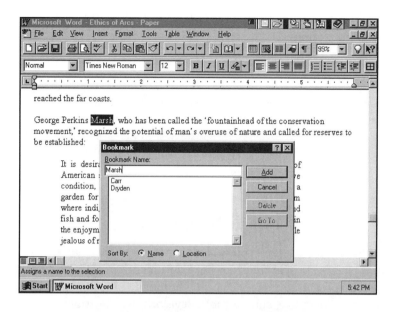

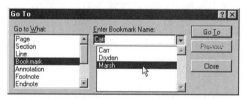

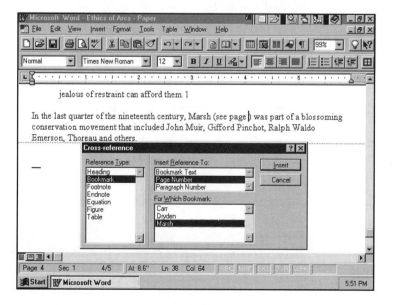

Troubleshooting

I can't delete my bookmark reference.

The cross-reference appears as a code in the document. You can't press Backspace to delete this code with the insertion point only. When your insertion point is on the code, it appears with a gray highlight. Select the entire highlight and press Delete to remove the cross-reference. If you want to delete the bookmark, choose Edit, Bookmark, select the bookmark name, and then choose the Delete command button.

Working with Revisions

◀ See "Changing Revision Options," p. 238

The Revision feature allows you to see when changes are made to a document. If multiple people are reviewing a document, each person's revisions can be formatted in a different color. To turn on the Revision feature so that changes are visible, choose Tools, Revisions. The Revisions dialog box appears, as shown in figure 10.28. To add revision marks, check the Mark Revisions While Editing checkbox and choose OK. By default, inserted text appears with an underline and deleted text appears with strikethrough formatting; all revisions are marked with a vertical line in the margin.

Fig. 10.28
To turn off revision marks, deselect the Mark Revisions While Editing checkbox.

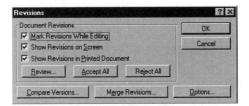

If you want to accept revisions and remove the revision marks from the document, choose Tools, Revisions and click the Accept All button. To reject all the revisions entered into the document, click the Reject All button. To review each revision, click the Review button.❖

Chapter 11

Working with Tables and Borders

by Patty Winter and Rick Winter

You can enhance your documents by adding tables to organize information. Using tables instead of aligning data with simple tabs allows you to apply enhancements that liven up the information you are presenting and make it more noticeable.

Create tables to organize columns of information, produce forms, or add simple spreadsheets to your documents. Word enables you to enter and format text in a table, and create calculations in the table, as well as format the table itself. You can add rows and columns, adjust spacing, perform calculations, add borders, adjust row height, and more.

Word also enables you to add graphics such as lines, borders, and shading to your documents to illustrate them and to add interest.

In this chapter, you learn to

- Insert a table into a document

- Enter, edit, and format the text in a table

- Modify row height and column width

- Add lines, borders, and shading to a document

- Create sums in a table

Working with Tables

A table is a convenient method of organizing text. You can use a table to create forms, reports, simple spreadsheets, and columns of numbers. You even can use tables to produce side-by-side paragraphs, such as those in a resume or an agenda.

Tables consist of columns and rows. *Columns* are the vertical divisions of the table; *rows* are the horizontal divisions. The box formed by the intersection of a column and row is called a *cell*. You can fill cells with text and graphics. When you type text into a cell, the text wraps from one line to the next, enlarging the cell as you enter more text.

When you insert a table, you enter the number of columns and rows you want the table to contain. After the table is inserted, you can modify the table and its contents by adding borders and shading, formatting the text, adjusting column width and row height, and so on. This section introduces table basics. For information about adding borders and shading to a table, see "Adding Lines, Borders, and Shading," later in this chapter.

Inserting a Table

You can insert a table by using the Table menu or the Insert Table button on the Standard toolbar. To use the menu, choose T<u>a</u>ble, <u>I</u>nsert Table. The Insert Table dialog box appears (see fig. 11.1).

Fig. 11.1
Enter the number of columns and rows in the Insert Table dialog box.

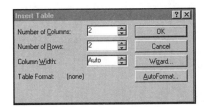

The following list describes the options in the Insert Table dialog box:

- *Number of <u>C</u>olumns.* Enter the number of columns for the table.

- *Number of <u>R</u>ows.* Enter the number of rows for the table.

- *Column <u>W</u>idth.* Set a specific column width for all columns, or leave the option at Auto. Auto column width divides the space between the left and right margins. You can adjust the width of any column at any time.

- *Table Format.* If you use AutoFormat to format the table, this option displays the predefined format.

- *Wizard.* Starts the Table Wizard; you answer the wizard's questions and choose options for formatting the table.

- *AutoFormat.* Displays the Table AutoFormat dialog box, in which you choose styles, borders, fonts, and so on from a list of predefined table formats. AutoFormat is very much like the Style Gallery.

◀ See "Using Template Wizards," p. 269

◀ See "Using AutoFormat," p. 264

Note

You always can add rows and columns by choosing Table, Insert Rows, or Table, Insert Columns. You can also delete rows and columns by choosing Table, Delete Rows, or Table, Delete Columns.

When you insert a table, Word normally displays table gridlines. If you do not see any gridlines, choose Table, Gridlines to display the nonprinting guides.

To insert a table, follow these steps:

1. Position the insertion point where you want to insert the table.

2. Choose Table, Insert Table. The Insert Table dialog box appears.

3. Enter the Number of Columns and the Number of Rows.

4. Optionally, enter a value in the Column Width box.

5. Optionally, choose Wizard or AutoFormat and answer all the queries in the dialog boxes.

6. Choose OK to insert the table and close the Insert Table dialog box.

Note

If you click the Insert Table button in the Standard toolbar, a grid appears. Drag the mouse pointer across the grid to specify the number of columns; drag down the grid to specify the number of rows. When you release the mouse button, Word inserts a table with the specified number of columns and rows.

Adding Text to a Table

After you insert the table, you can add text. You enter text in a table much the same way you enter text in any document. Moving around in a table, however, is a bit different. You can also edit the text in a table as you edit any

◀ See "Formatting Paragraphs," p. 194

◀ See "Format-
ting Text,"
p. 190

text. After you enter the text, you can select it to apply various types of formatting, such as type sizes and alignments.

Entering Text

To enter text in a table, position the insertion point in a cell and then type
the text. To move to another cell in the table, use the arrow keys. The arrow
keys move from cell to cell and from row to row. If a cell contains text, an
arrow key first moves one character or line at a time and then moves from
cell to cell.

Press the Tab key to move the insertion point to the right from one cell to
another, highlighting any text in a cell. Press Shift+Tab to move one cell to
the left. To actually insert a tab in a cell, press Ctrl+Tab and then set the tab
stop as you normally do.

Selecting Text in a Table

Selecting text in a table is similar to selecting text in any document. You can
drag the I-beam pointer over the text to select it, or click the selection bar to
select an entire row. In addition, you can use some techniques specific to
selecting text in a table. Following is a list of those techniques:

- To select one cell, triple-click that cell or click the left inside edge of
  the cell.

- To select an entire column, drag the mouse down the column. Alternatively, place the mouse pointer at the top of the column; the pointer
  changes to a black down arrow. Then click to select the column; click
  and drag across columns to select more than one column.

- Select an entire row by clicking the selection bar to the left of the table;
  drag up or down to select more than one row.

- To select the entire table, position the cursor in the table and press
  Shift+Alt+5 (on the numeric keypad). Alternatively, place the insertion
  point in the table and choose Table, Select Table.

Tip
Use the ruler to
adjust text
indents. For
more informa-
tion, see
Chapter 7.

After selecting the text, you can format it as you would any other text by
applying various fonts, font sizes, alignments, and so on. Figure 11.2 shows
a selected column, centered and bold headings, and right-aligned numbers.

Mouse pointer

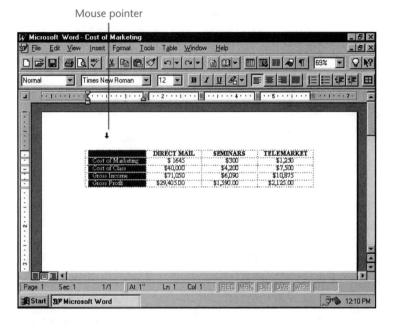

Fig. 11.2
Select text in a
table to format it.

Modifying a Table

You use commands in the Table menu to insert or delete rows and columns,
change cell height and width, and make other modifications. When you
modify a table element, you first must select that element. You select a row,
column, or cell the same way you select text in a table; refer to the preceding
section for more information.

Inserting and Deleting Columns and Rows

Inserting columns and rows is relatively simple, once you understand how
Word does it. To insert one row, select a row in the table and choose Table,
Insert Rows. Word inserts one row *before*, or above, the selected row. To insert
two or more rows, select two or more rows in the table and then choose
Table, Insert Rows. Word inserts as many rows as you selected before the
selected rows.

Tip
To add a row at the
bottom of a table,
position the inser-
tion point in the
bottom right cell
and press Tab.

> **Note**
>
> Depending on what you select, the Table menu commands change. Select a column,
> and the Table menu has the Insert Columns and Delete Columns commands. Select a
> cell, and the commands are Insert Cells and Delete Cells.

II

Using Word

Similarly, to insert one column, select one column and then choose T<u>a</u>ble, <u>I</u>nsert Columns. Word inserts one column *to the left of*, or before, the selected column. Select two or more columns to insert two or more rows before the selected columns.

To delete a row or column, select it and then choose T<u>a</u>ble, <u>D</u>elete Rows or T<u>a</u>ble, <u>D</u>elete Columns.

To insert or delete a column or row, follow these steps:

1. Select the column or row to be deleted, or select the column or row to the right of or below the place where you want to add a column or row.

2. Point the mouse at the column or row and press the right mouse button to display the shortcut menu.

3. Select Insert Columns/Rows or Delete Columns/Rows.

Note

Any shortcut menu will respond to a key pressed by selecting the first command that begins with that letter; if there is more than one command that begins with that letter, Word cycles through them each time you press that letter key. In other words, you can press the first letter of the desired command. If it's the only command beginning with that letter, the command is selected. If there's more than one command that starts with that letter, the first one is highlighted. Press Enter or press the letter key again to move to the next command beginning with that letter.

Adjusting Cell Height

You can change the height of a cell or the height of a row in the Cell Height and Width dialog box. Choose T<u>a</u>ble, Cell Height and <u>W</u>idth. Select the <u>R</u>ow or <u>C</u>olumn tab, depending on which area of the table you want to adjust. Figure 11.3 shows the Cell Height and Width dialog box with the Row tab displayed.

Fig. 11.3
Adjust the height of the rows and indent or align one row in the Row tab of the Cell Height and Width dialog box.

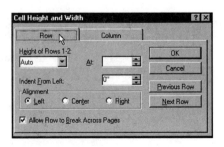

To adjust the height of the row, select one of the following options in the Height of Row drop-down list:

- *Auto.* Word adjusts the height of the row to accommodate the tallest font or graphic.

- *At Least.* Enter the minimum row height in the At box. However, Word adjusts the height of the rows to the contents of the cells.

- *Exactly.* Enter a row height in the At box. If the cell contents exceed the height you entered, Word prints only what fits in the cell.

To indent the selected rows or the entire table from the left margin, type a number in the Indent From Left box or use the scroll arrows to select a number.

To change the horizontal alignment of the selected rows or the entire table, choose Center or Right in the Alignment options.

To allow the text in a row to split across pages, choose the Allow Row to Break Across Pages option.

To adjust either the previous row or the next row, click the Previous Row or Next Row button. Choose either command button to move from row to row as you adjust the height of the rows. Click OK when you are finished adjusting the rows, or proceed with adjusting columns.

> **Note**
>
> If no row is selected when you open the Cell Height and Width dialog box, the Height of Row option applies to all rows in the table. When you select a row, the Height of Row option applies only to the selected row.

Adjusting Column and Cell Width

You also can adjust column and cell width in the Cell Height and Width dialog box. Choose Table, Cell Height and Width and then select the Column tab (see fig. 11.4).

To adjust the column width, enter a new width in the Width of Column text box. The Space Between Columns option specifies the amount of blank space between column boundaries and the contents of the cell. If you click the AutoFit button, Word automatically resizes all columns in the table to fit the contents of the cells.

II

Using Word

Fig. 11.4
Use the Column
tab to specify each
column's width
and to add space
between columns.

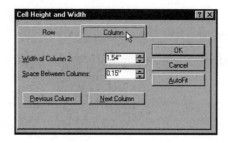

Troubleshooting

I inserted several rows or columns in the wrong place.

Click the Undo button in the Standard toolbar or choose Edit, Undo. Then select
some existing rows or columns, keeping in mind that the new rows or columns are
inserted before the selected ones.

I want to add a column to the right of a table.

Position the insertion point just outside the last column and choose Table, Select
Column. Then click the Insert Columns button in the Standard toolbar.

Adding Lines, Borders, and Shading

Word includes many graphic elements you can add to your documents, including lines, borders, and shading. Use these elements to attract attention to
your document, break the monotony of straight text, emphasize text, and
pique the reader's interest.

You can add a line above headings to make them stand out or add lines to a
table to help divide the data. Create a shaded border to attract attention to
text, or add clip art to a newsletter to make it more interesting.

Word enables you to add graphic lines and borders with the Borders toolbar
or with menu commands. The toolbar method is by far the easier method.
You can add borders and shading to text, tables, charts, and other elements
by using the Borders toolbar.

Displaying the Borders Toolbar

To display the Borders toolbar, place the mouse pointer on any toolbar that
currently appears on-screen and click the right mouse button. The Toolbar
shortcut menu appears. Click Borders, and the Borders toolbar appears; click
again and the toolbar disappears.

Figure 11.5 shows the Borders toolbar. Drop-down lists contain options for various line thicknesses (the Line Style drop-down list) and various fills and screens (the Shading drop-down list). The rest of the buttons help you specify the border's location.

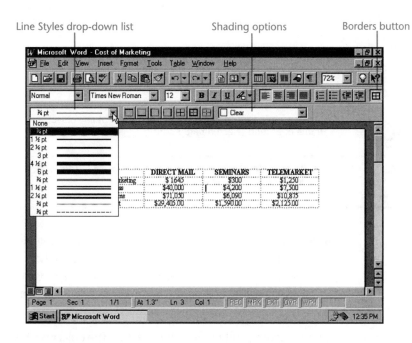

Line Styles drop-down list   Shading options   Borders button

Fig. 11.5

Use the Borders toolbar to assign borders to text, pages, tables, pictures, and other elements.

II

Using Word

Applying a Border

To apply a border, place the insertion point in the paragraph where you want the line or border to appear, or select the table, row, column, cell, picture, or frame. Choose the Line Style drop-down list from the Borders toolbar; select a line style. Then, in the Borders toolbar, click the border button you want to use. When you click a border button, Word inserts the border from left indent marker to right indent marker or side to side (for objects). If you click the same border button again, Word removes the border.

Following is a list of the border buttons:

Button	Description
	Top Border. Inserts a border along the top of a table, row, column, cell, frame, or picture, or above a paragraph of text.
	Bottom Border. Inserts a border along the bottom of a table, row, column, cell, frame, or picture, or below a paragraph of text.

(continues)

Button	Description
	Left Border. Inserts the border along the left side of the object or paragraph.
	Right Border. Inserts the border along the right side of the object or paragraph.
	Inside Border. Inserts a border along the inside lines of a table or between selected paragraphs.
	Outside Border. Applies a border to the outside of any object or frame or around selected paragraphs.
	No Border. Before you use this button to remove a border, select the bordered paragraph, table, or object.

Tip
Adjust the length of a border line by selecting it and moving the indent markers in the ruler.

You can apply more than one border to an object or text. For example, you can apply a $3/4$-point top border and a six-point bottom border. To that, you can add three-point left and right borders, creating a somewhat strange box around the object or text. You can also apply shading to the same text or object to which you have applied one or more borders.

You can apply various shading and patterns by selecting the object or the text, or by positioning the insertion point. Choose a shading from the Shading drop-down list in the Borders toolbar. The list provides shading that is stepped in percentages from 5 percent to 100 percent (or solid). Additionally, Word displays a variety of patterns you can apply to text or objects. The pattern list follows the shading list.

Figure 11.6 shows a table with a double 3/4-point outside border (around the outside of the table), a single 3/4-point inside border (outlining each of the cell's borders except the outside borders), and 20-percent shading for the heading row.

▶ See "Using Formulas," p. 369

Summing Up in Tables

You may find you have a table that requires some kind of total. Word provides the access to creating formulas in your Word tables and allows you to perform spreadsheet-type calculations in a table created in Word. If your table has a simple calculation, or you don't want to use Excel or a spreadsheet application, or if you want to keep everything in the same application, you can choose Table, Formula to add formulas to your tables.

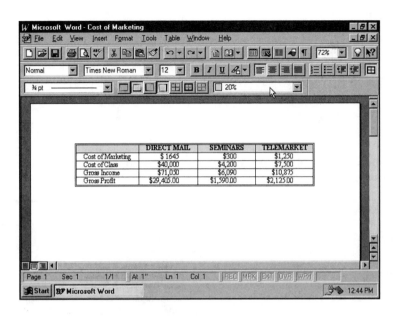

Fig. 11.6
You can choose
different borders
for the inside and
outside of a table,
and add shading to
specific areas of
the table.

Inserting a Formula in a Cell

Inserting a formula in a cell is similar to performing the same action in a spreadsheet application. If you know how to use spreadsheet programs, you can try what you already know. On the other hand, if you aren't familiar with spreadsheet programs, you can still use formulas in Word. Figure 11.7 shows the Formula dialog box, displayed when you choose T̲able, F̲ormula.

Tip
Spreadsheet-
type references
similar to
=SUM(A2:A9)
are valid in the
Word formula
field.

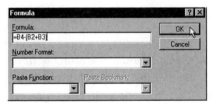

Fig. 11.7
The formula is
used to calculate
gross profit in the
Direct Mail
column.

II

Using Word

Note

Cell references in Word tables are the same as cell references in spreadsheet applications, with one major difference—you don't have any row or column headings telling you what cell you are using. To determine the cell reference, you need to keep track. Columns are letters beginning with "A." Rows are numbers beginning with "1." The intersection of the column and row is the cell reference.

(continues)

(continued)

In figure 11.6, the first column is A, the Direct Mail column is B, the Seminars column is C, and the Telemarket column is D. Cost of Marketing is row 2, Cost of Class is row 3, Gross Income is row 4, and Gross Profit is row 5. Therefore, if you are looking at the Gross Income for Direct Mail, the cell reference is B4.

The following table shows the formulas for the example table shown in figure 11.6:

To calculate	Formula
Gross Profit for Direct Mail (cell B5)	= B4-(B2+B3) B4=Direct Mail Gross Income, B2=Cost of Marketing, B3=Cost of Class
Gross Profit for Seminars (cell C5)	= C4-(C2+C3) C4=Seminars Gross Income, C2=Cost of Marketing, C3=Cost of Class
Gross Profit for Telemarket (cell D5)	= D4-(D2+D3) D4=Telemarket Gross Income, D2=Cost of Marketing, D3=Cost of Class

To insert a formula in a cell, follow these steps:

1. Position the insertion point in the cell to receive the formula.

2. Choose Table, Formula.

3. Either accept the default formula to sum the column, or delete the default formula and type a formula beginning with = (equal sign) and followed by a mathematical calculation using cell references in place of actual numbers, where needed.

   You could also use the functions that come with Word. Instead of typing a formula in the preceding step, click the Paste Function drop-down list to display the functions within Word's formula field. Some of the common functions include the following:

   - Average(). Calculates the average of the arguments; arguments are cell references inside the parentheses.

   - Count(). Counts the number of items within the arguments including the beginning and ending references.

- ■ MAX(). Finds the highest number within the arguments including the beginning and ending references.

- ■ MIN(). Finds the lowest number within the arguments including the beginning and ending references.

4. Choose the <u>N</u>umber Format you want to use. You can select from seven number formats:

   - ■ #,##0. Displays the number with commas and no decimal places.

   - ■ #,##0.00. Displays numbers with commas and two decimal places.

   - ■ $#,##0.00;($#,##0.00). Displays numbers with dollar signs, commas, two decimal places and negative numbers in parentheses.

   - ■ 0. Displays the whole number rounding up, no commas, no decimal places.

   - ■ 0%. Displays the number as a percent rounded up.

   - ■ 0.00. Displays numbers with two decimal places.

   - ■ 0.00%. Displays the number as a percent with two decimal places.

5. Choose OK.

Recalculating a Formula

One of the best reasons to use formulas in your table is the ease with which you can recalculate the formula when one of the values changes. You can enter the new value in the table and have Word perform the recalculation for you. If you have more than one formula to be calculated, you can update all the formulas at one time.

To recalculate formulas in a table, follow these steps:

1. Enter the new value or values in your table.

2. Do one of the following: move to the cell containing the formula, select the row or column containing all the formulas, or select the entire table.

3. Press F9, the calculation key.

II

Using Word

Troubleshooting

I tried to recalculate a formula in my table, but nothing changed.

When you move to the field with the formula, you must have the insertion point in the field code or select the entire cell or formula field before you press F9.

Part III

Using Excel

Chapter 12

Creating Worksheets

by Patrice-Anne Rutledge

In this chapter, you learn the basic techniques for creating worksheets in Excel. The chapter begins with an introduction to fundamental Excel terms and concepts. You then learn how to enter data, move to other areas in the worksheet, and select cells and ranges. Once you've mastered these skills, you'll have the confidence to create nearly any type of worksheet.

In this chapter, you learn to

- Move around the worksheet

- Enter text, numbers, and formulas

- Select cells and ranges

- Repeat and undo Excel commands

- Save a worksheet

Defining Excel Terms

When you start Excel, a blank workbook appears in the document window. The *workbook* is the main document used in Excel for storing and manipulating data. A workbook consists of individual worksheets, each of which can contain data. Initially, each new workbook you create contains 16 worksheets, but you can add more worksheets later. In addition to worksheets, you can create chart, macro, visual basic module, and dialog sheets.

Each worksheet is made up of 256 columns and 16,384 rows. The columns are lettered across the top of the document window, beginning with A through Z and continuing with AA through AZ, BA through BZ, and so on through column IV. The rows are numbered from 1 to 16,384 down the left side of the document window.

The intersections of rows and columns form *cells*, which are the basic units for storing data. Each cell takes its name from this intersection and is referred to as a *cell reference*. For example, the address of the cell at the intersection of column C and row 5 is referred to as cell C5.

At the bottom of each worksheet is a series of *sheet tabs*, which enable you to identify each worksheet in the workbook. The tabs initially are labeled Sheet1, Sheet2, and so on, as shown at the bottom of the screen in figure 12.1.

Fig. 12.1

An Excel workbook is made up of columns, rows, cells, and worksheets.

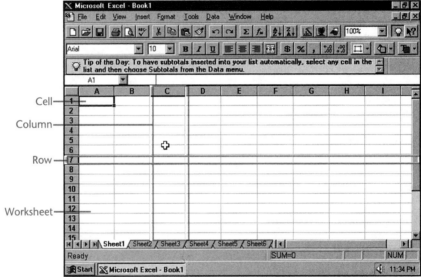

Moving Around in a Worksheet

In a new worksheet, the cell at the intersection of column A and row 1 is highlighted, indicating that cell A1 is the active cell. When you start typing, the data appears in the active cell. To enter data in another cell, first make that cell active by moving the cell pointer to it, using either the mouse or keyboard. You can also view another area of your worksheet and not move the active cell by using the scroll bars.

Mouse Movements

Using the mouse, you can activate a cell quickly by placing the cell pointer on the cell and clicking the left mouse button. Figure 12.2 shows the cell pointer highlighting the active cell.

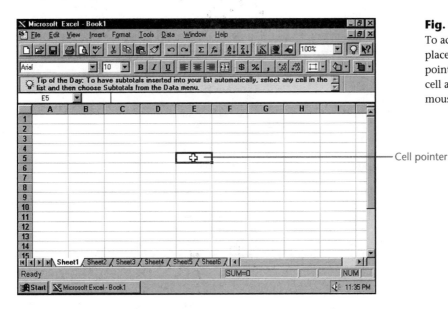

Fig. 12.2
To activate a cell, place the cell pointer on that cell and click the mouse.

Cell pointer

Keyboard Movements

You can use the arrow, Page Up, and Page Down keys on your keyboard, or various key combinations, to move to another cell. The keys that you use to move to new locations are listed in table 12.1.

Table 12.1   Using the Keyboard to Move Among Cells

Keys	Description
←, →, ↑, ↓	Moves one cell to the left, right, up, or down, respectively
Ctrl+ ←, →, ↑, ↓ End+ ←, →, ↑, ↓	Moves to the next nonblank cell
Tab	Moves one cell to the right
Enter	Moves one cell down

(continues)

III

Using Excel

Table 12.1 Continued	
Keys	**Description**
Shift+Tab	Moves one cell to the left
Shift+Enter	Moves one cell up
Home	Moves to column A of the active row
Ctrl+Home	Moves to cell A1 of the worksheet
Ctrl+End	Moves to the last cell used in the worksheet
Page Up	Moves up one screen
Page Down	Moves down one screen
Alt+Page Up	Moves one screen width to the left
Alt+Page Down	Moves one screen width to the right
Ctrl+Page Up	Moves to the following worksheet
Ctrl+Page Down	Moves to the preceding worksheet

Use the Go To command to move to a specific cell. Choose Edit, Go To, or press the F5 key to display the Go To dialog box (see fig. 12.3).

Fig. 12.3
The Go To dialog box enables you to move to a specific cell.

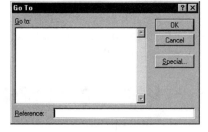

When the Go To dialog box appears, type the reference of the cell you want to move to in the Reference text box, and then press Enter. To move to cell D5, for example, type **D5** and then press Enter or click the OK button. The cell pointer moves to cell D5, which now becomes the active cell.

You also can move to a specific cell by using the *name box*, located at the left end of the formula bar. Click the box, type the address of the cell to which you want to move, and then press Enter. (The formula bar is discussed in "Entering Data" later in this chapter.)

Moving Around by Scrolling

To view another section of the worksheet without moving the active cell, use the vertical and horizontal scroll bars to reposition the screen. Using the mouse, click the up or down scroll arrow to scroll line by line. You also can scroll the screen by dragging the scroll box up and down the scroll bar. If you click the scroll bar above the scroll box, the screen scrolls up one screen. If you click the scroll bar below the scroll box, the screen scrolls down one screen.

To scroll through a worksheet by using the keyboard, press the Scroll Lock key on your keyboard, and use the arrow keys to scroll to the section of the worksheet you want to view. Scrolling moves the screen but does not change the active cell.

Entering Data

After you activate the cell in which you want to enter data, you can type text, numbers, dates, times, or formulas in the cell. As you type, the data appears in the active cell and in the area above the worksheet called the *formula bar* (see fig. 12.4). The formula bar displays the *insertion point*, a blinking bar that indicates where the next character you type will appear.

Tip
When you drag the scroll box, the row number or column heading is displayed for your reference.

Tip
To see the active cell when it's not visible in the current window, press Ctrl+ Backspace. The window scrolls to display the active cell, and selected ranges remain selected.

Click here to reject data   Click here to accept data   Click here to activate Function Wizard

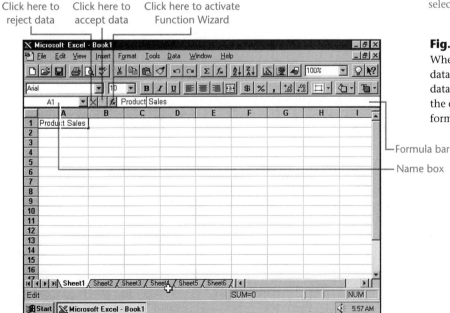

Fig. 12.4
When you enter data in a cell, the data appears in the cell and in the formula bar.

Formula bar
Name box

III

Using Excel

▶ See "Using the Function Wizard," p. 392

Three small boxes appear between the name box and the insertion point in the formula bar. The first two boxes enable you to reject or accept the data you entered. To reject your entry, click the X box or press Esc. To accept your entry, click the checkbox or press Enter. The third box in the formula bar activates the Function Wizard, a dialog box that enables you to build formulas by using Excel's built-in functions.

Entering Text

Text entries consist of alphanumeric characters such as letters, numbers, and symbols. You can enter up to 255 characters in a single cell, although Excel may not be able to display all the characters if the cell is not wide enough or if an entry appears in the cell to its right. When you enter text in a cell, Excel stores that entry as text and aligns it to the left edge of the cell.

When you enter data that consists of numbers and text, Excel evaluates the entry to determine its value. If you type an entry such as **1098 Adams Street**, for example, Excel automatically determines that it is a text entry because of the letters.

If you want to enter a number as text, such as a ZIP code, precede the entry with an apostrophe. For example, 46254 would be read as a number, but '46254 would be read as a text entry. You can use the apostrophe when you want to enter a number but do not want Excel to interpret it as a value to be used in calculations.

Entering Numbers

▶ See "Changing Column Width and Row Height," p. 349

▶ See "Formatting Numbers," p. 341

Numeric entries are constant values and consist only of numeric values. You can enter integers (such as **124**), decimal fractions (**14.426**), integer fractions (**1 1/5**), and values in scientific notation (**1.23E+08**).

> **Caution**
>
> If you enter a long number in a cell and the cell displays ##### or the number appears in scientific notation (1.23E+08), the current column width is too small to display the number in its entirety. To fix this, double-click the right edge of the column heading to widen it.

Entering Dates and Times

In addition to entering text and numbers, you can enter dates and times in a worksheet cell. When you enter a date or time, Excel converts the entry to a serial date number, so that it can perform calculations based on these dates and times. The information in the cell is displayed in a regular date or time format, however.

Because Excel converts dates and times to serial numbers, you can perform calculations on these values as you would with any number. For example, you could determine the number of days that have passed between two dates.

To enter a date, type the date using any of these formats:

8/12/95
12-Aug-95
12-Aug
Aug-12

To enter a time, use any of these formats:

14:25
14:25:09
2:25 PM
2:25:09 PM

Tip
To enter the current date in a cell quickly, press Ctrl+; (semicolon). To enter the current time, press Ctrl+: (colon).

Entering Formulas

One of the most valuable features of Excel is its capability to calculate values by using formulas. Excel formulas can range from the simple, such as adding a range of values, to the complex, such as calculating the future value of a stream of cash flows.

You can calculate values based on numbers that you type directly into the formula. For example, you can enter the formula **=4+5+7** to add the values 4, 5, and 7. However, the power of Excel's formula capability lies in the fact that formulas also can refer to data in other cells in the worksheet. The formula **=B2+B3+B4**, for example, adds the values in cells B2, B3, and B4. When the values in these cells change, Excel automatically updates and recalculates the formula, using the new data in these cells.

▶ See "Creating Formulas," p. 369

Excel recognizes a formula in a cell if the entry starts with an equal sign (=), a plus sign (+), or a minus sign (-). To enter a formula, first type = and then type the formula. The active cell and the formula bar display the formula as you enter it. After the formula is complete, press Enter; the active cell displays the result of the formula (see fig. 12.5). The formula bar continues to show the formula when the cell is the active cell.

III

Using Excel

Fig. 12.5
When you enter a
formula in a cell,
Excel displays the
result.

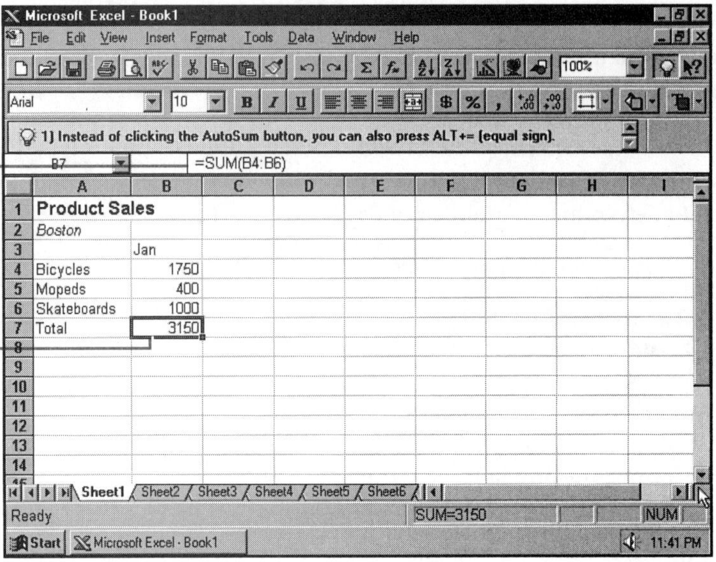

Formula ——

Result of formula ——

Troubleshooting

A formula used to calculate a range of cells does not calculate properly.

Make sure that values in the range have not been entered as text. To do so, highlight each cell in the range and check for the appearance of an apostrophe at the beginning of the entry. If an apostrophe appears, press F2 to enter Edit mode, press the Home key to move to the beginning of the entry, press the Delete key to remove the apostrophe, and press Enter. Continue with these steps until all cell entries have been checked. You can also use the AutoCalculate feature to check the sum, average, or count of a range of data, described in the next section, "Selecting Cells and Ranges."

Excel converted a date to a number.

You must enter dates in a format that Excel recognizes—for example, **3/12/94** or **12-Mar-94**. Other characters may not produce a valid date. Sometimes a cell in which you enter a date may already contain a numeric format. Choose F̲ormat, C̲ells to assign a different format.

A formula appears as text in a cell.

If you neglect to enter an equal, plus, or minus sign in front of a cell reference, Excel interprets the entry as text. To fix this problem, highlight the cell and press F2. Then press the Home key, type the equal sign, and press Enter.

Selecting Cells and Ranges

> **Note**
>
> Excel's new AutoCalculate feature displays the sum of selected cells in the status bar. This is a useful way to quickly calculate a range. For example, simply selecting cells A1 through A3 will show you the sum of this range. You can also display the average or count of a selected range by right-clicking the status bar and choosing either AVERAGE or COUNT from the menu.

Many commands in Excel require that you select a cell or range of cells. You already have learned how to select a single cell. You also can select several cells at the same time. A *range* is a group of cells that can be acted upon with Excel commands.

You can use the keyboard or the mouse to select a range. To select a range with the mouse, follow these steps:

1. Click a corner of the range you want to select.

2. Drag the mouse over the range.

3. When you reach the end of the selection range, release the mouse button.

To select a range with the keyboard, follow these steps:

1. Move to a cell at a corner of the range you want to select.

2. Press and hold down the Shift key, and then press the arrow keys to select the range.

Figure 12.6 shows a selected range.

> **Note**
>
> If you select a range of cells and then move the cell pointer, the range is deselected. If this happens, just select the range again.

Excel also enables you to select more than one range of cells at a time with the same ease as selecting a single range.

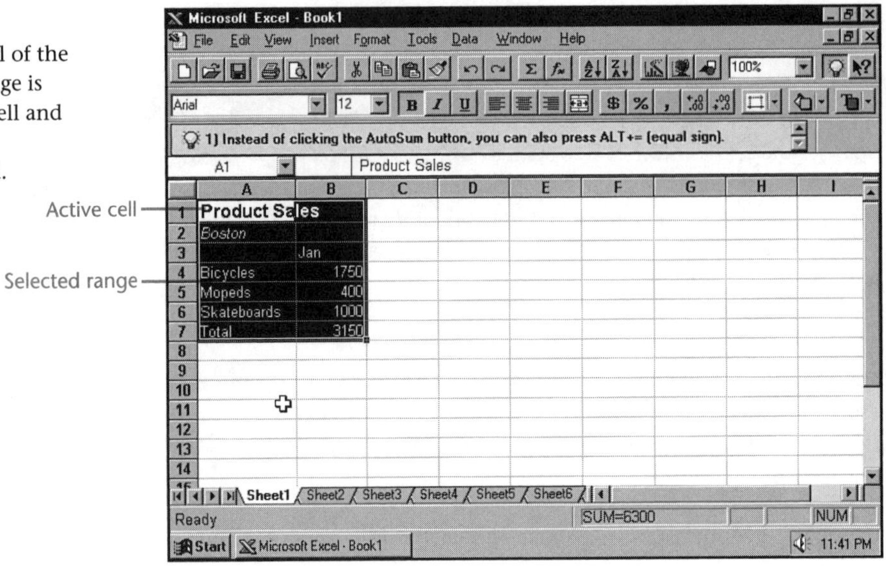

Fig. 12.6

The first cell of the selected range is the active cell and has a white background.

Active cell ——

Selected range ——

To select multiple ranges with the mouse, follow these steps:

1. Click and drag the mouse over the first range you want to select.

2. Press and hold down the Ctrl key, and continue selecting other ranges.

To select multiple ranges with the keyboard, follow these steps:

1. Press and hold down the Shift key, and use the arrow keys to select the first range.

2. Press Shift+F8. The indicator ADD appears in the status bar at the bottom of the screen indicating that you can extend a selection.

3. Move to a cell at a corner of the next range you want to select.

4. Press Shift and an arrow key to select the range. ADD disappears from the status bar. To add another range, press Shift+F8 to go back to Add mode, and repeat steps 3 and 4.

To select the entire worksheet, click the rectangle directly above the row numbers and to the left of the column headings, or press Ctrl+Shift+space bar. To deselect a range, click any cell outside the range.

Tip
To select nonadjacent columns or rows, press and hold down the Ctrl key as you make your selections.

To select an entire row, click the heading of the row you want to select. You also can position the pointer in the row you want to select and press Shift+space bar. Figure 12.7 shows two ranges selected in a worksheet.

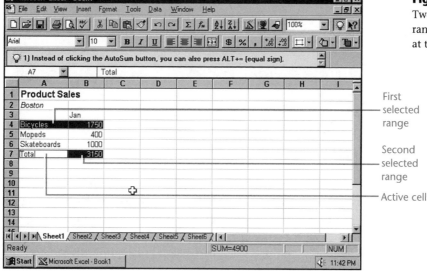

Fig. 12.7
Two nonadjacent ranges are selected at the same time.

First selected range

Second selected range

Active cell

To select an entire column, click the heading of the column you want to select. You also can position the pointer in the column you want to select and press Ctrl+space bar (see fig. 12.8).

III

Note

Some Excel commands require a specific action before you can use the command. If you do not cut or copy something to the Clipboard, for example, you cannot choose Edit, Paste (it appears grayed or dimmed). If an object is not selected, the commands that are relevant only to selected objects are dimmed and unavailable.

Fig. 12.8
Click a column
heading to select
an entire column;
click a row
heading to select
an entire row.

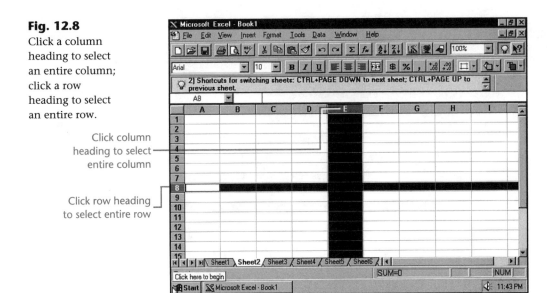

Click column
heading to select
entire column

Click row heading
to select entire row

Entering a Series of Text, Numbers, and Dates

When creating budgets and forecasts, you often need to include a series
of dates, numbers, or text. Excel relieves this tedious task by offering the
AutoFill feature, which enables you to create a worksheet quickly by filling a
range of cells with a sequence of entries. For example, you can fill a range of
cells with consecutive dates or create a series of column titles.

You can create a series of entries in two ways:

- Use the mouse to drag the AutoFill handle (the small square at the
  bottom right corner of the active cell).

- Choose Edit, Fill, Series.

Another feature useful in creating a series is AutoComplete. As you enter data
in a list, Excel memorizes each entry. If you begin to make an entry that
matches a previous entry, Excel will automatically complete it for you. You
can accept the entry or continue typing new data. For example, if you type
San Francisco in cell A3 and then begin entering the letter S in cell A4,
Excel will automatically enter **San Francisco** in A4. This helps cut down
on the time it takes to enter data as well prevent errors.

You can also choose potential entries from a list of your previous entries, just as you can in the database application Access. To do this, right-click your mouse and choose Pick From List from the shortcut menu. A list of all your previous entries pops up and you can choose your desired entry from it.

Creating a Series of Text Entries

Excel recognizes common text entries, such as days, months, and quarterly abbreviations.

To fill a range of cells with text entries, follow these steps:

1. Select the first cell that contains the data.

2. Drag the AutoFill handle over the range of adjacent cells that you want to fill (see fig. 12.9).

3. Release the mouse button. Excel fills the range of selected cells with the appropriate text entries (see fig. 12.10).

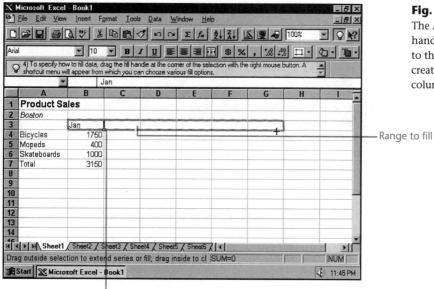

Fig. 12.9
The AutoFill handle is dragged to the right to create a series of column titles.

Range to fill

AutoFill handle
of the cell containing data

III

Using Excel

Fig. 12.10
Excel fills the
selected range of
cells with a series
of column titles.

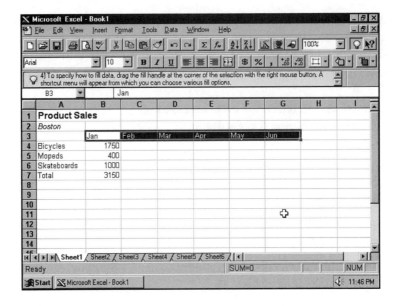

Excel's AutoFill feature recognizes numbers, dates, times, and key words, such as days of the week, month names, and quarterly abbreviations. Excel knows how these series run and extends the series to repeat correctly. Table 12.2 shows examples of series that Excel can use with AutoFill.

Table 12.2 Fill Sequences	
Data You Enter	**Sequence Returned**
Qtr 1	Qtr 2, Qtr 3, Qtr 4
Product 1	Product 2, Product 3, Product 4
1993	1994, 1995, 1996
Jan	Jan, Feb, Mar
Jan 93	Jan 94, Jan 95, Jan 96
Mon	Tue, Wed, Thu
North	South, East, West
2, 4	6, 8, 10, ...

Creating a Series of Numbers

You can enter a series of numbers that increment by 1 or by values you specify.

To fill a range of cells with a series of numbers, follow these steps:

1. Enter the starting number in the first cell of the range. If you want to increment the numbers by a value you specify, enter the first two values in adjacent cells.

2. Select the range containing the numbers.

3. Drag the fill handle over the range of adjacent cells you want to fill.

4. Release the mouse button. Excel fills the range of selected cells with the appropriate numeric entries (see fig. 12.11).

Tip

Excel uses these two values to determine the amount to increment in each step.

To increment by a value other than 1, enter desired values in the first two cells of the range

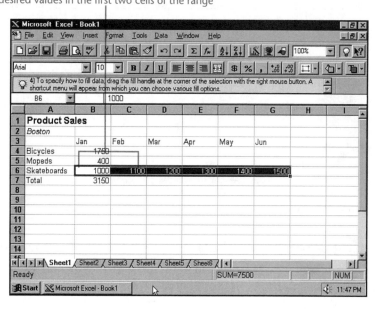

Fig. 12.11
The AutoFill handle creates this series of numbers in increments of 100.

Tip

To prevent a series from incrementing, hold down the Ctrl key as you drag the AutoFill handle.

Creating a Series of Dates

You can fill a range of cells with a series of consecutive dates that increment by a specific value.

To fill a range of cells with dates, follow these steps:

1. Enter the starting date in the first cell in the range. If you want to increment the date by a specific value, enter the appropriate date in the next cell in the range.

2. Select the range containing the dates.

3. Drag the AutoFill handle over the range of adjacent cells you want to fill.

4. Release the mouse button. Excel fills the range of selected cells with the appropriate dates (see fig. 12.12).

Fig. 12.12
The AutoFill handle created this series of dates in increments of one week.

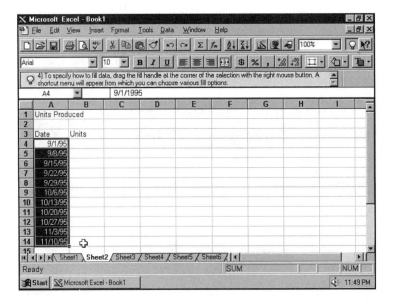

Entering a Series with the Edit Fill Series Command

Choosing Edit, Fill, Series enables you to fill a range of cells with greater precision than you can with the AutoFill handle. For example, when you choose Edit, Fill, Series, you can specify a stop value as well as a start value.

To fill a range of cells by choosing Edit, Fill Series, follow these steps:

1. Enter the starting number or date in the first cell of the range you want to fill.

2. Select the range of cells you want to fill.

3. Choose Edit, Fill, Series. The Series dialog box appears (see fig. 12.13).

Fig. 12.13
In the Series dialog box, select the type of series and the step and stop values.

4. Indicate whether you want to fill your series in Rows or Columns.

5. Specify the Type of series you want to create.

6. If you are creating a series of dates, specify the Date Unit.

7. Enter the Step Value. This value represents the amount by which the series changes from cell to cell.

8. Enter the Stop Value. This value represents the last value in the series.

9. Choose OK.

Troubleshooting

AutoFill filled the entire range with the same text entered in the first cell of the range.

When Excel cannot recognize the correct pattern for entering text, AutoFill copies the selected cells to the entire range. Make sure that the starting text is one that AutoFill can recognize—for example, Qtr 1 or January.

I tried to use AutoFill to extend a series, but numbers were not incremented by the difference of the first two numbers of my series.

If the increment in the AutoFill range was 1, you probably did not select the first two cells before using AutoFill. Be sure to select the two cells, because that is what Excel uses to determine the increment; otherwise, it defaults to 1. If the increment was not the difference between your first two cells or 1, you probably selected more than two cells and Excel averaged the difference to determine the increment. Again, be sure to just select two cells.

Repeating and Undoing a Command

Excel has a built-in safety net that enables you to reverse many commands or actions. The Edit, Undo command reverses the last command you selected or the last action you performed. To undo a command or action, choose Edit, Undo, or press Ctrl+Z.

> **Note**
>
> Excel retains only the last action or command. You must choose Edit, Undo immediately after the command or action.

Undo is not available for all commands. If you choose Edit, Delete Sheet and delete a worksheet from a workbook, for example, the Edit menu shows Can't Undo as a dimmed command. Although Undo can reverse many actions, you still must use certain commands with caution.

To reverse the Undo command, choose Edit, Undo again or press Ctrl+Z.

 Excel also enables you to repeat the last command or action you performed. To repeat a command or action, choose Edit, Repeat, or press F4.

Saving Workbooks

 When you create a new workbook, Excel assigns to it the name Book1 if it is the first workbook created, Book2 if it is the second, and continues to increment in this pattern. You must save the file to disk to make the workbook permanent. To save a file in Excel, choose File, Save, or press Ctrl+S. Enter a name for the file and specify the location to which the workbook should be saved.

In addition to saving new workbooks, you can also save files to other file formats, such as previous versions of Excel or Lotus 1-2-3. Excel also enables you to save workbook settings in a workspace file.

Saving Files to Other File Formats

When you save a file, Excel automatically assigns an extension to the file. If you are saving a workbook, the extension is XLS; the extension for a template is XLT; and the extension for a workspace is XLW.

You can use the Save as Type drop-down list to save an Excel file in another file format. To save an Excel file for use in Lotus 1-2-3, for example, drop down the Save as Type list, and then select the 1-2-3 Lotus file format you want (see fig. 12.14). Excel supports 1-2-3 Releases 1 (WKS), 2 (WK1), 3 (WK3), and 4 (WK4).

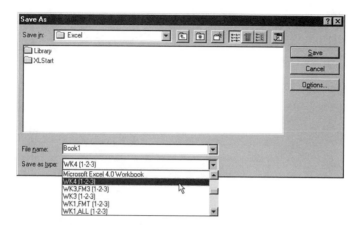

Fig. 12.14
You can save an
Excel file in a 1-2-3
file format.

If you use a worksheet feature that is not supported by earlier versions of
Excel or other spreadsheets, the value result of that feature is calculated and
saved with the worksheet.

Saving a Workspace File

If you work with the same set of workbooks on a daily basis, Excel enables
you to save information about what workbooks are open and how they are
arranged on-screen. The next time you want to work with these workbooks,
you only need to open the workspace file, and all the workbooks are opened
and arranged as they were when you saved the file.

The File, Save Workspace command creates a workspace file that contains the
name and location of each workbook in the workspace and the position of
each workbook when the workspace was saved.

To create a workspace file, follow these steps:

1. Open and arrange the workbooks as you want them to be saved in the
   workspace.

2. Choose File, Save Workspace. Figure 12.15 shows the Save Workspace
   dialog box that is displayed.

3. Type a name for the workspace file in the File Name text box.

4. Choose OK.

III

Using Excel

Fig. 12.15

Type a name for the workspace file in the Save Workspace dialog box.

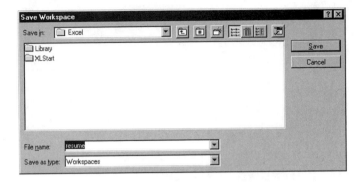

Caution

When you create a workspace file, do not move any of the workbook files to a new location. If you do, Excel will not be able to locate the files when you open the workspace file.

You can open a workspace file just as you would any other Excel file. After you have opened the file, you can save and close the individual workbooks in the workspace as you normally would. When you make changes to a workbook in the workspace, you must save the file by choosing File, Save. The File, Save Workspace command saves only information on which workbooks are open and how they are arranged on-screen.❖

Chapter 13

Editing Worksheets

by Patrice-Anne Rutledge

After creating a worksheet, you will spend the majority of your time editing the work you have done. You may need to move data from one area of the worksheet to another, or you may want to copy a range of data. This chapter presents the basics for editing a worksheet in Excel.

In this chapter, you learn to

- Edit the contents of a cell

- Clear the contents of a cell

- Copy, cut, and paste worksheet data

- Insert and delete columns, rows, and worksheets

- Find and replace worksheet data

- Spell check your worksheet

Editing Worksheet Data

After you enter data in a cell, you can edit the contents of the cell. You can edit the contents using the formula bar, or you can use the in-cell editing feature of Excel to edit the contents directly in the cell.

> **Note**
>
> To use the in-cell editing feature of Excel, you must make sure that the feature has been enabled. To double-check, choose Tools, Options, and select the Edit tab. The Edit Directly in Cell option should be selected. If it isn't, click the check box to the left of the option. Choose OK when you finish.

Editing an Existing Cell Entry

To edit the contents of a cell, first select the cell you want to edit, and then click the formula bar or press F2. The contents of the cell appear in the formula bar. You can also edit the contents of the cell directly in the cell by double-clicking it.

▶ See "Formatting Numbers," p. 341

To edit the entry, use the left and right arrow keys to reposition the insertion point in the formula bar, or move the mouse and use the I-beam pointer to reposition the insertion point in the formula bar. The vertical blinking bar appears where the I-beam is positioned when you click the mouse (see fig. 13.1). Then press Delete or Backspace to delete characters to the right or left of the insertion point, respectively.

Insertion point

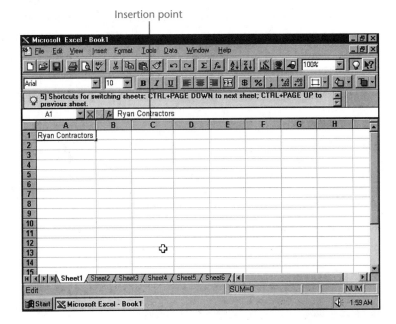

Fig. 13.1
The insertion point shows where the next character you type will appear.

When editing a cell, you can reposition the insertion point by using the mouse or the keyboard. Table 13.1 lists the editing keys on the keyboard.

Table 13.1 Editing Keys	
Key	**Action**
←	Moves one character to the left.
→	Moves one character to the right.

Key	Action
Ctrl+→	Moves to the next word.
Ctrl+←	Moves to the preceding word.
End	Moves to the end of the cell entry.
Home	Moves to the beginning of the cell entry.
Delete	Deletes next character to the right.
Backspace	Deletes preceding character.

Deleting Worksheet Data

In addition to editing the contents of a cell, you can delete the data in a cell. To replace an existing cell entry, select the cell and type the new entry. When you do, the new entry replaces the current contents of the cell. If you want to delete the contents of a cell or range altogether, the easiest way to do it is to select the cell or range of cells and then press the Delete key. When you do, Excel clears the contents of the cell or range.

Clearing Cell Contents

When you use the Delete key to clear a cell, Excel clears all data from the cell, but does not change cell formatting. The Edit Clear command, on the other hand, enables you to choose what you want to clear from the cell.

To clear the contents of a cell or range, select the cell or range and then choose Edit, Clear. From the Edit Clear cascading menu, select the command that represents the data you want to clear.

Choose All to clear everything from the cell, including cell formatting and cell notes. Choose Formats to clear only cell formatting from the cell. To clear the contents of a cell but leave formatting and cell notes intact, choose Contents. To remove only cell notes from a selected range of cells, choose Notes.

Tip

To clear the contents of a cell or range quickly, highlight the range, click the right mouse button, and choose Clear Contents from the shortcut menu.

III

Using Excel

> **Caution**
>
> A common error many new users make when clearing cells is selecting the cell and then pressing the space bar. Although the cell may appear to be blank, Excel actually stores the space in the cell. Spaces can cause problems in worksheet calculations. Do not press the space bar to clear a cell. Instead, use the methods outlined in this section.

▶ See "Changing Fonts, Sizes, and Styles," p. 357

▶ See "Annotating Worksheets," p. 458

Copying Worksheet Data

The quickest way to copy worksheet data is to use the drag-and-drop method. As its name implies, you simply drag the data you want to copy to another area of the worksheet.

◄ See "Copying and Moving Data," p. 78

To copy data with drag-and-drop, follow these steps:

1. Select the range of cells you want to copy.

2. Position the mouse pointer on the border of the selected data.

3. Hold down the Ctrl key, and click and drag the selection to the new location.

   As you move the mouse pointer, Excel displays an outline indicating the size and location of the copied data (see fig. 13.2).

4. Release the mouse button to drop the copied data in its new location.

Fig. 13.2
An outline indicates the location where the copied data will be placed.

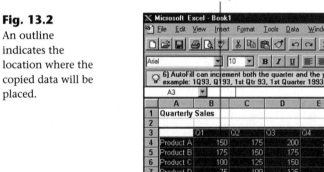

Copying Data with Copy and Paste

When you need to make multiple copies of worksheet data, the easiest way to accomplish this is to use the Edit Copy and Edit Paste commands. When you choose Edit, Copy, a copy of the selected data is stored on the Clipboard. You then can paste as many copies in the worksheet as you need.

To copy data by using Edit, Copy and Edit, Paste, follow these steps:

1. Select the range of data you want to copy.

2. Choose Edit, Copy, or press Ctrl+C. Alternatively, click the right mouse button and then choose Copy from the resulting shortcut menu.

A marquee surrounds the selection you copied, and the status bar at the bottom of the screen prompts you to select the location where you want to copy the data (see fig. 13.3).

◄ See "Copying and Moving Data," p. 78

A marquee surrounds the copied data

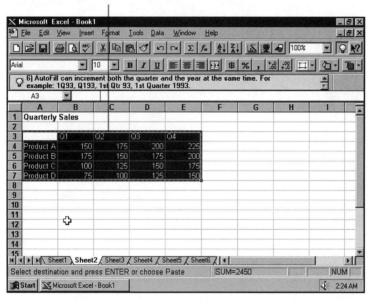

Fig. 13.3
A marquee surrounds the copied data.

3. Select the cell in which you want to paste a copy of the data.

4. Choose Edit, Paste, or press Ctrl+V. Alternatively, click the right mouse button and then choose Paste from the resulting shortcut menu. If you want to paste a single copy of the selection, press Enter.

III

Using Excel

> **Note**
>
> As long as the marquee surrounds the copied data, you can continue to use Edit, Paste to paste copies of the data in the worksheet. If you press Enter to paste a copy of the data in the worksheet, Excel clears the copied data from the Clipboard.

Copying Data with AutoFill

The AutoFill command enables you to copy cell contents to adjacent cells quickly. As a bonus, if the entry consists of a date, day of the week, or alphanumeric item such as Product 1, Excel automatically extends the series in the selected cells (see fig. 13.4).

AutoFill extends the series in the selected cells

Fig. 13.4
The AutoFill command fills the selected cells with a series.

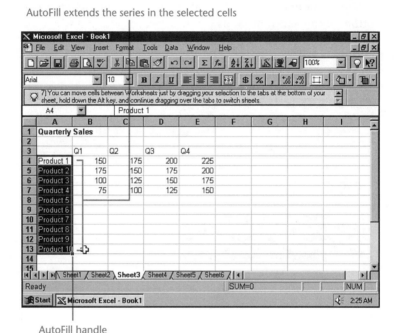

AutoFill handle

◄ See "Entering a Series of Text, Numbers, and Dates," p. 312

To use the AutoFill command to copy data, follow these steps:

1. Select the cell that contains the data you want to copy.

2. Position the mouse pointer on the fill handle that appears in the lower right corner of the cell.

3. Drag the fill handle over the adjacent cells in which the copied data will appear, and release the mouse button.

Copying and Applying Formats

► See "Creating and Applying a Style," p. 362

Another option for copying data in your worksheet is to copy cell formatting from one range to another. This feature is handy if you want to apply formatting to a range of cells but don't want to create a style.

To copy formatting from one range to another, follow these steps:

1. Select the range of cells that contains the formatting you want to copy.

2. Click the Format Painter button, or double-click the button if you want to apply the formatting to more than one range. Figure 13.5 shows the result of using the Format Painter.

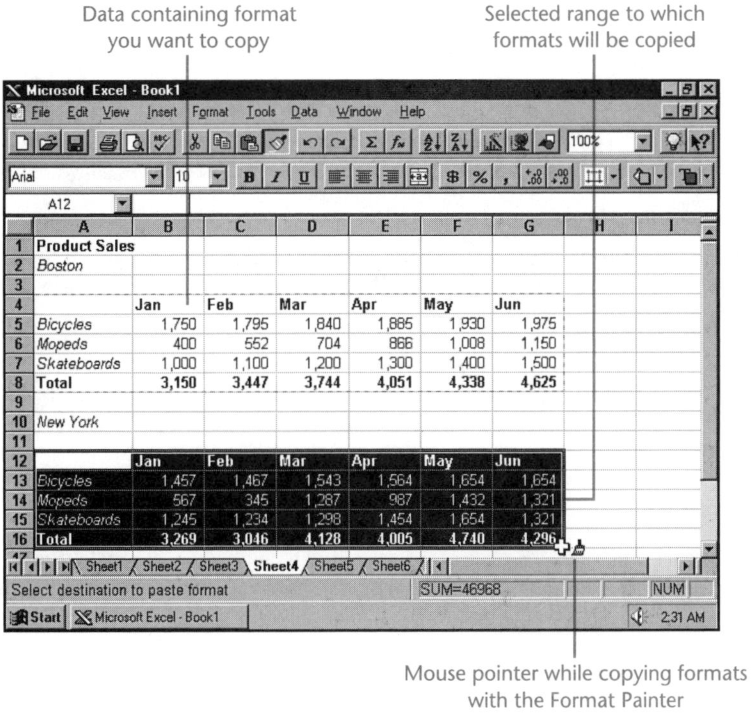

Data containing format
you want to copy

Selected range to which
formats will be copied

	A	B	C	D	E	F	G	H	I
1	Product Sales								
2	Boston								
3									
4		Jan	Feb	Mar	Apr	May	Jun		
5	Bicycles	1,750	1,795	1,840	1,885	1,930	1,975		
6	Mopeds	400	552	704	866	1,008	1,150		
7	Skateboards	1,000	1,100	1,200	1,300	1,400	1,500		
8	Total	3,150	3,447	3,744	4,051	4,338	4,625		
9									
10	New York								
11									
12		Jan	Feb	Mar	Apr	May	Jun		
13	Bicycles	1,457	1,467	1,543	1,564	1,654	1,654		
14	Mopeds	567	345	1,287	987	1,432	1,321		
15	Skateboards	1,245	1,234	1,298	1,454	1,654	1,321		
16	Total	3,269	3,046	4,128	4,005	4,740	4,296		

Select destination to paste format   SUM=46968   NUM

Mouse pointer while copying formats
with the Format Painter

Fig. 13.5
The Format Painter button enables you to copy formatting from one range of cells to another.

3. Select the cell or range of cells where you want to apply the formatting. When you release the mouse button, Excel applies the formatting.

4. Continue selecting each additional range of cells. If you double-clicked the Format Painter button, click the button again to turn off the feature or press Esc.

Troubleshooting

I tried to copy data using drag-and-drop, but it wasn't working. Excel would just select the range of cells rather than copy the data.

The cell drag-and-drop feature is probably turned off. To check, choose Tools, Options, and select the Edit tab. Make sure that the Allow Cell Drag and Drop check box is selected (if it is, an X appears in the check box). Choose OK.

If the drag-and-drop feature is enabled, remember that you must click the outer edge of the selected range and then drag the selection.

I used the Edit Copy and Edit Paste commands to copy a range of data in my worksheet. I pressed Enter to paste the data into the new location, and it worked without a hitch. But when I tried to choose Edit, Paste to paste another copy, Paste was unavailable.

When you choose Edit, Copy to move a range of data, Excel does indeed copy the data to the Clipboard. But when you press Enter to paste the data, Excel clears the contents of the Clipboard. Notice also that the marquee surrounding the data disappears.

If you want to paste multiple copies of the data in the worksheet, do not press the Enter key to paste the data. Instead, continue to choose Edit, Paste to paste the copies in the worksheet.

I tried to copy a range of data by using AutoFill, but I just moved the selected cell when I dragged it.

You probably dragged the edge of the cell rather than the AutoFill handle. The AutoFill handle is located on the lower right corner of the cell, and the mouse pointer changes to a solid plus sign (+) instead of an arrow when placed on the AutoFill handle.

Moving Worksheet Data

As with copying, you can move worksheet data from one area of the worksheet to another. You can use the drag-and-drop method to move a range of data quickly, or you can use the Edit Cut and Edit Paste commands to cut a range of data and paste it in another location.

Moving Data with Drag-and-Drop

When you use the drag-and-drop method to move data, you are physically moving the range of data from one area to another. This is different from copying, which keeps the source data intact.

To move a range of data with drag-and-drop, follow these steps:

1. Select the range that contains the data you want to move.

2. Position the mouse pointer on the border of the selected data.

3. Click and drag the selection to the new location. As you move the mouse, a border appears in the worksheet, indicating the location in which the data will appear.

4. Release the mouse button to drop the selected data in the new location.

> **Note**
>
> Excel does not allow you to overwrite existing data automatically when you use drag-and-drop. A message appears, warning you that you are about to overwrite existing data. Choose Cancel and indicate a new position, or choose OK if you want to over-write cells.

Moving Data with Cut and Paste

When you choose Edit, Cut (Ctrl+X) to move worksheet data, a copy of the data is stored on the Windows Clipboard. You then can paste the data in another area of the worksheet.

To move data by choosing Edit, Cut, follow these steps:

1. Select the range of data you want to move.

2. Choose Edit, Cut, or press Ctrl+X. Alternatively, click the right mouse button and then choose Cut from the resulting shortcut menu.

   A marquee surrounds the selection you cut, and the status bar at the bottom of the screen prompts you to select the location where you want to paste the data.

3. Select the cell in which you want the data to appear, and then choose Edit, Paste, or press Ctrl+V. Alternatively, click the right mouse button and choose Paste from the resulting shortcut menu. You also can press Enter.

> **Note**
>
> When using Edit, Paste to paste data from the Clipboard, indicate a single cell rather than a range of cells in which to paste the data. If you select a range of cells, the range you select must be the same size as the range you placed on the Clipboard.

III

Using Excel

Troubleshooting

I tried to move a range of data by using drag-and-drop, but the data I was trying to move was instead copied to the range of cells I wanted the data to move to.

You probably dragged the AutoFill handle rather than the edge of the cell. The AutoFill handle is located on the lower right corner of the cell and is used to quickly fill a range of cells with the data. When the mouse is positioned on the AutoFill handle, the mouse pointer changes to a solid plus sign (+) instead of an arrow.

To move the data, position the mouse pointer on an edge of the cell, and then drag the mouse to move the data.

When I used Edit, Paste to move a range of data, Excel pasted only a portion of the data in the selected range.

When pasting data, make sure that you select a single cell in which to paste the data. When you do, Excel pastes the entire range. If you select more than one cell and the selected range is smaller than the original range of cells, Excel pastes only the data that will fit in the selected range.

Note

▶ See "Referencing Cells in Formulas," p. 372

When copying and moving formulas, keep in mind that Excel may adjust cell references in the formula to reflect the new location. When you copy a formula, Excel adjusts the cell references. When you move a formula, Excel will not adjust cell references.

Inserting and Deleting Columns, Rows, and Cells

Another area of editing you'll perform in Excel is that of inserting and deleting columns, rows, and cells. Sometimes, restructuring a worksheet entails more than moving data to another location. For example, if you add another sales region to your sales tracking worksheet, you can insert a new column to hold the data. Likewise, if you remove a product from your product line, you can delete the rows that contain the data.

Inserting Columns, Rows, and Cells

When you need to insert additional space in your worksheet, you can insert columns, rows, and cells in the middle of existing data. When you insert columns, rows, and cells, existing data shifts to accommodate the insertion.

To insert a column, follow these steps:

1. Position the cell pointer in the column where the new column should appear.

2. Choose <u>I</u>nsert, <u>C</u>olumns, or click the right mouse button and then choose Insert from the shortcut menu. Excel inserts a new column, and existing columns shift to the right.

To insert a row, follow these steps:

1. Select a cell in the row below where the new row should appear.

2. Choose <u>I</u>nsert, <u>R</u>ows, or click the right mouse button and then choose Insert from the shortcut menu. Excel inserts a new row, and existing rows move down.

To insert a cell or range, follow these steps:

1. Select the cell or range where the new cells should appear.

2. Choose <u>I</u>nsert, C<u>e</u>lls, or click the right mouse button and then choose Insert from the shortcut menu. The Insert dialog box appears (see fig. 13.6).

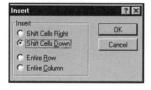

Fig. 13.6
The Insert dialog box prompts you to specify the direction in which the existing cells should move.

3. Select Shift Cells Right to insert the new cells to the left of the selection. Select Shift Cells <u>D</u>own to insert the new cells above the selection.

4. Choose OK. The selected cells move in the direction you specified.

Deleting Columns, Rows, and Cells

You can delete columns, rows, and cells from your worksheet when they contain data that is no longer needed. When you delete columns, rows, and cells, existing data moves to close the space.

To delete a column, follow these steps:

1. Click the letter of the column you want to delete. To delete multiple columns, highlight each additional column.

III

Using Excel

2. Choose <u>E</u>dit, <u>D</u>elete, or click the right mouse button and then choose Delete from the shortcut menu. The selected column is removed from the worksheet, and existing columns move to the left.

To delete a row, follow these steps:

1. Click the number of the row you want to delete. To delete multiple rows, highlight each additional row.

2. Choose <u>E</u>dit, <u>D</u>elete, or click the right mouse button and then choose Delete from the shortcut menu. The selected row is removed from the worksheet, and existing rows move up.

Caution

Use care when using <u>E</u>dit, <u>I</u>nsert and <u>D</u>elete in your worksheets. When you use these commands, the entire worksheet is affected by your action. If a formula refers to a cell that is deleted, for example, the cell containing the formula returns the #REF! error value. If this occurs, choose <u>E</u>dit, <u>U</u>ndo immediately after making a deletion.

To delete a cell or range of cells, follow these steps:

1. Select the range of cells that you want to delete.

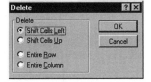

2. Choose <u>E</u>dit, <u>D</u>elete, or click the right mouse button and then choose Delete from the shortcut menu. The Delete dialog box appears (see fig. 13.7).

3. Select Shift Cells <u>L</u>eft, and the existing data will move to the left. Choose Shift Cells <u>U</u>p, and the existing data will move up.

4. Choose OK after you make your selection.

Fig. 13.7
In the Delete dialog box, specify the direction in which the existing cells should move.

Inserting and Deleting Sheets

Excel provides true 3D functionality, which enables you to create workbooks that contain multiple sheets of data. Each new workbook you create contains

16 worksheets, but you can add additional worksheets, as well as delete worksheets that you no longer need.

Inserting Sheets

When you insert a worksheet, Excel inserts the sheet before the current worksheet. To insert a worksheet, select the sheet to the right of where the new worksheet should appear, and choose Insert, Worksheet. Excel inserts a sheet and assigns a name to the sheet.

Deleting Sheets

To delete a sheet, move to the sheet you want to delete, and then choose Edit, Delete Sheet. Excel deletes the sheet.

Moving Sheets

In addition to inserting and deleting sheets, you can rearrange worksheets in the workbook by moving them to a new location.

Excel employs the drag-and-drop method for moving sheets. To move a sheet, click the tab of the sheet you want to move. Hold down the mouse button, and drag the sheet to the new position in the workbook. When you release the mouse button, the sheet is dropped in its new location.

Naming Sheets

Initially, Excel names each worksheet in the workbook Sheet1, Sheet2, and continues incrementing. You can, however, easily rename a sheet to reflect the data it contains. In a Monthly Sales worksheet, for example, you can use a separate sheet for each sales region. You then could name each sheet North, South, East, and West. Thereafter, anyone else who uses the worksheet will be able to tell what the worksheet contains just by looking at the name.

To rename a worksheet, double-click the sheet tab of the worksheet you want to rename. The Rename Sheet dialog box appears (see fig. 13.8).

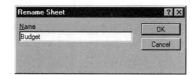

Fig. 13.8

Type a name for the worksheet in the Rename Sheet dialog box.

Enter a name for the worksheet in the text box, and choose OK. Excel displays the name in the selected sheet's tab.

Finding and Replacing Worksheet Data

Excel provides the capability to find and (optionally) replace specific data in your worksheet. You can, for example, search for all occurrences of the value 1994 and replace it with 1995.

Finding Worksheet Data

You can search the entire workbook, or you can search only a selected worksheet range. To search the entire workbook, select a single cell. To search a specified range, select the range that you want to search. Follow these steps to perform a search:

1. Choose Edit, Find, or press Ctrl+F. The Find dialog box appears (see fig. 13.9).

Fig. 13.9
The Find command enables you to locate specific data in your worksheets.

2. In the Find What text box, type the data you want to find. Then specify the search options, described in table 13.2.

3. Choose Find Next to begin the search. When Excel locates the characters, choose Find Next to find the next occurrence, or choose Replace to access the Replace dialog box (this option is discussed in the next section).

4. Choose Close to end the search and close the dialog box.

Tip
If the Find dialog box is obstructing your view of the worksheet, click and drag the title bar of the dialog box until you can see the active cell in the worksheet.

Table 13.2 Find Options	
Option	**Action**
Search	Specifies whether to search across rows or down columns.
Look In	Selects the location of the data: cell formulas, cell values, or cell notes.
Match Case	Finds only characters that match the case of the characters you specified.

Option	Action
Find Entire Cells <u>O</u>nly	Searches for an exact match of the characters you specified. It does not find partial occurrences.
<u>F</u>ind Next	Finds the next occurrence of the search string.
Close	Ends the search and returns to the worksheet.
<u>R</u>eplace	Opens the Replace dialog box (discussed in the next section).

Note

If you're not sure of the specific string you are looking for, you can specify wild-card characters in the search string to locate data that contains some or all of the characters. You can use an asterisk (*****) to search for any group of characters and a question mark (**?**) to search for any single character.

Replacing Worksheet Data

The Edit Replace command (Ctrl+H) is similar to the Find command in that it enables you to locate specific characters in your worksheet. The Replace command then enables you to replace the characters with new data.

To replace worksheet data, follow these steps:

1. To search the entire workbook, select a single cell. To search a specified range, select the range you want to search.

2. Choose <u>E</u>dit, R<u>e</u>place. The Replace dialog box appears (see fig. 13.10).

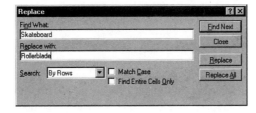

Fig. 13.10
You can use the Edit Replace command to replace formulas, text, or values.

3. In the Fi<u>n</u>d What text box, type the data you want to replace. In the R<u>e</u>place With text box, type the data with which you want to replace the current data.

4. Specify the replace options, as described in table 13.3.

> **Caution**
>
> Make sure that Find Entire Cells Only is activated if you are replacing values or formulas. If it is not selected, Excel will replace characters even if they are inside other strings. For example, replacing 20 with 30 will also make 2000 become 3000.

5. Choose Find Next to begin the search. When Excel locates the first occurrence of the characters, choose the appropriate replace option (see table 13.3).

6. Choose Close to close the dialog box.

Table 13.3	**Replace Options**
Option	**Action**
Search	Specifies whether to search across rows or down columns.
Match Case	Finds only characters that match the case of the characters you specified.
Find Entire Cells Only	Searches for an exact match of the characters you specified. It does not find partial occurrences.
Find Next	Finds the next occurrence.
Close	Closes the Replace dialog box.
Replace	Replaces the characters in the active cell with those specified in the Replace With text box.
Replace All	Replaces all occurrences of the characters with those specified in the Replace With text box.

> **Caution**
>
> When replacing data in your worksheet, use Replace All with care, because the results may not be what you expect. Whenever you use Replace, it's a good idea to first locate the data you want to replace to make sure that the data is correct.

Tip
If you make a mistake when replacing data, close the dialog box, and choose Edit, Undo (Ctrl+Z) immediately to reverse the replacement.

Spell Checking the Worksheet

Excel's Spelling command enables you to check worksheets, macro sheets, and charts for misspellings and to correct the errors quickly. The spelling feature offers a standard dictionary and also enables you to create an alternate customized dictionary to store frequently used words not found in the standard dictionary. When you check spelling, Excel looks in the standard dictionary and the custom dictionary for the correct spelling.

In addition to finding spelling errors, Excel finds repeating words and words that might not be properly capitalized. You can check spelling in the entire workbook, a single cell, or a selected range.

To check the spelling of data in your worksheet, follow these steps:

1. Specify the worksheet range you want to check. To check the entire worksheet, select cell A1. Excel starts checking from the active cell and moves forward to the end of the worksheet. To check a specific word or range, select the cell containing the word, or select the range.

2. Choose Tools, Spelling, or press F7. When Excel finds a spelling error, the Spelling dialog box appears (see fig. 13.11).

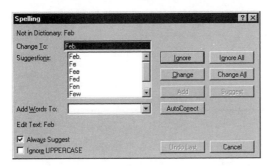

Tip

To check the spelling in more than one worksheet, select the tab of each sheet you want to check.

Fig. 13.11
The Spelling dialog box appears when Excel finds a spelling error in the worksheet.

The following options are available to correct a spelling error:

Table 13.4   Spelling Dialog Box Options

Option	Action
Change To	Types a replacement for the word.
Suggestions	Selects a replacement word from a list of suggested words.
Add Words To	Selects the dictionary to which you want to add words that are spelled correctly but not found in the standard dictionary.

(continues)

III

Using Excel

Table 13.4 Continued	
Option	**Action**
Ignore	Ignores the word and continues the spell check.
Ignore All	Ignores all occurrences of the word.
Change	Changes the selected word to the word displayed in the Change To box.
Change All	Changes all occurrences of the word to the word displayed in the Change To box.
Add	Adds the selected word to the custom dictionary.
AutoCorrect	Makes a correction based on AutoCorrect choices.
Suggest	Displays a list of additional suggestions based on a selection from the Suggestions list.
Always Suggest	Excel automatically displays a list of proposed suggestions whenever a word is not found in the dictionary.
Ignore UPPERCASE	Skips words that are all uppercase.
Undo Last	Undoes the last spelling change.
Cancel/Close	Closes the dialog box (the Cancel button changes to Close when you change a word or add a word to the dictionary).

◀ "Letting AutoCorrect Do Your Spelling for You," p. 95

The AutoCorrect feature allows Excel to correct common typing errors as you make them. For example, many people accidentally type two initial capital letters while holding down the Shift key, or routinely transpose letters in certain words such as *adn* for *and*. To set up AutoCorrect, follow these steps:

1. Choose Tools, AutoCorrect. The AutoCorrect dialog box opens, as displayed in figure 13.12.

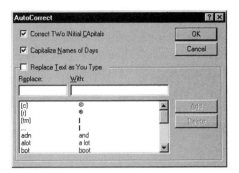

Fig. 13.12
AutoCorrect
corrects your
mistakes as soon
as you make them.

Caution

Deselecting the Replace Text As You Type box will deactivate AutoCorrect.

---

2. Check the appropriate boxes to activate any of the following options: Correct TWo INitial CApitals, Capitalize Names of Days, or Replace Text As You Type.

3. To add a common error to the AutoCorrect list, enter the incorrectly typed word in the Replace box and the correct version in the With box. Then click the Add button to add this entry to AutoCorrect.

4. Choose OK to return to your worksheet.

Tip
To remove an
AutoCorrect entry,
select it and click
Delete.

III

Using Excel

Chapter 14
Formatting Worksheets

by Patrice-Anne Rutledge

After you create a worksheet, the next step is to change the appearance of data in your worksheet to make it more visually appealing. Excel provides many features and functions that enable you to produce high-quality worksheets. You can include such formatting options as applying different fonts, and you can add graphics, colors, and patterns to worksheet elements.

In this chapter, you learn to

- Format numbers

- Change column widths and row heights

- Align text

- Change fonts, sizes, and styles

- Apply patterns and borders

- Create and apply a style

- Create and work with graphic objects

Formatting Numbers

When you enter numbers in the worksheet, don't be concerned with the way they look. You can change the appearance of numbers by applying a numeric format.

Excel provides many common numeric formats; you can create your own as well. For example, you can apply a predefined currency format that uses two decimal places or create a currency format that uses an international currency symbol.

To apply a numeric format, follow these steps:

1. Select the cells containing the numbers you want to format.

2. Choose Format, Cells; or press Ctrl+1. Alternatively, click the right mouse button and choose the Format Cells command from the resulting shortcut menu. The Format Cells dialog box appears (see fig. 14.1).

Fig. 14.1
The Format Cells dialog box displays a list of predefined number formats.

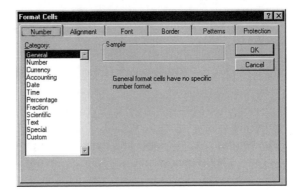

3. Select the type of number format you want to apply from the Category list. A list of sample formats displays in the Type list box for the Date, Time, Fraction, Special, and Custom categories. The Number, Currency, Accounting, Percentage, and Scientific categories include options for setting decimal places, and in some cases, for negative numbers. General and Text categories include no further options.

4. Select the number format you want to use from the choices displayed. A sample of the selected format appears in the Sample area of the dialog box.

5. Choose OK. Excel applies the selected number format to the selected cells in your worksheet.

◀ "Using Toolbars in Microsoft Office Applications," p. 44

Applying Number Formats Using the Toolbar

You can quickly apply commonly used number formats—such as Currency, Comma, and Percentage—by using the Formatting toolbar (see fig. 14.2). Use either the number format buttons that appear in the toolbar by default or the Style menu that you manually add to the toolbar.

Currency   Percentage   Comma

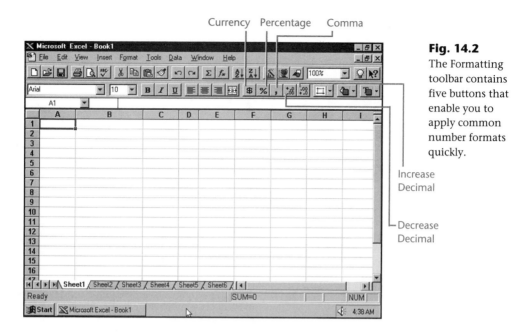

Fig. 14.2
The Formatting
toolbar contains
five buttons that
enable you to
apply common
number formats
quickly.

Increase
Decimal

Decrease
Decimal

To apply a number format by using the Formatting toolbar, select the cells
containing the numbers you want to format and then click the appropriate
button in the toolbar.

Formatting Numbers Using the Style Menu

You also can format numbers by using styles. To apply one of the predefined
number formats listed as a style, select the cells containing the numbers you
want to format and choose F̲ormat, S̲tyle. The Style dialog box appears (see
fig. 14.3). Select the desired style in the S̲tyle Name drop-down list, and then
choose OK.

III

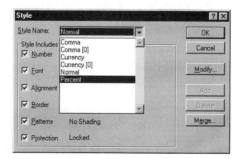

Fig. 14.3
Format numbers
using the pre-
defined styles in
the Style dialog
box.

Using Excel

Table 14.1 describes the predefined formatting choices.

Table 14.1	Number Formats Available in the Style Dialog Box
Format	**Description**
Comma	Adds two decimal places to the number, and adds commas to numbers that contain four or more digits. A number entered as **1000** is formatted as 1,000.00.
Comma (0)	Rounds decimals and adds commas to numbers that contain four or more digits. A number entered as **1000.55** is formatted as 1,001.
Currency	Adds a dollar sign and two decimal places to the number. Also adds a comma to numbers that contain four or more digits. A number entered as **1000** is formatted as $1,000.00.
Currency (0)	Adds a dollar sign to the number and rounds decimals. Also adds a comma to numbers that contain four or more digits. A number entered as **1000.55** is formatted as $1,001.
Normal	Applies the style that defines normal or default character formatting. A number entered as **1000** is formatted as 1000.
Percent	Multiplies the number by 100 and adds a percentage symbol to the number. A number entered as **.15** is formatted as 15%.

Note

► See "Customizing Application Toolbars," p. 759

To add the Styles box to the Formatting toolbar, choose View, Toolbars, and then choose Customize. Select Formatting from the Categories list. In the Buttons section of the dialog box, click and drag the Style button to the Formatting toolbar, and choose Close.

You also can use the following shortcut keys to format numbers:

Key	Format
Ctrl+Shift+~	General format
Ctrl+Shift+!	Comma format with two decimal places
Ctrl+Shift+$	Currency format with two decimal places

Key	Format
Ctrl+Shift+%	Percent format
Ctrl+Shift+^	Scientific notation format

Creating a Custom Number Format

Although Excel provides most of the common number formats, at times you may need a specific number format that the program does not provide. For example, you may want to create additional numeric formats that use various international currency symbols. Excel enables you to create custom number formats. In most cases, you can base your custom format on one of Excel's predefined formats.

To create a custom number format, follow these steps:

1. Choose Format, Cells; or press Ctrl+1. Alternatively, click the right mouse button and choose Format Cells from the resulting shortcut menu. If necessary, select the Number tab in the Format Cells dialog box.

2. Select Custom in the Category list box. Then select the predefined format in the Type list. Some common symbols used in these formats are listed in table 14.2. The formatting symbols appear in the Type text box, and a sample appears above the text box (see fig. 14.4).

3. Edit the selected format in the Type text box.

Table 14.2 Numeric Formatting Codes

Code	Description
#	Placeholder for digits.
0	Placeholder for digits. Same as #, except that zeros on either side of the decimal point force the numbers to match the selected format.
$	Currency symbol is displayed with the number.
,	Placeholder for thousands separator.
.	Placeholder for decimal point.
%	Multiplies number by 100 and displays number with a percent sign.

Fig. 14.4
You can define
your custom
format in the
Type text box.

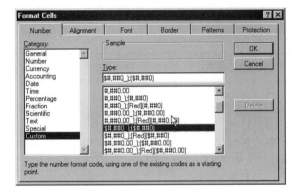

4. Choose OK. The custom format appears at the end of the list.

> **Note**
>
> You can select and delete custom formats from the list; however, you cannot delete
> any of Excel's predefined number formats.

Changing Date and Time Formats

Excel recognizes most dates and times entered in a worksheet cell. If you
enter **9-1-95** in a cell, for example, Excel assumes that you are entering a date
and displays the number in a date format. (The default date format is 9/1/95.)
If you enter 9:45, Excel assumes that you are referring to a time and displays
the entry in a time format. You can change to another date or time format.

◀ See "Entering
Dates and
Times," p. 306

To apply a date or time format, follow these steps:

1. Select the cell or range containing the data you want to format.

2. Choose Format, Cells; or press Ctrl+1. Alternatively, click the right
    mouse button and choose Format Cells from the resulting shortcut
    menu.

3. Select Date from the Category list to display the list of date formats (see
    fig. 14.5). To apply a time format, select Time from the Category list.

4. Select the format you want to use from the Type list box.

5. Choose OK. Excel applies the format to the data.

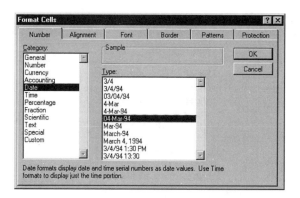

Fig. 14.5
A list of predefined date formats appears in the Date section of the Format Cells dialog box.

You also can use the following shortcut keys to enter and format the current date and time:

Key	Format
Ctrl+;	Current date (entering)
Ctrl+:	Current time (entering)
Ctrl+#	Date format d-mmm-yy (formatting)
Ctrl+@	Time format h:mm AM/PM (formatting)

Use the same procedure to create custom date and time formats as custom number formats; the only difference is that you use date and time format codes. Table 14.3 lists these codes.

Table 14.3	Date and Time Format Codes
Code	**Description**
m	Month as a number with no leading zero
mm	Month as a number with leading zero
mmm	Month as a three-letter abbreviation
mmmm	Month as a full name
d	Day of week with no leading zero
dd	Day of week with leading zero

(continues)

III

Using Excel

Table 14.3 Continued	
Code	**Description**
ddd	Day of week as a three-letter abbreviation
dddd	Day of week as a full name
yy	Year as a two-digit number
yyyy	Year as a four-digit number
h	Hour with no leading zero
hh	Hour with leading zero
m	Minute with no leading zero
mm	Minute with leading zero
AM/PM	AM or PM indicator

Troubleshooting

Excel fills a cell with ##### when I apply a numeric format to a number in my worksheet.

When a cell is not wide enough to accommodate a formatted number, Excel displays the number as #####. To display the complete number in the cell, you must adjust the column width of the cell. When you widen the column sufficiently, Excel displays the fully formatted number in the cell.

A few methods for changing the width of a column are available. You can double-click on the right side of the column heading to autofit the column to the data you entered. Or, you can adjust the width to a precise amount, using Format, Column, Width, or you can use the mouse to drag the column border until the column is the appropriate width.

To adjust the width of a column to a precise amount, position the cell pointer in the column and choose Format, Column, Width, or click the right mouse button and choose Column Width from the resulting shortcut menu. In the Column Width dialog box, enter the desired column width; then choose OK. To adjust the width of a column by using the mouse, position the mouse pointer on the right border of the column heading whose width you want to change. The mouse pointer changes to a two-headed horizontal arrow when positioned properly. Drag the arrow to the right or left to increase or decrease the column width. A dotted line in the worksheet

(continues)

(continued)

indicates the column width. Release the mouse button when the column is the width you want. For more information on changing column widths, see the following section, "Changing Column Width and Row Height."

I want to create a numeric format that uses an international currency symbol. I changed the International setting in the Windows Control Panel to reflect the country I wanted to use, but that changed the symbol for all currency formats. How can I use an international symbol in my custom format without changing the others?

To create a custom numeric format with an international currency symbol, choose Format, Cells, and select the Number tab. In the Category list, select Custom; then select the format that closely resembles the format you want to use from the Type list box. Select the Type text box, highlight the currency symbol used by that format, and press Delete to delete the symbol. You then can enter special characters to display the currency symbols. To use the pound symbol (£), press the Num Lock key, hold down the Alt key, and—using the numeric keypad—type **0163**, which is the ANSI character for that symbol. To use the yen symbol (¥), press the Num Lock key if it's not already active, hold down the Alt key, and type **0165** in the numeric keypad. The appropriate currency symbols are inserted into the text box when you release the Alt key. Choose OK to save the custom numeric format.

Changing Column Width and Row Height

When you enter data in a cell, the data often appears truncated because the column is not wide enough to display the entire entry. If a cell cannot display an entire number or date, Excel fills the cell with pound signs or displays the value in scientific notation (for example, 4.51E+08). After you adjust the width of the cell, the entire number or date appears.

You can change the column width by using the mouse or menu commands. When you use the mouse to change the column width, you drag the column border to reflect the approximate size of the column. When you choose Format, Column, Width, you can specify an exact column width.

Using the Mouse To Change Column Width

To change the column width by using the mouse, follow these steps:

1. Position the mouse pointer on the right border of the heading of the column whose width you want to change. The mouse pointer changes

III

Using Excel

to a double-headed horizontal arrow when positioned properly. To change the width of multiple columns, first select the columns by dragging the mouse over the additional column headings, and then position the mouse on the heading, as just described.

2. Drag the arrow to the right or left to increase or decrease the column width, respectively. A dotted line indicates the column width (see fig. 14.6).

3. Release the mouse button when the column is the width you want.

Double-headed arrow for changing column width

Fig. 14.6
Drag the double-headed arrow to change the column width.

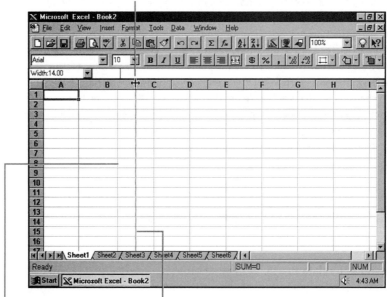

Original column width   New column width

Using the Column Width Command To Change Column Width

To change the column width by using the Column Width command, follow these steps:

1. Click the heading of the column whose width you want to change. To change the width of multiple columns, drag the mouse pointer over each additional column.

2. Choose F<u>o</u>rmat, <u>C</u>olumn, <u>W</u>idth. Alternatively, click the right mouse button, and choose Column Width from the shortcut menu. The Column Width dialog box appears (see fig. 14.7).

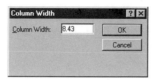

Fig. 14.7
Enter a specific column width in the Column Width dialog box.

3. Enter the column width in the Column Width text box.

4. Choose OK. Excel adjusts the width of the selected columns.

Adjusting Column Width Automatically

In addition to changing column width manually, Excel enables you to adjust the column width to accommodate any specific cell entry or the widest cell entry in a column.

To adjust the column width to the width of a specific entry, select the cell containing the entry, and then choose F<u>o</u>rmat, <u>C</u>olumn, <u>A</u>utoFit Selection. Excel adjusts the width of the column.

Adjusting the Row Height

Excel automatically adjusts the row height based on the font you are using, but you can change the row height to accommodate additional white space or to minimize the row height in your worksheet. You can use both the mouse and Excel commands to change the row height.

To adjust the row height by using the mouse, follow these steps:

1. Position the mouse pointer on the bottom border of the heading of the row whose height you want to change. The mouse pointer changes to a double-headed vertical arrow when positioned properly. To change the height of multiple rows, drag over the additional row headings.

2. Drag the arrow down or up to increase or decrease the row height, respectively. A dotted line indicates the row height (see fig. 14.8).

3. Release the mouse button when the row is the height you want.

Tip

To quickly change the column width to fit the widest entry, position the mouse pointer on the right border of the column heading and double-click the mouse.

III

Using Excel

Double-headed arrow for changing row height

Fig. 14.8
Drag the double-headed arrow to change the row height.

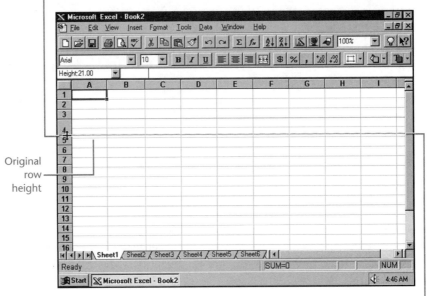

Original row height

New row height

To adjust the row height by using the Row Height command, follow these steps:

1. Click the heading of the row whose height you want to change. To change the width of multiple rows, drag the mouse pointer over each additional row.

2. Choose F<u>o</u>rmat, <u>R</u>ow, H<u>e</u>ight. Alternatively, click the right mouse button and choose Row Height from the shortcut menu. The Row Height dialog box appears (see fig. 14.9).

Fig. 14.9
Enter a specific row height in the Row Height dialog box.

> **Note**
>
> The row height is measured in points and is based on the size of the default font used in the worksheet. The default font used by Excel is 12-point Arial.

3. Enter the row height in the Row Height text box.

4. Choose OK. Excel adjusts the height of the selected rows.

Aligning Data

Excel provides several formatting options for changing the appearance of data in the worksheet. For example, you can change the alignment of text or numbers within a cell so that they appear left-aligned, right-aligned, or centered. You also can format lengthy text to wrap within a cell, center text across a range of columns, or align text vertically within a cell.

To align data, follow these steps:

1. Select the cell or range that contains the data you want to align.

2. Choose Format, Cells; or press Ctrl+1. Alternatively, click the right mouse button and choose the Format Cells command from the resulting shortcut menu. The Format Cells dialog box appears (see fig. 14.10). Select the Alignment tab.

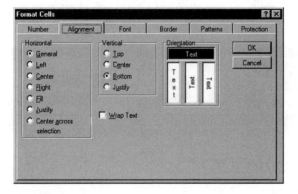

Fig. 14.10
Change the alignment of data in the Alignment tab of the Format Cells dialog box.

3. Specify the alignment you want to use. See table 14.4 for descriptions of alignment options.

4. Choose OK.

Table 14.4	Alignment Options
Option	**Description**
General	Aligns text to the left and numbers to the right
Left	Aligns text and numbers to the left edge of the cell
Center	Centers text and numbers within a cell
Right	Aligns text and numbers to the right edge of the cell
Fill	Repeats the contents until the cell is full
Justify	When text is wrapped within a cell, aligns text evenly between the cell borders

Wrapping Text within a Cell

You can align text entries to wrap within a single cell or a range of cells. To wrap text within a cell or range, select the cell or range of cells containing the entry, and then choose Format, Cells; or press Ctrl+1. You also can click the right mouse button and choose the Format Cells command from the shortcut menu. In the Format Cells dialog box, select the Alignment tab. Then select Wrap Text and choose OK. Excel wraps the text (see fig. 14.11).

Fig. 14.11
Column titles are wrapped within each cell.

Excel automatically adjusts row heights for rows with wrapped text in cells.

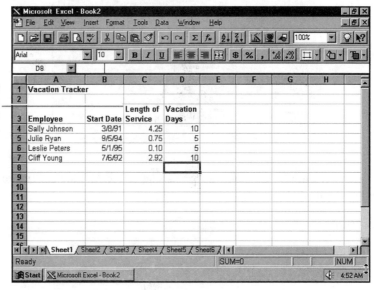

Centering Text across Columns

To center text over multiple columns, first select the cell that contains the text and the range of columns across which you want to center the text. Selected cells defining the range of columns must be blank.

Choose F_ormat, C_ells; or press Ctrl+1. Alternatively, click the right mouse button and choose the Format Cells command from the shortcut menu. The Format Cells dialog box appears. Select the Alignment tab. Then select Center A_cross and choose OK. Excel centers the text across the specified columns (see fig. 14.12).

Text centered across columns A-D

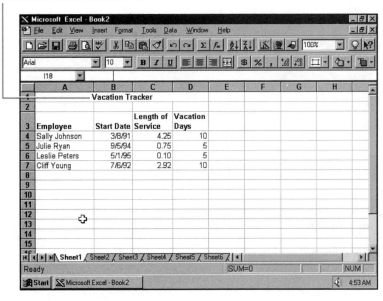

Fig. 14.12
Text is centered across the selected columns.

Aligning Text Vertically or Horizontally

Excel enables you to align text either vertically or horizontally in a cell. To format text vertically or horizontally, follow these steps:

1. Select the cell or range of cells containing the text you want to format.

2. Choose F_ormat, C_ells; or press Ctrl+1. Alternatively, click the right mouse button and choose Format Cells from the shortcut menu. The Format Cells dialog box appears. Select the Alignment tab.

Tip
When aligning text, use Excel's Format, Col_umn, A_utoFit and Format, Row, A_utoFit commands to adjust the column width or row height quickly.

III

Using Excel

3. In the Orientation section, select the vertical or horizontal orientation. If you select a vertical orientation, you also must select a specific vertical alignment (Top, Center, or Bottom) in the Vertical box.

4. Choose OK. Excel aligns the text (see fig. 14.13).

Fig. 14.13
Text is aligned vertically in row 3.

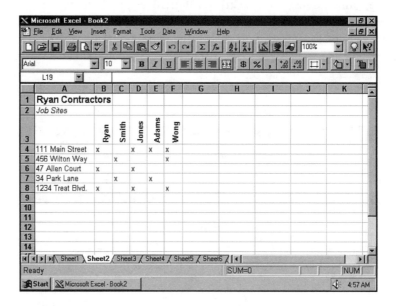

Troubleshooting

I used the Center Across Selection command to center a text entry across a range of columns, but the entry would not center.

One of the cells in the selection probably contains a space character or some other entry. To remove these characters, select the range of cells (except for the cell containing the entry you want to center) and then press Delete. The entry should be selected.

After I aligned text vertically in a cell, some of the characters did not display.

When a row height is set to the default row height, only a few characters of vertically rotated text display. To display the entire contents, position the mouse pointer on the bottom border of the row and double-click the left mouse button, or click the row heading and choose Format, Row, AutoFit to adjust the height to best fit the row's contents.

Changing Fonts, Sizes, and Styles

Excel provides several formatting options for changing the appearance of text in your worksheets. You can, for example, choose a different font, change the size of the selected font, and apply a font style to cells in your worksheet.

Changing Fonts

The list of fonts available in the Font dialog box depends on the type of Windows fonts you have installed and the type of printer you are using. You can quickly change the font and font size in the font and font size boxes on the Formatting toolbar. You can also change a font in the Format Cells dialog box. To do so, follow these steps:

1. Select the cell or range of cells that you want to change.

2. Choose Format, Cells; or press Ctrl+1. In the Format Cells dialog box, select the Font tab.

3. In the Font list box, select the font you want to use; to change the text size, select a size in the Size list or type any size in the Size text box (see fig. 14.14).

4. Choose OK.

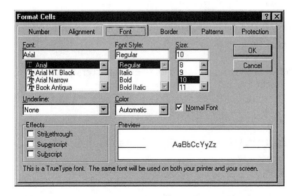

Fig. 14.14
The Font section of the Format Cells dialog box displays the currently installed Windows and printer fonts.

Applying Text Formats

In addition to changing the font and size of data in your worksheets, you can apply text attributes to the data. For example, you can assign such attributes as bold, italic, and underline, and change the color of text.

To apply one of these formatting attributes, select the bold, italic, underline, or font color buttons on the Formatting toolbar. You can also apply text formats in the Format Cells dialog box by following these steps:

1. Select the cell or range of cells you want to format.

2. Choose Format, Cells; or press Ctrl+1. In the Format Cells dialog box, select the Font tab.

> **Note**
>
> As you make changes in the dialog box, Excel applies the selections to the text in the Preview box. The changes aren't made to the selected cells until you choose OK.

3. Select the style you want to apply in the Font Style list box. Use the Underline drop-down list to select an underline style. To change the color of the data, click the Color drop-down list and select a color. Select Strikethrough, Superscript, or Subscript if you want.

4. When you finish, choose OK.

Formatting Characters in a Cell

Tip

When formatting characters in a cell, you also can use the buttons in the Formatting toolbar to change the appearance of text.

You can apply formatting to individual characters in a text entry. For example, you can assign the Bold format to a single character in a cell.

To format characters in a cell, follow these steps:

1. Double-click the cell containing the data you want to format, or select the cell and then press F2.

2. In the cell or formula bar, select the characters you want to format.

3. Choose Format, Cells; or press Ctrl+1. The Font tab displays automatically.

4. Select the attributes you want, and then choose OK.

Applying Patterns and Borders

In addition to formatting numbers or text, you can format cells. For example, you can add a border to a cell or range of cells and fill a cell with a color or pattern.

Applying a Border

Borders enhance a worksheet's appearance by providing visual separations between areas of the worksheet. Borders also improve the appearance of printed reports.

To apply a border, follow these steps:

1. Select the cell or range you want to format.

2. Choose Format, Cells; or press Ctrl+1. Alternatively, click the right mouse button and choose the Format Cells command from the shortcut menu. In the Format Cells dialog box, select the Border tab (see fig. 14.15).

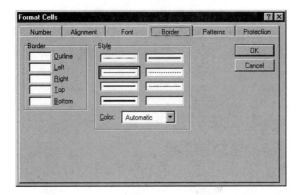

Fig. 14.15
In the Format Cells dialog box, select a border to add to a cell.

3. Choose the placement of the border by selecting Outline, Left, Right, Top, or Bottom in the Border box. The Outline option puts a border around the outer edges of the selection. The Left, Right, Top, and Bottom options place a border along the specified edges of each cell in the selection.

4. In the Style area, select the type of border you want. To change the color of the border, select the color from the Color drop-down list.

5. When you finish, choose OK.

Tip
To apply borders quickly, select the cell or range you want to format, and then click the arrow next to the Borders button to display the Border buttons.

III

Using Excel

Applying Patterns

You can enhance a cell with patterns and colors. The Format Cells Patterns command enables you to choose foreground and background colors as well as a pattern.

> **Note**
>
> To apply the same formatting to a different area, select the new area and then click the Repeat button or press F4 immediately after you apply the formatting.

To format a cell with colors and patterns, follow these steps:

1. Select the cell or range you want to format.

2. Choose Format, Cells; or press Ctrl+1. Alternatively, click the right mouse button and choose the Format Cells command from the shortcut menu. In the Format Cells dialog box, select the Patterns tab (see fig. 14.16).

Fig. 14.16
Apply patterns and colors to a cell with the Format Cells dialog box.

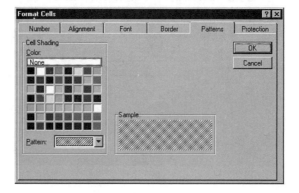

3. Select a background color for the cell in the Color section. The Sample box in the bottom right corner of the dialog box shows you what the color looks like.

4. Select a pattern in the Pattern drop-down list by clicking the down arrow. To specify a background color for the pattern, select a pattern color from the Pattern pull-down list. If the foreground and background colors are the same, the cell displays a solid color. The Sample box shows you what the formatting looks like.

5. Choose OK.

Using Automatic Range Formatting

If you aren't sure which colors and formats work well together, Excel's AutoFormat feature can eliminate much of the guesswork. AutoFormat enables you to make choices from a list of predefined formatting templates.

These formats are a combination of number formats, cell alignments, column widths, row heights, fonts, borders, and other formatting options.

To use the AutoFormat feature, follow these steps:

1. Select the range you want to format.

2. Choose Format, AutoFormat. The AutoFormat dialog box appears (see fig. 14.17).

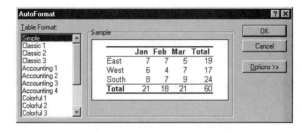

◄ See "Using Automatic Formatting," p. 88

Fig. 14.17
The AutoFormat dialog box displays formatting templates.

3. Select one of the format types in the Table Format list box. Excel displays the selected format in the Sample box.

4. Choose OK to apply the format.

Note

To copy the formats from a range of cells to another range in the worksheet, select the range of cells containing the formats and click the Format Painter button in the Standard toolbar. Then, using the mouse, highlight the range of cells to which you want to copy the formats. When you release the mouse button, Excel applies the formats to the selected range.

Troubleshooting

After I changed the color of a cell, the entry was no longer displayed.

When the background color of a cell is the same color used by the cell entry, you will not see the entry. To change the color of the cell entry, select the cell and choose Format, Cells. Select the Font tab, select a color from the Color drop-down menu, and choose OK.

After I choose the AutoFormat command, Excel displays an error message, stating that it cannot detect a table around the active cell.

You probably selected a single cell before choosing the AutoFormat command. You must select more than one cell for AutoFormat to work.

III

Using Excel

Creating and Applying a Style

When you find yourself applying the same worksheet formats over and over, you can save yourself some time by saving the formats in a style. Then, when you want to use the formats, you can apply all of them with a single command.

You can create a style based on cell formats that already appear in the worksheet, or you can create a new style by using the options in the Style dialog box.

Creating a Style by Example

You can define a style based on existing formats in your worksheet. When you create a style by example, Excel uses the formats of the selected cell to create the style.

To create a style by example, follow these steps:

1. Select the cell that contains the formats you want to name as a style.

2. Choose Format, Style. The Style dialog box appears (see fig. 14.18).

Fig. 14.18
The Style dialog box displays the options you can use to define a style.

3. Type a name for your new style in the Style Name text box, and then choose Add. The style appears in the Style Name drop-down list.

4. Choose OK.

Defining a Style

To create a new style, follow these steps:

1. Choose Format, Style to display the Style dialog box.

2. Type a name for the style in the Style Name text box. (Normal is the default style.) The current format appears in the Style Includes box.

3. Choose the <u>M</u>odify button. The Format Cells dialog box appears.

4. Select the tab for the attribute you want to change. The dialog box for the selected attribute appears.

5. Enter the changes you want to make. Choose OK to return to the Style dialog box.

6. After you make all the necessary style changes, choose OK. The dialog box closes, and Excel applies the style to any selected cells in the worksheet.

Applying a Style

To apply a style, follow these steps:

1. Select the cell or range to which you want to apply the style.

2. Choose F<u>o</u>rmat, <u>S</u>tyle to display the Style dialog box.

3. Select the name of the style you want to apply in the <u>S</u>tyle Name list.

4. Choose OK. Excel applies the style to the selected cell or range.

Creating and Working with Graphic Objects

Excel makes it easy to enhance your worksheets with graphic objects by providing a full set of drawing tools. You can create such objects as circles, squares, and rectangles and add them to your worksheet.

Creating an Object

To create a drawn object, click the Drawing button in the Standard toolbar to display the Drawing toolbar. Select the Drawing tool that represents the object you want to create.

Position the mouse pointer in the area of the worksheet where you want to start drawing (the mouse pointer changes to a small cross when you position it in the worksheet area). Click and hold down the left mouse button, and drag the mouse until the object is the size you want. Then release the mouse button. Excel adds the drawing to the worksheet (see fig. 14.19).

▶ See "Using Drawing Tools," p. 549

III

Fig. 14.19
A rectangle is
added to the
worksheet.

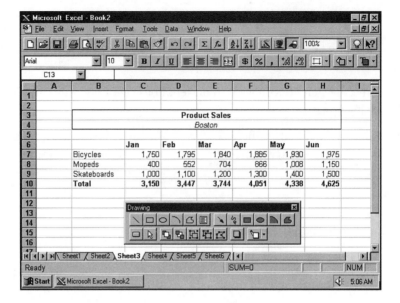

Selecting, Moving, and Resizing Objects

After placing an object in the worksheet, you can move that object to a new location or resize it.

To Select an Object

Before you can move or resize an object, first select it by placing the mouse pointer next to the object and clicking the left mouse button. The mouse pointer becomes an arrow when positioned on the border of the object. Handles appear around the object, indicating that it is selected (see fig. 14.20).

To Move an Object

► See "Manipulating Objects," p. 526

Select the object you want to move, and then position the mouse pointer inside the boundaries of the object. When the mouse pointer becomes an arrow, click and hold down the left mouse button, drag the selected object to the desired location, and release the mouse button.

To Resize an Object

Select the object you want to resize. Handles appear around the object; these handles enable you to resize the selected object.

Position the mouse pointer on one of the black handles. The mouse pointer changes to a double-headed arrow when properly positioned. To make the object wider or longer, position the mouse pointer on one of the middle handles. To resize the object proportionally, position the mouse pointer on one of the corner handles.

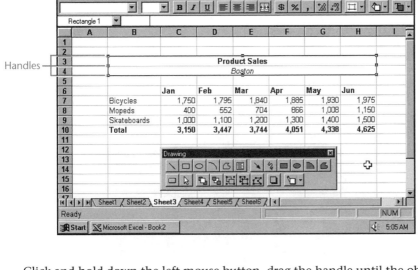

Fig. 14.20
Handles appear around this object, indicating that it is selected and can be moved or resized.

Click and hold down the left mouse button, drag the handle until the object is the size you want (see fig. 14.21), and then release the mouse button.

Left edge of original rectangle

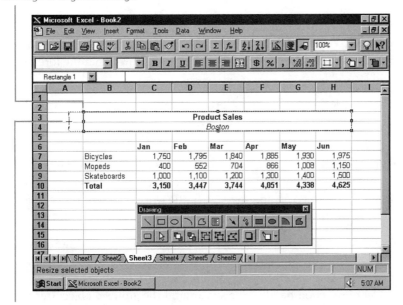

Fig. 14.21
The rectangular object is resized.

Left edge of resized rectangle

III

Using Excel

Formatting Objects

As you can with text, you can add color, patterns, and borders to drawn objects in your worksheet.

To format an object, follow these steps:

1. Select the object you want to format.

2. Choose F<u>o</u>rmat, Obj<u>e</u>ct; or press Ctrl+1. Alternatively, click the right mouse button and choose the Format Object command. The Format Object dialog box appears (see fig. 14.22).

Fig. 14.22
Change the appearance of a drawn object with the Format Object dialog box.

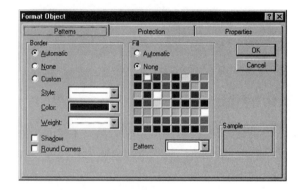

3. Select a border style in the Border section of the dialog box. Select a color and pattern in the Fill section of the dialog box. The Sample area in the bottom right corner of the dialog box shows what the formatting will look like.

4. Choose OK to close the dialog box and apply the selected formats.

Grouping Objects

In creating a graphic or picture, you might draw several separate objects. If you want to work with multiple objects at the same time—for example, if you want to move the object to another area in the worksheet or want to create a copy of the drawing—you can group the objects to form a single object.

To group objects, first select the objects. (You can use the Drawing Selection button in the Drawing toolbar or hold down the Shift key as you click each object.) Choose F<u>o</u>rmat, <u>P</u>lacement, <u>G</u>roup. Excel groups the objects together. A single set of selection handles appears around the grouped object (see fig. 14.23).

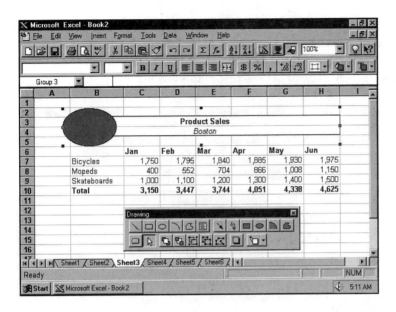

Fig. 14.23

All selected objects appear as one object, with handles outlining the area of the single grouped object.

To break a grouped object back into multiple objects, select the grouped object, and then choose F<u>o</u>rmat, <u>P</u>lacement, <u>U</u>ngroup. Individual objects appear, with handles surrounding each object.

Creating a Text Box

Excel enables you to create text boxes in your worksheets for adding paragraphs of text.

To create a text box, select the Text Box button and position the mouse pointer in the worksheet (the mouse pointer becomes a small cross). Click the left mouse button, and drag the pointer in the worksheet area. After you release the mouse button, the insertion point appears in the top left corner of the text box, ready to accept the text you type. The text wraps according to the size of the box (see fig. 14.24).

You can format, move, and resize a text box as you can any other object in a worksheet. When you resize a text box, the text automatically wraps to fit the new size of the box. You can apply formats to all the text in the text box or only to individual words. To make the entire text bold, for example, select the text box and click the Bold button in the Formatting toolbar. To make a single word of the text bold, place the mouse pointer inside the text box. The mouse pointer changes to an I-beam. Select the text you want to format by clicking and dragging the I-beam over the text. Then use standard formatting commands, tools, or shortcuts to format the selected text. As long as the insertion point appears inside the text box, you can use normal formatting and editing procedures. For information on formatting, refer to sections "Formatting Numbers," "Aligning Text Vertically or Horizontally," and "Changing Fonts, Sizes, and Styles," earlier in this chapter.

Fig. 14.24
Text fits within
this text box.

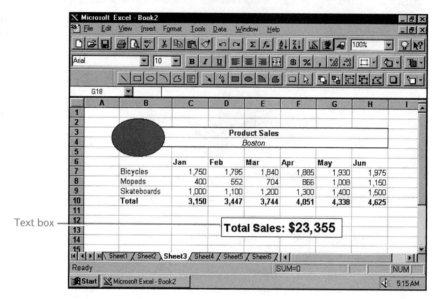

Text box

To select and move a text box, position the mouse pointer (arrow) on the border of the text box and then click the left mouse button.❖

Chapter 15

Using Formulas

by Patrice-Anne Rutledge

The greatest benefit of using an electronic spreadsheet program, such as Excel, is the program's power to calculate formulas based on values in the worksheet. You can, for example, create a formula that calculates the difference between sales figures on a quarterly basis or that totals the commissions each sales representative has received. Excel includes several tools to simplify creating formulas as well as resolving problems with them.

In this chapter, you learn to

- ■ Create a formula

- ■ Reference cells in formulas

- ■ Solve problems with formulas

- ■ Copy formulas

- ■ Name cells used in formulas

Creating Formulas

You can create formulas in Excel in two ways: type the formula directly in the cell, or point to the cells that you want the formula to compute.

Creating a Formula by Typing

To create formula by entering the cell addresses and numeric operators in a cell, follow these steps:

1. Select the cell in which you want to enter a formula.

◄ See "Entering Worksheet Data," p. 305

2. Type = (equal sign) to start the formula.

> **Note**
>
> You can enter a plus sign (+) or minus sign (–) to begin a formula; Excel will convert the formula to the appropriate format. If you enter **+B4+B5**, for example, Excel will convert the formula to =+B4+B5.

3. Type the cell references containing the values to be computed, entering the appropriate operator. To find the difference between the two values in cells B5 and B11, for example, enter **=B5–B11** in another cell, such as cell B14.

4. Press the check box in the formula bar. Excel displays the result of the formula in the active cell and the formula appears in the formula bar.

> **Note**
>
> To display formulas in a worksheet instead of their calculated values, select any cell in the worksheet and press Ctrl+` (accent grave). Press Ctrl+` a second time to display the formula result.

Creating a Formula by Pointing

You can, unfortunately, make errors when typing cell references in a formula. To minimize errors that occur when you use cell references in formulas, build a formula by pointing to cells rather than by typing the cell references.

> **Note**
>
> After you enter a complicated formula in your worksheet, you may want to protect it to make sure it can't accidentally be erased. To do so, choose Tools, Protection, Protect Sheet (or Protect Workbook) to enter a password for your work. To unprotect, choose Tools, Protection, Unprotect Sheet (or Unprotect Workbook).

Pointing to Cells with the Mouse

Suppose that you want to enter, in cell B14, a formula that subtracts the total in cell B11 from the total in cell B5. To build a formula by pointing to cells with the mouse, follow these steps:

◀ See "Moving Around in a Worksheet," p. 302

1. Select the cell in which you want to enter a formula.

2. Type = (equal sign) to start the formula. For this example, type = in cell B14.

3. Click the cell whose reference you want to add to the formula. For this example, click cell B5 to add the cell address in the formula bar.

4. Type – (minus sign).

5. Click the next cell you want to add to the formula. For this example, click cell B11.

6. Click the check box in the formula bar to complete the formula entry (see fig. 15.1). You can also press Enter to accept a formula entry.

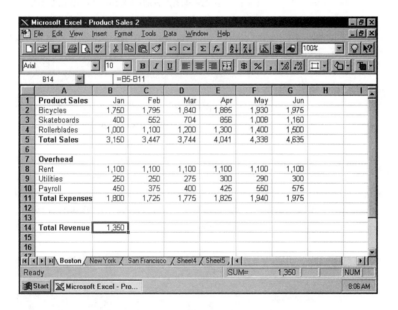

Fig. 15.1
The result of the formula appears in cell B14. The formula appears in the formula bar.

Entering Cell References with the Keyboard

Suppose that in cell D9 you want to build a formula that finds the difference between the totals in cells B9 and C9. To enter cell references with the keyboard, follow these steps:

1. Select the cell in which you want to enter a formula.

2. Type = (equal sign) to start the formula. For this example, type = in cell D9.

III

Using Excel

3. Use the arrow keys to highlight the cell that contains the data you want to use. For this example, press ← twice to select cell B9. Notice that the marquee is positioned in cell B9. Cell B9 is added to the formula.

4. Type – (minus sign).

5. Use the arrow keys to highlight the next cell you want to use. For this example, press ← to select cell C9. Cell C9 is added to the formula.

6. Press Enter to complete the entry.

Referencing Cells in Formulas

You will often refer to other cells in creating your formulas. Excel provides several options for referring to these cells; you can refer to cells that change for each row or column location, cells that remain absolute in every location, or cells that are located in other worksheets or even other workbooks.

Using Relative References

In most instances, you will want to use a *relative reference* when referring to other cells in a formula. This is the default reference; you won't need to enter any special commands to choose this option. Using relative reference, cell references will change depending on their column and row location (see fig. 15.2). When you copy a formula that contains cell references, the cell references adjust to their new location. For example, if you create a formula based on the data in column A, moving that formula to column B will reference the data in that column, rather than the original data.

Fig. 15.2
Using relative reference, copying the formula in cell A3 to cell B3 will change the cell references to the data in column B.

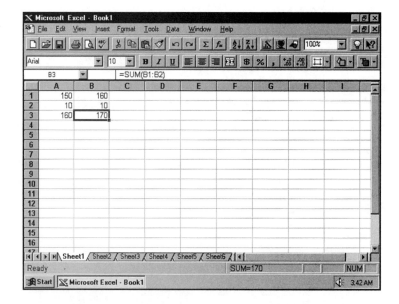

Using Absolute References

Absolute references are useful when you want your formula to refer to data in a specific cell, rather than allowing the reference to change based on the column or row. For example, say that the current commission rate for your sales staff is displayed in cell A3. Your worksheet also contains columns for sales representatives, total sales, and commissions. To calculate the commission each representative receives based on his or her sales, you would divide total sales by the commission rate. The sales figure would change in each row, but the commission rate would remain the same, or absolute. You can make a column, row, or cell reference absolute by placing a dollar sign (**$**) before the reference. A1, B7, and AB8 are all examples of absolute references.

To enter an absolute reference in a formula, follow these steps:

1. In the formula bar, type the equal sign (**=**) and the cell you want to make absolute.

2. Press F4 to activate the absolute reference key.

3. Continue pressing F4 until the appropriate combination of letters and dollar signs appear.

4. Enter the remainder of your formula and press Enter.

Figure 15.3 illustrates the use of an absolute reference.

Tip
You can also enter absolute references by entering the appropriate reference manually in the formula bar.

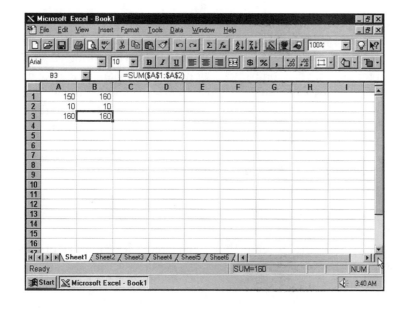

Fig. 15.3
The absolute reference in cell A3 remains the same when copied to B3.

III

Using Excel

Using Mixed References

You can also combine the use of relative and absolute references into a *mixed reference*. For instance, you may want the column to remain absolute but not the row, or vice versa. Entering **$A1** will allow the row to change if you copy data, but not the column. Use the absolute reference key, F4, to enter the appropriate mixed reference by scrolling through its options.

Editing Absolute and Relative References

To edit an existing reference, place the insertion point on the formula bar within the formula you want to change. Press F4 until the desired change takes place, and then press Enter.

Entering References to Other Sheets

▶ See "Linking Data Between Excel Work-sheets," p. 708

You can also include references to data in other worksheets in your workbook. To do so, enter the name of the sheet, an exclamation mark, and the cell reference. For example, typing **Sheet1!A1** would refer to cell A1 in Sheet1. If you've renamed your sheet, indicate the name you have given it.

> **Caution**
>
> If your new sheet name includes spaces, you must surround the sheet name with single quotation marks—for example, **'Budget 1995'!A1**.

Referencing Other Files

Sometimes you may want to refer to data that is located in another workbook. Suppose you have created separate workbooks containing sales information for each of your company's regions. You may want to refer to data in each of those workbooks when you create a new workbook that summarizes sales information for the entire corporation. To refer to cell C10 in the 1995 Sales sheet in the workbook named "Western," you would enter the following reference:

```
='[WESTERN.XLS]SALES 1995'!$C$10
```

Using Operators in Formulas

Excel's operators allow you to perform arithmetic calculations with formulas, manipulate text, perform comparisons, and refer to several different ranges in the worksheet with references.

Arithmetic Operators

In addition to using Excel's built-in functions to perform calculations, you can use arithmetic operators to perform a calculation on worksheet data. Following are the arithmetic operators used in basic calculations:

Operator	Purpose
+	Addition
–	Subtraction
*	Multiplication
/	Division
%	Percentage
^	Exponentiation

Text Operators

By using text operators, you can concatenate (or join) text contained in quotation marks or text in other cells. For example, entering the formula **="Total Sales: "&B4** returns Total Sales: 28 when cell B4 contains the value 28.

Comparative Operators

To compare results, you can create formulas with comparative operators, which return TRUE or FALSE, depending on how the formula evaluates the condition. For example, the formula **=A4>30** returns TRUE if the value in cell A4 is greater than 30; otherwise, it returns FALSE.

Following are the comparative operators you can use in a formula:

Operator	Purpose
=	Equal to
<	Less than
>	Greater than
<=	Less than or equal to
>=	Greater than or equal to
<>	Not equal to

III

Using Excel

Reference Operators

Reference operators enable you to refer to several different cells in a single formula. For example, entering the formula **SUM(A4:A24)** sums the values located in cells A4 through A24.

Order of Operators

Most formula errors occur when the arithmetic operators are not entered in the proper *order of precedence*—the order in which Excel performs mathematical operations. Following is the order of precedence for arithmetic operations in a formula:

Operator	Purpose
^	Exponentiation
*, /	Multiplication, division
+, −	Addition, subtraction

Exponentiation occurs before multiplication or division in a formula, and multiplication and division occur before addition or subtraction. For example, Excel calculates the formula =4+10*2 by first multiplying 10 by 2 and then adding the product to 4, which returns 24. That order remains constant whether the formula is written as =4+10*2 or 10*2+4.

Troubleshooting

I get an error message when I try to create a formula using parentheses.

When creating a long formula, each open parenthesis must be matched by a closed parenthesis, or Excel will not accept the formula. When you use parentheses in a formula, compare the total number of open parentheses with the total number of closed parentheses.

*I entered the formula **=5+10*2** and received the wrong result, 25 instead of 30.*

Remember that Excel will always perform multiplication before addition or subtraction. To force Excel to add the first two figures before multiplying, enter the following: **=(5+10)*2**.

Tip
If a formula includes arithmetic operators at the same level, the calculations are evaluated sequentially from left to right.

You can change the order of precedence by enclosing segments of the formula in parentheses. Excel first performs all operations within the parentheses and then performs the rest of the operations in the appropriate order. For example, by adding parentheses to the formula =4+10*2 to create =(4+10)*2, you can force Excel first to add 4 and 10 and then multiply the sum by 2 to return 28.

Entering Dates and Times in Formulas

You also can create formulas to calculate values by using dates and times. When you use a date or time in a formula, you must enter the date or time in a format that Excel recognizes, and you must enclose the entry in double quotation marks. Excel then converts the entry to its appropriate value. To find the number of days that elapsed between two dates, for example, you would enter a formula such as **="4/2/95"–"3/27/95"**. In this example, Excel returns 6, the number of days between March 27, 1995 and April 2, 1995.

◀ See "Entering Dates and Times," p. 306

If Excel does not recognize a date or time, it stores the entry as text and displays the #VALUE! error value.

> **Note**
>
> You can reduce the time you spend entering repetitive formulas by using arrays. *Arrays* are rectangular ranges of formulas or values that Excel treats as a single group. For more information on using arrays in Excel, see *Special Edition Using Excel for Windows 95*, also published by Que.

Converting Formulas to Values

In many cases, after you create the formula, you need only the result rather than the formula itself. After you calculate your monthly mortgage payment, for example, you no longer need the formula. In such a situation, you can convert the formula to its actual value.

To convert a single formula to a value, follow these steps:

1. Select the cell that contains the formula.

2. Press the F2 function key, or double-click the cell.

3. Press the F9 function key. Excel replaces the formula with the value.

To convert a range of formulas to values, follow these steps:

1. Select the range that contains the formulas you want to convert.

2. Choose <u>E</u>dit, <u>C</u>opy, or click the right mouse button and choose Copy from the shortcut menu. A marquee surrounds the selected range.

III

Using Excel

3. Choose Edit, Paste Special. The Paste Special dialog box appears (see fig. 15.4).

Fig. 15.4

Use the Paste Special dialog box to convert formulas to values.

4. Select the Values option.

5. Choose OK. Excel replaces the formulas in the selected range with values.

Solving Problems with Formulas

Excel formulas can be great time-savers, allowing you to quickly create worksheets that include calculations and references to the contents of other cells. On occasion, though, your formulas can produce errors, when you enter them incorrectly or refer to cells that are invalid. Fortunately, Excel offers several ways to locate and solve errors within your formulas.

Debugging Formulas

Several errors can occur when you enter formulas in Excel. In many cases, Excel displays an error value that enables you to debug your formulas based on that value. Following are the error values and their possible causes:

Error	Meaning
#DIV/0!	The formula is trying to divide by zero.
#N/A	The formula refers to a value that is not available.
#NAME?	The formula uses a name that Excel does not recognize.
#NUL!	The formula contains a reference that specifies an invalid intersection of cells.

Error	Meaning
#NUM!	The formula uses a number incorrectly.
#REF!	The formula refers to a cell that is not valid.
#VALUE!	The formula uses an incorrect argument or operator.

Note

When an error value appears in the worksheet, click the TipWizard button to see a description of the error value.

To access Excel's error values' Help screens, click the Help button, select the Index tab in the Help Topics dialog box, type **Error values**, and then click the Display button to show the help options for error values.

Using Edit Go To Special

The Edit, Go To, Special command provides an easy way to locate cells with errors. To use this feature, follow these steps:

1. Choose Edit, Go To, Special. The Go To Special dialog box appears (see fig. 15.5).

2. Select Formulas, Errors. Be sure all other options are deselected.

3. Choose OK to go to cells that contain errors.

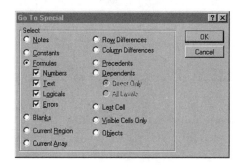

Fig. 15.5
The Go To Special dialog box assists in troubleshooting formula problems.

III

Using Excel

Using Auditing Features

Auditing is another useful feature that helps you trace errors, locate cells that refer to your current cell, and attach comment notes to your cells. You can use auditing to troubleshoot errors as well as prevent errors by reviewing and commenting on your work.

Definition of Terms

Excel's auditing tools allow you to accomplish three tasks:

- Trace precedents

- Trace dependents

- Trace errors

In a cell that contains a formula, tracing *precedents* will point to cells included in that formula. Tracing *dependents* will point to any cells that include a formula reference to the current cell.

For example, if cell A3 refers to the contents of cell A1 plus cell A2, then cell A3 would point to its precedents, cells A1 and A2. Cell A1, however, would point to cell A3 as its dependent. Figure 15.6 illustrates both precedents and dependents.

Fig. 15.6

Arrows trace both precedents and dependents in a worksheet.

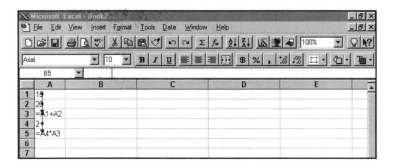

Choosing from the Menu or Auditing Toolbar

You can access Excel's auditing feature from either the menu or toolbar. To access from the menu, choose Tools, Auditing, and select your option from the menu that displays. Options include Trace Precedents, Trace Dependents, Trace Error, Remove All Arrows, or Show Auditing Toolbar.

To display the Auditing toolbar, choose Tools, Auditing, Show Auditing Toolbar. Table 15.1 illustrates each button on this toolbar.

Table 15.1	Auditing Toolbar
Button	**Name**
	Trace Precedents
	Remove Precedent Arrows
	Trace Dependents
	Remove Dependent Arrows
	Remove All Arrows
	Trace Error
	Attach Note
	Show Info Window

Auditing an Error

To audit an error, follow these steps:

1. Select the cell you want to audit.

2. Click the Trace Error button from the Auditing toolbar, or choose <u>T</u>ools, <u>A</u>uditing, and select Trace <u>E</u>rror from the menu.

3. View the precedents of the problem formula to help you determine a solution.

III

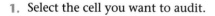

> **Caution**
>
> Be sure that the Show <u>A</u>ll or Show <u>P</u>laceholders option is selected in the View tab of the Options dialog box, or you won't be able to use the auditing features (the toolbar will beep or the menu options will be dimmed). To access this tab, choose <u>T</u>ools, <u>O</u>ptions.

Using Excel

Annotating Your Worksheet

Annotating or adding notes to your worksheet can become very important if you create complex, sophisticated formulas. They can help you determine both the sources of and the reasoning behind any formula, months or even years after you created it. Good notes can save time and energy spent auditing and tracing errors in your formulas. Excel offers the option of adding either text or voice notes to your cells.

To add a note, follow these steps:

1. Select the cell you want to annotate.

2. Click the Attach Note button on the Auditing toolbar, or choose Insert, Note to open the Cell Note dialog box (see fig. 15.7).

Fig. 15.7
The Cell Note dialog box lets you add extensive notes to each cell.

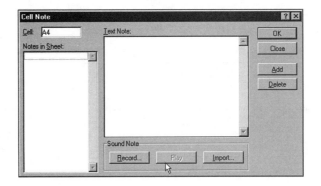

3. Enter a note in the Text Note area, if desired. This note will be listed in the Notes in Sheet list.

4. Click OK to return to the worksheet, or Add to add another note.

5. To add another note to a different cell, enter that cell name in the Cell box and repeat steps 3 and 4.

6. To attach a recorded sound note to the cell, click Record to open the Record dialog box (see fig. 15.8).

7. Click the Record button and begin speaking. The scale will show you how much time you have remaining, up to a total of 1:11 minutes.

8. When you are finished speaking, click Stop and then OK to return to the Cell Note dialog box.

Tip
In order to record voice messages, you must have a sound board and microphone installed.

Tip
You can also import sound files by clicking the Import button in the Cell Note dialog box.

Fig. 15.8
You can attach
recorded voice
notes to your
worksheet in the
Record dialog box.

9. Click Close to return to your worksheet.

After you finish annotating your worksheet, you will notice that all the cells with notes have a small red dot in the upper right corner. You can position the mouse pointer over any annotated cell to display the contents of the note. To edit the note, press Shift+F2. After you create a text or sound note, you can delete it in the Cell Note dialog box by selecting it in the Notes in Sheet list, and clicking the Delete button.

Working with Range Names

As you become more proficient in writing formulas, you will find that cell references are sorely lacking in describing the data that is being calculated. If you saw the formula =B9–C9 in a worksheet, it wouldn't be clear as to which data is being used.

> **Note**
>
> To display the cells to which a formula refers, select the formula in the worksheet and then click the Trace Precedents button in the Auditing toolbar, as detailed in the previous section, "Using Auditing Features."

By assigning a name to a cell or range of cells, you can describe the data in your worksheets. The formula +Total_Sales–Total_Expenses, for example, instantly tells you what data the formula uses.

Creating a Range Name

To create a range name, follow these steps:

1. Select the cell or range of cells you want to name.

2. Click the Name box located at the left end of the formula bar.

III

Using Excel

3. Enter the name you want to assign to the selected range.

4. Press Enter.

Tip

To move to a
range quickly,
type the range
name that you
want to go to
in the Name
box.

To create a range name using an alternative method, follow these steps:

1. Choose Insert, Name, Define. The Define Name dialog box appears.

2. Type a name in the Names in Workbook text box.

3. Choose OK.

To display a list of range names in the active workbook, click the arrow next to the Name box in the formula bar. The drop-down list displays all range names in the workbook (see fig. 15.9).

Fig. 15.9
This drop-down
list displays all
range names in
the workbook.

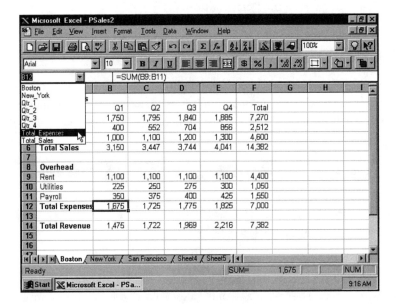

Note

You also can use the Name box to insert a name into a formula. Click the drop-down arrow next to the Name box, and select the range name you want to use.

Inserting Names

After you assign a range name, you can refer to that range name the way you refer to cell references.

To insert a name into a formula, follow these steps:

1. To create a formula that uses range names, type = (equal sign) to start the formula.

2. Choose Insert, Name, Paste. The Paste Name dialog box appears (see fig. 15.10).

Fig. 15.10
Insert a name into a formula in the Paste Name dialog box.

3. In the Paste Name drop-down list, select the name you want to insert.

4. Click OK to close the dialog box.

5. Type the rest of the formula, and press Enter or click the check box in the formula bar when you finish (see fig. 15.11).

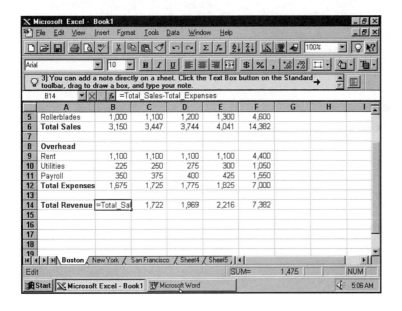

Fig. 15.11
This formula refers to two range names in the worksheet, Total_Sales and Total_Expenses.

III

Using Excel

Deleting Range Names

If you change the contents of a range, you may want to delete the range name if it no longer applies. To delete a range name, follow these steps:

1. Choose Insert, Name, Define. The Define Name dialog box appears (see fig. 15.12).

Fig. 15.12

You can delete range names in the Define Name dialog box.

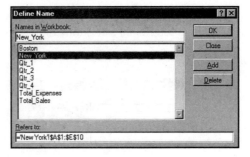

2. In the Names in Workbook drop-down list, select the range name you want to delete.

3. Click the Delete button.

4. Choose OK.

> **Note**
>
> When you define names in the Define Name dialog box, click the Add and Delete buttons to make multiple changes. Choose OK when you finish making changes.

Creating Range Names from Existing Text

Excel enables you to create range names by using existing text from a worksheet. You can, for example, use text that appears in a column to name the cells to the immediate right. Naming cells from existing data enables you to create many range names at one time.

To create range names from existing text, follow these steps:

1. Select the range of cells that contains the text and the cells to be named.

2. Choose Insert, Name, Create. The Create Names dialog box appears (see fig. 15.13).

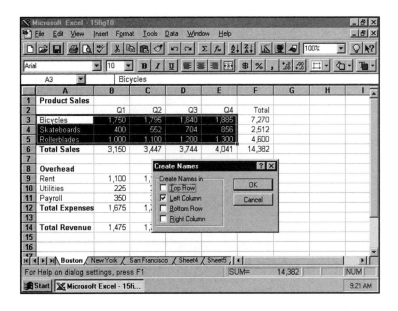

Fig. 15.13
Names will be created from the text that appears in the first column of the selected range.

3. Select the check box that shows the location of the cells containing the text you want to use for range names. Options include Top Row, Left Column, Bottom Row, or Right Column.

4. Choose OK.

Troubleshooting

After I deleted a range name, Excel replaced some of the formulas in the value #NAME?.

When you delete a range name, any formula that refers to the range name returns #NAME?. To correct a formula that refers to a deleted range name, replace the #NAME? reference with the appropriate cell address, or choose Insert, Name, Define to re-create the deleted range name.

After I create a formula that uses a name, Excel interprets the formula as a text entry.

When you use a range name as the first item in a formula, you must begin the formula with an equal sign (=), as in **=SALES*4.05**. Otherwise, Excel thinks that you are entering a text label.

Chapter 16

Using Functions

by Patrice-Anne Rutledge

Excel's functions are built-in calculation tools that perform complex financial, statistical, or analytical calculations; assist in decision-making; and create or manipulate text. Although you can enter many of these functions manually as a formula, using a built-in function can help reduce errors. To make creating a function even easier, Excel offers step-by-step guidance with the Function Wizard.

In this chapter, you learn to

- Create and edit a function

- Use the Function Wizard to enter a function

- Examine some sample functions

Understanding Functions

If you could not calculate complex formulas in Excel, creating worksheets would be quite difficult. Fortunately, Excel provides more than 200 built-in *functions*, or predefined formulas, that enable you to create formulas easily for a wide range of applications, including business, scientific, and engineering applications.

Excel comes with a large number of built-in worksheet functions, including mathematical, database, financial, and statistical functions. The program also includes date, time, information, logical, lookup, reference, text, and trigonometric functions.

Using Arguments

◀ See "Creating a Formula by Typing," p. 369

Each function consists of the equal sign (=), the function name, and the *argument(s)* (cells used for carrying out the calculation). The SUM function, for example, adds the numbers in a specified range of cells (see fig. 16.1). The addresses of the specified cells make up the argument portion of the function. The active cell shows the result of the function. The most common argument type is numeric, but arguments can also be text, values, dates, times, or arrays.

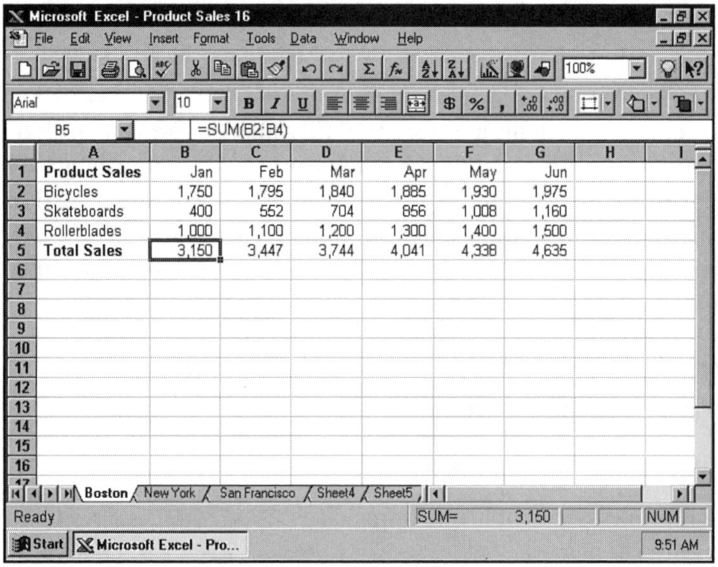

Fig. 16.1
This formula uses the SUM function to total the entries in cells B2, B3, and B4.

Functions can include both mandatory and optional arguments. Mandatory arguments are indicated in bold italic type; optional arguments are italic. For example, the format for the payment function is PMT(**rate**,**nper**,**pv**,*fv*,*type*). This indicates that in order to calculate a payment, you must include the rate, number of periods, and present value, but the future value and type are not required. Functions such as PMT ( ) will be explained in more detail later in this chapter.

Observing the Parts of the Screen that Help Create Functions

There are two toolbars that contain buttons or boxes that assist in the creation of functions: the Standard toolbar and the formula bar. The Standard toolbar is the default toolbar; the formula bar appears when you enter data into a cell. Figure 16.2 displays these main areas.

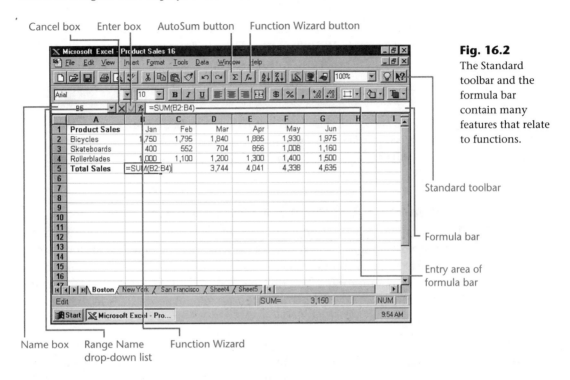

Cancel box   Enter box   AutoSum button   Function Wizard button

Fig. 16.2
The Standard toolbar and the formula bar contain many features that relate to functions.

Standard toolbar

Formula bar

Entry area of formula bar

Name box   Range Name   Function Wizard
              drop-down list

When you begin to enter a function into a cell, what you enter will display in the Entry area. To accept the function data, you can press Enter or click the Enter box on the formula toolbar. To cancel your entry, click the Cancel box. The formula bar also shows you the cell reference or name of the active cell in the Name box and the list of named cells or ranges in the Range Name drop-down list. For more automated function creation, you can use the AutoSum button to automatically total a range. The Function Wizard button is also available on both the Standard toolbar and the formula bar.

Entering Functions

There are several ways to enter a function in Excel. You can:

- Type the function in yourself.

- Use the AutoSum button to sum ranges of data.

- Use the Function Wizard to guide you in entering the function you need.

Typing Functions

Tip

If you're a Lotus 1-2-3 user, you can enter a 1-2-3 function, such as **@SUM(A1..A4)**, and Excel will convert it to the appropriate Excel function.

To enter a function in the active cell, type = (equal sign), followed by the function name (for example, SUM), followed by an open parenthesis. Then specify the cell or range of cells you want the function to use, followed by a closed parenthesis. When you press Enter to enter the function in the cell, Excel displays the result of the formula in the cell.

> **Note**
>
> You do not need to enter the last parenthesis if you are creating a formula with Excel's built-in functions. Excel automatically adds the last parenthesis when you press Enter.

Using the AutoSum Button To Sum Ranges

You can use the AutoSum button, located in the Standard toolbar, to sum a range of cells quickly. You can, for example, use the AutoSum button to total the values in adjacent columns or rows. To do so, select a cell adjacent to the range you want to sum, and then click the AutoSum button. Excel inserts the SUM function and selects the cells in the column above the selected cell or in the row to the left of the selected cell.

◀ See "Entering Data," p. 305

◀ See "Using Wizards," p. 162

You also can highlight the range of cells you want to sum. To do so, select the range of cells (including blank cells) to the right of or below the range, and then click the AutoSum button. Excel fills in the totals.

Using the Function Wizard

If you're not sure how a particular function works, the Function Wizard can guide you through the process of entering the function.

To display the Function Wizard, choose Insert, Function. The Function Wizard dialog box appears (see fig. 16.3).

The Function Category list displays Excel's built-in functions, and the Function Name list shows an alphabetized list of functions available for the highlighted category. To access the DATE function, for example, select Date & Time in the Function Category list, and then select DATE in the Function Name list. When you select a function, the function appears in the formula bar, and the formula bar is activated.

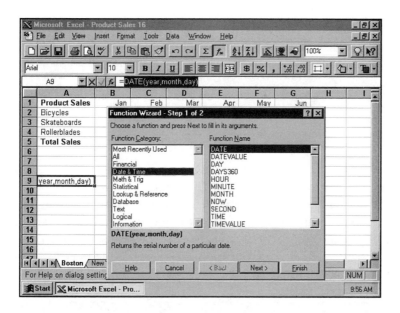

Fig. 16.3
In the Function
Wizard dialog box,
select the function
you want to use.

After you select the function you want, click Next or press Enter to display
the next Function Wizard dialog box. The Step 2 dialog box prompts you to
enter the arguments required for the function (see fig. 16.4). An argument
can be a single cell reference, a group of cells, a number, or another function.
Some functions require a single argument; others require multiple arguments.
Function arguments are enclosed in parentheses, and arguments are separated
by commas.

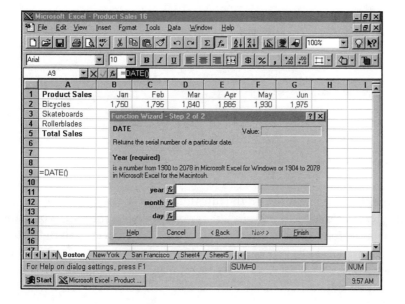

Fig. 16.4
Enter the required
arguments for the
function in the
Function Wizard
dialog box.

III

Using Excel

Each argument text box must contain a cell reference or data. If an argument is required, the label to the left of the text box is bold.

> **Note**
>
> If you know how to use the function, click Finish. After you click on Finish, the Function Wizard exits to the worksheet.

To enter argument data, click the mouse or press Tab to position the insertion point in the first argument text box. The Function Wizard displays a description of the argument in the display area above the text boxes. Enter the values to be used for the arguments, use the mouse to select the cell(s) in the worksheet to be used for the argument, or use the keyboard to enter the cell reference(s) or name(s). The Function Wizard displays the value to the right of the text box (see fig. 16.5).

Fig. 16.5
This dialog box contains multiple arguments for the Date function.

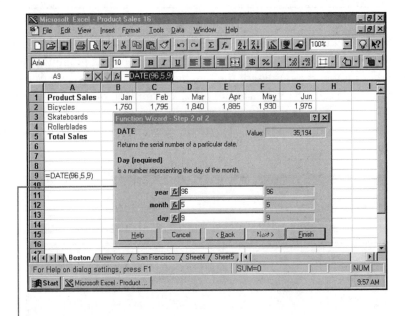

Argument description

Tip
If the Function Wizard dialog box is in the way, move the dialog box by clicking and dragging its title bar.

To enter the first argument for the function, select the cell that contains the data you want to use. To indicate a range of cells, select the range you want to use in the formula. You can also enter the cell references from the keyboard. If, for example, you want to sum the numbers in cells B1, B2, and B3, enter **B1:B3** or **B1,B2,B3** in the argument text box. Each argument appears between the parentheses in the formula bar.

When you finish entering the arguments required by the function, the result of the formula appears in the Value box in the top right corner of the Function Wizard dialog box. Click Finish to enter the function in the cell. The dialog box disappears, and the result of the formula appears in the cell. If the formula contains an error or is incomplete, either an alert box pops up (see fig. 16.6) or an error value, such as #NAME? or #NUM!, appears in the cell.

◀ See "Debugging Formulas," p. 378

Fig. 16.6
This alert box appears if your formula contains an error.

In some cases, Excel highlights the part of the function that contains the error. Edit the function in the formula bar, and when the formula is corrected or complete, click the check box or press Enter.

Editing Functions

After entering a function, you can edit it. You can use the Function Wizard to edit a function, or you can edit the formula and function directly in the cell.

◀ See "Editing Worksheet Data," p. 321

To use the Function Wizard to edit a formula, follow these steps:

1. Select the cell that contains the function you want to edit.

2. Choose Insert, Function. The Function Wizard appears, displaying the function used in the formula.

3. Change any of the arguments as necessary.

4. Click Finish when you complete the function. If the formula contains another function, click Next.

5. Repeat steps 3 and 4 for each function you want to edit.

To edit a function manually, follow these steps:

1. Select the cell that contains the function you want to edit.

2. Double-click the cell or click the formula bar.

3. Select the argument you want to change.

4. Enter the new argument.

5. Press Enter or click the check-mark button in the formula bar.

Getting Help with Functions

As you are using Excel's functions, you can use Excel's context-sensitive help system for assistance. To access Excel's on-line help for functions, choose the Help button on the toolbar and choose Microsoft Excel Help Topics. Double-click Reference Information in the Contents tab, and then double-click Worksheet Functions. This section includes a help topic for each function with detailed information and examples (see fig. 16.7).

Fig. 16.7
Excel's Help feature offers detailed information on many types of worksheet functions.

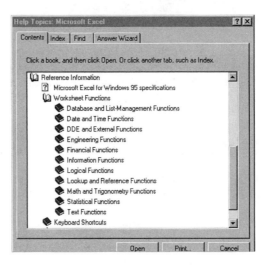

Troubleshooting

After I click the AutoSum button, Excel does not produce a total amount.

If you click the AutoSum button and there are no surrounding cells with numbers to add, the SUM function does not recognize a range address to sum. Select the range of cells you want to sum; the range address appears within the parentheses. Remember that to use the AutoSum button, you must select a cell adjacent to the values you want to sum, or you must select the range of cells (including any blank cells) and then click the AutoSum button.

After I enter a function, Excel displays the error value #NAME? in the cell.

There are two possible causes: you specified a range name that does not exist, or you misspelled the function name. To check, press the F2 function key, and remove the equal sign (=) from the beginning of the formula. Then double-check the spelling of the function. If this spelling is incorrect, correct it, and then type the equal sign. If the function name is spelled correctly, the next step is to make sure that the range to which you referred exists in the worksheet. To do this, click the arrow at the left end of the formula bar, and check the range names in the drop-down list. If the name does not appear in this list, choose Insert, Name, Define to create the range name. When you do, the formula will return the correct result.

Examining Some Sample Functions

The easiest way to learn to create functions in your worksheets is to see some examples of functions in action. The following section details some of the most common Excel functions and gives real-life examples of how they may be used.

For more detailed information on using functions, see *Special Edition Using Excel for Windows 95*, published by Que.

Financial

Financial functions are one of the most common functions used in Excel. With financial functions, you can calculate annuities, cash flow, depreciation, interest, and internal rate of return, among other things. Some common financial functions include:

- DDB(***cost,salvage,life,period***,*factor*). Returns the depreciation of an asset for a specified period using the double-declining balance method.

- FV(***rate,nper,pmt,pv***,*type*). Returns the future value of an investment.

- IPMT(***rate,per,nper,pv***,*fv,type*). Returns the interest payment for an investment for a given period.

- IRR(***values***,*guess*). Returns the internal rate of return for a series of cash flows.

- NPER(***rate,pmt,pv***,*fv,type*). Returns the number of periods for an investment.

III

Using Excel

- NPV(***rate,value1***,*value2,…*). Returns the net present value of an investment based on a series of periodic cash flows and a discount rate.

- PMT(***rate,nper,pv***,*fv,type*). Returns the periodic payment for an annuity.

- RATE(***nper,pmt,pv***,*fv,type,guess*). Returns the interest rate per period of an annuity.

- SLN(***cost,salvage,life***). Returns the straight-line depreciation of an asset for one period.

To be able to intelligently use these functions, you first need to understand the arguments they contain. Table 16.1 explains some of the arguments used in the common functions listed above whose definitions may not be readily apparent. Remember that the Function Wizard and online help also explain these arguments as they are used for each function.

Table 16.1 Arguments in Common Functions	
Argument	**Description**
Nper	Total number of payment periods in an annuity.
Pv	Present value—the total amount that a series of future payments is currently worth.
Fv	Future value—the amount of cash you want to attain after the last payment.

To see a real-life example of a financial function, let's examine the PMT function. You can use PMT to determine a potential monthly mortgage rate if you already know the loan amount, term of the loan, and interest rate. For example, if you wanted to purchase a house with a loan amount of $200,000 at 8 percent for 30 years, you could use the PMT function to learn that this house would require monthly payments of $1,480 (see fig. 16.8).

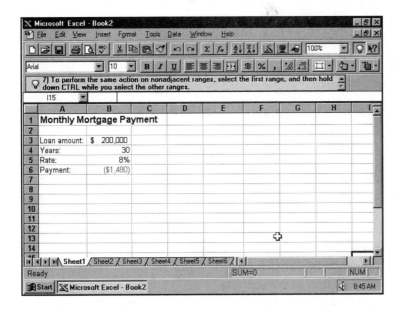

Fig. 16.8
The PMT function helps you determine a monthly mortgage.

Date and Time

Date and time functions are also very common. Some of the ones you'll see most often include:

- DATE(***year,month,day***). Returns the serial number of a particular date.

- NOW( ). Returns the serial number of the current date and time.

- TODAY( ). Returns the serial number of today's date.

Common examples of these functions include using TODAY( ) to enter a date such as **9/15/95** or NOW( )to enter **9/15/95 8:43**.

Math and Trigonometry

Math and trigonometry functions vary from simple formulas that perform basic calculations to complex ones that are more in the realm of the mathematician than the general spreadsheet user. Some examples include:

- ABS(***number***). Returns the absolute value of a number.

- COS(***number***). Returns the cosine of a number.

- INT(***number***). Rounds a number down to the closest integer.

III

Using Excel

- LOG(***number***,*base*). Returns the logarithm of a number to a specified base.

- ROUND(***number,num_digits***). Rounds a number to a specified number of digits.

- SUM(**number1**,number2...). Adds the arguments.

 SUM( ) is probably the most common function you will use in Excel, and one you are already familiar with. You can also summarize cells by using the AutoSum button on the toolbar, which will automatically create a formula using the SUM( ) function. This was discussed in more detail in the section "Using the AutoSum Button to Sum Ranges" earlier in this chapter.

Statistical

Statistical functions include ways to average and count as well as to determine the minimum and maximum in a range. Excel also offers more sophisticated statistical functions such as absolute and standard deviations, negative binomial distribution, and the inverse of the lognormal distribution. Here's a few examples:

- AVERAGE(***number1***,*number2*...). Average the arguments.

- COUNT(***value1***,*value2*...). Counts how many numbers are in the argument list.

- MAX(***number1***,*number2*...). Returns the maximum value in a list of arguments.

- MIN(***number1***,*number2*...). Returns the minimum value in a list of arguments.

- STDEV(***number1***,*number2*...). Estimates the standard deviation based on a sample.

A frequently used statistical function is AVERAGE. Suppose that you want to average the sales made in each of your company's regions. The sales totals for each region are listed in cells D4 through D10. You can enter the function **AVERAGE(D4:D10)** in cell D11 to find out the average sales per region.

Text

Text functions can be used to change case, trim text, or perform searches. Some common examples include the following:

■ CONCATENATE(***text1,text2***,...,*text30*). Joins up to 30 text arguments.

■ LOWER(***text***). Converts text to lowercase.

■ PROPER(***text***). Capitalizes the first letter of each word in a string of text.

■ REPLACE(***old_text,start_num,num_chars,nex_text***). Replaces characters within text.

■ SEARCH(***find_text,within_text***,*start_num*). Locates one text value within another.

■ TRIM(***text***). Removes spaces from text.

■ UPPER(***text***). Converts text to uppercase.

For example, you might want to title a sales report **Monthly Sales = $1,500,000**. "Monthly Sales =" is a text field, but the $1,500,000 is based on a formula located in cell B40. To create your title as described, you can use the CONCATENATE function—**CONCATENATE("Monthly Payment=",B40)**.

Logical

Logical functions are useful for testing and decision-making:

■ AND(***logical1***,*logical2*...). Returns TRUE if all the arguments are true.

■ IF(***logical_test,value_if_true***,*value_if_false*). Returns one value if true, another value if false.

■ OR(***logical1***,logical2...). Returns TRUE if one or more of the arguments is true; FALSE if all are false.

You can also use a combination of logical functions to assist in decision-making. For instance, in the mortgage example you looked at earlier, you could set up a function that would display "Within budget" or "Beyond budget", depending on what your maximum budgeted house payment is. The following function would set a budget limit at $1,500:

=IF(AND(B6>-1,500),"Within budget","Beyond budget")

Anything more than $1,500 would result in a text field that told you this particular loan was beyond your means.

III

Using Excel

Other Functions

Other functions include lookup and reference functions that manipulate references, cells, or ranges; database functions that return information about a database; and information functions that provide information about the Excel environment:

- DGET(***database,field,criteria***). Extracts the record that matches the criteria from the database, and returns TRUE if all the arguments are true.

- ISBLANK(***value***). Returns TRUE if the value is blank.

- ISNUMBER(***value***). Returns TRUE if the value is a number.

- LOOKUP(lookup_value,array). Looks up values in an array.❖

Chapter 17

Creating and Printing Reports

by Patrice-Anne Rutledge

Excel provides sophisticated charting capabilities that enable you to display your worksheet data in graphical form. When you create a chart, you can embed the chart in a worksheet alongside the data on which it is based, or you can create a separate chart sheet. When you're ready to print worksheet data and charts, you can create reports that consist of multiple worksheet areas.

In this chapter, you learn to

- Define the area to be printed

- Define page settings

- Preview and print worksheet data

- Create and print reports

Printing Worksheet Data

Excel provides many options that enable you to control the printed output of your worksheets. You can use the Print Preview command to preview worksheet data before printing. The Page Setup command enables you to define margin settings and to create headers and footers. Both commands can be found in the File menu.

◀ See "Printing All or Part of the Document," p. 134

Printing a Particular Area

You can print the entire workbook, a specific worksheet in the workbook, or a selected range of data. By default, Excel automatically selects and prints the current worksheet. You can, however, define a portion of the worksheet to be printed.

Printing a Specific Range

To print a specific range in the worksheet, follow these steps:

1. Select the range to be printed, using the mouse or the keyboard.

2. Choose File, Print, or press Ctrl+P. The Print dialog box appears, as shown in figure 17.1.

Fig. 17.1

The Print dialog box enables you to specify the data you want to print.

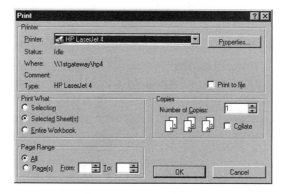

3. In the Print What section of the dialog box, select the Selection option.

4. Choose OK. Excel prints the selected worksheet range.

Defining a Print Area

Tip

You can also set the print area in the Sheet tab of the Page Setup dialog box (choose File, Page Setup).

If you are printing the same range in a worksheet over and over, you can define that range as the print area so that you no longer need to specify the range each time you print the worksheet.

To define the print area, follow these steps:

1. Select your specified area, either with the keyboard or the mouse.

2. Choose File, Print Area.

3. Select Set Print Area from the menu.

Removing a Defined Print Area

To remove a defined print area, choose File, Print Area, and select Clear Print Area from the menu. You can also remove a defined print area in the Page Setup dialog box. To do so, choose File, Page Setup, and click the Sheet tab. Delete the reference in the Print Area text box, and then choose OK.

Inserting and Removing Page Breaks

When you define a print area, Excel inserts automatic page breaks into the worksheet. *Automatic page breaks*, which appear as dashed lines in the worksheet, control the data that appears on each printed page. Excel also inserts automatic page breaks when a selected print range cannot fit on a single page. If you aren't satisfied with the location of the automatic page breaks, you can insert manual page breaks.

You can insert two types of page breaks:

- *Vertical page breaks*. Break the print range at the current column.

- *Horizontal page breaks*. Break the page at the current row.

Inserting a Vertical Page Break

To insert a vertical page break, follow these steps:

1. Click the heading of the column to the right of where the page break should occur.

2. Choose Insert, Page Break. A dashed line appears in the worksheet, indicating the page break.

Inserting a Horizontal Page Break

To insert a horizontal page break, follow these steps:

1. Click the heading of the row below where the page break should occur.

2. Choose Insert, Page Break. Excel adds the page break.

Figure 17.2 shows a horizontal page break added to a worksheet.

III

Using Excel

Fig. 17.2
A horizontal page
break has been
added to this
worksheet.

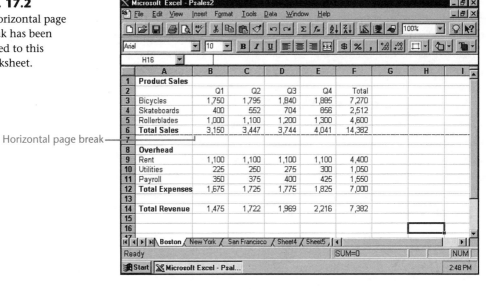

Horizontal page break

Removing Page Breaks

To remove a page break, position the cell pointer below or to the right of the page-break intersection, and then choose Insert, Remove Page Break.

Fitting the Print Range to a Single Page

If the specified print range is a few lines too long to print on a single page, you can fit the worksheet to the page. When you use this method, Excel scales the worksheet so that it fits on a single page.

To fit the print range on a single page, follow these steps:

1. Choose File, Page Setup.

2. If necessary, select the Page tab.

3. Select the Fit To option. By default, the Fit To option is one page wide by one page tall.

4. Choose OK. When you print, Excel scales the worksheet range to a single page.

Tip

To remove all page breaks from the worksheet, click the Select All button in the top left corner of the worksheet frame (the rectangular button next to cell A1), and choose Insert, Remove Page Break.

Troubleshooting

While attempting to remove a page break, I chose the Insert menu, but the Remove Page Break command was not displayed in the menu.

To remove a manual page break, you first must select the cell that contains the manual page break setting. When the cell pointer is correctly positioned, the Remove Page Break command appears in the Insert menu. To minimize the chance for error, select a range of cells surrounding the page break. When you open the Insert menu, the Remove Page Break command should appear.

After selecting the entire worksheet, I chose Insert, Remove Page Break, but Excel removed only some of the page breaks.

A print area must be defined for the worksheet. When you define a print area, Excel automatically inserts page breaks into the worksheet. Although these page breaks appear similar to the manual page breaks that you insert into the document, you cannot use the Remove Page Break command to delete them; instead, you must clear the defined print area.

To clear a defined print area, choose File, Print Area and select Clear Print Area. When you return to the worksheet, the page breaks no longer appear.

Modifying the Page Setup

The Page Setup command enables you to define the page settings for the printed output. You can change the orientation of the page, change the margins and text alignment, and set print titles.

Changing the Worksheet Page Orientation

The default setting for printed output arranges the data in *portrait orientation*—that is, the data is arranged vertically on the page. You may, however, want the data to print in *landscape orientation*—arranged horizontally on the page. If the data range is wide, for example, you may want to print it in landscape orientation, across the width of the page.

To change the page orientation, follow these steps:

1. Choose File, Page Setup.

2. Select the Page tab.

3. Select the Landscape option to print the range across the width of the page.

4. Choose OK.

III

Using Excel

Changing Worksheet Page Margins

The margins define the distance between the printed output and the edge of the page. Excel enables you to change the top, bottom, left, and right margin settings. In addition, you can specify margins for the headers and footers, as well as center the print range between the margins, either horizontally or vertically.

To change the margins, follow these steps:

1. Choose File, Page Setup.

2. Select the Margins tab.

3. Enter the measurements, in inches, in the appropriate text boxes. You also can click the up and down arrows to change the margin settings by increments. Figure 17.3 shows the margins for the current print range.

Fig. 17.3

Use the Margins tab of the Page Setup dialog box to change the margins and alignment of data on a page.

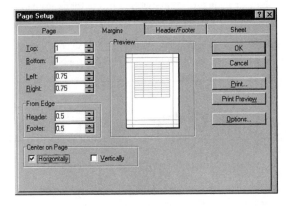

4. To indicate the header and footer margins, specify the measurement in the From Edge section of the dialog box.

> **Note**
>
> You also can change the margins from within Print Preview by dragging the margin borders. For more information, see "Changing Worksheet Page Margins and Other Settings in Print Preview" later in this chapter.

5. To center the data between the top and bottom margins on the page, select the Vertically option. To center the data between the left and right margins, select the Horizontally option. To center the text both horizontally and vertically on the page, select both options.

6. Choose OK.

Setting and Removing Print Titles

When you print large worksheets, you can set print titles so that information such as worksheet titles, column headings, and row headings appears on each page in the printout.

To create print titles, follow these steps:

1. Choose File, Page Setup.

2. Select the Sheet tab, if necessary.

3. If you want to define titles across the top of each page, select the Rows To Repeat At Top box. If you want to define titles down the left side of each page, select the Columns To Repeat At Left box (see fig. 17.4).

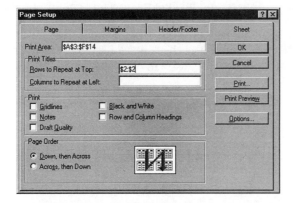

Fig. 17.4
In the Page Setup dialog box, define the area to be used as the print title.

4. If you are defining titles to appear across the top of each page, select the row headings containing the data you want to use as titles, or enter the row references.

   If you are defining titles to appear down the left side of the page, select the column headings containing the data you want to use as titles, or enter the column references.

5. Choose OK.

Note

When you print a worksheet that contains print titles, do not select the range containing the titles when you define the print area. Otherwise, the titles will appear twice on the first page of the printout.

III

Using Excel

To remove print titles, follow these steps:

1. Choose File, Page Setup.

2. Select the Sheet tab, if necessary.

3. Delete the cell references in the Print Titles section of the dialog box.

4. Choose OK.

Setting Other Print Options

◄ See "Changing Printing Options," p. 134

You can define additional print settings in the Page Setup dialog box. You can include the worksheet gridlines in the printout; print notes that have been added to cells; print the data in black and white, even if color has been applied to the worksheet; and include the row and column headings.

Choose File, Page Setup, and select the Sheet tab. In the Print section of the dialog box, select or deselect the check box adjacent to the appropriate print option. Figure 17.5 shows the Sheet tab of the Page Setup dialog box.

Fig. 17.5
Select the appropriate print options in the Sheet tab of the Page Setup dialog box.

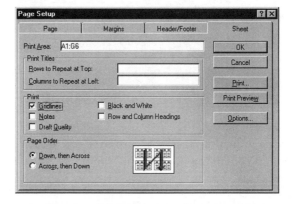

Creating Headers and Footers

Headers and footers enable you to add text—such as the current date, page number, and file name—to the top and bottom of the printed page. Excel provides default header and footer information (the name of the current sheet is centered in the header, and the current page number is centered in the footer). You also can select additional options and define your own header and footer information.

Using Predefined Headers and Footers

To select one of Excel's predefined header and footer options, follow these
steps:

1. Choose <u>F</u>ile, Page Set<u>u</u>p.

2. Select the Header/Footer tab. Figure 17.6 shows the predefined header
   and footer options.

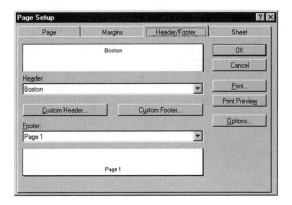

Fig. 17.6
Select the text you
want to use in the
header and footer
area of the printed
page.

3. Click the arrow next to the He<u>a</u>der box, and select a header from the
   drop-down list.

4. Select the data you want to use as a footer from the <u>F</u>ooter list.

5. Choose OK.

Tip
To remove a
header or
footer, select
None from the
appropriate list.

Creating Custom Headers and Footers

Instead of using a predefined header and footer, you can define your own
custom header and footer. Follow these steps:

1. Choose <u>F</u>ile, Page Set<u>u</u>p.

2. Select the Header/Footer tab, if necessary.

3. If appropriate, select an existing header or footer that resembles the
   header or footer you want to create.

4. Select the <u>C</u>ustom Header or C<u>u</u>stom Footer option to display a new
   dialog box. Figure 17.7 shows the Header dialog box.

   Each text box that appears in the dialog box controls the alignment of
   the text in the header or footer. Data can be left-aligned, centered, or

III

Using Excel

right-aligned. Excel uses codes to create certain types of text in the headers and footers. The Page Number code, for example, is used to insert page numbering. The buttons that appear above the text boxes are used to insert the codes. Table 17.1, which follows these steps, describes the code buttons you can use in the header and footer.

Fig. 17.7
Create custom headers and footers by using the text boxes and buttons that appear in this dialog box.

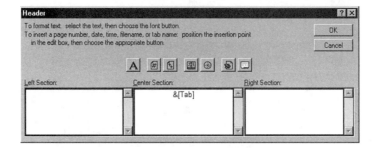

5. Select one of the three text boxes, and then type the header or footer text, or choose a button to enter a header or footer code. To apply text formatting to the header or footer information, click the Font button to display the Font dialog box, and select the appropriate options.

6. Choose OK.

Table 17.1 Header and Footer Codes			
Button	**Name**	**Code**	**Description**
A	Font	None	Displays the Font dialog box.
#	Page Number	&[Page]	Inserts the page number.
	Total Pages	&[Pages]	Inserts the total number of pages.
	Date	&[Date]	Inserts the current date.
	Time	&[Time]	Inserts the current time.

Button	Name	Code	Description
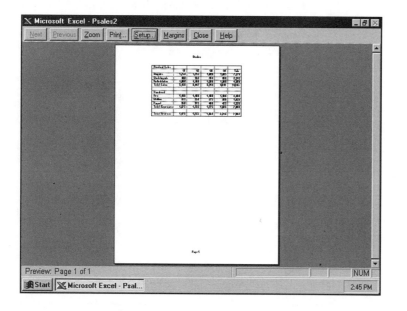	Filename	&[File]	Inserts the file name.
	Sheet Name	&[Tab]	Inserts the name of the active sheet.

Previewing a Worksheet

You can preview the data to make sure it appears the way you want before you print the worksheet. You also can change the margin settings and column widths, if necessary.

◀ See "Using Print Preview," p. 135

To preview the data, follow these steps:

1. Choose File, Print Preview. Excel switches to Print Preview and displays the print range, as shown in figure 17.8.

Fig. 17.8
Print Preview shows what the worksheet will look like when printed.

2. Click the Next and Previous buttons to move from page to page. Notice that these buttons appear dimmed if the data you are previewing fits on a single page.

III

Using Excel

Zooming In and Out on the Worksheet

For a closer look at data, you can zoom in and view an enlarged display; when you want to see more of the data, you can zoom out.

Tip
Press Page Up and Page Down to display each page in the document. Press Home to move to the first page; press End to move to the last page.

To zoom in on the worksheet, click the Zoom button, or position the mouse pointer over the section you want to view and click the left mouse button. The mouse pointer changes to a magnifying glass when positioned over the page. To view other areas of the page, use the vertical and horizontal scroll bars. To zoom out, click the Zoom button again, or click the left mouse button.

Changing Worksheet Page Margins and Other Settings in Print Preview

If, while previewing the worksheet, you find that the current margins or column widths are not adequate, you can change them in Print Preview. When you click the Margins button, light gray boundaries indicating the margins appear around the page. Black handles also appear to indicate the top, bottom, left, and right margins. Square handles appear along the top of the page, with lines indicating the width of each column. Figure 17.9 shows margin and column markers in Print Preview.

Margin markers   Column marker

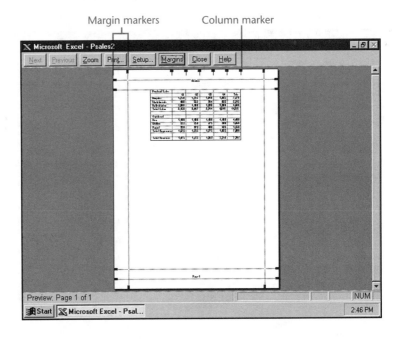

Fig. 17.9
You can change the margins and column widths by dragging the markers.

To adjust the margins, click the handle that represents the margin you want to change. When you do, the mouse pointer changes to a crossbar, and the status bar shows the actual margin setting. Drag the handle to the appropriate location. When you release the mouse button, the margin adjusts, and the data is repositioned on the page.

To change a column width, click the square handle that indicates the column width you want to change. The status bar displays the current column width. Drag the marker to increase or decrease the column width. When you release the mouse button, the column width and data adjust to fit the new size.

When you're satisfied with the way the data appears, click the Print button to print the worksheet. To return to the worksheet, click the Close button.

◀ See "Changing Column Width and Row Height," p. 349

Printing the Worksheet

After you define the print settings and preview the data, you're ready to print the worksheet. The File, Print command enables you to specify the number of copies you want to print, as well as the number of pages (if the print range spans multiple pages). You also can specify the data you want to print, if you have not already defined a print area.

To print the worksheet, follow these steps:

1. Choose File, Print, or press Ctrl+P. The Print dialog box appears.

2. If you have not defined a print area, you can specify the data you want to print by selecting options in the Print What section of the dialog box (refer to fig. 17.1).

3. Select the Selection option to print the selected range of cells; select the Selected Sheet(s) option to print the selected worksheets in the workbook; or select the Entire Workbook option to print every worksheet in the current workbook.

4. To specify the number of copies to be printed, enter the amount in the Copies box.

5. To specify a specific range of pages to be printed, enter the range in the Page Range section of the dialog box.

6. When you're ready to print, choose OK.

Tip
Click the Print button in the Standard toolbar to bypass the Print dialog box and send the output directly to the printer with the default print settings.

III

Using Excel

Note

The Print dialog box also includes a button that enables you to access the Properties box. To change any of these settings, click the Properties button and make the necessary selections.

Troubleshooting

My data won't fit on the page when I print it.

You have several options to get your worksheet data to fit on one page—you can reduce the font size, decrease the margin width, or change from portrait to land-scape orientation if you haven't already done so.

I created a custom header, and the header overflows onto my data when I print it.

To adjust the space between a custom header and your worksheet data, choose File, Page Setup to open the Page Setup dialog box. Select the Margin tab and decrease the size in the Header box in the From Edge section. For example, if you reduce the size from .5 (the default) to .25, you will increase the space between the header and your data. You can also adjust the footer in this section as well.

Using Views and Reports

Excel provides two add-ins that enable you to create and generate printed reports:

- *View add-in.* Enables you to assign names to worksheet ranges and to include the print settings and display options for the ranges.

- *Report Manager add-in.* Enables you to create a report consisting of named views and scenarios.

Installing the View and Report Manager Add-Ins

Before you can define a named view or create a report, you must install the View Manager and Report Manager add-ins.

To install the add-ins, follow these steps:

1. Choose Tools, Add-Ins. The Add-Ins dialog box appears (see fig. 17.10).

2. Select Report Manager and View Manager from the Add-Ins Available list.

3. Choose OK. The Report Manager and View Manager commands are added to the View menu.

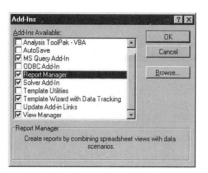

Fig. 17.10
Use the Add-Ins dialog box to install Excel add-ins.

Creating a View

Choosing View, View Manager enables you to define multiple print ranges, with different display and page setup characteristics, in a single worksheet. Normally, every print area of a worksheet must contain the same display characteristics. By using named views, however, you can print multiple ranges with different print settings at the same time.

To create a view, follow these steps:

1. Select the range of cells you want to define as a view.

2. Choose View, View Manager. The View Manager dialog box appears (see fig. 17.11).

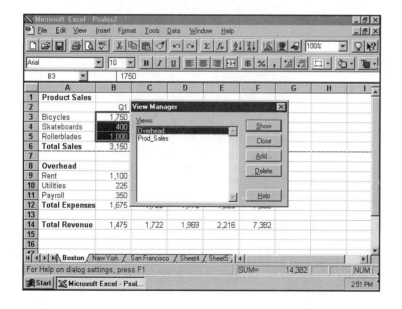

Fig. 17.11
Create multiple views of worksheet data in the View Manager dialog box.

III

Using Excel

3. Click the Add button. The Add View dialog box appears (see fig. 17.12).

Fig. 17.12
Enter a name for
the view in the
Add View dialog
box.

4. Enter a name for the view in the Name text box.

5. Choose OK.

Creating a Report

If your worksheet consists of multiple views of your worksheet, or scenarios of data, you can print those different views and scenarios as a report.

To create a report, follow these steps:

1. Choose View, Report Manager. The Report Manager dialog box appears.

2. Click the Add button to create the report. The Add Report dialog box appears (see fig. 17.13).

Fig. 17.13
Select the views
and scenarios to
be added to the
report.

3. Enter a name for the report in the Report Name text box.

4. Select the view you want to add to the report from the View drop-down list, and then click Add. The view you added appears in the Sections in This Report list.

5. Select the scenario you want to add to the report from the Sce*n*ario drop-down list, and then click *A*dd. The scenario you added appears in the S*e*ctions in This Report list.

6. To change the order of the views and scenarios in the S*e*ctions in This Report list, select a view or scenario and then choose the Move *U*p or Move *D*own button to rearrange the order.

7. Repeat steps 4 through 6 until you finish adding views and scenarios to the report.

8. Select Use *C*ontinuous Page Numbers to number the pages consecutively.

9. Choose OK. You return to the Report Manager dialog box.

10. Choose *P*rint to print the report, or *C*lose to close the dialog box without printing the report.

Editing and Printing a Report

If you want to change the contents of a report or print a report, you can use the View Report Manager command to do so.

To edit a report, follow these steps:

1. Choose *V*iew, *R*eport Manager. The Report Manager dialog box appears.

2. Select the name of the report you want to edit from the *R*eports list, and then choose *E*dit.

3. Change the views and scenarios, as outlined in the preceding section.

4. Choose OK.

To print a report, follow these steps:

1. Choose *V*iew, Report Manager. The Report Manager dialog box appears.

2. Select the report you want to print from the *R*eports list.

3. Click the *P*rint button. The Print dialog box appears.

4. Specify the number of copies to be printed.

5. Choose OK to print the report.

Troubleshooting

I want to create a report, but the Report Manager command does not appear in the View menu.

When the Report Manager command does not appear in the View menu, it means that the Report Manager add-in has not been installed. To install the Report Manager add-in, choose Tools, Add-Ins. In the Add-Ins Available list, check marks appear next to the names of the add-ins that are currently installed. Select Report Manager to add a check mark to the left of the name, and choose OK. The Report Manager command now appears in the View menu.

When I print a report, Excel numbers each page in the report page 1.

To use consecutive page numbers in the report, choose View, Report Manager, select the name of the report from the Reports list, and choose Edit. Select the Use Continuous Page Numbers option, and choose OK. The next time you print the report, Excel will number the pages consecutively.

Chapter 18

Managing Data

by Patrice-Anne Rutledge

With Excel, you easily can manage data by creating a list. After you organize information into a list format, you can find and extract data that meets certain criteria. In addition, you can sort information in a list to put data in a specific order, and you can extract, summarize, and compare data. You also can create a Pivot Table to summarize information in an Excel list.

Excel for Windows 95 provides many tools that enable you to analyze and perform more complex calculations than the typical worksheet formula allows. The Goal Seeker command and Solver add-in enable you to calculate an answer based on one or more calculations. When you need to generate different answers for what-if analysis, the Scenario Manager enables you to do just that. Annotating worksheet cells helps you and others who use your spreadsheet to understand formulas and logic.

In this chapter, you learn to

- Create a list

- Use a data form to enter and edit records

- Sort and filter data in a list

- Generate subtotals and grand totals

- Create pivot tables

- Use the Goal Seeker to calculate a defined result

- Find answers to problems using the Solver

- Annotate formulas with notes

III

Using Excel

Creating and Editing a List

A *list* is information in worksheet cells that contain similar sets of data. When you organize information in a list, you can sort, filter, and summarize data with subtotals. Each *column* in a list represents a category and determines the type of information required for each entry in the list. Each row in a list forms a *record*.

To create a list, enter a column title for each column in the section of the worksheet where you want to start the list. You can create a list in any area of the worksheet. Just make sure that the area below the list is clear of any data so the list can expand without interfering with other data in the worksheet.

You enter data in the rows immediately following the column titles to form a record. Every record must have the same fields, but you do not have to enter data in all fields. Figure 18.1 illustrates a sample list.

Fig. 18.1
In this sample list, product sales are tracked by product, store, region, month, and amount.

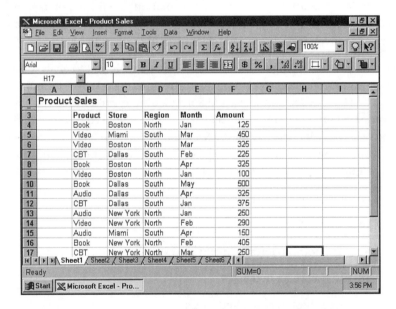

◄ See "Using Wizards," p. 162

To facilitate entering and editing records in a list, Excel provides a *data form* that presents an organized view of the data and makes data entry easier and more accurate. The form displays field names, text boxes for data entry, and buttons for adding, deleting, and finding records. You can enter new records, edit existing records, find records, and delete records using the data form.

> **Note**
>
> The Template Wizard with Data Tracking is an add-in that creates a template linking selected workbook cells to fields in a database. This feature is useful, for example, in a networked environment where more than one user will enter data into a database. To open this wizard, choose <u>D</u>ata, Te<u>m</u>plate Wizard.

Adding Records with the Data Form

The data form provides text boxes, using the column titles or the field names from your list. You enter the data for each field in each text box on the form.

To add a record and enter data using the data form, follow these steps:

1. Position the cell pointer in any cell in your list.

2. Choose <u>D</u>ata, F<u>o</u>rm. The Data Form dialog box appears, as shown in figure 18.2.

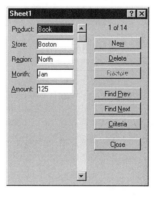

Fig. 18.2
The data form displays the field names and text box to the right of each field name.

3. To add a new record to the list, click the Ne<u>w</u> button. A new blank form appears.

> **Note**
>
> If you type data for a new record in the list and then decide you don't want to add the record, click the <u>R</u>estore button to erase the entry from the form. You must click <u>R</u>estore before pressing Enter to save the record.

4. Enter the appropriate data in each text box on the form.

Press Tab to move forward to the next text box. Press Shift+Tab to move to the previous text box.

5. When you finish entering data for the record, press Enter to add the new record to the list. Another blank form appears, enabling you to enter another new record.

6. Click the Close button to return to the worksheet.

Viewing Records with the Data Form

You can use the data form to view records in your list. Position the cell pointer in a cell in your list and choose Data, Form.

Use the following procedures to view records in a list:

To	Do this
View the next record	Choose Find Next or press down arrow
View the previous record	Choose Find Prev or press up arrow
Move to a new record form	Press Ctrl+Page Down
View the first record	Press Page Up

You also can use the scroll bar to view each record in your list.

If you press the Find Next key to view the next record in the list and Excel beeps, you are viewing the last record in the database. To view the first record in the list, press the Page Up key. As you view each record in the list, the data form displays the current record number in the top right corner of the dialog box, as shown in figure 18.3.

Fig. 18.3
This screen displays the fourth record in a list of 14 records.

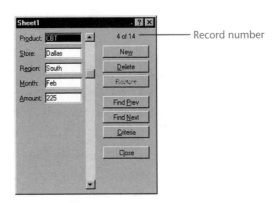

Deleting Records with the Data Form

You also can use the data form to delete records from your list. When you use the form to delete records, you are able to delete only one record at a time.

To delete a record from the data form, follow these steps:

1. Position the cell pointer in any cell in your list.

2. Choose Data, Form. The data form appears.

3. Click the Find Next or Find Prev button, or press the up arrow or the down arrow, to move to the record you want to delete.

4. When the record you want to delete appears in the form, click the Delete button to delete the record.

   The records below the deleted record are renumbered to account for the deleted record. Excel prompts you with the dialog box shown in figure 18.4 to verify that you want to delete the record.

Fig. 18.4
A message box appears reminding you that the record will be permanently deleted.

5. Choose OK or press Enter to delete the record, or click Cancel to keep the record.

6. Click the Close button to return to the worksheet.

Finding Records with the Data Form

You can use the data form to find particular records in your database. When you use the data form, you can view only one found record at a time.

To find records from the data form, follow these steps:

1. Select a cell in the list.

2. Choose Data, Form.

3. Click the Criteria button.

4. Select a text box and enter the criteria or pattern for which you want to search, as shown in figure 18.5.

Tip
You can use multiple criteria when searching for records. Just enter the criteria values in the appropriate text boxes.

III

Using Excel

Fig. 18.5
In this example,
the search
criterion is an
amount greater
than 450.

5. Click the Find Next button or press the down arrow after you have entered the criteria. If no matches exist, you hear a beep. Click the Find Prev button or press the up arrow if you want to search backward through the database to find a match.

6. Click the Close button to clear the dialog box.

Troubleshooting

After I choose Data, Form, Excel displays an error message stating that no list was found.

Before choosing Data, Form, you must first select any cell within the list you want to modify.

When I choose New to add a new record to the list in the data form, Excel displays the message Cannot extend list or database, *and I can't enter a new record.*

The data form does not allow you to add new records to the list if there are not enough blank rows below the current list range. Choose OK to close the dialog box and then click Close to close the data form. If any data is below the list range, choose Edit, Cut and Edit, Paste to move the data to a new location. When you create a list, remember to select a location in the worksheet with enough room to expand the list.

Sorting and Filtering Data in a List

An Excel list provides you with flexibility so you can organize data to meet your needs. You can sort the list to display data in a certain order, just as you can sort table data in both Word and Access. You also can filter the list so it displays only certain records.

Sorting Data in a List

Excel sorts lists based on fields; it can use any field name you have created in the list as a sort field for reorganizing the list.

Note

To quickly sort a list, select a cell in the column by which you want to sort, then click the Sort Ascending or the Sort Descending button.

To sort a list, follow these steps:

1. Position the cell pointer in the list you want to sort. Or, if you want to sort only selected records in a list, highlight the records you want to sort.

2. Choose Data, Sort. The Sort dialog box appears, as shown in figure 18.6.

Fig. 18.6
You can sort a list based on multiple field names.

3. To prevent the column titles from being sorted with the rest of the list, choose Header Row in the My List Has section of the dialog box.

4. The Sort By text box is selected and displays the first field name from the list. Use the drop-down list box to replace the field name in this text box with the field name by which you want to sort. Choose the Ascending or Descending option for the order in which you want to sort the selected records.

5. To sort records using additional fields, press Tab or select the Then By text box and specify the field. Select the next Then By text box if you want to sort by a third field.

6. Choose OK or press Enter. Excel sorts the data in the list, as shown in figure 18.7.

Tip
If you perform an incorrect sort, choose Edit, Undo Sort or press Ctrl+Z immediately to reverse the sort and return to the original list.

III

Using Excel

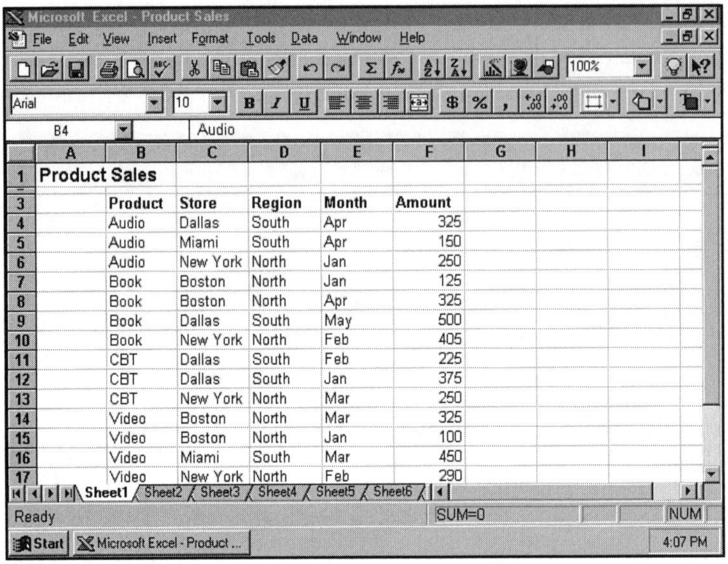

Fig. 18.7
The selected records are sorted according to the options in the Sort dialog box.

> **Note**
>
> If you select only certain data in your list, a Sort Warning appears. You can choose to Expand the selection or Continue with the current selection. If you don't expand, remember that only that section will be sorted, and not any of its related columns or rows.

Filtering Data in a List

When you need to work with a subset of data within the list, you can filter the list so only certain records appear. After you have filtered a list, you can modify the records, generate subtotals and grand totals, and copy the data to another area of the worksheet.

Tip
To remove the AutoFilter drop-down arrows from your list, choose Data, Filter, AutoFilter again.

When you filter a list, Excel displays only those records that meet the criteria; Excel hides the other records from view. Two methods are available for filtering the records in a list. You can use the AutoFilter command to quickly filter data in a list. Or, to filter data using additional criteria, you can use a custom AutoFilter.

Using AutoFilter To Filter Records

To filter a list with the AutoFilter command, follow these steps:

1. Select a cell in the list you want to filter.

2. Choose <u>D</u>ata, <u>F</u>ilter, Auto<u>F</u>ilter. Excel inserts drop-down arrows next to each column heading in your list, as illustrated in figure 18.8.

3. Click the drop-down arrow in the column that contains the data you want to display. Excel displays a listing of all the unique items in the column, as shown in figure 18.9.

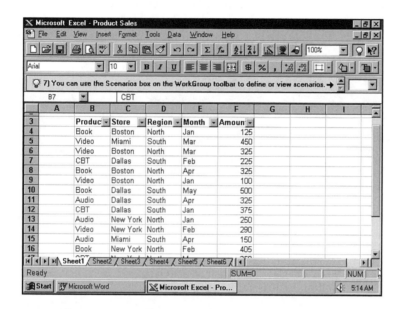

Fig. 18.8
Drop-down arrows appear next to each column title.

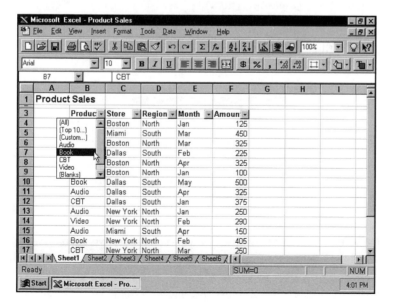

Fig. 18.9
Select the item you want to display from the drop-down list.

III

Using Excel

4. Select the item you want to display. Select Blanks to display empty cells or NonBlanks to display cells that have value.

5. Repeat steps 3 and 4 for each additional column you want to filter.

Excel displays only those records that meet the filter criteria. Excel displays in a different color the row headings of records that match.

To return the list to its original state, select All from the drop-down list of each column.

Creating a Custom AutoFilter

Note

To automatically filter the top (or bottom) 10 items in your list, select Top 10 from your AutoFilter list to open the Top 10 AutoFilter dialog box. In this dialog box, you can set criteria for filtering a certain number of items.

You can define a custom AutoFilter when the data you want to filter must meet a specified criteria.

To create a custom AutoFilter, follow these steps:

1. Select a cell in the list you want to filter.

2. Choose Data, Filter, AutoFilter.

3. Click the drop-down arrow in the column that contains the data you want to filter, and choose Custom. Excel displays the Custom AutoFilter dialog box, shown in figure 18.10.

Fig. 18.10
Define a custom filter in the Custom AutoFilter dialog box.

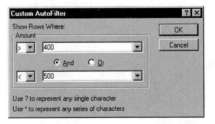

4. Click the arrow in the drop-down list of comparative operators, and select the comparative operator with which you want to compare the data. Enter the data you want to compare in the text box, or click the arrow to display a list of items and select an item.

5. To add a second set of criteria, choose <u>A</u>nd to indicate that the records must meet both sets of criteria. Choose <u>O</u>r to indicate that the records must match either set of criteria. Define the second set of criteria.

6. Choose OK or press Enter. Excel filters the list and displays those records that match the criteria (see fig. 18.11).

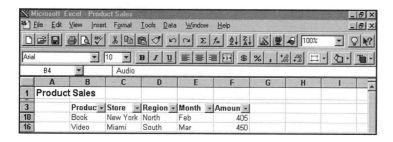

Fig. 18.11
The filtered list displaying records where Amount is greater than 400 but less than 500.

Troubleshooting

After sorting the database, Excel sorts the column titles along with the data in the list.

To prevent the column titles from sorting with the rest of the list, choose Header <u>R</u>ow in the My List Has section of the Sort dialog box.

I selected multiple filters, but my list doesn't display any records.

Select All from the AutoFilter drop-down list to redisplay the records. When you use multiple filters, each record in the list must contain each of the specified criteria. If a record contains one of the specified criteria but not the other, that record does not display.

Adding and Removing Subtotals

When you sort data in a list, Excel enables you to summarize the data with subtotals. When you summarize a list, Excel calculates subtotals based on subsets of the data and also calculates a grand total.

Creating Subtotals

To add subtotals to a list, follow these steps:

1. Sort the data according to the order in which you want to create subtotals. To generate subtotals based on sales region, for example, first sort the list by Sales Region.

2. Select a cell in the list you want to summarize.

3. Choose Data, Subtotals. The Subtotal dialog box appears, as shown in figure 18.12.

Fig. 18.12
You can generate subtotals for a list in the Subtotal dialog box.

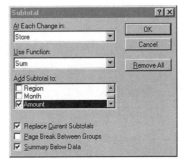

4. Select the group to define the subtotals. To generate automatic subtotals by store, for example, select the Store field from the At Each Change In drop-down list.

5. Select the Subtotal function from the Use Function drop-down list. To create subtotals, make sure that Sum is selected.

6. Choose the data you want to subtotal in the Add Subtotal To box. To subtotal the data found in the Amount field, for example, select Amount.

7. Press Enter or choose OK to add the subtotals to your list, as shown in figure 18.13.

> **Note**
>
> If your list is not sorted prior to selecting the Subtotal command, Excel creates a subtotal for each entry in the list. To prevent this occurrence, sort the list before you choose the command.

Hiding and Displaying Data in a Subtotaled List

When you add automatic subtotals to a list, Excel displays the list in Outline view. You can expand and contract the level of detail in the list to display only the subtotals and grand totals of data.

Figure 18.13 shows the list displayed in Outline view. The icons that appear along the left edge of the worksheet window enable you to expand and contract the level of detail.

Level 1,2,3 buttons

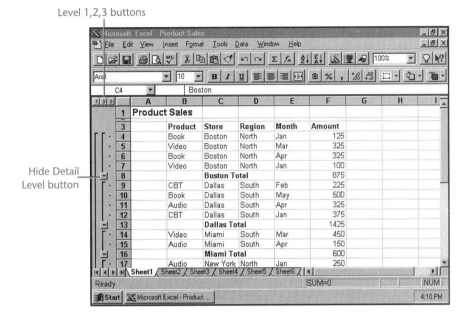

Hide Detail
Level button

To hide detail level, select a subtotal cell and click the Hide Detail Level button. Excel contracts the list to display the subtotal detail only (see fig. 18.14).

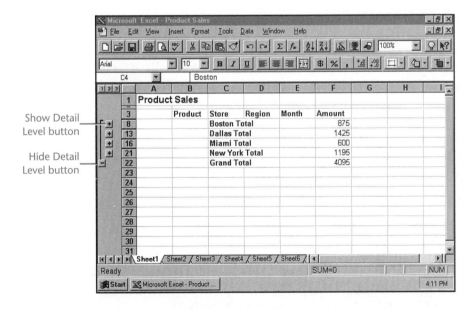

Show Detail
Level button

Hide Detail
Level button

To display a detail level, select a subtotal cell and click the Show Detail Level button. Excel expands the list to show the detail level.

Using Excel

Removing Subtotals from a List

To remove subtotal data from a list, select a cell in the subtotaled list and choose the Data, Subtotals command. Choose the Remove All button from the Subtotals dialog box.

Summarizing Data with Pivot Tables

Excel for Windows 95 includes a capability called the *pivot table* that enables you to quickly and easily summarize and compare data found within a list. When you want to summarize your data in another way, you only need to drag and drop fields to create a whole new report, without changing the structure of the data in your worksheets.

You use the automated PivotTable Wizard to create pivot tables in Excel. The PivotTable Wizard guides you step by step through the process of creating a pivot table. The PivotTable Wizard prompts you to define the pivot table information, using the fields defined in a list.

> **Note**
>
> Position the cell pointer in a list in your worksheet prior to choosing the PivotTable command. Excel pastes the range of the list in the Range text box. Click Next if that's the list you want to use.

Creating a Pivot Table with the PivotTable Wizard

When you create a pivot table from a list, the column titles in the list are used as Row, Column, and Page fields. The data in the columns becomes items in the pivot table. When the data in your list contains numeric items, Excel automatically uses the Sum function to calculate the values in the pivot table. If the data in your list contains text items, Excel uses the Count function to calculate a count of the source items in the pivot table.

Tip
Don't spend too much time deciding where to place the fields. You can always rearrange the fields after you add the pivot table to your worksheet.

To create a pivot table from a list in your worksheet, follow these steps:

1. Choose Data, PivotTable. Step 1 of the PivotTable Wizard appears, as shown in figure 18.15.

2. Specify the data you want to use in the Pivot Table. Select Microsoft Excel List or Database, and click the Next button. Step 2 of the PivotTable Wizard appears, as shown in figure 18.16.

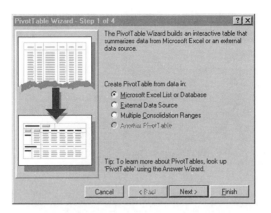

Fig. 18.15
Specify the data to
use for the pivot
table in Step 1 of
the PivotTable
Wizard.

Fig. 18.16
Specify the range
of data in Step 2 of
the PivotTable
Wizard.

3. Specify the location of the list in the <u>R</u>ange text box (type the range
   address or highlight the range with the mouse), and then click Next.
   Step 3 of the PivotTable Wizard appears, as shown in figure 18.17.

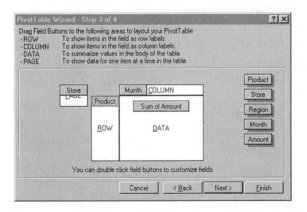

Fig. 18.17
Define the pivot
table layout in
Step 3 of the
PivotTable Wizard.

4. Define the layout of the pivot table by dragging the field names displayed on the right side of the dialog box to the Row, Column, or Page
   area. Fields placed in the <u>R</u>ow area appear in each row in the pivot
   table. Fields placed in the <u>C</u>olumn area appear in each column of the
   pivot table. Fields placed in the <u>P</u>age area filter the data shown in the
   pivot table.

5. Click Next to display the final step in the PivotTable Wizard (see fig. 18.18).

Fig. 18.18
Specify the location of the pivot table in Step 4 of the PivotTable Wizard.

6. Enter a cell reference in the PivotTable Starting Cell text box. If you leave this text box empty, Excel creates a new worksheet and adds the pivot table to it. In Step 4, you can also create a name for your pivot table in the PivotTable Name box as well as choose from the following options—Grand Totals for Columns, Grand Totals for Rows, Save Data With Table Layout, or AutoFormat Table.

7. Choose Finish. The PivotTable Wizard displays the results in a table on the worksheet (see fig. 18.19).

When you add a pivot table to the worksheet, Excel automatically displays the Query and Pivot toolbar. The toolbar contains buttons for the most frequently used pivot table commands (see fig. 18.19.)

Note

To display each page in the data table on a separate worksheet in the workbook, click the Show Pages button on the Query and Pivot toolbar.

Editing and Updating a Pivot Table

After you have added a pivot table to your worksheet, you can quickly rearrange the fields in the pivot table to display an entirely different view of your data. Each field in the list is represented by a shaded cell in the pivot table. Figure 18.20 shows the fields. You change the view of the data by dragging the fields to other areas in the pivot table.

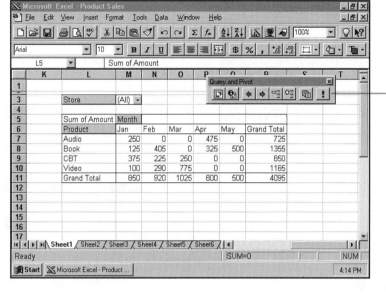

Fig. 18.19
This pivot table summarizes sales by Product, Store, and Month.

Query and Pivot toolbar

Page area field
Row area field
Column area field

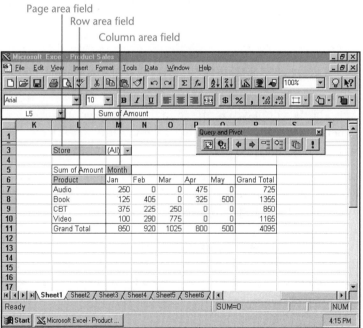

Fig. 18.20
Change the view in a pivot table by dragging fields to the Row, Column, and Page areas.

III

Rearranging a Pivot Table

To change the data displayed on the current page, click the drop-down arrow displayed in the Page area of the pivot table. A list of items for the current field appears. Select an item from the list to filter the data in the pivot table to display data for that item only (see fig. 18.21).

Fig. 18.21

The pivot table displays sales data for Boston sales only.

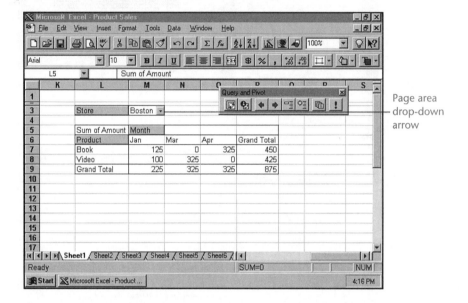

Page area drop-down arrow

To change the data displayed in the columns of the pivot table, drag a Row or Page field to the Column area of the pivot table. When you do, the pivot table displays a columnar view of the data (see fig. 18.22).

To change the data displayed in the rows of the pivot table, drag a Page or Column field to the Row area of the pivot table. The pivot table displays data in a Row field in each row (see fig. 18.23).

Adding and Removing Fields in a Pivot Table

You can change the data used in a pivot table by adding new fields to the pivot table or by removing fields that you no longer need. When you add a new field to the pivot table or delete an existing field, Excel automatically updates the pivot table.

> **Note**
>
> When you add and remove data from a pivot table, the action has no effect on the source data in the list.

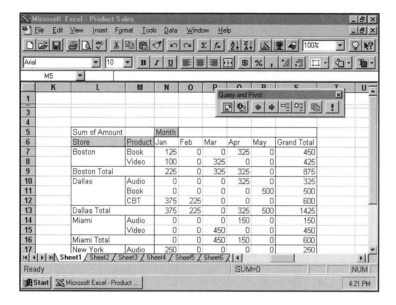

Fig. 18.22
The columns in
the pivot table
show sales by
Store and Month.

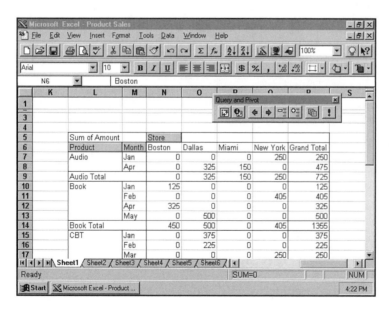

Fig. 18.23
The rows in the
pivot table show
sales by Product
and Month.

III

Using Excel

To add a field to the pivot table, follow these steps:

1. Position the cell pointer in the area of the pivot table where you want
to add a field. To add a field to the Row area, for example, select a cell
in the Row area of the pivot table.

2. Click the right mouse button to display the PivotTable shortcut menu and choose Add, Row Field.

3. The fields in the list used to generate the pivot table appear in a cascade menu. Select the field you want to add to the pivot table.

Figure 18.24 shows the pivot table after adding an additional field.

Fig. 18.24
The Region field is added to the pivot table layout.

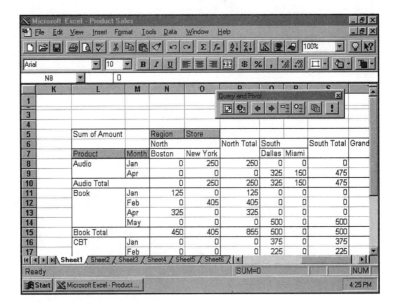

You can remove a pivot table field directly from the pivot table in the worksheet. To remove a field, drag it outside the pivot table area. Excel then removes the data from the table.

Modifying the Appearance of a Pivot Table

Excel provides special formatting commands for modifying the appearance of a pivot table. When you use these commands, Excel retains the format, even when you reorganize and recalculate the data in the pivot table.

You can change the numeric format of the data displayed in the data area, format an entire pivot table, and rename fields and items in the table.

> **Note**
>
> When you update a pivot table, Excel recalculates and reformats the data in the table. Therefore, you should avoid manually formatting the table.

Applying a Numeric Format

To change the numeric formatting in the data area of the pivot table, follow these steps:

1. Select a cell in the pivot table.

2. Choose <u>D</u>ata, PivotTable F<u>i</u>eld, or click the right mouse button and choose PivotTable Field from the shortcut menu. The PivotTable Field dialog box appears (see fig. 18.25).

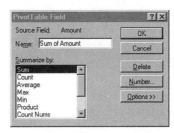

Fig. 18.25
The PivotTable Field dialog box offers several options for modifying the appearance of your pivot table.

3. Click the <u>N</u>umber button from the PivotTable Field dialog box. The Format Cells dialog box then appears (see fig. 18.26).

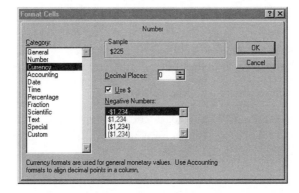

Fig. 18.26
Change the numeric format of cells in the Format Cells dialog box.

III

4. Select the numeric format you want to apply to the data area from the Category list.

5. Choose OK twice to return to the worksheet.

Formatting the Pivot Table

When you create a pivot table and select the AutoFormat Table check box in the PivotTable Wizard, Excel automatically formats the table for you. To use another format, select a cell in the pivot table and choose Format, AutoFormat. Select the format you want to use from the AutoFormat dialog box, and choose OK (see fig. 18.27).

Fig. 18.27
You can choose from several predefined formats in the AutoFormat dialog box.

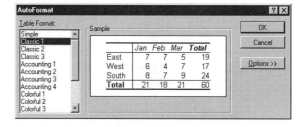

Changing the Calculation Used in a Pivot Table

When the items displayed in the data area of a pivot table are numeric, Excel automatically uses the Sum function to summarize the data in the list. When the items are text, Excel uses the Count function to summarize the text items. You can change the summary function a data field uses to calculate an average or maximum value, for example. You also can change the calculation type used in the data area.

Changing the Summary Function

To change the summary function the pivot table uses, follow these steps:

1. Select a cell in the data area of the pivot table.

2. Choose Data, PivotTable Field, or click the right mouse button and choose the PivotTable Field command from the shortcut menu.

3. In the Summarize By list box, select the function you want to use to summarize the data.

4. Choose OK or press Enter.

The results are shown in figure 18.28.

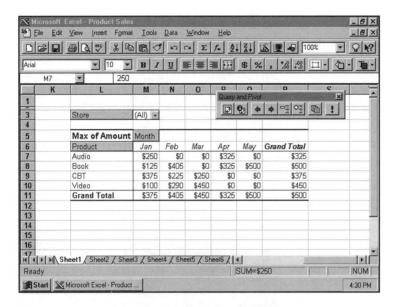

Fig. 18.28
The data area
displays the
maximum price.

Changing the Summary Type

Excel can calculate values used in the data area based on the values of other
cells. You can calculate the difference between items in a field, for example,
or calculate the items as percentages of the total.

To change the summary type used by the data field in the pivot table, follow
these steps:

1. Select a cell in the data area of the pivot table.

2. Choose Data, PivotTable Field, or click the right mouse button and
   choose the PivotTable Field command.

3. Click the Options button in the PivotTable field dialog box (see
   fig. 18.29).

4. Click the arrow in the Show Data As list box to display the calculation
   types available (see fig. 18.30) and choose your desired option.

5. Select the summary method you want to use from the Summarize By
   list box, and then select the fields and items you want to use.

6. Choose OK or press Enter.

III

Using Excel

Fig. 18.29
The PivotTable
Field dialog box
expands to display
the summary type
options.

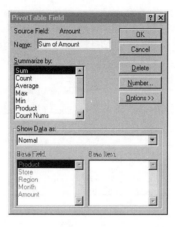

Fig. 18.30
The PivotTable
Field dialog box
displays the
calculation type
options.

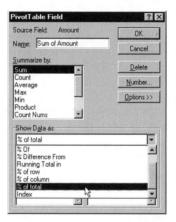

Refreshing Data in a Pivot Table

When you update the data in the source list in your worksheet, you must refresh the pivot table to include the new information. To refresh data in the pivot table, select any cell in the pivot table and choose Data, Refresh Data or click the right mouse button and choose the Refresh Data command from the shortcut menu.

If you add new records to your source list, you must redefine the source range used to create the pivot table, using the PivotTable Wizard.

To extend the source range to include additional records in the pivot table, follow these steps:

1. Select a cell in the pivot table.

2. Choose <u>D</u>ata, <u>P</u>ivotTable, or click the right mouse button and choose the PivotTable command from the shortcut menu.

   Excel displays Step 3 of the PivotTable Wizard.

3. Click <u>B</u>ack to display Step 2.

4. Respecify the source data range and click <u>F</u>inish. Excel adds the new records to the pivot table.

Forecasting with the Goal Seeker

Excel's Goal Seek command enables you to perform simple forecasting in your worksheets. You can find a specific value for a defined result by adjusting the value of other cells in the worksheet. For example, you can find out how many houses you need to sell to generate a total sales figure of $1.6 million. The benefit of using the Goal Seek command is that Excel uses the data known—in this case, the total sales amount and the amount per product—and performs the calculation instantaneously, without your having to calculate multiple iterations to come up with the answer.

To use the Goal Seeker, begin by setting up the problem and entering the known variable in the worksheet. The worksheet shown in figure 18.31 contains the data variable for a sales forecasting worksheet.

Tip

To proceed through the Goal Seeker one calculation at a time, click the Pause button and then click the Step button until you finish.

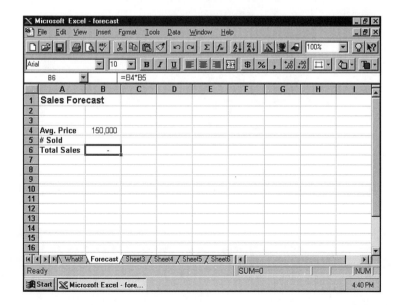

Fig. 18.31
Goal Seek adjusts the amount in cell B4 to meet the proposed sales amount.

III

Using Excel

To use the Goal Seeker, the variable you want to adjust must be a formula, and the formula must refer to the other cells in the worksheet. You specify the cell containing the formula as the Set Cell. Then the formula in the Set Cell refers to the cell to adjust. In the worksheet in figure 18.31, the Total Sales cell contains the formula =B4*B5. In this case, you know the average price of a house is $150,000. You want to see how many houses must be sold.

To forecast with the Goal Seeker, follow these steps:

1. Choose Tools, Goal Seek. The Goal Seek dialog box appears, as illustrated in figure 18.32.

Fig. 18.32
Indicate three input cells in the Goal Seek dialog box: the cell containing the formula, the goal you want to seek, and the cell to adjust.

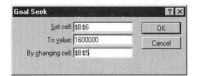

2. Specify the cell containing the formula as the Set Cell.

3. In the To Value text box, enter the value the cell must reach.

4. Specify the cell to adjust in the By Changing Cell text box.

5. Choose OK or press Enter after you specify the cells. Figure 18.33 shows the Goal Seek Status dialog box, which informs you of the status of the operation.

Fig. 18.33
The Goal Seek Status dialog box shows the status of the problem.

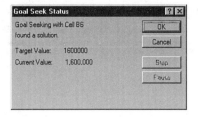

6. Choose OK or press Enter. Excel displays the results in the worksheet cells (see fig. 18.34).

Finding the Best Solution with Solver

The Goal Seek command enables you to generate values based on a single input cell. By contrast, the Solver add-in enables you to calculate the values needed to reach a particular result by adjusting the value of one or more cells. Furthermore, you can define constraints, which Solver must meet when generating the optimum solution.

In the case of the real estate agency determining the number of houses it must sell to meet its annual sales forecast, you must take other considerations into account besides the average price of the house and the goal to meet.

Loading the Solver Add-In

Before you can use the Solver, you must first load the Solver add-in into memory. When you installed Excel, you were given the option of installing the add-ins that ship with Excel. If you chose to install the add-ins, you can use the Tools, Add-Ins command to load Solver into memory. If you did not install the add-ins, you must do so before you can use Solver.

To load Solver into memory, follow these steps:

1. Choose Tools, Add-Ins. Figure 18.35 shows the currently installed Add-ins.

2. From the list of installed add-ins, select Solver Add-In.

3. Choose OK or press Enter. The Solver command appears in the Tools menu.

Fig. 18.35
The currently installed add-ins appear in the Add-Ins dialog box.

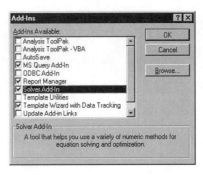

Setting Up the Problem

To use the Solver in your worksheets, you must first define the problem you need to solve. With Solver, each of the constraint cells are based on formulas. The changing values are the values to which each of the constraint cells refer. Therefore, to set up the problem, determine which of the cells will be used as the constraints and make sure they contain formulas. The worksheet shown in figure 18.36 illustrates a problem that the Solver will help solve.

Fig. 18.36
Solver will adjust the data in range B5:D5 until the total sales value in cell E8 equals $1.6 million.

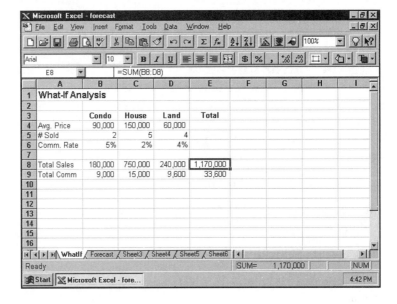

Running Solver

After you have set up the worksheet and located the cells to use, follow these steps to run Solver:

1. Choose Tools, Solver to start the Solver add-in. Figure 18.37 displays the Solver Parameters dialog box.

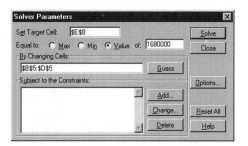

Fig. 18.37
Use the Solver
Parameters dialog
box to define the
optimal cell, the
cells to adjust, and
the constraints.

2. Indicate the cell that contains the formula you want to solve in the
   Set Target Cell text box.

3. Use the Equal To section of the dialog box to indicate the optimum
   value for the cell: choose the maximum value, minimum value, or a
   specific value. To meet a specific value, select the Value option and type
   the value in the text box.

4. In the By Changing Cells text box, indicate the cell or range of cells
   that the Solver will need to adjust to reach the optimum value.

5. To specify constraints, click the Add button to add each constraint to
   the problem. Figure 18.38 shows the Add Constraint dialog box.

Fig. 18.38
Specify the con-
straint to use for
the problem in the
Add Constraint
dialog box.

6. To create a constraint, follow these steps:

   ■ Specify the cell containing the formula on which the constraint
     is based in the Cell Reference text box.

   ■ Click the drop-down arrow to display the list of constraint
     operators and select the appropriate operator.

   ■ In the final text box, type the value the constraint must meet.

   ■ Choose the Add button to add the current constraint to the
     problem and create another, or choose OK to add the constraint
     and return to the Solver Parameters dialog box. The constraints
     you have defined appear in the Subject to the Constraints list box.

III

Using Excel

7. Choose <u>S</u>olve to start the Solver. The Solver begins calculating the optimal solutions. When Solver finds a solution, the Solver Results dialog box appears, as shown in figure 18.39.

Fig. 18.39
The Solver Results dialog box gives you options for using the solution that the Solver found.

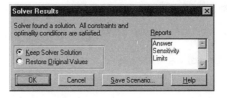

8. Excel adds the solutions to the worksheet. Choose <u>K</u>eep Solver Solution to use the offered solutions. Choose Restore <u>O</u>riginal Values to return to the original worksheet values. Figure 18.40 shows the worksheet after the Solver found the solutions for the problem.

Fig. 18.40
The results of the Solver show that two condos, eight houses, and five plots of land must be sold to generate $1.68 million in sales and $45,000 of commission.

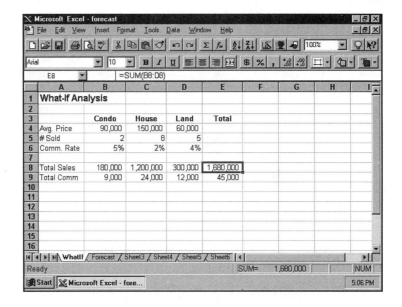

Creating Solver Reports

Solver enables you to generate reports summarizing the results of its solutions. You can create three types of reports:

■ *Answer.* Shows the original and final values for the target cell and the adjustable cells, as well as the status of each constraint.

■ *Sensitivity*. Shows the sensitivity of each element of the solution to changes in input cells or constraints.

■ *Limits*. Shows the upper and lower values of the adjustable cells within the specified constraints.

Tip
You can create more than one Solver report by pressing Ctrl while you select the report names.

To create a report, select the report from the list that appears in the Solver Results dialog box (refer to fig. 18.39). Choose OK. Excel creates the report in a separate sheet.

Performing What-If Analysis with Scenarios

For most spreadsheet users, a large portion of analysis involves performing what-if analysis. What effect does changing the average price of home sales have on my forecast? If I sell more condos than houses, will that have a negative impact on total sales?

◀ See "Working with Range Names," p. 383

The solution to each of these questions requires that input values in the worksheet change. When these values change, however, the original results also change, making it difficult to compare one outcome with another. To account for these changing variables, many users construct multiple data tables to test the outcome of each variable, comparing the original result to the new result.

One of the pitfalls in creating various solution tables is that monitoring the difference between the tables becomes increasingly difficult. When multiple people use the worksheet, keeping track of the ranges proves to be an exercise in frustration. Finally, as you create each additional table to test a scenario, the worksheet grows larger and more unwieldy with each addition.

Excel for Windows 95 provides a tool that enables you to track these scenarios with ease. The Scenario Manager feature provides a mechanism that saves each iteration of a problem and then enables you to view one solution at a time.

Creating a Scenario

Before you create a scenario, you must first identify the worksheet range that contains the data, as well as the input cells that will change for each scenario. The worksheet shown in figure 18.41 illustrates a sales worksheet that enables you to track the change in Total Sales and Total Commission, based on the number of properties sold.

Fig. 18.41

In this Sales
worksheet, you can
perform what-if
analysis using the
Sold cells.

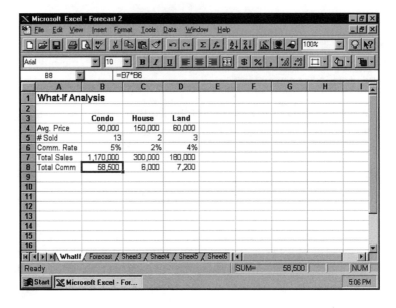

After you have identified the data, follow these steps to create a scenario:

1. Choose Tools, Scenarios. The Scenario Manager dialog box appears, as shown in figure 18.42.

Fig. 18.42

You use the
Scenario Manager
dialog box to
create scenarios.

2. Click the Add button to display the Add Scenario dialog box, as shown in figure 18.43.

3. Type a name for the scenario in the Scenario Name text box.

4. In the Changing Cells text box, indicate the cell or range of cells that will change for each scenario.

Fig. 18.43
The Add Scenario
dialog box enables
you to name the
scenario and
define the cells
that will change.

5. In the Comment field, Excel automatically enters your name and the
   date the scenario was created. Type additional information in the text
   box as necessary.

6. To prevent changes from being made to the cells in the worksheet,
   select the Prevent Changes option in the Protection section of the dialog box. To hide the cell data from view, select the Hide option.

7. Choose OK when you have finished defining the Scenario. Figure 18.44
   shows the Scenario Values dialog box, in which you enter the data for
   each of the cells in the scenario.

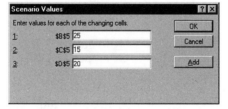

Fig. 18.44
Enter the data for
each of the cells
in the Scenario
Values dialog box.

III

Note

When creating scenarios, choose Insert, Name, Define to assign a name to
each cell in the scenario. Excel then uses those names in the Scenario Values
dialog box and in scenario reports.

Each of the displayed text boxes relates to each of the specified cells for
the scenario. The cell reference of each cell appears for reference.

8. Type the data that represents the data to be used for the scenario.

Using Excel

9. When you're finished, choose OK or press Enter. The Scenario Manager dialog box reappears, as shown in figure 18.45.

Fig. 18.45

The Scenario Manager dialog box displays each of the defined scenarios.

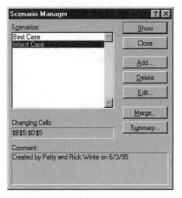

The name of the newly defined scenario appears in the Scenarios list box. When you select a scenario from the list, the Changing Cells field displays the cell addresses of the scenario. The Comments field displays the comments you entered to describe or annotate the scenario.

10. To view the scenario, select the scenario name from the list and click the Show button. Excel displays the values in each of the cells in the worksheet. If the dialog box prevents you from seeing the data, click and drag the title bar of the dialog box to move it out of the way.

11. At this point, you can click the Add button to define a new range of values as a scenario, or click the Edit button to edit the values used by the current scenario.

12. To return to the worksheet, click the Close button. Excel displays the values defined by the scenario in the worksheet.

Note

Click the Scenario button on the Workgroup toolbar to quickly switch between scenarios in the worksheet. To display the Workgroup toolbar, choose the View, Toolbars command, select Workgroup from the Toolbars list, and choose OK. To display a scenario, click the drop-down arrow in the Scenario button and select the scenario you want to view.

Editing and Deleting Scenarios

You can edit an existing scenario or delete a scenario altogether. When you edit a scenario, you can rename the scenario, specify other worksheet cells as the changing cells, and edit the comment. Furthermore, you can change the values defined by the scenario.

To edit a scenario, follow these steps:

1. Choose Tools, Scenarios to display the Scenario Manager dialog box. Select the scenario you want to edit from the Scenarios list box, and click the Edit button. Excel displays the Edit Scenario dialog box, shown in figure 18.46.

Fig. 18.46
Excel automatically adds the modification date to the Comment field.

2. Make any modifications necessary to the data shown in the text boxes, and choose OK. The Scenario Values dialog box opens.

3. Enter the new values and choose OK.

To delete a scenario, select the scenario you want to delete in the Scenario Manager dialog box and click the Delete button. Excel removes the scenario from the Scenario listing.

Summarizing Scenarios with Reports

Excel provides two methods of displaying scenarios in a concise report. The Scenario Summary creates a simple report in table form, showing the data for the changing cells and their effect on the results of formulas in a range. You also can generate a Pivot Table Summary from a multiple scenario set.

III

Using Excel

Creating a Summary Report

To create a summary report, follow these steps:

1. Choose Tools, Scenarios.

2. Click the Summary button to display the Scenario Summary dialog box, as shown in figure 18.47.

Fig. 18.47
Choose the type of summary report to create.

3. Choose Scenario Summary, if it is not already selected, from the Report Type area of the dialog box.

4. In the Result Cells text box, indicate the range of cells that contain formulas based on the input cells.

5. Choose OK. Excel displays a new sheet with a summary table of the scenario inputs and results, as illustrated in figure 18.48.

Fig. 18.48
This summary report shows current values as well as the Best Case and Worst Case scenarios and their results.

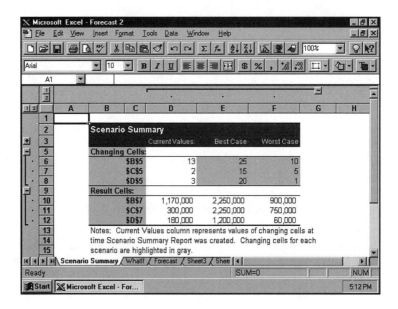

Creating a Scenario Pivot Table Report

To create a pivot table from the scenarios in your worksheet, follow these steps:

1. Choose Tools, Scenarios.

2. Click the Summary button.

3. In the Scenario Summary dialog box, select the Scenario PivotTable option.

4. In the Result Cells text box, indicate the range of cells that contain formulas based on the input cells.

5. Choose OK. Excel displays a new sheet with a pivot table of the scenario inputs and results, as illustrated in figure 18.49.

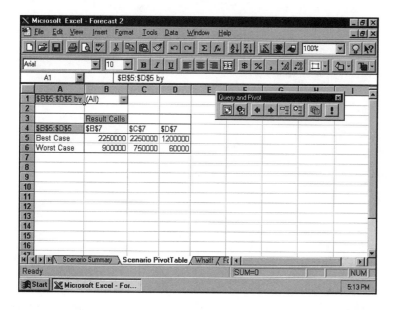

Fig. 18.49
A summary pivot table report showing scenarios by creator, Best Case, and Worst Case scenarios and their results.

You can manipulate the pivot table summary report as you would any pivot table. If you change a scenario, however, the pivot table is not updated. You must create a new pivot table to account for the changes.

Annotating Worksheets

◄ See "Anno-
tating Your
Work," p. 281

◄ See "Annotat-
ing Your
Worksheet,"
p. 382

When you use many formulas and functions for analysis in your worksheets, it can become difficult to remember exactly what each formula is calculating and what data it is using in its calculations. Excel enables you to annotate cells with notes so you can enter descriptive data about a formula. When you share your worksheets with other users, the notes provide a handy mechanism for describing the contents of a cell or for additional information.

Adding a Note

To annotate a cell, follow these steps:

1. Select the cell and choose Insert, Note. The Cell Note dialog box appears, as shown in figure 18.50.

Fig. 18.50
Annotate formulas
and other data in
your worksheets
with notes.

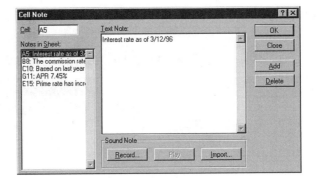

2. Enter the cell address (or point to it with the mouse) of the cell you want to annotate in the Cell text box.

3. Type the data of the note in the Text Note text box.

4. Click the Add button to add the note to the worksheet. The Notes in Sheet list box displays the cell address, as well as the first few words of the note.

5. Choose OK to return to the worksheet.

Viewing a Note

When a cell in the worksheet has a note attached to it, a small red box appears in the upper right corner of the cell. To display the contents of the note, pause the mouse pointer over the cell and the note, or cell tip will appear in a rectangular box. You can also select the cell and choose Insert, Note to view the note. The text of the note appears in the Text Note text box, shown in figure 18.51. Choose OK when you have finished viewing the note.

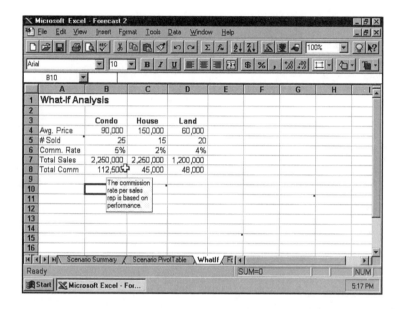

Fig. 18.51
The note attached to the current cell appears in the Text Note text box.

Note

If the note indicators do not appear in the worksheet, choose Tools, Options, select the View tab, choose the Note Indicator option in the Show portion of the dialog box, and choose OK.

Removing a Note

To remove a note from a worksheet cell, select the cell and choose Edit, Clear. Choose the Notes command from the cascade menu to delete the note from the cell.❖

Part IV

Using Multimedia in Microsoft Office

Chapter 19

Using Microsoft Graph

by Carman Minarik

A graph, or *chart*, is an effective tool for clearly presenting data in a way that provides instant visual impact. In other words, charts are easier to understand at a glance than are rows and columns of data. Because of the high impact that charts provide, Microsoft Office includes two tools for chart creation— Microsoft Excel's charting capabilities and Microsoft Graph version 5.0. Chapter 20, "Creating and Printing Excel Charts," describes Excel's charting functions, whereas this chapter is devoted to the use of Microsoft Graph to create charts in PowerPoint presentations and Word documents.

In this chapter, you learn to

- ◼ Start Microsoft Graph

- ◼ Enter and edit data in the Datasheet window

- ◼ Choose a chart type and add chart elements

- ◼ Choose colors, patterns, borders, and fonts

- ◼ Use Graph to edit an existing chart

Starting Microsoft Graph

Microsoft Graph is a charting application, separate from PowerPoint or Word, that is accessible from within PowerPoint or Word. When you start Graph, a sample chart appears in the current document, and a datasheet appears on top of the chart. The chart appears in the document as an object; the datasheet appears in a separate window with its own title bar. The datasheet and chart are displayed on-screen simultaneously and are dependent on each other. When you change data in the datasheet, Graph automatically updates the chart to reflect the new data.

> **Note**
>
> In PowerPoint and Microsoft Graph, the nomenclature for the terms *chart* and *graph* is confusing. Most commands use the word *chart*, except those that refer to graph placeholders. The word *chart* is used almost exclusively in this book, except when reference is made to the program Microsoft Graph. Also, when you create a new slide from AutoLayouts, one AutoLayout type is called Graph as well. In almost all other areas of PowerPoint (including Help), the word *chart* is used.

Microsoft Graph is a standalone application and is not, therefore, designed to run on its own. Instead, you access Graph from within another application such as Word or PowerPoint. Before accessing Microsoft Graph, then, you must be working in another application which supports embedded objects, such as PowerPoint or Word.

If you are working in Word, follow these steps to start Graph:

1. Position the insertion point at the desired location for the new chart.

2. Choose Insert, Object. In the Create New tab of the Object dialog box, select Microsoft Graph 5.0 from the Object Type list and click OK.

3. Microsoft Graph will start, and a chart and datasheet will appear.

▶ See "Creating a Presentation Using a Template," p. 579

If you are working in a PowerPoint presentation, follow these steps to start Graph:

1. Display the slide in which you want to insert a chart, or add a new slide to the presentation. The slide should either be blank or contain a placeholder for a chart.

2. As you learn in Chapter 25, "Creating, Saving, and Opening Presentations," whenever you add a new slide to a presentation, PowerPoint automatically displays the New Slide dialog box, in which you select a slide layout (see fig. 19.1). Three of the 24 available slide layouts include placeholders for graphs (indicated by pictures of bar graphs on the slide layout). Select a layout that includes a graph placeholder.

> **Note**
>
> If you access Microsoft Graph from a slide that contains objects or placeholders other than for a graph, the graph you create appears on top of other objects (such as text or drawn objects). To avoid obscuring other objects with a chart, select a blank slide layout or a slide layout that contains a graph placeholder before you access Microsoft Graph.

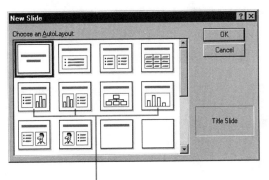

IV

Using Multimedia

Layouts with graph placeholder

Fig. 19.1
The New Slide
dialog box
includes three
layouts that
contain graph
placeholders.

PowerPoint displays a slide similar to the one shown in figure 19.2. A
dotted frame defines the boundaries of the graph placeholder. Inside
the placeholder is a small picture of a bar graph with the instruction
`Double click to add graph`.

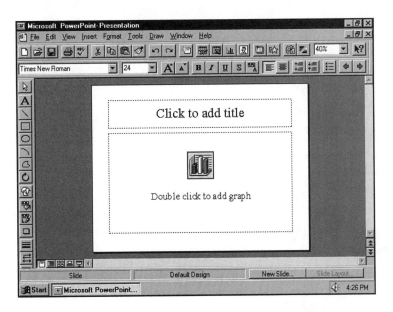

Fig. 19.2
Graph placehold-
ers contain a small
picture of a bar
graph.

3. Starting Microsoft Graph is as easy as the instructions indicate: `Double-click the graph placeholder`. After a few seconds, a sample bar chart
   appears in the graph placeholder in your slide. The datasheet appears
   on top of the chart in a separate window (see fig. 19.3). The sample data
   in the datasheet is used to create the sample bar chart.

Fig. 19.3

The chart and Datasheet window appear in PowerPoint.

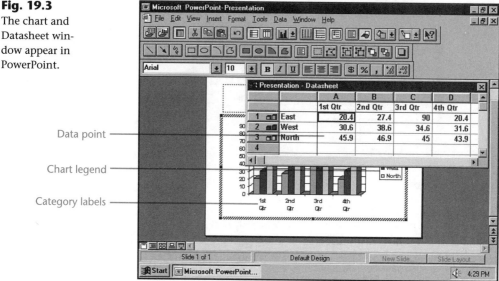

Data point

Chart legend

Category labels

4. To access Microsoft Graph when your slide is blank or does not contain a graph placeholder, simply click the Insert Graph button in the Standard toolbar, or choose Insert, Microsoft Graph. The sample chart and Datasheet window appear.

Troubleshooting

I don't want to use any of the PowerPoint AutoLayouts that include graphs. How can I add a graph to my slide and arrange other objects on the slide myself?

Choose the blank AutoLayout for your slide. When you create a chart using Microsoft Graph, the chart will be centered in the middle of the slide. You can resize the chart object, move it, and add other objects to the slide where you want them.

The Datasheet window covers up the chart. How can I see what the chart looks like?

The datasheet is contained in its own window, which has standard window controls. You can therefore move and resize the datasheet to make the chart visible.

I closed the Datasheet window in Microsoft Graph before I was finished using it. How can I redisplay it?

In Microsoft Graph, choose View, Datasheet, or click the View Datasheet button in the Graph toolbar.

Looking at the Microsoft Graph Menus and Toolbar

Notice in figure 19.3 that the PowerPoint menu and toolbars are replaced by the Graph menu and toolbars when Microsoft Graph is active. This menu and toolbar replacement takes place when Graph is started in Microsoft Word, as well. Graph's Standard, Drawing, and Formatting toolbars are displayed.

The buttons in Graph's Standard toolbar greatly simplify working with charts. For example, you can change the color or pattern of a set of bars in a bar chart by clicking the Color or Pattern button. This chapter emphasizes the use of these buttons, and it also explains menu command techniques. Table 19.1 explains the functions of the buttons in the Graph Standard toolbar.

Table 19.1	**Microsoft Graph's Standard Toolbar**	
Button	**Button Name**	**Purpose**
	Import Data	Imports data from another application into the Graph datasheet.
	Import Chart	Imports a chart from an Excel worksheet.
	View Datasheet	Displays or hides the datasheet for the current chart.
	Cut	Cuts selected objects.
	Copy	Copies selected objects to the Clipboard.
	Paste	Inserts the contents of the Clipboard.
	Undo	Reverses the last action taken.
	By Row	Causes Graph to use rows of data as data series.

Tip

If you forget the purpose of a toolbar button, position the mouse pointer on the button. A ToolTip appears with the button's name.

(continues)

Table 19.1 Continued		
Button	**Button Name**	**Purpose**
	By Column	Causes Graph to use columns of data as data series.
	Chart Type	Displays a drop-down list of chart types.
	Vertical Gridlines	Inserts/removes vertical gridlines into the current chart.
	Horizontal Gridlines	Inserts/removes horizontal gridlines into the current chart.
	Legend	Turns the chart legend on or off.
	Text Box	Inserts a new text box into a chart.
	Drawing	Displays or hides a Drawing toolbar for drawing objects in a chart.
	Color	Displays a drop-down fill-color palette.
	Pattern	Displays a drop-down color and pattern palette.

Working with the Datasheet

A Microsoft Graph datasheet, made up of rows and columns, is similar to a Microsoft Excel worksheet. Rows are numbered 1 through 3,999, and columns are labeled A, B, C...AA, AB, AC, and so on, through column EWU. The intersection of each row and column is a *cell*, in which you enter text or a number. Unlike an Excel worksheet, however, a Microsoft Graph datasheet cannot use formulas.

Understanding How Data Is Plotted

In figure 19.3, the sample datasheet shows three rows, or *series*, of data: East, West, and North. A *data series* contains individual *data points* that are plotted along the y-axis (vertical axis) of a chart as columns, lines, or pie slices. The first column of the datasheet contains the series names that identify each data series. These headings are translated to the chart's *legend*. The category labels in the first row of the datasheet (the row above row 1) represent *categories* of data. These column headings are translated to the x-axis (horizontal axis) of the chart as category labels. Thus, categories appear as groups in a chart.

Arranging Data by Rows or Columns

By default, Microsoft Graph assumes that data series appear in rows and that categories appear in columns, so Graph plots all charts accordingly. In figure 19.3, this series-in-rows arrangement emphasizes time spans: Qtr 1, Qtr 2, Qtr 3, and Qtr 4.

If you prefer, however, you can reverse the data series arrangement so that Graph uses columns as data series and rows as categories of data. In figure 19.4, the series-in-columns arrangement emphasizes regions—East, West, and North—rather than time spans. The arrangement you use depends on personal preference and on the data you want to emphasize. Unless otherwise indicated, the examples in this chapter use the series-in-rows arrangement.

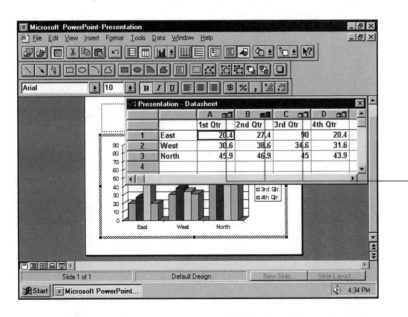

Fig. 19.4
Switching from series in rows to series in columns changes the way a chart is plotted.

These indicate that data series appear in columns

By glancing at the datasheet, you can tell whether rows or columns are represented as data series. When rows are plotted as the data series, miniature graphic representations of the chart type (such as bars or lines) appear next to the row headings. When columns are plotted as the data series, the graphics appear next to the column headings. You can see examples of these miniature graphics in figures 19.3 and 19.4.

  To specify the arrangement of data in a chart, click the By Row or By Column button in the Graph toolbar, or choose Data, Series in Rows or Series in Columns. You can switch back and forth between the two arrangements to decide which one represents your data most effectively.

Entering Data

When you're ready to enter data in the datasheet, type over the existing sample data. You can add more data to the datasheet by filling in blank rows and columns.

◀ See "Entering Data," p. 305

To highlight a cell in the datasheet, use the arrow keys or click a cell. The *active*, or highlighted, cell is outlined with a bold border. Any entry you type in a cell automatically replaces the current contents of a cell. To complete an entry, press Enter or press any of the arrow keys to move to another cell.

Editing Data

Editing refers to changes that you make in data after it is entered in the datasheet. You change data in a datasheet the same way you do in other spreadsheet programs. Editing includes changing individual entries; cutting, moving, and copying entries; and inserting and deleting rows and columns. Before you can edit cells, however, you must know how to select them.

Selecting Cells, Rows, and Columns

As you enter and edit data in the datasheet, you may want to work with a group of cells rather than just one. You might want to move a group of cells to a new location, for example. In the datasheet, you can select a range of cells, entire rows, or entire columns.

A *range* of cells is any rectangular group of cells. To select a range, click the cell in the top left corner of the range and drag the mouse to the cell in the bottom right corner of the range. The entire range is highlighted.

Selecting an entire row or column is accomplished by clicking the row or column heading. To select all cells in row 3, for example, click the row number 3; to select all cells in column D, click the column label D. You also can select multiple rows or columns by dragging the mouse across row and column headings.

◄ See "Selecting Cells and Ranges," p. 309

To cancel any selection, whether you have selected a range of cells or a group of columns or rows, press Esc or click any single cell.

Editing an Entry

Editing a cell entry enables you to change only selected characters in an entry. To edit a cell entry, double-click the cell. An insertion point appears in the cell. Use the standard text editing techniques to make the desired changes. When you finish editing, press Enter.

◄ See "Editing Worksheet Data," p. 321

Clearing Cells

Clearing refers to removing the contents, format, or both from cells. You clear cells to remove unwanted data from a datasheet.

The Clear command gives you the option of clearing the contents of a cell, the format of a cell, or both. *Contents* refers to the data contained in a cell, such as a number or text character. The *format* of the cell refers to a variety of characteristics, such as the font, number format, and so on.

To clear a cell, follow these steps:

1. Select the cell or cells you want to clear.

2. Choose Edit, Clear, or click the right mouse button and choose Clear from the shortcut menu. Select All to clear the contents and formats; Contents to clear the entries but retain the formatting; or Formats to clear the format assigned to the cell, but retain the contents.

Inserting and Deleting Rows and Columns

As you enter your own data into the datasheet, you may find it necessary to insert a new row or column, or to delete an existing row or column.

◄ See "Inserting and Deleting Columns, Rows, and Cells," p. 330

If you want to insert a row, select the row below the place where you want a new row. To insert a row above row 4, for example, select row 4. If you want to insert a column, select the column to the right of the place where you want the new column. To insert a new column to the left of column D, you would select column D. When you have selected the desired row or column, choose Insert, Cells, or Insert from the shortcut menu.

Microsoft Graph enables you to insert several rows or columns at once. Highlight the number of rows or columns you want to insert; then choose Insert, Cells. Microsoft Graph automatically inserts the number of rows or columns you highlighted.

To remove rows or columns from the datasheet, select the appropriate rows or columns; then choose Edit, Delete, or choose Delete from the shortcut menu.

Cutting, Moving, and Copying Data

◀ See "Moving around the Document," p. 75

Microsoft Graph enables you to rearrange data in the datasheet using several standard editing methods. Graph fully supports use of the Clipboard and the associated Edit menu commands Cut, Copy, and Paste.

◀ See "Copying Worksheet Data," p. 324

Excluding Rows or Columns

◀ See "Moving Worksheet Data," p. 328

Sometimes instead of deleting rows or columns, you simply want to exclude them from a chart. Suppose that your datasheet contains sales figures for 20 departments, but you want to plot the sales performance of only the first five departments. To plot this chart, you need to exclude rows 6 through 20.

To exclude rows or columns from a chart, follow these steps:

1. Select the rows or columns that you want to exclude from a chart.

2. Choose Data, Exclude Row/Col.

Tip
You can also double-click row or column headings to include or exclude rows or columns.

When you exclude cells from a chart, the entries in the cells are grayed, and the buttons for the row or column headings lose their three-dimensional attributes, as shown in figure 19.5. At the same time, the current chart is updated to reflect the excluded data.

To restore excluded cells to a chart, select the appropriate rows or columns and then choose Data, Include Row/Col. The normal attributes return to the entries in the cells, and the row and column heading buttons.

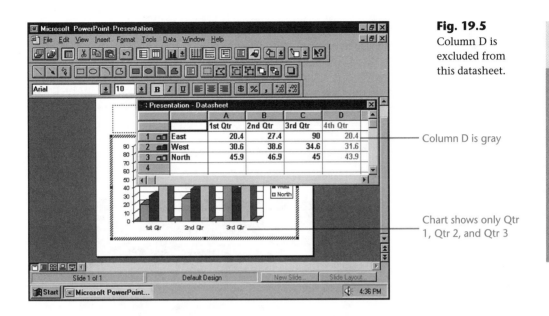

Fig. 19.5
Column D is excluded from this datasheet.

Column D is gray

Chart shows only Qtr 1, Qtr 2, and Qtr 3

Choosing a Chart Type

When you start Microsoft Graph, a three-dimensional column chart is created from the sample data in the datasheet. A column chart, however, is not the only type of chart you can create in Microsoft Graph. You also can create the following types of two-dimensional charts:

- Area
- Bar
- Column
- Line

- Pie
- Doughnut
- Radar
- Scatter

To create charts with depth, select any of the following three-dimensional chart types:

- Area
- Bar
- Column

- Line
- Pie
- Surface

▶ See "Changing a Chart Type," p. 488

You may choose any of these chart types by clicking the Chart Type button on the toolbar.

If you need additional charting options, use the Format Chart Type dialog box. In the dialog box, choose either the 2-D or 3-D option in the Chart Dimension area; then the available chart types appear below the Chart Dimension area.

Figure 19.6 displays three-dimensional chart types in the Chart Type dialog box.

Fig. 19.6
Select the chart type in the Chart Type dialog box.

Tip

If you double-click the kind of chart you want in the Chart Type dialog box, you select the default subtype for the chart and close the dialog box without choosing OK.

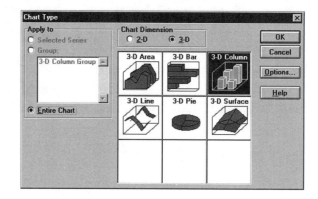

For most chart types, Microsoft Graph offers at least one or two variations, or *subtypes*. If you select the 3-D column chart type, for example, you then can select one of four subtypes.

To display a chart's subtypes, choose the Options button in the Chart Type dialog box. The Format 3-D Column Group dialog box appears as shown in figure 19.7. Choose the desired subtype and click OK.

Fig. 19.7
The Subtype tab displays subtypes and a sample chart using your data.

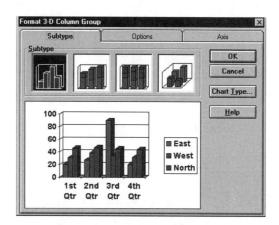

Using AutoFormats

AutoFormats are predefined formats that specify a chart type and subtype. AutoFormats also control other chart characteristics, such as color, font, and patterns. Using an AutoFormat can greatly reduce the time spent creating professional-looking charts.

To use an AutoFormat, follow these steps:

1. Choose Format, AutoFormat, or click the right mouse button and choose AutoFormat from the shortcut menu. The AutoFormat dialog box appears, as shown in figure 19.8.

    ▶ See "Using AutoFormats," p. 496

2. In the Formats Used area, select the Built-in option.

3. In the Galleries list, select a chart type.

4. In the Formats area, select a chart subtype.

5. Click OK. Microsoft Graph applies the AutoFormat to the current chart.

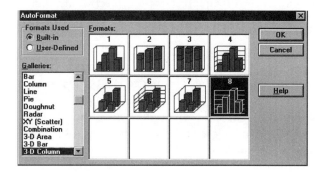

Fig. 19.8
Select a format in the AutoFormat dialog box.

Adding Visual Elements to a Chart

Charts often contain additional elements that make the chart easier to read and interpret. For example, you may want to add titles, a legend, axis labels, data labels, or gridlines.

▶ See "Enhancing a Chart," p. 491

Adding Titles

To add a chart title, x-axis title, or y-axis title, choose Insert, Titles, which displays the dialog box shown in figure 19.9.

Fig. 19.9
The Titles dialog box allows you to add titles to the named options.

> **Note**
>
> The options in the Titles dialog box vary, depending on the type of chart you are using.

To add titles to a chart, follow these steps:

1. Choose Insert, Titles, or click the right mouse button and choose Insert Titles from the shortcut menu. The Titles dialog box appears.

2. Check each title type you want to add to your chart.

3. Choose OK. Microsoft Graph adds text objects to the chart.

4. Click a text object to select it.

5. Enter the correct text for the title.

6. Click any blank area of the chart to deselect the text object.

If you add a title to a chart and then decide you don't want to use it, select the text object and then choose Edit, Clear; choose Clear from the shortcut menu; or press the Delete key.

Adding a Legend

A *legend* uses color-coded or pattern-coded boxes to identify the data series in a chart. Microsoft Graph automatically adds a legend to every new chart. If you prefer not to include a legend in a chart, you can remove or add the legend to the chart by clicking the Legend button on the Toolbar.

Adding Data Labels

Data labels mark the exact value or percentage represented by a data point. Data labels are often used in bar or column charts to pinpoint values when data points are close together. These labels also are commonly used in pie charts to identify the exact percentage represented by each pie slice.

To add data labels to a chart, follow these steps:

1. Choose Insert, Data Labels, or click the right mouse button and choose Insert Data Labels from the shortcut menu. The Data Labels dialog box appears (see fig. 19.10).

2. Select an option.

3. If you want the legend key to appear with the data label, check the Show Legend Key Next to Label check box.

4. Choose OK.

Fig. 19.10
Add data labels in this dialog box.

Adding Gridlines

Gridlines are horizontal and vertical lines that overlay a chart. These lines help you follow a point from the x- or y-axis to identify a data point's exact value. Gridlines are useful in large charts, charts that contain many data points, and charts in which data points are close together. The sample column chart that Microsoft Graph creates includes horizontal gridlines.

To turn gridlines on or off in a chart, follow these steps:

1. Choose Insert, Gridlines, or click the right mouse button and choose Insert Gridlines from the shortcut menu. The Gridlines dialog box appears, as shown in figure 19.11.

Fig. 19.11
Use the Gridlines dialog box to choose gridline options.

2. For each axis, turn major and minor gridlines on or off. Major gridlines appear at axis labels, and minor gridlines appear between axis labels.

3. Choose OK.

 You also can add or delete major gridlines by clicking the Vertical Gridlines and Horizontal Gridlines buttons on the Standard toolbar.

Specifying Colors, Patterns, Borders, Fonts, and Other Formatting

You can apply colors, patterns, and other formatting to almost any element in a chart. To change a chart element's formatting, follow these steps:

1. Double-click the element you want to change.

2. The Format [*element*] dialog box appears, as shown in figure 19.12.

Fig. 19.12
Use the Format [*element*] dialog box to change element attributes.

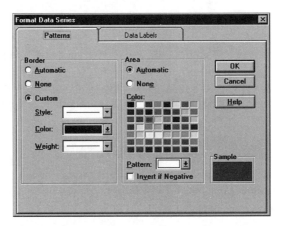

Tip
If you make a change to a chart format and don't like the results, you can choose Edit, Undo to change it back.

> **Note**
>
> The name of the Format dialog box varies depending on what element you are changing. If you are changing a data series, the [Element] is Data Series, and the dialog box is titled Format Data Series.

3. Select the desired options.

4. Look at the Sample box in the bottom right corner of the dialog box for a preview of the changes. Repeat steps 3 and 4 to change any additional colors or styles.

5. Choose OK.

The options available in the Format [*element*] dialog box change depending on the chart element you have selected. For example, figure 19.13 shows the Format [*element*] dialog box for a chart axis. Note the variety of formatting tabs available.

▶ See "Enhancing Text," p. 627

▶ See "Working with Colors and Line Styles," p. 632

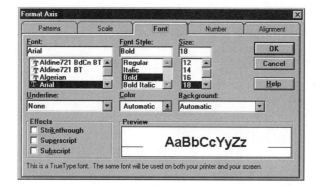

Fig. 19.13
The Format [*element*] dialog box allows many formatting options.

Inserting a Chart into a Document

While you are working in Microsoft Graph and making changes in your chart, the changes you make are updated in your document. As long as you continue working in Graph, the Graph menu bar and toolbars remain active. When you are finished creating your chart and want to return to your document, click any blank area of the document window outside the chart area. The chart becomes an object in the document, and the menus and toolbars of the application from which you launched Microsoft Graph return.

Editing a Chart

To edit an existing Microsoft Graph chart, double-click it in the document in which it appears. This launches Microsoft Graph and enables you to edit any attributes as previously discussed.❖

▶ See "Editing a Chart," p. 507

Chapter 20

Creating and Printing Excel Charts

by Carman Minarik and Jan Snyder

A chart is a graphic representation of worksheet data. Excel offers 15 types of charts to choose from—nine two-dimensional (2D) chart types and six three-dimensional (3D) chart types. By selecting from a number of built-in formats for each chart type or by adding custom formats, you can produce an unlimited number of charts.

Charts can be created on an existing worksheet or as a separate sheet within a workbook. If you change data represented by the chart, Excel updates the chart automatically. After creating a chart, you can add titles and gridlines.

In this chapter, you learn to

- Create a chart using the ChartWizard

- Enhance a chart

- Format a chart automatically

- Create a data map

- Print a chart

Creating a Chart with the ChartWizard

The ChartWizard provides an automated, step-by-step approach to creating charts from worksheet data. You can create the chart on the current worksheet, or you can place it on a new sheet in the current workbook. The following sections describe each step in the ChartWizard process.

Select the Data

The first step in creating a chart is to select the data on the worksheet. Although you can select data to be charted before or after the ChartWizard starts, the data is typically selected first. Use these guidelines when selecting data for a chart:

- Chart data must be placed in columns and rows, but does not need to be in adjacent columns and rows.

- Position labels to be used on a chart in the top rows and leftmost columns of the chart data.

- Select the labels along with the chart data.

- Select nonadjacent cells by holding down the Ctrl key.

Figure 20.1 illustrates sales data for three departments in a layout suitable for charting.

Fig. 20.1

Labels in row 3 and column A are selected along with chart data.

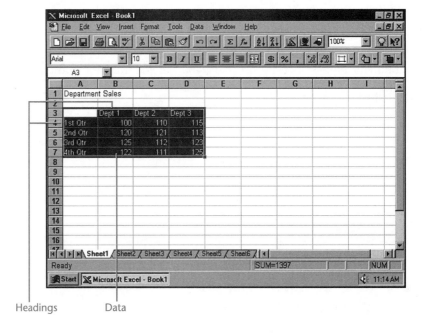

Headings   Data

When the data is selected, click the ChartWizard button. The mouse pointer changes to a plus sign with a chart object appearing as a subscript of the plus sign. Click and drag a box on the worksheet to indicate the position and size of the chart. You can also just click to place the top-left corner—Excel will automatically size the chart. Step 1 of the ChartWizard is displayed, as shown in figure 20.2.

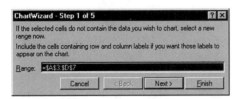

Fig. 20.2
Step 1 of the ChartWizard allows you to confirm or change the range of cells to be charted.

The Step 1 dialog box indicates which cell range or ranges will be charted. If the desired range is not indicated, you can enter or select a new range at this time by dragging in the worksheet. ChartWizard displays the range coordinates.

Tip
Don't worry about the exact size and position of the chart. You can resize and move it.

> **Note**
>
> The chart is linked to the cell range indicated in Step 1 of the ChartWizard. If data in this cell range changes, the chart is updated automatically.

To move from step to step in the ChartWizard, use the action buttons as defined in table 20.1.

Tip
You can create a chart on a separate sheet by choosing Insert, Chart, As New Sheet.

Table 20.1   ChartWizard Buttons

Choose This Button	To Do This
Next>	Move to the next step.
<Back	Return to the previous step.
Finish	Create a chart using the options selected so far and exit the ChartWizard.
Cancel	Cancel the ChartWizard and return to the worksheet.

If the data range indicated in the Step 1 dialog box is correct, click the Next button to move to the Step 2 dialog box.

Chart Type

Step 2 in the ChartWizard allows you to select a basic chart type. The Step 2 dialog box is shown in figure 20.3.

Fig. 20.3
Use this dialog box to select the desired chart type.

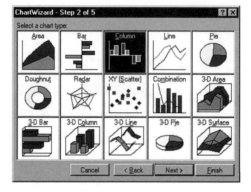

Some chart types work better for particular types of data. For example, a pie chart might be the best choice to view the percentage of total revenue produced by each department in a company. In the Department Sales example, a line or column chart will be used to compare departmental performance over time. Click the desired chart type from the 15 available options and then click the Next button.

Chart Format

◀ See "Choosing a Chart Type," p. 473

Step 3 in the ChartWizard lets you select a specific format for the chosen chart type. The Step 3 dialog box is shown in figure 20.4. This dialog box offers different options depending on which chart type you selected in the previous step.

Fig. 20.4
Select chart formatting on this dialog box.

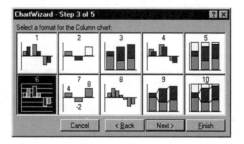

Click the desired chart format and then click the Next button.

Data Series

Step 4 of the ChartWizard shows a sample of the chart you are creating and allows you to select additional charting options.

The Data Series In options allow you to choose the orientation of the chart— that is, whether the data series (information that is represented on the chart as columns, lines, data points, and so on) is entered on the spreadsheet in rows or columns. Figure 20.5 shows the worksheet data charted using the Data Series In Columns option. Compare this figure to the sample chart in figure 20.6, which shows the appearance of the chart with the Data Series In Rows option selected. Notice that the data series names appear in the legend for each figure.

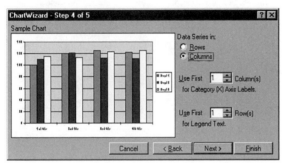

Fig. 20.5
This sample chart shows data from the worksheet charted with the data series in columns.

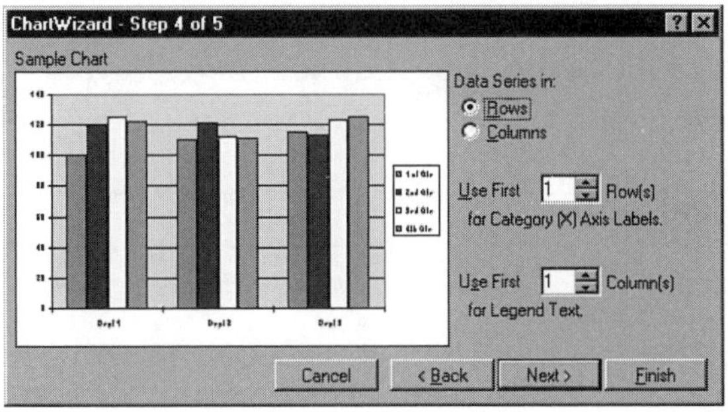

Fig. 20.6
Using the same worksheet data, this sample chart shows the data series in rows.

Step 4 of the ChartWizard also allows you to specify in two other ways how data should be used in the chart: for axis labels and for legend text (or for pie and doughnut charts, the chart title). In figure 20.5, ChartWizard is using the first column for the axis labels and the first row for legend text; therefore, the settings in the dialog box are

- Use First 1 column(s) for Category (X) Axis Labels
- Use First 1 Row(s) for Legend Text

If the worksheet data you selected does not include axis labels or legend text, the corresponding option should be set to 0 (zero). When you specify **0** for one of these options, the first row or column is displayed as a data series or data point. You can enter numbers for these options by typing or by using the up and down arrows to the right of each number.

Click the Next button to proceed to Step 5.

Titles and Legend

You can add titles to the chart and each of the axes, and you can add a legend in Step 5 of the ChartWizard, as shown in figure 20.7.

Fig. 20.7
Titles and a legend appear in the final ChartWizard dialog box.

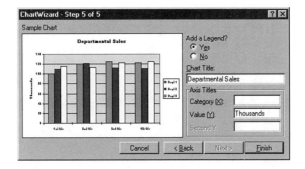

Choose the desired legend option, enter a chart title and axis titles if desired, and then click the Finish button to end the ChartWizard and create the chart. Figure 20.8 shows the completed chart embedded in the Excel worksheet.

Tip
The Chart toolbar appears automatically when you activate a chart. You can also right-click any toolbar and then choose Chart in the shortcut menu to display the Chart toolbar.

Troubleshooting

I want to access the chart commands when I embed a chart in my worksheet.

To access the chart commands for an embedded chart, you must double-click the chart you want to edit. When you do, Excel changes the menu commands in the Format and Insert menus to reflect commands for editing charts. When you create a chart in a separate chart sheet, the Insert and Format menus automatically contain these commands.

My chart has only one data series, so I do not want to display the legend with the chart.

To remove the legend box from a chart, select the chart and then click the Legend button in the Chart toolbar. Excel removes the legend box from the chart.

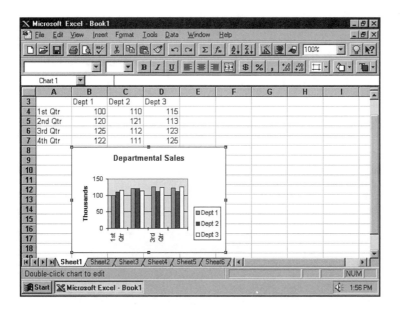

Fig. 20.8
ChartWizard places the finished chart in the worksheet.

Moving and Sizing a Chart Object

The initial size and shape of a completed chart is determined by the size of the area dragged after clicking the ChartWizard. Once a chart is created, you can make it larger or smaller or move it to a new location on the worksheet.

To size a chart, complete the following steps:

1. Select the chart by clicking it. Selection handles appear as small black handles around the chart.

2. Position the mouse pointer over a handle. The mouse pointer becomes a double-headed arrow.

   ◄ See "Selecting, Moving, and Resizing Objects," p. 364

3. Click and drag the handle to make the chart larger or smaller. To proportionally size the chart, hold down the Shift key while dragging one of the corner handles.

   ► See "Resizing and Scaling Objects," p. 612

Figure 20.9 shows the dotted lines that appear to indicate the increase or decrease as a chart is being resized. While you are resizing the chart, the pointer changes to a crosshair.

To move a chart to a new location on the worksheet, complete the following steps:

Fig. 20.9
The dotted lines
show the new size
as you drag a
handle to resize
a chart.

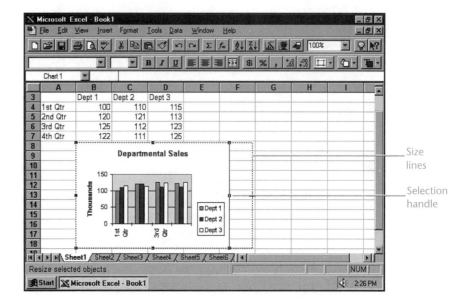

Size
lines

Selection
handle

Tip
To move an
object only hori-
zontally or verti-
cally, hold down
the Shift key
while dragging.

1. Select the chart.

2. Click inside the chart boundary (not on one of the handles) and drag
   the chart to a new position.

Changing a Chart Type

Tip
To keep an object
aligned with the
cell gridlines
when moving or
resizing, hold
down the Alt key.

Excel has options available for displaying data in various chart types, as discussed in the earlier section "Choosing a Chart Type." A completed chart of
any type can easily be changed to a different chart type at any time.

Complete these steps to change the chart type:

1. Select the chart.

2. Click the arrow next to the Chart Type button on the Chart toolbar.

3. Select the type of chart you want from the displayed palette (see
   fig. 20.10).

The chart type can also be changed using menu choices. Follow these steps:

1. Double-click the chart to activate it or choose Edit, Object. You should
   see a dashed border around the chart rather than the selection handles
   discussed earlier (see fig. 20.11).

Fig. 20.10
Choose a chart type from the palette.

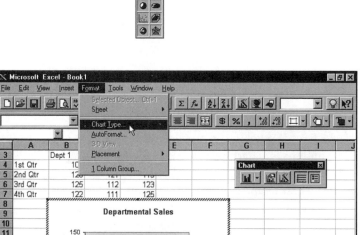

Fig. 20.11
The heavy dashed border indicates the chart has been activated.

Tip
To edit a chart, you also can click the right mouse button on the chart and choose Edit Object from the shortcut menu.

2. Choose F**o**rmat, Chart **T**ype to display the dialog box shown in figure 20.12.

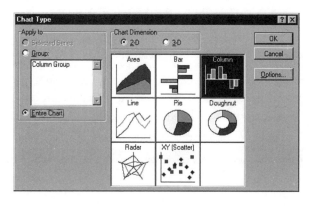

Fig. 20.12
Use the Chart Type dialog box to change the basic chart appearance.

3. Select either 2-D or 3-D in the Chart Dimension area.

4. Choose a chart type for the entire chart.

> **Note**
>
> If a single data series is selected in the chart, choose Selected Series. If the chart includes more than one chart type, choose the one you want to change in the Group list in the Chart Type dialog box.

5. Click OK.

Chart Type Options

Additional options for chart types are available by clicking the Options button in the Chart Type dialog box. The Format [Column Group] dialog box shown in figure 20.13 appears. (The exact name of the dialog box varies depending on your selection in the Chart Type dialog box.)

Fig. 20.13

Use the Format Column Group dialog box to choose a chart subtype for the column chart type.

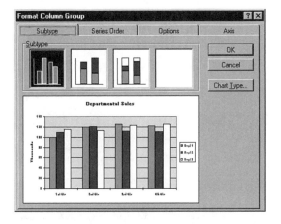

The tabs available in this dialog box include:

■ *Subtype tab*. Here you can choose the desired chart subtype. Different subtypes are available depending on the selected chart type. The subtypes for a column chart, as shown in figure 20.13, include regular column, stacked column, and percentage stacked column.

■ *Series Order tab*. Select this tab at the top of the dialog box to change the order in which the chart series are plotted.

■ *Options tab*. This tab displays varying controls dependent on the chart type. In the Department Sales example, column overlap and gaps between column groups can be changed using this tab.

■ *Axis tab*. Select this tab to specify which axis the column group is using in a multiple-axis chart.

Choose OK when you have finished making changes in all tabs. Excel applies the changes to your chart.

3-D View Options

When working with a 3-D chart type, additional controls for chart appearance are available by choosing Format, 3-D View. The dialog box shown in figure 20.14 opens.

Elevation controls

Rotation controls

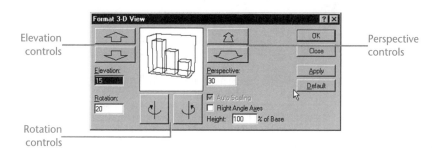

Perspective controls

Fig. 20.14

Use the Format 3-D View dialog box to change the angle, elevation, and perspective of the chart type.

Elevation controls the relative level at which the chart is viewed. Enter a value or use the arrow buttons to adjust the value.

Rotation controls the view angle of the chart around the vertical axis. Enter a rotation value in degrees, or click the rotation arrows to change the view angle.

Use the perspective controls to set the amount of depth in the chart view. Select the Right Angle Axes option to remove all perspective from the chart view.

To return to the standard 3-D view, click the Default button.

Enhancing a Chart

Nearly every part of an Excel chart can be formatted. This flexibility gives you complete control over the appearance of your chart. Before an individual chart item can be formatted, it must be selected. Chart items in an active

◄ See "Adding Visual Elements to a Chart," p. 475

chart can be easily selected with the mouse. Table 20.2 lists mouse procedures for selecting various items on an active chart.

Table 20.2 Selection Options	
To	**Do This**
Select an item	Click the chart item. Black handles appear around the edges or at the ends of the item.
Select a data series	Click any marker in the chart data series. Handles appear on each marker in the series.
Select a single data marker	Select the entire series, then click again on the desired marker. Handles appear around the edges of the item. The top (larger) handle can be dragged to change the value of a single marker.
Select gridlines	Click a gridline. Make sure the tip of the mouse pointer is exactly on the gridline.
Select an axis	Click the axis or the area containing the axis labels.
Select the legend	Click the legend. Click again to select an individual legend entry or legend key.
Select the entire plot area	Click any area in the plot area not occupied by another item, including gridlines.
Select the entire chart	Click anywhere outside the plot area not containing another item.

Note

A *marker* is an object that represents a data point in a chart. Bars, columns, pie wedges, and symbols are examples of markers. All the markers that belong to the same data series appear as the same shape, symbol, and color.

Each component of an Excel chart can be individually formatted to change its appearance, and other options. To display the formatting options available for a specific chart item, select the chart item and then press Ctrl+1 or choose Format, Selected [Object] (where [Object] is the name of the selected item). You can also double-click the desired chart item. Either of these methods will open a formatting dialog box with options relating to the selected chart item. Figure 20.15 shows an example of this dialog box. Note the tabs for various formatting options.

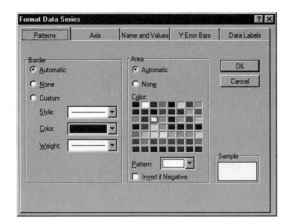

Fig. 20.15
The Format Data
Series dialog box
enables you to
change the appear-
ance of each data
series.

The following sections describe additional enhancement options available for
various chart components.

Data Labels

You can add data labels to a chart to annotate the chart elements. To add
data labels to a chart, follow these steps:

1. Double-click the chart you want to enhance, or activate the chart sheet.

2. Choose Insert, Data Labels, or click the right mouse button and then
   choose Insert, Data Labels from the shortcut menu. The Data Labels
   dialog box appears (see fig. 20.16).

Tip
You can add data
labels to a specific
data series by
selecting it before
choosing Insert,
Data Labels.

Fig. 20.16
Use the options in
the Data Labels
dialog box to
annotate the
chart elements.

3. Select the type of data labels you want to display.

4. Choose OK. Excel adds the data labels to each data series in the chart
   (see fig. 20.17).

> **Note**
>
> If the data markers appear crowded, you can resize the chart. Or change the font size or alignment of the data label by double-clicking them and making changes in the Format Data Labels dialog box.

Fig. 20.17
The actual data values appear above each marker.

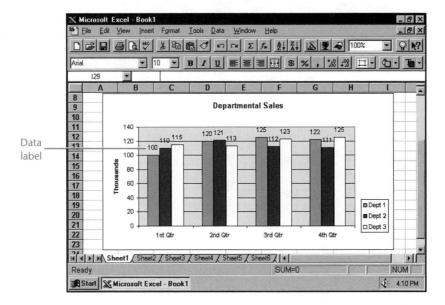

Data label

Gridlines

Gridlines are horizontal and vertical lines that overlay a chart. These lines help you follow a point from the x- or y-axis to identify a data point's exact value. Gridlines are useful in large charts, charts that contain many data points, and charts in which data points are close together.

Tip
To add horizontal gridlines to a chart, click the Horizontal Gridlines button. Click this button again to remove the gridlines.

To add gridlines to a chart, follow these steps:

1. Double-click the chart you want to enhance, or activate the chart sheet.

2. Choose the Insert, Gridlines, or click the right mouse button and then choose Insert Gridlines from the shortcut menu. The Gridlines dialog box appears (see fig. 20.18).

3. Select the type of gridlines you want to display.

   Major gridlines occur at the major intervals on the axis. Use minor gridlines if you also want gridlines between the major intervals on the axis.

4. Choose OK. Excel adds the gridlines to the chart (see fig. 20.19).

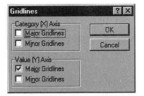

Fig. 20.18
Use this dialog box to add major and minor gridlines to a chart.

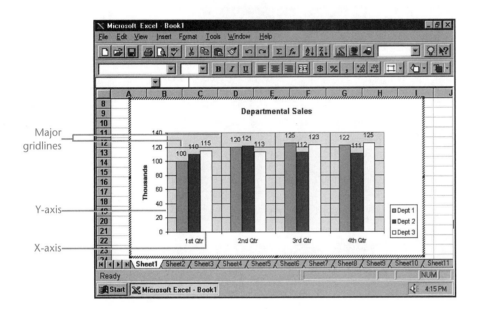

Fig. 20.19
Major gridlines have been added to both the x- and y-axes.

Chart Titles

Excel allows you to add an overall chart title and titles for each chart axis. To add titles to a chart, follow these steps:

1. Double-click the chart to which you want to add titles, or activate the chart sheet.

2. Choose Insert, Titles, or click the right mouse button and then choose Insert Titles from the shortcut menu. The Titles dialog box appears (see fig. 20.20).

Fig. 20.20
Use the Titles dialog box to add titles.

3. Select the chart and axis titles you want to add, and then choose OK. The dialog box closes, and you return to the chart, in which the title objects now appear.

4. Select each object to type the title text, and then press Enter. The titles appear in the chart (see fig. 20.21).

5. Press Esc to deselect the title objects.

Fig. 20.21
A chart can be enhanced with both a chart title and a y-axis title.

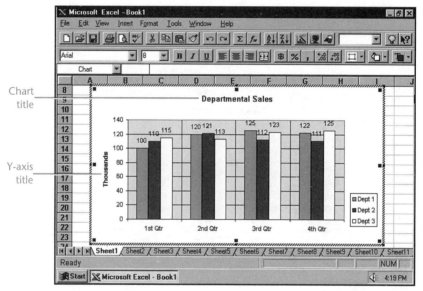

Using AutoFormats

Excel provides several built-in chart formats that you can use to enhance your charts. For each chart type, there are several autoformats that you can apply. In addition, you can create your own autoformats based on existing charts that you created.

To apply an autoformat to a chart, follow these steps:

1. Double-click the chart you want to format.

2. Choose Format, AutoFormat, or click the right mouse button and then choose AutoFormat from the shortcut menu. The AutoFormat dialog box appears (see fig. 20.22).

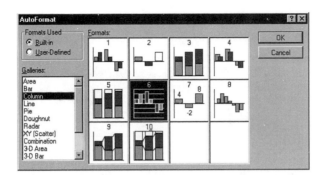

Fig. 20.22
Select a built-in
autoformat to
apply to a chart.

3. Choose the Built-In option to use one of Excel's built-in autoformats.

4. Select the type of chart you want from the Galleries list box.

5. Select the format you want to use from the Formats area, which gives you a sample of the appearance of formats available for the chart type selected in the Galleries list box.

6. Choose OK. Excel applies the autoformat to the chart.

To create a custom chart format, follow these steps:

1. Double-click the chart that contains the formats you want to define as a custom chart format, or activate the chart sheet.

2. Choose Format, AutoFormat, or click the right mouse button and then choose AutoFormat from the shortcut menu. The AutoFormat dialog box appears (refer to fig. 20.22).

3. Select the User-Defined option. After you select that option, the buttons in the dialog box change.

4. Choose the Customize button. The User-Defined AutoFormats dialog box appears (see fig. 20.23).

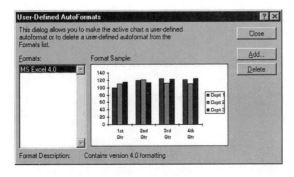

Fig. 20.23
Customized chart
formats appear in
the Format Sample
area.

5. Click the Add button. The Add Custom AutoFormat dialog box appears, as shown in figure 20.24.

Fig. 20.24
Enter a name
and description
for the custom
autoformat.

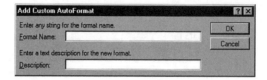

6. Enter a name for the autoformat in the Format Name text box and a description in the Description text box.

7. Choose OK. You return to the User-Defined AutoFormats dialog box, where the custom autoformat now appears in the Formats list (see fig. 20.25).

8. Choose Close.

Fig. 20.25
The custom
autoformat has
been added to the
Formats list.

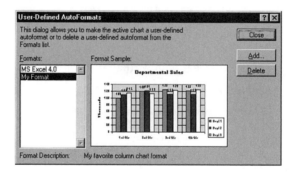

To apply a custom autoformat, follow these steps:

1. Double-click the chart you want to format, or activate the chart sheet.

Tip
To remove an
autoformat and
return to the de-
fault chart format,
click the Default
Chart button on
the Chart toolbar.

2. Choose Format, AutoFormat, or click the right mouse button and then choose AutoFormat from the shortcut menu. The AutoFormat dialog box appears.

3. Select the User-Defined option.

4. Select the format you want to use from the Formats list.

5. Choose Close.

Troubleshooting

When I use the AutoFormat command to change the chart type, I lose some of the formats from my chart.

When you choose Format, AutoFormat in a chart that has already been custom formatted, you lose some or all of the chart's formatting. To change the chart type of an existing chart—yet retain the custom formatting—choose Format, Chart Type, or click the Chart Type button and then select a chart type from the palette.

Creating a Data Map

Data Map is an impressive new feature of Excel that is useful for charting geographic data. You can create a map linked to your worksheet data, which provides an effective visual tool for analyzing demographic data. Suppose that you have sales figures for each state in the United States. Instead of comparing data in a simple bar chart, which may not be so simple for 50 states, use a data map to represent ranges of sales data on a color-coded or shaded map of the United States.

Setting Up the Data To Map

Included with Excel is an assortment of statistical data from which you can create maps. The Mapstats workbook, located in the Program Files\Common Files\Datamap\Data folder, contains demographic data that you can illustrate on maps. You can also embed a map based on data you enter in the worksheet.

A requirement for creating a Data Map is that geographic regions, such as country or state names, must be in one column in the range you select in the worksheet. The geographic data originates from any of the following maps: Australia, Canada, Europe, Mexico, North America, UK Standard Regions, US with AK & HI Insets, United States in North America, and World Countries.

Before you create a map, you need to prepare data in the worksheet by performing the following steps:

1. In a column of your worksheet, enter data that contains names or abbreviations of geographic regions, such as states, countries, or provinces.

   Excel also accepts numeric postal codes, which you should format as text to prevent loss of leading zeros.

> **Note**
>
> You must use geographic regions that the data map feature recognizes. You can find the correct spelling and abbreviations for the allowable region names in the Mapstats workbook.

◄ See "Copying Worksheet Data," p. 324

2. In another column, enter numeric values for each geographic region. Figure 20.26 shows sample data for creating a data map. This data was copied from three columns of the USA worksheet in the Mapstats workbook.

Fig. 20.26
Geographic regions and data are prepared in the worksheet before creating a map.

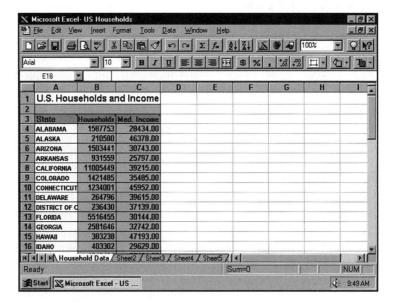

3. (Optional) Enter additional columns of numeric data related to each geographic region if you want to represent them on the map.

4. (Optional) Enter column headings at the top of each column of data if you want them to be automatically included in the legend on the map.

Plotting the Map

Similar to the method of creating an Excel chart, you first prepare your worksheet data, and then you create the map. After you prepare the geographic data you want to use in the data map, follow these steps:

1. Select the range of data to map, including the geographic regions, numeric values, and headings.

2. Choose Insert, Map. Or click the Map button on the Standard toolbar. The mouse pointer turns into a crosshair.

3. Drag on the worksheet where you want the map to appear—from the upper-left corner to the lower-right corner of the map area.

   You can change the size and position of the map later.

4. If Excel cannot create the map from the range you selected, a dialog box prompts for more information. For example, if you selected state names, the Multiple Maps Available dialog box appears (see fig. 20.27). Select the map you want and then click OK.

Tip
Create a blank map by selecting only a column of geographic regions.

Fig. 20.27
A dialog box appears if Excel needs more information to create the map.

Troubleshooting

When I try to create the map, I get the Unable to Create Map dialog box. What am I doing wrong?

If you have used a geographic name that Excel does not recognize, then Excel does not know which map to create. You can choose a map from the list and click OK, or choose Cancel to return to the worksheet and correct your data.

5. The map is displayed on the worksheet. The Data Map toolbar and menu appear, and the Data Map Control dialog box opens. Drag the dialog box (using its title bar) to another location if it is covering the map (see fig. 20.28).

6. In the Data Map Control dialog box, drag column buttons and format buttons to the white box. The buttons in the white box determine how data is presented on the map.

   When you drag a button, the mouse pointer turns into a hand pulling a handle. In figure 20.29, the Med. Income column button has been dragged into the white box. The Dot Density format button appears next to it automatically; however, you can drag another format button to replace the Dot Density button.

Tip
You can drag buttons out of the white box to remove features from the map. The mouse pointer turns into a recycling bin while you are dragging.

Fig. 20.28
Microsoft Data
Map transforms
your Excel menu
and toolbar when
a map is inserted
in the worksheet.

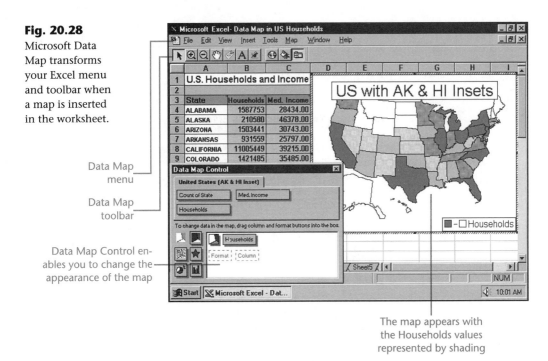

Data Map
menu

Data Map
toolbar

Data Map Control en-
ables you to change the
appearance of the map

The map appears with
the Households values
represented by shading

Fig. 20.29
Choose the
columns and
formats that will
appear on the map
by dragging them
in the Data Map
Control dialog
box.

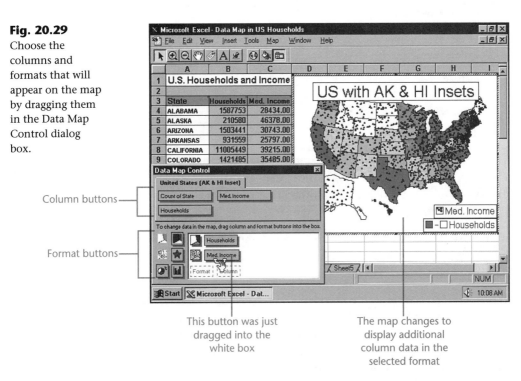

Column buttons

Format buttons

This button was just
dragged into the
white box

The map changes to
display additional
column data in the
selected format

Table 20.3 shows the format buttons you can choose in the Data Map Control dialog box:

Table 20.3 Format Buttons for Data Map Control	
Choose This Format Button	**To Produce This Effect**
Value Shading	Shades map features according to the numeric values.
Category Shading	Colors map features according to their category.
Dot Density	Shows numeric data as a quantity of small dots.
Graduated Symbol	Shows numeric data as various sizes of symbols.
Pie Chart	Displays a pie chart in each map area, which shows data for that area.
Column Chart	Displays a column chart in each map area, which shows data for that area.

7. Drag other column and format buttons as needed in the Data Map Control dialog box, and then close the dialog box by clicking its X button.

To redisplay the Data Map Control dialog box, click the Show/Hide Data Map Control button on the toolbar or choose <u>V</u>iew, Data Map <u>C</u>ontrol on the Data Map menu.

After you create a map, you probably will want to make a few changes to it. You do this by using options in the Data Map menu and toolbar, as described in the following section.

Customizing the Map

Data Map in Excel offers many ways for you to change the appearance of your map. If your map is not activated in Excel, you must double-click it to start Data Map, which displays the Data Map menu and toolbar. An activated map has a hatched border (refer to fig. 20.29).

Following are suggested changes for the map shown in figure 20.29. Each change is illustrated in figure 20.30:

Tip
The Data Map Help menu offers detailed topics on changing your map. Choose Help, Data Map Help Topics, Contents, How to Use Maps, and then find the feature you want to add, remove, or change.

■ Stretch the map frame by dragging its selection handles.

■ Change the title by double-clicking it to position the insertion point, and then edit the title. Change the font of the title by right-clicking the title. In the shortcut menu, choose Format Font, and then make selections in the Font dialog box.

■ Edit each legend by double-clicking to display the Edit Legend dialog box. Clear the Use Compact Format check box to show numeric information in the legend. You also can change the legend title and subtitle.

Click the Edit Legend Entries button if you want to change the numbers in the value ranges.

■ Notice that the legend in figure 20.30 shows six value ranges. The original map displayed five ranges (five shades on the map) and was changed by choosing Map, Value Shading Options and then changing the Number of value ranges. You also can change the Color of the shading in the Value Shading Options dialog box.

Fig. 20.30
You can make few or many changes to improve the readability of your map.

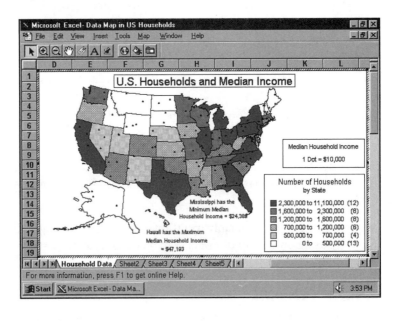

- Change the number of units represented by each dot by choosing Map, Dot Density Options. In figure 20.29, the dot density was 1,000. In figure 20.30, the dot density is 10,000 Units (or dollars), making the map less cluttered, although less precise in illustrating median household income.

- Resize a legend by clicking to select and then dragging the selection handles. Move a legend by selecting and then dragging the legend or its border.

- Reposition the map in its frame by clicking the Grabber button in the toolbar. Position the hand-shaped mouse pointer on the map and drag to relocate the map in its frame.

- Add text to the map by clicking the Add Text button on the toolbar. Click anywhere on the map to position the insertion point, and start typing. Press Enter to complete the text, or click elsewhere to type more text.

- Change to the normal mouse pointer by clicking the Select Objects button. Click text to select the text box, and then drag to reposition the text. Or right-click the text and choose Format Font to change its font.

As you can see in figure 20.30, a few changes can greatly enhance the basic map first created. Other changes you can make on maps are:

- Add map labels by clicking the Map Labels button on the toolbar. In the Map Labels dialog box, choose labels you want to use. To place state names on the map, for example, choose Map Feature Names. Or to put values on the map as labels, choose Values From and select the name of the column that contains the values. After you choose OK, the mouse pointer becomes a crosshair and labels appear as you point to map features. To make the label stick on the map, click where you want to place it. Click the Select Objects button when you finish placing map labels.

- Magnify an area of the map for closer viewing by clicking the Zoom In button and then clicking the part of the map that will become the center when the map is enlarged. Click the Zoom Out button and then click the map to shrink the map in the frame. To return the map to its full display, click the Display Entire button on the toolbar.

> ### Note
>
> If you change worksheet data that is represented in the map, an exclamation point appears in the upper-left corner of the map. You should refresh the map by clicking the Exclamation point button or by choosing Refresh from the Map menu.

- Delete titles, legends, added text, or map labels by selecting them and then pressing Delete.

- Add additional data to the map by choosing Insert, Data and specifying the worksheet range to include in the map.

- Add map pins to the map by clicking the Custom Pin Map button on the toolbar. Type a name for the pin map and click OK. Then click the location on the map where you want to place a map pin, type a description, and then press Enter.

- Add features such as airports, cities, lakes, and highways, by choosing Map, Add Features. In the Add Map Features dialog box, select features and then choose OK.

- Hide map features by choosing Map, Features. Clear the Visible check box next to the feature and then choose OK.

When you finish making changes to the map, click outside the map to close the Data Map program and return to the Excel worksheet. The map is embedded in the worksheet, and the Excel menus and toolbars return. Be sure to save the workbook—the map is saved with the workbook. To edit the map again, you must double-click it to activate it and to turn on Data Map features.

> ### Note
>
> Microsoft Data Map was developed by MapInfo Corporation as a subset of the MapInfo desktop mapping software system. You can purchase additional maps and demographic data files from MapInfo Corporation. See the Data Map Help topic "Purchasing additional maps" for more information. You can create maps in MapInfo and then use the maps with Excel after you first set up the map by running the Data Installer (Datainst.exe).

Editing a Chart

When you use the ChartWizard to create charts, Excel plots the data according to the selected worksheet range. You can use several commands to edit an existing chart. For example, you can delete a data series from a chart, add a new data series to a chart, and change the order in which the data series appear.

To delete a data series from a chart, select the data series you want to remove, and then press the Delete key. Excel removes the data series and redraws the chart to reflect the deletion.

To add a data series, follow these steps:

1. Double-click the chart to which you want to add new data, or switch to the chart sheet that contains the chart.

2. Choose Insert, New Data. The New Data dialog box appears.

3. Enter or select the range in the worksheet that contains the data you want to add.

4. Choose OK. Excel adds the data series to the chart.

To change the order of the data series, follow these steps:

1. Double-click the chart you want to modify, or switch to the chart sheet.

2. Choose Format, Chart Type, or click the right mouse button and then choose Chart Type from the shortcut menu. The Chart Type dialog box appears.

3. Choose the Options button.

4. Select the Series Order tab.

5. Select the series you want to change, and then choose the Move Up or Move Down button until the series are listed in the order you want.

6. Choose OK.

Printing Charts

When you print a worksheet that contains an embedded chart, the chart prints along with the other worksheet data, just as it is displayed on the screen. You can also print the chart only, without other worksheet data.

◄ See "Editing a Chart," p. 479

► See "Editing Objects," p. 546

◀ See "Printing
Worksheet
Data," p. 403

Printing charts in Excel is no different from printing any worksheet range. You can specify print options for charts in much the same way that you do for data that appears in the worksheet. You can, for example, specify the size of the chart and the printing quality, and preview the chart before printing.

Tip

To print the chart with the default print settings, click the Print button in the Standard toolbar.

Before you print a chart, you need to specify the chart print settings. Follow these steps:

1. Double-click the chart you want to print, or move to the chart sheet that contains the chart you want to print.

2. Choose File, Page Setup.

3. Select the Chart tab to view special options for printing charts. Figure 20.31 shows the printing options that are available for a chart.

Fig. 20.31

The Chart tab of the Page Setup dialog box includes options for printing charts.

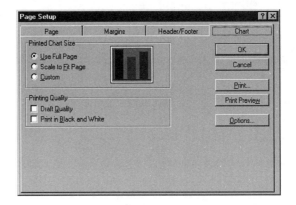

4. Select the appropriate chart size in the Printed Chart Size area of the dialog box.

5. To print the chart in black and white, select the Print in Black and White option in the Printing Quality area.

6. When you finish specifying the print settings, you can print the chart. Choose Print in the Page Setup dialog box. The Print dialog box appears.

7. Choose OK to accept the print settings and begin printing the chart.

IV

Troubleshooting

I want to print a chart that is embedded in a worksheet. But when I select the chart and choose File, Print, Excel prints the entire worksheet.

To print an embedded chart, first double-click the chart to select it, and then choose File, Print. Excel will print only the selected chart. To print an embedded chart along with a selected range of cells, you must highlight the range of worksheet cells that contain the data and the chart.

Chapter 21

Inserting Microsoft Visual Objects

by Carman Minarik

All the applications in the Microsoft Office package allow you to add objects of various types to your documents. You might, for example, add a company logo to a budget created in Excel, or a clip art image to a newsletter created in Word, or a sales chart to a slide in a PowerPoint presentation. These items, called *visual objects*, can add impact and appeal to your documents.

In this chapter, you learn to

■ Insert visual objects from menus and toolbars

■ Insert object files into your documents

■ Create new objects using applications such as Equation and WordArt

■ Move, resize, and manipulate objects that have been inserted into documents

Getting Started

Visual objects can be inserted in different ways, depending on the application in use and your own personal preferences. The following sections describe some of the methods used to insert visual objects.

Using the Insert Object Command

Primary access to the full range of visual objects is available through the Insert menu in any Office application. Choose Insert, Object to open the dialog box shown in figure 21.1.

Fig. 21.1
The Object dialog box allows you to choose the type of visual object you want to insert into your document.

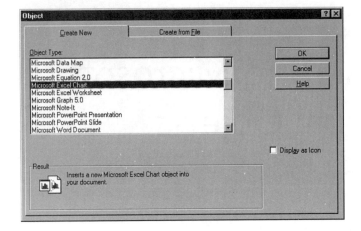

This dialog box has two tabs: Create New and Create from File. These represent the two options for adding a visual object to your document. You can create a new object, or use an object already created and saved as an existing file.

Also note the Display as Icon check box. If you select this option, the actual visual object you insert isn't displayed in your document. Instead, you see an icon representing the visual object type you inserted. If you double-click this icon, the actual object is displayed.

Using the Toolbar Buttons

Some Office applications provide toolbar buttons as an alternative method for inserting particular types of visual objects. Table 21.1 summarizes these buttons.

Table 21.1 Object Insertion Buttons		
Button	**Application**	**Function**
	Word	Inserts Excel worksheet
	PowerPoint	Inserts Word table
	PowerPoint	Inserts Excel worksheet

Button	Application	Function
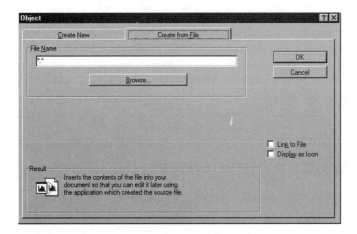	PowerPoint	Inserts Microsoft Graph chart
	PowerPoint	Inserts clip art image

IV

> **Note**
>
> The Object dialog box described earlier doesn't appear when you use a toolbar button to insert an object. Instead, you're taken directly to the screen for the object type you're inserting. This may be much faster than using the Insert menu, but you won't have the range of options available in the Object dialog box.

Fig. 21.2
The Create from File tab allows you to select the existing object file to insert.

Inserting an Object from a File

If you want to insert an existing object, such as a company logo created in WordArt, into your document, choose the Create from File tab in the Object dialog box. The dialog box changes as shown in figure 21.2.

If you know the path and file name for the object you wish to insert, you can type it in the File Name box. If you don't know the path and file name, click the Browse button. The Browse dialog box appears, as shown in figure 21.3.

Office applications can automatically update documents which contain inserted objects if the original object file is changed. Just click the Link to File check box in the Object dialog box.

► See "Inserting a New Object into Your Document," p. 711

Fig. 21.3
Click the <u>B</u>rowse button to open this dialog box. Select the desired file in the file list.

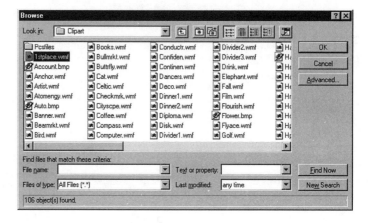

Troubleshooting

I want to add my company logo without looking for the file every time.

You can add the logo file as an AutoCorrect entry by selecting the inserted graphic and choosing <u>T</u>ools, <u>A</u>utoCorrect. In the AutoCorrect dialog box, the file name of your selected clip art appears in the <u>W</u>ith box. Type a text entry, such as **ourlogo** in the <u>R</u>eplace box. Click <u>A</u>dd to put the entry on the list. Be sure the Replace <u>T</u>ext as You Type check box is selected, and then choose OK. Now, when you type **ourlogo**, the text will be replaced by the graphic.

Creating a New Object

The <u>C</u>reate New tab in the Object dialog box allows you to create a new visual object for insertion into your document. The <u>O</u>bject Type list displays all available visual object options. The choices available in this list vary depending on the software installed on your computer. For example, if you don't have Microsoft Excel installed on your system, the options for Microsoft Excel Chart and Microsoft Excel Worksheet won't appear in the <u>O</u>bject Type list.

The actual steps used to insert an object vary with the type of object selected for insertion. Some objects, such as clip art, require only a simple selection process to insert. Other object types, such as WordArt and Equation objects, require more complex operations. The following sections describe some of the commonly used visual object types and the steps used to create and insert them.

Using Microsoft ClipArt Gallery 2.0

One of the best ways to spice up a document is to insert a clip-art drawing. The ClipArt Gallery contains many drawings that cover a wide range of topics. When you choose Microsoft ClipArt Gallery in the Object dialog box, the Microsoft ClipArt Gallery 2.0 application window appears. Figure 21.4 shows the window maximized.

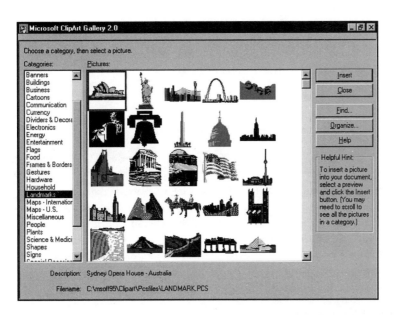

Fig. 21.4
The ClipArt Gallery window allows you to choose from a variety of pictures.

> **Note**
>
> The first time you attempt to access clip art, you may be asked whether you want to add clip-art files from Office. Responding Yes to this question makes the clip-art files available for you to insert into your documents.

A list of categories appears at the top of the ClipArt Gallery window. The box to the right of the category list displays a sample of each clip-art file in the current category. Use the scroll bar, Page Up/Page Down keys, or the arrow keys to see each picture in a category. If you prefer to scroll through the entire selection of clip-art files, select the (All Categories) option in the Categories list box.

To add a clip-art drawing to your document, follow these steps:

1. Indicate the desired location for the clip-art object:

Tip
In PowerPoint, you can click the Insert Clip Art button on the Standard toolbar to open the ClipArt Gallery.

IV

Using Multimedia

Tip
Click the Organize
button to add or
update pictures.
To delete a picture
from the Gallery,
right-click the
picture and choose
Delete Picture.

- In PowerPoint, display the slide you want to insert clip art into.

- In Word, position the insertion point where the clip art should be inserted.

- In Excel, activate the cell that will be the upper left corner of the inserted clip art.

2. Choose Insert, Clip Art. The Microsoft ClipArt Gallery 2.0 window appears.

3. Select a category in the Categories list.

4. Select a picture, and then choose Insert.

The selected picture appears in your document.

▶ See "Inserting
Clip-Art
Pictures,"
p. 598

> **Note**
>
> With the new AutoClipArt feature of PowerPoint, you can add suggested clip-art images based on what you type. Choose Tools, AutoClipArt to open the AutoClipArt dialog box. Click the View ClipArt button to view the clip-art that PowerPoint suggests for your presentation based on the word associated with the clip-art. To run AutoClipArt in the background, select the Run in Background check box.

Troubleshooting

I get an error when I try to run ClipArt Gallery and then the window appears with no categories and no pictures.

You haven't properly installed ClipArt Gallery. Run Office Setup from your original disks or CD to install the program, located in PROGRAM FILES\COMMON FILES.

I want to add clip-art files from other programs to the ClipArt Gallery.

To do this, click the Organize button in the ClipArt Gallery window. Choose Add Pictures and select the clip-art file you want to add in the Add Pictures to Gallery dialog box. Click Open. When the Picture Properties dialog box appears, enter a Description and select a check box in the Categories list. Or choose a New Category. Choose OK to add the picture to the ClipArt Gallery.

Using Microsoft Equation 2.0

Microsoft Equation 2.0 is a supplemental application that is a part of Microsoft Office. Equation provides you with typographical capabilities for complex mathematical equations. If you need to incorporate any type of mathematical expression into your documents, Equation provides the tools for creating it.

> **Note**
>
> Microsoft Equation doesn't *solve* equations. It's designed to allow you to represent equations typographically on a page.

When you choose Microsoft Equation 2.0 in the Object dialog box, the current application's menus and toolbars are temporarily replaced by Equation's menus and toolbar.

You'll use the toolbar for most of your work in Equation. The top row of the toolbar contains individual mathematical symbols, while the bottom row contains templates for common mathematical expressions. Each button on the toolbar opens a palette of options. Figure 21.5 shows Equation's toolbar.

Equation also allows you to type text, numbers, and symbols directly into the expression. Any combination of templates, symbols, and typing can be used to create your mathematical expression.

As an example of a use of Equation 2.0, suppose you're writing an essay on the history of mathematics. You want to include the fundamental theorem of calculus in the essay, as shown in figure 21.6.

$$\int_a^b f(x)\,dx$$

Tip

Microsoft Equation automatically formats text and numbers you type to match commonly used mathematical conventions. You can change the formatting of selected text, however, by choosing <u>S</u>tyle, <u>O</u>ther.

IV

Using Multimedia

Fig. 21.5
The Microsoft Equation 2.0 toolbar assists you in creating complex equations.

Fig. 21.6
The fundamental theorem of calculus is easier to construct than to understand.

Follow these steps to create such an expression:

1. Indicate the desired location for the Equation object:

   - In PowerPoint, display the slide into which you want to insert the equation.

   - In Word, position the insertion point where the equation should be inserted.

   - In Excel, activate the cell that will be the upper left corner of the inserted equation.

2. Choose Insert, Object, then click Microsoft Equation 2.0 in the Object dialog box. When you click OK, the Equation menu and toolbar open.

3. Open the integral palette on the toolbar and select the desired template as shown in figure 21.7.

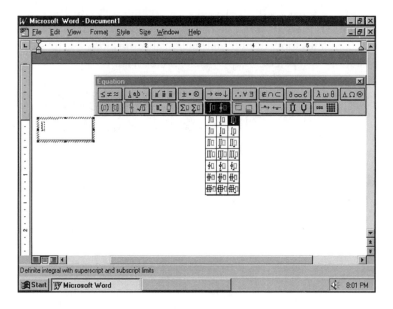

4. Figure 21.8 shows the resulting template. Notice the insertion point position within the template. Type the character **f**.

5. Choose the parentheses template as shown in figure 21.9 to achieve the expression shown in figure 21.10. Note the position of the insertion point, inside the parentheses.

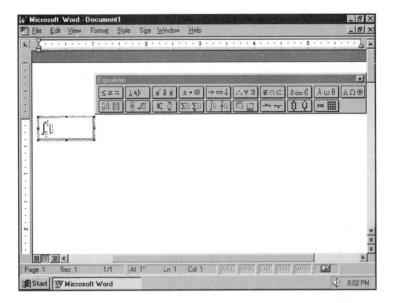

Fig. 21.8
The selected integral template appears in a Word document.

IV

Using Multimedia

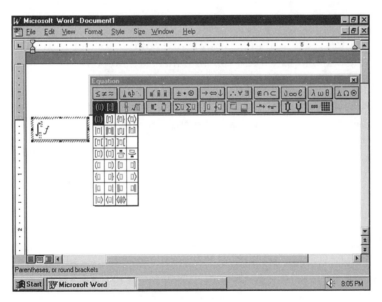

Fig. 21.9
Many options for mathematical fences such as parentheses are available in Equation 2.0.

Fig. 21.10

A parentheses
template is added
to the expression.

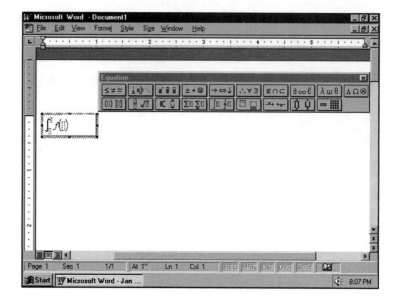

6. Type the character **x**.

7. The Tab key is used to move from one position to another within an Equation template. Press Tab until the insertion point is positioned after the right parenthesis. Type the characters **dx**.

8. Press the Tab key to move the insertion point to the upper- and lower-limit fields, entering the **a** and **b** characters in the appropriate fields.

9. Click anywhere outside the Equation object border to close the Equation toolbar and menu.

Using Microsoft Organization Chart 2.0

Microsoft Organization Chart 2.0 is a separate application program bundled with Microsoft Office, specifically designed to create organization charts. The chart is the customary organization tree of a company or department, and can be very basic or branch out with complex relationships. Elements of an organizational chart can be customized with different box and line styles and color fills, and boxes of various kinds can be added with the click of a mouse.

To create an organization chart, follow these steps:

1. Indicate the desired location for the Organization Chart object:

- In PowerPoint, display the slide into which you want to insert the object.

- In Word, position the insertion point where the object should be inserted.

- In Excel, activate the cell that will be the upper left corner of the inserted object.

2. Choose Insert, Object, then click MS Organization Chart 2.0 in the Object dialog box. When you click OK, the Microsoft Organization Chart window appears (see fig. 21.11)

    In Excel, you must double-click the inserted object to open the Organization Chart window.

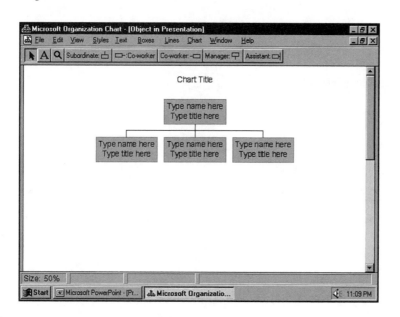

Fig. 21.11
A basic organization chart appears, ready for editing.

3. Click the Chart Title and type a title for your chart. You can press Enter to type more than one centered line.

4. Enter text in boxes by clicking the box and typing. The boxes prompt you for a name, title, and comments; however, you can type anything you want to appear in each box.

    Press Esc or click outside of a box to complete it.

Tip
In PowerPoint, you can choose the Organization Chart in Autolayout on a new slide, and then double-click the slide to open Microsoft Organization Chart.

Tip
Create multiple boxes of the same type by holding down the Shift key when you click the box tool. Click the Selection Arrow tool to deactivate the box tool when you have finished creating boxes.

5. To create a new box, click the box tool for the type of box you want, and then click the box in the chart where you want to attach the new box.

The box tools are in the toolbar; each tool illustrates the type of box object it creates (see fig. 21.12).

Co-worker   Manager box   Chart Title   New boxes are selected
left box   from the toolbar

Fig. 21.12
The Organization
Chart takes the
shape of the
elements you
choose.

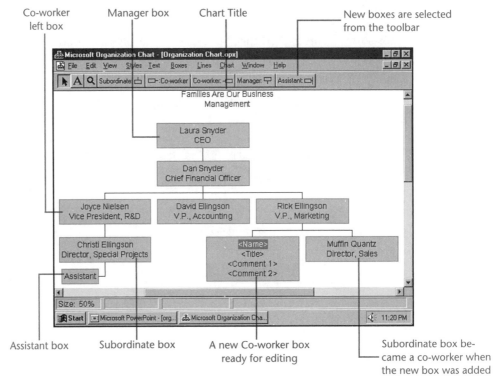

Assistant box   Subordinate box   A new Co-worker box   Subordinate box be-
                                    ready for editing   came a co-worker when
                                                               the new box was added

Tip
To choose all
boxes to apply
formatting, choose
Edit, Select All, or
press Ctrl+A.

▶ See "Inserting
an Organiza-
tion Chart,"
p. 602

6. Continue to add boxes and text in the structure you want. You can use the Styles menu to add groups of boxes. Figure 21.12 illustrates some of the organization chart elements.

7. Change the appearance of the text and boxes by selecting the objects and choosing options from the Text and Boxes menus. Change the background color by choosing Background Color in the Chart menu.

8. Choose File, Update to update the current organization chart in the document, slide, or worksheet.

9. Choose File, Exit and Return to close the Microsoft Organization Chart window and return to Word, PowerPoint, or Excel.

Using Microsoft WordArt 2.0

Office comes with a supplementary application called WordArt 2.0 that allows you to create interesting text effects to enhance newsletters, flyers, brochures, and so on. Using WordArt, you can arrange any TrueType or Adobe Type Manager (ATM) font into a variety of shapes and alignments, add 3-D effects and more.

To create a special effect with WordArt, complete the following steps:

1. Indicate the desired location for the WordArt object:

    ■ In PowerPoint, display the slide into which you want to insert the object.

    ■ In Word, position the insertion point where the object should be inserted.

    ■ In Excel, activate the cell that will be the upper left corner of the inserted WordArt object.

2. Choose Insert, Object, then click Microsoft WordArt 2.0 in the Object dialog box. When you click OK, the WordArt dialog box, menu, and toolbar open (see fig. 21.13).

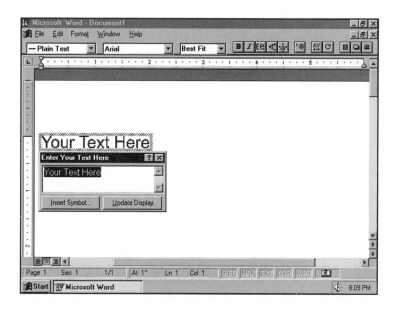

Fig. 21.13
Type your text in
this dialog box.

3. Type the text you want to apply special effects to in the space indicated.

4. If you want to use a special symbol in your text, such as a bullet, place the insertion point where you would like to place the symbol. Then click Insert Symbol, click a symbol, and click OK (see fig. 21.14).

Fig. 21.14
Choose a symbol to insert in your text.

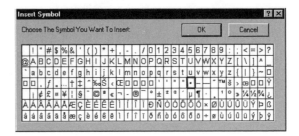

5. Select the text effect options you want to try from the pop-up menu on the far left of the WordArt toolbar shown in figure 21.15.

Fig. 21.15
Choose the desired text effect.

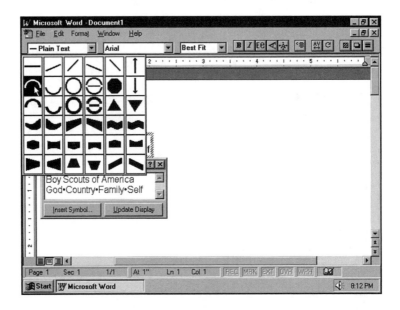

Tip
Various combinations of text effects, fonts, and sizes provide dramatically different results. With WordArt, you can experiment with many combinations and find exactly what you want.

6. Change the font and size using the pop-up menus along the toolbar. Arial MT Black in a size that best fits the curve are used in figure 21.16.

7. Click the desired effect to apply it to the object. The object is automatically inserted into your document where the insertion point was placed (see fig. 21.16).

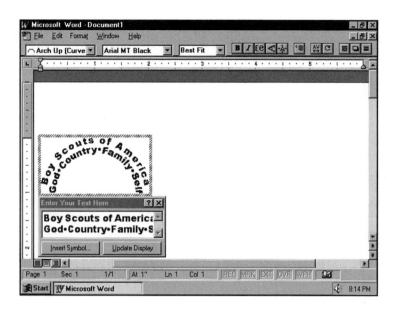

Fig. 21.16
The Arch Up
(Curve) effect has
been applied to
the text.

Additional effects can be applied to the text using the buttons along the
WordArt toolbar (or the corresponding Forma<u>t</u> menu choices if you prefer).
Table 21.2 summarizes WordArt's toolbar buttons.

Table 21.2 Buttons on WordArt's Toolbar	
Button	**Description**
B	Changes text to bold
I	Changes text to italic
Ee	Changes case of the text
◁	Arranges text vertically on the page
⊹A⊹	Stretches text to fit frame
⌐≡	Determines text alignment

(continues)

Table 21.2 Continued	
Button	**Description**
	Adjusts spacing between characters
	Adjusts rotation and angle of text
	Controls shade of text
	Places custom shadows behind text
	Controls border width around characters

Applying various combinations of the effects available in WordArt 2.0 can create interesting, attention-getting text to be used in any Office application.

Troubleshooting

WordArt isn't listed in the Object dialog box.

The exact entry is Microsoft WordArt 2.0. If you don't see that either, WordArt isn't installed. Install it by running the Office Setup program on your original disks or CD.

My screen looks funny when I start WordArt.

WordArt replaces Word's menus and toolbar.

How do I get out of WordArt?

Just click the page outside the WordArt image or the Enter Your Text Here dialog box.

Manipulating Objects

◀ See "Typing and Editing," p. 68

The previous sections of this chapter described various methods of inserting visual objects into your documents. Once the object has been inserted, you may need to edit, move, size, or position the object.

Editing an Object

All visual objects used in Office are *embedded objects*. This means double-clicking any visual object causes the source application to open, allowing you to edit the object. For example, if you double-click a chart inserted from Microsoft Graph, Microsoft Graph opens. When the source application opens, use that application's tools to modify the object as needed.

Resizing with Handles

To resize any of the objects described in this chapter, first click the object to select it, and then drag any of the resize handles surrounding the object to a new position.

The resize handles on the sides of the selection box resize in one dimension only. For instance, if you click the resize handle at the top of the selection box, you can stretch or shrink the height of an object on its top only; the bottom remains anchored. If you click the right resize handle, you can stretch or shrink the width of an object on its right side only; the left side remains anchored. Release the mouse button when the object is the size you want.

The resize handles at the corners of an object enable you to resize an object in two dimensions at once. If you click the resize handle in the upper-right corner of an object, for instance, you can change the height or width of the object by dragging the handle in any direction. When you drag a corner handle, the handle in the opposite corner remains anchored while you expand or contract the object's height and width.

When you resize in two dimensions at once, you may want to maintain an object's height-to-width ratio. To do so, hold the Shift key as you drag any corner resize handle. The handle in the opposite corner remains anchored while you resize the object.

You might also want to resize in two dimensions at once, from the center of the object outward. Hold down the Ctrl key as you drag any corner handle. By holding both the Shift and Ctrl keys as you drag a corner handle, you can maintain an object's height-to-width ratio *and* resize from the center outward, all in one step.

▶ See "Resizing and Scaling Objects," p. 612

Using Cut, Copy, and Paste

Visual objects can be moved from place to place within a document, and from one document to another. Follow these steps to move a visual object:

1. Select the visual object you want to move.

2. Choose Edit, Cut, or click the right mouse button and choose Cut from the Shortcut menu. The selected object is removed from its current location and placed on the Clipboard.

◀ See "Copying and Moving Data," p. 78

3. Select the destination for the object. If necessary, open the desired document. Then, indicate the desired location for the object:

◀ See "Selecting, Moving, and Resizing Objects," p. 364

   ■ In PowerPoint, display the slide into which you want to insert the object.

   ■ In Word, position the insertion point where the object should be inserted.

▶ See "Moving and Copying Objects," p. 611

   ■ In Excel, activate the cell that will be the upper left corner of the inserted object.

4. Choose Edit, Paste, or click the right mouse button and choose Paste from the Shortcut menu.

To duplicate the selected object rather than move it, choose Copy rather than Cut in step 2.

Using Drag-and-Drop

As an alternative to Cut and Paste, you can also move visual objects by using drag-and-drop. To move an object using drag-and-drop, you simply point at the object, hold down the mouse button, and drag the mouse pointer to the new location. Keep these additional points in mind when using drag-and-drop:

■ Drag-and-drop works within a document, between documents of the same Office application, or between Office applications.

■ If you want to copy the object rather than move it, hold down the Ctrl key while you drag the object.

■ If you're dragging from one document to another, the destination location must be visible on your screen before you start dragging.

> **Note**
>
> Drag-and-drop moves information, even when dragging from one application to another. Be careful to hold down the Ctrl key if you want to copy the information.

Using Frames in Word

Visual objects placed in a Word document from any of the sources discussed previously in this chapter can be positioned in the same way. Objects can be centered, and left- or right-aligned with the text using the text alignment tools on the toolbar. When more control over an object's position is necessary, a *frame* can be used. To position an object using a frame, it's easiest to work in Page Layout view. Switch to Page Layout view if necessary, and complete these steps:

1. Select the desired object.

2. Choose Insert, Frame.

3. Drag the framed graphic to the desired position. When you release the mouse button, the graphic moves to its new position. Figures 21.17 and 21.18 show an Equation 2.0 object before and after a frame has been added. Notice that text wraps around an object which has been framed.

▶ See "Framing a Picture," p. 681

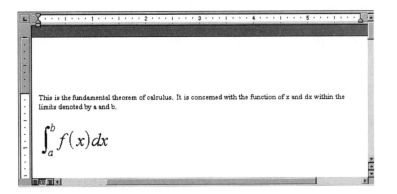

Fig. 21.17
The Equation object in a Word document before a frame is added.

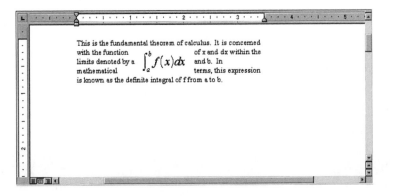

Fig. 21.18
The object has now been resized and dragged into position using a frame.

IV

Using Multimedia

Chapter 22

Inserting Sound and Motion Pictures

by Carman Minarik

Windows 95 provides full multimedia functionality, supporting devices such as sound cards, CD-ROM drives, audio and video input and output devices, and others. Windows 95 also provides software support for many multimedia features, such as audio CD playback, sound recording, and video clip manipulation. You can use a wide range of Windows multimedia functions in your Microsoft Office applications.

You learned in Chapter 21, "Inserting Microsoft Visual Objects," that you can add many types of objects, such as clip art and organizational charts, to a document created in a Microsoft Office application. This chapter explains how to insert other types of objects, such as sound files, video clips, and PowerPoint presentations.

In this chapter, you learn to

- Use Media Player to insert sound and video objects in your documents
- Use Media Player options to control sound and video objects
- Use Sound Recorder to add sound to your documents
- Incorporate PowerPoint presentations in Office documents
- Move, edit, and resize multimedia objects in your documents

Understanding Sound and Video in Microsoft Office

Using sound and video objects can add enormous impact to your documents. Sound and video are especially effective for presentations. You can, for example, include a sound or video clip that plays during your PowerPoint presentation. Or, if you have equipment to record sound, add a sound recording to a Word document or Excel worksheet to introduce yourself and explain the contents.

You incorporate sound and video files into a document as objects, much like a simple clip-art image. You can set the sound or video object to play the object once or continuously. You also can move and edit the object within the document, just like any other object.

Sound and video files tend to be large in size, adding significantly to the memory and disk space requirements for the file in which they are incorporated. Keep this point in mind as you design your documents. Although it may be fun and impressive to add a video clip to all your word processing documents, this practice may not be efficient. In general, use sound and video when it can enhance the message you are trying to send.

Windows 95 supports a variety of multimedia playback and editing software. One of the most flexible examples of this type of software is Microsoft Media Player, which is included in Windows 95. This application enables you to insert, play, and perform basic editing on sound and video files. By default, Media Player is the application launched when you insert most types of multimedia objects. An exception is audio CD, which starts the new Microsoft CD Player when you insert an audio CD in the CD-ROM drive. For more details on using the Media Player, read the topics on Media Player's Help menu.

Inserting an Object from a File

Multimedia objects are stored in files which you can select for insertion in a document or presentation. These objects files are inserted similar to the way you insert visual objects, discussed in Chapter 21, "Inserting Microsoft Visual Objects."

To insert any multimedia object, you use these steps:

1. Choose Insert, Object, which opens the Object dialog box (see fig. 22.1).

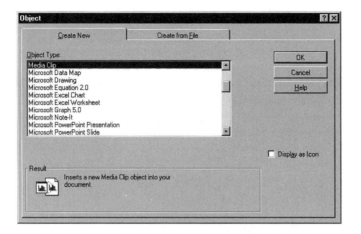

IV

Using Multimedia

Fig. 22.1
The Object dialog box enables you to choose the type of object you want to insert into your document.

2. If you want to insert an existing video or sound object into your document, choose the Create from File tab in the Object dialog box. A new dialog box appears, enabling you to enter the name of the file to insert.

3. If you know the path and file name for the object, type it in the File Name box. If you do not know the path and file name, click the Browse button to open a dialog box that lists the contents of your folders. Choose the file you want from the list.

4. Microsoft Office applications provide the capability to automatically update documents containing inserted objects if the original object file changes. To use this capability, check the Link To File check box in the Create from File tab of the Object dialog box.

5. Choose OK to close the Object dialog box.

◀ See "Inserting an Object from a File," p. 513

▶ See "Inserting a New Object into Your Document," p. 711

Creating New Objects

You use the Create New tab in the Object dialog box to insert new sound or video objects into your documents (refer to fig. 22.1). As you scroll through the Object Type list, you see several multimedia object types, including Media Clip, MIDI Sequence, and Video Clip. Select the object type you want to insert and click the OK button. You will find more detailed steps for inserting motion pictures, sound, and PowerPoint presentations later in this chapter.

◀ See "Creating a
New Object,"
p. 514

▶ See "Embed-
ding Informa-
tion in Your
Documents,"
p. 711

> ### Note
>
> You are not actually creating a *new* sound or video file when you use the Create New tab. You are still inserting an existing sound or video file into your document. The advantage of using the Create New tab is that you can exercise more control over the behavior of the multimedia object, since the application which controls the object file is started. Many options are available through the Create New tab that are not available when you use the Create from File tab.

The following sections provide details on the use of various types of multi-media objects.

Inserting Movies, Animations, and Video Clips

You insert movies, animations, and video clips all in the same way. In fact, you can think of these three types of objects as belonging to the general category of *motion pictures*. Video comes from a few sources: you can put a video-capture board into your computer and hook up a portable video camera or a VCR to it, or you can buy video clips on CD-ROM. Microsoft's Video for Windows is one of several software standards for video.

Inserting Motion Pictures

To insert a motion picture into a document, follow these steps:

1. Indicate where you want the motion picture object:

   - In PowerPoint, display the slide into which you want to insert a motion picture.

   - In Word, position the insertion point where you want to insert the motion picture.

   - In Excel, activate the cell in the upper left of the area where you want to locate the motion picture.

2. Choose the Insert, Object command, and click the Create New tab. In the Object Type list, click Media Clip or Video Clip in the Object dialog box, and then click OK. The Microsoft Media Player menu and tools appear, as shown in figure 22.2.

Media Player menu bar

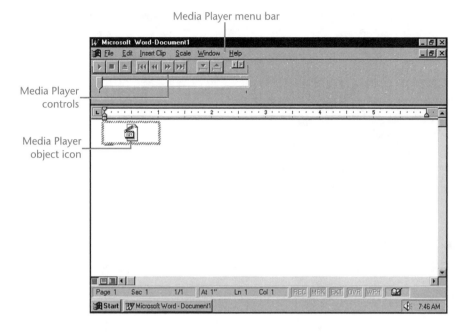

Media Player controls

Media Player object icon

Fig. 22.2
The Media Player controls appear when you insert a media clip or video clip.

3. Select the Insert Clip, Video for Windows menu option. An Open dialog box appears (see fig. 22.3). Video clips using the Video for Windows file standard have the extension AVI. This extension may not show on-screen, depending on your View, Options settings in Windows Explorer.

Fig. 22.3
Choose the video file you want from the Open dialog box.

4. Select the video file you want in the list box, or type its path and name in the File Name text box, and click the Open button. The Media Clip icon is replaced with the actual video clip you selected, as illustrated in figure 22.4.

Fig. 22.4
A video clip has
been inserted
into this Word
document.

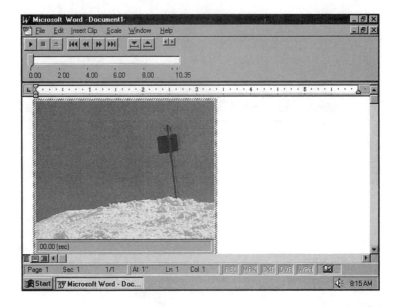

5. Click anywhere in the document outside the video object to return to
   the original document. The normal application menu bar and toolbars
   return, as shown in figure 22.5.

Fig. 22.5
Word's menu bar
and toolbars
return after
clicking outside
the video object.

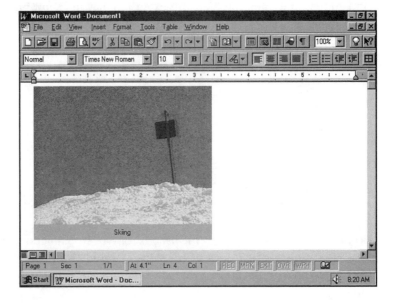

Playing Motion Pictures in a Document

To play a motion picture in a document, position the mouse pointer over the motion picture object and double-click. The application's normal menus and toolbars disappear, and a control bar appears beneath the motion picture. You can click the Stop and Play buttons on the bar to control playback of the motion picture. Figure 22.6 shows a motion picture during playback.

Pause button

Stop button

Fig. 22.6
You control playback of the motion picture using buttons on the control bar.

Setting Motion Picture Options

You can use several settings to control a motion picture's behavior in a document. Access these settings by choosing Edit, Options in the Media Player to open the Options dialog box (see fig. 22.7).

Fig. 22.7
Use the Options dialog box to adjust various object settings.

This dialog box provides these options:

- ■ Auto Rewind causes the motion picture to automatically return to the first frame after playback is complete.

- ■ Auto Repeat sets the motion picture to replay continuously until you click the Stop button.

- ■ Control Bar On Playback determines whether the control bar, with the Play and Stop buttons, is visible.

- ■ The Caption box enables you to enter a label for the motion picture. This label appears beneath the motion picture object.

- ■ Border Around Object determines if the object border, including the caption, is visible.

- ■ Play in Client Document enables the motion picture to play without actually launching Media Player.

- ■ Dither Picture to VGA Colors enhances playback on some video systems.

Figure 22.8 shows the motion picture inserted earlier, with the control bar and borders deactivated.

Fig. 22.8
The motion picture has the control bar and borders deactivated.

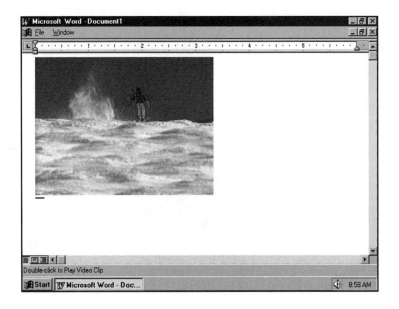

Media Player provides other controls for enhancing motion pictures in a document. Some of these controls are available as buttons in the Media Player window, as described in table 22.1.

Table 22.1 The Media Player Controls	
Button	**Function**
▶	Play
■	Stop
⏏	Eject
⏮	Previous Mark
⏪	Rewind
⏩	Fast Forward
⏭	Next Mark
⏷	Start Selection
⏶	End Selection
◀	Scroll Backward
▶	Scroll Forward

Most of the Media Player buttons work the same way as a cassette tape player. The Start Selection and End Selection buttons, however, may be unfamiliar. Use these buttons to select a portion of a motion picture to play in a document. To play just a portion of a motion picture, follow these steps:

Tip
You also can drag
the slider to the
position you want
on the clip.

1. Move to the beginning of the desired portion of the motion picture. Use the Play, Fast Forward, and Rewind buttons to locate the exact position you want.

2. Click the Start Selection button.

3. Move to the end of the desired portion of the motion picture. Use the Play, Fast Forward, and Rewind buttons to locate the exact position you want.

4. Click the End Selection button. The selected portion of the motion picture is highlighted on the time bar as shown in figure 22.9.

Fig. 22.9
The highlight
indicates a portion
of this motion
picture is selected
for playback.

Selected portion

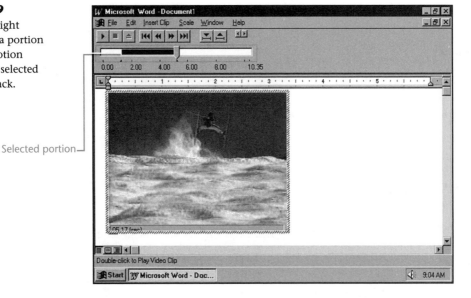

You also can set a specific portion of a motion picture for playback by choosing Edit, Selection when Media Player is active. The Set Selection dialog box opens (see fig. 22.10). You can enter the start and end time in this dialog box.

Fig. 22.10
The Set Selection
dialog box enables
you to enter start
and end positions
of the motion
picture.

Troubleshooting
My video clip plays continuously and I don't have any control buttons to stop it. You need to change the media player settings for the video clip. Right-click the video clip and select Edit Media Clip. In the menu, choose Edit, Options. In the Options dialog box, deselect the Auto Repeat check box. If you want controls to show, select the Control Bar On Playback check box. Choose OK.

Inserting Music and Sound

If your computer system has sound capabilities, you can insert sound and music files into your documents. Microsoft Windows includes an application called Sound Recorder that enables you to record and play back sound files. You also can use Media Player to insert sound files, as well as MIDI sequences.

Using Sound Files

Sound files sometimes are called Wave files, because they normally have the extension WAV as part of their file names. Follow these steps to insert sound files into your documents using Sound Recorder:

1. Indicate where you want the sound object:

    - In PowerPoint, display the slide into which you want to insert the sound object.

    - In Word, position the insertion point where you want to insert the sound.

    - In Excel, activate the cell in the upper left of the area where you want to locate the sound.

2. Choose the Insert, Object command and click the Create New tab. In the Object Type list, click Wave Sound in the Object dialog box, then click OK. The Sound Object dialog box appears, as shown in figure 22.11.

3. If you want to record a new sound, click the Record button, record the sound, and click the Stop button when finished.

Fig. 22.11
Use Sound Re-
corder to record
and play back
sounds.

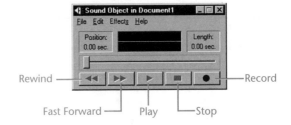

Rewind   Fast Forward   Play   Stop   Record

4. If you want to insert an existing sound, choose Edit, Insert File in the
   Sound Object dialog box. In the Insert File dialog box, locate the folder
   where the sound file is stored. Select a file from the list box or type in
   the File Name text box (see fig. 22.12).

Fig. 22.12
The Insert File
dialog box enables
you to select a
sound file for use
with Sound
Recorder.

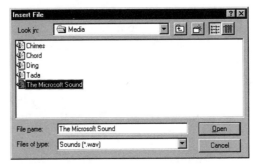

Tip
Click the right
mouse button on
top of an audio
file icon or video
clip. The shortcut
menu pops up.
Choose Edit Media
Clip from the
shortcut menu,
and the Media
Player appears,
ready for editing.

5. Click Open to choose the file. The Insert File dialog box closes.

6. Close the Sound Object dialog box. Sound Recorder inserts the sound
   file as an icon into your document.

7. Double-click the sound file icon to play the sound file.

Using MIDI Sequences

MIDI sequences are digitized musical files created by connecting electronic
instruments to a computer. As the musician plays, the music is digitized as a
computer file. The musician can then modify the computer file to alter the
music. You can insert MIDI sequences into Microsoft Office applications
using Media Player. To insert a MIDI sequence, follow these steps:

1. Indicate where you want the MIDI sequence object:

- In PowerPoint, display the slide into which you want to insert a MIDI sequence.

- In Word, position the insertion point where you want to insert the MIDI sequence.

- In Excel, activate the cell in the upper left of the area where you want to locate the MIDI sequence.

2. Choose Insert, Object and click the Create New tab. In the Object Type list, click MIDI Sequence in the Object dialog box, and then click OK. The Media Player menu and controls appear, as shown earlier in figure 22.2.

3. Choose the Insert Clip, 1 MIDI Sequencer menu option. An Open dialog box appears.

4. Select the folder where your MIDI file is stored. Select a file from the list box and click the Open button. The Media Clip icon appears, as illustrated in figure 22.13.

5. Click anywhere in the document outside the video object to return to the original document. The normal application menu and toolbars return.

Media Player enables you to insert existing sound and MIDI files, as well as motion picture files. Sound Recorder enables you to work with sound files only, but you can record new sound files as well as use existing files.

The icons that these two programs produce are illustrated in figures 22.13 and 22.14.

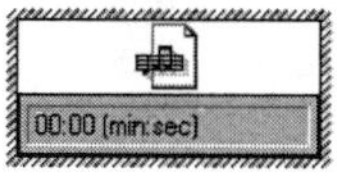

Fig. 22.13
This icon represents a Media Player MIDI Sequence sound file.

Fig. 22.14
This icon represents a Sound Recorder sound file.

Inserting a PowerPoint Presentation

Suppose you have explained in a Word document the agenda for an upcoming meeting, where you plan to include a PowerPoint presentation. You can add an entire PowerPoint presentation to a document created in Word or Excel, allowing the planners of the meeting to read the document and view the inserted presentation at their own workstations.

To use a presentation in a document, follow these steps:

1. Indicate where you want to insert the PowerPoint presentation object:

   - In Word, position the insertion point where you want to insert the PowerPoint presentation.

   - In Excel, activate the cell in the upper left of the area where you want to locate the PowerPoint presentation.

2. Choose Insert, Object and select the Create from File tab in the Object dialog box. A new dialog box appears, enabling you to enter the name of the file to insert.

3. If you know the path and file name for the PowerPoint presentation, type it in the File Name box. If you do not know the path and file name, click the Browse button to open a dialog box that lists the contents of your folders. Choose the file you want from the list.

4. To link the object to the original presentation, which enables automatic updating of the document when the original file changes, check the Link To File check box in the Create from File tab of the Object dialog box.

5. Choose OK to close the Object dialog box. The PowerPoint presentation is added to your document. The first slide in the presentation is visible, as shown in figure 22.15.

6. Double-click the slide to start the presentation. PowerPoint launches in Slide Show mode, enabling you to play the presentation by clicking each slide to move to the next slide.

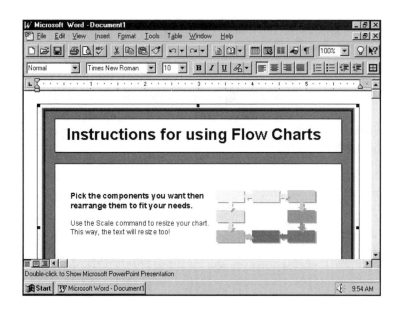

Fig. 22.15
A PowerPoint
presentation has
been inserted
into this Word
document.

Moving Objects

You can move sound and motion picture objects from place to place within a
document, and from one document to another. Follow these steps to move or
duplicate a sound or motion picture object:

1. Select the object you want to move.

2. Choose Edit, Cut, or click the right mouse button and choose Cut from
   the shortcut menu. The selected object is removed from its current
   location and placed on the Clipboard.

   To duplicate the selected object rather than move it, choose Copy
   rather than Cut in this step.

3. Select the destination for the object. If necessary, open a different document. Then indicate where you want to insert the object:

   ▪ In PowerPoint, display the slide into which you want to insert the
     object.

   ▪ In Word, position the insertion point where you want to insert
     the object.

   ▪ In Excel, activate the cell in the upper left of the area where you
     want to locate the object.

Tip
When you cut and
paste multimedia
objects that have
play settings ap-
plied to them, the
settings migrate
with the objects.

4. Choose Edit, Paste, or click the right mouse button and choose Paste from the shortcut menu.

◄ See "Selecting, Moving and Resizing Objects," p. 364

► See "Moving and Copying Objects," p. 611

As an alternative to Cut and Paste, you can move sound and motion picture objects by using drag-and-drop. To move an object using drag-and-drop, you simply point to the object, hold down the mouse button, and drag the mouse pointer to the new location. Keep these additional points in mind when using drag-and-drop:

■ Drag-and-drop works within a document, between documents of the same Office application, or between Office applications.

■ If you want to copy the object rather than move it, hold down the Ctrl key while you drag the object.

■ If you are dragging from one document to another, the destination location must be visible on your screen before you start dragging.

> **Note**
>
> Drag-and-drop moves information, even when dragging from one application to another. Be careful to hold down the Ctrl key if you want to copy the information.

Editing Objects

You may want to change some of a sound or motion picture object's properties. To edit an object in a document, follow these steps:

1. Click the sound or motion picture object to select it.

2. Choose Edit, Media Clip Object, Edit.

   Media Player or Sound Recorder opens, depending on the object type you selected.

3. Make the changes you want to the object, using the Sound Recorder or Media Player controls and menu options.

4. Click anywhere outside the object to return to the normal application menus and toolbars.

To resize any of the objects described in this chapter, you first click the object to select it and then drag any of the resize handles surrounding the object to a new position.

The resize handles on the sides of the selection box resize in one dimension only. For instance, if you click the resize handle at the top of the selection box, you can stretch or shrink the height of an object on its top only.

The resize handles that appear at the corners of an object enable you to resize an object in two dimensions at once. If you click the resize handle in the upper right corner of an object, for instance, you can change the height or width of the object by dragging the handle in any direction. The handle in the opposite corner remains anchored.

Another option is to resize in two dimensions from the center of the object outward. Hold down the Ctrl key as you drag any corner handle. You can maintain an object's height-to-width ratio *and* resize from the center outward, all in one step, by holding both the Shift and Ctrl keys as you drag a corner handle.

Tip

To maintain an object's height-to-width-ratio, hold down the Shift key as you drag any corner resize handle.

Caution

Use caution when resizing motion picture clips. Depending on the recording method used, you may significantly degrade the image by resizing.

▶ See "Resizing and Scaling Objects," p. 612

IV

Using Multimedia

Chapter 23

Drawing Shapes, Curves, and Lines

by Carman Minarik

One of the easiest and most effective ways to enhance a document is to add a drawn object. In Microsoft Office applications, you can draw common shapes, such as ovals and rectangles, or more unusual shapes, such as stars, arrows, and cubes. You also can draw lines, arcs, and freeform shapes by using various drawing tools.

In this chapter, you learn to

- Use the drawing tools in Office applications

- Draw various shapes, such as rectangles and ovals, and perfect shapes, such as squares and circles

- Draw lines, arcs, and freeform shapes

- Modify shapes after they are drawn

Using Drawing Tools

Drawing tools are available in Word, Excel, and PowerPoint. To use them, you must first display one or both of the Drawing toolbars.

You may be familiar with the Drawing toolbar in PowerPoint because it is displayed in the PowerPoint window (the leftmost toolbar) automatically whenever you start the program. Additional drawing tools available in

PowerPoint are called the *Drawing+ tools*. To display the Drawing+ toolbar, follow these steps:

1. Choose <u>V</u>iew, <u>T</u>oolbars.

2. Click the box next to Drawing+, placing a check in the box, as shown in figure 23.1.

3. Click OK to display the additional drawing tools to the left of the standard Drawing toolbar.

Fig. 23.1
Choose here
to display the
Drawing+ toolbar.

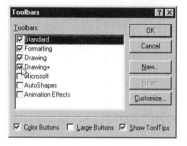

The Drawing toolbar is displayed along the bottom of the window in Word by clicking the Drawing button.

To display the Drawing toolbar in Excel, you also can click the Drawing button, or follow these steps:

1. Choose <u>V</u>iew, <u>T</u>oolbars.

2. Click the box next to Drawing, placing a check in the box.

3. Click OK to display the standard Drawing toolbar in its own mini window.

Notice that the Drawing toolbars in each Office application contain many common tools. Table 23.1 illustrates each of these common tools and describes its function.

Table 23.1   Common Drawing Tools

Button	Drawing Tool	Function
	Line	Draws straight lines in any direction from the point at which you click the mouse.
	Rectangle	Draws rectangles of any dimension.
	Ellipse	Draws curved shapes, including ellipses and circles.
	Arc	Draws arched or curved lines. When filled, the shape becomes a quarter-ellipse.
	Freeform	Draws any irregular shape.

To activate a Drawing tool, simply click it. When you click the Line, Rectangle, Ellipse, Arc, or Freeform tool, the mouse pointer changes to a crosshair. To activate any of the remaining tools, you must select an object before you click the tool.

◀ See "Drawing Toolbars," p. 49

Drawing Shapes

In the context of this chapter, a *shaped object*, or *shape*, is defined as a closed object that you draw using a drawing tool.

To draw a shape, follow these steps:

1. In the Drawing toolbar, click the tool corresponding to the shape you want to draw.

2. Move the mouse pointer to the approximate location on the page where you want to draw the object. The mouse pointer changes to a crosshair.

3. Click and drag the mouse in any direction. As you drag the mouse, a solid outline of the shape appears in the document, worksheet, chart, or slide.

4. When the object is the shape and size you want, release the mouse button.

As you draw, don't feel that you must position your object perfectly the first time; you can relocate, resize, or adjust the object later.

Drawing AutoShapes

The AutoShapes tool is a drawing tool unique to PowerPoint. It displays its own toolbar when you click it. The toolbar, shown in figure 23.2, contains 24 predefined shapes that you can draw instantly simply by clicking and dragging the mouse. The AutoShapes toolbar makes it easy for you to draw shapes that you frequently might include in your PowerPoint slides, but you can also move them to documents in other applications.

Fig. 23.2
Add predefined shapes instantly with PowerPoints AutoShapes toolbar.

To draw an AutoShape, use the same technique listed previously for other shapes, except select an AutoShape tool before you begin drawing. Follow these steps:

1. Click the AutoShapes tool in the Drawing toolbar. The AutoShapes toolbar appears.

2. Click an AutoShape to activate it.

3. Place the mouse pointer in the slide where you want to draw the object. The mouse pointer changes to a crosshair.

4. Click and drag the mouse in any direction. As you drag, a solid outline of the shape appears.

5. When the object is the shape and size you want, release the mouse button.

Drawing Perfect Shapes

To draw a perfect or *uniform* shape, you follow the same basic steps for drawing a shape, except that you use the Shift key as the "constraint" key. Holding down the Shift key maintains the horizontal and vertical distance from the mouse pointer as you draw, so that you can use the Ellipse tool, for example, to draw a perfect circle. Figure 23.3 shows a perfect circle and a perfect square drawn using the Rectangle tool and the Ellipse tool.

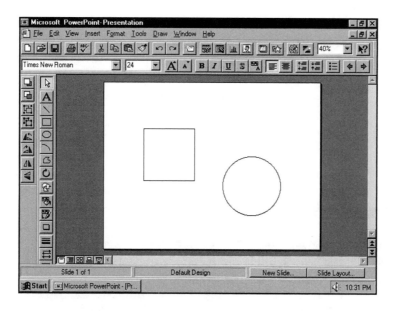

Fig. 23.3
Perfect shapes are
drawn by dragging
with the Shift key
held down.

IV

Using Multimedia

To draw a uniform shape, follow these steps:

1. Click the drawing tool you want to use.

2. Place the mouse pointer in the document where you want to draw the object. The mouse pointer changes to a crosshair.

3. Press and hold down the Shift key.

4. Click and drag the mouse pointer in any direction.

5. When the object is the uniform shape and size you want, release the mouse button.

Drawing from the Center Outward

You have learned how to draw a shape by starting at one of the corners and drawing in any direction. Sometimes, you might want to draw a shape from the center outward. To draw an object from the center outward, you use another constraint key: Ctrl. When you press the Ctrl key as you draw a shape, the center of the object remains anchored at the point where you place the crosshair when you begin drawing.

To draw from the center outward, follow these steps:

1. Click the drawing tool you want to use.

Tip
You can use the Shift and Ctrl keys together for the combined effect of drawing a perfect circle or square from the center outward.

2. Position the crosshair in the slide where you want the center of the object to be located.

3. Press and hold down the Ctrl key.

4. Click and drag the mouse in any direction. As you draw, the center point of the object remains anchored.

5. When the object is the shape and size you want, release the mouse button.

Drawing Lines and Arcs

The technique for drawing lines and arcs is similar to that used for drawing shapes. The only difference between drawing lines and arcs and drawing other types of shapes is that lines and arcs are not enclosed objects. Lines and arcs have a beginning point and an end point, with resize handles at each of those points. Figure 23.4 shows items drawn with the Line tool and the Arc tool.

Fig. 23.4
Draw simple shapes, such as a line or an arc.

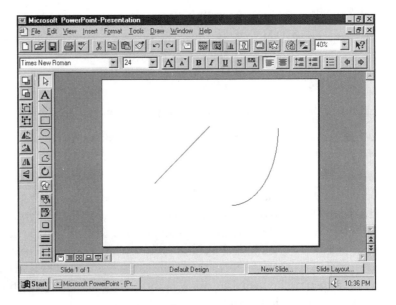

To draw a line or arc, follow these steps:

1. Click the Line or Arc tool in the Drawing toolbar.

2. Place the mouse pointer in the slide area. The mouse pointer changes to a crosshair.

3. Click where you want the line or arc to begin, and then drag the mouse until the line or arc is completed as you want.

4. Release the mouse button.

Drawing Perfect Lines and Arcs

In the "Drawing Perfect Shapes" section earlier in this chapter, you learned that the Shift key can be used to draw uniform objects. Used in conjunction with the Line tool, the Shift key enables you to draw vertical lines, horizontal lines, and lines at a 45-degree angle.

To draw a vertical line, press and hold down the Shift key, and then drag the mouse vertically from the starting point of the line. To draw a horizontal line, press and hold down the Shift key, and then drag the mouse horizontally from the starting point. To draw a line at a 45-degree angle, press and hold down the Shift key, and then drag the mouse diagonally in the direction you want to draw the line.

> **Note**
>
> Experiment with the various angles by holding down the Shift key and moving the mouse in a circle around the beginning point of the line. A straight line appears at 45, 90, 135, 180, 225, 270, 315, and 360 degrees from the starting point.

When you use the Shift key in conjunction with the Arc tool, you can draw a *uniform arc*—that is, the shape of the arc you draw (regardless of the size) always is a quarter-circle. A *perfect arc* is one in which two lines drawn perpendicular to the arc's end points form a right angle (90 degrees).

Drawing Lines and Arcs from a Center Point

Just as you can use the Ctrl key to draw shapes from the center outward, you also can use the Ctrl key to draw lines and arcs from a center point outward. The point at which you place the crosshair in the slide becomes the center point for the line or arc. As you drag the mouse in any direction, this center point remains anchored.

You also can use the Ctrl and Shift keys in conjunction with the Line and Arc tools to draw uniform lines and arcs outward from a center point.

Drawing Freeform Shapes

Using the Freeform tool, you can draw any type of freeform shape or polygon. A *freeform shape* can consist of curved lines, straight lines, or a combination of the two. You might use the Freeform tool to draw a cartoon, create an unusual shape, or write your name. A freeform shape can be *open* (that is, the beginning point and end point don't meet) or *closed* (the beginning point and end point meet to form an object). A closed shape made up of straight lines is called a *polygon*.

To draw a shape (open or closed) consisting of straight lines, click and release the mouse button at each vertex in the shape. A *vertex* is the point at which you click and release the mouse button while drawing a freeform shape. To draw freehand shapes, drag the Freeform tool and then double-click where you want the shape to end. The Freeform tool remains active until you complete the shape you're drawing by double-clicking or by pressing Enter. To create a closed object, click near the beginning point of the shape, which automatically connects the beginning and end points to create an object.

To draw an open or closed shape consisting of straight lines, follow these steps:

1. Click the Freeform tool in the Drawing toolbar.

2. Place the mouse pointer at the point where you want to begin drawing. The mouse pointer changes to a crosshair.

3. Click the mouse button, and then release it.

4. Place the crosshair where you want the first line to end and the second line to begin, and then click and release the mouse button.

5. Repeat step 4, clicking and releasing the mouse button at each vertex.

6. To make the object an open shape, double-click after you draw the last line. To close the shape, place the mouse pointer near the beginning point, and then click the mouse button. A straight line connects the beginning and end points.

To draw an open or closed freeform shape, follow these steps:

1. Click the Freeform tool in the Drawing toolbar.

2. Place the mouse pointer at the point where you want to begin drawing. The mouse pointer changes to a crosshair.

3. Click and drag the mouse in any direction, drawing the shape you want.

4. To create an open object, double-click when you finish drawing, or press Enter. To create a closed shape, double-click near the point where you began drawing, which automatically connects the beginning and end points.

As you draw freehand shapes, you can pause at any point by releasing the mouse button. Before beginning to draw again, place the crosshair where it was located before you paused, and then click and drag to continue drawing. To mix straight and curved lines in the same drawing, alternate between clicking a vertex and dragging the mouse.

Editing Freeform Shapes

When you click a freeform shape to select it, it displays the usual eight resize handles. You can drag any of the resize handles to make a freeform shape larger or smaller. Freeform shapes, unlike other shapes, also contain *control handles* (see fig. 23.5). Control handles enable you to modify the freeform shape in addition to simply resizing it.

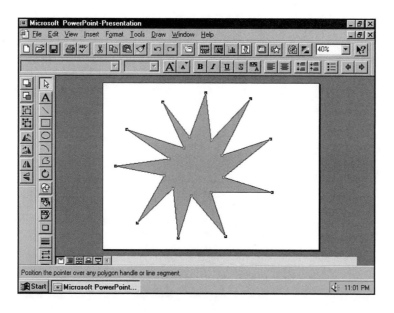

Fig. 23.5
A freeform shape displays control handles.

To display an object's control handles in Word or Excel, click the Reshape button on the toolbar. In PowerPoint, double-click the object. When you place the mouse pointer on a control handle, the pointer changes to a crosshair. To move a control handle, position the crosshair over the control handle, and then click and drag the handle in any direction. To add a control handle, press and hold down the Shift and Ctrl keys; then click on the original line where you want to add the handle. To delete a control handle, press and hold down the Ctrl key; then click the handle.

A control handle appears at each vertex of a freeform shape or polygon. If you look closely at the control handles of a freeform shape, you can see that the curves of a shape created by dragging the mouse are not actually curves; they are a series of short lines connected to one another.

You can adjust the shape of a freeform object by dragging an existing control handle to a new position, deleting a control handle, or adding a control handle. Curves that you draw slowly often contain more control handles than are necessary; deleting some handles can make working with the curve easier. If an object contains straight lines that you want to convert to gentle curves, add a few control handles so that you can curve the line.❖

Part V

Using PowerPoint

Chapter 24

Getting Aquainted with PowerPoint

by Donna Minarik

PowerPoint is the component of Microsoft Office used to create professional-quality overhead transparency, paper, 35mm slide, photoprint, or on-screen presentations. This chapter familiarizes you with the layout of the PowerPoint window and its tools and capabilities.

In this chapter, you learn to

- Start and exit PowerPoint

- Look at PowerPoint window elements

- Examine components of PowerPoint presentations

- Understand templates, masters, objects, and layouts

- Add visuals to PowerPoint slides

Starting and Exiting PowerPoint

Like other applications in Microsoft Office, PowerPoint can be started in more than one way, allowing you to choose the method that is most convenient. Following are the ways in which PowerPoint can be started:

- Click the Start button and choose the PowerPoint shortcut, usually found in the Programs menu.

- Double-click the PowerPoint icon in the Microsoft Office folder (found in your hard disk window).

Tip

Create a shortcut to PowerPoint by dragging the PowerPoint icon from the PowerPoint folder to the desktop; then double-click the shortcut to open the program.

After a few seconds, the PowerPoint window appears. Like other Microsoft Office applications, PowerPoint displays the Tip of the Day dialog box, which contains a new tip each time you start PowerPoint. If you don't want to see the Tip of the Day each time you start PowerPoint, select the Show Tips at Startup check box in the Tip of the Day dialog box to remove the X from the box; then click OK. (You can display tips at any time by choosing Help, Tip of the Day.)

When you want to exit PowerPoint, choose File, Exit. If the current file is unsaved, PowerPoint displays a dialog box asking if you want to save the changes you made to the current file. Choose Yes if you want to save, No if you don't want to save, or Cancel to return to your file without saving.

Getting Familiar with the PowerPoint Window

► See "Creating a New Presentation," p. 578

After you close the Tip of the Day, PowerPoint automatically displays the dialog box shown in figure 24.1. This dialog box lets you choose how you want to create a presentation. PowerPoint offers a variety of methods for creating presentations, including use of a template or a wizard.

Fig. 24.1
Your first choice is a foundation on which you base your presentation; alternately, you can open an existing presentation.

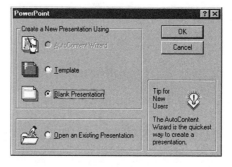

Tip

If your presentation window is smaller than that in the figure, click the Maximize button to enlarge the window.

Figure 24.2 shows what a typical PowerPoint presentation screen might look like. PowerPoint's standard menu bar, Standard toolbar, and Formatting toolbar are shown below the window's title bar. The Drawing toolbar is displayed down the left side of the window. Surrounded by a gray background, the first slide in the presentation is represented by the white area in the middle of the screen. The individual "pages" in a presentation that become overheads, 35mm slides, or an on-screen slide show are considered slides. Notice that vertical and horizontal scroll bars are now visible on-screen (compare to fig. 24.1). At the left end of the horizontal scroll bar are View buttons, used for displaying different views of your presentation.

> **Note**
>
> For more information about displaying different views in PowerPoint, see Chapter 25, "Creating, Saving, and Opening Presentations."

Formatting toolbar   Title bar   Menu bar   Standard toolbar

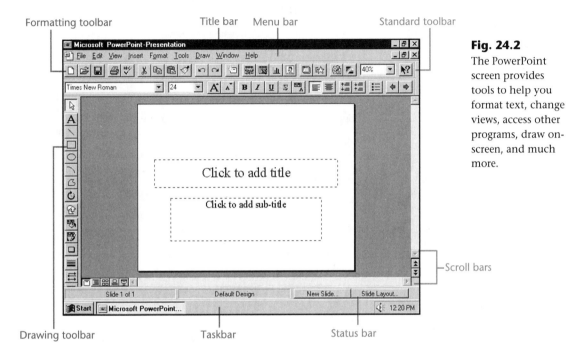

Drawing toolbar   Taskbar   Status bar

Fig. 24.2
The PowerPoint screen provides tools to help you format text, change views, access other programs, draw on-screen, and much more.

V

Using PowerPoint

Window Elements

The menus in PowerPoint are similar to the menus in other Microsoft Office applications. Menus such as File, Window, and Help are standard across all applications. PowerPoint's menus are most similar to Word's, but the Draw menu is unique to PowerPoint. Table 24.1 describes each PowerPoint menu and the types of commands found on each.

Table 24.1	PowerPoint Menus
Menu	**Description**
File	Contains standard Microsoft Office application File menu and commands specific to PowerPoint, such as Pack and Go and Send to Genigraphics. Additionally, if you're using the Microsoft Exchange that installs with Windows 95, an extra section adds mail commands such as Send and Add Routing Slip.

(continues)

Menu	Description
Table 24.1 Continued	
Edit	Contains commands for Undo, Cut, Copy, and Paste. Duplicate (Ctrl+D) and Delete Slide are found on this menu, along with commands for creating Links to other files, Find and Replace, and editing an Object.
View	Contains commands to choose the presentation view you want to display on your screen or to display masters. This menu also contains commands for turning on and off the display of toolbars, rulers, and guides. (You learn about rulers and guides in the "Displaying Rulers and Guides" section of this chapter.) Use this menu also to control the zoom percentage used in a particular view.
Insert	Contains commands that let you insert a variety of elements in a presentation, from a simple date or time to clip art, graphs, or other objects.
Format	Contains commands for changing all aspects (font, alignment, spacing, color, shadow) of how text and objects look in a presentation. Also contains commands for selecting templates, color schemes, and layouts.
Tools	Contains typical Microsoft Office tools (such as Spelling) as well as tools that are unique to PowerPoint. Use the commands on this menu to create transitions between slides, hide slides, or recolor or crop a picture. You also find commands for customizing toolbars and setting PowerPoint options, as well as commands for setting animation, reminding you of meetings, interactive settings, and so on.
Draw	Contains commands to manipulate objects in a presentation. For instance, you can group several objects as one; rearrange the "stacking order" or layers of objects; and rotate, flip, and change the scale of objects.
Window	Contains standard Microsoft Office application Window menu, such as New Window and Arrange All, as well as a Fit to Page command.
Help	Standard Microsoft Office application Help menu plus an Answer Wizard and Tip of the Day.

▶ See "Creating a New Presentation," p. 578

▶ See "Enhancing Text," p. 627

▶ See "Working with Templates," p. 621

Along the lower edge of the PowerPoint window is the status bar, which displays the number of the current slide or other element you're working on (Slide Master, Outline Master, Handout Master, or Notes Master) at the left end. The center of the status bar shows the design template currently being used; you can also double-click this area to apply a new design template. The right end contains two buttons. The New Slide button makes it easy for you to add a new slide to your presentation without choosing Insert, New Slide (or pressing Ctrl+M). When you click the Slide Layout button, the Slide Layout dialog box appears from which you can choose a specially designed slide layout. Layouts and templates are described in detail in the "Understanding Masters and Templates" and "Understanding Objects and Layouts" sections later in this chapter.

Above the status bar is the horizontal scroll bar. At the left end are four View buttons. Each button displays a different view of the current presentation. The four buttons are pointed out in figure 24.2 and described in the section "Examining the Components of a PowerPoint Presentation," later in this chapter.

PowerPoint's Standard Toolbar

Table 24.2 describes each of the buttons on PowerPoint's Standard toolbar. Each button represents a PowerPoint menu command. You learn how to use most of these buttons in subsequent chapters. Refer to Chapter 23, "Drawing Shapes, Curves, and Lines," for an explanation of the tools on the Drawing toolbar.

Tip
Right-click any toolbar to display a list of available toolbars; select a toolbar to display or to hide from the list.

V

Using PowerPoint

Table 24.2 Buttons on PowerPoint's Standard Toolbar	
Button	**Description**
	Creates a new presentation and displays the New Presentation dialog box.
	Displays the File Open dialog box, from which you can choose a presentation file to open (or Design Template or Outline).
	Saves the current presentation under the current name and file type. If the presentation has not yet been saved, displays the File Save dialog box.
	Prints the active presentation.
	Checks the spelling in the current presentation. Displays the Spelling dialog box if errors are found.
	Removes the selected text or object from the slide and places it on the Windows Clipboard.
	Places a copy of the selected text or object on the Windows Clipboard, leaving the original text or object unchanged.
	Pastes the contents of the Clipboard into the current slide.

(continues)

Table 24.2 Continued

Button	Description
	Records all attributes (color, font, shadow, pattern, and so on) of the selected object or text selection so that you can copy all attributes to another object or text selection.
	Reverses the most recent action taken. Note that not all actions (commands) can be reversed.
	Redoes or repeats (depending on the action) the most recent action taken. Not all actions can be redone or repeated.
	Opens the New Slide dialog box from which you can choose an AutoLayout for the new slide.
	Embeds a Microsoft Word table of the size (rows and columns) you specify in your presentation.
	Embeds an Excel worksheet of the size (rows and columns) you specify in your presentation.
	Embeds a graph in your presentation using the data you specify.
	Allows you to insert clip art into your presentation using Microsoft's ClipArt Gallery.
	Applies a selected design template to the slide show.
	Transfers the content of the current presentation to Microsoft Word.
	Displays the presentation in black and white, rather than in color. Clicking the tool again toggles the view back to color.
	Lets you zoom in and out of your presentation.
	The mouse pointer changes to a question mark, which you can use to click any PowerPoint menu command, button, or toolbar for which you want help. You can double-click the icon to open Help Topics.
	Shows the current font and displays a drop-down list of available fonts.
	Shows the current font size and displays a list of available font sizes.
	Increases font size of selected text to the next larger available size.

Button	Description
A	Decreases font size of selected text to the next smaller available size.
B	Adds or removes boldface to and from selected text (this button toggles on and off with each click).
I	Adds or removes italic to and from selected text (this button toggles on and off with each click).
U	Adds or removes underlining to and from selected text (this button toggles on and off with each click).
S	Adds or removes text shadow to and from selected text (this button toggles on and off with each click).
A	Displays eight colors for text in a palette. To choose a different color, click the Other Color option, which displays the Other Color dialog box.
≣	Left-aligns selected text.
≣	Centers selected text.
≔	Adds bullets to selected text (this button toggles on and off with each click).
⬅	Promotes selected text to next higher level in an outline.
➡	Promotes selected text to next lower level in an outline.

Displaying Rulers and Guides

When you work with text documents in Word, it's helpful to display horizontal and vertical rulers in the Word window. Because some slides contain text, rulers can be useful in PowerPoint as well. Rulers give you a reference point within a slide so that you can see at what point (in inches) a text or drawn object appears. They also help you plan the use of space on a slide by providing guides for object and text placement.

To display rulers in the PowerPoint window, choose View, Ruler. Rulers appear in one of two states—*drawing* or *text*—depending on the objects currently selected on the slide. In figure 24.3, rulers are shown in the *drawing state*, which places the zero point at the *center* of each ruler. This allows you to position objects from the center point to the outer edges of a slide. The position of the mouse is indicated on each ruler by a dashed line. In figure 24.3, the mouse position on each ruler is at approximately 2.5 inches. You also can see that the slide is 10 inches wide and 7.5 inches long.

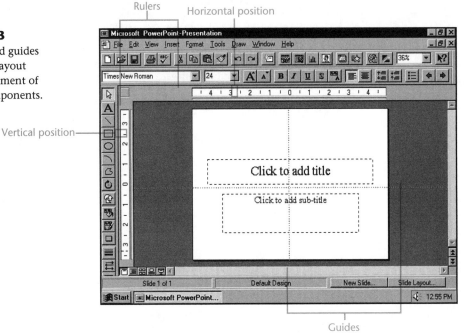

Fig. 24.3
Rulers and guides assist in layout and alignment of slide components.

Tip
You can also reposition a guide by dragging it to a new location.

When it's important to position slide elements precisely or to align certain elements vertically or horizontally, you can choose <u>V</u>iew, <u>G</u>uides. This command displays dotted lines vertically and horizontally through the center point of a slide. Use the guides to help you visually align elements on a slide. Guides are shown in figure 24.3.

> **Note**
>
> Guides do not appear on printed copies of your slide; they only appear only on-screen while you are working in PowerPoint.

Examining the Components of a PowerPoint Presentation

At first you might think that PowerPoint is an application used only to create slides for a presentation, but PowerPoint offers much more. It helps you plan, create, and deliver a presentation in a practical way. Think about how a speaker gives a presentation: she might plan the presentation by first creating the outline; then completing the "look" and content of the slides; and finally by printing them. While she speaks, the speaker might refer to printed copies of the slides that contain her own handwritten notes. She might also provide copies of her slides to the audience so that they can follow along or take notes.

Key components of a PowerPoint presentation include the following:

- Slides

- Outlines

- Speaker's notes

- Audience handouts

Creating each of these components could take a great deal of extra time, but PowerPoint simplifies the task by creating each one automatically. You can use just one component or any combination of the four, depending on your particular requirements.

You can view any of the components on-screen or print copies. PowerPoint displays slides, as illustrated earlier in figure 24.2, by default. Outline pages look like a typical outline, with main headings aligned at the left margin and lower-level headings indented (see fig. 24.4). Speaker's note pages contain a reduced version of the slide at the top of the page with space at the bottom of the page for the speaker's notes (see fig. 24.5). Audience handouts can contain two, three, or six slides per printed page, as shown in figure 24.6. Notice that you can't view audience handouts on-screen. When you view the Handout Master, you see dotted frames that outline the location of the slides on the page.

To view slides, the outline, or note pages, choose <u>V</u>iew, <u>S</u>lides; <u>V</u>iew, <u>O</u>utline; or <u>V</u>iew, <u>N</u>otes Pages. To view handout pages, choose <u>V</u>iew, <u>M</u>aster; then choose Han<u>d</u>out Master from the submenu that appears. After you choose a view, the status bar indicates which view is displayed.

V

Using PowerPoint

Tip
You can edit an outline in Word by changing to Outline view and clicking the Report It icon.

◀ See "Outlining a Document," p. 252

Fig. 24.4
Use Outline view to create a presentation and to organize your slides.

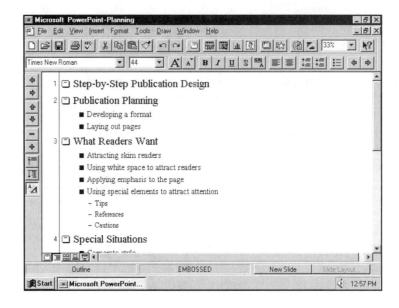

Fig. 24.5
Enter speaker's notes to help you remember important items during your presentation.

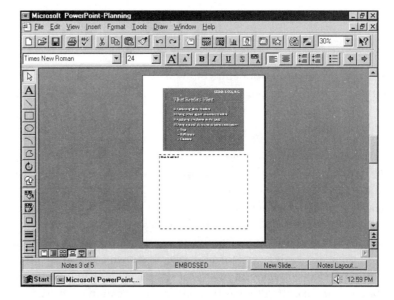

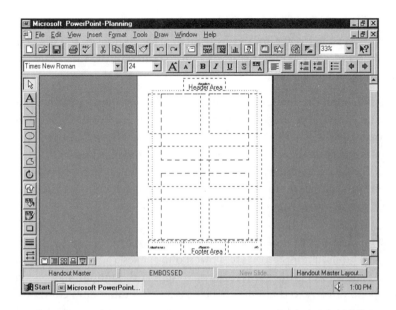

Fig. 24.6
The layout options for audience handout pages are indicated by dotted lines on the Handout Master.

V

Using PowerPoint

Note

You can quickly display a presentation component by clicking the View buttons at the left end of the horizontal scroll bar. Click the Slide View, Outline View, or Notes Pages View button to display any of these elements. To display the Handout Master, press and hold down the Shift key; then click the Handout Master button.

Understanding Masters and Templates

PowerPoint provides features that help you create attractive, eye-catching slides: Design Templates and Masters. Design templates contain color schemes and design elements that provide a background for a slide. The color schemes employ matching colors for text, lines, background, and so on; design elements are lines, shapes, or pictures added to the background to enhance the text and graphics you add to a slide. A design template also includes masters with pre-formatted styled fonts that complement the "look" the template represents; for example, the Embossed template looks formal and sophisticated. The use of the Times New Roman font and the bullet styles add to the look.

The Slide Master controls the font styles, formatting, and placement of text on a slide. A slide master, for example, may place all titles in the top center of each slide and use a 48-point Univers font to represent the titles. The text formatting and placement appears on the Slide Master.

Using slide masters and design templates create consistency within a presentation. When you choose a design template, the color scheme, layout, and formatting are applied to all slides in the presentation. Similarly, the elements and formatting of the master slide apply to all slides in the presentation. For added flexibility, PowerPoint enables you to change any of the elements of a design template: text formatting, color scheme, layout, master elements, and so on.

Using Masters

Tip
The Slide Master controls the formatting on all slides except title slides, which are controlled by the Title Master.

For every presentation you create, PowerPoint makes a set of *masters* available: a Slide Master, Title Master, Notes Master, and Handout Master. Masters correspond directly to the slides, speaker's notes, and handout components of a presentation. Masters contain the elements (text or pictures) that you want to appear on every component page. For instance, if you want your company logo to appear on each of your slides, it isn't necessary to insert the logo on individual slides. You add the logo to the Slide Master, and it automatically appears on every slide. Other elements you might add to a master include pictures or clip art, page numbers, the date, the title of the presentation, or reminders such as "Company Confidential."

To display a master, choose View, Master, which displays a submenu. From the submenu, choose Slide Master, Title Master, Handout Master, or Notes Master. Notice that the left end of the status bar indicates which master is currently displayed. The Slide Master shown in figure 24.7 includes areas for a master title, bulleted text, date, and footer text, included as parts of a master slide. Additionally, the company's name: Design Docs, Inc. has been added as a header on the master slide, and therefore to all slides in the presentation.

Note

You can quickly display a master by using the View buttons at the left end of the horizontal scroll bar. Press and hold down the Shift key; then click the Slide View (for Slide Master), Outline View (for Title Master), Slide Sorter View (for Handout Master), or Notes Pages View (for Notes Master) button. To return to slide, outline, slide sorter, or notes view, choose the appropriate command from the View menu, or click the View button at the lower left corner of the window.

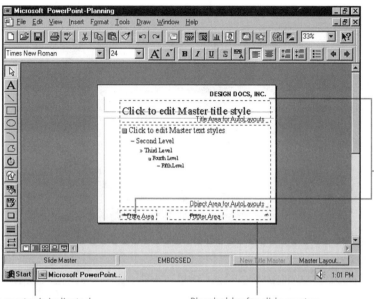

Fig. 24.7
A Slide Master
contains all the
elements that you
want to appear on
each slide.

Elements added to
the slide master

Slide master is indicated   Placeholder for slide master

Using Design Templates

A *design template* is a saved presentation file that contains predefined slide
and title masters, color schemes, and graphic elements. The design templates
provided with Microsoft are designed by professional graphic artists who
understand the use of color, space, and design. Each template is designed to
convey a certain look, feel, or attitude. Figure 24.8 shows how the EMBOSSED
template looks.

You select a design template based on the look you want for your presentation, and then apply the template to your new or existing presentation file.
The template applies to all slides in the presentation, and you can apply a
new template to a presentation at any time. Keep in mind that if you want
selected slides in a presentation to have a look different from the template,
you can change any aspect of any slide on an individual basis.

When you create a new "blank" presentation, you use PowerPoint's default
template called Default Design. It appears not to be a template at all because
it contains no color (except black and white), no graphic elements, and no
stylistic formatting. Figure 24.3, shown earlier in this chapter, illustrates the
Default Design template. This is the template you use if you want complete
control over your presentation's design, color scheme, and graphic elements,
because it lets you start as much "from scratch" as possible. You can, however, modify aspects of *any* template, not just the Default Design template.

▶ See "Working
with Templates,"
p. 621

▶ See "Working
with Color
Schemes,"
p. 639

V

Using PowerPoint

Fig. 24.8

The *EMBOSSED* template conveys a formal, sophisticated image.

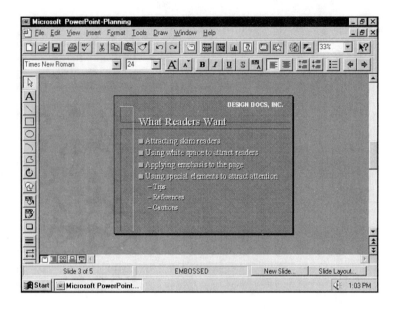

Understanding Objects and Layouts

PowerPoint slides are made up of *objects*; they are the key elements in any slide. Any time you add text, a graph, a drawing, an organization chart, clip art, a Word table, an Excel spreadsheet, or any other inserted element into a slide, it becomes an object. To work with an object, you select it and then change its content or size, move, copy, or delete it. You also can change *attributes* of an object, such as its color, shadow, border, and so on.

If you don't feel confident positioning or arranging objects on a slide, you can let PowerPoint do the work for you by using AutoLayouts. AutoLayouts save you the time and trouble of creating new objects for a new slide, and then arranging, positioning, and aligning them. Each AutoLayout contains placeholders for various kinds of objects such as text, clip art, organization charts, and so on. Placeholders appear as faint dotted lines on the slide and contain identifying text, such as "double-click to add clip art" or "click to add text."

Each AutoLayout contains different object placeholders in different arrangements. For instance, the AutoLayout for a presentation title page contains two text placeholders: one for a slide title and one for a subtitle. The title page AutoLayout is shown earlier in figure 24.3. The AutoLayout in figure 24.9 shows three placeholders: one for a slide title, one for text, and one for clip art.

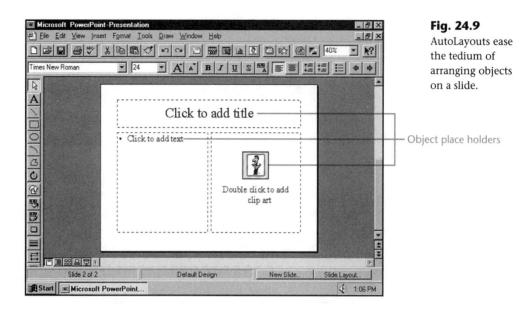

Fig. 24.9
AutoLayouts ease
the tedium of
arranging objects
on a slide.

Whenever you add a new slide to a presentation, PowerPoint automatically
displays the New Slide dialog box (see fig. 24.10). Use this dialog box to select
the desired AutoLayout. If you want to change the AutoLayout for an existing
slide, click the Slide Layout button on the status bar.

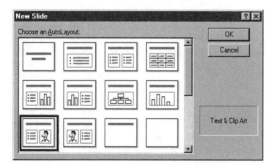

Fig. 24.10
The New Slide
dialog box dis-
plays a variety of
AutoLayouts.

Adding Objects to PowerPoint Slides

There is no reason for a PowerPoint presentation to contain dull slides full of
nothing but text. PowerPoint lets you add many different types of objects to
your slides to grab an audience's attention, add interest or humor, or to illustrate a particular point. Some objects can be created from within PowerPoint;
others can be imported from other applications.

V

Using PowerPoint

To insert an object from another application onto a PowerPoint slide, choose an option on the Insert menu or use one of the buttons on the Standard toolbar. Table 24.3 summarizes the options available on the Insert menu.

Note

Refer to Chapter 26, "Entering Slide Content," for more information about inserting objects in a presentation.

Table 24.3   Objects You Can Insert in PowerPoint Slides

Object Type	Description
Clip Art	A tool that provides access to a collection of prepared illustrations that depicts a wide variety of items and topics. ClipArt is an excellent choice if you don't feel confident about your drawing abilities.
Picture	If you have access to other prepared artwork, such as a bitmap file, you can insert it in a PowerPoint slide. (PowerPoint recognizes many different picture file formats.)
Movie	If you have access to movie files, such as Microsoft AVI files or Quicktime for Windows files, you can insert them onto a slide.
Sound	Allows you to insert sound files onto a slide.
Microsoft Graph	An embedded application that lets you create a chart or graph from tabular data. You create the graph in much the same way as you create a graph from spreadsheet data in Excel.
Microsoft Word Table	Because Microsoft Word is part of Microsoft Office, you have quick and easy access to Word if you want to insert a table in a slide. The Word table can contain up to 26 columns and up to five rows.
Object	Gives you access to a wide variety of object types such as Microsoft Excel spreadsheets and charts, Word documents, Paintbrush pictures, and Microsoft WordArt.

Chapter 25

Creating, Saving, and Opening Presentations

by Donna Minarik

To work with PowerPoint, you need to understand how to create a new presentation, save a presentation you want to keep, and open an existing presentation when you want to work with it again. PowerPoint provides a variety of methods for starting a presentation—from a template or wizard, for example. Alternatively, you can start with a blank presentation and add your own colors and graphic elements.

As you work on your presentation, you can choose to view one slide at a time or many slides at once. If you choose to view one slide at a time, you can work on the details of that slide, such as text entry and formatting, adding pictures, changing colors, and so on. When you have several slides completed, you can view them as small pictures, or *thumbnails*, on-screen at the same time so you can organize them.

Finally, you'll want to save your presentation for later editing, printing, or viewing. After saving a presentation, you can open it at any time for modification.

In this chapter, you learn to

- Create a new presentation using a variety of methods
- Change your view of a presentation
- Add, insert, and delete slides
- Save and close a presentation and open an existing one

Creating a New Presentation

To give you the greatest amount of flexibility, PowerPoint offers a variety of ways to create a new presentation. You can create a "blank" presentation that contains no color or style enhancements; you can copy the appearance of an existing presentation; or you can get step-by-step help in creating a presentation by using a wizard (wizards are described in the following section, "Creating a Presentation Using a Wizard").

◀ See "Starting and Exiting PowerPoint," p. 561

When you open the PowerPoint application, the dialog box pictured in figure 25.1 appears, allowing you to choose the method by which you will create your presentation. The only time you see this dialog box is when you first open PowerPoint.

Fig. 25.1
Use this dialog box to choose a method for creating a presentation.

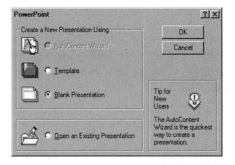

Each of the possible methods is discussed in the following sections.

Creating a Presentation Using a Wizard

A *wizard* is a guided online script that asks you to respond to questions related to the task you are performing. In PowerPoint, you create the framework for a new presentation by responding to questions presented in a series of dialog boxes. Using your answers, the wizard creates the new presentation file.

The AutoContent Wizard makes it easy for you to create a presentation from an outline. The Wizard asks you questions about the content of the presentation and, based on your answers, the Wizard creates an outline. The Wizard's outline uses each slide's title as the main heading; the heading appears next to a slide number and slide icon. You can then enter body text for the slide— using up to five levels if necessary. The Wizard helps you rearrange points in the outline and even rearrange slides within the outline. Editing is also easy using the Wizard's outline.

Creating a Presentation Using a Template

If you want to select a template, specify options for the slide masters and use suggested topics for a presentation; you will probably want to use one of the wizards discussed earlier to create the presentation. Sometimes, however, you want to apply only a template to a presentation. In such a case, select the Template option in the New Presentation dialog box.

◀ See "Understanding Masters and Templates," p. 571

To use a template to create a presentation, follow these steps:

1. Choose File, New. PowerPoint displays the New Presentation dialog box.

2. Select the Presentation Designs tab. PowerPoint displays the dialog box as seen in figure 25.2. In this figure, the Presentation design names are shown in Large Icons view. Other possible views are List and Details. You can select them by clicking the appropriate button in the dialog box, as labeled in the figure.

Tip
View the Presentation Designs by List to see more file names at a time; then you can choose any file name to preview.

V

Using PowerPoint

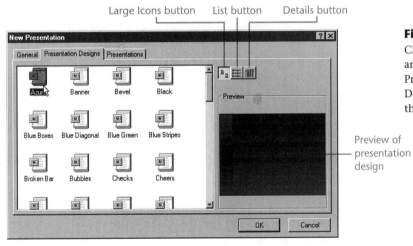

Fig. 25.2
Choose from among several Presentation Designs shown in this dialog box.

Preview of presentation design

3. Click any Presentation Design to see a preview of that design in the lower right corner of the dialog box. You can scroll the window to view more designs.

4. When you have selected a design, click OK to apply it to the presentation.

Creating a Blank Presentation

Tip
You can add colors, lines, and objects to a blank presentation to create your own template.

When you create a blank presentation, PowerPoint uses the DEFAULT.PPT template. The default template uses no color (black and white only) and includes no styles or enhancements. Creating a blank presentation puts you in complete control of the color scheme, layout, and style characteristics of your slides. You can leave the presentation blank, or you can add a template, colors, and other enhancements selectively at any time by using menu or toolbar commands. Use the blank presentation method when you want the maximum degree of flexibility.

▶ See "Working with Colors and Line Styles," p. 632

▶ See "Working with Color Schemes," p. 639

To create a blank presentation, follow these steps:

1. Choose File, New, or press Ctrl+N. PowerPoint displays the New Presentation dialog box (refer to fig. 25.2).

2. Select the Presentations tab and then choose the Blank Presentation icon. Choose OK. PowerPoint displays the New Slide dialog box, seen in figure 25.3.

Fig. 25.3
Choose the layout for your first slide in a blank presentation.

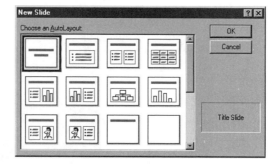

3. Select the layout you want to use for the first slide and then click OK. PowerPoint displays the first slide in your new presentation, using the layout you specify.

▶ See "Working with Templates," p. 621

Note

You can use a template from another presentation, whether the template is one of PowerPoint's or one of your own. (If the template is your own, be sure to save the presentation as a Design Template in the Save as Type list box in the File Save dialog box.) To apply an existing template to a presentation, choose Format, Apply Design Template. Choose the folder containing the template and in the Name list, select the template. Click Apply to close the dialog box and apply the template to the existing presentation.

Moving through a Presentation

When a presentation contains more than one slide, you must be able to display the slide you want easily. The left end of the status bar displays the number of the current slide. To move from one slide to another in Slide view or Notes Pages view, use the vertical scroll bar. To display the preceding slide, click the Previous Slide button. Click the Next Slide button to display the slide that follows. The Next and Previous Slide buttons are labeled in figure 25.4.

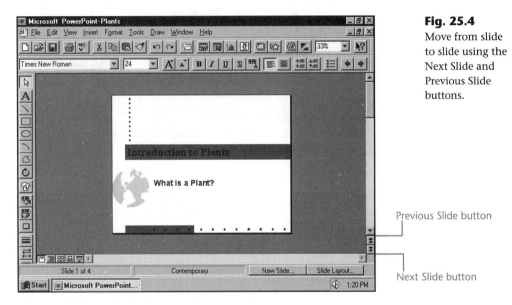

Fig. 25.4
Move from slide to slide using the Next Slide and Previous Slide buttons.

Previous Slide button

Next Slide button

V

Using PowerPoint

When a presentation contains a large number of slides, the Previous Slide and Next Slide buttons are not efficient for moving from a slide near the beginning to a slide near the end of a presentation. Instead, you can move to a specific slide quickly by dragging the scroll box in the vertical scroll bar. As you drag the box up or down, PowerPoint displays a slide number and title to the left of the scroll bar, as shown in figure 25.5. When the number of the slide you want to view is displayed, release the mouse button. PowerPoint moves directly to the slide you specify without having to move through each slide in-between.

Tip
If you prefer, you can use the Page Up and Page Down keys to move from one slide to another.

Fig. 25.5
Dragging the scroll box allows you to move to a specific slide quickly.

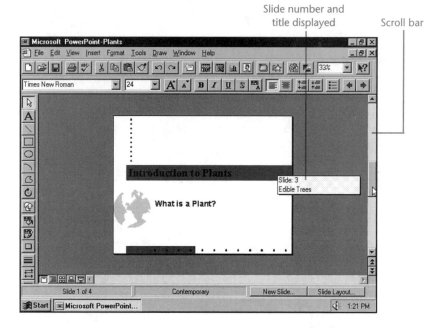

Slide number and title displayed

Scroll bar

Another way to quickly move from slide to slide is to switch to Slide Sorter view, and then double-click the slide you want to view. PowerPoint automatically switches back to Slide view and displays the slide you select. See the section "Viewing a Presentation," later in this chapter.

Adding, Inserting, and Deleting Slides

After you create your presentation file, you can add, insert, or delete slides whenever necessary. To add a slide, follow these steps:

1. Click the Insert New Slide button on the Standard toolbar or the New Slide button on the right of the status bar. You can also add a new slide by choosing Insert, New Slide or by pressing Ctrl+M. The New Slide dialog box appears (refer to fig. 25.3).

2. Choose the format of the new slide.

3. Click OK.

The new slide is inserted after the slide currently being displayed.

You can delete a slide at any time by displaying the slide you want to delete and choosing Edit, Delete Slide.

Note

You can also select the slide in Slide Sorter view and press the Delete key to delete a slide. See the section "Viewing a Presentation," later in this chapter.

Troubleshooting

I accidentally deleted a slide from my presentation. How can I restore it?

In any of the views (Slide, Outline, Slide Sorter, and Notes Pages), you can click the Undo button in the toolbar, choose Edit, Undo, or press Ctrl+Z. Remember that you must use Undo *immediately* after deleting the slide. If you take any other actions first, the slide cannot be restored.

I inserted a new slide in the wrong location in my presentation. Can I move it?

Yes. It's best to use Slide Sorter view to rearrange slides in a presentation. For specific instructions, see "Using Slide Sorter View" later in this chapter.

Tip

If you want to add your own objects and text blocks to a slide, choose the Blank slide AutoLayout in the New Slide dialog box.

▶ See "Inserting Clip-Art Pictures," p. 598

▶ See "Inserting Other Objects," p. 603

V

Using PowerPoint

Viewing a Presentation

PowerPoint offers several ways to view your presentation. Each view has a particular purpose and advantage. The five views are summarized in Table 25.1 and described in detail in the sections that follow.

The quickest way to switch views is to click the view buttons, pictured in table 25.1, which are found in the bottom left corner of the PowerPoint window. Simply click the button for the view you want to use to change the view of the current presentation.

Table 25.1 PowerPoint Views		
View		**Description**
	Slide	Displays individual slides in Full-Slide view, which enables you to see the slide in detail.
	Outline	Displays the text from all slides in the presentation, giving you an overview of the content of the presentation.
	Slide Sorter	Displays a miniature version of every slide in the presentation in proper order; an overview of the look and flow of the presentation.
	Notes Pages	Displays a miniature version of an individual slide at the top of the screen and speaker's notes below the slide; enables you to review your notes while viewing the slide.
	Slide Show	Displays slides as they would appear during an on-screen slide show by using the entire screen area. Press Page Down and Page Up to switch from slide to slide. Press Esc to end Slide Show view.

Zooming In and Out

Regardless of the view you choose, PowerPoint displays your presentation at a preset percentage of its full size. The display percentage is the zoom setting that PowerPoint uses. The percentage PowerPoint uses varies, depending on your video driver, the screen resolution you use, and the size of your monitor.

Tip
Choose the Zoom Control list and select Fit to make the slide fit completely on the page.

PowerPoint uses a different zoom percentage in each view. The default percentages are designed to provide an optimized view within the window. If you zoom in closer by setting a higher zoom percentage, you reduce the portion of the page that you are able to view.

To change the zoom percentage in any view, select an option from the Zoom Control drop-down list in the Standard toolbar shown in figure 25.6, or type a new percentage in the Zoom Percentage box.

To change the percentage by using a menu command, choose View, Zoom to display the Zoom dialog box; select a zoom option or type a custom percentage in the Percent box; then click OK.

Using Slide View

Slide view displays individual slides in the current PowerPoint window. Figure 25.7 shows a presentation displayed in Slide view. This view is the best way to get a detailed picture of each slide. Slide view also is useful when you are entering or changing slide content. To switch from one slide to another, press the Page Up and Page Down keys or use the scroll bar, as described in "Moving through a Presentation" earlier in this chapter.

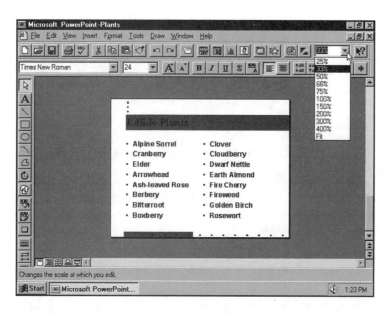

Fig. 25.6
Choose a percentage from the Zoom Control drop-down list, or just type a percentage in the Zoom Control text box.

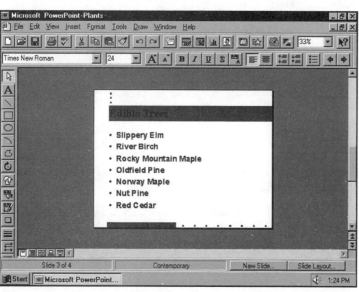

Fig. 25.7
Use Slide view to enter and edit text in individual slides.

V

Using PowerPoint

Using Outline View

Outline view displays only the text of multiple slides in outline form, as shown in figure 25.8. A numbered slide icon appears to the left of each slide's title. When a slide contains no pictures or graphics, the slide icon is empty except for a narrow line near the top indicating the title. When a slide contains a picture or other object, the slide icon also contains a graphical representation. This difference helps you identify at a glance which slides contain objects and which slides contain only text.

Fig. 25.8
A presentation shown in Outline view makes organization and rearrangement of slides easy.

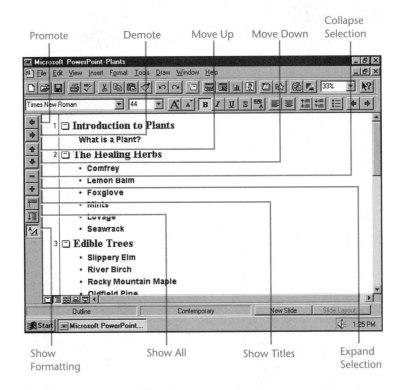

Tip
To view only the titles of each slide, click the Show Titles icon; to view all titles and text, click the Show All icon.

Note

You can move slides and their contents around in Outline view by clicking and dragging the slide icon to the left of the slide title. To make sure all of a slide's contents move with the title, collapse the outline first. To collapse an outline to just the titles, click the Show Titles icon on the toolbar.

Using Slide Sorter View

Slide Sorter view gives you an overall perspective of your presentation by displaying a miniature version of each slide on a single screen. The number of slides you can view at one time depends on your video card, driver, and monitor, as well as on the zoom percentage used. The lower the zoom percentage, the more slides you can view.

In Slide Sorter view (see fig. 25.9), the slide number appears near the bottom right corner of each slide. When your presentation output is intended to be a slide show, the amount of time each slide is displayed during the slide show appears near the bottom left corner of each slide.

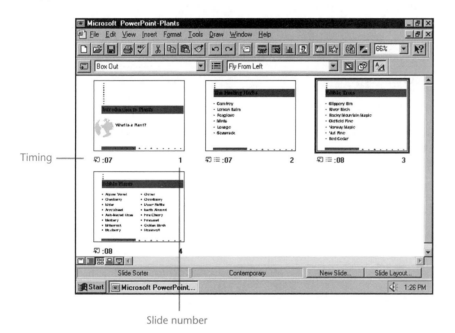

Timing

Slide number

Fig. 25.9
Use Slide Sorter view to get an overall picture of your slide presentation and to reorganize slides in the presentation.

V

Using PowerPoint

You can change the order of slides and copy slides in Slide Sorter view. First, you must select a slide.

To select a slide in Slide Sorter view, use the arrow keys to highlight a slide, or click the slide you want to select. A bold outline surrounds the selected slide. To select multiple slides, press and hold down the Shift key while clicking all the slides you want to select. Another way to select multiple slides is to click and hold down the left mouse button as you drag an outline around the slides you want to include. To cancel any selection, click any blank area of the Slide Sorter view window.

In Slide Sorter view, rearranging slides is as simple as selecting a slide, and then dragging it to a new location. As you drag the mouse, the mouse pointer changes to a miniature slide with a down arrow. When you move the pointer between two slides, a vertical bar appears to mark the location where the slide will be inserted if you release the mouse button. If you have selected more than one slide, you can move them all at once using this method as well. PowerPoint automatically renumbers rearranged slides.

Slide Sorter view is the best view to use when copying slides. Select the slide (or slides) you want to copy; then press and hold down the Ctrl key as you drag the slide to the copy location. The mouse pointer changes to a miniature slide with a plus symbol (+), and a vertical bar appears between slides to mark the location where the slide will be inserted. When you release the mouse button, a copy of the selected slide is inserted in the new location.

Troubleshooting

I can't select the text on a slide in Slide Sorter view.

You cannot edit text or otherwise manipulate individual slide elements when in Slide Sorter view. You can, however, double-click the slide you want to edit to change to Slides view so you can edit.

I can't move slide 2 to slide 1's spot in slide sorter view.

To move a slide to another spot, you must click and drag the mouse pointer all the way to the left of the slide until the vertical bar appears. Release the mouse button, and the slide will move.

Using Notes Pages View

PowerPoint provides special notes pages on which you can type notes to be used as you make the presentation. The top half of the page displays a reduced version of the slide; the bottom portion of the page contains a text object in which you can type the text of your notes (see fig. 25.10).

At PowerPoint's default zoom percentage, Notes Pages view displays an entire page on-screen. When you are typing or editing speaker's notes, however, it's difficult to read the text at the default percentage. If you use a larger percentage (such as 66 or 75), the text you type is more readable, and you still can view part of the slide content as you type.

To change the view to Notes Pages, click the Notes Pages View icon on the horizontal scroll bar, or choose View, Notes Pages.

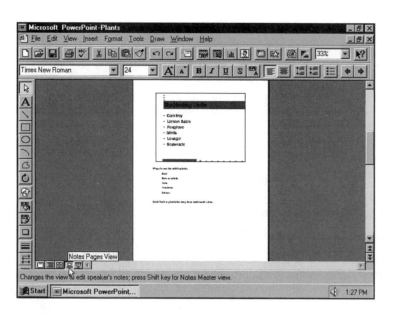

Fig. 25.10
A slide presenta-
tion can be shown
in Notes Pages
view; to better see
the notes on-
screen, zoom to
75% or 100%.

Using Slide Show View

Slide Show view enables you see each slide in your presentation at maximum
size. When you use this view, the PowerPoint window is not visible; each
slide occupies the complete screen area, as shown in figure 25.11. If your final
output is intended to be an on-screen slide show, Slide Show view is useful
for previewing your slides to see how they will look during the actual slide
show.

▶ See "Running
a Slide Show,"
p. 651

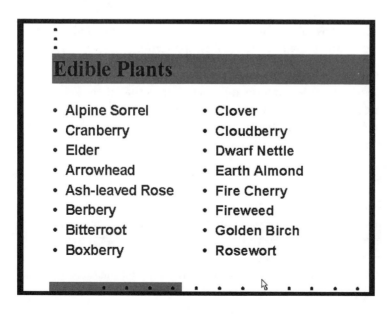

Fig. 25.11
A presentation
shown in Slide
Show view can be
run on-screen for
customers to see.

V

Using PowerPoint

> **Note**
>
> Slide Show view displays your slides starting with the slide displayed before you switch views. If you want the slide show to begin at slide 1, be sure to select slide 1 before switching to Slide Show view. You can also press Home to move to the first slide and End to move to the last slide in a presentation.

Saving a Presentation

When you save a presentation, PowerPoint saves *all* components of the presentation (slides, outline, speaker's notes, and handout pages) in one file.

Tip
To quickly save changes to an existing file, press Ctrl+S.

You save a file in PowerPoint the same as you save a file in any other Microsoft Office application. The first time you save a file, PowerPoint displays the File Save dialog box, regardless of whether you choose File, Save, or File, Save As. When you want to save an existing file under a different name, on a different disk or directory, or as a different file type, choose File, Save As. When you want to save changes to an existing file, choose File, Save, or click the Save icon.

You can name the file using long file names as you would in any other Windows 95 application.

Opening an Existing Presentation

◀ See "Working with Files," p. 102

You open a PowerPoint presentation using the same method you use to open any file in any of the Microsoft Office applications.

As in many applications, you can open several presentations at the same time. The active presentation appears on top of the others, and its title bar is highlighted. As with all Windows applications, the names of all open presentation files are listed in the Window menu and appear on the taskbar.

Closing a Presentation

To close an existing presentation, choose File, Close, or double-click the presentation window's Control menu box. If you have made changes in the file since you last saved it, PowerPoint asks whether you want to save those changes. Choose Yes to save the changes, No to ignore the changes, or Cancel to return to the presentation without saving the file.❖

Chapter 26

Entering Slide Content

by Donna Minarik

PowerPoint slides can contain much more than just text. You can insert clip art, pictures, tables, worksheets, graphs, organization charts, and many other types of objects into your slides. This chapter begins by teaching you how to choose a slide layout and how to enter and edit slide text. You also learn the steps required for entering information other than text (such as pictures, tables, and graphs).

In this chapter, you learn to

- ■ Work with AutoLayout

- ■ Enter and edit text

- ■ Insert clip art, tables, and worksheets

- ■ Insert graphs, organization charts, and other objects

Reviewing AutoLayout

In Chapter 24, "Getting Acquainted with PowerPoint," you were briefly introduced to AutoLayout, a PowerPoint feature that includes 21 prepared slide layouts with different object placeholders and arrangements. Using AutoLayout, you can choose a slide layout that contains the object placeholders you need for your current slide. A title slide, for example, contains two text object placeholders: one for a title and one for a subtitle. After you select a slide layout, you insert the actual content of your presentation—text, pictures, and graphs—into the placeholders on the slide.

Whenever you add a new slide to a presentation, PowerPoint automatically displays the Slide Layout or New Slide dialog box, which contains the 24 AutoLayouts (see fig. 26.1).

Tip
Scroll in the window to display more slide layouts than the first 12 you see on-screen.

Fig. 26.1

Use the Slide Layout/New Slide dialog box to choose a layout for a slide.

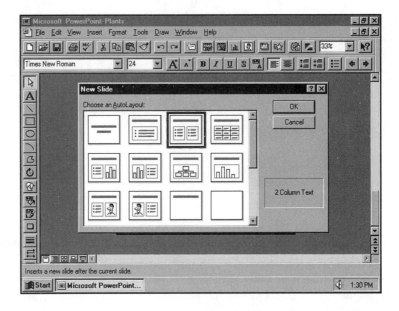

Note

The dialog box shown in figure 26.1 is titled Slide Layout or New Slide, depending on the method you use to display it. The contents of the dialog box are always the same regardless of the name shown in the title bar. To avoid confusion, this chapter refers to this dialog box as the Slide Layout dialog box from here on.

As you select the different AutoLayouts, a description of the highlighted layout appears in the bottom right corner of the dialog box. This description names the types of objects included in the layout, such as title slide, table, bulleted list, organization chart, and so on.

The solid gray lines at the top of each slide layout represent the slide title. Other text in a slide layout is represented by faint gray lines. Text nearly always is formatted with bullets. The placeholders that contain vertical bars represent graphs, and those with pictures represent clip art or pictures. The empty boxes represent placeholders for other objects, usually imported from other applications, such as Excel.

Highlight the layout you want to use for your new slide and then choose Apply, or double-click the layout you want to use. PowerPoint automatically applies the selected layout to the new slide, complete with placeholders for objects. After you choose a layout, replace the sample in each placeholder with actual text or another object, such as a graph or table.

> **Note**
>
> Notice that one slide layout in the Slide Layout dialog box is blank; it contains no placeholder. Use this layout when you want to create and place text and the objects in a slide.

The slide layout can be changed at any time. You can display the Slide Layout dialog box by clicking the Slide Layout button at the bottom of the PowerPoint window or by choosing F_ormat, Slide L_ayout.

> **Caution**
>
> After you enter information in a placeholder, be careful about changing the slide layout. The objects that contain information remain in the slide while the placeholders for the new layout are added. PowerPoint tries to rearrange objects so that all of them will fit, but this isn't always possible. The slide can become cluttered with overlapping objects and placeholders, and sometimes an object will be deleted.

Entering and Editing Text

Virtually every slide in a presentation contains text of some kind, even if it's just a title. Entering and editing text in PowerPoint is similar to entering and editing text in any Office application. The following sections describe how to enter the text content of your slides and how to edit the text when necessary.

◀ See "Typing and Editing," p. 68

◀ See "Using Undo," p. 75

Typing the Content for Your Slides

One method of entering slide text involves replacing the sample text in a slide placeholder with your own text. The slide shown in figure 26.2, for example, includes two placeholders for text: one that contains a sample title and one that contains a bulleted list. The third placeholder is for clip art. A faint dotted line appears around each placeholder.

Click anywhere within a placeholder to select it. The faint outline is replaced by a wide hashed border, shown in figure 26.3. This border indicates that the current placeholder is selected. The sample text disappears, and an insertion point appears inside the placeholder, indicating that you can enter text. In a title or subtitle placeholder, the insertion point can be centered or left-aligned. In a bulleted-list placeholder, the sample text disappears and the bullet remains, with the insertion point positioned where the text will begin.

V

Using PowerPoint

Fig. 26.2

This slide layout contains two placeholders for text and one placeholder for clip art.

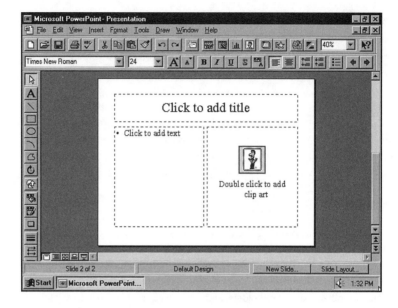

Fig. 26.3

A selected text placeholder is indicated by a wide-hashed border.

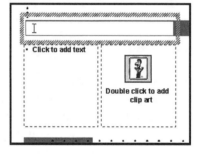

Type the actual text for your slide inside the selected placeholder. In the case of titles and subtitles, press Enter only when you want to begin a new centered line of text. In the case of bullets, press Enter only when you want to begin a new bulleted item. If your bulleted text is too long to fit on one line, PowerPoint automatically wraps the text to the next line and aligns the text appropriately.

When you finish entering text, deselect the object by clicking a blank area of the slide or the gray border around the slide. Notice that the object no longer is defined by the faint dotted line (see fig. 26.4). The absence of the dotted line gives you a more realistic idea of how the completed slide will look.

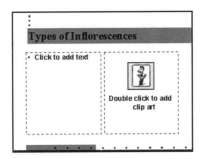

Fig. 26.4
When a text object
contains actual
text, it is no longer
surrounded by a
dotted border.

Creating New Text Objects

You may need to add a label or other text that is not part of a placeholder. Suppose that your slide contains a title and a bulleted list like the one shown in figure 26.5. If you want to add a note that is not formatted like the bulleted list, you must add the note as a separate object.

To create a text object, follow these steps:

1. Click the Text Tool button in the Drawing toolbar.

2. Position the pointer (now a vertical bar) where you want the text box to be.

3. Click the mouse button. A text box the size of one character appears. An insertion point is visible in the text box.

4. Type the desired text. The text box expands to accommodate the text you enter. If you want to type on a new line, press Enter.

Tip
You can also drag
the text tool to
create a rectangle
in which the add-
ed text will go.

Troubleshooting

I selected an AutoLayout that contains bullets, but I've decided not to use bullets. How do I get rid of them?

Click the Bullet On/Off button on the Standard toolbar to add or remove bullets. To change the type of character used for the bullet, choose Format, Bullet, or choose Bullet from the shortcut menu.

V

Using PowerPoint

Fig. 26.5
Text notes can be
added anywhere
on a slide.

Bulleted list from
placeholder

Text object created
with Text tool

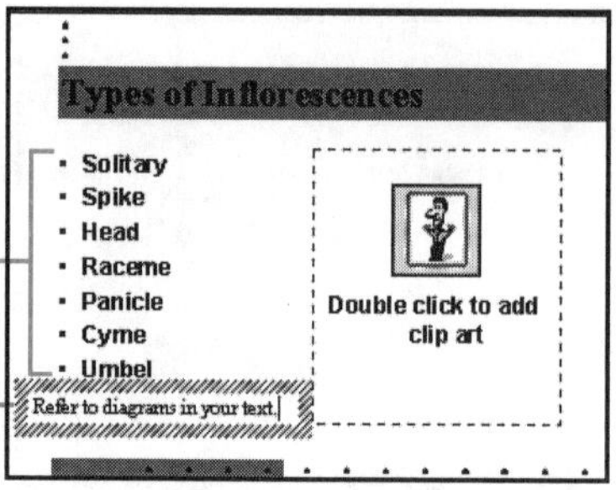

Changing Text and Correcting Errors

◀ See "Selecting
Text," p. 74

Text in any text object can be changed by clicking the object. An insertion
point appears, indicating that you are able to edit the text. Use standard editing conventions to change text, as summarized in table 26.1.

Table 26.1   Editing Conventions for Text Objects

Action	Result
Arrow keys	Move the insertion point right, left, up, or down within the text
Backspace or Delete	Erases characters (to the left and right, respectively) of the insertion point. Also clears selected text from the object without placing it in the Clipboard.
Click and drag the mouse	Selects a string of characters
Double-click a word	Selects the entire word
Triple-click a line	Selects the entire line
Ctrl+A	Selects all text in a selected text object
Ctrl+click	Selects an entire sentence
Ctrl+X	Cuts selected text and places it in the Clipboard
Ctrl+C	Copies selected text to the Clipboard
Ctrl+V	Pastes text from the Clipboard

In addition to the keyboard shortcuts listed in table 26.1, you can use the
Cut, Copy, Paste, Clear, and Select All commands (in the Edit menu) to edit
text. When text is selected on a slide, the Cut, Copy, and Paste commands
also appear in the shortcut menu.

When you finish editing text in a text box, be sure to click any blank area of the slide or the gray area surrounding the slide to deselect the text box.

Tip
You can click the border of a selected text block to reveal handles; drag a corner or side handle to resize the text block.

Checking Your Spelling in PowerPoint

The spelling checker in PowerPoint compares all the words in your document with a dictionary file, much the way any Microsoft Office application does. When the spelling checker finds a word that's not in the dictionary file, it highlights the word in your slide and displays the word in the Spelling dialog box, shown in figure 26.6.

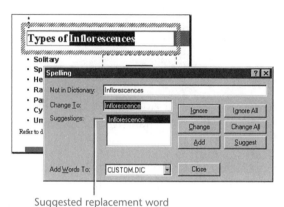

Suggested replacement word

Fig. 26.6
The Spelling dialog box displays unrecognized words.

V

Using PowerPoint

> **Note**
>
> The spelling checker checks text in all objects in a presentation file *except* those objects that contain text imported from other applications.

◀ See "Checking Spelling," p. 90

The spelling checker moves through your presentation one slide at a time, and then checks the speaker's notes (if any) before closing the Spelling dialog box. You can stop using the spelling checker at any time by clicking the Close button in the Spelling dialog box.

To check the spelling in a presentation file, follow these steps:

1. Choose Tools, Spelling or click the Spelling button on the Standard toolbar to display the Spelling dialog box. The spelling checker highlights the first unrecognized word in the presentation file and displays the word in the Not in Dictionary box.

2. Choose the appropriate command button (Ignore, Ignore All, Change, Change All, or Add). The spelling checker takes the indicated action and then highlights the next unrecognized word.

3. Repeat step 2 until the spelling checker displays a message saying that the entire presentation has been checked.

4. Choose OK.

> **Note**
>
> You can use PowerPoint's AutoCorrect (Tools, AutoCorrect) to automatically correct common typing errors. If, for example, you constantly type "wrod" instead of "word," you can add this to the AutoCorrect list and as you type the wrong letters, PowerPoint automatically corrects your typing.

◄ See "Letting AutoCorrect Do Your Spelling for You," p. 95

Inserting Clip-Art Pictures

One of the best ways to spice up a slide show is to insert a clip-art drawing. The ClipArt Gallery contains many drawings that cover a wide range of topics.

You can insert clip art into a slide in several ways. If you have selected a slide layout with a clip-art placeholder, simply double-click the placeholder to choose a clip-art file to insert.

> **Note**
>
> The first time you attempt to access clip art, PowerPoint asks whether you want to add clip-art files from Microsoft Office. Responding Yes makes the clip-art files available for you to insert into your slides.

You can also insert clip art on a slide without a clip-art placeholder by choosing Insert, Clip Art, or clicking the Insert Clip Art button on the Standard toolbar. Regardless of the method used to access clip art, the next step is to select a file in the ClipArt Gallery 2.0 dialog box, shown in figure 26.7.

Tip
If you want the clip art on every slide in the presentation, insert it on the Slide Master.

A list of categories appears at the top of the ClipArt Gallery dialog box. The box below the category list displays a sample of each clip-art file in the current category. Use the scroll bar, Page Up/Page Down, or the arrow keys to see each picture in a category. If you prefer to scroll through the entire selection of clip-art files, select the (All Categories) option in the category list box.

To add a clip-art drawing to your slide, follow these steps:

1. Display the slide into which you want to insert clip art.

2. Choose Insert, Clip Art; click the Clip Art button on the standard toolbar; or, if your slide contains a clip-art placeholder, double-click it. The Microsoft ClipArt Gallery dialog box appears.

3. Select a category in the category list.

4. Select a picture, and then click OK. PowerPoint closes the ClipArt Gallery dialog box and inserts the picture into your slide. Figure 26.8 shows a slide with a clip-art picture.

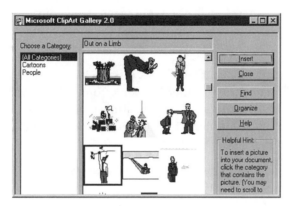

Fig. 26.7
The ClipArt Gallery dialog box allows you to choose from a variety of pictures.

V

Using PowerPoint

Fig. 26.8
Add clip art to a slide to make the presentation more interesting and to make it look more professional.

Inserting a Word Table or Excel Worksheet

A table of data can convey useful information on a slide. Although PowerPoint's text-editing tools don't provide the means to create a table, PowerPoint enables you to use Word or Excel to create the tables you need.

To create a worksheet or table, click the Insert Microsoft Excel Worksheet button or the Insert Microsoft Word Table button in the Standard toolbar.

A drop-down grid of cells appears. This grid enables you to define the size of your table or worksheet, as shown in figure 26.9. Click and drag the mouse pointer across the cells in the grid to indicate how many rows or columns you want in your table or worksheet. The cells you select are highlighted, and the dimensions are listed below the grid.

When you release the mouse button, PowerPoint inserts a special object into your slide. In the case of a Microsoft Word table, the object looks like the one shown in figure 26.10. Notice that PowerPoint's Standard toolbar and menu bar are temporarily replaced by the Word menus and toolbar, so that all Word features and commands are available to you while you create your table. In effect, you are using Word inside a PowerPoint window.

◀ See "Working with Tables," p. 286

To create the content of your table, click the area in which you want to add text, or press Tab to move the insertion point from left to right across the cells in the table. Press the up- and down-arrow keys to move the insertion point from one row to another. Use standard editing conventions to enter and edit text in the table.

◀ See "Editing Worksheet Data," p. 321

When your table is complete, deselect it by clicking any blank area outside the table or the gray area that surrounds the slide. When the table no longer is the selected object, the PowerPoint menus and toolbar return. You can make changes in the table at any time by double-clicking inside the table. When the table is selected again, the Word menus and toolbar return automatically. Figure 26.11 shows a completed Word table on a PowerPoint slide.

Insert Microsoft Word Table button ——— ┌— Insert Microsoft Excel Worksheet button

Fig. 26.9
Use the grid to choose the number of rows and columns for the Word table to be inserted.

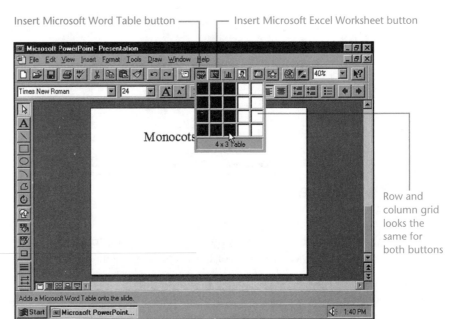

Row and column grid looks the same for both buttons

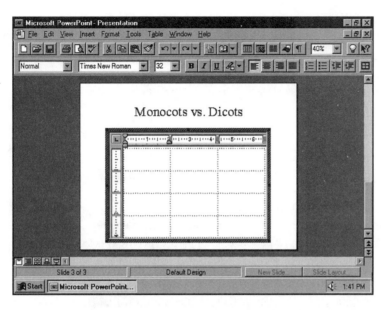

Fig. 26.10
Inserting a Word table provides Word's formatting flexibility.

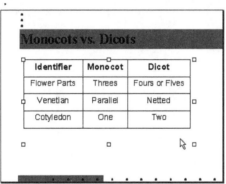

Fig. 26.11
Move a completed Word table by selecting it and then dragging it to a new position.

Tip
Resize the table by dragging one of the corner or side handles.

The same principles that govern Word tables hold true for Excel worksheets: when you insert a worksheet, you enter, edit, and format the data in Excel and then click outside of the worksheet to return to PowerPoint. When you click the Insert Excel Worksheet button in the PowerPoint toolbar, a drop-down grid appears. Click and drag the mouse pointer across the cells in the grid to indicate the number of rows and columns for your worksheet. PowerPoint inserts a special worksheet object into your slide, and Power-Point's standard menus and toolbar are replaced by the Excel menus and toolbar.

Use Excel's commands and tools to create and edit your worksheet. When the worksheet is complete, deselect it by clicking any blank area of the slide or the border of the slide; the standard PowerPoint menus and toolbar return.

Tip
Select the text in the table and change the type-face, size, attributes, alignment, and so on, just as you would any text in Word.

V

Using PowerPoint

◀ See "Formatting
Text," p. 190

◀ See "Entering
Data," p. 305

◀ See "Editing
Worksheet
Data," p. 321

◀ See "Formatting
Numbers,"
p. 341

◀ See "Starting
Microsoft
Graph," p. 463

> **Note**
>
> Graphs, or *charts*, are graphic representations of data in worksheets. In a presentation, a bar, pie, or area chart often can depict data much more clearly than words can. In PowerPoint, you can insert a graph into a slide by using an application called Microsoft Graph.

Inserting an Organization Chart

Organization charts can be added to PowerPoint presentations. An organization chart can convey information about new management, a group or department reorganization, or people to contact for specific types of information.

To insert an organization chart into a PowerPoint slide, you can use a slide layout that includes a placeholder for an organization chart. Choose Format, Slide Layout, or click the Slide Layout button at the bottom of the PowerPoint window to display the Slide Layout dialog box (see fig. 26.12).

Fig. 26.12
The Organization
Chart layout is
selected in the
Slide Layout dialog
box.

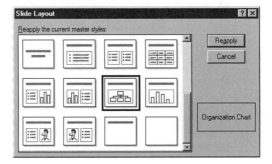

Tip
You can also add
an organization
chart by choosing
Insert, Object, and
then choosing
Microsoft Organization Chart from
the resulting dialog box.

In the dialog box, highlight the layout that includes the organization chart; then click OK. PowerPoint applies the layout to the current slide, inserting an organization-chart placeholder. To access Microsoft Organization Chart, double-click the placeholder. After a few seconds, the Microsoft Organization Chart window appears. Figure 26.13 shows a sample organization chart.

Enter the appropriate information in the sample organization chart, using Microsoft Organization Chart commands. Because Microsoft Organization Chart is a separate application, it contains its own help files. If you are not familiar with this application, select any of the topics listed in the Help menu or press F1.

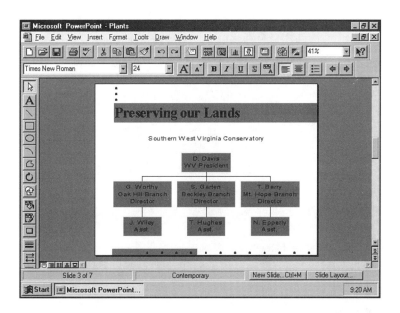

Fig. 26.13
The MS Organization Chart application enables you to create simple or complex charts for your presentation.

When the organization chart is complete and you're ready to return to your PowerPoint presentation, choose File, Update [*file name*] and then choose Exit and Return to [*file name*] command from the Microsoft Organization Chart File menu. The organization chart is inserted into the current slide. To deselect the organization chart, click any blank area of the slide or the gray area surrounding the slide.

Tip
Double-click the chart to open the MS Organization Chart application and edit the chart.

Inserting Other Objects

In this chapter, you have learned how to insert clip art, a Word table, an Excel worksheet, and an organization chart into a PowerPoint slide. You can insert many other types of objects by choosing Insert, Object. This command opens another application on top of your PowerPoint window, enabling you to create a new file or open an existing file within that application.

To insert a new file from another application, follow these steps:

1. Display the PowerPoint slide into which you want to insert an object.

2. Choose Insert, Object. PowerPoint displays the Insert Object dialog box (see fig. 26.14). The Object Type list displays all the types of files you can insert into a PowerPoint slide.

Fig. 26.14
The Insert Object
dialog box lists
several types of
objects that can be
inserted onto a
slide.

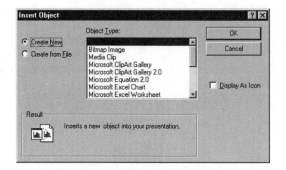

> **Note**
>
> Because the Insert Object feature of PowerPoint works by opening another
> application, you must have that application installed on your computer.

3. Select the Create New option.

4. (Optional) Select the Display As Icon option if you want to display the
   object as an icon.

5. In the Object Type list, select the object you want to insert; then click
   OK. The Insert Object dialog box closes, and the window for the appropriate application opens on top of the PowerPoint window.

6. Use the application as you normally would. That is, create a new file if
   necessary, or simply select an item (such as an equation or a clip-art
   file). For cases in which you select an item, PowerPoint inserts the item
   and closes the application. For cases in which you create a new file,
   return to PowerPoint by choosing the Exit and Return to [File Name]
   command from the open application's File menu. The application
   window closes, and the file you created is inserted into the current
   PowerPoint slide.

7. Click any blank area of the slide or the gray area surrounding the slide
   to deselect the object.

If you want to insert an existing file created in another application onto
your slide, select the Create From File option in the Insert Object dialog box.
When you insert an existing file from another application, the file is inserted
onto the PowerPoint slide directly; PowerPoint does not open the application
that was used to create the file. If you want to modify the file, you must open
the application by double-clicking the object after it is inserted into your
PowerPoint slide.

To insert an existing file from another application, follow these steps:

1. Display the PowerPoint slide into which you want to insert an object.

2. Choose Insert, Object. PowerPoint displays the Insert Object dialog box.

3. (Optional) Select the Display As Icon option if you want to display the object as an icon.

4. Select an item in the Object Type box.

5. Select the Create from File option. PowerPoint modifies the Insert Object dialog box to match the one shown in figure 26.15.

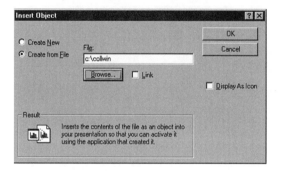

Fig. 26.15
The Insert Object dialog box changes if you choose to create from file instead of creating a new object.

6. If you know the name of the file, type the complete path name in the File box. If not, click the Browse button, which displays the Browse dialog box with a directory tree. Select the correct file name, and then click OK. The Browse dialog box closes, and you return to the Insert Object dialog box, where the file name you selected now appears in the File box.

7. Click OK in the Insert Object dialog box. The file you specified is inserted into your PowerPoint slide *without* opening the application used to create the file.

8. Click any blank area of the slide or the gray area surrounding the slide to deselect the inserted object.

Troubleshooting

I can't select the text or object on my slide.

The text or object is on the slide master. Choose <u>V</u>iew, <u>M</u>aster, and then choose <u>S</u>lide Master of <u>T</u>itle Master. After editing the text or object, choose <u>V</u>iew, <u>S</u>lides.

I inserted a clip art image and now I can't replace it with another clip art by double-clicking the object.

If the clip art gallery doesn't appear when you double-click a clip art image, you've converted the image to a PowerPoint object. To replace the object, select it, delete it, and then insert a new clip art object.

Chapter 27

Working with Objects

by Donna Minarik

You were introduced to objects in Chapter 24, "Getting Acquainted with PowerPoint," and you learned more about entering content in objects in Chapter 26, "Entering Slide Content." Objects are the building blocks of slides that contain primarily text, graphics, or pictures, but also can contain other elements such as tables, spreadsheets, or organization charts. You need to understand how to work with objects because they are the key components of a PowerPoint slide.

In this chapter, you learn to

- Select and group objects
- Move, copy, resize, and delete objects
- Align objects
- Use the grid
- Rotate and flip objects
- Stack objects

Selecting and Grouping Objects

◀ See "Drawing
Shapes," p. 551

◀ See "Under-
standing
Objects and
Layouts,"
p. 574

Before you can make any kind of change to an object such as adding color, changing size, moving, or deleting it, you must select the object. Selecting a single object is as simple as clicking it. When you click an object such as a chart, ClipArt drawing, or organization chart, *resize handles* surround the object in a rectangular shape. When you click a text object, a gray border appears; click the border to display the handles (see fig. 27.1). Resize handles are small boxes that appear at the four corners and on each of the four sides of the rectangle. Resize handles indicate that an object has been selected. In "Resizing and Scaling Objects" later in this chapter, you learn how to use these handles to change the size of an object.

Fig. 27.1
An object is selected when its resize handles are visible.

Resize handles ——

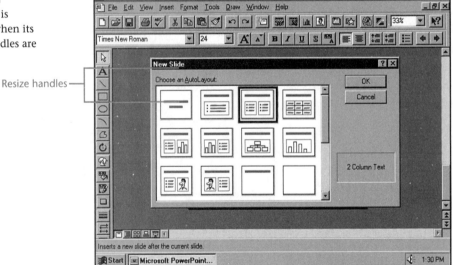

Selecting Multiple Objects

In PowerPoint, you generally select an object to move, copy, or resize it, or to change one or more of its attributes. An *attribute* is any characteristic that is applied to an object, such as color, border, fill, and shadow. Sometimes you may want to select more than one object at a time. Selecting multiple objects can save you the time of applying the same attribute to several objects individually. When you select multiple objects, any attribute you change is applied to *all* selected objects. To change the fill color of several objects to blue, for instance, select all objects and then apply the blue fill color.

To select multiple objects at once, press and hold down the Shift key and then click each object you want to include in the selection. The resize handles appear around each object you select (see fig. 27.2). If you select an object by mistake and want to remove it from your selection, continue holding down the Shift key while you click the object again. PowerPoint removes that object from the selection. Release the Shift key when you have selected all objects.

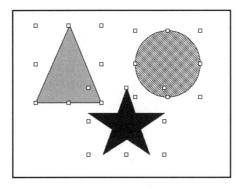

Fig. 27.2
In a multiple selection, resize handles appear around each selected object.

Another way to select multiple objects is to use the Selection Tool button on the Drawing toolbar. Click the Selection Tool button, and drag the mouse across all objects you want to include in the selection. As you drag the mouse, PowerPoint draws a dashed rectangle that encloses all selected objects. When you release the mouse button, the rectangle disappears, and the resize handles of each object in the selection are visible.

◀ See "Getting Familiar with the PowerPoint Window," p. 562

V

Using PowerPoint

Note

You must fully enclose all objects within the selection rectangle you draw. If a portion of any object is not enclosed within the rectangle, that object is excluded from the selection. You can add an object to any selection by holding down the Shift key and clicking the object.

To quickly select every object on a slide, choose Edit, Select All, or press Ctrl+A. PowerPoint immediately displays the selection handles of all objects on the slide.

Troubleshooting

When I draw a selection box around several objects, some objects are not selected. Why?

Remember that you must fully enclose all objects you want to select in the selection box. If a portion of an object falls outside the selection box, it isn't selected.

(continues)

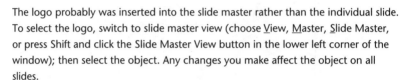

(continued)

Can I select objects on multiple slides at once?

No. The only way to view multiple slides at once is to use slide sorter view, and you cannot select objects in this view.

I try to select the company logo on my slide, but nothing happens. Why?

The logo probably was inserted into the slide master rather than the individual slide. To select the logo, switch to slide master view (choose <u>V</u>iew, <u>M</u>aster, <u>S</u>lide Master, or press Shift and click the Slide Master View button in the lower left corner of the window); then select the object. Any changes you make affect the object on all slides.

◄ See "Viewing a Presentation," p. 583

Grouping Objects

Grouping objects enables you to treat several objects as a single object. Suppose, for example, that you use PowerPoint's drawing tools to draw a company logo made up of more than one object (see fig. 27.3). Each object comprising the logo can be manipulated independently. Once designed, however, the logo will be used as a single object. Grouping these objects allows any attributes you choose, such as size, position, or rotation, to be applied to the grouped object as a whole.

Fig. 27.3
You can use PowerPoint tools with drawings comprised of more than one object.

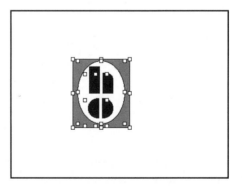

Tip
To select an object that's beneath another object, hold the Ctrl key while clicking the top object; the selection handles indicate which object is selected.

To group several objects, select the objects by using one of the methods you just learned (by pressing the Shift key or Selection Tool button, or by choosing <u>E</u>dit, Select A<u>ll</u>). The resize handles for each object are displayed. Now choose <u>D</u>raw, <u>G</u>roup. The object is now surrounded by an invisible rectangle, indicated by resize handles at the four corners and along each side of the rectangle. When you select the object in the future, it appears as a single object with one set of resize handles (see fig. 27.4).

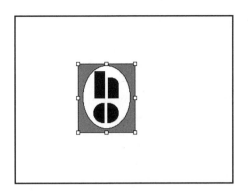

Fig. 27.4
Multiple objects
are grouped as a
single object for
easier editing and
formatting.

Sometimes you only want to group multiple objects temporarily. Suppose that you have moved or resized your company logo and now you want to apply different attributes to its various components. To separate grouped objects, select the grouped object; then choose Draw, Ungroup. PowerPoint separates the objects, and each object's selection handles are visible once again on the slide, as they appeared in figure 27.3.

Moving and Copying Objects

Moving an object on a slide is as simple as clicking and dragging the object to a new location. As you drag the mouse to a new location, the object stays in its original location on the slide while a dotted-line silhouette of the object follows your mouse movements around the screen. Release the mouse button when the silhouette of the object is positioned correctly. PowerPoint then moves the object to its new location.

Tip
You can right-click an object to reveal the quick menu and then choose Cut, Copy, or Paste.

To move an object from one slide to another or from one presentation to another, follow these steps:

1. Select the object to be moved.

2. Choose Edit, Cut, or press Ctrl+X. The selected object is removed from the current slide and placed on the Clipboard.

3. If you are moving the object to another slide in the same presentation, display that slide. If you are moving the object to another presentation, open the presentation and display the correct slide.

4. Choose Edit, Paste, or press Ctrl+V. PowerPoint pastes the object on the slide being viewed.

V

Using PowerPoint

5. Position the object as desired on the slide by clicking and dragging the object.

6. Click any blank area of the slide to deselect the object, or press Esc.

The steps for copying an object are similar to those for moving an object except that you choose Edit, Copy rather than Edit, Cut. As when moving an object, you can also copy an object within a slide, within a presentation, or to another presentation.

To copy an object, follow these steps:

1. Select the object to be copied.

2. Choose Edit, Copy, or press Ctrl+C. The selected object remains unchanged on the current slide, and a copy is placed on the Clipboard.

3. If you are copying the object to another slide in the same presentation, display that slide. If you are moving the object to another presentation, open the presentation and display the correct slide.

4. Choose Edit, Paste, or press Ctrl+V. PowerPoint pastes the object on the current slide.

5. Position the object as desired on the slide by clicking and dragging the object.

6. Click any blank area of the slide to deselect the object, or press Esc.

Resizing and Scaling Objects

Throughout this chapter you have seen several examples of the resize handles that become visible when an object or group of objects is selected. To resize an object, you first click the object to select it, and then drag any resize handle to a new position.

Tip
When you're resizing an object, position the mouse pointer over a handle until it changes to a double-headed arrow, and then drag the handle.

The resize handles that appear on the sides of the selection box resize in one dimension only. For instance, if you click the resize handle at the top of the selection box, you can stretch or shrink the height of an object on its top only; the bottom remains anchored. If you click the right resize handle, you can stretch or shrink the width of an object on its right side only; the left side remains anchored. Release the mouse button when the object is the size you want.

The resize handles that appear at the corners of an object enable you to resize an object in two dimensions at once. If you click the resize handle in the upper-right corner of an object, for instance, you can change the height or width of the object by dragging the handle in any direction. Whenever you drag a corner handle, the handle in the opposite corner remains anchored while you expand or contract the object's height and width.

When you resize in two dimensions at once, you may want to maintain an object's height-to-width ratio. To do so, hold down the Shift key as you drag any corner resize handle. The handle in the opposite corner remains anchored while you resize the object. Or you might want to resize in two dimensions at once, from the center of the object outward. To do so, hold down the Ctrl key as you drag any corner handle. By holding both the Shift and Ctrl keys as you drag a corner handle, you can maintain an object's height-to-width ratio *and* resize from the center outward, all in one step.

Another way to resize an object is to scale it. *Scaling* enables you to specify an object's size by percentage. If you want an object to be half its current size, for example, you scale it by 50 percent. To scale an object, choose the Draw, Scale, which displays the Scale dialog box shown in figure 27.5.

Fig. 27.5
Adjust the size of an object using the Scale dialog box.

To scale an object, follow these steps:

1. Select the object.

2. Choose Draw, Scale. The Scale dialog box appears.

3. In the % box, enter a number greater than 100 to enlarge the object; type a number smaller than 100 to reduce the object. You can either type a number or click the up- or down-arrows to change the setting.

4. (Optional) To preview the object, click Preview. If necessary, repeat step 3 to resize the object.

5. Click OK.

As an alternative to the preceding steps, you can have PowerPoint determine a scale for you by selecting the Best Scale for Slide Show option in the Scale dialog box. This option automatically chooses the best scale for an object to ensure optimal viewing during an on-screen slide show.

Select the <u>R</u>elative to Original Picture Size option to maintain the height-to-width ratio when adjusting the scale of the object.

Troubleshooting

My object is a rectangle one inch wide by two inches high. How can I use the resize handles to add approximately 1/2 inch to the top and bottom of the object uniformly?

Hold down the Ctrl key as you drag either the top or bottom resize handle. You also can use the Ctrl key with a side resize handle to add or subtract width uniformly. When used with a corner resize handle, the Ctrl key enables you to resize in two dimensions from the center of the object outward.

*I entered **100** in the % box to restore an imported picture to its original size, but the picture is still the wrong size, and its dimensions are not correct.*

When the original dimensions of an imported picture have been altered, choosing 100% scale does not restore them. You must select the <u>R</u>elative to Original Picture Size option as well. This option restores the picture's original height-to-width ratio to the scale you specify (use 100% for the original picture size). If, for example, you select the <u>R</u>elative to Original Picture Size option and enter **200** in the % box for the scale, the original dimensions are restored, and the object is twice its original size.

Aligning Objects

To achieve a neat, professional appearance on your slides, it is helpful to be able to precisely align objects. PowerPoint takes the guesswork out of aligning objects by offering a variety of automatic alignment options. You can use the traditional left-, center-, or right-alignment styles; or you can align the tops, bottoms, or middles of objects. Each of these alignment options is illustrated in the slide sorter view shown in figure 27.6.

In the figure, slide 1 shows how the objects were originally arranged. Slides 2, 3, and 4 illustrate how the objects are aligned along the left edges of the objects, the horizontal center, and the right edges of the objects. Slides 5, 6, and 7 show how the objects are aligned at the top, vertical midpoint, and bottom in relationship to each other.

To use any of PowerPoint's alignment options, follow these steps:

1. Select the objects you want to align.

2. Choose <u>D</u>raw, <u>A</u>lign. The Align cascading menu shown in figure 27.7 appears.

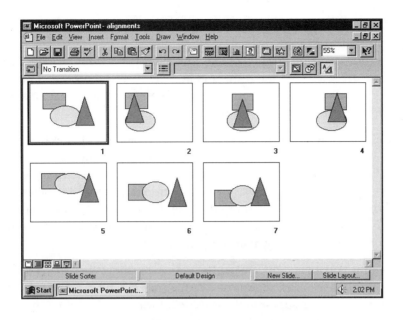

Fig. 27.6
PowerPoint offers
six automatic
alignment styles.

V

Using PowerPoint

Fig. 27.7
Choose an
alignment from
the cascading
Align menu.

Caution

If you do not select two or more objects, the Draw, Align command will appear dimmed. To select more than one object, hold the Shift key as you click each object.

Tip
To deselect one
object of several,
hold the Shift key
and click the
object you want
to deselect.

3. From the cascading menu, choose an alignment option. PowerPoint realigns the selected objects.

Using the Grid

◄ See "Getting Familiar with the PowerPoint Window," p. 562

Tip

You cannot apply an alignment to one group of objects but you can align two or more selected groups.

Tip

The Snap to Grid command is only available in Slides and Notes views.

To help you align and position objects on a slide, PowerPoint includes three tools—*guides*, *rulers*, and *grids*—that can be toggled on and off with a simple menu command. Guides and rulers are visible markers that appear on a slide to give you a visual reference point.

Unlike visible guides and rulers, the grid is an invisible set of lines that runs horizontally and vertically on a slide. The lines (approximately every 1/8 inch) form a grid similar to that of a very fine graph paper. When the grid is turned on, the corners of objects that you draw or move snap into alignment at the nearest intersection of the grid. Using the grid helps to make alignment of objects an easier task. The grid is best used when you do not need to align objects more precisely than approximately 1/8 inch.

To turn the grid on and off, choose Draw, Snap to Grid. When the grid is turned on, a check mark appears next to the Snap to Grid command on the menu (no indicators appear in the PowerPoint window). You also can turn the grid off temporarily by holding down the Alt key as you drag an object to a new location on a slide. If you experiment with pressing the Alt key as you drag an object, you can see for yourself how the grid works as you watch the object track smoothly across the screen or snap into place.

Rotating and Flipping Objects

Tip

You cannot flip text objects, although you can rotate text.

One way to add visual interest to your slides is to rotate or flip an object. *Rotating* refers to turning an object around a 360-degree radius. *Flipping* refers to turning an object over, either horizontally or vertically, to create a mirror image of that object. You can rotate or flip any PowerPoint object.

> **Caution**
>
> A PowerPoint object is defined as an object created within PowerPoint using a PowerPoint tool (such as the drawing tools) or an object imported from another program and then converted to a PowerPoint object. To convert an object to a PowerPoint object, you must be able to ungroup its components and then regroup them by choosing Draw, Group. If you cannot do this, the object cannot be converted to a PowerPoint object and, therefore, cannot be rotated or flipped.

PowerPoint enables you to rotate an object in either of two ways:

- You can rotate an object to any position in a 360-degree radius.

- You can rotate an object in 90-degree increments to the left or right, which has the effect of turning the object 1/4 turn.

When you flip an object, you flip it either horizontally or vertically 180 degrees. These choices are illustrated on the Rotate/Flip cascading menu, shown in figure 27.8.

Fig. 27.8
Rotation and flipping options are shown in the Rotate/Flip cascading menu.

To rotate an object by 90 degrees or flip an object 180 degrees, follow these steps:

1. Select the object to rotate.

2. Choose Draw, Rotate/Flip.

3. From the cascading menu, choose Rotate Left or Rotate Right to rotate the object, or Flip Horizontal or Flip Vertical to flip the object. PowerPoint immediately rotates or flips the object in the direction selected.

4. To rotate the object another 90 degrees, repeat steps 2 and 3.

5. Click any blank area of the slide to deselect the object.

To rotate an object to any angle in a 360-degree radius, use the Free Rotate Tool button on the Drawing toolbar or the Free Rotate command on the Rotate/Flip cascading menu. The appearance of the mouse pointer changes to reflect which tool is chosen.

To rotate an object to any position on a 360-degree radius, follow these steps:

V

Using PowerPoint

1. Select the object to rotate.

2. Click the Free Rotate Tool button on the Drawing toolbar, or choose Draw, Rotate/Flip; then choose the Free Rotate command. The mouse pointer changes to two curved arrows that form a circle with a cross in the center.

3. Position the cross in the mouse pointer on top of any of the object's resize handles. The mouse pointer changes again to a cross in the center with four outward-pointing arrows.

4. Click and hold down the left mouse button as you rotate the object either left or right until it is positioned correctly; then release the mouse button.

5. Click any blank area of the slide to deselect the object.

You can rotate or flip several objects at once, and you can rotate or flip grouped objects. When you select multiple objects to rotate or flip, each object rotates or flips independently of the others around its own center point; and each object rotates to the same angle as all others. When you rotate or flip grouped objects, however, the individual objects *do not* rotate or flip independently; they rotate or flip *as a whole*. This difference is illustrated in figure 27.9.

Fig. 27.9
Multiple objects rotate differently depending on how they are grouped.

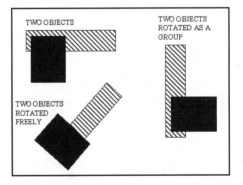

Changing the Stacking Order of Objects

As you add objects to a slide and overlap them, you quickly discover that the object drawn first appears underneath, and the object drawn most recently appears on top of the others. Think of the objects being stacked on the slide as you draw them. The most recently drawn object appears and remains at the top of the stack unless you change the stacking order. In figure 27.10, the circle was drawn first, then the triangle, and then the star. No matter where you move the objects on the slide, the circle is on the bottom, the triangle in the middle, and the star on top.

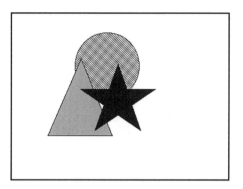

Fig. 27.10
Objects overlap each other in the order they are drawn.

PowerPoint lets you change the stacking order of objects in two ways. The Draw, Bring Forward, and Draw, Send Backward commands let you move an object one step at a time forward or backward through a stack of objects. So, if you have six objects stacked on top of one another and the sixth object is selected, that object becomes the fifth object in the stack if you choose Draw, Bring Forward. If you choose Draw, Send Backward, nothing happens because the selected object is already at the bottom of the stack.

The other way to move objects is by choosing Draw, Bring to Front, and Draw, Send to Back. These commands move a selected object to the top or to the bottom of the entire stack, regardless of its current position or the total number of objects in the stack. In figure 27.11, the circle was selected and brought to the front.

Fig. 27.11
The circle has been brought to the front of the stack.

V

Using PowerPoint

Note

Small objects can easily become completely obscured by others. If you cannot find an object to select it, select any object on the slide; then press the Tab key until the object you want is selected. Each time you press the Tab key, a new object on the current slide is selected.

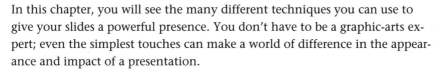

Chapter 28

Enhancing a Presentation

by Donna Minarik

In this chapter, you will see the many different techniques you can use to give your slides a powerful presence. You don't have to be a graphic-arts expert; even the simplest touches can make a world of difference in the appearance and impact of a presentation.

In this chapter, you learn to

- Work with templates
- Enhance text by changing the font, style, and color
- Work with line spacing, bullets, and alignment of text
- Work with colors, fills, and line styles of objects
- Add patterns, shading, borders, and shadows to objects
- Work with color schemes

Working with Templates

In Chapter 24, "Getting Acquainted with PowerPoint," you learned that templates are saved presentation files for which special graphic elements, colors, font sizes, font styles, slide backgrounds, and other special effects have been defined. PowerPoint includes templates designed for black-and-white overheads, color overheads, and on-screen slide shows.

◀ See "Under-
standing
Masters and
Templates,"
p. 571

Using a template is the quickest and easiest way to create professional-
looking presentations, because it takes the guesswork and experimentation
out of designing a presentation. PowerPoint templates are designed by
graphic-arts professionals who understand the elements required to achieve a
certain effect and to convey a particular attitude.

Choosing a Template

To specify a template when you create a new presentation, select the Template option in the PowerPoint dialog box that appears automatically when
you start the program.

Figure 28.1 shows a presentation using the blank presentation design.

Fig. 28.1
The blank design
creates a basic
black-and-white
template.

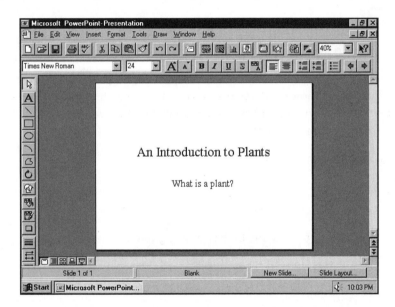

In the New Presentation dialog box, you can choose one of the following
tabs:

- *General.* Contains the blank presentation or default format. Using this
  presentation template, you can set your own format by making changes
  to the master template.

- *Presentation Designs.* Contains over 50 professionally designed templates
  on which you can base a presentation. Each presentation design

includes a color scheme, graphics such as lines or art, and a master with complete text formatting.

■ *Presentations*. Contains specific pre-set presentation templates that include color schemes and font formatting, in addition to slide layouts with suggestions for slide content. For example, one presentation is titled "Training" and another is titled "Selling a Product." Select the presentation that best suits your needs.

If you choose one of the presentation designs—such as Azure, Banner, Bevel, and so on—PowerPoint displays the New Slide dialog box from which you choose an AutoLayout. After you choose the layout, PowerPoint applies it to the slide template. Figure 28.2 illustrates the Banner template used with a Title slide.

◀ See "Reviewing AutoLayout," p. 591

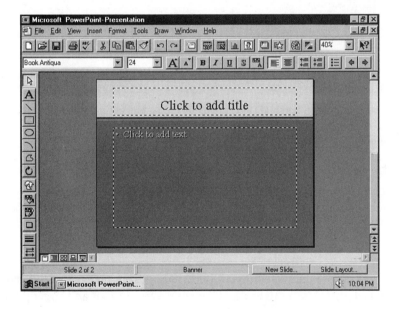

Fig. 28.2
Use a template when you already have an idea of the content of your presentation.

V

Using PowerPoint

Figure 28.3 illustrates one pre-set slide presentation available, "Reporting Progress." Notice the second slide suggests you define the subject as a title for the slide, then break the subject into smaller topics and list them with the bullets. Other slides in this presentation suggest overall status, background information, key issues, and future steps.

Fig. 28.3
PowerPoint's preformatted presentations guide you by suggesting slide content and format.

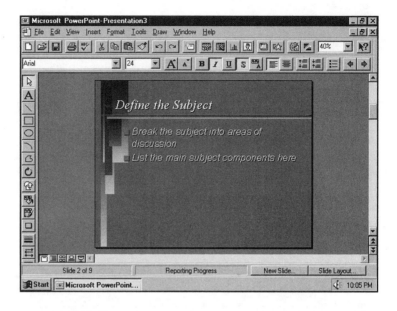

> **Note**
>
> If your presentation doesn't fit into one of the pre-set formats in the New Presentation dialog box, choose the General presentation for basic formatting and good suggestions for content.

◄ See "Inserting Clip Art Pictures," p. 598

To enter text into any of the Presentation text blocks, click the text block, delete the text, and then enter your own. You also can add new slides, objects, and other enhancements to the presentation.

Altering a Template

After you select a template for your presentation, you might want to change its characteristics. You might decide to use a different font and larger point size for your slide titles or to add a graphic element to the template. You can choose to change items on just one slide or on all slides. You might change, for example, the font on just one slide's title to set it apart from the other slides. On the other hand, you can make changes to all slides, for consistency, by changing the slide master.

Tip
The Slide Master looks very much like a presentation slide, but any changes made here affect all slides in the presentation.

To make changes that affect all slides in the presentation quickly and easily, change the slide master. To access the Slide Master, choose <u>V</u>iew, <u>M</u>aster, and select <u>S</u>lide Master from the submenu that opens.

You can change the text in a slide by modifying the font, style, color, and so on. Additionally, you can change fill and line colors of objects, or change entire color schemes. Refer to the sections "Enhancing Text" and "Working with Colors and Line Styles" later in this chapter.

Applying a Different Template

One major change you can make to a slide presentation is to change the template, or presentation design, you're using. When you change the template, you change color schemes, some graphic elements, and the master template. Changing templates does not change "Click here" box contents, added objects such as text blocks, charts, or drawings, slide layouts, or the number of slides in the presentation.

◀ See "Understanding Masters and Templates," p. 571

> **Caution**
>
> Sometimes when changing from one template to another, you may gain an extra "Click here" box or lose a title or subtitle because of individual designs. Check all slides carefully after changing templates to make sure all of your slide contents are there. If you're missing something, you can either go back to the original template or add the missing text.

To change the template of the active presentation, follow these steps:

  1. Choose F**o**rmat, Apply Design Te**m**plate to open the dialog box shown in figure 28.4.

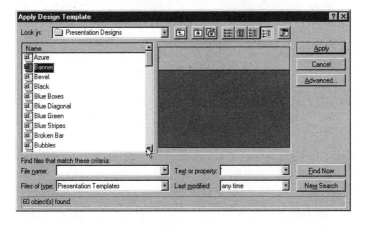

Fig. 28.4
Choose the desired template from the Name list in the Apply Design Template dialog box.

  2. Choose Presentation Designs in the Look **I**n box, if it is not already selected.

> **Note**
>
> To preview templates, click each template in the Name list. A sample of the highlighted template appears to the right in the dialog box.

3. Select a template name, click <u>A</u>pply, or press Enter to select the highlighted template. The dialog box closes, and PowerPoint applies the new template to the active presentation.

Figure 28.5 illustrates how a template can create an overall impression for your slide presentation. PowerPoint includes over 50 templates for you to try.

Fig. 28.5

Use a template that best suits the contents of your presentation.

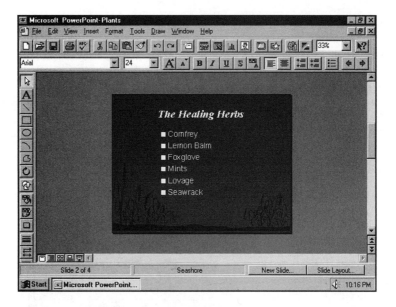

Troubleshooting

How can I use more than one template in a presentation?

Templates apply to all slides in a presentation; you cannot use more than one template in a single presentation. You can, however, change colors, fonts, shadows, patterns, and other enhancements in individual slides, as described throughout this chapter.

How can I create a custom template so I don't have to alter a PowerPoint template each time I create a new presentation?

First, choose the PowerPoint template on which you want to base your custom template. Make the desired changes to the template. When the template looks the way you want it, choose File, Save As. Give the file a unique name, and save it into the appropriate template directory. Be sure to choose Presentation Templates in the Save As Type box.

If I make changes to the slide master in my presentation, how is the PowerPoint template I'm using affected?

Any changes you make to a presentation master affect the current presentation only; the PowerPoint template file you are using is not altered.

Enhancing Text

V

Using PowerPoint

When you enter text in a slide, the font, style (regular, bold, or italic), size, color, and special effects (underline, shadow, and so on) of the text conform to the settings specified in the master assigned to the current template. The Forest template, for example, uses the 44-point Book Antiqua font in gray underlined shadowed for slide titles and the 28-point Book Antiqua font in blue shadowed for slide text. If you want to use a different font, style, size, color, or effect, you can change these settings (collectively called *font settings*) for all slides in a presentation by altering the slide master, or you can change font settings only for selected text objects.

Choosing a Font, Style, and Color for Text

To change font settings, select the text you want to change, then choose Format, Font, or the Font command on the shortcut menu, to display the Font dialog box (see fig. 28.6). The Font, Font Style, Size, and Color settings are self-explanatory; these options appear in most word processing, spreadsheet, and graphics programs.

◀ See "Formatting Documents," p. 81

The Effects area, however, contains some options with which you might not be familiar. The Shadow option adds a shadow at the bottom and the right side of each character. The Emboss option gives the text the appearance of raised letters by using a light color for the characters and a faint shadow behind each character. The Subscript option drops a selected character slightly below the normal line level, as in H_2O, whereas the Superscript option raises a selected character, as in 10^5. When you choose either of these options, you can specify the Offset percentage.

Fig. 28.6
The Font dialog box allows you to choose a font, size, style, color, and text effects.

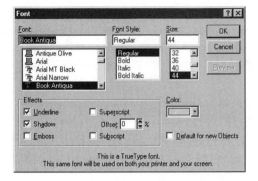

Choose the desired formatting and click OK.

You also can change specific format settings by clicking the following buttons in the Formatting toolbar:

Button	Button Name	Description
	Font Face	Changes the font of selected text
	Font Size	Changes the font size of selected text
A▲	Increase Font Size	Increases the font size
A▼	Decrease Font Size	Decreases the font size
B	Bold	Makes selected text bold
I	Italic	Makes selected text italic
U̲	Underline	Underlines selected text

Button	Button Name	Description
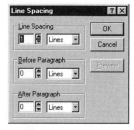	Text Shadow	Adds a drop shadow to selected text
	Text Color	Changes the color of selected text

Changing Line and Paragraph Spacing

Just as the template defines color schemes, graphics, and other characteristics for a presentation, the master attached to the template defines the line spacing for text in a text object. PowerPoint enables you to set the spacing between lines, as well as the amount of space before and after paragraphs. In most templates, the default spacing is 1 line, the space after paragraphs is 0, and the space before paragraphs is 0.2 or 0.

You might want to change line or paragraph spacing, depending on the content of your slides. To change line and paragraph spacing, follow these steps:

1. Select the text for which you want to adjust line or paragraph spacing, either in the master or on one individual slide.

2. Choose Format, Line Spacing. PowerPoint displays the Line Spacing dialog box, as shown in figure 28.7.

Fig. 28.7
Use the Line Spacing dialog box to set line and paragraph spacing.

3. In the Line Spacing, Before Paragraph, and After Paragraph boxes, enter the number of lines or points to be used. If you prefer to use points rather than lines, be sure to choose the Points setting in each drop-down list.

4. Click OK. PowerPoint returns to your slide and reformats the selected text.

Caution

When setting paragraph spacing, specify a setting for <u>B</u>efore Paragraph or <u>A</u>fter Paragraph, but not both. If you set both options, the actual space between paragraphs will be the sum of the two settings.

Aligning Text

Alignment refers to the horizontal positioning of text within a text object. In presentation slides, text generally is left-aligned for paragraphs or bullets and centered for titles. However, you can also justify or right-align text. Table 28.1 describes the alignment options.

Table 28.1   Alignment Options

Button	Alignment	Result
	Left Alignment	Aligns text along the left edge of a text object.
	Right Alignment	Aligns text al ong the right edge.
	Center Alignment	Aligns text at the center point of the text object so that an equal number of characters appear to the right and left of the center point.
	Justify	Aligns text along both the right and left edges so that the characters in a line cover the entire width of a text object.

Because alignment involves horizontal positioning of text at margins or at the center point of a text object, alignment affects entire paragraphs. In other words, you cannot align a single word or line in a paragraph.

Note

Use center-aligned or right-aligned text for headings or short lists or phrases. Use left-aligned text for heads, bulleted lists, or paragraphs of text.

You don't have to select any text to align a single paragraph; PowerPoint aligns the entire paragraph in which the insertion point is located. To align several paragraphs, select a portion of text in each paragraph, and then choose an alignment style.

To change the alignment of text, follow these steps:

1. Select the object that contains the text you want to align.

2. Place the insertion point anywhere in the paragraph you want to align, or select a portion of each paragraph you want to align.

3. Choose Format, Alignment, or choose Alignment from the shortcut menu. The Alignment cascading menu appears.

4. Choose Left, Right, Center, or Justify. PowerPoint immediately realigns the current paragraph or selected paragraphs.

Adding Bulleted Text

In addition to assigning styles, sizes, and spacing to various fonts you use in your slides, you also can format text to include bullets. In PowerPoint, you can use the default "Click here" bullet lists, or you can create a list in a text block and assign a custom bullet.

When working with bullets, use the Bullet On/Off icon to show/hide the bullets. You can turn off, for example, bullets for several items on a list or just one item, if you want to skip some text between bulleted items.

To add bullets to text or to customize the bullet used, follow these steps:

1. Select the text to be bulleted or position the insertion point on the first line of text.

2. Choose Format, Bullet. The Bullet dialog box appears (see fig. 28.8).

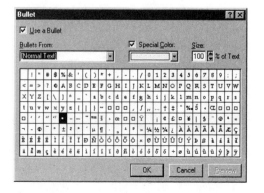

Tip

For left, right, or center alignment, you can also use the toolbar buttons shown in table 28.1.

Tip

Use a bulleted list to show equal importance for each item in the list. Use a numbered list to show the first item as the most important.

V

Using PowerPoint

◄ See "Inserting Other Objects," p. 603

Fig. 28.8
You can use any available font, such as Symbol or Wingdings, to create a bullet.

Tip
Click any bullet
in the dialog box
to display an
enlarged view of
the bullet.

3. In <u>B</u>ullets From, choose the font you want to use for the bullet.

4. You can use the color assigned in the template (and displayed in the Special <u>C</u>olor box), or you can choose a new color.

5. Size the bullet by changing the percentage in the <u>S</u>ize box.

6. Choose OK to apply the bullet to the text.

Working with Colors and Line Styles

All objects that you draw in PowerPoint (except lines) have a fill color, line color, and line style. The *fill color* is the color inside an object; the *line color* is the frame that defines the boundaries of an object; and the *line style* defines the width or style of the object's frame.

For any given object, you can turn off the fill color and line color. In most templates, for example, the line that frames a text object is turned off, because text generally looks better in the slide without a frame. For other objects (such as shapes that you create with the drawing tools), the object's frame usually is visible, and the object has a fill color.

In most templates, an object's line style is a narrow solid line. You can choose any of five wider line styles or any of four double or triple lines. In addition, you can change a solid line to a dashed, dotted, or mixed line by choosing one of the four dashed-line options. If an object is a straight line or arc rather than a shape, you can add arrowheads to either end or to both ends of the line or arc.

Choosing Fill and Line Colors and Line Styles

You will use the Colors and Lines dialog box (see fig. 28.9) to set line, fill, and line-style options.

Fig. 28.9
Use the Colors and
Lines dialog box
to define an
object's color and
frame style.

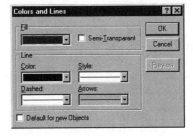

To change an object's fill color, follow these steps:

1. Select the object.

2. Choose Format Colors and Lines, or choose Colors and Lines from the shortcut menu. The Colors and Lines dialog box appears, displaying the current fill color in the Fill box.

3. Click the arrow to open the Fill drop-down list and display the available fill color options. Then choose from the following options:

   ■ Select the No Fill option to remove the fill color from the object.

   ■ Select one of the colors (derived from the current template).

   ■ Choose Background to set the fill color of the selected object to match the slide background color.

   ■ Select the Other Color option to open the dialog box shown in figure 28.10. Select the desired color from the palette. Choose OK to return to the Colors and Lines dialog box.

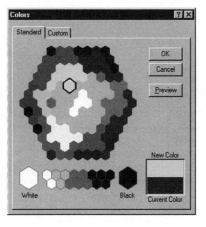

Fig. 28.10
The Colors dialog box displays a color palette.

4. Choose OK in the Colors and Lines dialog box. PowerPoint returns to your slide and changes the fill color or pattern of the selected object.

5. Click any blank area of the screen to deselect the object.

To change an object's line color or line style, or to add dashed lines or arrow-heads, follow these steps:

1. Select the object.

2. Choose Format, Colors and Lines, or choose Colors and Lines from the shortcut menu. The Colors and Lines dialog box appears, displaying the current line color in the Line box.

3. Click the arrow to open the Line Color drop-down list and display the available options. Then choose from the options:

   ■ Select the No Line option to remove the object's line color.

   ■ Select one of the colors (derived from the current template).

   ■ Select the Other Color option, which displays the Colors dialog box (refer to fig. 28.10). Select a color in the Color palette, and then choose OK.

4. To select a different line style, highlight a style in the Line Style list.

5. To use a dashed line, highlight a style in the Dashed list.

6. To add arrowheads to a line or arc, select an option in the Arrows list.

7. Click OK in the Colors and Lines dialog box. PowerPoint returns to your slide and changes the line color and style for the selected object.

8. Click any blank area of the screen to deselect the object.

A quick way to change an object's fill, line color, line style, dashed lines, or arrowheads is to use the respective tools in the Drawing toolbar. Select the object, and then click any of the tools shown in table 28.2. In each case, a drop-down list appears, enabling you to select a new color or style.

Table 28.2 Color and Line Tools	
Tool	**Tool Name**
	Fill Color
	Line Color
	Line Style

Tool	Tool Name
⇄	Arrowheads
▦	Dashed Lines

Using Shading and Patterns

Two effective variations for filled objects are shaded color and two-color pattern. A *shaded color* is a dark-to-light or light-to-dark variation of an object's color. This variation can run vertically, horizontally, diagonally, from the center outward, or from any corner. You also can adjust the intensity of the color.

To shade an object, follow these steps:

1. Select the object you want to shade.

2. Choose Format, Colors and Lines. The Colors and Lines dialog box appears. The current fill color is shown in the Fill box.

3. Click the down arrow to open the Fill drop-down list.

4. Select the Shaded option. The Shaded Fill dialog box appears, as shown in figure 28.11.

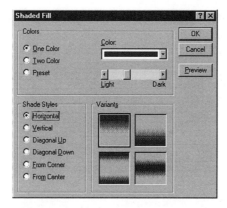

Fig. 28.11
Use the options in the Shaded Fill dialog box to create a gradient fill pattern.

5. Select an option in the Shade Styles list.

6. In the Variants box, highlight one variant. The Variants box reflects the choice you make.

7. To adjust the brightness, drag the scroll box in the Dark/Light scroll bar.

8. Use the Color option in the Shaded Fill dialog box if you want to change the fill color. If you wish to blend two colors for the gradient, choose the Two Color option. Choose the Preset option to display sets of predefined color gradients, such as Nightfall or Sapphire.

9. If you want, click the Preview button to preview the shade in the selected object.

10. Choose OK in the Shaded Fill dialog box. You return to the Colors and Lines dialog box.

11. Choose OK to close the dialog box. PowerPoint applies the shaded color to the selected object.

An alternative to shading an object is patterning. A *pattern* is a design (such as lines, dots, bricks, or checkerboard squares) that contains two colors: a foreground color and a background color.

To add a pattern to a filled object, follow these steps:

1. Select the object to which you want to add a pattern.

2. Choose Format, Colors and Lines, or choose Colors and Lines from the shortcut menu. The Colors and Lines dialog box appears.

3. Click to open the Fill drop-down list.

4. Select the Pattern option. The Pattern Fill dialog box appears, as shown in figure 28.12.

Fig. 28.12
Use the Pattern
Fill dialog box
to select a fill
pattern.

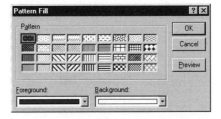

5. In the Pattern box, highlight the pattern you want to use.

6. In the Foreground and Background lists, select the colors for your pattern.

7. If you want, click the Preview button to preview the pattern in the selected object.

8. Click OK to close the Pattern Fill dialog box. You return to the Colors and Lines dialog box.

9. Click OK to close the dialog box. PowerPoint applies the two-color pattern to the selected object.

10. Click any blank area of the screen to deselect the object.

You can also use any of several more complex texturized patterns for your objects. Select the Textured option rather than Patterns from the Fill drop-down list to open the dialog box shown in figure 28.13. Choose from a variety of predesigned textured fill patterns in this dialog box.

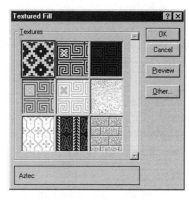

Fig. 28.13
Predefined fill textures are available in the Textured Fill dialog box.

Adding Shadows to Objects

Shadowing can enhance an object's visibility on a slide and make the object more noticeable.

To apply a shadow to an object, follow these steps:

1. Select the object.

2. Choose Format, Shadow. The Shadow dialog box appears, as shown in figure 28.14.

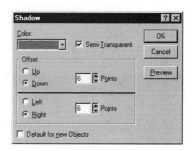

Fig. 28.14
Use the Shadow dialog box to specify shadow color, direction, and offset.

3. To change the color of the shadow, select a color in the Color drop-down list.

4. To set a vertical shadow offset, select the Up or Down option, and then enter the number of points in the Points box.

5. To set a horizontal shadow offset, select the Left or Right option, and then enter the number of points in the Points box.

6. If you want, click the Preview button to preview the shadow on the selected object.

7. Click OK or press Enter to apply the shadow to the selected object.

8. Click any blank area of the screen to deselect the object.

 You can add or remove a shadow for an object quickly by clicking the Shadow On/Off tool on the Drawing toolbar.

Copying Attributes from One Object to Another

 Suppose that you have taken care to apply a special color, shade or pattern, line width, line style, and shadow to a particular object. You can apply all these attributes to another object quickly by using the Format Painter button in the Standard toolbar.

To use the Format Painter button, follow these steps:

1. Select the object which contains the desired formatting.

2. Click the Format Painter button. The mouse pointer changes to a paint-brush.

3. Click the object you wish to apply the formatting to. The clicked object will be reformatted to match the original object.

Using the Format Painter button is equivalent to choosing Format, Pick Up Object Style, and Format, Apply Object Style.

To use the menu commands to apply attributes from one object to another, follow these steps:

1. Select the object from which you want to copy attributes.

2. Choose Format, Pick Up Object Style, or choose Pick Up Object Style from the shortcut menu.

3. Select the object to which you want to copy the attributes.

4. Choose Format, Apply Object Style.

Working with Color Schemes

A *color scheme* is a set of colors that are chosen because they complement one another. Every template has a predefined color scheme that consists of specific colors for the slide background, title text, other text, lines, fills, shadows, and accent colors. You can use the colors defined in a template, choose a different color scheme, or change individual colors in a color scheme.

Changing Individual Colors in a Color Scheme

You can change an individual color in the current color scheme and apply the new color to the current slide or to all of the slides in the presentation. Follow these steps:

1. Choose Format, Slide Color Scheme, or choose Slide Color Scheme from the shortcut menu. The Color Scheme dialog box appears, as shown in figure 28.15.

2. Click the Custom tab to change the dialog box options to those illustrated in figure 28.16.

V

Using PowerPoint

Fig. 28.15
The Color Scheme dialog box allows you to modify the presentation's colors.

Fig. 28.16
The Custom tab in the Color Scheme dialog box allows you to change individual colors.

3. Select the color you want to change, and click Change Color.

4. The Fill Color dialog box appears, looking the same as the Color palette shown in figure 28.10. Choose the desired color and click OK.

5. Repeat steps 3 and 4 to change other colors in the current color scheme.

6. In the Slide Color Scheme dialog box, click the Apply button to apply the change to the current slide. Click Apply to All to apply the new color to all slides in the current presentation.

Choosing a Different Color Scheme

Suppose that a template contains all the graphic elements you want to use, but the color scheme is not appropriate for the topic you are presenting. Rather than change individual colors in the template's color scheme, you can choose a different color scheme for the current template. When you choose a new color scheme, you are choosing a new set of predefined colors. As always, you can change individual colors in the scheme later if you choose.

To choose a color scheme, follow these steps:

1. Choose Format, Slide Color Scheme, or choose Slide Color Scheme from the shortcut menu (when no objects are selected). PowerPoint displays the Color Scheme dialog box (refer to fig. 28.15).

2. Available color scheme options are shown in the Color Schemes section of this dialog box.

3. Select the desired color scheme.

4. Click Apply to apply the new color scheme to the current slide. Click Apply to All to apply the new color scheme to all slides in the current presentation.❖

Chapter 29

Creating Output

by Donna Minarik

As you learned in Chapter 24, "Getting Acquainted with PowerPoint," you can print a variety of components of a PowerPoint presentation, including slides (on paper or overhead transparencies), audience handouts, outlines, and speaker's notes. You can also prepare an on-screen slide show as a special kind of output.

In this chapter, you learn to

- Check slides for consistency

- Build slide text

- Choose a setup for presentation components

- Set up your printer

- Print presentation components

- Create and run an on-screen slide show

Checking Slides before the Presentation

Before you output your presentation, you'll want to make sure the presentation is as good as it can be. You can check your slides by running the Style Checker. Style Checker checks for inconsistencies that you set in the Style Checker Options dialog box—inconsistencies such as case, punctuation, and number of fonts used in the presentation.

V

Using PowerPoint

To run the Style Checker, follow these steps:

1. Choose Tools, Style Checker. The Style Checker dialog box appears (see fig. 29.1).

2. Click the Options button to change any of the case, punctuation, or clarity options, as described in table 29.1.

Table 29.1   Style Checker Options

Option	Description
Case and End Punctuation Tab	
Case	
Slide Title Style	Choose to apply sentence case, lowercase, upper-case, or title case to the title style throughout your presentation. Choose Toggle Case if you've accidentally typed your titles with the Caps Lock on.
Body Text Style	Choose to apply from the same cases you chose for the title style.
Punctuation	
Slide Title Periods	Choose whether to Remove, Add, or Ignore periods in the slide titles.
Body Text Periods	Choose whether to Remove, Add, or Ignore periods in the body text.
Slide Title text box	Enter any other end punctuation marks you want to check the consistency of in slide titles.
Body Text	Enter any other end punctuation marks you want to check the consistency of in the body text.

Option	Description
Visual Clarity Tab	
Fonts	
Max Number of Fonts	Choose whether to limit the number of fonts used in one presentation, and enter the number to limit to in the text box.
Min Font Sizes	Enter the minimum size you want to use for the Slide Titles and for the Body Text.
Legibility	
Max Number of Bullets	Choose whether to limit the number of bullets used in the body text and if so, enter the number in the text box.
Max Number of Words	Choose whether to limit the number of words Per Slide Title and/or Per Bullet and enter the limiting number in the text box.
Check For Text Off Slide	Choose to select any added or imported text.

3. Choose OK to close the Style Checker Options dialog box.

4. Click the Start button. The Style Checker examines the slide presentation and then displays a summary, as shown in figure 29.2.

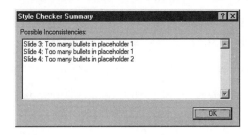

5. After reading the list of inconsistencies, you can go back through your presentation and make changes if you want. Choose OK to close the Summary box.

Choosing a Setup for Presentation Components

Before you output a presentation, indicate the type of output in the Slide Setup dialog box. You can output a presentation as an on-screen slide show, as 35mm slides, as overheads, or as some other type of output. In addition, you can specify other properties of the presentation, and then PowerPoint adjusts the presentation to best suit your selections.

To display the Slide Setup dialog box, choose File, Slide Setup. Figure 29.3 displays the Slide Setup dialog box.

Fig. 29.3
Specify your output and other components for the presentation in the Slide Setup dialog box.

The Orientation section of the Slide Setup dialog box offers Portrait and Landscape as options. When you choose Portrait, the slide is taller than it is wide. Landscape creates slides that are wider than they are tall. Slides are often printed in landscape orientation, whereas notes, handouts, and outlines are most often printed in portrait orientation. Therefore, PowerPoint offers separate orientation options for slides and notes, handouts, and outlines.

To choose a setup for slides, notes, handouts, and outlines, follow these steps:

1. Open the presentation you want to specify a setup for.

2. Choose File, Slide Setup. The Slide Setup dialog box appears (refer to fig. 29.3).

3. Choose the appropriate option in the Slides Sized For drop-down list. Options include:

   ■ *On-Screen Show.* Uses an area 10 inches wide by 7.5 inches tall so the slides fill the screen.

   ■ *Letter Paper.* Sets the width to 11 inches and the height to 8.5 inches.

   ■ *A4 Paper (210 x 297mm).* Sets the width to 10.83 inches (26 cm) and the height to 7.5 inches (18 cm).

- *35mm Slides*. Sets the width to 11.25 inches and the height to 7.5 inches so that the content fills the slide area.

- *Overhead*. Sets the width to 10 inches and the height to 7.5 inches so that the content fills the typical overhead transparency area.

- *Custom*. Allows you to choose the dimensions you want when you are printing on nonstandard paper.

4. To begin numbering slides with a number other than 1, enter a number in the Number Slides From box.

5. To change the print orientation for slides, choose either Portrait or Landscape.

6. To change the print orientation for notes, handouts, or an outline, choose either Portrait or Landscape.

7. When all settings are correct, choose OK.

Note

It's best to complete the slide setup before you create a new presentation. If you change the slide setup after your slides are created, you might need to make adjustments to your slides, depending on the setup dimensions you choose.

Setting Up Your Printer

Your printer is probably already set up for printing from other Microsoft Office or Windows applications. If you want to use a printer you don't normally use, you can change the printer setup using these steps:

1. Open the presentation you want to print.

2. Choose File, Print. PowerPoint displays the Print dialog box. The current printer is displayed at the top of the dialog box.

3. Click the arrow next to the current printer box to open a list of all installed printing devices.

4. To choose a printer, highlight the desired device in the Printer box.

5. Click OK to close the Print dialog box and return to the active presentation.

Printing Presentation Components

Tip
To print the cur-
rent presentation
using the default
settings in the
Print dialog box,
click the Print
icon.

PowerPoint allows you to print any component of a presentation: slides,
notes pages, handouts, and an outline.

To print any component, choose File, Print. The Print dialog box appears, as
shown in figure 29.4. In this dialog box, you choose the component you
want to print, the number of copies, the specific pages to print, and other
printing options. Table 29.2 describes the options in the Print dialog box.

Fig. 29.4
Use the Print
dialog box to
choose printing
options.

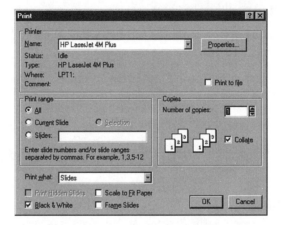

Table 29.2 Options in the Print Dialog Box

Option	Description
Properties	Click this button to set properties specific to the printer, such as paper size, orientation, graphics, fonts, and so on.
Print to File	Select this option if you want to print to a named file rather than to a printer. Slides are generally printed to file when they will be produced by a service bureau.
Print Range	This area allows you to print All slides, only the Current Slide, a Selection of slides, or specific ranges of slides you specify. In the Slides box, use a hyphen (as in **5-8**) to specify a continuous range. To specify individual pages, use commas (as in **12, 14, 17**). For multiple ranges, use a combination of the two (as in **5-8,12,17-21,25**).
Copies	This area enables you to specify the Number Of Copies to print, and whether to collate the copies as they print.
Print What	This drop-down box lists the PowerPoint components you can print.

Option	Description
Print Hidden Slides	When slides are set to Hidden, select this option to include hidden slides in the printing.
Black & White	This option changes all fill colors to white and adds a thin black border to all objects that are not bordered or do not contain text.
Scale to Fit Paper	If you choose a different paper size in the Slide Setup dialog box, this option scales each slide to fit the paper.
Frame Slides	This option adds a frame to the slides when printed.

Printing Slides

Using the options in the Print Range area of the Print dialog box, you can print all slides, only the current slide, the slides selected in the presentation, or a range of slides you specify. Be sure to select the Print Hidden Slides check box if your presentation contains slides that are set to Hidden and you want to include them in the printed output.

To print slides, follow these steps:

1. Open the presentation you want to print slides for.

2. Choose File, Print, and the Print dialog box appears.

3. In the Print Range area, select the appropriate option, as described in table 29.2.

4. In the Copies area, specify the number of copies to print.

5. In the Print What drop-down list, choose Slides.

6. In the lower portion of the dialog box, select any of the check boxes as appropriate.

7. When all settings are correct, click OK.

Printing Notes Pages

Notes pages contain a reduced slide at the top of the page and speaker's notes at the bottom of the page, as shown in figure 29.5. Since notes pages print one slide per page, you follow the same basic steps for printing notes pages as for printing slides.

Tip

The Print Hidden Slides option in the Print What area appears dimmed unless you have hidden slides in your presentation.

V

Using PowerPoint

Fig. 29.5
A notes page displays a reduced slide at the top of the page and speaker's notes at the bottom.

Tip
In the Print dialog box, choose Notes Pages in the Print What area.

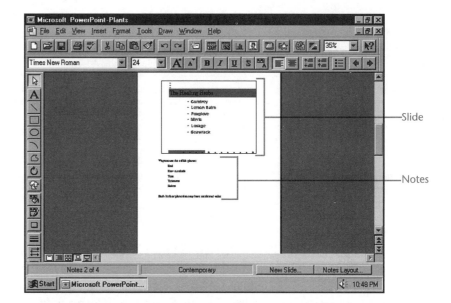

◄ See "Viewing a Presentation," p. 583

> **Note**
>
> When you plan to use speaker's notes, you can choose a layout for the notes and then create your notes in a Word document. Choose Tools, Write-Up and select the slide layout you want in the Write-Up dialog box. You can choose to link or embed the notes in the Paste Format area of the dialog box. When you choose OK, Word opens, ready for you to create your speaker's notes. Update and exit Word using the File menu to return to PowerPoint.

Printing Handouts

PowerPoint lets you print handouts using one of three different layout styles: two, three, or six slides per page. The first layout includes two slides per page. Other layouts let you print three or six slides per page. To see how a handout page looks with each of these layout options, display the Handout Master by holding the Shift key and clicking the Slide Sorter button. Alternatively, choose View, Master; then select the Handout Master option. You see a slide like the one shown in figure 29.6. The small dotted lines outline the three- and six-slides-per-page layouts. The long dotted lines outline the two-slides-per-page layout.

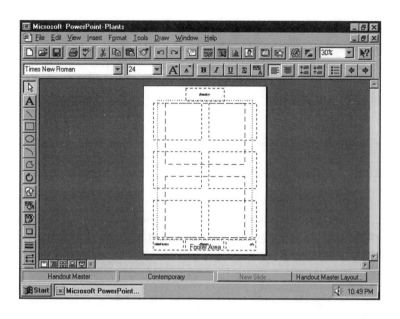

Fig. 29.6
Layout options for
handouts include
two, three, or six
slides per page.

Tip
If you choose to
print three slides
per page, the slides
are printed on the
left slide of the
page; the right
side is blank.

To print handouts, you use the same basic steps for printing slides. In the
Print <u>W</u>hat area of the Print dialog box, choose Handouts (2 Slides Per Page),
Handouts (3 Slides Per Page), or Handouts (6 Slides Per Page).

To print selected handout pages, it isn't necessary to determine on which
page a slide will print. Just specify the *slide numbers*—set in the Slide Setup
dialog box—that you want to print in the Slides box. If, for example, you
choose three slides per page and you want to print slides four, five, and six,
enter **4-6** in the Slides text box of the Print dialog box. PowerPoint prints the
second handout page.

For more information, see "Choosing a Setup for Presentation Components"
earlier in this chapter.

Printing an Outline

When you print a presentation outline, it is printed just as it was last displayed in Outline view. If you click the Show Titles button on the Outlining
toolbar to display only titles (no body text), for example, PowerPoint prints
only the slide titles. If you change the display scale using the Zoom Control
button on the Standard toolbar, the outline prints in the current scale percentage. If you click the Show Formatting button on the Outline toolbar to
display the outline text without formatting, the outline is printed exactly as
displayed on-screen.

◀ See "Viewing a
Presentation,"
p. 583

To print an outline, follow the steps outlined previously for printing slides, except select the Outline View option in the Print <u>W</u>hat section of the Print dialog box. In the Slides box, enter the slide numbers that you want to include on the outline page. If, for example, you type **1, 4, 5-9,** PowerPoint includes only those slides on the printed outline page.

Setting Up and Running a Slide Show On-Screen

One of the most effective ways to present your slides is to use your computer screen as an output medium. When you use your computer for an on-screen slide show, the entire screen area is used; PowerPoint's title bar, menu, and toolbars are cleared from the screen, and each slide is displayed using the full screen.

An on-screen slide show offers several advantages over transparencies or 35mm slides. An on-screen slide show:

- ■ Saves you the expense of producing slides.

- ■ Requires no projection equipment.

- ■ Allows you to use your computer's color capability to its fullest extent.

You also can annotate your slides as you give your presentation. (See the later section "Annotating a Slide Show" for more information.)

> **Note**
>
> You can use PowerPoint's Meeting Minder—<u>T</u>ools, <u>M</u>eeting Minder—to take notes and record items in Slide view or during a presentation. The notes you take are added to your notes pages; recorded items appear on the last slide of your presentation.

You can run a PowerPoint slide show manually (using the mouse or keyboard to advance to the next slide when you're ready); you can set up a slide show to run in a continuous "loop" for demonstration purposes; or you can set up a slide show to advance slides automatically.

Running a Slide Show

Several methods exist to run a PowerPoint slide show. To run a slide show
from within PowerPoint, use these steps:

1. Open the presentation for which you want to run a slide show.

2. Choose any view.

3. Choose View, Slide Show. The Slide Show dialog box appears, as shown
   in figure 29.7.

Fig. 29.7
Use the options in
the Slide Show
dialog box to set
timing, pen color,
and other slide
show features.

4. In the Slides area of the dialog box, select All or enter a range of slides
   to display.

5. In the Advance area, select Manual Advance or, for automatic slide
   advance, select Use Slide Timings. Alternately, choose Rehearse New
   Timings to display the slides and set the timing as you go.

6. For a continuously looping presentation, activate the Loop Continuously Until 'Esc' check box.

7. Click the Show button. Your slide presentation begins running.

Tip
Use the Rehearse
New Timings to
practice your
presentation
speech along with
each slide.

> **Note**
>
> If you choose Manual Advance in step 5, click the mouse, press Enter or press Page
> Down when you're ready to advance to the next slide. If you choose Use Slide Tim-
> ings, the slides advance automatically using the current timings.

Table 29.3 lists the methods for controlling your movements through a slide
show.

V

Using PowerPoint

Table 29.3 Methods for Controlling a Slide Show	
Function	**Method**
Show the next slide	Click the left mouse button or press any of the following keys: the space bar, N, right arrow, down arrow, or Page Down.
Show the preceding slide	Click the right mouse button or press Backspace, P, left arrow, up arrow, or Page Up.
Show a specific slide	Type the slide number and press Enter.
Toggle the mouse on or off	Type **A** or equal sign (=) (Show or pointer Hide).
Toggle between a black screen and the current slide	Type **B** or period (.).
Toggle between a white screen and the current slide	Type **W** or comma (,).
End the slide show and return to PowerPoint	Press Esc, hyphen (-), or Ctrl+Break.
Pause and resume an automatic slide show	Type **S** or plus sign (+).

 Another method for running a slide show is to simply click the Slide Show button along the lower-left side of the PowerPoint window. When you click this button, PowerPoint immediately runs the slide show, beginning with the slide that is currently selected. The slide show runs using current slide timings. If there are no timings set, you must advance each slide manually.

> **Caution**
>
> To run a slide show from the beginning using this method, be sure to select the first slide in the presentation before you click the Slide Show button.

Setting Transitions and Slide Timings

You can specify a transition style between slides. The transition style determines how one slide is removed from the screen and the next one is presented. When you set up a slide show to automatically advance to the next slide, you can also set the amount of time each slide remains on-screen.

To set transitions and timings, use the Transition dialog box shown in figure 29.8. From any of PowerPoint's display views, you can display this dialog box by choosing Tools, Slide Transition. When using Slide Sorter view, you can display the Transition dialog box by clicking the Transition button at the far left end of the toolbar.

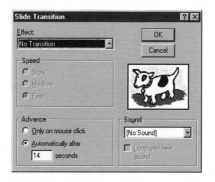

Fig. 29.8
Add transitions to the slide show in the Slide Transition dialog box.

To set timing between slides and specify transitions, follow these steps:

1. Display your presentation in Slide Sorter view.

2. Select the slide for which you want to set timing and transition options. If you want to use the same settings for multiple slides, select those slides as a group.

3. Click the Transition button at the far left end of the toolbar, choose Tools, Slide Transition, or choose Transition from the shortcut menu. PowerPoint displays the Transition dialog box in figure 29.8.

4. Select a transition style from the Effect drop-down list.

5. Select the appropriate option in the Speed area.

6. Choose whether you would like to advance the slide with a click of the mouse or automatically at a selected time interval in the Advance area. Add sound to the transition by choosing a sound from the Sound drop-down box.

7. Click OK.

Tip
When you choose an effect, the picture of the dog changes to a picture of a key using the selected effect.

Figure 29.9 shows a transition icon and a transition time displayed under each slide in Slide Sorter view indicating that transitions and slide times have been applied. You can click any transition icon to see a demonstration of the transition effect.

V

Using PowerPoint

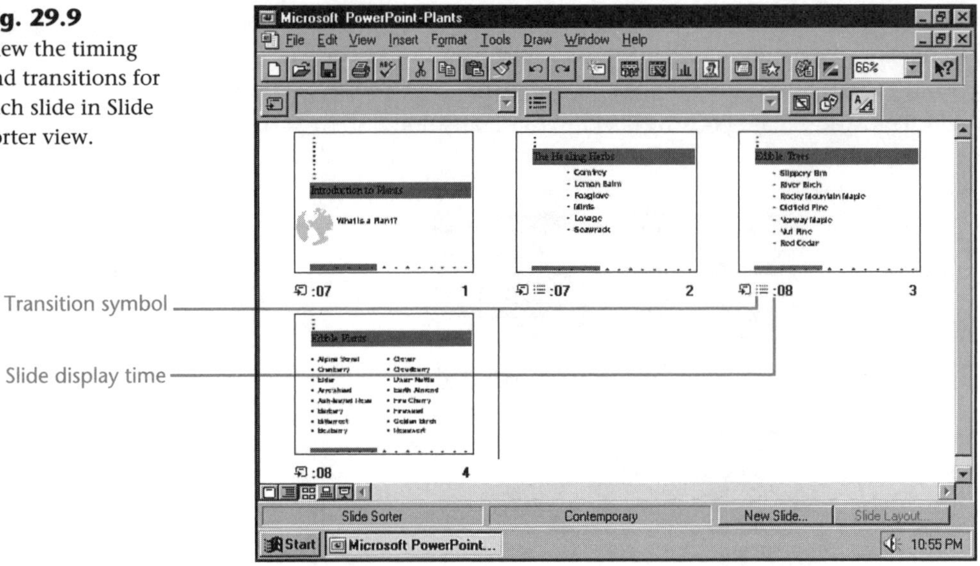

Fig. 29.9
View the timing
and transitions for
each slide in Slide
Sorter view.

Transition symbol ⎯

Slide display time ⎯

You can change transitions or timing at any time by repeating these steps.
You also can change slide timing when you rehearse a slide show, as described in the next section.

Automating a Slide Show

As discussed earlier, you can choose to advance to successive slides automatically during your presentation, and you can set slide timings to control ad-
vancement to successive slides. You can also set slide timings as you rehearse
a presentation by following these steps:

1. From any view, choose View, Slide Show. The Slide Show dialog box
    appears.

2. In the Slides area, choose All or specify the slides you want to rehearse
    in the From and To boxes.

3. In the Advance area, select the Rehearse New Timings option; then
    click Show. Your slide presentation begins running, and a clock timer
    appears in the lower-left corner of the screen, counting seconds.

4. Begin rehearsing your presentation. When you are ready to advance to
    the next slide, click the mouse button, press Enter, or press Page Down.

5. Repeat step 4 until all slides are shown. A message appears telling you
    the total time for the new slide timings.

Choose <u>Y</u>es to record the new timings; choose <u>N</u>o to ignore the new timings and retain the previous timings.

Annotating a Slide Show

When you deliver a presentation using overhead transparencies, you may often circle or underline a specific point, or write notes on the slide in response to audience questions or comments. If you use a dry-erase marker, you can easily wipe off your annotations so that the transparencies are not permanently marked.

When you run an on-screen slide show, PowerPoint gives you the ability to *electronically* annotate your slides in freehand form using the mouse. For instance, you might want to draw a check mark beside an important point or underline it. As with overhead transparencies and dry-erase markers, electronic annotations are not permanent. They are automatically removed when you move to the next slide in a slide show, or you can remove annotations manually as you present your slides.

To annotate slides during a slide show, follow these steps:

1. Start your slide show.

2. Click the annotation icon, which appears in the lower left corner of your screen.

3. Choose Pen from the resulting pop-up menu. The pointer will turn into a pen.

    Tip
    To display the pen during a slide show, press Ctrl+P.

4. Press and hold the mouse button as you write or draw on-screen by moving the mouse. Release the mouse button to stop drawing or writing.

5. Repeat step 4 to write or draw again on the slide.

6. (Optional) Type **E** to erase all annotations to the current slide, so you can circle or check other areas of the slide.

7. When you are finished annotating the current slide, click the annotation icon again and choose the Arrow command from the pop-up menu to restore the mouse pointer.

    Tip
    You can change from the Pen to the Arrow by pressing Ctrl+A.

If you don't type **E** to erase all annotations on the current slide (see step 5), PowerPoint erases all annotations automatically when you move to the next slide in the slide show.

V

Using PowerPoint

Building Slide Text

You can apply an interesting build effect to a slide with a bulleted list, so that the items on the list appear one at a time. Using build effects makes the show more interesting and keeps the viewers from reading ahead of the speaker.

To add build effects to a presentation, follow these steps:

1. In Slides view, select the text block you want to apply build effects to.

2. Choose Tools, Build Slide Text. A check mark appears beside the option. To turn build effects off, choose the command again to remove the check mark and hide build effects.

To change the way the text builds, follow these steps:

1. In Slide Sorter view, select the slide with the build effects; notice a build icon appears beside the transition and timing icons (see fig. 29.10).

Fig. 29.10
Choose a build effect from the Text Build Effects drop-down list.

Tip
If you choose to advance the slide show manually, the text builds on-screen each time you click the mouse; otherwise, the build is automatic.

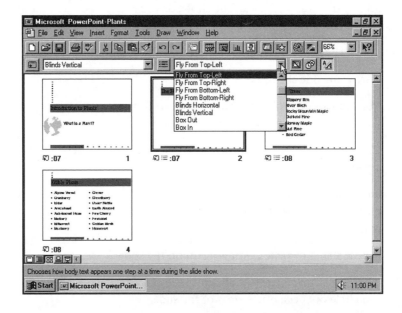

2. Click the down arrow beside the Text Build Effects button on the toolbar to display build options. Select one of the options as the method the text will appear on-screen.

Note

You can also use the Animation Settings dialog box to govern how your builds look on-screen. Select the slide and choose <u>T</u>ools, A<u>n</u>imation Settings. Set the build options, order of the build, and effects using this dialog box.

Troubleshooting

In Slide Sorter view, I applied a build effect using the Text Build Effects drop-down list. Now all bullets build at the same time during a slide show instead of one at a time. What did I do wrong?

You must first choose <u>T</u>ools, <u>B</u>uild Slide Text from Slide view to make each bulleted item appear separately; then you can choose the build effect in Slide Sorter view.

In Slide Sorter view, the Slide Transition Effects and Text Build Effects buttons are blank. How can I use them?

The buttons are blank unless a slide is selected. Select the slide you want to apply an effect to and the buttons appear.

Note

You can take the on-screen slide show with you to show on another's computer. The Pack and Go Wizard prepares and copies the presentation for you. To pack and go, choose <u>F</u>ile, Pack And <u>G</u>o. Follow the directions on-screen to copy the presentation to a disk.

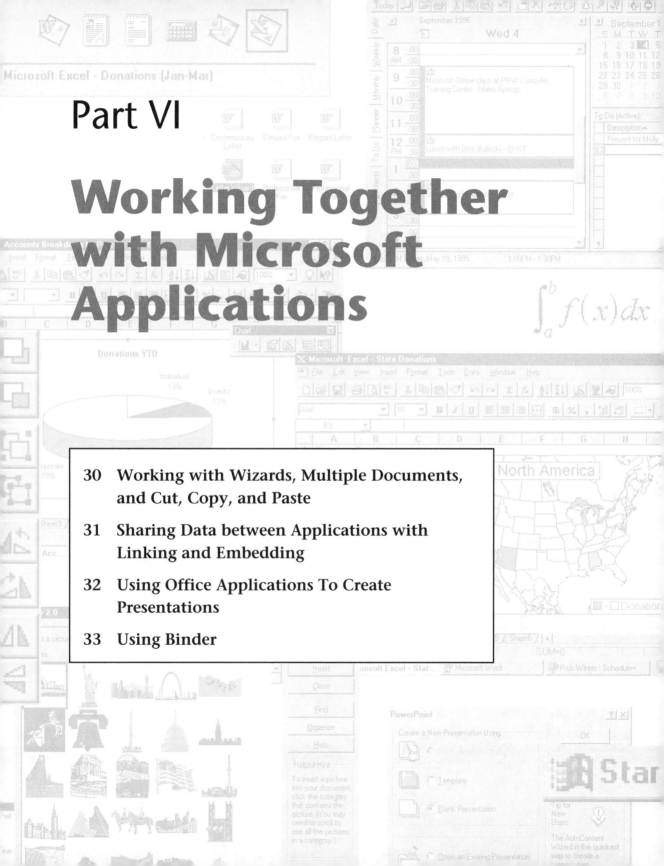

Part VI

Working Together with Microsoft Applications

Chapter 30

Working with Wizards, Multiple Documents, and Cut, Copy, and Paste

by Rick Winter and Patty Winter

One of the nicest time-saving features in Microsoft Office is wizards. You can start a new document by selecting the type of document you need to create, and working through wizard dialog boxes to set up the document. The benefit of wizards is that you don't need to know *how* to create the document, you just answer the questions on the dialog boxes.

Information within your organization probably is scattered throughout your hard drive and everyone else's. Instead of typing the information over and over, you can use the Cut, Copy, and Paste commands to reuse existing information. This not only saves time but also saves potential errors when retyping information. To start your documents and save time, try the wizards that come with the Office applications.

In this chapter, you learn to

- Use wizards to start letters
- Switch between programs
- Copy text, data, and pictures between programs

Starting a Letter with the Letter Wizard

◄ See "Using Wizards," p. 162

◄ See "Using Template Wizards," p. 269

As mentioned in Chapter 5, "Using Help," a *wizard* is a subset of templates that walks you through creating a document by asking you a series of questions about what you want to do. Through your answers, the wizard creates a format for your document and adds some text to get you started.

To start the Letter Wizard, follow these steps:

1. Choose File, New. The New dialog box appears, displaying a series of tabs that organize the templates and wizards.

2. Click the Letters & Faxes tab. The tab shows letter and fax templates and the Letter and Fax Wizards, as shown in figure 30.1. The wizard is indicated by the Letter Wizard name and the wand icon.

Fig. 30.1
Letter templates and the Letter Wizard appear in the New dialog box.

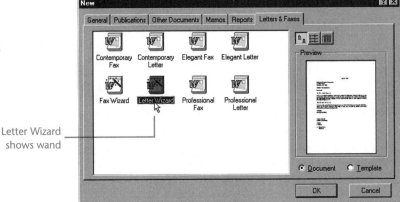

Letter Wizard shows wand

3. Select the Letter Wizard.

4. Choose OK.

Note

You can choose the three buttons to the right of the list of templates to see different views of the list:

■ Details shows large icons.

■ List shows small icons and a list of file names.

■ Large Icons shows file details such as name, size, document type, and when the document was last modified.

After you choose OK in the New dialog box, the first dialog box of the Letter Wizard appears, shown in figure 30.2. The dialog box asks whether you want to select a prewritten business letter, write a business letter, or write a personal letter. Below the options is a tip message that changes when you choose an option, giving you more information about your choice.

If you select a prewritten business letter, a list of 15 letters appears (see fig. 30.3). This list has various letters, including a press release, a collection letter, a resume cover letter, various thank-you letters, and even a letter to Mom.

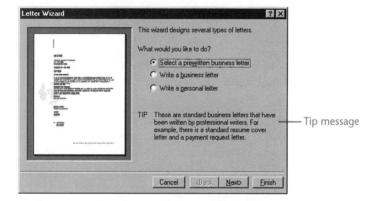

Fig. 30.2
The first Letter Wizard dialog box enables you to select different types of letters.

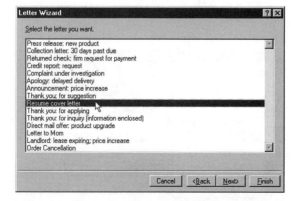

Fig. 30.3
You can select a prewritten business letter from the list box.

VI

Working Together

If none of the prewritten letters is appropriate, choose <u>B</u>ack to return to the Letter Wizard dialog box, shown in figure 30.2. Select the Write a <u>B</u>usiness

Letter option and choose <u>N</u>ext. The next Letter Wizard dialog box, shown in figure 30.4, asks which items you want to appear in your letter, including page numbers and the date. Put a check mark next to the items you want in your letter.

Fig. 30.4
Click a check box to select an item (with a check mark) or deselect an item (without a check mark).

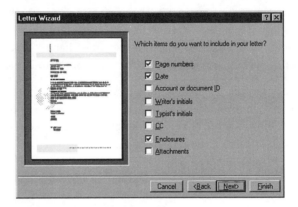

The next dialog boxes ask whether your letter is on letterhead and, if it is, where to place the letterhead on the page.

Copying Information into a Dialog Box

The dialog box shown in figure 30.5 requests your name and address and the recipient's name and address. You can type the information or copy it from somewhere else, if it is available. Your name and address should already be filled in if you created a previous letter with a wizard, or if you entered the information in the <u>T</u>ools, <u>O</u>ptions, User Info tab of the Options dialog box. The recipient's name and address already appear in your Notepad document (see fig. 30.6).

Fig. 30.5
To copy the recipient's name and address in the Letter Wizard, highlight the existing information.

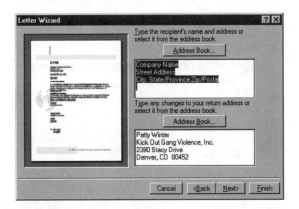

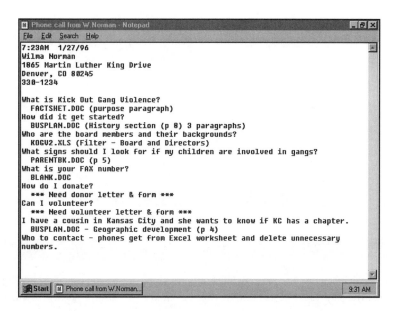

Fig. 30.6
This Notepad document shows requested information and potential sources for the answers.

To copy information from the Notepad into the Letter Wizard dialog box, follow these steps:

◄ See "Copying and Moving Data," p. 78

1. Drag the I-beam mouse pointer over the existing information in the recipient's text box to highlight all the information you will replace, as shown in figure 30.5.

2. Switch to the open Notepad document by clicking the button that reads `Phone call from W. Norman` on the taskbar at the bottom of the screen. If a document is not open, you can use the Start button on the taskbar to open programs or documents.

◄ See "Switching between Documents," p. 138

◄ See "Modifying User Info," p. 240

3. In the Notepad window, highlight the information you want to copy.

4. To copy the highlighted text, choose <u>E</u>dit, <u>C</u>opy, or press Ctrl+C.

5. Click the Word button on the taskbar to return to the Letter Wizard dialog box in Word.

6. The old entry in the recipient's text box should still be highlighted. Press Ctrl+V to paste the information from the Clipboard to the text box. Figure 30.7 shows the completed text box.

◄ See "Opening a Document from the Taskbar," p. 29

VI

Working Together

Fig. 30.7
The information
from the Clip-
board is pasted
into the text box.

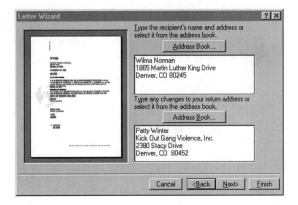

> ### Note
>
> You cannot use the Edit menu or any button in a toolbar while you are in this dialog box. The only way to paste from the Clipboard is to press Ctrl+V or use the shortcut menu by pressing the right mouse button. The same holds true when you are trying to cut or copy from a dialog box. Press Ctrl+X to cut or Ctrl+C to copy highlighted text in a text box or use the shortcut menu.

Finishing the Letter Wizard

To finish the interactive portion of creating a letter, fill out other dialog boxes in the Letter Wizard by following these steps (choose Next to move to each successive step):

1. After you insert the names and addresses, choose Next to continue to the next dialog box.

2. Select an option button to specify the style you want for your letter: Professional, Contemporary, or Elegant.

3. The Letter Wizard dialog box, which displays a checkered finish flag, asks whether you want to create an envelope or mailing label, display help, or display the letter (see fig. 30.8). For example, to display a Help window with topics related to your letter, select the Display Help as I Work option. To just see the letter without help, select Just Display the Letter.

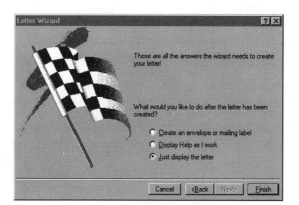

Fig. 30.8
The Letter Wizard
dialog box gives
you three options
from which to
choose after the
letter is finished.

4. If you select the Create an Envelope or Mailing Label option, the Envelopes and Labels dialog box appears (see fig. 30.9). The name of the recipient appears in the Delivery Address text box, and your address appears in the Return Address text box. If necessary, edit these entries in the dialog box.

Tip
You also can enter
the Envelopes and
Labels dialog box
by choosing Tools,
Envelopes and
Labels.

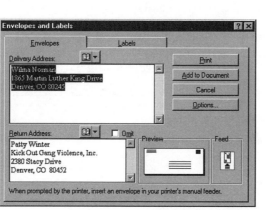

Fig. 30.9
The Wizard takes
you to the
Envelopes and
Labels dialog box,
where you can edit
addresses.

5. Your name and address automatically appear in the Return Address text box. If you have preprinted envelopes, check the Omit check box to remove the return address.

6. To create an envelope, choose the Envelopes tab.

7. To create a label, choose the Labels tab. In the Labels tab, you can specify the label size, which label to print on a label sheet, and whether a bar code prints on the label.

VI

Working Together

When the Delivery Address and Return Address appear as you want, you may choose from the following options:

■ Choose Options to change the envelope size, add or remove a bar code, change the fonts for the delivery or return addresses, or change the placement of the addresses on the envelope.

■ Choose Add to Document to add the envelope as a separate page in your document. This option also enables you to preview the envelope before you print it.

■ Choose Print to go directly to the printer.

■ Choose Cancel to exit the Envelopes and Labels dialog box without saving.

Regardless of whether you print an envelope, your letter appears with the current date and the recipient's information. Throughout the letter, information that you need to replace is indicated by brackets, as shown in figure 30.10. Click the bracketed area and type your replacement text.

Fig. 30.10

Select [Click here and type recipi-ent name] and type the salutation for the letter.

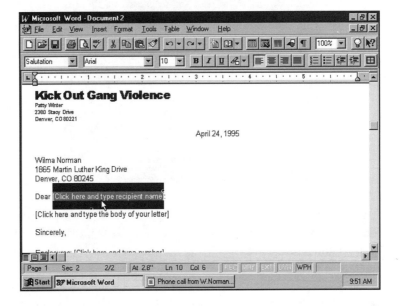

Copying Information from Notepad to Word

You can copy items from a Notepad document into your letter. Click the Notepad button on the taskbar to open the Notepad document. If the program is not open, click the Start button on the taskbar, choose the Programs icon, and then choose the Accessories icon. Click the Notepad icon from the Accessories group and choose File, Open to open your Notepad document.

◀ See "Launching Programs," p. 28

To place the information in the Clipboard, follow these steps:

1. In the Notepad document, highlight the text you want to copy.

2. Choose Edit, Copy, or press Ctrl+C.

> **Note**
>
> To remove the information from the Notepad and place it in the Clipboard, choose Edit, Cut, or press Ctrl+X.

To copy the information from the Clipboard to your Word document, follow these steps:

1. Return to the Word document by clicking the Word button on the taskbar or by pressing Alt+Tab.

2. In your document, position the insertion point where you want to place the copy.

3. Choose Edit, Paste, or press Ctrl+V.

Using the Styles from the Letter Wizard

When you use a template or wizard, more than text comes with the document. Styles, AutoText entries, and macros are added to the Normal template entries to give you added flexibility in creating your documents. The first item in the Formatting toolbar shows you the current style for the highlighted text. Figure 30.11 shows that Return Address is the style when the insertion point is in the letter's return address.

◀ See "Formatting with Styles," p. 259

VI

Working Together

Fig. 30.11
The Letter Wizard adds a Return Address style and uses it for the return address.

Style box ———

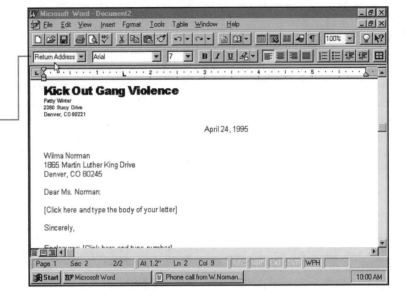

If you display the style area by choosing Tools, Options and increase the size of the style area to .7 or larger, you can then view the different styles applied to each section of the letter: Wilma's address, or the body of the letter, the style changes to Date, Inside Address, or Body Text, respectively. You can apply a style by highlighting the text, clicking the Style box down arrow, and selecting the style from the drop-down list. In this case, references to the documents and other notes from the Notepad document were first deleted, and then the Lead-in Emphasis style was selected.

In this example, Enter was pressed between each question and the style changed back to Body Text. To return to Normal style, press Ctrl+space bar.

Copying Text between Word Documents

The information for your documents may be scattered throughout existing documents. Learning how to copy text between documents saves valuable time, especially if you want to retype the same text repeatedly.

Opening Word Documents

◀ See "Working with Files," p. 102

Part of the process of working with multiple documents in Word is opening those documents. You can open each document separately by choosing File, Open, and you can have more than one document open at a time.

To open more than one document, follow these steps:

1. Choose File, Open. The Open dialog box appears.

2. If necessary, select the file location in the Look In drop-down list.

3. Do one of the following:

   ■ In the file name list, press Ctrl and then click each of the files you want to open, as shown in figure 30.12.

   ■ To select adjacent file names, click the first file name, hold down the Shift key, and click the last file name.

   ■ In the File Name text box, type the names of the files you want to open, separating file names with spaces.

4. Choose OK. All the selected files open.

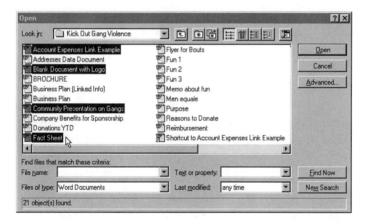

Fig. 30.12
Press Ctrl and click file names to open nonadjacent files.

Switching between Documents

When you have several documents open, you need to switch between the documents to copy information between them.

◄ See "Switching Between Documents," p. 138

To switch between open documents in Word, do one of the following:

■ Choose one of the documents from the bottom of the Window menu, as shown in figure 30.13.

■ Press Ctrl+F6 to cycle through the open documents.

VI

Working Together

Fig. 30.13
To go to the
Business Plan
document, type **2**
or click Business
Plan.

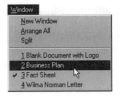

Copying Information from One Word Document to Another

◄ See "Copying
and Moving
Data," p. 78

After you open your documents, you can copy information between them. Use the Clipboard method described in this section or the drag-and-drop feature mentioned later in the section "Using Drag-and-drop to Copy Information between Documents."

To copy information between documents, follow these steps:

1. Highlight the text you want to copy.

2. Choose Edit, Copy, or press Ctrl+C.

3. Switch to the document that is to receive the copy and position the insertion point where you want to place the copy.

   If you know the target page number, double-click the left portion of the status bar to open the Go To dialog box; type that page number and choose Next.

4. Choose Edit, Paste, or press Ctrl+V.

◄ See "Copying
the Format
with Format
Painter," p. 87

After you copy the text into your document, you may need to reformat the text so that it matches the surrounding text.

Note

The Format Painter button is handy for copying formats. Position the insertion point within the text that has the format you want; click the Format Painter button. Drag the mouse-pointer paintbrush across the text you want to change. When you release the mouse button, the highlighted text changes format.

> **Note**
>
> When you use the normal paste procedure in step 4 of the preceding steps, the text retains some formatting from the original document. If you want the text to assume the formatting of the text at the insertion point in your target document, choose Edit, Paste Special. Then select the Unformatted Text option in the As list in the Paste Special dialog box.

Arranging Documents

If you want to see more than one document at a time, you can display parts of each document window.

To arrange the documents, follow these steps:

1. Open the documents you want to view.

2. Choose Window, Arrange All. The documents are tiled within the window, as shown in figure 30.14.

Tip
Close or minimize any documents you don't want to view. If you have too many documents open, you can see only a small portion of each document.

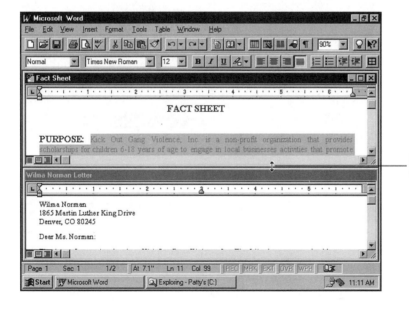

Fig. 30.14
Two documents, Fact Sheet and Wilma Norman Letter, are open and visible here.

Use mouse pointer to change window size

Use these options to adjust the windows:

- To change the size or shape of the window, point to a window border and drag the double-headed mouse pointer.

- To move a window, drag the title bar.

VI

Working Together

Using Drag-and-Drop To Copy Information between Documents

◄ See "Moving with Drag-and-Drop," p. 79

When you have more than one document visible, you can drag text between the two documents. To move or copy information with drag-and-drop, follow these steps:

1. Highlight the text you want to move or copy.

2. Position the mouse pointer in the middle of the highlighted text.

Tip
You can use the same drag-and-drop procedure when you move or copy text within the same document.

3. To move the text, drag the mouse pointer. The mouse pointer changes to a gray rectangle as you drag, and a gray dashed line indicates where the text will be placed.

To copy text, hold down the Ctrl key and drag the mouse pointer. A plus sign (+) appears with the mouse pointer (see fig. 30.15).

Fig. 30.15
When you copy text, a plus sign (+) appears with the mouse pointer.

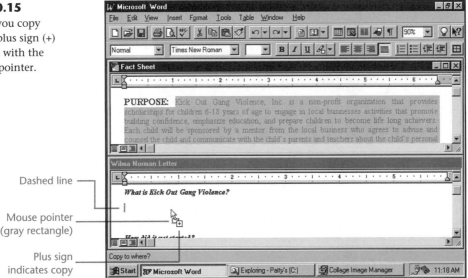

Dashed line

Mouse pointer (gray rectangle)

Plus sign indicates copy

4. Drag the text into the new window to receive the copy.

5. Release the mouse button to complete the copy procedure.

Troubleshooting

When I copy information with drag-and-drop, the original document loses its information.

You used the move feature instead. Make sure that you hold down the Ctrl key throughout the process. After you drag the information, release the mouse button first, and then release the Ctrl key.

My copied text appears in the middle of existing text.

Don't forget to watch the gray dashed line that is part of the mouse pointer. This line shows where the copied text will be inserted.

I get a black circle with a slash through it when I try to copy.

When it is on the title bar or status bar, the black circle with the slash indicates that you cannot drop as you drag the mouse with a copy. Make sure that you go all the way into the other document before you release the mouse button.

Copying Spreadsheet Information

The procedure for copying information from an Excel spreadsheet to a Word document is essentially the same as copying between two Word documents. You highlight the area you want to copy and choose Edit, Copy, then move to the location where you want the copy to appear and choose Edit, Paste.

Copying from Excel to Word

To copy information from an Excel worksheet to a Word document, follow these steps:

1. Start Excel by clicking the Start button on the taskbar and choosing Programs, Microsoft Excel.

2. Choose File, Open, or press Ctrl+O.

3. Select the name of the file you want to open and choose OK.

◀ See "Selecting Cells and Ranges," p. 309

4. To highlight the range you want to copy, do one of the following things:

    ■ With the thick white-cross mouse pointer, drag across the range to copy, as shown in figure 30.16.

    ■ Hold down the Shift key and use the arrow keys to highlight the range.

Fig. 30.16
In the Excel work-sheet, highlight the range you want to copy.

White cross mouse pointer

Caution

When you drag the mouse pointer, make sure that it is a thick white cross and not an arrow (used for drag-and-drop) or a black plus sign (used for automatic fill).

5. Choose Edit, Copy, or press Ctrl+C. A marquee surrounds the range to be copied.

6. Return to the Word document by clicking the Word button on the taskbar or by pressing Alt+Tab.

7. Position the insertion point where you want the spreadsheet information to appear.

8. Choose Edit, Paste, or press Ctrl+V.

Note

When you perform a normal paste operation in step 8, the information goes into a table in Word, as shown in figure 30.17. The light gray grid lines do not print. If you want lines to appear, choose Format, Borders and Shading. To change your columns in Word, drag the column marker.

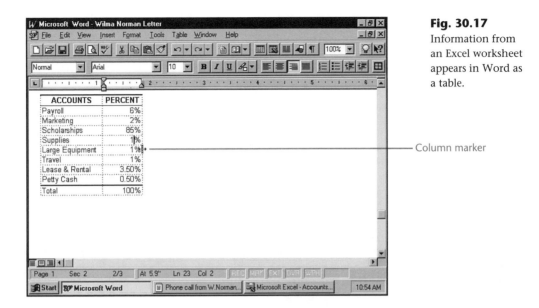

Fig. 30.17
Information from
an Excel worksheet
appears in Word as
a table.

Column marker

Using Paste Special with a Spreadsheet

If you don't want text to appear in a table in your Word document, you can
use the Paste Special option. To use Paste Special with spreadsheet data in the
Clipboard, choose Edit, Paste Special. The Paste Special dialog box appears, as
shown in figure 30.18.

◀ See "Working
with Tables,"
p. 286

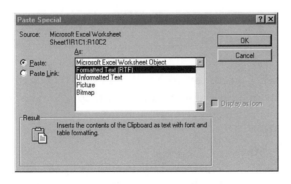

Fig. 30.18
Select one of the
options in the
Paste Special
dialog box to
format your text.

The options in the Paste Special dialog box enable you to link, embed, or
specify a format for the spreadsheet. To link information to the spreadsheet,
select Paste Link.

In the As list box, select from the following options how you want your Excel
worksheet to appear.

▶ See "Linking an
Excel Work-
sheet to a Word
Document,"
p. 697

VI

Working Together

■ To insert the Excel spreadsheet as an object, select Microsoft Excel Worksheet Object.

■ To insert the spreadsheet as a table in your Word document (the default when you choose Edit, Paste), select the Formatted Text (RTF) option.

◄ See "Setting Tabs," p. 199

■ To insert the spreadsheet with tabs separating data that was in columns, as shown in figure 30.19, select the Unformatted Text option. If you select this option, you probably will need to highlight the data and change the tab stops if you want the information to align.

Fig. 30.19

When you copy information from the spreadsheet by using the Unformatted Text option, set a tab stop to separate the items that were in columns in the worksheet.

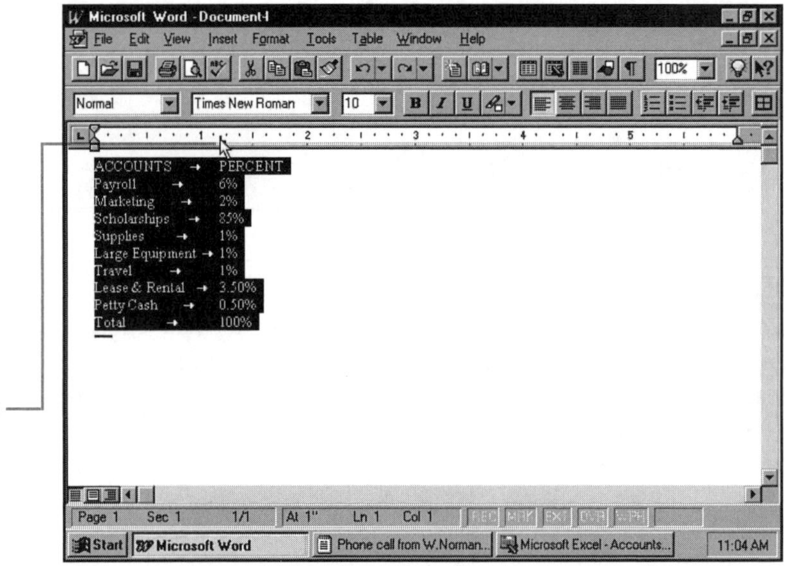

New tab stop ──

■ To insert the spreadsheet as a graphic, as shown in figure 30.20, select the Picture or Bitmap option in the As list box. Both options insert the spreadsheet as a diagram, but Picture takes up less room in the file and prints faster.

To edit the picture, first select the picture to display the small black handles. To resize the picture, point to one of the handles until the mouse pointer changes to a double-headed black arrow, and then drag. To move the picture up or down in the document, drag the drag-and-drop white arrow and rectangle mouse pointer.

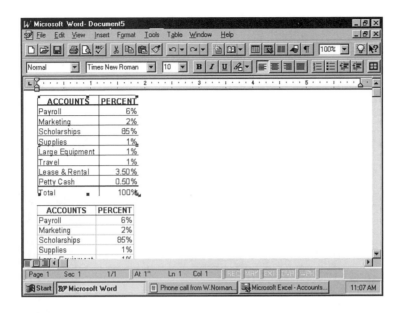

Fig. 30.20
The top table shows the Picture format, and the bottom table shows the Bitmap format.

Troubleshooting

I can't see much of my document after I move a table.

When you move a table, the right margin of the document may move so that it no longer is visible. To correct the problem, click the horizontal scroll bar after the scroll box, and then before the scroll box. This action repositions your document so that you can see both margins. If you still cannot see both margins, you may need to use the Zoom Control (the third item from the right in the Standard toolbar).

Copying Pictures from PowerPoint

In addition to copying text or data, you may want to copy a slide or picture from PowerPoint or a chart from Excel. The procedure is essentially the same: select the object; choose Edit, Copy; then choose Edit, Paste.

To copy a PowerPoint picture, follow these steps:

1. Start PowerPoint by clicking the Start button on the taskbar and choosing Programs, Microsoft PowerPoint.

VI

Working Together

2. On the initial screen, choose <u>O</u>pen an Existing Presentation, and choose the name of the file.

◀ See "Moving through a Presentation," p. 581

3. Go to the slide, as shown in figure 30.21, by clicking the Next Slide or Previous Slide buttons (double arrows) in the scroll bar. Or you can use the Slide Sorter View button and double-click the slide you want.

Fig. 30.21
You can copy a sample PowerPoint picture into your document.

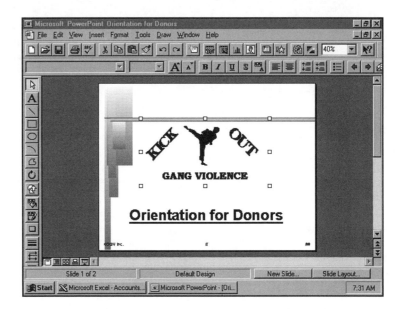

4. Click the object or objects to copy. White handles surround the object to show that it is selected (refer to fig. 30.21).

5. Choose <u>E</u>dit, <u>C</u>opy, or press Ctrl+C.

6. Return to the position in your Word document where you want to place the copy.

7. Choose <u>E</u>dit, <u>P</u>aste or press Ctrl+V. The object appears in your Word document.

Choosing <u>E</u>dit, Paste <u>S</u>pecial does not do anything different than choosing <u>E</u>dit, <u>P</u>aste. You cannot link or embed the object with Paste <u>S</u>pecial.

To select the picture, click the object. To change the size of the picture in Word, drag a handle. To move the picture vertically in the document, drag it to the new position. To move the picture horizontally or have text wrap around the object, however, you need to frame the picture first, as described in the following section.

Framing a Picture

When you paste a PowerPoint picture or an Excel chart, or you select Picture or Bitmap in the Paste Special dialog box, the graphic is one object in your Word document. For better control in positioning the object, you can frame it. Figure 30.22 shows an unframed object in page layout view. Text does not wrap around the picture, and you cannot move the picture horizontally on the page.

Fig. 30.22
In this example, the picture had to be made smaller. Notice that the text does not wrap around the picture.

To frame a picture, follow these steps:

1. Select the object.

2. Click the Insert Frame button in the Drawing toolbar or choose Insert, Frame.

3. Choose Yes if the program prompts you to go to page layout view.

When the object is framed, you can move it horizontally on the page and position text to the left or right of the object. To edit the properties of the frame, choose Format, Frame. You can specify whether you want text to wrap around the picture, set the size and location of the picture, and remove the frame. Figures 30.23 and 30.24 show the completed letter.

◀ See "Using Frames in Word," p. 529

VI

Working Together

Fig. 30.23
The first page of a letter is created by using the Letter Wizard command.

Pasted from PowerPoint and inserted into frame

Pasted from Notepad

Pasted from other Word documents

Pasted from Excel database

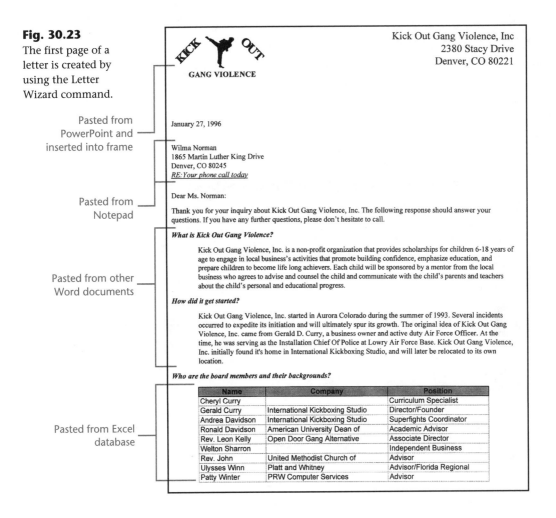

Kick Out Gang Violence, Inc
2380 Stacy Drive
Denver, CO 80221

GANG VIOLENCE

January 27, 1996

Wilma Norman
1865 Martin Luther King Drive
Denver, CO 80245
RE: Your phone call today

Dear Ms. Norman:

Thank you for your inquiry about Kick Out Gang Violence, Inc. The following response should answer your questions. If you have any further questions, please don't hesitate to call.

What is Kick Out Gang Violence?

Kick Out Gang Violence, Inc. is a non-profit organization that provides scholarships for children 6-18 years of age to engage in local business's activities that promote building confidence, emphasize education, and prepare children to become life long achievers. Each child will be sponsored by a mentor from the local business who agrees to advise and counsel the child and communicate with the child's parents and teachers about the child's personal and educational progress.

How did it get started?

Kick Out Gang Violence, Inc. started in Aurora Colorado during the summer of 1993. Several incidents occurred to expedite its initiation and will ultimately spur its growth. The original idea of Kick Out Gang Violence, Inc. came from Gerald D. Curry, a business owner and active duty Air Force Officer. At the time, he was serving as the Installation Chief Of Police at Lowry Air Force Base. Kick Out Gang Violence, Inc. initially found it's home in International Kickboxing Studio, and will later be relocated to its own location.

Who are the board members and their backgrounds?

Name	Company	Position
Cheryl Curry		Curriculum Specialist
Gerald Curry	International Kickboxing Studio	Director/Founder
Andrea Davidson	International Kickboxing Studio	Superfights Coordinator
Ronald Davidson	American University Dean of	Academic Advisor
Rev. Leon Kelly	Open Door Gang Alternative	Associate Director
Welton Sharron		Independent Business
Rev. John	United Methodist Church of	Advisor
Ulysses Winn	Platt and Whitney	Advisor/Florida Regional
Patty Winter	PRW Computer Services	Advisor

What signs should I look for if my children are involved in gangs?

Be aware if your child:
1. Wants to buy an excessive amount of blue and red for his or her wardrobe.
2. Wears sagging pants on hips or waist.
3. Wears an excessive amount of gold jewelry.
4. Uses excessive amounts of gang language.
5. Withdraws from family members.
6. Associates with undesirables.
7. Stays out later than usual.
8. Desires too much privacy.
9. Develops major attitude problems with parents, teachers or those in authority.
10. Starts to use drugs and alcohol.
11. Uses hand signs.
12. Receives money or articles without your permission or awareness.
13. Suddenly using racial slurs or hateful comments about other religions.
14. Wants to wear boots, shave his/her head, wear suspenders of a specific color.
15. Lacks identification or has false identification.
16. Wears beepers and begins using cellular phones.

What is your FAX number?

555-3317

How do I donate? & if I do, where do my funds go?

ACCOUNTS:	PERCENTAGE OF DONATION
Payroll	6%
Marketing	2%
Scholarships	85%
Supplies	1%
Large Equipment (over $500)	1%
Travel	1%
Lease & Rental	3.50%
Petty Cash	0.50%
Total	100%

Can I volunteer?

Certainly, we need office workers and volunteers to recruit sponsors, participating organizations, and scholarship candidates. Call us at (303)555-3646. Thank you for your interest in our organization and for your concern about our children and violence.

Sincerely,

Patricia L. Winter

PW/rw

Enclosures: 1

Fig. 30.24
The second page of the letter shown in figure 30.23.

Pasted from other Word document

Pasted from Excel spreadsheet

VI

Working Together

Chapter 31

Sharing Data between Applications with Linking and Embedding

by Rick Winter and Patty Winter

Earlier chapters showcased the nonprofit organization Kick Out Gang Violence and suggested ways that you can use Microsoft Office. Many parts of the existing documents may be useful for information requests and for other reports and documents you may need to create. People who might need the information include prospective donors, sponsors, participating organizations, the press, parents, schools, prospective scholarship recipients, event attendees, paid staff, volunteers, the director, and the board of directors. Trying to provide information to everyone is a huge task. By using Microsoft Office's capabilities to link and embed information, you can streamline the task of supplying information to a diverse audience.

In this chapter, you learn to

- ■ Link information between documents
- ■ Update links
- ■ Edit links
- ■ Embed information within documents

Moving beyond Copy and Paste To Link Information

Tip

To copy and paste information, use your shortcut menu or the keyboard shortcuts—Ctrl+C for copy and Ctrl+V for paste.

◄ See "Copying Text between Word Documents," p. 670

You may have documents or portions of documents that you need to use over and over. With Microsoft Office applications, you have different options to accomplish the same task. The first option is a simple copy and paste. Whenever you need information from one document, open the document, and select and copy the information. Then open the second document and paste the information at the appropriate point.

Although the copy and paste procedure is the easiest to master, it has two drawbacks. First, if the original information changes, you need to continually repeat the procedure if you want to keep your documents current. The second drawback is that you need to remember the application that created the information and where you put the files. If you want to edit the data, you may need to return to the original application.

To overcome these drawbacks, you have two additional options for sharing data between files (and applications). One option is to create a link between two files. Whenever the data in the source file changes, the destination file receives the update. The technical term for this is *dynamic data exchange* or DDE.

> **Note**
>
> This chapter references the *source* application and document as the application and file on disk that supply data. The *destination or target* application and document are the application and file on disk that receive the data.

Using Embedding To Link Information

Another option is to embed the information into your destination document. When you *embed* the information, you can use the source application's tools to update the information. Depending on the source application, you have two ways to get to the tools (menus and toolbars) of the source application. You can launch the source application from within the destination document, and a separate window appears with the source application showing the information to edit.

The second way to use embedded application tools is called *in-place editing*. When you select the object to edit, your menu and toolbar change to the source application, but you remain in the document and can see the surrounding text or data. The technical term for this kind of sharing is *object linking and embedding* (OLE). If the source application starts when you edit the data, it is OLE 1.0 compliant. If you can edit the data without leaving the destination, the source application is OLE 2.0 compliant. Embedding is discussed in more detail in the section "Embedding Information in Your Documents," later in this chapter.

> **Note**
>
> This chapter mentions objects. An *object* can be text, a chart, table, picture, equation, or any other form of information that you create and edit, usually with an application different from your source application.

One difference between linking and embedding is where the information is stored. Linked (DDE) information is stored in the source document. The destination contains only a code that supplies the name and location of the source application, document, and the portion of the document. Embedded (OLE) information is stored in the destination document, and the code associated with OLE points to a source application rather than a file.

In some cases, you cannot launch the source application by itself; you need to use your destination application to start the application. These applications are called *applets* (small applications) and include WordArt, ClipArt, Microsoft Graph, and others. You generally launch the source application by choosing Insert, Object.

You may want to look at your existing documents and see whether you will continually use different portions in other documents. Table 31.1 lists the existing available documents for Kick Out Gang Violence. Suppose that, as office manager, you use Excel to list the original document and divide the document into parts that may be used repeatedly in other documents. You decide it would be better to create separate documents for each frequently used piece required in multiple documents. You also include a column for the application that may be best for the subdocuments.

Table 31.1 Portions of Documents You Can Link to Other Applications

Portion of Document You Can Use Elsewhere	Proposed Application	Notes and Where Else Needed
Business Plan Word document		
Logo	PowerPoint	Use for many documents
Purpose	Word	Queries, brochure, many documents
New-chapter networking	Word	Also instruct new chapters
Timeline for development	Word	Goals, manage timeline, board notes
Geographic development	Word	Goals, board notes
Distribution of funds	Excel	Goals, board notes
Reasons to donate	Word	Donors, sponsors presentations, brochure
Benefits to your company	Word	Sponsors presentation, brochure
History	Word	Queries, press release, brochure
Equipment needed for startup	Excel	Need to update as new numbers, info received
Orgchart	Organization Chart	Will change; board notes
Budget board notes	Excel	Summary, internal management
Fact Sheet Word document		
Logo	PowerPoint	Use for many documents
Purpose documents	Word	Queries, brochure, many
Eligibility queries	Word	New-chapter notices, scholarship
Scholarship amount	Word	New-chapter notices, scholarship queries
Submission process	Word	New-chapter notices, scholarship queries

Using Common Steps To Link Documents

The procedure for linking any kind ofdocu application to any other application is essentially the same regardless of the source or destination application. You copy the source into the Clipboard and then use the Link option in the Paste Special dialog box to create the link. In the Paste Special dialog box, you also can specify the type of format in which the information is presented.

In some cases, you may not be able to use the Paste Special dialog box to create the link. To link a PowerPoint slide to a Word document, for example, you may need to use the Insert Object dialog box to create the link. This procedure is described in "Linking a PowerPoint Picture to a Word Document" later in this chapter.

To copy an item to the Clipboard and link the item to another document, follow these steps:

1. Select the item in the source document.

2. Choose Edit, Copy or press Ctrl+C.

3. Move to the target application and document. Position the insertion point where you want the link to appear.

4. Choose Edit, Paste Special. The Paste Special dialog box appears, as shown in figure 31.1.

   Several format types may be available, depending on the source application. Two options usually are available: Paste and Paste Link. The Link option is grayed if you cannot link the source document for the selected format. Choosing Paste copies the item from the Clipboard but does not create a link.

   A check mark in the Display as Icon check box places a small picture symbol in your document.

   The Result area gives more detail on what happens with your choices.

5. Select a format option in the As list box as described in the following paragraphs.

6. Choose Paste Link.

7. Choose OK.

Tip

Don't forget that you can use the Start button on the taskbar and the Documents icon to locate the files you most recently worked on.

Tip

Alt+Tab will cycle through the applications you currently have running. If the target application was running before you opened the source application, Alt+Tab will allow you to fast-switch back to that application.

VI

Working Together

Fig. 31.1
In the Paste
Special dialog box,
you can choose
Paste and Paste
Link.

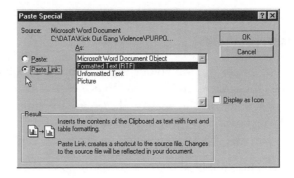

The As list box shows different formats. These formats change, depending on the source and target applications. In general, four different formats appear in most links. One of the formats usually is Object. In figure 31.1, the specific format is Microsoft Word Document Object. When you insert, or embed, an object, you can double-click the object or its icon (if the Display as Icon option is active) and then edit the object with the source application. Embedding is described in the section "Embedding Information in Your Documents" later in this chapter.

Another format option is Formatted Text. This option means that the object appears in your target document with most of the formatting (fonts, borders, and so on) from the source document. This option is different from Unformatted Text, in which the text takes on the format of the target document.

The last option is to add a picture of the document. Picture creates a picture of the object. Whether the original document is a picture or text, the link becomes a picture, and you can size and move the picture as one item.

Troubleshooting

I linked my documents, but the source document isn't there. Where did it go?

You may have moved your source document. Check the links by turning on the field codes. Choose Tools, Options, and in the View tab, select Field Codes. Then make sure your source file is in the right location. You can use Windows Explorer to find your files.

Linking Two Word Documents

When you want to link two Word documents, you can use Paste Special to create the link, or you can use the Insert, File feature. To insert a portion of a file, use the Paste Special feature, which is helpful if the source document is not a complete file. To insert an entire document, choose Insert, File. In the Insert File dialog box, make sure that you select the Link To File option under the command buttons.

To link two Word documents, follow the steps in the preceding section, "Using Common Steps To Link Documents." Select and copy the text you want to link and then move to your target document and choose Edit, Paste Special. In the Paste Special dialog box, select the Unformatted Text option in the As list box to enable the linked text from the source document to assume the format of the target document.

Table 31.1 shows that the purpose for Kick Out Gang Violence is mentioned in the business plan, fact sheet, and in most other documents. As office manager for Kick Out Gang Violence, you may want the changes to be updated in all documents containing the purpose. Therefore, you might create the separate Word document called PURPOSE to describe the purpose of Kick Out Gang Violence. Because the text is formatted differently in diverse target documents, you want to link the text using the Unformatted Text option in the As list box of the Paste Special dialog box.

Displaying the Link

When you move within the linked section, as shown in figure 31.2, the link is highlighted in gray. Although you can edit the linked text, the editing changes disappear when the link is updated (when you open the file again, print the file, or press F9, the Update Field shortcut key). The gray highlight reminds you not to edit this part of the document.

> **Note**
>
> If the linked text is not highlighted, choose Tools, Options and then select the View tab. In the Field Shading drop-down list, select When Selected or Always.

If you want to see the name of the source document, you can display the field name codes rather than the actual text. Choose Tools, Options. In the View tab, choose the Field Codes option. (To display the text, deselect Field Codes.) Figure 31.3 shows field codes used in place of text. You can see that

◀ See "Changing General Settings," p. 231

◀ See "Modifying Viewing Options," p. 233

◀ See "Customizing Printing," p. 237

VI

Tip
To toggle between the field code and display the text, press Shift+F9.

Working Together

the file is linked to PURPOSE.DOC, and Word 6 is the format for the file, so the source application could be Word 6 or Word 7. The file also is linked to LOGO.PPT, and PowerPoint is the source application.

Fig. 31.2
The linked area in the document is highlighted in gray.

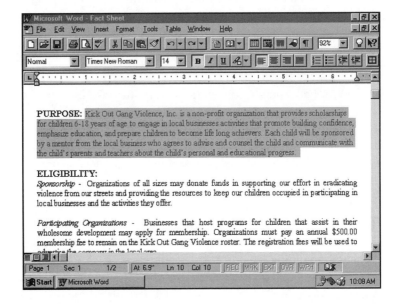

Note

The Microsoft Word 7 application uses Word 6 files to maintain compatibility with the previous version of Microsoft Word.

Troubleshooting

Changes in my source document aren't reflected in my destination document.

The link may be an automatic link or may require manual updating (see the following section, "Editing Links"). You can also do the following:

■ To update any manual links, you can go to each field code by pressing F11. To update the code or link, press F9.

■ To make sure that your document updates any automatic links when you open the file, choose Tools, Options. In the General tab, make sure that Update Automatic Links on Open is selected.

■ To make sure that your document prints with the latest information, choose Tools, Options. In the Print tab, make sure that Update Links is selected.

Tip
To go to the previous field code, press Shift+F11.

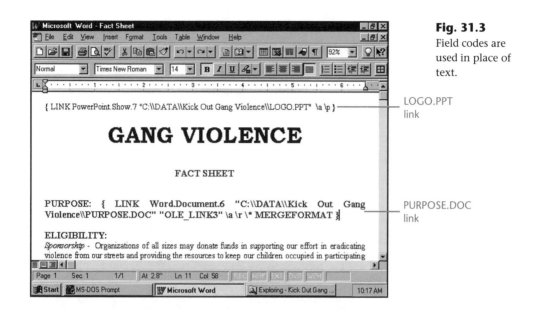

Fig. 31.3
Field codes are used in place of text.

Editing Links

When you link a document, you must keep both the document name and the document in the same location (drive and directory). If you rename, delete, or move a document, the link is broken, and you get an error in your destination document. In some cases, you can break the link so that the source document is inserted into the target document without a link; in other cases, you can change the name of the source document.

To change links, follow these steps:

1. Choose Edit, Links. The Links dialog box appears, as shown in figure 31.4.

2. Select the file(s) in the Source File list box.

3. Do one or more of the following things:

   ■ Choose Automatic to have the link updated every time the data is available.

   ■ Choose Manual to require updating through the Update Now choice or by selecting the link and pressing F9.

   ■ Choose Locked to prevent updates to the link.

   ■ Choose the Update Now button to update a manual link with any changes from the source file.

Tip
To get out of a dialog box quickly without saving your changes, press Esc.

■ Click the Change Source button to change the file name or location of the linked file in the Change Source dialog box.

■ Click the Break Link button to insert the object into the document and unlink it. When Word displays a message box asking whether you are sure that you want to break the selected links, choose Yes.

Fig. 31.4
The Links dialog box enables you to update, change, or break links.

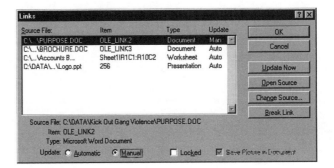

4. Click OK when you finish.

Troubleshooting

I linked an Excel spreadsheet to my Word document, but the link won't update.

You may have locked the linked document, which means you want to prevent updates to the link in your Word document. To unlock the link, press Ctrl+Shift+F11, and then update the field by pressing F9.

Inserting a File into a Document

You also can link documents by using the Insert, File command, which enables you to insert an entire file. When you use Paste Special to link a file, only the text you select before the Copy command is part of the target file. If you later go back and insert text before or after the source document selection, the target document does not include the entire text. Insert, File alleviates this problem. The file that you insert can be from the same application or a different application.

To insert a file into a document, follow these steps:

1. Move to the position in the target document where you want to insert the file.

2. Do one of the following:

   ■ In Word, choose Insert, File. The Insert File dialog box appears, as shown in figure 31.5.

   ■ In Excel, choose Insert, Object. The Object dialog box appears. Choose the Create from File tab; then enter the file name in the File Name text box.

   ■ In PowerPoint, choose Insert, Object. The Insert Object dialog box appears. Choose the Create from File option; then enter the file name in the File text box.

◀ See "Using File Dialog Boxes," p. 102

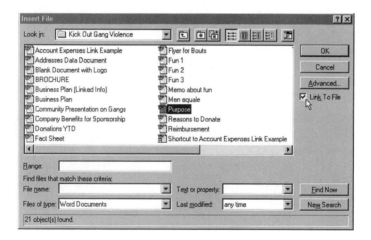

Fig. 31.5
The Insert File dialog box enables you to create a link between the files.

3. Identify the file you want to insert, including the drive and directory if necessary.

4. Choose the Link to File option in Word, the Link to File option in Excel, or the Link option in PowerPoint.

5. Choose OK.

As in the Paste Special example earlier in this chapter, you can display the linked document with a gray highlight or show the field codes. In figure 31.6, the revised business plan document shows field codes for the linked documents.

VI

Working Together

Fig. 31.6

The field code
INCLUDETEXT
appears for the
Word documents
NEWNET.DOC,
TIMELINE.DOC,
and
GEOGDEV.DOC,
and the
spreadsheet
FINDIST.XLS.

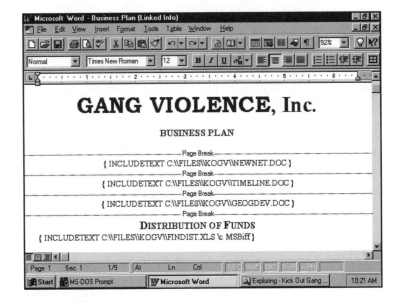

Note

If you want to insert several documents into a single larger document, give your documents a consistent appearance by using the same formats for each one. You also can use templates and styles to help ensure consistency among documents. For more information, see "Formatting with Styles" in Chapter 10, "Working with Large Documents."

Troubleshooting

When I make editing changes in my document, why are my changes gone when I open the document again? I know I saved the file.

You may be editing a document with a linked file. When you make changes in the linked field, Word will not save them. You need to change the source document to save the changes. To view the field codes, choose Tools, Options and in the View tab select Field codes to view the field codes.

To be able to always see field codes, choose Tools, Options and on the View tab, in the Field Shading option, select Always or When Selected.

Linking an Excel Worksheet to a Word Document

The procedure for linking a range or an entire Excel worksheet to a Word document is the same as for linking Word documents. You can use either the Paste Special command or choose Insert, File, although formatting a document is easier when you use the Paste Special command. When you use Insert, File, the resulting table sometimes is hard to center on the page because of extra space for the last column or extra cells. In the As list box of the Paste Special dialog box, you have the same formatting choices when you Paste Link as when you Paste (see fig. 31.7).

◀ See "Copying Text between Word Documents," p. 670

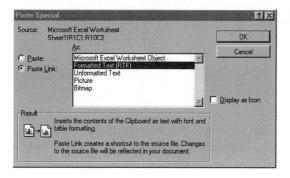

Fig. 31.7
Choose the Paste Link option to link the spreadsheet to the Word document.

The following list describes the formatting options in the Paste Special dialog box shown in figure 31.7. The results appear in figure 31.8.

- To insert the Excel spreadsheet as an object, select Microsoft Excel Worksheet Object. In a Word document, when you double-click the object, you activate the application's tools that created the object. You then can edit the object, using the source application's menus, toolbars, and other commands.

- To insert the spreadsheet as a table in your Word document (the default choice when you choose Edit, Paste), select Formatted Text (RTF). You may need to change the column widths for the table to line up properly, as is the case in figure 31.8.

- To insert the spreadsheet with tabs separating data, choose Unformatted Text. You may need to highlight the data and change the tabs for the selection if you want the information to align.

VI

Working Together

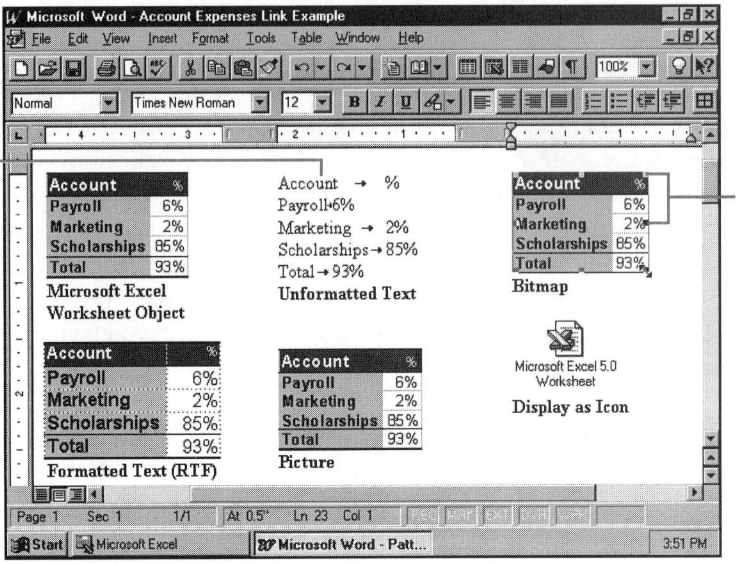

Fig. 31.8

You can insert the spreadsheet as various types of objects.

Unformatted text does not retain formatting

Selection handles used for sizing the picture

- To insert the spreadsheet as a graphic, select Picture or Bitmap. Both options insert the spreadsheet as a diagram, but Picture generally takes up less room in the file and prints faster. In figure 31.8, however, there is almost no discernible difference between Microsoft Excel Worksheet Object, Picture, and Bitmap. In fact, these three options do the same thing. They all insert a picture into the Word document, and you can double-click all three options to go to Excel to edit the object.

  To edit the picture, first select the picture to show the small square selection handles. To resize the picture, point to one of the handles until the mouse pointer changes to a small double-headed black arrow; then drag. To move the picture up or down in the document, drag the drag-and-drop white arrow and rectangle mouse pointer. To go to Excel to change the data, double-click the picture.

◄ See "Moving Objects," p. 545

- Put a check mark in the <u>D</u>isplay as Icon check box on the right side of the dialog box to place a small symbol that represents the program (or any other icon you select).

Suppose that now you need to create a quarterly report that contains text, Excel worksheets, and Excel charts. To do this, you begin by inserting some introductory text at the beginning of the report that includes the purpose and history of the organization. You then link the PURPOSE.DOC and HISTORY.DOC Word documents to the quarterly report file. To report on the donations for the first three months, you probably want to show the amount in a table, a pie chart by type of donation, and a bar chart of donations by month.

Figure 31.9 shows a formatted Excel worksheet. Because the numbers will change, you want to link rather than paste the worksheet and the charts.

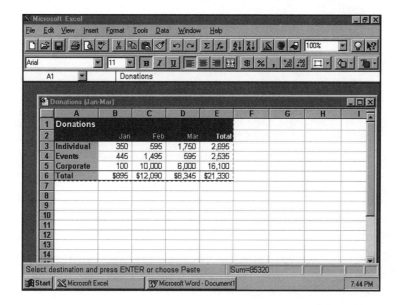

Fig. 31.9
Highlight the range in Excel and choose Edit, Copy.

To copy this worksheet into a Word document, follow these steps:

1. In Excel, highlight the range you want to link (A1:E6).

2. Choose Edit, Copy, or press Ctrl+C.

3. Switch to Word.

4. Choose Edit, Paste Special. The Paste Special dialog box appears.

5. Choose Paste Link and As Picture. Choose OK. The result appears in figure 31.10. Notice that the picture is left-justified.

◀ See "Switching between Documents," p. 138

6. If you want to center the worksheet, select the picture and then click the Center button.

Fig. 31.10
The worksheet picture appears left-justified in the Word document.

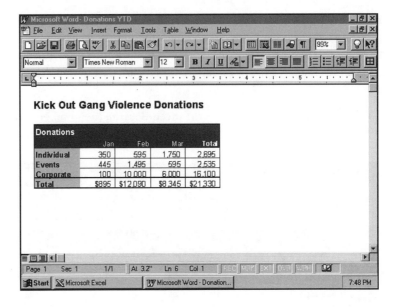

Troubleshooting

We are working in a workgroup, and I know that my coworkers have changed the Excel document. Why aren't the links updating when I open or print the Word document?

You may have one of two options turned off. Check Tools, Options, and in the General tab, make sure the Update Automatic Links at Open option is on. In the Print tab, check to make sure the Update Links option is on.

Linking an Excel Chart to a Word Document

◄ See "Creating a Chart with the ChartWizard," p. 481

Suppose that you want to add a pie chart and bar chart to this page in your quarterly report document. You can create charts quickly by clicking the ChartWizard button in Excel's Standard toolbar.

Creating a Pie Chart

To create a pie chart, follow these steps:

1. Drag the white-cross mouse pointer to highlight the titles in A3 to A5.

2. Hold down the Ctrl button and drag to highlight E3 to E5.

3. Click the ChartWizard button. The mouse pointer changes to a graph and a plus sign.

4. Click Sheet2 to draw the chart in that location (see fig. 31.11).

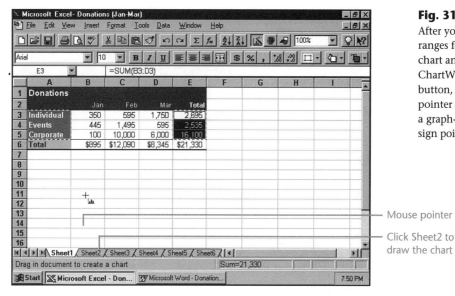

Fig. 31.11
After you select the ranges for your chart and click the ChartWizard button, the mouse pointer changes to a graph-and-plus-sign pointer.

— Mouse pointer

— Click Sheet2 to draw the chart

5. Drag from the top-left corner to the bottom-right corner of the range where you want the chart to appear. The ChartWizard dialog box appears, displaying five steps.

6. Click Next to go to the Step 2 ChartWizard dialog box.

7. Select 3-D Pie and then click the Next button, as shown in figure 31.12.

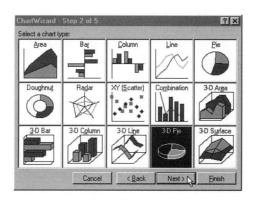

Fig. 31.12
The ChartWizard dialog boxes enable you to select chart types and other settings.

VI

Working Together

8. Choose Next until you get to the Step 5 ChartWizard dialog box. Type **Donations YTD** in the Chart Title text box and then click Finish. The chart appears in the second sheet of the workbook, as shown in figure 31.13.

Fig. 31.13

The chart appears in Sheet2, surrounded by handles.

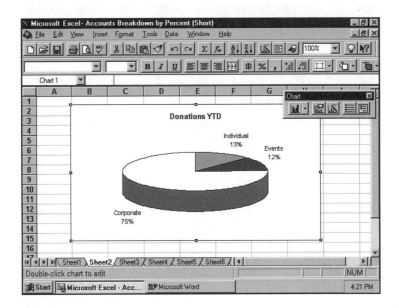

9. You can copy the chart the same way you do a range. Because the chart already is selected (handles surround the chart), choose Edit, Copy, or press Ctrl+C.

10. Return to the quarterly report document in Word.

11. Choose Edit, Paste Special. The Paste Special dialog box appears.

12. Select Picture, and then choose the Paste Link option. Click OK. The chart appears in the Word document, surrounded by handles. If the handles do not appear, click the picture.

13. Choose Format, Paragraph. In the Indents and Spacing tab, select Center from the Alignment drop-down list or press Ctrl+E to center the picture.

Creating a Bar Chart

To create a bar chart, follow these steps:

1. Drag the white-cross mouse pointer to highlight the range A2 through D5 on the spreadsheet shown earlier in figure 31.11.

2. Click the ChartWizard button.

3. Move to Sheet2 and highlight the range where the chart will appear. The ChartWizard dialog box Step 1 of 5 will be displayed.

4. Fill in the ChartWizard dialog boxes as they come up, including:

    ChartWizard Step 2 of 5: select the 3-D Column chart

    ChartWizard Step 3 of 5: select Format 4

    ChartWizard Step 5 of 5: in the Chart Title text box, type **Donations by Month**

    After you finish the ChartWizard dialog boxes, make sure that you click the Finish button; the chart appears with selection handles.

5. Choose Edit, Copy, or press Ctrl+C.

6. Return to the quarterly report document.

7. Choose Edit, Paste Special. The Paste Special dialog box appears.

8. In the As list box, select Picture and choose the Paste Link option. Choose OK. The chart appears in the Word document, with handles.

The third diagram in the quarterly report is shown in figure 31.14. When the final numbers come in, simply go to the Excel range and edit them. Figure 31.15 shows an updated Word document with the new number (15,000) for March corporate donations.

> **Note**
>
> To remove the border surrounding the charts, change the charts in Excel rather than Word. In Excel, click to select the chart. In the middle of the chart, click the right mouse button and choose Format Object from the pop-up menu. In the Patterns tab, choose None in the Border section.

> **Troubleshooting**
>
> *I paste-linked an Excel worksheet into my Word document. Word inserted an extra paragraph mark above the link. Why can't I delete the extra paragraph mark?*
>
> You can't delete the paragraph mark, but you can make it very small by changing the line spacing. Make sure the insertion point is on the extra line, choose Format, Paragraph, and in the Line Spacing option, change the setting to Exactly and At to **0.01**".
>
> The paragraph mark doesn't appear if you paste the worksheet instead of linking.

VI

Working Together

Fig. 31.14

The Excel range and two charts appear in the Word document.

Kick Out Gang Violence Donations

Donations				
	Jan	Feb	Mar	Total
Individual	350	595	1,750	2,695
Events	445	1,495	595	2,535
Corporate	100	10,000	6,000	16,100
Total	$895	$12,090	$8,345	$21,330

Donations YTD

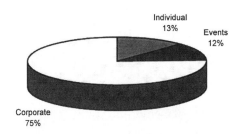

Donations by Month

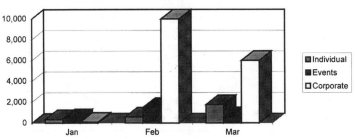

Kick Out Gang Violence Donations

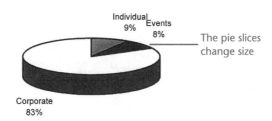

Donations	Jan	Feb	Mar	Total
Individual	350	595	1,750	2,695
Events	445	1,495	595	2,535
Corporate	100	10,000	15,000	25,100
Total	$895	$12,090	$17,345	$30,330

New number
in March

Fig. 31.15
After you update the
Excel worksheet, the
changes occur
in the Word
document.

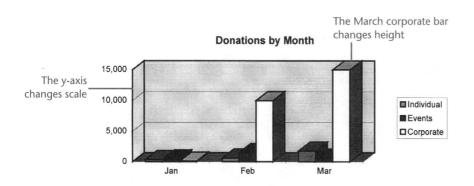

Donations YTD

Individual
9%   Events
      8%

The pie slices
change size

Corporate
83%

The March corporate bar
changes height

Donations by Month

The y-axis
changes scale

15,000

10,000

5,000

0

Jan   Feb   Mar

■ Individual
■ Events
□ Corporate

VI

Working Together

Linking a PowerPoint Picture to a Word Document

◀ See "Adding, Inserting, and Deleting Slides," p. 582

Suppose that you went through your documents and noticed that the organization logo was on almost every document. If your organization is established, pasting the logo may be appropriate. But you may want to link the logo if the logo may change and you want all documents with the logo updated. The Paste Special command, however, does not include PowerPoint as a Paste Link option. Insert, File also does not have a PowerPoint option. To do the link, you need to choose Insert, Object, and the first slide of the presentation must be the picture you want to link.

To create your PowerPoint slide, follow these steps:

1. Go to PowerPoint.

2. To insert pictures into your slide, choose Insert, Clip Art (if the picture is part of Microsoft ClipArt Gallery) or Insert, Picture (if you obtained the picture from another source).

3. To type text, click the Text tool. Then click the location in the document where you want to add text, and type.

4. To create rotated text, click the Free Rotate tool and drag the mouse pointer as shown in figure 31.16.

5. Save the document.

Fig. 31.16
Click the Free Rotate Tool and drag the top-right handle to change the orientation of the text.

Free Rotate tool

To link a PowerPoint slide to Word, follow these steps:

1. Create a PowerPoint slide with a picture and/or text you want to link to your Word document.

2. Save the PowerPoint presentation.

3. Go to the location in your Word document where you want to position the picture.

4. Choose Insert, Object. The Object dialog box appears, as shown in figure 31.17.

5. Click the Create from File tab and type the File Name or select the file using the Browse button.

6. Choose the Link to File option and then choose OK.

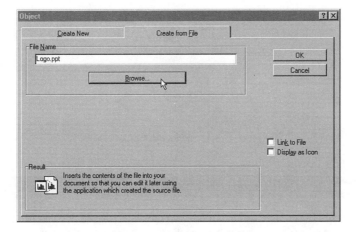

Fig. 31.17
Use the Object dialog box to select the type of infor-mation you want to insert.

The picture appears in your Word document. You can resize the picture by dragging the handles. To move the picture horizontally, you need to frame the picture. Choose Insert, Frame. If you are prompted, choose Yes to go to Page Layout view. When the picture is in a frame, you can drag the frame to position the picture. You also can choose Format, Frame to indicate where you want to position the picture (such as centered horizontally or vertically on the page) and whether text should wrap around the picture. Figure 31.18 shows the picture in a document.

◀ See "Using Frames in Word," p. 529

VI

Working Together

Fig. 31.18
The PowerPoint
slide is inserted
into a Word
document.

GANG VIOLENCE

Superfights

Saturday, February 3rd, 1996
7:00 pm

EIGHT EXCITING KICKBOXING BOUTS

Tournament Information
Where: Aurora Central High School
11700 East 11th Avenue
Aurora, Colorado 80010

For information call: 745-3646
General Admission: $5.00 per person donation
Ring Side: $10.00 per person

All Proceeds Will Be Donated to Kick Out Gang Violence, Inc.

Note

If your PowerPoint presentation is more than one slide, you can double-click the picture in Word to launch PowerPoint or the PowerPoint presentation. If you launch PowerPoint, you can edit the slide. If you launch the presentation, you can play the presentation by clicking each slide to move to the next slide.

Linking Data between Excel Worksheets

In some cases, you may want to repeat text or data in an Excel worksheet. For example, you may want to include a summary of actual numbers on a separate sheet of the workbook. You can copy the labels and numbers, or you can create a formula to copy the text and values. If you link through a formula, when the numbers or labels in the source part of the document change, they also change in the target part of the document.

The formula is easy: type an equal sign (=) in the cell to receive the link; move to the cell you want to link and click the mouse; then press Enter. The cell you want to link can be in the same sheet, in a different sheet of the same workbook, or in a different workbook file. Figure 31.19 shows an example. The budget worksheet on the left contains monthly numbers. To see only the categories and the year totals, you can hide columns or create the formula.

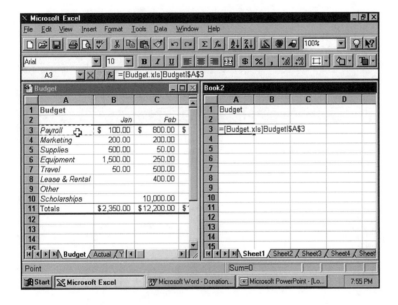

Fig. 31.19
After you link the cell, the reference contains the file name, the sheet name, and an absolute reference to the cell (A3).

To link the worksheets, follow these steps:

1. Choose File, New to create a blank workbook and type **Budget** in cell A1.

2. Move to cell A3 and type =.

3. Move to the source worksheet (identified as BUDGET in the Kick Out Gang Violence example).

4. Click A3 in the BUDGET worksheet and then press Enter.

Notice in figure 31.19 that when you use this method, the reference to the cells includes the file name (BUDGET.XLS), the sheet name (BUDGET!), and an absolute reference to the cell (A3). If you want to copy the information,

Tip
You can remove the dollar sign by pressing F4 three times.

◄ See "Referencing Cells in Formulas," p. 372

as in this example, remove the dollar signs to make the reference relative. Then you can copy cell A3 from A4 through A11 to link the other cells. Notice in figure 31.20 that the cell reference has no dollar signs (A3).

> **Note**
>
> To arrange your worksheets side by side, as shown earlier in figure 31.19, choose Window, Arrange and then choose the Tiled option in the Arrange Window dialog box. You don't need to arrange your worksheets this way, however. You could move to the other worksheet by choosing the document name from the bottom of the Window menu.

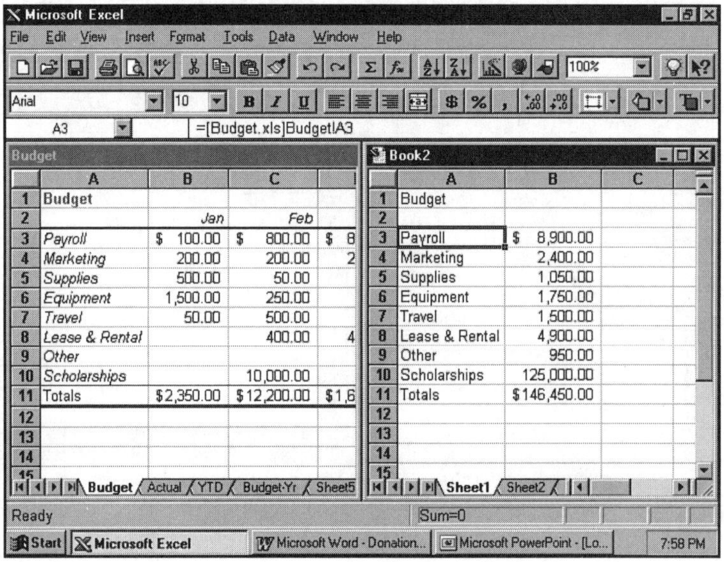

Fig. 31.20
To copy the cell information, change the reference so that no dollar signs appear, as shown in the edit line (A3).

◄ See "Creating a Formula by Pointing," p. 370

The formula automatically contains the file name (if the reference is to a cell in a different workbook), the sheet name (if the reference is to another sheet), and the cell name. The default formula includes dollar signs, which means that if you copy the formula, the reference does not change. In the example, Payroll would be in every cell in column A. Delete the dollar signs so that the copy will work correctly.

Embedding Information in Your Documents

As mentioned at the beginning of the chapter, in addition to linking information, you can embed information within a document. When you embed an object, the information resides in the destination document, but the source application's tools are available for use in editing.

You can use any of the following methods to embed information in a document:

- Copy the information to the Clipboard; choose <u>E</u>dit, Paste <u>S</u>pecial; and select an object format. (This method was discussed earlier in the section "Using Common Steps To Link Documents," along with other Paste Special formats.)

- Arrange two windows side by side and use drag-and-drop to copy information between the applications.

  ◀ See "Moving with Drag-and-Drop," p. 79

- Choose <u>I</u>nsert, <u>O</u>bject, and open an existing file. (This method was discussed in "Inserting a File into a Document" earlier in this chapter.)

- Choose <u>I</u>nsert, <u>O</u>bject, and create a new object. This section describes this method.

Inserting a New Object into Your Document

If you want to use the features of another application in your document, you can choose <u>I</u>nsert, <u>O</u>bject and select an application from a list. In addition to the standard Microsoft Office applications, the list contains applets and other Windows applications. Applets are small applications that cannot be run by themselves. When you purchase an application, one or more applets may be available.

Following is a list of applets that come with Microsoft Office. If you purchased your applications separately, you may not have all the applets.

Applet	Use
Calendar Control	Inserts a new calendar control object
Microsoft ClipArt Gallery	Inserts clip-art pictures

(continues)

VI

Working Together

Applet	Use
Microsoft Data Map	Inserts a map showing different levels associated with data
Microsoft Equation	Creates mathematical expressions
Microsoft Graph	Inserts charts from data in a Word table
MS Organization Chart	Creates organization charts
Microsoft Word Picture	Inserts a picture and the tools associated with the Word drawing toolbar
Microsoft WordArt	Creates logos and other special text effects

To use the tools from another application or applet within your document to create a new object, follow these steps:

1. Position the insertion point in the destination document.

2. Choose <u>I</u>nsert, <u>O</u>bject. The Object dialog box appears, as shown in figure 31.21.

Fig. 31.21
The Insert Object dialog box lists applets as well as Windows applications.

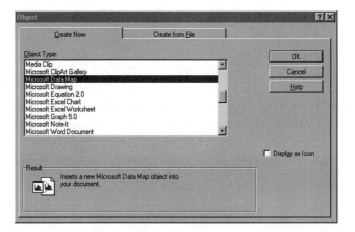

3. In the <u>C</u>reate New tab, select an application or applet from the <u>O</u>bject Type list.

4. If you want to see only an icon for the object, put a check mark in the Dis<u>p</u>lay as Icon check box.

5. When you finish with the Object dialog box, choose OK.

After you complete these steps, one of two things will occur. You may enter a separate window for the application or the applet, as shown in figure 31.22. The other possibility is that you will remain in your destination document window, but the menu bar and toolbar will change to reflect the source application, as shown in figure 31.23. For example, when you choose Microsoft Excel Worksheet, the menu bar and toolbar change to Microsoft Excel, enabling you to use Excel features such as the AutoSum button.

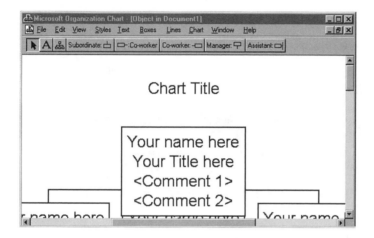

Fig. 31.22
When you choose MS Organization Chart Data Map, a separate window opens. After you finish with the chart program, choose File, Exit to return to the Word document.

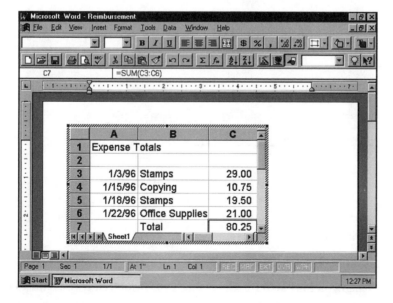

Fig. 31.23
When you choose Microsoft Excel Worksheet, in-place editing enables you to use Excel features.

VI

Working Together

When you finish creating the object, you can exit the object in either of two ways. If you launched a separate window for the application or applet, choose File, Exit. If you stayed in your destination document, click outside the object.

Editing an Embedded Object

Regardless of which of the four methods you use to embed information into your document, you can edit the embedded object with the tools of the source application.

To edit the object, follow these steps:

1. Click the object. Handles appear around the object, and the status bar tells you to double-click the object (see fig. 31.24).

Fig. 31.24

The status bar displays instructions on how to get to the source-application tools.

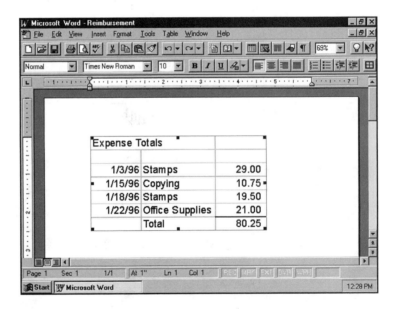

2. Double-click the object. Depending on the source and destination applications, a separate window for the program appears, or the current window's toolbar and menu bar change to those of the source application.

3. Edit the object, using the application's toolbar and menus.

4. When you finish editing the object, exit the object. If you launched a separate window for the application or applet, choose File, Exit. If you stayed in your destination document, click outside the object.

In some cases, you may be prompted if you want to update the object in your destination document. If you want to save the editing changes, choose Yes, otherwise choose No.

Troubleshooting

Sometimes when I open a Word document with an embedded object, the object returns to its original size instead of staying the size I want.

When you embed an object in Word, Word inserts the Embed field code in the document. In the Embed field code, there could be a switch **/s** which means return the object to its original size. To fix this problem, you need to modify the Embed field code for the object. To view the field code instead of the object, click the object and then press Shift+F9 to switch to the field code. Delete **/s** at the end of the Embed code.

VI

Working Together

Chapter 32

Using Office Applications To Create Presentations

by Rick Winter and Patty Winter

The focus of Chapter 31 was integrating Microsoft Office applications through embedding and linking information mostly into Word documents. This chapter focuses on using Microsoft Office applications to create a presentation. If you need overhead transparencies, 35mm slides, a graphical report, or a computer-driven presentation, you can use PowerPoint to create the presentation. If you have information in other sources, such as Word or Excel, you can copy or link the information from the source application to PowerPoint.

In this chapter, you learn to

- ■ Organize a presentation
- ■ Use the Word Outline feature to create slides
- ■ Copy or link information to PowerPoint
- ■ Embed a presentation in a Mail message

Organizing the Presentation with a Word Outline

If you are accustomed to using Word, you can create an outline of your presentation in Word and use the outline to create slides in PowerPoint.

◀ See "Format-
ting with
Styles," p. 259

Suppose that you have to create a presentation for community groups about gangs. You have the basics of the presentation in a Word document. PowerPoint uses Word's heading styles for the title and bullets of slides. Therefore, you first reformat the Word document to include Heading 1 for the planned title of the slide, Heading 2 for each major bullet item, and Heading 3 for each minor bullet item.

◀ See "Outlining
a Document,"
p. 252

If you use Heading 1, Heading 2, and Heading 3 styles, you also can use the Outline feature of Word to organize and view your slides. To change to the Outline view in a Word document, choose <u>V</u>iew, <u>O</u>utline; alternatively, click the Outline View button in the horizontal scroll bar directly above the status bar. The view changes to show indents for each heading level (see fig. 32.1).

Fig. 32.1
Word's Outline
view enables you
to organize your
presentation.

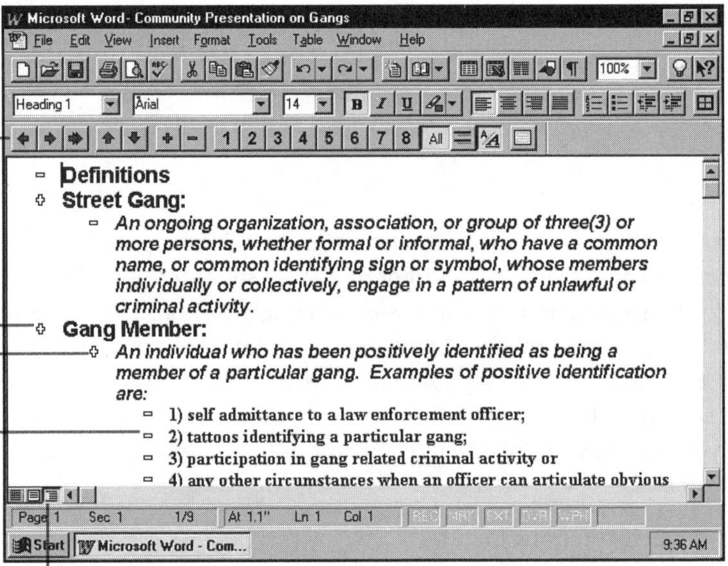

Outlining toolbar ⌐

Heading 1 is the
first-level indent ⌐

Heading 2 is the
second-level indent ——

Heading 3 is the
third-level indent ——

Outline View button

> **Note**
>
> When you convert to PowerPoint, Heading 1 becomes the slide title. Heading 2 is the second-level indent, which becomes first-level bullets in PowerPoint. Heading 3 is the third-level indent, which becomes second-level bullets in PowerPoint.

When you choose <u>V</u>iew, <u>O</u>utline, the document changes to show different levels, and the Outlining toolbar becomes available. You can use the Outlining toolbar to show one or more levels in the outline. In the toolbar, the buttons numbered 1 through 8 enable you to show from one to eight levels of your outline. The 1 button corresponds to Heading 1 style, the 2 button corresponds to Heading 2 style, and so on. When you show Heading 2 styles by clicking the 2 button, Heading 1 styles also appear, and so on. Figure 32.2 shows the outline when you click the Show Heading 1 button. Click the All button to show your entire document. You also can use the Outlining toolbar to promote or demote levels in the outline.

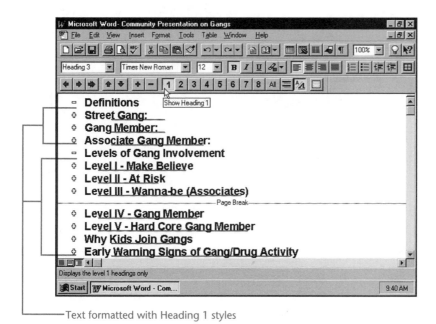

Fig. 32.2
Word's numbered Outlining toolbar buttons enable you to see one or more heading styles.

Text formatted with Heading 1 styles

If a Heading 1 contains no supporting text (that is, the heading is followed by no Heading 2), a minus sign appears to the left of the text. If a Heading 1 contains supporting text, a plus sign appears to the left of the text. Double-click the plus sign to show the supporting headings and body text. Double-click the plus sign again to collapse the text.

◀ See "Moving with Drag-and-Drop," p. 79

To move a heading (and all text below the heading), place the mouse pointer on the plus or minus sign in front of the heading you want to move. The mouse pointer changes to a black four-headed arrow (see fig. 32.3). Drag the mouse up or down to where you want to position the selected text. You also can use the Move Up or Move Down button in the Outlining toolbar. The Move Up button moves the selected text up in the outline. The Move Down button moves the selected text down in the outline. To change a level in the outline, use the Promote and Demote buttons in the toolbar, or change the

◀ See "Editing a Style," p. 262

VI

Working Together

style to a different heading. The Promote button changes the selection to a higher level (for example, from Heading 2 to Heading 1). The Demote button changes the selection to a lower level.

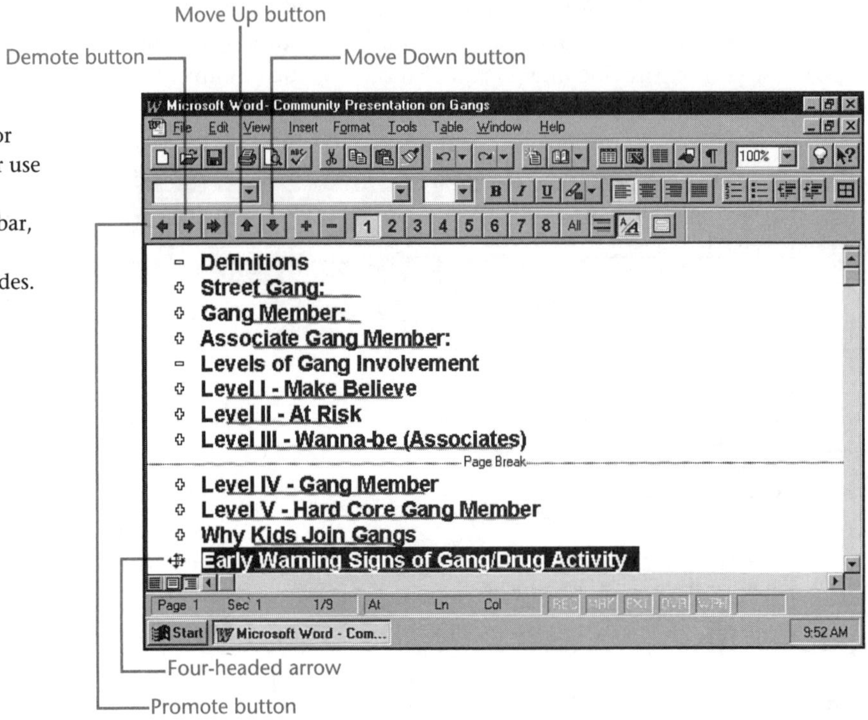

Fig. 32.3
Drag the plus or minus signs, or use buttons in the Outlining toolbar, to change the order of the slides.

When you finish organizing your outline, save and close the document.

Using a Word Outline To Create Slides

When you want to use the Word document in PowerPoint, you can create a new presentation or add to an existing presentation. The Word Heading 1 style becomes the title of each slide. Heading 2 style becomes the first-level bullet for each slide, and so on.

To start a new presentation, follow these steps:

1. Within PowerPoint, choose File, Open, press Ctrl+O, or click the Open button on the Standard toolbar. The Open dialog box opens with a list of files or folders.

2. Change the drive and folder, if necessary.

3. In the Files of <u>T</u>ype drop-down list, select All Outlines to display Word documents, if necessary.

> **Note**
>
> You also can use Excel worksheets to create slides (the All Outlines file type will display Excel worksheets as well).

4. Type the file name in the File <u>N</u>ame text box, or click the desired file in the list box to select the file.

5. Choose OK.

Figure 32.4 shows the outline view of the presentation in PowerPoint. Slide number 3 (shown in fig. 32.5) shows the definition of a Gang Member. To switch between views, click the buttons in the bottom-left corner of the presentation window or use the <u>V</u>iew menu. Compare the slide in figure 32.5 with figure 32.1. Notice that the Heading 1 style became the title of the slide, the Heading 2 style became the first bullet, and the Heading 3 styles became subpoints of the bullet.

Tip
Instead of doing steps 4 and 5, double-click the desired file name in the list box to open the file.

◄ See "Viewing a Presentation," p. 583

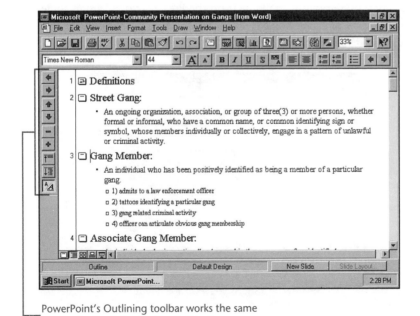

Fig. 32.4
Opening a Word document brings you into a PowerPoint outline.

PowerPoint's Outlining toolbar works the same way as the Outlining toolbar in Word

VI

Working Together

Fig. 32.5
The heading styles, shown in figure 32.1, create each slide.

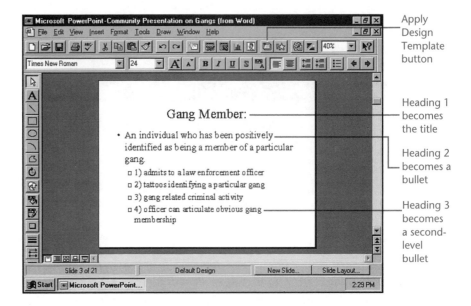

Apply Design Template button

Heading 1 becomes the title

Heading 2 becomes a bullet

Heading 3 becomes a second-level bullet

◀ See "Creating a Presentation Using a Wizard," p. 578

After you open a Word file to create a PowerPoint presentation, you can select a more interesting format than simple black text on a white background. To change the format, click the Apply Design Template button, or use the Format, Apply Design Template command. The Apply Design Template dialog box lists the templates available from the Presentations Design folder and shows a preview of each choice (see fig. 32.6). Figure 32.7 shows the formatted and edited slide from figure 32.5.

Fig. 32.6
Use the Apply Design Template to change the formatting of your presentation.

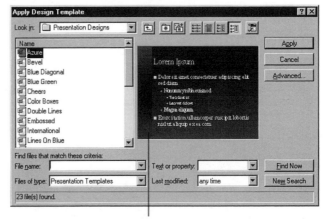

The preview area shows you what the design of the presentation will look like

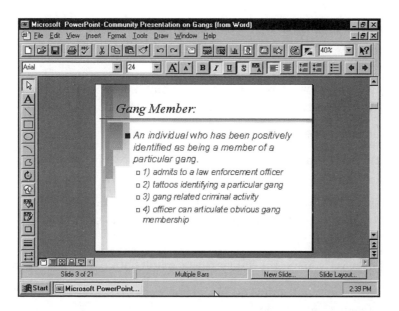

Fig. 32.7
The slide shown
originally in figure
32.5 is formatted
and the Black and
White view is
selected.

> **Note**
>
> You can insert the Word outline into an existing presentation. The Word outline
> assumes the format of the existing PowerPoint presentation. To insert a file into the
> presentation, move to the location in an existing PowerPoint presentation where you
> want to insert slides and choose Insert, Slides from Outline and select the file name
> and location.

Troubleshooting

I can't open or insert my Word Outline file into a PowerPoint presentation.

You may not have closed the Word document before you returned to PowerPoint.
Click the Word button on the task bar. If necessary, choose the Window command
and select the document name. Choose File, Close to close the document. Click the
PowerPoint button to return to PowerPoint.

Automating the Process from Word to PowerPoint

Buried within Word is a wonderful button that automates the process
of going from a Word outline to presentation slides. After you attach a

presentation template as a global template, you can use the Present It toolbar button or macro whenever you want to convert a Word outline to a PowerPoint presentation.

The first time you want to use the Present It button, you need to attach the template where it is located. To attach the template, follow these steps:

1. From any open document, choose File, Templates.

2. On the Templates and Add-ins dialog box that opens, choose the Add button.

Tip
You also can run the Present It macro by choosing Tools, Macro, Run.

3. Within the Add Template dialog box, change the folder to the MSOFFICE\WINWORD\MACROS, choose the PRESENT7 template file, and choose OK.

Now whenever you want to display the Present It button, follow these steps:

1. Open the Word outline document you want to convert to a PowerPoint presentation.

2. If the Microsoft toolbar does not appear, place the mouse pointer on any toolbar, click the right mouse button, and then select Microsoft.

3. Click the Present It button (see fig. 32.8). After a few moments, PowerPoint opens, and the document converts from the Word outline to a PowerPoint presentation.

Fig. 32.8
The Microsoft toolbar has a PowerPoint button and a Present It button to allow you to go to PowerPoint or to convert a Word outline to a PowerPoint presentation.

Click the Present It button to convert the outline

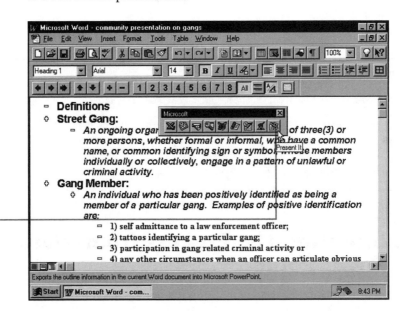

Summarizing Data in Excel and Linking a Range to PowerPoint

If you have information in Excel that you want to bring to the presentation, you can copy and paste the information or link the information. If you want the data in the presentation to be updated every time the Excel worksheet changes, link the information from Excel.

◀ See "Adding, Inserting, and Deleting Slides," p. 582

You first must create a new slide to accept the data. To create a new slide that accepts data from Excel, follow these steps:

1. Choose Insert, New Slide, press Ctrl+M, or click the Insert New Slide button.

2. Select the graph layout, and then choose OK (see fig. 32.9). A new slide appears, with instructions on where to add the title and graph, as shown in figure 32.10.

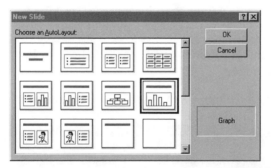

Fig. 32.9
Select the graph style when you add a new slide to a PowerPoint presentation.

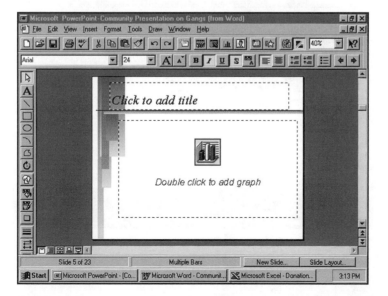

Fig. 32.9
Click the graph area and press Delete to remove the instruction to add a graph.

VI

Working Together

3. Click the middle of the slide once (where the slide tells you to double-click), and press the Delete key to remove the graph.

> **Note**
>
> If you double-click in the graph area, you will launch Microsoft Graph. Instead, this procedure uses this layout to keep the area available for Microsoft Excel data (whether it is an Excel worksheet or chart).

◄ See "Copying and Moving Data," p. 78

◄ See "Copying Spreadsheet Information," p. 675

Now you are ready to copy information from Excel into the slide. To copy or link the information from Excel, follow these steps:

1. From the PowerPoint slide in the preceding steps, choose the Start button on the taskbar, and choose Programs, Microsoft Excel.

2. Open the file containing the information you want to copy or link.

3. Drag the mouse pointer (a white cross) to select the range of data in Excel that you want to place as a graph in PowerPoint (see fig. 32.11).

4. Choose Edit, Copy, press Ctrl+C, or click the Copy button in Excel's standard toolbar.

5. Click the PowerPoint button in the taskbar to return to PowerPoint.

Fig. 32.11
Select the range you want to copy in Excel.

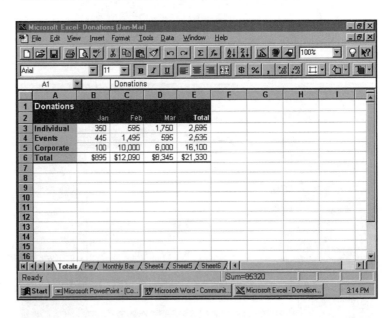

> **Note**
>
> If both applications are windowed and tiled, just click the slide you want, or use Alt+Tab to switch applications.

6. Choose Edit, Paste Special in PowerPoint. The Paste Special dialog box appears (see fig. 32.12).

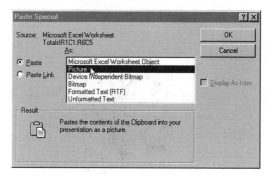

Fig. 32.12
The Paste Special dialog box enables you to paste or link information from Excel.

7. Do one of the following things:

   ■ To paste a picture of the Excel worksheet, choose the Paste option button and then select Picture from the As list box.

   ■ To link the information so that the slide updates when the Excel worksheet updates, choose the Paste Link option button. Select the only option in the As list box when you link: Microsoft Excel Worksheet Object. When you use this option, you can double-click the worksheet data to enter Excel and edit the worksheet.

> **Note**
>
> If you click the Paste button in the toolbar, choose Edit, Paste, or press Ctrl+V, the selected data from Excel comes into the slide unformatted. It is better to use the Paste Special options. The Unformatted Text and Formatted Text options bring the information from the worksheet as text; the columns are not lined up. You can reformat the text, if you want.

◄ See "Entering and Editing Text," p. 593

◄ See "Resizing and Scaling Objects," p. 612

VI

Working Together

8. Choose OK in the Paste Special dialog box. The selected data from Excel appears in your slide (see fig. 32.12). Complete the slide as necessary by adding titles and sizing and moving the figure.

Fig. 32.13
The selected data
from Excel appears
in the slide.

Click the title area
and type a title

Drag the handles to
resize the graph

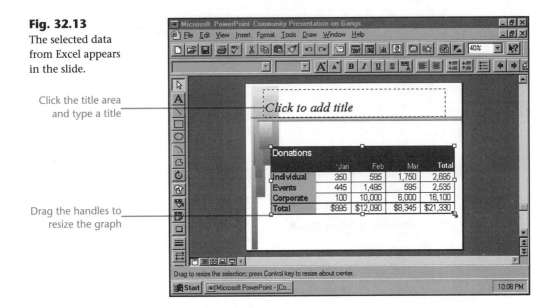

Troubleshooting

When I copy to PowerPoint, the data from my Excel spreadsheet is not lined up.

Make sure that you select the Picture option in the Paste Special dialog box. Do not choose Edit, Paste, click the Paste button, or press Ctrl+V to bring into PowerPoint the copy of the Excel data.

The Excel worksheet is too big for my PowerPoint slide.

Try simplifying the worksheet before you copy it into PowerPoint. You also can change the size of the worksheet in PowerPoint by dragging the picture handles, but remember that your viewers have to be able to read the slide.

Creating Charts in Excel and Copying to PowerPoint

Adding an Excel chart to a PowerPoint presentation is essentially the same as adding a worksheet.

To add an Excel chart to a slide, follow these steps:

1. Click the middle of a chart in an Excel worksheet to display handles on the chart (see fig. 32.14).

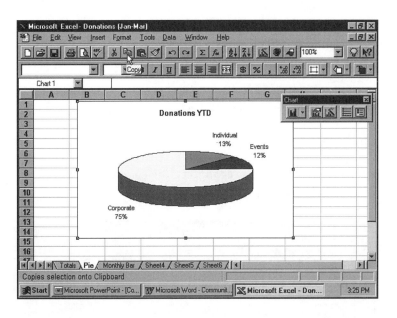

Fig. 32.14
Select the Excel
chart you want
to copy into
PowerPoint.

2. Choose Edit, Copy, press Ctrl+C, or click the Copy button in Excel's
   standard toolbar.

3. Click the PowerPoint button on the task bar and go to the PowerPoint
   slide where you want to copy information.

4. Choose Edit, Paste Special from PowerPoint. The Paste Special dialog
   box appears (see fig. 32.15).

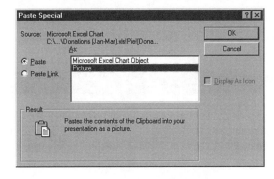

Fig. 32.15
Fill out the Paste
Special dialog box
to display the
chart in the slide.
There are fewer
options here than
in figure 32.11
because an Excel
chart is being
pasted rather than
a worksheet
selection.

VI

Working Together

5. Do one of the following things:

   ■ Choose the Paste option button; from the As list box, select the
     Microsoft Excel Chart Object option. This option enables you to
     double-click the chart to return to Excel and edit the object.

■ Choose the <u>P</u>aste option button; from the <u>A</u>s list box, select the Picture option to see only the chart.

■ Choose the Paste <u>L</u>ink option button; from the <u>A</u>s list box, select the Microsoft Excel Chart Object option to link and embed the slide with the Excel worksheet.

6. Choose OK from the Paste Special dialog box.

You also may have to resize the chart (drag the handles) and add a title to the slide. Figure 32.15 shows the completed slide.

Fig. 32.16

The edited slide appears with the Excel chart.

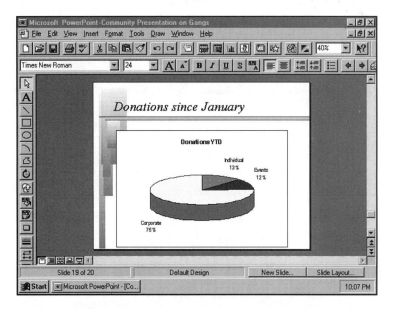

> **Note**
>
> If you want the Excel chart background to match the existing PowerPoint slide background, make sure you format the chart in Excel before copying the slide to PowerPoint by using Excel's F<u>o</u>rmat, Ob<u>j</u>ect command; select <u>N</u>one for Borders and No<u>n</u>e for Fill.

Embedding the Presentation in an Electronic Mail Message

As with any document, you should frequently save your presentation so that your updates are protected. When you finish the presentation, make sure that you save it. If you want to send the presentation to others on your network for review, embed the presentation in an electronic mail message.

To create a message that includes the presentation, follow these steps:

1. From PowerPoint with the presentation open, choose File, Send.

2. Choose the Profile Name for your electronic mail if prompted in the Choose Profile dialog box. Then click OK.

3. Address the message by filling out the To and Cc text boxes.

4. Type a short summary in the Subject text box.

5. Type any message you want in the message area. Your screen should resemble figure 32.17.

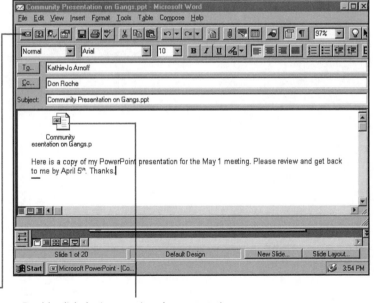

Send button

Double-click the icon to view the presentation

Fig. 32.17
The PowerPoint presentation appears as an icon in the message text area. Your mail program may look different from this version of WordMail depending on your electronic mail package.

VI

Working Together

6. Click the Send button to send the message.

When the recipients get the message, they can double-click the PowerPoint icon to see the presentation on their computers.❖

Chapter 33

Using Binder

by Robert Garrison

With the Windows GUI (graphical user interface), you have become familiar with the idea of folders and files. Much like the folder in a standard file cabinet, the computer folder has become a collecting place for all sorts of papers and documents. The trouble is, the more documents and folders you create on your computer, the harder it is to find anything, no matter how neat and tidy you try to be.

Using the Microsoft Office Binder, you can become better organized on the computer. The Binder takes the concept of computer organization one step further than using a folder to store related files. The Binder enables you to organize Microsoft Office documents into a specific order, called *sections*, just like you do with papers in the sections of a real three-ring binder.

In this chapter, you learn to

■ Create a Binder and add sections

■ Rearrange sections

■ Remove the section view

■ Work in the outside view

■ Print options

■ Open an existing Binder

Looking at an Example Binder

The Binder can hold all your files and folders on nearly any subject. The examples in this chapter show you how to use the Binder to put together information for a book on depression glass for Collector's Loot as in figure 33.1.

Fig. 33.1
Use Binder to or-
ganize your work
with sections in
the book.

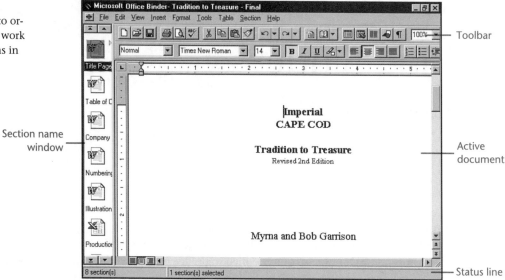

Section name
window

Toolbar

Active
document

Status line

Creating a New Binder

By navigating the taskbar's Start button, you can select Microsoft Binder from
the Program group. When Binder opens, it automatically displays a new,
blank binder (see fig. 33.2).

Fig. 33.2
Consider an empty
Binder as another
document type
waiting for you
to add sections
that are Office
documents.

Show/Hide
Binder icon

These areas will be useful to you as you build your binder:

- The *toolbar* contains File, Section, and Help menus.

- The window on the left contains *section names*.

- The window on the right contains the document of the *active section*.

- The *status line* shows the number of sections and the number of currently selected sections.

- Hide or display the left window pane by clicking the Binder icon.

Adding Sections

The Binder opens with no sections in it—you see just an empty binder. Remember, a section can be any of the Office documents such as Word or Excel. When you are adding a section, the created document is empty. To add a section, complete the following steps:

1. Choose Section, Add.

2. Select the correct document type from the Add Section dialog box (see fig. 33.3). For this example, choose Microsoft Word Document, then click OK.

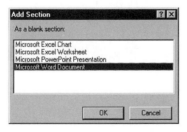

Fig 33.3
Organize your work by placing Office documents in sections of the binder.

3. Notice in figure 33.4 that the section window now looks like Microsoft Word and that the menu bar contains the Word Menu options as well as the binder's Section menu. A section in a binder assumes all the capabilities of the Office application.

VI

Working Together

Fig. 33.4

The active section is now a Word document. All the functionality of Word is available.

Word icon shows the type and name of this section

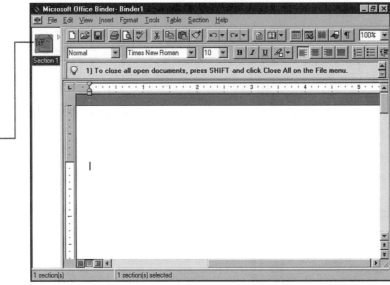

Tip

To rename a section, right-click the section's icon and choose Rename, or you can choose Section, Rename.

4. The default section name, Section 1, is not particularly helpful. Fortunately, you can easily rename a section: just click the existing name, Section 1, and the name will be outlined (see fig. 33.5).

Fig. 33.5

Edit the section title by double-clicking the title.

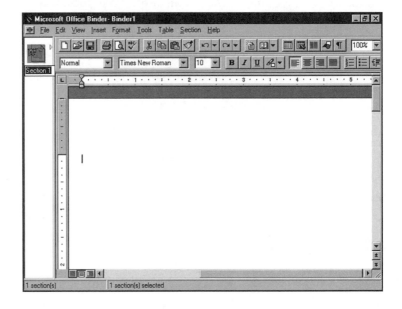

5. Type **Title Page**. Your binder should now look like figure 33.6.

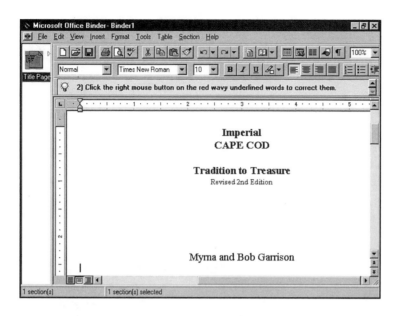

Fig. 33.6
Change the title of
the Binder section
to label the new
document.

Any new document can be added as a section to a Binder. You have all the
capabilities of Office available within the Binder. For example, you can cut
and paste between sections or link between documents.

Adding Text from Existing
Documents

If you already have some Office documents created, you can add them to the
Binder. You can add a table of contents to the binder, for example, by following these steps:

1. Choose Section, Add from File to open the Add from File dialog box
   (see fig. 33.7).

2. The Binder presents a standard Windows File Open dialog box. You can
   navigate to the correct folder if necessary, and then highlight the file
   you want to add. You can add the file Table of Contents by selecting
   the file and clicking OK.

VI

Working Together

Fig. 33.7
Adding existing documents to the Binder shows the organization of your work.

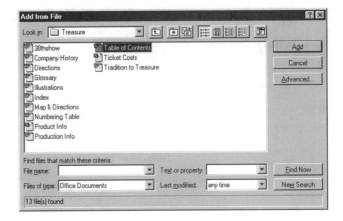

Note

You can use Shift+click or Ctrl+click to select multiple files to add to the binder. When you add files this way, they will appear as sections in the binder in alphabetical order. They will be added to the binder after the active section. Just reorganize them by moving the sections to the desired location.

3. Repeat steps 1 and 2 for each file you want to add to the binder. Figure 33.8 shows a binder with the files added as sections in the binder.

Fig. 33.8
Adding a file does not change the selected section. The last active section remains highlighted.

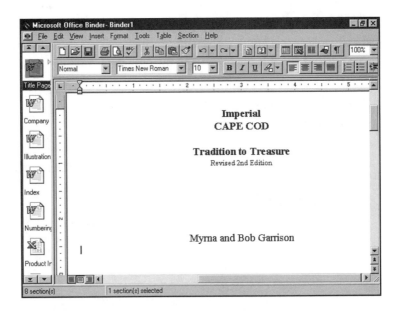

Rearranging Sections

As you review your section orders, you may realize that you have a section in the wrong place. (Remember, these sections were just loose in the folder before.) Suppose that you want to rearrange the sections so the Illustration section follows the Numbering section. Follow these steps:

1. Choose Section, Rearrange. The Rearrange Sections dialog box appears, showing the sections you can reorder (see fig. 33.9).

Fig. 33.9
Use the Move Up and Move Down buttons to rearrange the placement of sections.

2. Highlight the section you want to move.

3. Click Move Up or Move Down to move the sections.

4. When you have rearranged the sections as needed, click OK to close the dialog box. The sections appear in the same order as they were listed in the dialog box.

Hiding the Section Window

You may feel a bit crowded working on a document in the binder with the sections showing in the left pane of the Binder window. If you want to make the section full-screen, click the Show/Hide Binder icon on the menu bar. Figure 33.10 shows the result of hiding the left pane.

The Show/Hide Binder icon works as a toggle. Click the icon again to make the left window pane reappear.

VI

Working Together

Fig. 33.10
Get the big
picture—hide the
section titles.

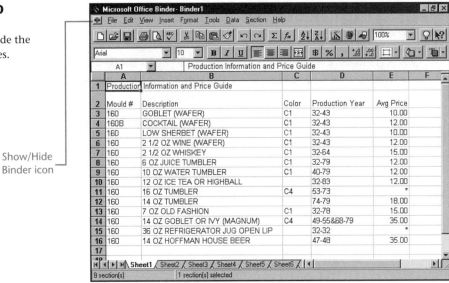

Show/Hide
Binder icon

Working in Outside View

In the binder, only the currently active section is displayed. You cannot display more than one window by tiling the sections. By choosing Section View Outside, however, you can reference one document while working on another. Follow these steps:

1. Make the Excel spreadsheet section, Product Info, active by clicking it.

2. Choose Section, View Outside. The current section now becomes a separate window, as in figure 33.11. You can move the window like you do any other window.

3. Make the binder active and select the section you want to work on by clicking the section icon.

4. Arrange the windows as needed so that you can see both documents.

5. To return from Outside view, just close the Outside View document. You return to the active Binder window.

Tip
You can see the Outside view of a section using the standard Windows steps of clicking and dragging the windows' title bar.

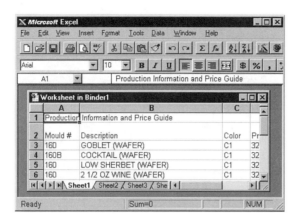

Fig. 33.11
By viewing a
section outside of
the binder, you
can work on two
sections at once.

Printing Options

The Binder gives you three options for printing: you can print the active
section, all the sections in the Binder, or a single section.

Printing the Active Section

Printing the active section is similar to printing a document from the normal
Office application, except that you find the Print command in the Section
menu rather than in the File menu. To print a section, follow these steps:

1. Choose Section, Print.

2. Complete the Print dialog box as needed. (For details about printing,
   see Chapter 4, "Managing Files and Work Areas.")

3. Click OK to print.

These steps enable you to print a document as if you were printing from the
application itself. You can also print sections from the Print Binder dialog
box, as described in the next section.

Printing from the Binder

You can print all binder sections at one time or just print selected sections.
To print, follow these steps:

1. To print selected sections, you use normal mouse actions such as click,
   Shift+click, or Ctrl+click to highlight the sections you want to print.

2. Choose File, Print Binder. The Print Binder dialog box appears (see
   fig. 33.12).

VI

Working Together

Fig. 33.12
Choosing the
correct options
allows you to print
the binder the way
you want.

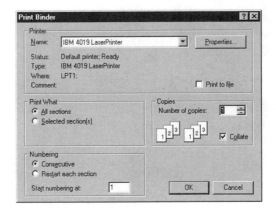

This list contains some of the important print options:

- Use the Print What section to choose All Sections or Selected Section(s). Selecting All Sections allows you to print the entire binder as a complete document in the order of the sections.

- Numbering enables you to select whether each section's page numbers restart or all sections are numbered consecutively. The starting page number is set by entering a value in Start Numbering At.

- Clicking Collate prints the indicated number of copies in complete sequential sets.

3. Fill in the appropriate options, and then click OK to begin printing.

Using the Binder adds a new dimension to Office. You can now organize your document, edit it, and save it as a complete collection of related files. You save a binder just like any other Office document. See Chapter 4, "Managing Files and Work Areas," for general information on saving.❖

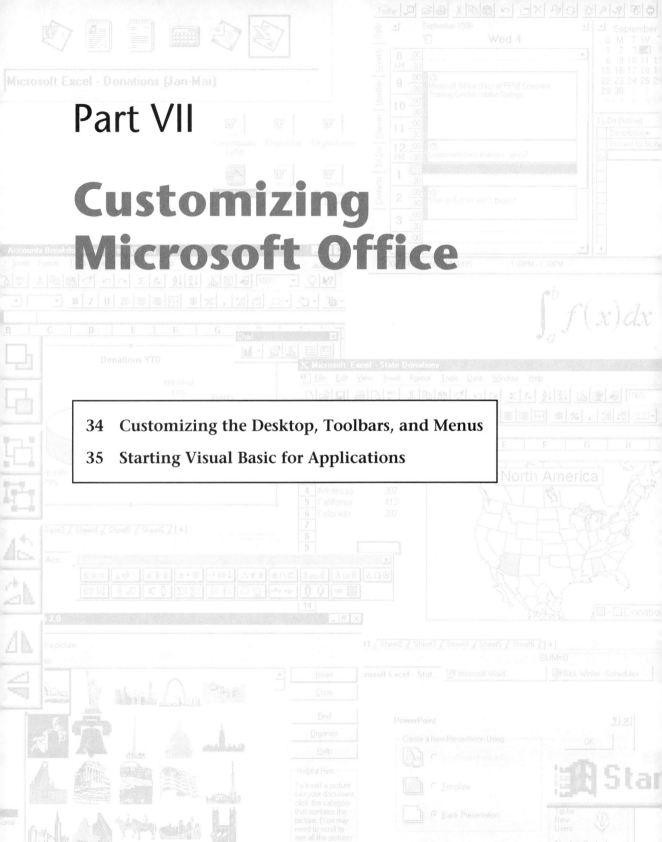

Part VII

Customizing Microsoft Office

Chapter 34

Customizing the Desktop, Toolbars, and Menus

by Diane Tinney

Part of the power of Microsoft Office comes from its flexibility; you can change its appearance and structure to fit your work habits. You can create and modify toolbars, buttons, and menus. You can add commands that don't usually appear on the toolbar or menu. You can even assign macros to menu items, tools, and buttons. This flexibility enables you to create your own customized user interface, such as a customized toolbar and menu. And, true to the design goals of Microsoft Office and the "suite" approach, after you learn how to customize one application, you can use that knowledge to customize the other Office applications.

In this chapter, you learn to

- Modify the Windows 95 interface

- Customize the Microsoft Office Shortcut Bar

- Add and change toolbar buttons

- Create and modify toolbars

- Customize application menus

- Add custom menus

Customizing the Windows 95 Interface

The first place you can start customizing your Office installation is the Windows 95 interface. Figure 34.1 shows a customized toolbar and menu.

Fig. 34.1
Office enables you to customize menus, toolbars, and startup options.

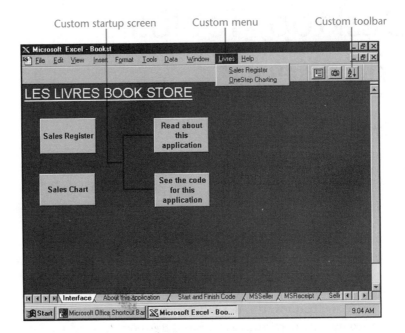

Custom startup screen   Custom menu   Custom toolbar

Windows 95 enables you to modify the taskbar, the Start menu, and the icons that appear on the Windows 95 desktop. In Windows 95, you can modify the Start menu program listings, customize the taskbar, and create shortcuts to your favorite Office programs and documents. Figure 34.2 shows a customized Windows 95 Start menu, taskbar, and some shortcut icons on the desktop.

> **Note**
>
> For more information on Windows 95, see Que's *Special Edition Using Windows 95* and Que's *Windows 95 Installation and Configuration Handbook*.

Modifying the Windows 95 Taskbar

The Windows 95 taskbar is a handy tool that enables you to start applications and switch between minimized applications with a single click. In Windows 95, you can change the location and appearance of the taskbar.

To move the taskbar to another location on your screen, drag the taskbar to the location you want. You can drag the taskbar to the top, bottom, right, or left side of your screen.

Customized Start menu   Shortcut icon   Customized Shortcut Bar

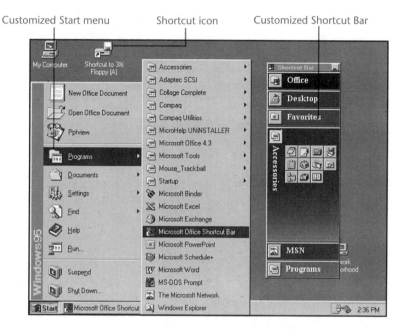

Fig. 34.2
Windows 95 enables you to modify the taskbar, the Start menu, and the desktop.

To customize the Windows 95 taskbar, follow these steps:

1. Right-click an unused area of the taskbar to display the shortcut menu.

2. Choose Properties to display the Taskbar Properties sheet.

3. Select the taskbar options you want (see fig. 34.3). Table 34.1 describes the taskbar options you can set to control the appearance of the taskbar.

4. Choose Apply to activate changes immediately and close the sheet.

Tip
Point to the clock to display the day and date.

Tip
If you are hiding the taskbar, be sure to select Always on Top so that you can see the taskbar when running a full-screen program.

Table 34.1 Taskbar Options	
Option	**Description**
Always on Top	Ensures that the taskbar is visible even when running a full-screen program.

(continues)

Table 34.1 Continued	
Option	**Description**
Auto Hide	Reduces taskbar to a thin line. To redisplay full taskbar, point to line.
Show Small Icons in Start Menu	Displays smaller icons in Start menu, which reduces the width of the menu.
Show Clock	Displays digital time on taskbar.

Fig. 34.3
Using the Taskbar
Properties sheet,
you can control
the appearance of
the taskbar.

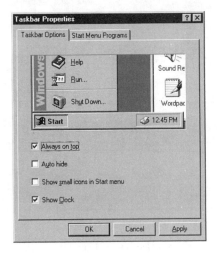

Customizing the Start Menu

Clicking the Start button on the taskbar displays a menu, called the Start menu, which lists applications and files you can load. The Start menu is organized into groups called folders. For example, the Start menu folder called Programs contains another folder called Accessories that contains a menu item called Calculator. You can customize the Start menu by adding your own menu items to the existing folders, by editing the names of existing folders and menu items, or by adding new folders.

To add a new menu item or folder to the Start menu, follow these steps:

1. Right-click the taskbar to display the shortcut menu.

2. Choose Properties to display the Taskbar Properties sheet.

3. Select the Start Menu Programs tab (see fig. 34.4).

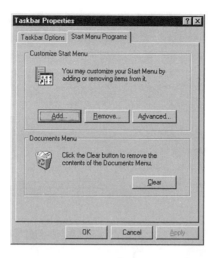

Fig. 34.4
Using the Taskbar
Properties sheet,
you can modify
the Start menu.

VII

Customizing Office

4. Choose Add. The Create Shortcut dialog box appears (see fig. 34.5).

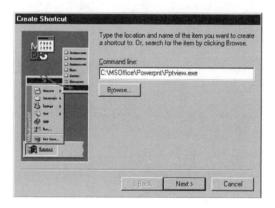

Fig. 34.5
The Create
Shortcut dialog
box assists you in
adding a program
to the Start menu.

5. Type the full file path name of the program you want to add to the
   menu, or choose Browse to select a file. Click Next> to continue.

6. Select the program folder in which you want to list the new program
   (see fig. 34.6). Or choose New Folder to create a new folder in the Start
   menu. Click Next> to continue.

7. Type a name for the new menu choice (see fig. 34.7). Choose Finish to
   add the new program menu item to the Start menu. The result is shown
   in figure 34.8.

Fig. 34.6
You can place shortcuts in an existing folder, or create a new folder on the Start Menu.

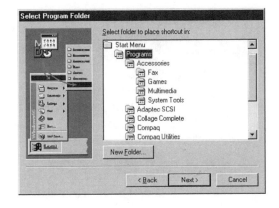

Fig. 34.7
When naming a shortcut, use a brief, but descriptive, name.

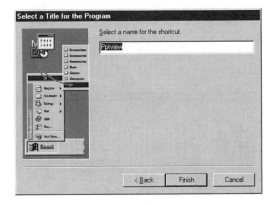

Fig. 34.8
You can add new menu items to any folder on the Start menu, even the Start menu itself.

Custom Start menu item —

To remove a menu item from the Start menu, follow these steps:

1. Right-click the taskbar to display the shortcut menu.

2. Choose Properties to display the Taskbar Properties sheet.

VII

3. Select the Start Menu Programs tab.

4. Choose Remove. The Remove Shortcuts/Folders dialog box appears (see fig. 34.9).

Fig. 34.9
Using the Remove Shortcuts/Folders dialog box, you can delete menu items and folders from the Start menu.

5. Select the program folder or program item you want to delete.

6. Choose Remove.

Running Applications on Startup

You can specify that you want Windows 95 to automatically run certain applications when you start up Windows 95. For example, if you use Word and Schedule+ every day, you may want to instruct Windows 95 to automatically load them for you when Windows 95 first opens. To do this, add the programs to the Startup folder (located in the Programs folder on the Start menu, see fig. 34.10).

Tip
Don't add too many programs to your startup group, only those you really use. Otherwise, you will slow down your system and waste resources.

Fig. 34.10
Programs listed in the Startup folder of the Start menu automatically load when Windows 95 starts.

Creating a Shortcut Icon

Tip

You also can drag-and-drop a program from a browse list onto the desktop to quickly create a shortcut icon.

You can create a shortcut icon to place on your Windows 95 desktop for easy access to a program or document. By default, Windows 95 places several shortcut icons on your desktop such as My Computer, Network Neighborhood, and My Briefcase. Double-clicking the shortcut icon launches the associated program and loads any specified documents.

To create a shortcut icon, follow these steps:

Tip

Remove shortcut icons you rarely use. Add shortcut icons for the documents and programs you use everyday.

1. Right-click the desktop to display the shortcut menu.

2. Choose Ne<u>w</u>, <u>S</u>hortcut. The Create Shortcut dialog box appears.

3. Type the full file path name of the program you want to add to the menu, or choose B<u>r</u>owse to select a file. Click Next to continue.

4. Type a name for the new shortcut icon and choose Fin<u>i</u>sh. The shortcut icon now appears on your desktop (see fig. 34.11).

> **Note**
>
> Notice that shortcut icons you create on the desktop have a small arrow in the bottom-left corner of the icon.

Fig. 34.11
You can add new shortcut icons to your desktop to quickly access programs and documents.

New shortcut icon

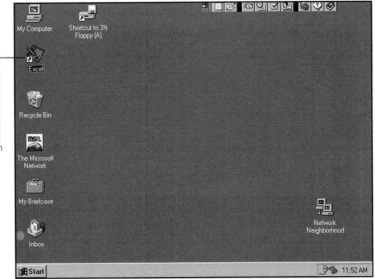

Customizing the Office Shortcut Bar

By default, when Office 95 installs, it places the Microsoft Office Shortcut Bar in your Startup folder. Therefore, every time you start Windows 95, the Office Shortcut Bar displays at the top of your screen (see fig. 34.12). The Office Shortcut Bar gives you quick access to common Office tasks such as opening and creating documents. Using the Office Shortcut Bar, you can also add and remove Office programs and control Office settings such as the location of workgroup templates.

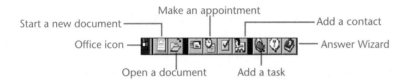

Start a new document — Make an appointment — Add a contact
Office icon — — Answer Wizard
Open a document   Add a task

Fig. 34.12
The Office Short-cut Bar provides quick access to Office tasks.

You can customize many features of the Office Shortcut Bar to better meet your needs. For example, you can do the following:

- Change the size, location, and appearance of the toolbar
- Change the names and order of buttons on the toolbar
- Hide or display toolbar buttons
- Add a button to the toolbar to load a file or program
- Add more toolbars to the Office Shortcut Bar

◄ See "What's New with Office 95," p. 10

◄ See "Looking at Microsoft Office Shortcut Bar," p. 34

◄ See "Using Dialog Boxes," p. 55

One of the most useful features of the Office Shortcut Bar is that it can display and manage numerous toolbars. As shown in figure 34.13, the Office Shortcut Bar comes with six default toolbars that you can select to display or hide: Office, Desktop, Accessories, Favorites, MSN, and Programs. You can customize any one of these toolbars or add your own custom toolbars.

Customizing the Office Shortcut Bar is organized into four areas: customizing the view, modifying the buttons, customizing and creating toolbars, and changing settings. The following sections explain how to customize each area of the Office Shortcut Bar.

Customizing the View

The View tab of the Customize dialog box enables you to control the color and other display options of the Office Shortcut Bar (see fig. 34.14). For example, by default, the toolbar buttons are set to a small size. You can change the button size to a larger size by clicking the appropriate checkbox. You can also activate features such as ToolTips, sound, and animation.

Fig. 34.13
The Office Shortcut Bar can display numerous toolbars.

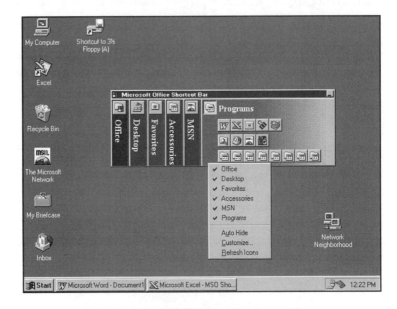

Fig. 34.14
Using the View tab of the Customize dialog box, you can modify the display of the Office Shortcut Bar.

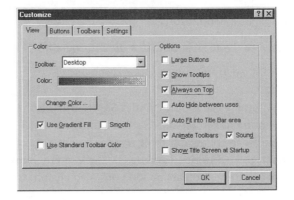

Tip
To change the position of the Office Shortcut Bar, drag it to a new location.

To customize the view features of the Office Shortcut Bar, follow these steps:

1. Right-click the Office Shortcut title bar or on the background of a toolbar (not the toolbar button, but between the toolbar buttons) to display the shortcut menu.

2. Choose Customize. The Customize dialog box appears with the View tab selected by default (again see fig. 34.14).

3. Select the desired settings. Table 34.2 describes each of the view settings and options.

4. Click OK when you are done to save changes.

Table 34.2 Options for Customizing Office Shortcut Bar View	
Setting	**Description**
Toolbar	Specify the toolbar name for which you want to customize the color settings.
Change Color	Displays color palette from which you can select a color.
Use Gradient Fill	Specifies to use gradient coloring.
Use Standard Toolbar Color	Changes color settings back to default colors. When selected, other color options are grayed out.
Large Buttons	Specifies to use large buttons and icons.
Show Tooltips	Specifies to show ToolTip text that describes what the button does.
Always on Top	Specifies that the toolbar displays on top of any open windows.
Auto Hide Between Uses	Hides the toolbar when not in use.
Auto Fit into Title Bar Area	Adjusts toolbar size to fit inside the current application's title bar.
Animate Toolbars	Activates any animation features of the toolbar.
Sound	Activates any sound features of the toolbar.
Show Title Screen at Startup	Displays the title screen when first started.

Tip

Dragging the Office Shortcut Bar to the center of your screen helps you better navigate the shortcut menus.

VII

Customizing Office

Note

To change the position of the Shortcut Bar when the View option Auto Fit into Title Bar is selected, use an editor, such as WordPad, to edit the MSOFFICE.INI file in the Windows folder. In the [OPTIONS] section, change the RightPos = line to a number higher than the default, which varies by the resolution of your display.

Customizing the Buttons

The Buttons tab of the Customize dialog box enables you to customize toolbar buttons in the Office Shortcut Bar (see fig. 34.15). You can select which files to display as buttons, arrange the order of buttons, add new files and folders as buttons, delete existing entries, and add spaces between buttons on a toolbar.

Fig. 34.15
Using the Buttons tab, you can modify the contents and layout of toolbars in the Office Shortcut Bar.

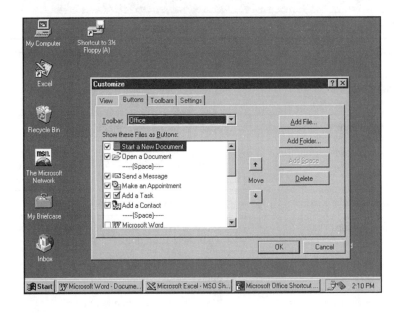

Tip
Add the MS-DOS prompt button to the Office Shortcut Bar for quick access to the prompt from any application.

To customize the button features of a toolbar in the Office Shortcut Bar, follow these steps:

1. Right-click the Office Shortcut title bar or the background of a toolbar (not the toolbar button, but between the toolbar buttons) to display the shortcut menu.

2. Choose Customize.

3. Select the Buttons tab (see fig. 34.15).

4. Modify and add toolbar buttons as needed. Table 34.3 describes each of the button settings and options on the Buttons tab.

5. Click OK when you are done to save changes.

Table 34.3 Options for Customizing Office Shortcut Buttons	
Setting	**Description**
Toolbar	Select the toolbar to customize.

Setting	Description
Show These Files as Buttons	Select (check) the buttons to include on the toolbar.
Add File	Select a file to add to the toolbar as a button.
Add Folder	Select a folder to add to the toolbar as a button.
Add Space	Insert a space between buttons.
Delete	Delete the selected button or space.
Move ↑	Move the selected button up in the toolbar button list (to the left in the toolbar itself).
Move ↓	Move the selected button down in the toolbar button list (to the right in the toolbar itself).

Note

By default, a new button displays the icon included in the program's executable file. For files and folders without a defined icon, the Office Shortcut Bar uses the standard file and folder icons. You can change the icon on a button by modifying the button properties:

1. Right-click the button and choose Properties.

2. Select the Shortcut tab and choose Change Icon.

3. Select the icon file name and icon to use, and then click OK.

Customizing the Toolbars

The Toolbars tab of the Customize dialog box lists the files available to show as toolbars on the Office Shortcut Bar (see fig. 34.16). The checked folders will be displayed and the unchecked folders will be hidden. The Toolbars tab also enables you to add your own custom toolbars or remove toolbars.

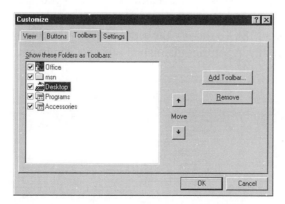

Fig. 34.16
The Toolbars tab of the Customize dialog box enables you to hide, add, or remove toolbars.

Tip
Create your own
toolbar for quick
access to fre-
quently used tools
such as spread-
sheets, documents,
or databases.

To add toolbars to the Office Shortcut Bar, follow these steps:

1. Right-click the Office Shortcut title bar or the background of a toolbar
   (not the toolbar button, but between the toolbar buttons) to display the
   shortcut menu.

2. Choose Customize.

3. Select the Toolbars tab (again see fig. 34.16).

4. Select Add Toolbar. The Add Toolbar dialog box appears (see fig. 34.17).

Fig. 34.17
The Add Toolbar
dialog box enables
you to create new
toolbars.

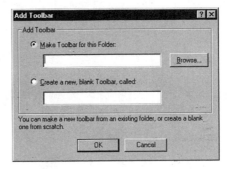

5. To make a toolbar for a folder, type the folder name in the text box
   labeled Make a Toolbar for This Folder (or use the Browse button to
   select a folder)

   or

   Type a new name in the text box labeled Create a New, Blank Toolbar.

6. Click OK when you are done to save changes.

Customizing Settings

The Settings tab of the Customize dialog box enables you to change Office
Shortcut Bar settings, such as where the user and workgroup templates are
stored (see fig. 34.18). To modify the settings, select the Item you want
and choose Modify. A Settings dialog box prompts you to enter a new file
location.

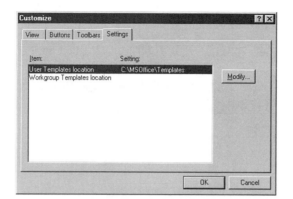

Fig. 34.18
You can change
the location of
User and Work-
group templates
files via the
Settings tab in the
Customize dialog
box.

Customizing Application Toolbars

The process of customizing toolbars in Microsoft Office applications is much
the same as customizing the toolbars in the Office Shortcut Bar. In most applications, however, you have even more options.

Customizing Predefined Toolbars

Each application comes with several built-in toolbars, some of which display
automatically. For example, by default, Microsoft Word displays the Standard
and Formatting toolbars. In addition to these, you can display a number of
predefined toolbars:

- Borders

- Database

- Drawing

- Forms

- Microsoft

- Word for Windows 2.0

- TipWizard

Excel and PowerPoint provide sets of predefined toolbars. Excel has 13 built-
in toolbars, and PowerPoint has 8. You can customize any of the built-in
toolbars to better meet your needs. You could have a toolbar for every type
of task you perform (for example, one for mail merges and one for desktop
publishing) or for each user of a computer.

To customize a built-in toolbar, follow these steps:

1. Choose <u>V</u>iew, <u>T</u>oolbars. The Toolbars dialog box appears (see fig. 34.19).

Fig. 34.19
The Toolbars
dialog box enables
you to customize
the view and con-
tents of toolbars.

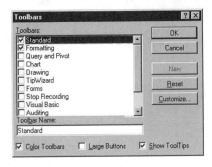

Tip
To quickly custom-
ize toolbars, right-
click a blank area
of any toolbar and
select Customize
from the shortcut
menu.

2. Choose the <u>C</u>ustomize button. The Customize dialog box appears (see fig. 34.20). In PowerPoint, this is called the Customize Toolbars dialog box.

3. To add items to a built-in toolbar, click the category that contains the buttons or other items you want to add.

4. Drag the buttons or items you want from the Buttons section to the toolbar.

Fig. 34.20
The Customize
dialog box enables
you to drag
buttons and other
items to or from
any toolbar
displayed on the
desktop.

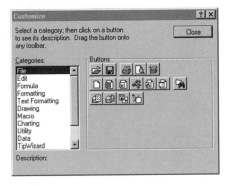

5. To remove items from the toolbar, drag the buttons or items off the toolbar.

6. To move buttons or items, drag them to a new location on the same toolbar or to a different toolbar.

7. Click Close to close the Customize dialog box.

Creating a Custom Toolbar

In addition to modifying the default toolbars of Microsoft Office applications, you can create your own custom toolbar. For example, you could have a toolbar for every type of task you do, such as one for mail merge and one for desktop publishing.

> **Note**
>
> For information about each application's Standard toolbar, see Chapter 2, "Getting Started and Identifying Screen Parts," or see the chapters pertaining to the individual applications.

To create a custom toolbar, follow these steps:

> **Note**
>
> Although Excel screens are used in this section to illustrate the process of creating custom toolbars, the screens in Word and PowerPoint are similar. Any exceptions are noted.

1. Choose <u>V</u>iew <u>T</u>oolbars to display the Toolbars dialog box.

2. In Excel, enter a name for the toolbar in the Toolbar Name text box (doing so enables the <u>N</u>ew button) and choose the <u>N</u>ew button (see fig. 34.21).

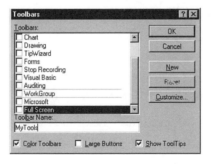

3. In PowerPoint, choose the <u>N</u>ew button to display the New Toolbar dialog box. Type a name for the toolbar in the Tool<u>b</u>ar Name text box and choose OK.

◀ See "Formatting with Styles," p. 259

◀ See "Using AutoFormat," p. 264

◀ See "Using Templates Wizards," p. 269

VII

Customizing Office

Fig. 34.21
In Excel, you must enter a name for the new toolbar before choosing New.

4. In Word, choose the <u>N</u>ew button to display the New Toolbar dialog box. Type a name for the toolbar in the Tool<u>b</u>ar Name text box. Select the template in which you want to store the toolbar from the Make Toolbar Available To drop-down list and choose OK.

5. The Customize dialog box appears, along with the new (empty) toolbar.

6. Select the category that contains the buttons or other items you want to add to the new toolbar.

7. Drag the buttons or items you want from the Buttons section to the new toolbar (see fig. 34.22).

Fig. 34.22

The custom toolbar named MyTools contains three buttons.

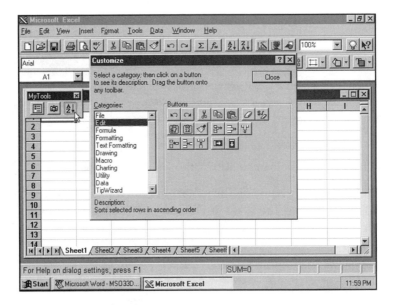

8. Repeat steps 6 and 7 until you fill your custom toolbar with the features you want (the toolbar expands to accommodate your selections).

9. Click the Close button to close the Customize dialog box.

Troubleshooting

The new toolbar I created contains no buttons.

A new toolbar is empty until you add buttons. With the new toolbar visible on-screen, return to the Customize dialog box. Select the category containing the buttons you want to use and drag the button images to your custom toolbar.

Someone customized the default toolbar. I need to get the Standard toolbar back.

Choose the <u>V</u>iew Toolbars command, select a toolbar, and choose the <u>R</u>eset button to return to the built-in version of the selected toolbar.

The colored toolbars are hard to see on my black-and-white monitor.

Choose the <u>V</u>iew Toolbars command and deselect the Color Toolbars checkbox at the bottom of the Toolbars dialog box. Deselecting this option gives the toolbar buttons better contrast.

Customizing Application Menus

Consistency among products lacks a little when it comes to customizing the application menus. No interactive method of modifying the application menus exists in Excel or PowerPoint. In Excel, you can create a macro using Visual Basic for Applications (VBA) and add it to the <u>T</u>ools menu via the Macro Options dialog box or <u>T</u>ools, <u>M</u>enu Editor (only available on Module sheets). You can use the Menu Editor to create new menu bars and menus, but you must use VBA to display a custom menu. Currently, only Word provides an interactive method of customizing built-in menus and creating custom menus.

Customizing Word Menus

You can change the organization, position, and content of default Word menus. To do so, follow these steps:

1. Choose the <u>T</u>ools, <u>C</u>ustomize command. Alternatively, place the mouse pointer on the toolbar, click the right mouse button, and choose <u>C</u>ustomize from the shortcut menu. The Customize dialog box appears.

2. Select the Menus tab (see fig. 34.23).

3. Select the category that contains the command you want to use.

4. In the C<u>o</u>mmands list, select the command.

5. To assign a command to another menu, select the menu name from the Change What Men<u>u</u> drop-down list.

6. To change the position, select the position you want from the <u>P</u>osition on Menu drop-down list. (Select Auto if you want Word to position the menu item for you.)

Fig. 34.23
Word enables you
to customize its
built-in menus.

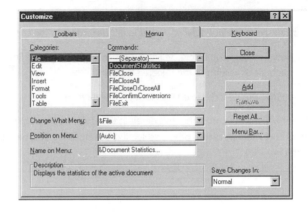

7. To change the name of the menu item or the shortcut key, edit the text in the Name on Menu text box. Put an ampersand (&) before the key you want to designate as the shortcut key.

8. In the Save Changes In drop-down list, select the template in which you want to save the customized menu.

9. Choose the Add button to add the selected command to the menu.

◄ See "Using
Templates
Wizards,"
p. 269

10. Click the Close button when you complete your changes.

Creating Custom Menus

In addition to modifying the built-in menus, you can add your own custom menus to Word's built-in menu bar. You could, for example, create a custom menu which lists common tasks you perform such as mail merges, drawing callouts, and applying font changes. The Menus tab of the Customize dialog box provides easy access to this helpful feature.

To create custom menus, follow these steps:

1. Choose the Tools, Customize command. Alternatively, place the mouse pointer on the toolbar, click the right mouse button, and choose Customize from the shortcut menu. The Customize dialog box appears.

2. Select the Menus tab.

3. Choose the Menu Bar button. The Menu Bar dialog box appears (see fig. 34.24).

4. In the Name on Menu Bar text box, type the name of the first menu item. To assign a shortcut key, type an ampersand (&) in front of the letter you want to be underlined.

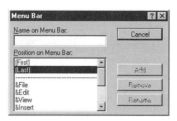

Fig. 34.24
Using the Menu
Bar dialog box,
you can create a
custom menu.

5. Select a position from the Position on Menu Bar list. The menu item will appear before the item selected.

6. Choose the Add button.

7. Repeat steps 4 through 6 until you finish creating your menu.

8. Click Close to exit the Menu Bar dialog box. You return to the Customize dialog box.

9. Close the Customize dialog box. The new menu should appear on-screen (see fig. 34.25).

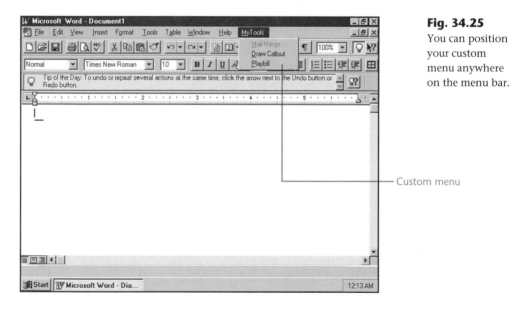

Fig. 34.25
You can position
your custom
menu anywhere
on the menu bar.

Custom menu

Troubleshooting

I find the default Edit Links menu command name misleading. I need to change it to something more meaningful.

Choose the Tools, Customize command and select the Menus tab. Select the Edit category and the EditLinks menu item. In the Name on Menu text box, type a new name for the menu item. Choose the Rename button to save your change.

Someone customized the default menus. I need to get the standard menus back.

Choose the Tools, Customize command. Select the template you want from the Save Changes In drop-down list. Choose the Reset All button to return to the built-in versions of all menus in the selected template.

I pressed Alt+Ctrl+minus sign (–), and I lost a menu item.

You pressed a special shortcut-key combination that deletes menu items. Word provides shortcut keys that help you add and delete menu items as you work. Rather than open the Customize dialog box, you can press Alt+Ctrl+minus sign (–) to delete an item from the selected menu, or Alt+Ctrl+equal sign (=) to add a menu item to the selected menu. See the preceding troubleshooting item for directions on resetting the menus.

Chapter 35

Starting Visual Basic for Applications

by Jeff Bankston

The applications of Microsoft Office provide a varied and divergent set of environments for accomplishing business tasks. The binder that ties all these environments together is OLE 2.0 (object linking and embedding), and the program that controls OLE 2.0 is Visual Basic for Applications (VBA). VBA is a programming environment that eventually will be the macro language for all the applications in Microsoft Office. OLE is an extension of the Windows environment that allows one application to link another application's data file directly into its own data file. This merging of data files is a powerful tool you can use in VBA.

In this chapter, you can learn about these topics:

- Understanding Visual Basic for Applications

- Understanding the difference between Visual Basic for Applications and other Basic languages

- Using Visual Basic for Applications to automate tasks

- Creating small programs in the Visual Basic for Applications language

Understanding Visual Basic for Applications

Visual Basic for Applications is a programming environment based on the Visual Basic for Windows programming language. VBA takes the place of the rudimentary macro programming languages usually found in applications.

Although it is a powerful application development tool, VBA bridges the gap between the ease of macro languages and the need for object-oriented programming languages. New users can record their actions and create macros without having to learn the complexities of the language. In fact, recording actions and then looking at the recorded code is the easiest way to start learning VBA on your own.

Currently in Microsoft Office for Windows 95, VBA is fully developed only in Excel. Word contains its own programming language called Word Basic, which is a bit different from VBA. PowerPoint does not currently contain a programming language.

Eventually, Microsoft plans to integrate VBA into all its mainstream applications including MS Access for Windows 95. Microsoft has made a very credible start with the current releases of its products. As VBA is implemented in other applications, you can move the procedures developed here to those other applications with few, if any, changes.

Understanding Objects

The difference between Visual Basic for Applications and other Basic programming languages is that VBA is object-oriented. You already have seen objects in action in Microsoft Office. In Chapter 30, "Working with Wizards, Multiple Documents, and Cut, Copy, and Paste," you embedded graphics (Graphic objects) and Excel ranges (Range objects) into Word documents. These objects know how to manipulate and display themselves, even when they are embedded in another application's document. Visual Basic for Applications takes advantage of this capability to control those objects.

Visual Basic for Applications uses an object-oriented programming model. If you understand object-oriented programming (OOP), understanding VBA's implementation of it is easy. If you don't, don't worry—the concept is not as complicated as it sounds.

◀ See "Linking an Excel Worksheet to a Word Document," p. 697

VBA *objects* are just a convenient way of storing and hiding data and code in a program. Instead of writing a program to manipulate some data values, you encapsulate the data and the code that manipulates that data in an object. From then on, you need only to access the object to use or display its data.

◀ See "Linking Data between Excel Worksheets," p. 708

You see this capability in action when you embed an object from one application into another. The embedded object takes care of itself, and the embedding object needs only to give the embedded object a place to display itself. When you attach a Visual Basic button to a worksheet, for example, the worksheet does not need to know how to make the button work when you click it—the button handles that. In code, you do much the same thing. You don't try to manipulate an object's data directly; you send messages to the object and let it do the work.

VBA objects include such things as buttons, menu items, ranges of worksheet cells, and even a worksheet itself. Almost everything you can see on-screen while an application is running is an object.

Understanding Objects in Visual Basic for Applications

You can visualize the objects of Visual Basic as a series of containers (see fig. 35.1). The largest container is the Application object, which is the current program you are running, such as Excel. In Excel, the Application object contains Menu objects, Control objects, Workbook objects, and so forth. Within the Workbook objects are Sheet objects (worksheets, macro sheets, modules, dialog sheets, and so on), and within the Sheet objects are Range objects (cell ranges.) Other applications have similar objects to cover their particular needs. See the documentation and the online help for the different applications of Microsoft Office for a list of the objects in each application.

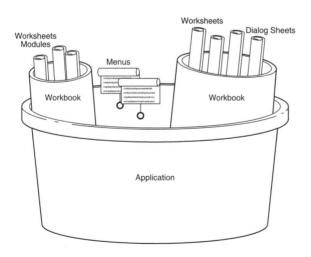

Fig. 35.1
The Visual Basic for Applications object model: containers within containers.

Note

Individual cells are not objects in Excel but are accessed as Range objects, which contain a cell or cell range.

Accessing Objects

To access a specific object in Visual Basic for Applications, you start with the outermost container object, followed by a period, followed by the next inner container object, followed by a period, and so on, until you reach the object you want. To access cell B5 in an Excel worksheet named Sheet3 in a workbook named Book2, for example, you could use the following reference:

```
Application.Workbooks("Book2").Worksheets("Sheet3").Range("B5")
```

Because Visual Basic for Applications deals with objects, any application that registers its objects with the Windows operating system makes those objects available to Visual Basic for Applications. Thus, even if you are running Visual Basic for Applications in another application, you still can access an object in Excel in much the same way as you would if you were in Excel itself. The only difference is that you must include the name the other application used when registering itself, to specify which Application object to use. For example, you could use the following reference in Project to access a cell in Excel:

```
Excel.Application.Workbooks("Book2").Worksheets("Sheet3").Range("B5")
```

This reference is somewhat cumbersome, so Visual Basic for Applications makes an assumption that enables you to leave out some of these containers. For each container not included on the left side of a reference to an object (such as the workbook or worksheet reference), Visual Basic for Applications assumes that the currently active object of that type is the one being referenced.

Thus, you almost always can leave out the application, as well as the workbook. Be careful, though, and make sure you know what objects are active before you leave them out of the specification. Leaving out the containers has the positive effect of making your procedures more portable. If you leave out all but the Range object, your code always applies to the currently active sheet, so you don't have to change the sheet name to apply your code to a different sheet. In addition to the named sheets and workbooks, you can use the objects ActiveWorkbook, ActiveSheet, ActiveCell to reference the currently active objects without having to know their names.

> **Note**
>
> Keep in mind that if you use specific workbook and sheet names in your procedures, the procedures will work only in those named workbooks and procedures. By leaving out parts of an object's specification, you make your code applicable to all objects of the class you left out.

Understanding Classes and Collections

A *class* of objects is a reference to a general type or classification of objects. In Visual Basic for Applications, for example, each cell or cell range in a worksheet is a Range object, which is an example of the Range class.

If you combine all the objects of a specific class into a group, that group is known as a *collection*. Thus, all the workbooks in the Application object are in the collection Workbooks, and all the worksheets in a workbook are in the collection Worksheets. All the worksheets also are in the collection Sheets, which includes all types of sheets (worksheet, chart, module, and dialog) in a workbook.

Accessing Collections

Collections are what you use to access most objects. To access a specific member of a collection, follow the collection name with either a string containing the object name or an integer in parentheses. Thus, Worksheets("Sheet1") refers to the sheet named Sheet1, and Worksheets(2) refers to the second worksheet in the collection of all worksheets in the active workbook. If you want to access cell B5 in the third worksheet in a workbook named Book2, you could use the following reference:

```
Workbooks("Book2").Worksheets(3).Range("B5")
```

If you leave out the number and parentheses in the reference to a collection, the reference is to all the members of the collection.

> **Caution**
>
> Be careful when using numbers to select objects in a collection. If you add or delete members of a collection, the numbering of all the other members of that collection can change, and your number may select a different object.

Understanding Properties

An object's data is called the *property* of that object. Most properties are readable, but not all can be written or changed. See the Visual Basic for Applications section of online help for a description of each of the properties. In the description of each object is a list of the properties that apply to it.

Tip

Each object has size, shape, and color properties.

For a Range object (one or more worksheet cells), the font, color, font size, contents, and so on are read/write properties, but the location is read-only (cells don't move.) Properties can refer to the direct data contained in an object, such as the value of a cell, or to data values that control how an object looks and behaves, such as color.

Property values can be strings of text, numbers, logicals (`True` or `False`), or enumerated lists. An *enumerated list* is a numbered list of options, where the number is used to select a specific option. For example, the `Color` property of most objects is an enumerated list in which 0 is none, 1 is black, 2 is white, 3 is red, 4 is green, 5 is blue, and so on.

For the enumerated lists, VBA and the other compliant applications in Microsoft Office contain lists of predefined constants to use in place of the numbers. Using the constants is much more informative than using the numbers. The constants that are applicable to a property are listed in the description of the property in online help. You can see a list of constants by searching for *constants* or *variables* in online help and selecting the "Variables and Constants Keywords Summary" and "Visual Basic Constants" topics.

Accessing Properties

The easiest way to see what properties to set, and what values to set them to, is to start the Macro Recorder, perform whatever changes you want to perform, turn off the recorder, and then copy the recorded property changes into your program. Both Excel and Word currently have macro recorders.

Following is the syntax for accessing an object's properties:

```
object.property
```

In this example, `object` is the object whose properties you want to change or view, and `property` is the name of the property. If the preceding construct is on the right side of a statement, you are reading the value of the property from the object. If the construct is on the left side of a statement, you are setting the value of the property. To set the value of the `Formula` property (the contents of the cell) of cell B5 to `=ABS(B4)` when cell B5 is in the `Sheet1` worksheet (which is in the `Book2` workbook), you could use the following statement:

```
Workbooks("Book2").WorkSheets("Sheet1").Range("B5").Formula =
"=ABS(B4)"
```

To read the same property from the same cell and store it in the variable myFormula, you could use this statement:

```
myFormula = Workbooks("Book2").WorkSheets("Sheet1").Range("B5").Formula
```

The rules concerning omitting container objects (described in "Accessing Objects" earlier in this chapter) apply here. Because you must include an object with the property, you cannot leave off the Range object to get the formula in whatever cell is the active cell. For these and similar cases involving other objects, some special properties return the currently active or selected object. Table 35.1 lists these special properties.

Table 35.1 Special Properties That Return the Active Objects	
Property	**Description**
ActiveCell	The active cell in the active window
ActiveChart	The active chart in a workbook
ActiveDialog	The active dialog sheet in a workbook
ActiveSheet	The active worksheet, chart, module, or dialog sheet in a workbook
ActiveWorkbook	The active workbook in an application
Selection	The currently selected object in the currently selected sheet

Caution

Be sure that an object of the expected type is the active object before you try to use the active properties, such as ActiveSheet, in a procedure. If an object of the specified type is not the active object, these properties return nothing, and a procedure that uses them is likely to crash.

To get the formula contained in the active cell of the Sheet3 worksheet, for example, you could use the following statement:

```
myFormula = Workbooks("Book2").WorkSheets("Sheet3").ActiveCell.Formula
```

If `Book2` and `Sheet3` are the currently active workbook and worksheet, you could use this statement:

```
myFormula = ActiveCell.Formula
```

If `Book2` is the active workbook, but `Sheet3` is not necessarily the active worksheet, you could use this statement:

```
myFormula = WorkSheets("Sheet3").ActiveCell.Formula
```

If you wanted to access cell B5 in whatever worksheet is active in `Book2`, you could use this statement:

```
myFormula = WorkBooks("Book2").ActiveSheet.Range("B5").Formula
```

Everything to the left of the last period must evaluate to an object or a collection of objects.

Understanding Methods

Visual Basic for Applications *methods* are the blocks of code stored in an object that know how to manipulate the object's data. For the `Range` object, for example, the `Calculate` method causes the formulas in the selected cells to be recalculated, and the `Clear` method clears the cell's contents. Methods do things to objects and the data they contain, as opposed to properties, which set values. To learn more about the specifics of different methods, and to find out what methods apply to what objects, see the Visual Basic for Applications section of online help.

Accessing Methods

Tip
Methods carry out an object's task.

You access or execute an object's methods in nearly the same way that you access an object's properties. The main difference is that you always access a property as part of a formula, but a method must be part of a formula only if it returns a value. The `Rows` method, for example, returns a collection containing all the rows in the range. To use this method to set the `RowHeight` property of all the rows in the currently selected range to 20, use a formula like the following:

```
Selection.Rows.RowHeight = 20
```

To get the number of rows in the current selection, you could use the `Rows` method to return a collection and the `Count` property to return the number of items in the collection, as follows:

```
numRows = Selection.Rows.Count
```

Some methods require arguments to make them work. For example, the Insert method, when applied to a range object, needs an argument to tell it how to move the cells that are already in the selection; the Rows method needs an index number to select a single row in the collection of rows. If the method is part of a formula, the arguments must go in parentheses. To get the RowHeight of the second row in the collection of rows, you could use the following statement:

```
theHeight = Selection.Rows(2).RowHeight
```

If the method is only being executed and is not part of a formula, place the arguments to the right of the reference to the method. To use the Insert method to insert blank cells for the current selection and to move the current selection down to make room, you could use this statement:

```
Selection.Insert xlDown
```

The argument actually is an integer, but the built-in constant is used here to make the code more readable. You can get the built-in constants that apply to a method in the description of the method in online help, or you can search for *constants* or *variables* in online help and then select the "Variables and Constants Keywords Summary" or "Visual Basic Constants" topic.

Creating Procedures with the Macro Recorder

The best way to learn to use Visual Basic for Applications is to create procedures with it, by using the Macro Recorder. When you turn on the Macro Recorder and create a worksheet, the recorder writes the Visual Basic code that performs the same actions you are performing by hand. By examining that code, you learn how to use VBA to access and change an application's objects.

In the following sections, you create a simple worksheet that calculates the tax on the cost of an item and then calculates the total cost. The worksheet has an input cell and two calculated output cells. The input cell accepts a cost, and the output cells display the tax and the total cost.

Starting the Recorder

To prepare the worksheet and display the Record New Macro dialog box, follow these steps:

1. Start Excel if you haven't already done so.

2. Open a new workbook by choosing File, New, select the Workbook and click OK.

3. Choose Tools, Record Macro, Record New Macro, and then choose the Options button. The Record New Macro dialog box appears (see fig. 35.2).

4. In the Macro Name field, type **FigureTax**.

5. In the Description field, type this line:

   Create a worksheet to calculate the tax on an item.

6. Leave the other fields at the default values shown in figure 35.2, and choose OK.

Fig. 35.2
The Record New
Macro dialog box
enables you to set
the name and
other options for a
new procedure.

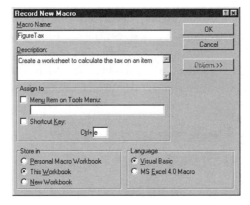

The Stop Macro button appears in a floating toolbar, and the Macro Recorder records what you do, recording all your keystrokes and mouse clicks until you click the Stop Macro button.

Recording a Procedure

You can create the procedure simply by creating the worksheet as you normally do. To create the worksheet, follow these steps:

1. Select cell B4 and type **Cost**.

2. Select cell B5 and type **Tax**.

3. Select cell B6 and type **Total**.

4. Select cell C4 and type **12.43**.

5. Select cell C5 and type **=C4*0.0825**.

6. Select cell C6 and type **=C4 + C5**.

7. Select cell C4, choose Format, Cells, and select the Number tab. Select the Currency format type, select the ⁻$1243.10 format, and choose OK. Repeat this step for cell C6 exactly. Repeat this step again for cell C5, but use the Number format.

8. Select cell C5, choose the Format, Cells command, and select the Border tab.

9. In the Borders dialog box, on the left side click Bottom for the placement of the border, and on the right side click the lower left box for the style. Click OK to continue.

◄ See "Entering Data," p. 305

◄ See "Selecting Cells and Ranges," p. 309

◄ See "Formatting Numbers," p. 341

The worksheet now should look like figure 35.3.

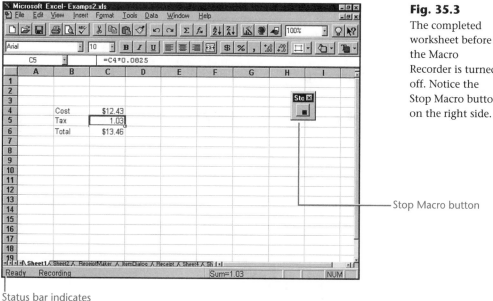

Fig. 35.3
The completed worksheet before the Macro Recorder is turned off. Notice the Stop Macro button on the right side.

Stop Macro button

Status bar indicates that macro is recording

Stopping the Recorder
Stopping the recorder is easy: simply click the Stop Macro button.

Examining the Procedure

To examine your newly created procedure, find the Module1 tab at the bottom of the screen and click it. Your procedure appears on-screen and looks like figure 35.4.

Fig. 35.4

The Excel Macro Recorder places the recorded commands in a module, as shown here for the `FigureTax` procedure.

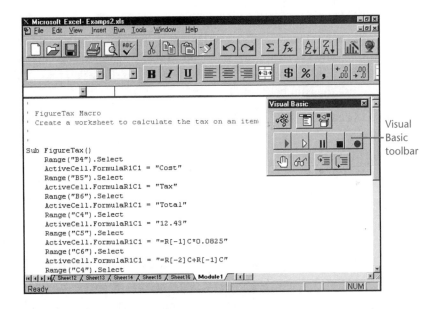

Visual Basic toolbar

Tip

The code for each module and procedure is stored within each worksheet and saved with it. If you're having problems understanding some code, try Que's *Special Edition Using Visual Basic*.

The listing of the procedure is shown in listing 35.1.

Listing 35.1 The FigureTax Procedure

```
'
' FigureTax Macro
' Create a worksheet to calculate the tax on an item.
'
'
Sub FigureTax()
    Range("B4").Select
    ActiveCell.FormulaR1C1 = "Cost"
    Range("B5").Select
    ActiveCell.FormulaR1C1 = "Tax"
    Range("B6").Select
    ActiveCell.FormulaR1C1 = "Total"
    Range("C4").Select
    ActiveCell.FormulaR1C1 = "12.43"
    Range("C5").Select
```

```
        ActiveCell.FormulaR1C1 = "=R[-1]C*0.0825"
        Range("C6").Select
        ActiveCell.FormulaR1C1 = "=R[-2]C+R[-1]C"
        Range("C4").Select
        Selection.NumberFormat = "$#,##0.00"
        Range("C6").Select
        Selection.NumberFormat = "$#,##0.00"
        Range("C5").Select
        Selection.NumberFormat = "0.00"
        Selection.Borders(xlLeft).LineStyle = xlNone
        Selection.Borders(xlRight).LineStyle = xlNone
        Selection.Borders(xlTop).LineStyle = xlNone
    With Selection.Borders(xlBottom)
        .Weight = xlThick
        .ColorIndex = xlAutomatic
    End With
        Selection.BorderAround LineStyle:=xlNone
    End Sub
```

If you examine this listing and compare it with the steps you just took, you see that each step results in one or more lines of code inserted into the procedure. Many extra lines also are in the procedure; these lines set parameters that you did not explicitly set when you created the worksheet. These extra lines result when you choose OK in a dialog box that sets several parameters. Although you may change only one parameter in the dialog box, closing the box sets all the parameters displayed in that box and inserts corresponding lines into the procedure being recorded.

> **Note**
>
> In the Borders dialog box, for example, you set only the Bottom option (step 9), but eight lines were inserted into the procedure, setting the values of all the other options. In many cases, you can delete these extra lines from the procedure without changing its results.

The procedure appears in color, with comments in green, keywords in blue, and everything else in black. Floating on the right half of the procedure window is the Visual Basic toolbar. The toolbar can be floating or docked on any side. Figure 35.5 shows the function of each button in the Visual Basic toolbar. The first three buttons are for module insertion, Object Browser, and Menu Editor, in that order from left to right; the next five are for module execution and handling; the last four are for module debugging.

Fig. 35.5
The Visual Basic toolbar contains controls for executing and debugging a program.

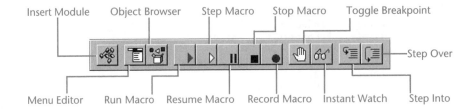

Insert Module — Object Browser — Step Macro — Stop Macro — Toggle Breakpoint — Step Over

Menu Editor — Run Macro — Resume Macro — Record Macro — Instant Watch — Step Into

Running the Procedure

To run this procedure, follow these steps:

1. Select an unused worksheet. Make sure that the sheet is unused or has nothing useful in the B4:C6 range because the procedure overwrites that area.

2. Choose the Tools, Macro command. The Macro dialog box shown in figure 35.6 appears, showing all procedures available in this sheet and in the global sheet (currently, none).

3. In the dialog box, select the FigureTax procedure and choose Run. The worksheet appears and the procedure runs, setting the contents and formatting the worksheet cells.

   The completed worksheet is identical to the one that you created by hand.

Fig. 35.6
The Macro dialog box enables you to select and execute procedures. The dialog box also provides an easy way to locate, edit, or delete procedures.

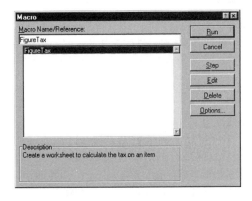

Understanding the Procedure

Now go back and take a closer look at the listing of the procedure by selecting the Module1 tab. The first few lines of the procedure are comments. Comments are ignored by an executing procedure and can contain any text.

Any text following a single quotation mark is a comment. Comments can appear at the beginning of a line or to the right of any valid VBA statement:

```
'
' FigureTax Macro
' Create a worksheet to calculate the tax on an item.
'
'
```

Following the comments is the procedure header, which names the procedure:

```
Sub FigureTax()
```

Following the procedure header are 12 statements that alternately select each cell in the range B4:C6 and insert text, a number value, or a formula. The last four lines insert formulas, but they are written in the R1C1 style rather than the A1 style of cell addressing. This method is the default for saving inserted formulas, no matter what method was used to create the worksheet while the recorder was running. When this procedure is played back, the formulas are automatically converted into whatever style is the default in the active worksheet. The 12 statements look like this:

```
Range("B4").Select
ActiveCell.FormulaR1C1 = "Cost"
Range("B5").Select
ActiveCell.FormulaR1C1 = "Tax"
Range("B6").Select
ActiveCell.FormulaR1C1 = "Total"
Range("C4").Select
ActiveCell.FormulaR1C1 = "12.43"
Range("C5").Select
ActiveCell.FormulaR1C1 = "=R[-1]C*0.0825"
Range("C6").Select
ActiveCell.FormulaR1C1 = "=R[-2]C+R[-1]C"
```

The next two statements select the range C4 and apply the currency format to that cell. The same thing is repeated for cell C6.

```
Range("C4").Select
Selection.NumberFormat = "$#,##0.00"
Range("C6").Select
Selection.NumberFormat = "$#,##0.00"
```

The last nine lines of the procedure are the result of selecting cell C5 and making changes in the Borders dialog box. Notice that you selected only the Bottom box, but the procedure set values for all the options in the dialog box. The values xlNone, xlBottom, xlThin, and so on are built-in Excel constants. See online help for a list of the constants available for use with different properties and methods. These lines look like this:

```
Range("C5").Select
Selection.Borders(xlLeft).LineStyle = xlNone
Selection.Borders(xlRight).LineStyle = xlNone
Selection.Borders(xlTop).LineStyle = xlNone
With Selection.Borders(xlBottom)
    .Weight = xlThick
    .ColorIndex = xlAutomatic
End With
Selection.BorderAround LineStyle:=xlNone
```

Note

The With, End With structure in the procedure is a method of decreasing the size of a procedure and arranging together all statements that apply to a specific object. The With statement works by inserting the object that follows the word *With* just before the period in each line below it. Thus, the following two blocks of code are equivalent:

```
With Selection.Borders(xlBottom)
    .Weight = xlThin
    .ColorIndex = xlAutomatic
End With

Selection.Borders(xlBottom).Weight = xlThin
Selection.Borders(xlBottom).ColorIndex = xlAutomatic
```

The last statement in the procedure is the procedure footer, which marks the end of the procedure:

```
End Sub
```

Creating an Application

Tip
Learning a new skill is usually best done with a project in mind. Think of some repetitious task in Excel that you've always wanted to automate, and you've got your application goal!

Now that you know about objects, properties, and methods, you can start putting some of that information together to create an application. The application you are going to create is a receipt maker, such as you might use at a checkout stand where you don't have a regular cash register. The program inputs data with a dialog box, inserts the data into a form in an Excel worksheet, and prints the form.

The basic structure of this program—input data, store it, do something with it—forms the basis of many programs, such as an inventory program or a personal organizer. You should be able to adapt the methods shown here for many different applications.

The program uses a worksheet and a module. The worksheet contains the receipt form that stores the data until you are ready to print it. The module contains the code that gets the data, stores it in the sheet, and prints it. First, create the worksheet. Don't worry if you don't understand what the code does; it is explained in the next few sections.

To create the worksheet, follow these steps:

1. Select an unused worksheet. Choose F̲ormat, S̲heet, R̲ename, or double-click the tab at the bottom of the sheet and change the sheet's name to **Receipt** in the dialog box, and click OK.

2. Select cell A2 and type **The XYZ Stationers**.

3. Select cell A3 and type **1127 Somewhere St**.

4. Select cell A4 and type **Righthere, CA 12345**.

5. Select cell B6 and type **Item**.

6. Select cell C6 and type **Cost**.

7. Select cell A7 and type **1**.

8. Select cell A8 and type **2**.

9. Select cells A7:A8, select the fill handle at the bottom right corner, and drag it down to A16 to create the series of numbers from 1 to 10.

10. Select C16, choose F̲ormat, C̲ells, select the Border tab, select a thick line style, click the Bottom box, and choose OK.

11. Select cells C7:C19, choose F̲ormat, C̲ells, select the Number tab, select the Currency type, select the format -$1,234.10, and choose OK.

12. Select the bar between the B and C column headings, and drag it until the column width is 27.00 characters.

13. Select cell B7 and name it **TopOfList**, using the I̲nsert, N̲ame, D̲efine command.

14. Select cells A1:D20 and name them **PrintRange**.

15. Choose the F̲ile, Page Set̲up command, select the Header/Footer tab, and set both the header and footer to none. Select the Sheet tab, deselect all the check boxes, and choose OK.

The worksheet should look like figure 35.7.

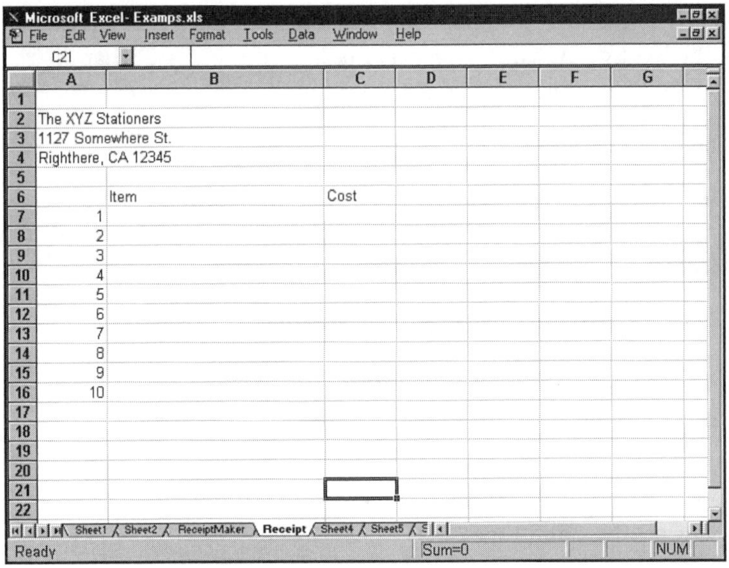

Fig. 35.7
Layout of the
Receipt worksheet.

The next step is to create the procedures in a module and attach those procedures to two buttons in the form.

To create the procedures, perform the following steps.

1. Choose the Insert, Macro, Module command to insert a new module.

2. Select the module and rename it **ReceiptMaker** by choosing the Edit, Sheet, Rename command or by double-clicking the module's name tab.

3. Type the procedures shown in listing 35.2 into the module.

Listing 35.2 The Receipt Maker Program

```
'
' Receipt Maker
' A program to make receipts.
'
Option Explicit    'Force the declaration of all variables.
Dim theSheet As Object    'Pointer to the worksheet.
Dim OutputRange As Object 'Pointer to the list of items.
Const MaxNumItems = 10    'Maximum number of items allowed.
'
' Get entries.
'
```

```
Sub GetEntries()
  Dim theItem As String, theCost As Currency
  Dim theRow As Integer, NumItems As Integer
  'Define the pointer to the worksheet.
  Set theSheet = Application.Workbooks("Examps.xls").
        Worksheets("Receipt")
  'Define the pointer to the top of the table of items.
  Set OutputRange = theSheet.Range("TopOfList")
  ClearRange OutputRange        'Clear the table of items.
  NumItems = 1
  'Ask for the name and cost for up to 10 items.
  Do While NumItems <= MaxNumItems
    'Get the name.
    theItem = InputBox("Item Name:", "Make Receipt")
    'If the user didn't enter anything, _ he must be done, so quit.
If theItem = "" Then Exit Do
    'Get the cost.
    theCost = Val(InputBox("Item Cost:", "Make Receipt"))
    'Insert the items name and cost on the worksheet.
    OutputRange.Cells(NumItems, 1).Formula = theItem
    OutputRange.Cells(NumItems, 2).Formula = Str(theCost)
    NumItems = NumItems + 1  'Increment the number of items.
Loop
TotalIt     'Calculate and print the totals.
'Make the TotalIt procedure an event procedure
'attached to the worksheet.
theSheet.OnEntry = "TotalIt"   'Retotal it if the user makes
changes.

End Sub
'
' Calculate subtotal and total.
'
Sub TotalIt()
  Dim theRow As Integer
  Dim SubTotal As Currency, ItemTax As Currency
  Dim theTotal As Currency
  SubTotal = 0
  'Calculate the total by extracting the values from the worksheet.
  For theRow = 1 To MaxNumItems
    SubTotal = SubTotal + Val(OutputRange.Cells(theRow, 2).Value)
  Next theRow
  'Insert the subtotal, tax, and total on the worksheet.
  With OutputRange
    .Cells(MaxNumItems + 1, 1).Formula = "Subtotal"
    .Cells(MaxNumItems + 1, 2).Formula = Str(SubTotal)
    .Cells(MaxNumItems + 2, 1).Formula = "Tax"
    ItemTax = theTax(SubTotal)  'Calculate the tax.
    .Cells(MaxNumItems + 2, 2).Formula = Str(ItemTax)
    theTotal = SubTotal + ItemTax
    .Cells(MaxNumItems + 3, 1).Formula = "Total"
    .Cells(MaxNumItems + 3, 2).Formula = Str(theTotal)
  End With
End Sub
```

(continues)

Listing 35.2 Continued

```
'
' Clear the output range.
'
Sub ClearRange(theRange As Object)
  Dim theRow As Integer
  For theRow = 1 To MaxNumItems + 3
    'Clear the cells. Use ClearContents to only clear the values
    'and not the formatting.
    theRange.Cells(theRow, 1).ClearContents
    theRange.Cells(theRow, 2).ClearContents
  Next theRow
End Sub
'
' Print the receipt.
'
Sub PrintReceipt()
  theSheet.OnEntry = ""  'Turn off the automatic retotaling.
  theSheet.Range("PrintRange").PrintOut  'Print the worksheet.
End Sub
'
' Calculate the tax on an item.
'
Function theTax(Cost As Currency) As Currency
  Const TaxRate = 0.0825
  theTax = Cost * TaxRate
End Function
```

4. Switch to the Receipt worksheet and display the Drawing toolbar by choosing the View, Toolbars command.

5. Click the Create Button tool in the Drawing toolbar and draw the Make Receipt button as shown in figure 35.8. When the Assign Macro dialog box appears, select GetEntries for the macro and choose OK.

6. The button should still be selected; if not, click the Drawing Selection tool in the Drawing toolbar and select the button. Select the text on top of the button and change it to **Make Receipt**.

7. Create the Print Receipt button, attach it to the macro PrintReceipt, and make the title **Print Receipt**.

8. Close the Drawing toolbar by clicking the X in the upper right corner of the toolbar.

9. Save the workbook as EXAMPS.XLS.

The worksheet should look like figure 35.8. If you did everything correctly, you can use the program to create a receipt:

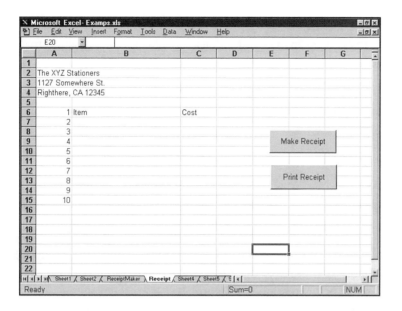

Fig. 35.8
The Receipt Maker
program finished.

1. Switch to the Receipt worksheet and click the Make Receipt button.

2. In the first dialog box that appears, type the name of an item and press Enter.

3. In the second dialog box, type the cost of the item and press Enter.

4. Continue typing names and costs until you have entered all the items you want to use in this receipt.

5. To end the list, press Enter or click the Cancel button in the Item Name dialog box. The totals are calculated and displayed in the receipt.

6. Click the Print Receipt button to print the receipt.

Branching and Decision-Making

As you read down the listing of some programs, you may come across the following line:

```
If theItem = "" Then Exit Do
```

The line is an `If` statement that tests the value of `theItem` to see whether it contains an empty string. The variable `theItem` contains the text name of the item to be added to the receipt. If the variable is empty, the user is finished entering data, and you execute the `Exit Do` statement to exit from the `Do/Loop` structure. Thus, the `If` statement controls a branch in the structure of the program.

Block If Structures

A block If structure enables you to use a logical condition equation to decide which block of code to execute. The block If structure follows:

```
If condition1 Then
    statements1
ElseIf condition2
    statements2
Else
    statements3
End If
```

When the If statement is executed, *condition1* is tested, and if the result is True, the block *statements1* is executed. If *condition1* is False, *condition2* is tested, and if the result is True, the block *statements2* is executed. The structure may have multiple ElseIf clauses, and each is tested in turn, looking for a clause whose condition is True. If none of the conditions is True, the statements following the Else clause are executed. Only the block of statements following the first condition that returns True is executed; all the others down to the End If statement are skipped, even if their conditions would have returned True.

Logical Formulas

The conditions used in the If statements are logical values, formulas that result in a logical value, or numeric formulas that result in a value of zero (False) or nonzero (True). Logical formulas usually are created by comparing two values, using one of the comparison operators shown in table 35.2. You can combine logical expressions with the Boolean operators listed in table 35.3. For more information, search for *comparison operators* and *logical* in the Visual Basic for Applications section of online help.

Table 35.2   The Comparison Operators

Operator	Description
=	Equal to
<>	Not equal to
>	Greater than
<	Less than
>=	Greater than or equal to
<=	Less than or equal to

Table 35.3 The Logical Operators	
Operator	**Description**
And	Logical and
Eqv	Logical equivalence
Imp	Logical implies
Not	Logical negation
Or	Logical or
Xor	Logical exclusive or

Select Case

The `Select Case` structure performs a function similar to that of the block `If`
structure, in that an expression is used to select a particular block of statements. In `Select Case`, the expression returns a value, and that value is used
to determine which block of statements to execute. The syntax of the `Select
Case` structure follows:

```
Select Case expression
Case list1
    statements1
Case Else
    statements2
End Select
```

When the `Select Case` statement is executed, `expression` is evaluated. Following the `Select Case` statement are one or more `Case` statements. The value of
`expression` is compared with the comma-delimited list of values in *list1*.
If one of the values matches, the block *statements1* is executed. Otherwise,
that block is skipped, and the next `Case` statement is checked for a match. If
none of the `Case` statements results in a match, the block *statements2* following the `Case Else` statement is executed. As with the block `If` structure, only
one of the blocks of statements is executed.

Accessing Worksheet Cells

In the Receipt Maker example, after the user provides an item's name and
cost, that information is inserted into cells in the worksheet. Following is the
code that performs the insertion:

```
Set theSheet = Application.Workbooks("Examps.xls").
   Worksheets("Receipt")
'Define the pointer to the top of the table of items.
Set OutputRange = theSheet.Range("TopOfList")
   .
   .
   .
'Insert the item's name and cost on the worksheet.
OutputRange.Cells(NumItems, 1).Formula = theItem
OutputRange.Cells(NumItems, 2).Formula = Str(theCost)
```

You use a range reference and a Set statement to define an object variable that points to the cell named TopOfList in the worksheet. That range reference is used with the Cells method to select worksheet cells in positions relative to the cell TopOfList. After obtaining a range reference to a cell, use the Value and Formula properties to get or set the value of a cell. Notice that the Value property contains the value of a cell—that is, the number displayed in the worksheet—whereas the Formula property contains what was typed in the cell. In this case, because none of the cells contains a formula, the Value and Formula properties are the same.

Note

The range reference in the OutputRange variable refers to a named cell. This reference is preferable to referencing an explicit cell because you can rearrange the worksheet, and the code still gets the value from the correct cell.

You can reference the cells by using a cell reference, or you can reference a cell by row and column using Cell, which also returns a Range object. The following three statements reference the contents of cell C7 in the example:

```
theCost = theSheet.Range("C7").Value
theCost = theSheet.Range("TopOfList"). Cells(1, 2).Value
theCost = theSheet.Cells(7, 3).Value
```

The TotalIt procedure demonstrates both reading and changing the values of worksheet cells. The first part of the procedure gets the value in each cell in column C that contains a value and calculates a subtotal. This is shown in the code fragment below:

```
SubTotal = 0
   'Calculate the total by extracting the values from the worksheet.
   For theRow = 1 To MaxNumItems
      SubTotal = SubTotal + Val(OutputRange.Cells(theRow, 2).Value)
   Next theRow
```

The For and Next statements form a loop that executes the SubTotal statement one time for each row in the data range of the receipt. The value of the cell is obtained and totaled in the variable SubTotal.

> **Note**
>
> Notice how the Val( ) function is applied to the contents of the cell to ensure that a number is passed to the variable. Without the Val( ) function, the user could type into a cell a string that would crash your code if you attempted to store it in a numeric variable. The Val( ) function converts a string to a number and prevents that potential problem.

The second half of the procedure writes the labels and values for the subtotal, the tax, and the total in the worksheet:

```
With OutputRange
    .Cells(MaxNumItems + 1, 1).Formula = "Subtotal"
    .Cells(MaxNumItems + 1, 2).Formula = Str(SubTotal)
    .Cells(MaxNumItems + 2, 1).Formula = "Tax"
    ItemTax = theTax(SubTotal)   'Calculate the tax.
    .Cells(MaxNumItems + 2, 2).Formula = Str(ItemTax)
    theTotal = SubTotal + ItemTax
    .Cells(MaxNumItems + 3, 1).Formula = "Total"
    .Cells(MaxNumItems + 3, 2).Formula = Str(theTotal)
End With
```

This block of statements also demonstrates the use of the With statement to block cells together and to save some typing. The statements are logically blocked together because they refer to the same object, and they save some typing because you have to type the first object only once. The object following the With clause (OutputRange) is assumed to attach before the period to all the statements between the With and End With statements.

Calling Procedures

The TotalIt procedure is an example of a subprocedure that is called by other procedures. The GetEntries procedure needs to be able to calculate and display the totals in the worksheet, and it calls the TotalIt procedure to do so. Both procedures can be found in the ReceiptMaker worksheet.

At the beginning of the GetEntries procedure, you must clear any old entries from the receipt. The ClearRange procedure is called to perform that action:

```
Sub ClearRange(theRange As Object)
  Dim theRow As Integer
  For theRow = 1 To MaxNumItems + 3
    'Clear the cells. Use ClearContents to only clear
    'the values and not the formatting.
    theRange.Cells(theRow, 1).ClearContents
    theRange.Cells(theRow, 2).ClearContents
  Next theRow
End Sub
```

The procedure needs one object for an argument named `theRange` in the `ClearRange` procedure. In the `GetEntries` procedure, the `ClearRange` procedure is called with the following statement:

```
ClearRange OutputRange      'Clear the table of items.
```

Because this procedure call is not part of a formula, no parentheses around the argument are required.

The function procedure `theTax` is another procedure that is called from elsewhere in the program.

```
'
' Calculate the tax on an item.
'
Function theTax(Cost As Currency) As Currency
  Const TaxRate = 0.0825
  theTax = Cost * TaxRate
End Function
```

Notice that in this procedure, the argument is a Currency-type variable named `Cost`. The function is called as part of a formula in `TotalIt`:

```
ItemTax = theTax(SubTotal)   'Calculate the tax.
```

In `TotalIt`, the function `theTax` is passed the variable `SubTotal` as an argument. This variable points to a memory location, and that memory location is passed to the `theTax` function, where it is named `Cost`. Both names point to the same memory location, so if the value of `Cost` were changed in `theTax`, the value of `SubTotal` would change in `TotalIt` when the function completes executing.

In some cases, you want to make sure that a procedure does not change an argument, so you must pass the argument as a value instead of a memory address. You can do this in the procedure heading or in the calling program. In a procedure heading, for example, precede the argument with the keyword `ByVal`, as follows:

```
Function theTax(ByVal Cost As Currency) As Currency
```

The other way is to turn the argument in the calling program into a formula. The address where the result of the formula is stored is sent to the procedure instead of the addresses of any of the variables. You make a variable into a formula simply by enclosing the variable name in parentheses, as follows:

```
ItemTax = theTax((SubTotal))   'Calculate the tax.
```

The `TotalIt` procedure also is an event procedure attached to the worksheet. This attachment is done at the end of the `GetReceipt` procedure, as follows:

```
'Make the TotalIt procedure an event procedure attached
'to the worksheet.
theSheet.OnEntry = "TotalIt"    'Retotal it if the user makes changes
```

Later in the program, the `TotalIt` procedure is unattached from the
worksheet in the `PrintReceipt` procedure, as follows:

```
theSheet.OnEntry = ""    'Turn off the automatic retotaling.
```

The `OnEntry` property of a worksheet contains the name of a procedure to
be executed whenever the user changes the contents of a worksheet cell.
By making the `TotalIt` procedure an event procedure, the user can make
changes in the receipt before printing, and those changes will immediately
be included in the totals at the bottom of the receipt.

Using Loops

The `TotalIt` procedure has to search through the cells in the worksheet and
add the contents to calculate the subtotal. If you were to write range references to all 10 of the cells in the worksheet, you could add them up that way,
but you probably don't want to spend your time typing the same statement
over and over. To handle cases like this, you use loops.

For/Next

The most common loop is the `For/Next` loop, which executes a block of statements a specified number of times. The syntax of the `For/Next` loop is as
follows:

```
For loopvariable = start To end Step stepval
.
.statements
.
Next loopvariable
```

In the `For/Next` loop, `loopvariable` is a standard variable. The first time the
loop executes, `loopvariable` has the value `start`, and all the statements down
to the `Next` statement are executed. The second time the loop executes,
`stepval` is added to `loopvariable`, and that value is compared with `end`. If
`loopvariable` is greater than `end`, the loop terminates; otherwise, the statements within the loop are executed again. The `Step stepval` clause can be
omitted, in which case the `stepval` is 1. If `stepval` is negative, the loop counts
down rather than up until `loopvariable` is less than `end`.

The `TotalIt` procedure uses a `For/Next` loop to select all the cells that might
contain values in the worksheet, then the procedure calculates a total for all
the values found:

Tip
Plan out your
loops on paper
before doing so in
code. It'll save you
hours in debug-
ging infinite loops.

```
For theRow = 1 To MaxNumItems
   SubTotal = SubTotal + Val(OutputRange.Cells(theRow, 2).Value)
Next theRow
```

In this example, `theRow` is the loop variable, and it ranges from 1 to `MaxNumEntries`. Each time the loop executes, a different worksheet cell is selected, using the `Cells` method.

Do/Loop

The `Do/Loop` loop uses a condition to determine how many times to execute the loop. You can test the condition at the beginning or the end of the loop, and the loop can continue `While` the condition is `True` or `Until` the condition becomes `True` (while it is `False`.) Thus, the syntax has four variations, as follows:

```
Do While condition            Do Until condition
.                             .
.statements                   .statements
.                             .
Loop                          Loop

Do                            Do
.                             .
.statements                   .statements
.                             .
Loop While condition          Loop Until condition
```

The `GetEntries` procedure uses a `Do/Loop` structure to loop over the 10 allowed lines of input in the receipt. In this case, the `Do While` construction is used with a condition that remains `True` until the value of `NumItems` is less than or equal to `MaxNumItems`:

```
Do While NumItems <= MaxNumItems
   'Get the name.
   theItem = InputBox("Item Name:", "Make Receipt")
   'If the user didn't enter anything, he must be done, so quit.
   If theItem = "" Then Exit Do
   'Get the cost.
   theCost = Val(InputBox("Item Cost:", "Make Receipt"))
   'Insert the item's name and cost on the worksheet.
   OutputRange.Cells(NumItems, 1).Formula = theItem
   OutputRange.Cells(NumItems, 2).Formula = Str(theCost)
   NumItems = NumItems + 1   'Increment the number of items.
Loop
```

All the statements between the `Do` statement and the `Loop` statement are executed until the condition becomes `False`. An exception occurs if the user presses Cancel and the `If` statement within the loop has a `True` condition.

```
If theItem = "" Then Exit Do
```

If the condition is `True`, the `Exit Do` statement is executed, immediately terminating the loop and starting execution at the statement following the `Loop` statement. An `Exit For` statement also exists for exiting a `For/Next` loop early.

For Each

The `For Each` loop is used to perform some action for all the elements of an array or collection. The syntax is as follows:

```
For Each element In group
    statements
Next element
```

The `For Each` loop applies to arrays and collections only. The loop executes one time for each element in the array or collection. This loop is useful when you don't know (or don't care) how many elements are in a collection. The loop variable *element* is the same data type as the elements in the *group* collection. Each time the loop is calculated, *element* takes on the value of another member of the collection.

Accessing Disk Files

If you have been playing with the example, you may have noticed that each time you create a new receipt, all the data values go away. What is missing is a way to save the data so you can retrieve and use it. You may want to know how many items of what type were sold, or you may want to calculate the total receipts for the day to compare with receipts in the cash box.

You have a couple of options: you can store the data in another worksheet so that the data is saved with the workbook, or you can open a disk file and store the data immediately. These methods have different advantages, depending on what you plan to do with the data. If you save the data in a worksheet, you can apply all Excel database functions to it. If you save the data in a disk file, other programs can open it directly. In this example, you are going to save the data in a disk file. Add code to the `PrintRange` procedure to add the data to the end of a data file, as shown here (the added lines are in bold):

```
'
' Print the receipt.
'
Sub PrintReceipt()
  Dim theRow As Integer
    theSheet.OnEntry = ""  'Turn off the automatic retotaling.
    theSheet.Range("PrintRange").PrintOut  'Print the worksheet.
```

```
'Save the data from the receipt.
Open "c:\data\examps.dat" For Append As #1
For theRow = 1 To MaxNumItems
   Write #1, OutputRange.Cells(theRow, 1).Value,
   Write #1, OutputRange.Cells(theRow, 2).Value
Next theRow
'Write the subtotal, tax, and total.
With OutputRange
   Write #1, "Subtotal",
   Write #1, .Cells(MaxNumItems + 1, 2).Value
   Write #1, "Tax",
   Write #1, .Cells(MaxNumItems + 2, 2).Value
   Write #1, "Total",
   Write #1, .Cells(MaxNumItems + 3, 2).Value
End With
Close #1
End Sub
```

Tip

It's generally not a good idea to place files in the root level of any hard drive.

In the added lines, the file is opened for appending, using a file number of 1. Appending places each new entry at the end of the file. The loop then copies the data from the worksheet and writes it to the file. The program still appears to work the same, but now the data is saved every time the Print Receipt button is clicked. After you enter the data and click the Print Receipt button, the following text is in EXAMPS.DAT:

```
"Pencils",2.35
"Accounting pad",1.8
"Printer paper - box",18.95
,
,
,
,
,
,
,
"Subtotal",23.1
"Tax",1.9058
"Total",25.0058
```

Notice that the Write statement delimits the data in the file by placing quotation marks around the strings of text and placing commas between items written to disk. These delimiters make it easy for you to use the Input statement to read the data back into a program for further processing. If you use Print rather than Write, the text and strings are written to the file without delimiters, creating a text file suitable for printing rather than for reading back into another program.

For more information about reading and writing files, search for *input* in the Visual Basic for Applications section of online help, and select the topic "Input and Output Keyword Summary."

Using Built-in Dialog Boxes

Visual Basic for Applications has two built-in dialog boxes that you can use in your programs to send data to the user and to get data from the user. The two dialog boxes are created with the MsgBox() and InputBox() functions. You already have used the InputBox() function to get data from the user in the Receipt Maker program. The MsgBox() function displays a dialog box containing a message and one or more buttons to be clicked to close the dialog box. Both functions take one or more arguments to set the prompt text, box title, number and type of buttons, and so on. See online help for a complete list of arguments.

In addition to these two dialog boxes, you can use two Excel dialog boxes to enhance your programs when opening and saving files. The two dialog boxes are displayed with the GetSaveAsFilename and GetOpenFilename methods.

The GetSaveAsFilename method displays the standard File Save As dialog box and gets a file name from the user. The dialog box does not really save anything; it only gets you a path and file name to use. You then must use the Open statement to actually create the file and save something in it. The GetOpenFilename method operates in the same way, but it displays the standard File Open dialog box instead.

Creating Custom Dialog Boxes

In addition to the built-in dialog boxes, you can create your own custom dialog boxes and attach them to a Visual Basic for Applications program. For example, the Receipt Maker program could use a data-entry form to replace the two dialog boxes necessary to input a single entry.

To make this change, perform the following steps:

1. Open the EXAMPS.XLS workbook, and save it as EXAMPS2.XLS.

2. Choose the Insert, Macro, Dialog command. Your worksheet should look like figure 35.9, with a blank custom dialog box and the Forms toolbar. The Forms toolbar can be floating or docked at the top or bottom of the page. The tools in the Forms toolbar are listed in table 35.4.

Fig. 35.9
A custom dialog box before editing. The Forms toolbar is floating at the top of the screen.

Forms toolbar —

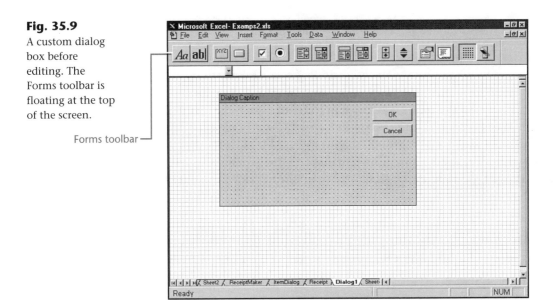

Tool	Tool Name	Description
Table 35.4	**Tools in the Forms Toolbar**	

Tool	Tool Name	Description
Aα	Label	Creates a text label.
ab|	Edit Box	Creates an edit box for inputting data.
xyz	Group Box	Creates a group frame to visually group other controls and to functionally group option buttons.
▭	Create Button	Creates a command button that can execute a procedure.
☑	Check Box	Creates a checkbox with a label for selecting nonexclusive options.
◉	Option Button	Creates an option button with a label for setting exclusive options. (Creates an option-button group within the Group frame.)

Tool	Tool Name	Description
	List Box	Creates a list box for selecting a value from a list of values in a scrollable box.
	Drop-Down	Creates a drop-down list box for selecting a value.
	Combination List-Edit	Creates a list-edit box (a combination of a list box and an edit box).
	Combination Drop-Down Edit	Creates a drop-down edit box (a combination of a drop-down listbox and an edit box).
	Scroll Bar	Creates a scroll bar for inputting a value by sliding a slider, or for using as an indicator of a value.
	Spinner	Creates a spinner for quickly stepping through a list of integer values.
	Control Properties	Displays the Properties dialog box for setting the properties of the selected control.
	Edit Code	Jumps to the procedure attached to the selected control.
	Toggle Grid	Turns on or off a grid to simplify the alignment of controls in a dialog box.
	Run Dialog	Activates the dialog box so that changing values or clicking buttons executes the attached procedures.

3. Select the dialog caption, type **Receipt Maker**, and click a blank portion of the dialog sheet.

4. Choose the Format, Sheet, Rename command and change the dialog sheet name to **ItemDialog**. Click OK.

5. Using the Label button in the Forms toolbar, draw two labels in the dialog box, as shown in figure 35.10. Select the caption of the first and type **Item Name:**. Select the caption of the second and type **ItemCost:**.

Fig. 35.10

Layout of the
Receipt Maker
dialog box.

6. Using the Edit Box button, draw two edit boxes in the dialog box, as shown in figure 35.10.

7. Select the edit box next to the Item Name label and change its name to **ItemNameBox**.

> **Note**
>
> To change the name of a control in a dialog sheet, select the control. Then click the name box on the left side of the edit bar, type the new name, and press Enter.

8. Select the edit box next to the Item Cost label and name it **ItemCostBox**.

9. Choose the Tools, Tab Order command. Select the ItemNameBox and move it to the top of the list; select the ItemCostBox, and move it just below the ItemNameBox. This procedure makes ItemNameBox the first thing selected when the dialog box appears. ItemCostBox is selected second, when the user presses the Tab key. Choose OK to complete the change in tab order.

10. Switch to the ReceiptMaker module, make the following changes in the GetEntries procedure (the changes are in bold), and save the workbook:

```
'
' Get entries.
'
Sub GetEntries()
  Dim theItem As String, theCost As Currency
  Dim theRow As Integer, NumItems As Integer
  Dim theDialog As Object
  'Define the pointer to the worksheet.
  Set theSheet = Application.Workbooks("Examps2.xls")
    Worksheets("Receipt")
  'Define the pointer to the top of the table of items.
  Set OutputRange = theSheet.Range("TopOfList")
  Set theDialog = Application.Workbooks("Examps2.xls")
    DialogSheets("ItemDialog")
```

```
        ClearRange OutputRange      'Clear the table of items.
    NumItems = 1
    'Ask for the name and cost for up to 10 items.
    Do While NumItems <= MaxNumItems
      'Clear the edit boxes.
      theDialog.EditBoxes("ItemNameBox").Text = ""
      theDialog.EditBoxes("ItemCostBox").Text = ""
      theDialog.Show
      'Get the name.
      theItem = theDialog.EditBoxes("ItemNameBox").Text
      'If the user didn't enter anything, he must be done, so quit.
      If theItem = "" Then Exit Do
      'Get the cost.
      theCost = Val(theDialog.EditBoxes("ItemCostBox").Text)
      'Insert the item's name and cost on the worksheet.
      OutputRange.Cells(NumItems, 1).Formula = theItem
      OutputRange.Cells(NumItems, 2).Formula = Str(theCost)
      NumItems = NumItems + 1  'Increment the number of items.
    Loop
    TotalIt   'Calculate and print the totals.
    'Retotal it if the user makes changes.
    theSheet.OnEntry = "TotalIt"
End Sub
```

The first change in the procedure defines a new object named `theDialog` that references the dialog sheet. That object then is used with the `EditBoxes` collection to clear the two edit boxes. The `Show` method is used to display the dialog box. After the user chooses the OK button, the contents of the two edit boxes are returned to the procedure and processed as before.

When you run the program by clicking the Make Receipt button in the worksheet, the dialog box appears, as shown in figure 35.11. Type the item's name, press Tab, type the item's cost, and press Enter. The first item is inserted into the receipt, and the dialog box appears again. To end entry, press Enter without typing anything in the dialog box. The totals are calculated.

Fig. 35.11
The Make Receipt dialog box.

Using the Debugging Tools

Program bugs are a fact of life for computer programmers. No matter how careful you are, bugs almost always appear; you must find them and remove them from your codes. The simplest bugs are *syntax errors*, in which the required parameters for the call were incorrect. VBA normally finds syntax errors as soon as you type them. Next are *run-time errors*, which are caused by using the wrong type of variable or by performing an improper numeric calculation (for example, taking the square root of -1). VBA also finds these errors as soon as the improper statement is executed. Last are *logical errors*, in which a program does not do what you want it to do. Logical errors are the most difficult to find because the program code compiles, but the program itself just doesn't do what you intended for it to do.

Visual Basic for Applications has a set of powerful debugging tools to help you find and correct program bugs. You can set breakpoints anywhere in your programs to force them to stop executing at that point. After you stop your program, choose Tools, Instant Watch to view the value of any variable or expression. You then can continue executing a program or step through it one statement at a time until you find your problem. You also can set watchpoints that automatically break a program when a variable or expression reaches a certain value.

Break Mode

Break mode is where an executing program is halted with all its variables still intact. Normally, when you end a program, the contents of all the variables are lost. However, break mode actually is a pausing of the executing program, so the contents of the variables that have been assigned values during program execution still are available.

> **Note**
>
> A running program enters break mode when you press Ctrl+Break, when it encounters an error, or when it encounters a breakpoint or watchpoint.

When a program enters break mode by encountering an error, or when you press Ctrl+Break, the Macro Error dialog box appears, giving you the choice to quit, continue, or open the Debug window.

Breakpoints and Watchpoints

Breakpoints and watchpoints also put a program into break mode. A *breakpoint* is a marker in a line of code that forces a program to stop executing when Visual Basic for Applications attempts to execute the marked line. A *watchpoint* is a marker in the value of a variable or a simple formula. When the value of a watchpoint changes in some specific way, the program is stopped and placed in break mode. Look at figure 35.12 at the *Sub* GetEntries() breakpoint. When this procedure is entered, break mode is entered. Because a breakpoint is entered, there is no data in the *Watch Pane*. There's no data to watch for!

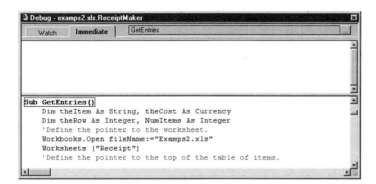

Fig. 35.12
The Debug
Window with a
breakpoint set.

To set a breakpoint, open the module containing your procedure and select
the line of code where you want the program to stop. Choose the Run, Toggle
Breakpoint command to set a breakpoint. Choose the command again to
remove a selected breakpoint, or choose the Run, Clear All Breakpoints command to remove all breakpoints. Then run your code. When it reaches a
breakpoint, the code stops and enters break mode. When a program enters
break mode by encountering a breakpoint or watchpoint, it goes directly to
the debug window, which is discussed in the following section.

The Debug Window

If you choose Debug in the Macro Error dialog box, or you encounter a
breakpoint or watchpoint, the Debug window appears (see fig. 35.13). The
Debug window is a split window, with the currently executing procedure in
the bottom half and the Immediate pane or the Watch pane at the top. In the
bottom half of the window, you can select lines of code, add or remove
breakpoints, and select code for watchpoints.

Tab to select Immediate pane   Calls window   Watch pane

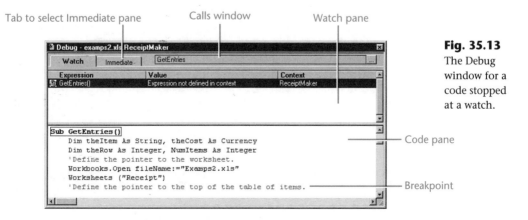

Fig. 35.13
The Debug
window for a
code stopped
at a watch.

Code pane

Breakpoint

The Debug window shown in figure 35.13 shows the code stopped at a breakpoint set in the `If` statement highlighted in the Code pane. The Watch pane shows the current value of `theItem`, `theCost`, and `theDialog.EditBoxes("ItemCostBox").Text` as watch variables. Notice that `theCost` has no value yet because it has not yet been passed the value in `theDialog.EditBoxes("ItemCostBox").Text`. At this point, you can continue execution of a procedure, set or delete more watchpoints, examine the value of variables, or step through the procedure one statement at a time.

The Immediate Pane

In the Immediate pane of the Debug window, you can type and execute almost any Visual Basic for Applications command. The only restriction is that the command must be only one line long. The Immediate pane also receives any printed values caused by the `Debug.Print` statement, used to print values from a running program.

The Watch Pane and Watch Expressions

The Watch pane displays the current value of watchpoints and watch expressions. Watchpoints, and watch expressions displayed in the Watch pane, continuously show the current value of the variables and expressions. The difference between these two is that although both show a value, a watch point can stop your code if the selected value changes in some specified way. You use the Instant watch to show the current value of a variable or expression without placing it in the Watch pane.

Figure 35.14 shows the result of selecting the variable `theItem` in the Debug window and choosing the Tools, Instant Watch command. If you choose the Add button, the Instant watch variable is changed into a watch expression and added to the Watch pane.

Fig. 35.14

An Instant Watch pane.

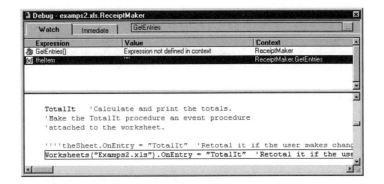

The Step Commands

At this point, you can use two step commands to execute one line of your program and stop again in break mode. Those commands are Run, Step Into and Run, Step Over. The Run, Step Into command makes the program execute one line at a time. If the program reaches a procedure, the next step occurs inside of that called procedure.

The Run, Step Over command is similar, but when it reaches a procedure call, it executes the procedure completely before stopping and going into break mode again. Thus, the Step Over command appears to step over procedure calls in the procedure you are executing.

The Calls Window

The window on the top right side of the Debug window shown in figure 35.13 shows the procedure that has been entered. If you click the ellipses box at the upper right of the DEBUG window, just below the X for the window itself, the Calls windows is opened. The Calls window shows the name of the procedure that contains the current point of execution. If you select the Calls window, it expands and lists all the active procedures in this program. Active procedures are those that are either performing the current task, or could have called some other procedure for another task.❖

Part VIII

Using Microsoft Office in a Group

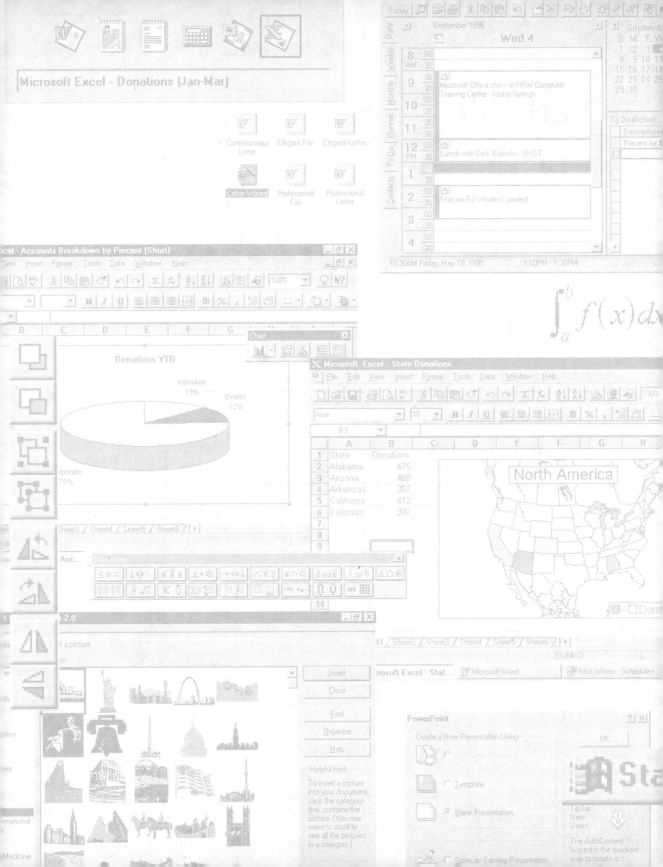

Chapter 36

Using Microsoft Exchange

by Robert Garrison

Microsoft Exchange enables you to send messages to people you work with. They don't even have to be connected to your network. In fact, you don't even have to be on a network either. You don't have to use any paper; your message appears on the recipients' computer screens, addressed to them. If you have a Microsoft Office product, you also can send or route documents to selected people. In addition, you can copy portions of a document or attach entire documents to a message.

The software for Microsoft Exchange is part of Windows 95. Microsoft Exchange is a tool that enables you to communicate with other people. Even if you don't have a network, this chapter may be relevant to you because Microsoft Exchange lets you communicate with others through service providers such as The Microsoft Network or CompuServe.

> **Note**
>
> Exchange messages sent to non-Exchange users may appear differently if they don't support the rich text format.

In this chapter, you learn to

- Start Exchange and create a message
- Copy information from a Word document and an Excel document to Exchange
- Attach Office files to a document in Exchange

■ Send a document through Exchange

■ Route a document

> **Note**
>
> The figures in this chapter reflect the use of Microsoft Exchange used on a system running Windows 95. Your figures may vary slightly if you run Windows NT or Windows for Workgroups.

Starting Exchange and Addressing the Message

Starting Exchange is similar to starting any other Windows program. You load Microsoft Exchange by double-clicking the Inbox on your desktop. Choosing the Inbox starts the Exchange program with the Inbox as the active folder. If Exchange is already running, you can switch to it by selecting its icon on the taskbar. Opening Exchange displays the window shown in figure 36.1. To open another message folder, double-click the folder. To start a message, click the New Message button or choose Compose New Message.

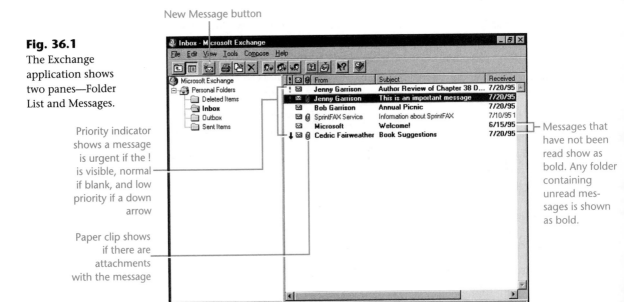

New Message button

Fig. 36.1
The Exchange application shows two panes—Folder List and Messages.

Priority indicator shows a message is urgent if the ! is visible, normal if blank, and low priority if a down arrow

Paper clip shows if there are attachments with the message

Messages that have not been read show as bold. Any folder containing unread messages is shown as bold.

Like all other Windows applications, the Exchange window has a menu bar and toolbar. You can use the toolbar to compose, reply to, read, move, or delete a message. The following table lists the Exchange toolbar buttons:

Button	Name
	Up one level
	Show\Hide Folders List
	New Message
	Print
	Move Item
	Delete
	Reply to sender
	Reply to all
	Forward
	Address Book
	Inbox
	Help
	Show Schedule

Tip

Click Show\Hide Folder List to toggle the Folder List pane. This expands the width of the message list when the Folder List is hidden.

VIII

Using Office in a Group

Creating a Personal Distribution List

Suppose as office manager of Collector's Loot, you want to send messages to other collectors, your staff, and your publisher. You know that they have various methods of receiving messages. You want to be able to send messages to these individuals as a group or to send to their individual addresses. You decide to create a personal distribution list for Collector's Loot so that you don't have to include multiple names when you address a message.

To create a distribution list, follow these steps:

1. Choose Tools, Address Book, or click the Address Book button. Then click the New Entry button. A New Entry dialog box appears, showing a list of entries you can create, as shown in figure 36.2.

Fig 36.2

You can maintain your Address Book by adding fax, mail, or Personal Distribution Lists.

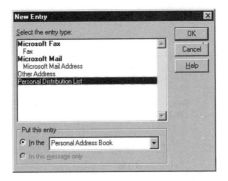

2. To create a new distribution list, select the Personal Distribution List. After you click OK, the New Personal Distribution List Properties sheet appears, as in figure 36.3.

Fig. 36.3

The New Personal Distribution List Properties sheet includes the personal distribution list that makes it easy to send messages to selected groups of people.

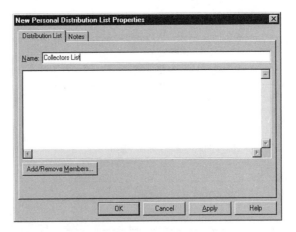

3. Type the name of the distribution list, **Collectors List**, in the Name: text box.

4. Click the Add/Remove Members button. The Edit Members of Collectors List appears, as shown in figure 36.4.

> **Note**
>
> If you don't type a distribution list name in step 3, the menu title will read New Personal Distribution List Members.

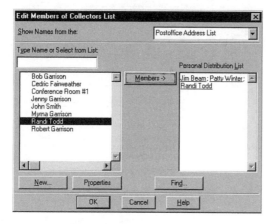

Fig 36.4
The personal distribution list lets you add names of people you regularly correspond with as a group.

5. Choose the correct address book from the Show Names from the list box.

6. Type the individual's name or select it from the list. You can double-click the name or click the Members button.

7. Repeat steps 5 and 6 as desired. When you finish adding names, click OK. You return to the New Personal Distribution List Properties sheet.

8. Choose OK.

9. Close the Address Book.

Tip
You can select names from more than one address book source for your distribution list.

Creating a Message

Creating a message is just like preparing a typed memo. You have to address the message to someone, indicate who you want copies to go to, and then type the message.

VIII

Using Office in a Group

To create and address the message, follow these steps:

1. Click New Message or choose Compose, New Message. The New Microsoft Exchange window appears, as shown in figure 36.5.

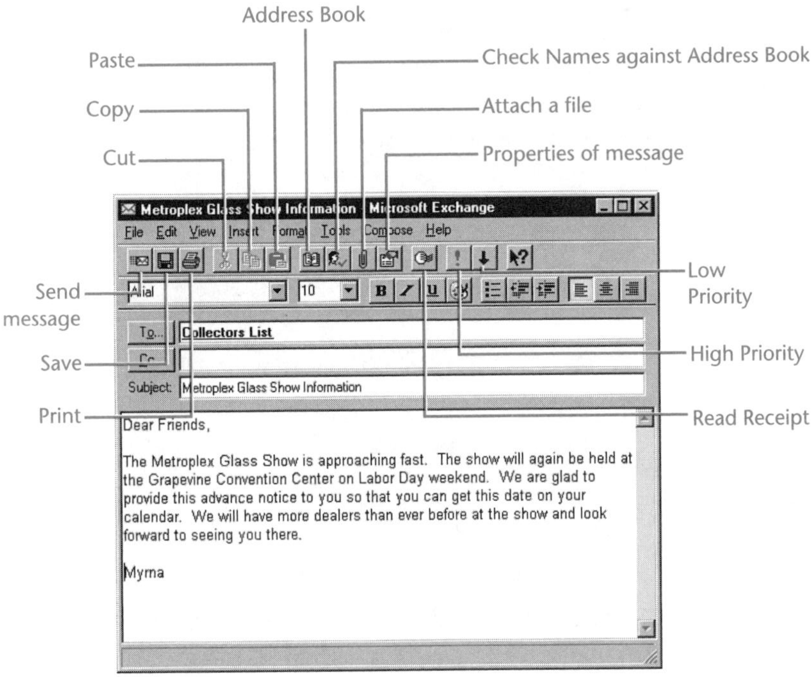

Address Book

Paste

Copy

Cut

Check Names against Address Book

Attach a file

Properties of message

Fig. 36.5
Use the Message window to complete a fill-in-the-blank form similar to a paper memo pad, but with lots more powerful options for sending the message almost anywhere.

Send message

Save

Print

Low Priority

High Priority

Read Receipt

> Metroplex Glass Show Information Microsoft Exchange
>
> File Edit View Insert Format Tools Compose Help
>
> Arial   10   B I U
>
> To...   Collectors List
>
> Cc
>
> Subject: Metroplex Glass Show Information
>
> Dear Friends,
>
> The Metroplex Glass Show is approaching fast. The show will again be held at the Grapevine Convention Center on Labor Day weekend. We are glad to provide this advance notice to you so that you can get this date on your calendar. We will have more dealers than ever before at the show and look forward to seeing you there.
>
> Myrna

2. To address the message, click the To box and do one of the following:

- Type the names of the individuals or groups. If you have more than one entry you must separate the entries with semicolons.

- Click the To button or choose select names from the Tools menu. An Address Book dialog box will appear. Select a name from the appropriate address book and choose either To or Cc. (By pressing the Cc button as needed, you can skip step 3.)

3. If necessary, move to the Cc text box and repeat step 2 for other recipients.

4. You should check names to see whether they are spelled correctly and that they are part of the current address list if you typed them manually. To do so, click the Check Names button. Names that were originally typed are not underlined. If they pass the Check Names and are valid, Exchange will underline the addressee.

5. Click the message input area, or press Tab to get to the message input area. Then type your message.

6. When you finish and are ready to send the message, press Ctrl+Enter or click Send.

Copying Information from a Document to an Exchange Message

Suppose that you want to use text from existing documents in your invitation to exhibit at your next show. To copy information into an Exchange message, you follow the same procedures as in any Office application. The following sections explain how to use the Paste command to copy text with default formatting from the source application, and how to change formatting from other applications with the Paste Special command.

Copying Text with Default Formatting

To copy information from an existing document, follow these steps:

1. Address the Exchange message and type any desired text in the Exchange text window.

2. Click the appropriate application icon in the Program Bar on the Microsoft Office Shortcut bar, and open the document.

3. Select the information you want to copy, as shown in figure 36.6.

4. Choose Edit, Copy, or press Ctrl+C.

5. Press Alt+Tab until the message name you want to paste into appears.

6. Move the insertion point to the place in the Exchange message where you want to insert the text.

7. Choose Edit, Paste, or press Ctrl+V. The text or object appears in the message, as shown in figure 36.7.

Fig. 36.6
Windows makes it
easy to copy text
from a Word
document to
Exchange. Just
select the portion
of the text or
graphics you want
to copy.

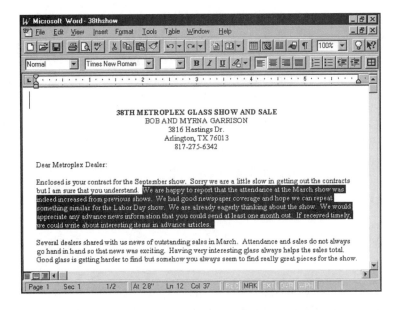

Fig. 36.7
This message text
was pasted from a
Word document
and Excel
worksheet.

Pasted from a Word
document. The de-
fault for paste is to
retain the format of
the document, but
it's inserted as text.
It does not maintain
a link to Word.

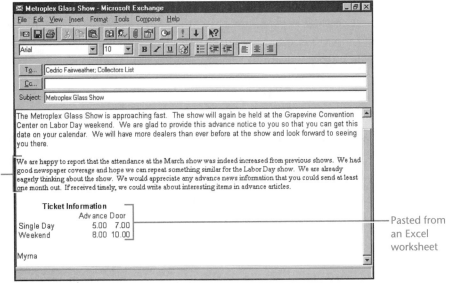

Pasted from
an Excel
worksheet

Using Paste Special to Change Formatting

In figure 36.7, notice that the text from the Word document retained its
formatting, but is a part of the Exchange text and that the data from the
Excel worksheet is an object with full Excel functionality. You can use Paste

<u>S</u>pecial to change the default formatting from other applications when you paste into Exchange. Try the following to see how to use Paste <u>S</u>pecial:

Click <u>E</u>dit, Paste <u>S</u>pecial. The Paste Special dialog box appears, displaying formatting options for the source application, as shown in figure 36.8.

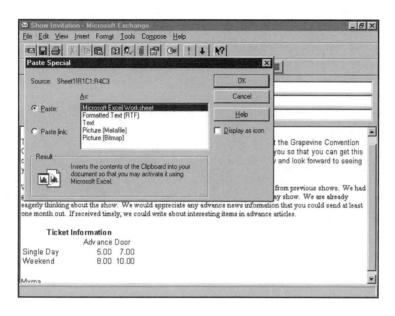

Fig. 36.8
In this example, the Paste Special dialog box contains Excel formatting options.

Select one of the formats, as described in the following list:

■ To insert the selection without formatting, choose Text in the <u>A</u>s box.

> ### Caution
>
> If the selected text was an Excel worksheet, tabs will separate the data but columns may not align correctly. If you select Text, you probably will have to add tabs for the selection if you want the information to align properly. Place your cursor in front of the text to be aligned and press Tab.

■ To insert the copy from the Clipboard as an object, select the choice that identifies the object. In figure 36.8, the list box indicates Microsoft Excel Worksheet. If you double-click the object, you enter the application that created the object; you then can edit the object using the source application's menu, toolbar, and other commands.

VIII

Using Office in a Group

■ To insert the selection as a graphic, choose Picture (Metafile) or Picture (Bitmap). Both options insert the selection as a diagram, but a metafile generally takes less room in the file and prints faster.

> **Note**
>
> For information on linking to a file, see "Attaching Word, Excel, or PowerPoint Files to Your Message" later in this chapter. The options available depend on your source application.

In figure 36.9, a formatted spreadsheet is inserted as a picture into the Exchange message.

Fig. 36.9
A formatted spreadsheet is inserted into the message.

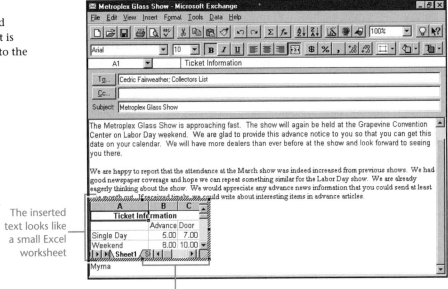

The inserted text looks like a small Excel worksheet

If you click within the spreadsheet area, small handles enable you to change the size

Choosing Edit, Paste Special after copying from a Word document gives you four formatting choices: Microsoft Word Document, Formatted Text (RTF), Text and Picture (Metafile). Figure 36.10 shows text pasted using the picture format.

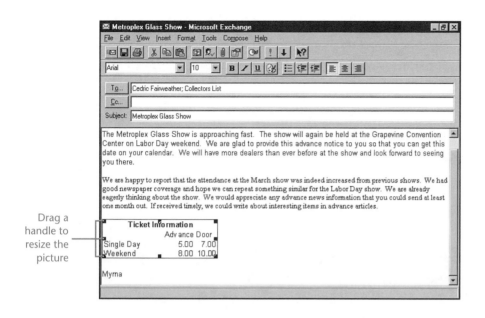

Fig. 36.10
Text or graphics
are pasted from a
Word document
into an Exchange
message.

Drag a
handle to
resize the
picture

VIII

Using Office in a Group

Attaching Word, Excel, or PowerPoint Files to Your Message

If a document is longer than you want in the message, or is a file you want
the recipient to use in an application, you can add it as an attachment to
your message with the Attach button. You can attach more than one document to each message. The attachments can be any type of file you might
have on your computer, not just Office documents.

To attach a file to your message, follow these steps:

1. In the Exchange message, move the cursor to where you want to attach
   the document.

2. Click the Attach button, or choose Insert, File. The Insert File dialog box
   appears.

3. Identify the name and location of the file. You navigate the Insert File
   just as you would on a File Open.

4. A document icon appears in your message, showing the file name and
   icon of the application that created the file, as shown in figure 36.11.

> **Note**
>
> If the file extension isn't recognized by Windows, the icon will be a generic file icon.

5. Repeat steps 3 and 4 for each file you want to attach.

6. When you finish attaching files, click OK.

7. Finish typing the message, and send it by clicking the Send button.

Figure 36.11 shows a completed message with multiple files attached.

Fig. 36.11
An exchange message can be used to send multiple files to a recipient as attachments.

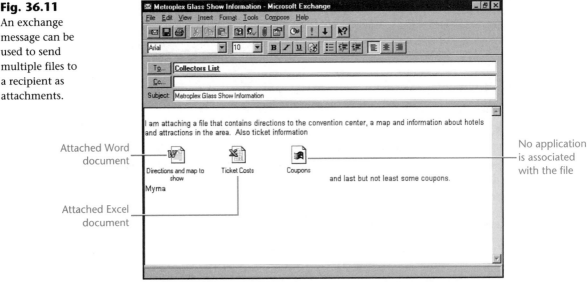

Attached Word document

Attached Excel document

No application is associated with the file

> **Note**
>
> If Windows does not recognize the extension, no application is associated with the file, and a Microsoft icon appears with the file name.

Troubleshooting

I tried double-clicking an icon, and I received the message that no application is associated with the file.

If no association exists, you might be able to figure out the type of file by looking at it with Quick View. Right-click on the icon and then click Quick View. If the document is in a compatible format, you will be able to read the text. If you can't read it, you need to ask the sender to provide more information about what program you need to use with the file.

If you type file extensions (up to three characters after a period) when you create file names, Windows may not know what application created the file, and the recipient cannot double-click the icon to open the file. You will also have this problem if you type a period at the end of the file name and type no extension—this prevents the application from adding its default extension.

Moving or Deleting an Attached File

Sometimes you might make a mistake and attach the wrong file to your message, or decide you want it in another place. It's easy to move or delete the attached file. Follow these steps:

1. Select the attached file by clicking its icon. A box will appear around the attached file. Click the right mouse button, and a pop-up menu will appear as in figure 36.12. Choose Cut to remove the document so that you can paste it in another location. If you don't need to paste the file somewhere else you can press the Delete key and the attachment will be removed.

2. If you want to move the document to a different place, click the mouse at the new point, then right-click the mouse and choose Paste.

Caution

The placement of files within the message is only preserved in Microsoft Exchange messages. If your recipient is on an information service that doesn't support the Exchange format, the attachments will appear differently.

Fig. 36.12
An attached file
can be moved
within, or deleted
from, a message.

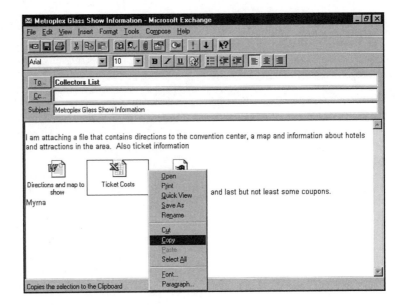

Sending a Document

If you are working in a Microsoft Office application, you do not have to switch to Exchange to send that document. When you send a document from within an Office application, you are asked for the recipients' names, the subject of the message, and additional message text.

To send a document from Word, Excel, PowerPoint or the Binder to an Exchange recipient, follow these steps:

1. Open the application and the file you want to send.

2. Choose File, Send. The application will launch Microsoft Exchange.

3. In the Exchange message dialog box, fill in the address and subject boxes, and type a message if desired, as shown in figure 36.13. (At this point, you're in the full Exchange program and can use all its features.)

4. Click the Send button or press Ctrl+Enter to send the file. After sending the file, you return to the source application.

Troubleshooting

My File menu does not show Send or Add Routing Slip.

You probably don't have Exchange loaded correctly, or you may be missing the MAP1=1 entry in the [MAIL] section of your WIN.INI file. Contact your system administrator for help.

My mail message shows the text of my document instead of an icon.

Choose Tools, Options and select the General tab. Be sure Mail As Attachment is checked.

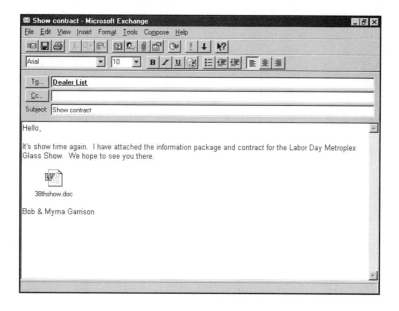

Fig. 36.13
After you choose File, Send, a Compose Mail window appears, enabling you to identify the recipient(s) and type a subject. There is an icon of your document already present.

VIII

Using Office in a Group

Reading a Sent Document

Now that we know how to send messages, what do we do when we receive one? To read any message, including one with an attached document, follow these steps:

1. Start or switch to the Exchange program. If Exchange is minimized then click its button on the taskbar. If you need to start it, then double-click the Inbox icon on the desktop.

2. If the Inbox folder is not highlighted, double-click the Inbox folder.

3. You want to read the message with the attached file. Double-click that unread message as shown in figure 36.14. When you open the message, you see an icon for the attached file.

Fig. 36.14
An unread message shows as a bold line. The paper clip indicates that there is an attached file.

Double-click the message icon or message subject to open the message

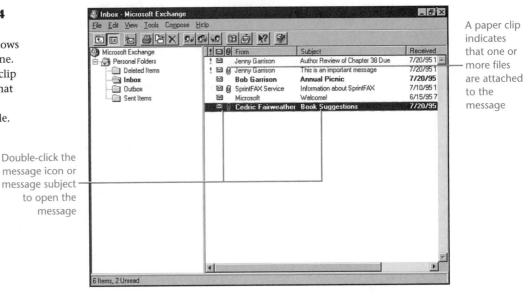

A paper clip indicates that one or more files are attached to the message

4. Double-click the file icon to open the application that is associated with the file type.

5. Read or edit the document. Close the document when you finish.

6. To return to the Exchange message, click the Microsoft Exchange button in the Program Bar of the Microsoft Office Shortcut bar.

7. When you finish reading the message, choose File, Delete, or click the Delete button. If you want to save and close your message by clicking the Close button.

If you want to reply to the message, you have two options:

■ You can send a normal message.

■ You can click the Reply button to show the original sender a copy of the original message and provide room for a reply. When you use the Reply button, you don't have to address the message; it is already addressed for you.

To reply to the message, follow these steps:

1. With the message open, click the Reply button, or press Ctrl+R. The message and address change, as shown in figure 36.15.

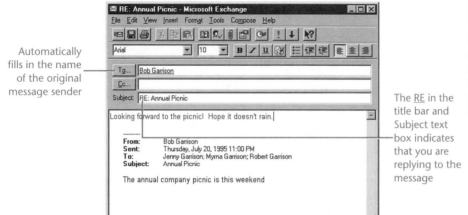

Automatically fills in the name of the original message sender

Fig. 36.15
When you click the Reply button, an extra line appears before the message, enabling you to insert your response.

The RE in the title bar and Subject text box indicates that you are replying to the message

2. Type your message at the insertion point before the message.

3. When you finish your reply, click Send, or press Alt+S.

Routing a Document

As an alternative to sending a document, you can route it to selected parties if you have this option enabled in Office. With routing, you can track the document's location; you also can send it simultaneously to all recipients or to one recipient after the other.

Creating a Routed Mail Message

To route a document from an Office application, follow these steps:

1. In the application, choose File, Add Routing Slip. The Routing Slip dialog box appears.

2. Choose Address, and select the names of the people to whom you want to send your document. When you click OK the Routing Slip shows who the document will be routed to, as shown in figure 36.16.

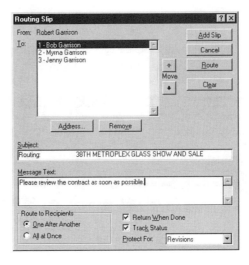

3. To change the order of the list, select a name and use the Move up or down arrow beside the list box.

4. To remove a name from the list, click Remove.

5. The Subject text box automatically includes Routing and the name of the document. To change what appears in the recipient mail folder, edit the text in this box.

6. In the Message Text box, add any information that appears in the message text area before the document.

7. In the Route to Recipients area, specify whether you want to route this file simultaneously to every recipient All at Once or to One After Another.

8. If you want to be notified via your Exchange Inbox of the status every time someone reads the document, select Track Status.

9. If you want the final document returned to you at the end of the routing, select Return When Done.

10. In the Protect For drop-down list box, specify whether you want to protect part or all of your document so that recipients can only view the document, and not make any changes.

11. When you finish, click the Route button to begin routing the document.

Working with Routed Mail

When the recipients open Exchange, they see a message indicating that they have new mail. When they double-click the unread message, they see your correspondence with the attached file and any instructions you include, as well as instructions on how to continue the routing, as shown in figure 36.17.

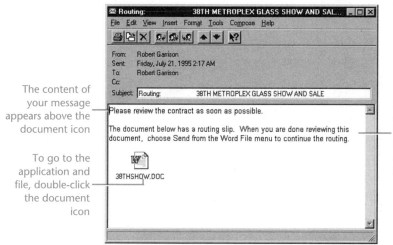

The content of your message appears above the document icon

To go to the application and file, double-click the document icon

Exchange instructs you to choose File Send from the Word menu to continue the routing (or return to the originator at the end of the line)

Fig. 36.17
The recipient sees the message and attached file.

VIII

Using Office in a Group

> **Note**
>
> Unless you add a note in the message text or subject area, the recipients of a sequential routing (except the first one in the list) won't know who originally routed the document. Make sure that you include a message informing recipients that you sent the document if it's important for them to know.

Each recipient can make notes in the document. When you receive the document, you will see the annotations and revision changes, as shown in figure 36.18. To see annotation marks, click the Show/Hide button in the toolbar. To see the annotations themselves, choose View, Annotations, or double-click one of the annotation marks.

> **Note**
>
> Revision markings for inserted and deleted text can be in different colors for up to eight authors. Do the following: Set Color: By Author in Tools, Options Revisions.

▶ See "Using Microsoft Office on a Network," p. 859

Fig. 36.18
When the document is returned to you, the comments and corrections reveal how others think your document should be changed.

Added or deleted text

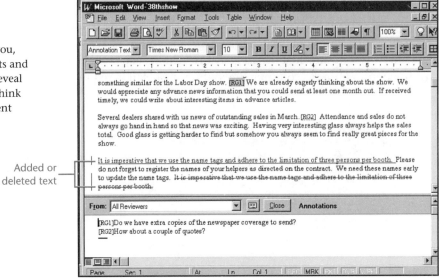

Chapter 37

Using Schedule+

by Robert Garrison

What was it I said that I would do the day after tomorrow? In today's fast-paced work environment, it is difficult to keep track of all your commitments. You can think of Schedule+ as being a Personal Information Manager, but it is really much more. With features like appointments, tasks, contacts, events, and the Seven Habits Wizard, you'll find Schedule+ to be an excellent assistant.

In this chapter, you learn to

- Start Schedule+

- Use the Schedule+ Screen

- Schedule an appointment

- Maintain a contact list

- Maintain a To Do list

- Print a schedule

- Use the Seven Habits Wizard

Starting Schedule+

There are five ways to start the Schedule+ program, which you will learn here. Which one you use will depend on the way you use Schedule+.

You can start Schedule+ in one of the following ways:

- Choose Start from the taskbar and then choose Programs, Microsoft Schedule+.

- Choose one of the buttons from the Microsoft Office Shortcut bar to access any of three parts of Schedule+:

To open Schedule+ and go directly to inserting a new appointment. For more information, see the following section, "Making Appointments."

 To open Schedule+ and go directly to adding a To Do item. For more information, see the section "Creating Tasks."

 To open Schedule+ and go directly to adding a new contact. For more information, see the section "Managing Contacts."

- In Word, you can click on the Insert Address button if you want to insert an address from your Schedule+ Contact List.

- If you are on a network and use Microsoft Exchange, you do not have to start Exchange first. Schedule+ will ask if you want to work in a group or alone. You choose <u>Y</u>es, Work in Group-Enabled Mode if you want to perform group meeting scheduling. If you simply want to work in your personal calendar and don't need any group meetings scheduled, you can click the <u>N</u>o, Work Alone button. Click OK to continue.

> **Note**
>
> After selecting Yes or No, you can click <u>D</u>on't Ask Me This Question Again. Schedule+ will use this setup in the future.

- If you are not already running Exchange, you will be asked to log in to the Microsoft Exchange. The Choose Profile dialog box allows you to select the MS Exchange Settings you want to use.

Following completion of the Choose Profile, you will be asked to log in to Microsoft Mail. During the login process, you may be prompted for the location of your postoffice, your mailbox name, and a password.

> **Caution**
>
> Using <u>R</u>emember Password will allow anyone to start and access your Microsoft Exchange if they have access to your computer.

You have now started Schedule+ and can begin reaping the benefits of technology in organizing your time.

Exploring the Screen

When you start Schedule+, you see the Schedule+ window on-screen (see fig. 37.1). Table 37.1 describes the buttons on the Schedule+ toolbar.

Note

If you used one of the Microsoft Office Shortcut Bar buttons to start, then the dialog box in figure 37.1 will appear on top of the Schedule+ window.

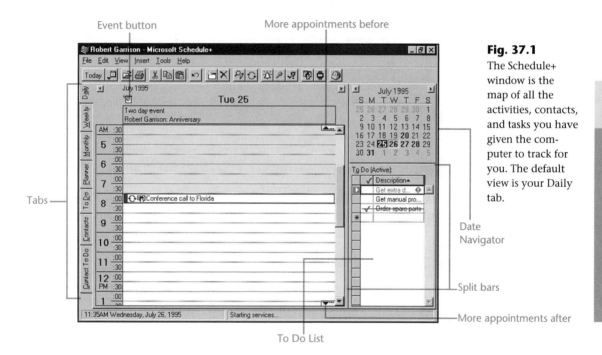

Fig. 37.1

The Schedule+ window is the map of all the activities, contacts, and tasks you have given the computer to track for you. The default view is your Daily tab.

VIII

Using Office in a Group

Moving the split bars allows you to change the size of the Appointment Book, Date Navigator, and To Do list. Making the Date Navigator larger can show more days before or after the current month.

Note

If you have appointments late in the day, the appointment may not be visible because they will be scrolled off the screen. If there is an appointment below the bottom of the screen, a down arrow with an ellipsis (...) after it next to the scroll bar will indicate you have appointments below.

Table 37.1 Buttons on the Schedule+ Standard Toolbar		
Button	**Name**	**Description**
Today	Select Today	Moves to today's date
	Go To Date	Use Date Navigator to change dates
	Open	Displays the Open Other's Appt. Book
	Print	Displays the Print dialog box
	Cut	Removes the selected text or object, placing it on the clipboard
	Paste	Pastes the clipboard contents at the current cursor location
	Undo	Reverses the most recent action. Not all actions (commands) can be reversed.
	Insert New Appointment	Inserts New Appointment
	Delete	Deletes the selected item
	Edit	Edits the item's detail information
	Recurring	Makes an item recurring or creates a new item
	Reminder	Sets a reminder for the item
	Private	Toggles the Private status of an item

Button	Name	Description
	Tentative	Toggles an appointment's tentative status
	Meeting Wizard	Activates Meeting Wizard
	Timex Watch Wizard	Activates Timex Wizard
	View mail	Starts or changes Microsoft Exchange
	Events	Inserts an event or annual event

VIII

Using Office in a Group

Note

When you are in each of the tabs (Appointments, To Do tasks, Contacts), the Insert button on the toolbar changes to Insert New Appointment, Insert New Task, Insert New Contact.

The tabs along the left side of the window enable you to select different views of your personal information manager. The tabs are described briefly in table 37.2.

Table 37.2   Tabs on the Schedule+ Window

Tab	Description
Daily	Gives a schedule for the current day, the Date Navigator, and a list of the active To Do's you have.
Weekly	Shows the next five days of appointments.
Monthly	Shows the entire month of your appointments.
Planner	Shows the meetings you have scheduled and who is attending them.

(continues)

Table 37.2 Continued	
Tab	**Description**
To Do list	Shows an expanded view of all your tasks and projects.
Contacts	Reveals your contact information for business and friends.

The tabs are explained later in this chapter.

Scheduling Your Time

If you are in a hurry, you can create a quick appointment. If you can take more time, however, you can tell Schedule+ more about your appointment by using the Insert New Appointment button. More information is retained to help you keep track of details.

Adding an Appointment

To quickly schedule your appointments, follow these short steps:

Tip
If you right-click the Date Navigator, you can move quickly to Today or Go To a date that you enter in the Date box.

1. Using the Date Navigator, click the day that you want to make the appointment. You can use the left- and right-arrow buttons to change months.

2. Select the appointment time by clicking the beginning time and dragging through the ending time of your appointment.

   Note

   You can make an appointment with someone in your contact list. See the section "Managing your Contacts" later in this chapter.

3. Type the information for your appointment. Be sure to include the name of the person with whom you are meeting. Your completed appointment will look similar to figure 37.2.

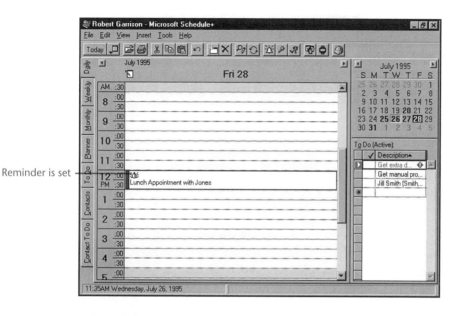

Reminder is set

Fig. 37.2
This shows an appointment entered by typing directly into the Appointment Book. The entry is completely free form.

VIII

Using Office in a Group

Note

If the Reminder icon appears, your defaults have a Set Reminder turned on. See "Customizing Schedule+" for more information.

If you later want to expand the information about this appointment you can double-click the appointment or click the Edit button if the appointment is already selected. See "Editing an Appointment" later in this chapter.

You can choose to use the Insert New Appointment button on the toolbar to gather more detail about your appointment at the time you are making it. Just follow these steps:

1. Click Insert New Appointment. The Appointment dialog box opens (see fig. 37.3).

   The Attendees tab, Notes tab, and Planner tab are discussed later in the chapter. Note the icons next to Where, Set Reminder, Private, and Tentative. These icons will show in the appointment item if they are checked.

2. Set the Start and End dates and times. The down arrows next to the Start and End dates pop up a Date Navigator calendar.

Tip
To change the ending time of an appointment, click and drag the bottom border of the appointment to the new ending time.

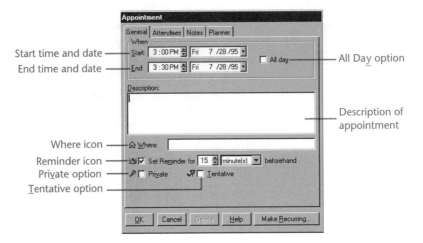

Start time and date / End time and date / All Day option / Description of appointment / Where icon / Reminder icon / Private option / Tentative option

3. Click the Description box and type in the information you want to show in the appointment.

4. Complete the other options. Table 37.3 shows the function of each option.

Table 37.3 Appointment Options

Option	Purpose
Where	Shows location where the appointment will be held
Set Reminder	Sets the number of minutes (hours, days, weeks, or months) to notify you before the appointment
Private	Prevents others from viewing the appointment text
Tentative	Indicates that this appointment is "penciled in"

5. Click OK to accept the appointment.

Editing an Appointment

To edit an appointment, select the appointment by either clicking it and then clicking the Edit button or by double-clicking the appointment. This will open the Appointment dialog box (see previous section). When you have made the changes needed, click OK.

Troubleshooting

Sometimes I double-click the appointment but it doesn't open the Appointment dialog box.

If you double-click in the text portion, you are editing just the Description. Double-click the border or an icon within the appointment.

Deleting an Appointment

To delete an Appointment, select the appointment and click Delete or <u>E</u>dit <u>D</u>elete Item.

> **Note**
>
> Pressing the Delete key will delete only a character of the Description.

Moving an Appointment

If you need to reschedule the appointment to a different day or time, you can choose one of the following methods:

- Edit the Start and Stop times and dates.

- Drag and drop the appointment to a new date on Date Navigator if the appointment will be at the same time.

- Drag and drop to a new time on the current date.

- Choose <u>E</u>dit, <u>M</u>ove Appointment and change the time and date.

◄ See "Moving around the Document," p. 75

> **Note**
>
> You can move an appointment between two schedules by using drag and drop. See "Managing the Schedule+ File" for information on multiple schedules.

Tip

If you are already editing an appointment, you can use the Make <u>R</u>ecurring button to change it from a single appointment to a recurring appointment.

Making Recurring Appointments

Often an appointment will be scheduled at regular intervals. You can change an appointment to a recurring meeting. Say that you have a meeting today with your boss. He now wants to meet every Tuesday and Thursday. To make the appointment recurring, follow these steps:

1. Select the appointment you want to make into a recurring appointment by clicking on it. Then you may perform one of these actions to open the Appointment Series When tab, as in figure 37.4:

   ■ Choose Insert, Make Recurring.

   ■ Click the Recurring button.

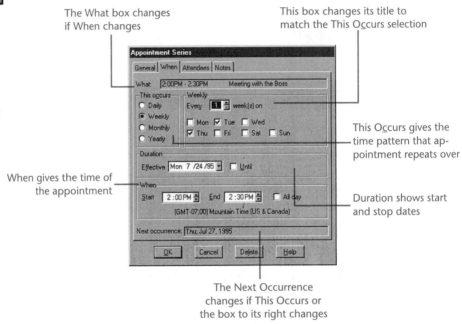

The What box changes if When changes

This box changes its title to match the This Occurs selection

Fig. 37.4
Convert an appointment to a recurring appointment by changing the pattern of the schedule in the Appointment Series.

This Occurs gives the time pattern that appointment repeats over

When gives the time of the appointment

Duration shows start and stop dates

The Next Occurrence changes if This Occurs or the box to its right changes

Tip
Choose Insert, Recurring Appointment to create a new appointment and make it recurring at the same time.

2. The Appointment Series When is flexible enough to schedule a recurring appointment on a daily, weekly, monthly or annual basis. Click This Occurs Weekly radio button. The right box will show Weekly.

3. Click Tue and Thu to check their boxes.

4. Click OK to schedule the recurring appointment.

Note

If you need to change the recurring appointment, click Edit on one of the appointments, then click Edit Series. The When tab of the Appointment Series will be displayed. You can make any changes then. If you want to stop having the recurring appointment click Delete.

Changing an Appointment into a Meeting

Sometimes you might make an appointment with someone and then decide
it should be a full-blown meeting. If that happens you can change an appointment to a meeting by doing the following steps:

1. Click Edit, then click the Attendees tab (see fig. 37.5).

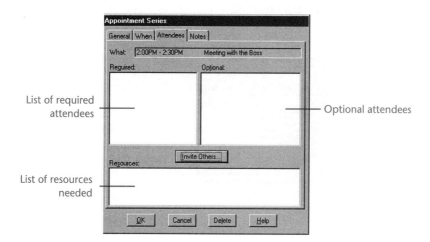

List of required
attendees

Optional attendees

List of resources
needed

Fig. 37.5
You can use the
Attendees tab to
invite other people
to a previously
scheduled
appointment.

2. Click Invite Others, and the Meeting Attendees dialog box opens (see
fig. 37.6).

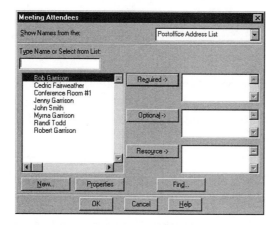

Fig. 37.6
Select the indi-
viduals to attend
the meeting.
Attendance can
be required or
optional.

3. Highlight a name from the Select List and click one of the following:

■ Required. The individual must come.

■ Optional. The individual is invited, but doesn't have to attend.

■ Reso<u>u</u>rce. The name represents a resource, such as a conference room and is needed for the meeting.

◄ See "Creating a Message," p. 813

4. Click OK. You return to the Attendees tab, and the newly invited attendees are listed in their respective boxes.

5. Click OK again and a Meeting Request window opens and allows you to send a message via Microsoft Exchange to invite others to the meeting (see fig. 37.7).

Fig. 37.7
Schedule+ automatically composes a Meeting Request to meeting invitees. All you add is the text of the message.

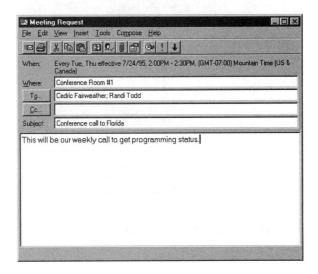

6. Add any additional information about the meeting and click the Send button.

You now have made your appointment an official meeting with others invited. You can check the status of the attendees by selecting the meeting, clicking Edit and then clicking Planner. The Appointment Planner tab opens (see fig. 37.8).

Troubleshooting

I don't have an <u>I</u>nvite button on the Attendees tab.

When you started Schedule+, you selected to work in stand-alone mode. You must exit Schedule+ and restart in group-enabled mode.

Fig. 37.8
The Attendees list
shows the status
of the meeting's
attendees and
resources.
A question mark
indicates they
have not re-
sponded to the
invitations.
A checkmark is a
confirmation and
an X is a decline.

Creating Events

During the course of the year, you probably have several events that you
want to remember. These may be birthdays for your family or an anniversary.
Or it could be a special occasion you want to remember. You can add an
event to Schedule+ by choosing one of the following methods:

- Choose Insert, Event or click the Events button to add an event that
  occurs over a specific time. Set the start and end date of the event, type
  a description of the event, and indicate whether you need a reminder
  and if the event is private.

- Choose Insert, Annual Event to add an event that occurs annually.

- Enter birthdays and anniversaries in the Contacts tab. See "Managing
  Contacts" later in this chapter.

Note

If there are more than two events on a day, then you will see a down arrow that
indicates more events are present. Click within the event box to see the additional
events.

Troubleshooting

I have entered events in the Schedule. Why can't I see them?

Choose Tools, Options and Display tab. Show Events must be checked for the events
to appear.

Using the To Do List

Tip
If you are on the
To Do tab or the
Daily To Do List,
you can click Add
a Task to create a
new task.

A task is any specific activity that you want to do and track to its completion. It could be work related or personal. Tracking a task in Schedule+ can be as simple as "is it done" to monitoring percent completion and setting reminders about the task. Tasks are visible on any Appointment Book tab that has a To Do list on it. You can also group related tasks into projects.

Creating a Task

The simplest way to create a task is to be on the Daily tab. Just right-click the To Do list, and then click New Task to display the dialog box shown in figure 37.9.

Fig. 37.9
Creating a task on
the To Do list helps
you remember
those little things
that you tend to
forget.

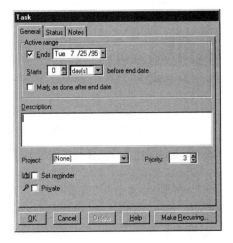

You can assign a task to a project by typing a project name in Project or by selecting it from the Project selection list.

Creating Projects

Tip
You assign a task
to a project by
entering the
project name in
the Task dialog
box's Project box.

A project is a collection of related tasks that you want to track. You can create a project from the beginning and add tasks as you go, or you can decide you have a number of tasks that you want to track as a project. To create a project, do one of the following:

■ Click Insert, Project.

■ Right-click the To Do list if you are on either the Daily tab or To Do tab, and then click New Project.

The Project dialog box opens. Type the project name in the Name box, set the Priority level to the desired number, and click Private if you don't want the project visible to others. Then click OK.

Assigning Tasks

Usually when you have an appointment, you have some type of preparation you need to do. Schedule+ can help you remember what task(s) you need to accomplish before your appointment. You can assign a task to no particular contact, to all contacts, or to a specific contact. Click the Contact To Do tab and perform the following steps:

1. From the Contacts list, select the individual with whom you want to associate a task.

2. Click the right mouse button to open the shortcut menu.

3. Select Task from the Contact shortcut menu. The Task dialog box opens with basic information filled in (see fig. 37.10).

4. Set a date for Active Range, which indicates when the task should end.

5. The Description area shows the contact you selected and the company name as a default. Add text to the default Description to further clarify the purpose or requirements of the task.

6. In the Project list box, you can group this task with similar tasks by assigning it to a specific project in the pull-down list.

7. Check the Set Reminder box if you want Schedule+ to remind you of the task a day before you should start it.

Tip
You can add the Contact To Do tab from the Tab Gallery. See "Customizing Schedule+" in this chapter.

Tip
You can click the row with All as the contact and view or add a task that applies to all of your contacts.

VIII

Using Office in a Group

Fig. 37.10
The Task dialog box automatically enters the contact name and sets a default priority of 3.

8. Click OK to accept your task information. The task is added to your To Do list. Repeat steps 2 through 8 if you have additional tasks for this individual.

> **Note**
>
> Note that the only tasks displayed are the ones assigned to the selected individual. If the Contact item selected is (All), then tasks assigned to all contacts are displayed.

You have now added a task to remind you of the things you need to do to prepare for contact. Figure 37.11 shows an example of the Contact and To Do tab with tasks listed.

Fig. 37.11
Adding a task to the Contact helps you do the right thing for the right person and at the right time.

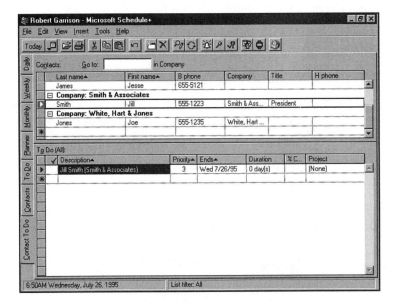

Managing Contacts

The following examples show you how to use your appointment book to keep track of clients, appointments, and tasks you need to do for them.

Adding a New Contact

To begin, add a new client to your contact list by following these steps:

1. From the Microsoft Office Shortcut Bar, click the Add a Contact button; or from Schedule+, choose Insert, Contact. The Contact dialog box opens (see fig. 37.12). Notice the tabs:

■ Business tab includes mailing and other information, such as the department and assistant's name.

■ Phone tab has business, home, fax, and other phone numbers. Each phone number, except FAX, has a Dial Phone icon that allows you to use your modem to dial phone numbers.

■ Address tab has personal information, home address, and phone.

■ Notes is a text box for notes about the client and four user-defined boxes.

Tip

If you don't want other people on the network to see information about this contact, check the Pri_v_ate checkbox on the Business tab.

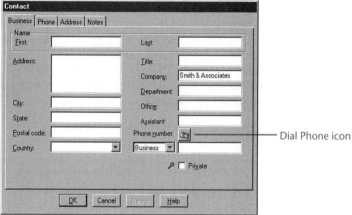

Fig. 37.12
The Contact dialog box stores address, phone, and more information about your contacts.

VIII

Using Office in a Group

Dial Phone icon

Tip

If you already are on the Contacts tab, click the Insert New Contact button or click the right mouse button and choose New Contact.

2. Fill in the information that is important for this contact. If you fail to put in both a first and last name, Schedule+ reminds you. (If you want to use only one name, just click _Y_es.) The other text boxes are optional.

3. Click OK to add the contact to your list.

Note

You can use your Contacts list to create an address for a letter or envelope or for a mail merge in Word. To use a name in a letter, click the Insert Address button on Word's Standard toolbar. To use names in a mail merge, choose _G_et Data on the Mail Merge Helper, choose Use _A_ddress book, and then choose the Schedule+ Contact List.

▶ See "Using the Address Book for Merging," p. 925

Making an Appointment with a Contact

If you want to enter an appointment with an individual in your contact list, follow these steps:

1. If your Contacts tab is not showing on-screen, click the appropriate tab for the type of contact list you want.

> **Note**
>
> You can have more than one tab for viewing contacts. There are tabs for Contacts, Contact List, and Contacts and To Do List. See "Customizing Schedule+" in this chapter for more information.

2. Highlight the contact you want. An arrow points to that row.

   If your list is lengthy, using the Go To box may be faster than scrolling down through the list in search of the person. Click in the Go To: box and type enough letters to bring you to the desired contact.

3. Press the right mouse button. A shortcut menu appears that allows you to cut, copy and paste, edit, delete, and add contacts and create appointments and tasks relating to the contact.

4. Click Appt. from Contact. The Appointment dialog box opens (see fig. 37.13).

5. Fill in the information for the appointment. If you want a reminder from Schedule+, click the Set Reminder checkbox. If you do not know what times are available, Schedule+ can help by showing your planner information.

Fig. 37.13
When you use the Appt. from Contact option from the shortcut menu, the contact's default name and company appear in the Description text box.

6. Click the Planner tab in the Appointment dialog box. A smaller version of the planner replaces the appointment information. Select an open time block for the appointment by clicking and dragging through the times you want (see fig. 37.14).

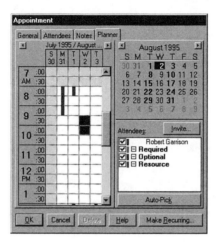

Fig. 37.14
Check your planner for a time that is not marked out in blue so that you are not in two places at once.

7. Click OK to accept the blocked time. If the time changes from the initial time, you get a dialog box asking to confirm the change. Click Yes to accept the change.

Creating Meetings in Planner

The Planner tab allows you to see your schedule over a several day period. If you are working in the group-enabled mode, you can also view the schedules of others. By using the Planner tab, you can find free days in which to schedule meetings. To schedule a meeting, do the following:

1. Click the Planner tab to make the planner active, as in figure 37.15.

> **Note**
>
> Clicking on the busy block places an X beside the names of attendees that are busy. To see what an individual is doing, double-click the busy block and then click the individual's name. The schedule description, if not private, is displayed.

VIII

Using Office in a Group

Fig. 37.15
The Planner tab
shows your free
and busy times to
help you schedule
meetings.

Date Navigator

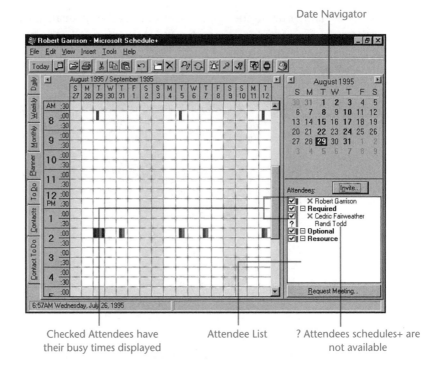

Checked Attendees have
their busy times displayed

Attendee List

? Attendees schedules+ are
not available

2. Click Invite. The Select Attendees dialog box opens (see fig. 37.16).

Fig. 37.16
The attendees you
select can be
required to attend
or the meeting can
be optional. You
can also reserve
resources, such
as rooms
or equipment.

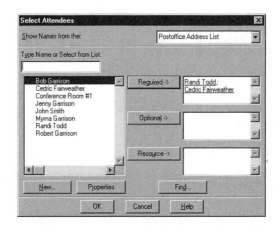

3. Highlight a name from the Select List and click one of the following:

   ◼ Required. The individual must come.

   ◼ Optional. The individual is invited, but doesn't have to attend.

■ Reso<u>u</u>rce. The name represents a resource, such as a conference room, and is needed for the meeting.

4. Click OK. You return to the Planner tab and the invited attendees are listed in their respective groups.

◄ See "Creating a Message," p. 813

5. Click <u>R</u>equest Meeting. The Meeting Request window opens and allows you to send a message via Microsoft Exchange to invite others to the meeting (see fig. 37.17).

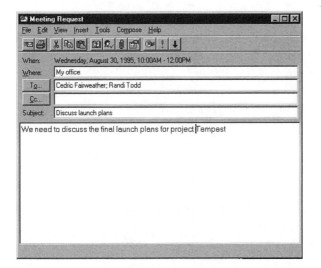

Fig. 37.17
Schedule+ automatically composes a Message Request to meeting invitees. All you add is the text of the message.

VIII

Using Office in a Group

6. Add any additional information about the meeting and click the Send button.

If you need to send additional information to the attendees of a meeting, use Tools, Send Mail. This opens a blank mail message addressed to all the attendees.

Note

The Meeting Wizard makes setting up a meeting easy. You don't have to know the steps, as the Wizard will prompt you to provide the information needed to schedule a meeting. Click <u>T</u>ools, Meeting Wizard to schedule your next meeting.

Troubleshooting

I don't have an Invite button on the Attendees tab.

When you started Schedule+, you selected to work in standalone mode. You must exit Schedule+ and restart in group-enabled mode.

Sorting Tasks and Contacts

You can view the various To Do tabs and the Contacts tabs in different sorted orders and groups. This allows you to look at the big picture or focus in on smaller details.

Working with the To Do Tab

Click the To Do tab (see fig. 37.18).

Up arrow shows this column is sorted in ascending order

Down arrow shows this column is sorted in descending order

The current filter

Fig. 37.18
The To Do tab reveals a wealth of information when you use the View commands.

Right arrow indicates selected task

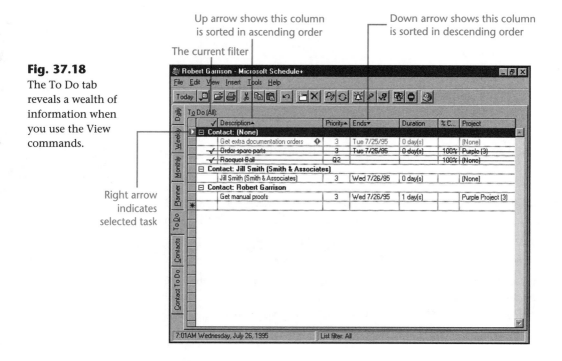

Table 37.4 shows the commands found under View.

Table 37.4 View Command Options	
Command	**Purpose**
<u>C</u>olumns	You can choose which columns to show in the To Do List.
<u>G</u>roup By	You can group the projects and tasks in up to three levels and sort by the grouping.
<u>S</u>ort	Set the order that tasks are listed. If you use <u>G</u>roup By, then the order is within each group.
A<u>u</u>tosort	Sort the list automatically if a change occurs.
Sort <u>N</u>ow	If A<u>u</u>tosort is not checked, then you can force a sort of the list.

Working with the Contact Tab

Click the <u>C</u>ontacts tab (see fig. 37.19).

Up arrow shows this column
is sorted in ascending order

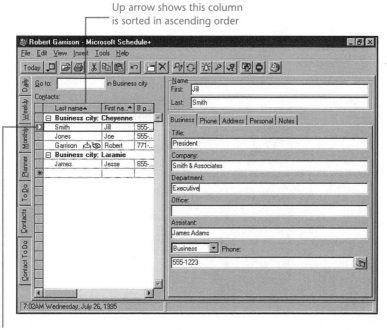

Right arrow indicates
selected contact task

VIII

Using Office in a Group

Fig. 37.19
The <u>C</u>ontacts tab
reveals a wealth of
information when
you use the View
commands.

Table 37.5 shows the commands found under View.

Table 37.5	View Command Options
Command	**Purpose**
Columns	You can choose which columns to show in the Contacts tab.
Group By	You can arrange the contacts in groups of up to three levels.
Sort	Set the order that contacts are listed. If you use Group By, then the order is within each group.
Autosort	Sort the list automatically if a change occurs.
Sort Now	If Autosort is not checked, then you can force a sort of the list.

Searching for Information in Schedule+

Schedule+ can contain lots of information—Appointments, Contacts, Tasks, and Events—making it difficult to find a specific item. You can use Edit, Find to search Schedule+. Choose Edit, Find to open the Find dialog box, as in figure 37.20, and complete these steps:

Fig. 37.20
Looking for the needle in the haystack is easier when you use Schedule+ Edit, Find to do the work for you.

Search is not available if Search in Contact List is selected

Result box

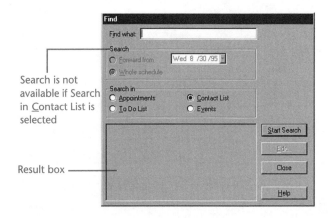

1. Enter the text to search for in Find What.

2. Select Search Forward From or Whole Schedule. This is not available if Search in Contact List is selected.

3. Select the type item to Search In.

4. Choose Find Next. If a match is found, you are shown additional information.

5. Choose Edit. You are placed in the correct dialog box for editing the object.

6. Repeat steps 2 through 5 as needed. Click OK when you are done.

Printing in Schedule+

If you plan to be away from your computer, you can print various parts of your Schedule+ information as needed. You can print your calendar, To Do items, your contact list, and even choose different layouts and paper formats:

1. Choose File, Print to open the Print dialog box (see fig. 37.21).

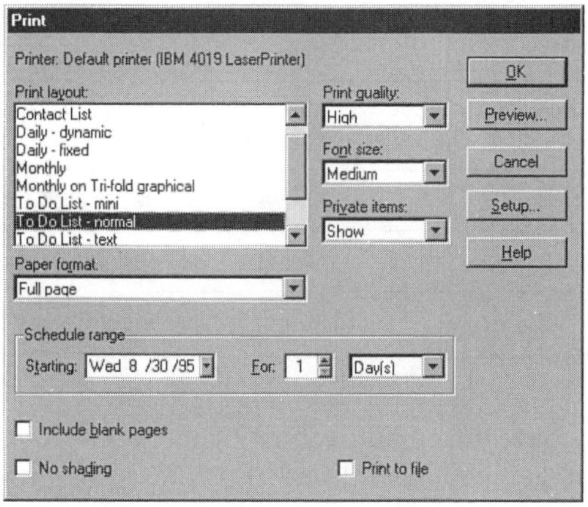

2. Select Print Layout by clicking the desired style.

3. Select Paper Format for your organizer.

4. In the Schedule Range area, select the date you want the printed schedule to begin with.

5. Click OK to print on your default printer.

What kind of daily planner do you use? You can even print pages to fit many popular products' page layouts. Print out your schedule for next week:

Tip
You can change the sort order, grouping, and filter for specific conditions to create reports for Tasks and Contacts. See "Sorting Tasks and Contacts."

VIII

Using Office in a Group

Fig. 37.21
The Print layout list box and Paper format drop-down list give many options for printing out your Appointments, To Do list, and Contacts.

From the Print dialog box, choose one of the Print layout options. See table 37.6 for a description of the different choices.

Table 37.6 Print Layout Options	
Name	**Description**
All Text	All information in your schedule
Contact List	Your contact list
Daily - dynamic	The daily appointments, without the To Do List
Daily - fixed	The daily appointments, with To Do List and Other Appointments (outside your normal work day)
Monthly	Monthly—one month per page
Monthly on Tri-fold graphical	Monthly—Appointments on two outside 1/3 and a one year calendar in center
To Do List - mini	Shows only priority, task description, and due date
To Do List - normal	Shows the priority, task description, start date, and end date
To Do List - text	Shows only the task description
Weekly - 5 day	Shows a 5 day appointment calendar
Weekly - 7 day	Shows a 7 day appointment calendar

Most organizers have information about blank paper products that can be used in their product. You want to use the Paper format that your organizer was designed for. The current Paper formats supported by Schedule+ are the manufacturers paper product are:

- Full page (8 1/2-by-11-inch plain paper)
- Avery 41-206 (small)
- Avery 41-256 (small)
- Avery 41-307 (medium)
- Avery 41-357 (medium)
- Filofax-#106 (small)

You're now ready to hit the road and meet all your appointments.

> **Note**
>
> Make notes on the printed calendar and make sure to update Schedule+ when you return to the office. Remember, getting organized with Schedule+ means you need to keep it up-to-date.

Using the Timex Wizard

If you are really intent on not missing a scheduled item, then you want to get a Timex Data Watch. Schedule+ can download selected information to your watch using the Timex Data Link Wizard or by choosing File, Export Timex Data, Link Watch. The watch gets the downloaded information by using an optical link to a bar code pattern displayed on your monitor. When the data has been downloaded, your watch will remind you of those appointments.

Managing Your Life with the Seven Habits Tool

Mircosoft has incorporated the Seven Habits Tool into Schedule+. The concepts of the Seven Habits come from Dr. Stephen R. Covey's books *The Seven Habits of Highly Effective People* and *First Things First*.

Microsoft's incorporation of the Seven Habits Tools emphasizes the following:

> *Habit 2: Begin with the End in Mind*. Helps you create and use a personal mission statement.
>
> *Habit 3: Put First Things First*. Guides you in setting priorities to organize what you do, rather than reacting to the urgent.
>
> *Habit 7: Sharpen the Saw*. Encourages you to plan daily and organize for self-improvement.

Choose Tools, Seven Habits Tools to access the Seven Habits.

You can access the Seven Habits Tutorial by choosing Tools, Seven Habits Quick Start.

Customizing Schedule+

Schedule+ is your personal electronic time manager. Because it is your personal tool, there are many ways that you can customize the looks and actions of Schedule+ to fit your own needs and desires.

Using the Tab Gallery

Schedule+ enables you to customize your appointment book, adding new categories and arranging the information. Choose View, Tab Gallery. The Tab Gallery dialog box appears (see fig. 37.22).

Fig. 37.22
The Tab Gallery dialog box allows you to add many more different kinds of views to manage your schedules.

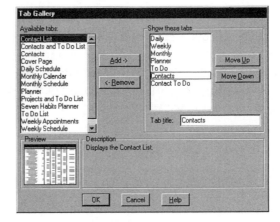

You can change the appearance of your Appointment Book using these areas of the Tab Gallery dialog box:

- The Available Tabs list shows the different window layouts from which you can select. These are described in detail in table 37.7.

- Show These Tabs are the tabs currently shown in the appointment book.

- When you select a tab, the Preview and Description areas give you an idea of what this particular tab does.

- In the Tab Title text box, you can change what the tab actually says.

Table 37.7 Available Tabs Options	
Tab	**Description**
Contact List	Displays the Contact List.

Tab	Description
Contacts and To Do List	Displays the Contact List and related tasks.
Contacts	Displays the Contact List and the card view of the selected contact.
Cover Page	Displays a cover-page bitmap.
Daily Schedule	Displays daily appointments, the Date Navigator, and the To Do List. Additional days can be added to this tab.
Monthly Calendar	Displays a month of appointments.
Monthly Schedule	Displays a month of appointments and the To Do List.
Planner	Displays the Planner showing free and busy times, the Date Navigator, and the meeting attendees list.
Projects and To Do List	Displays the Project List and related tasks.
Seven Habits Planner	Displays daily appointments for as many as seven days, as well as the To Do List grouped by Seven Habits roles.
To Do List	Displays the To Do List.
Weekly Appointments	Displays daily appointments for as many as seven days.
Weekly Schedule	Displays daily appointments for as many as seven days, as well as the To Do List.
Yearly Calendar	Displays up to twelve calendar months, which you can scroll to view past or future dates. Days on which an appointment occurs appear in bold.

To add a tab for the Contacts and To Do list, for example, follow these steps:

1. Highlight the Contacts and To Do List in the Available Tabs list. The Preview window shows you how the layout looks.

2. Click Add. Contact To Do appears in the Show These Tabs list.

3. To move the tab up so that it appears as the second tab on the list, highlight the Contact To Do item and then click the Move Up and Move Down buttons as necessary.

VIII

Using Office in a Group

Tip
You can click the Remove button to remove unneeded tabs from the Appointment Book.

Tip
Right-click on a tab
in the Appoint-
ment Book to get a
menu for the Tab
Gallery, to rename
or remove the tab,
or to reorder the
tabs.

4. Enter a title for the tab in the Tab title.

5. Click OK. You then can select the Contact To Do page by clicking its tab.

Tools Options

Schedule+ has many options that can be customized. To change these options, choose Tools, Options to open the Options dialog box. You can make changes to Options in five areas represented by the tabs:

- *General tab.* Affects a mixture of options in Schedule+. You can set the start and stop times of your day from this tab.

- *Defaults tab.* Allows you to set the defaults that are used in other Schedule+ windows.

- *Display tab.* Lets you control the visual look of your appointment book. Included in this tab are settings for the background colors of the Appointment Book and Planner. You also can set the color of the category of attendees in the planner. There are check boxes for a number of additional elements that can be shown in your views.

Tip
You may show
both time zones in
appointments if
you work with
others in a differ-
ent time zone, or
you yourself work
in two time zones.

- *Time Zone tab.* Allows you to set a primary and secondary time zone.

- *Synchronize tab.* Allows you to control how often your local schedule updates the master schedule file on the network.

Managing the Schedule+ File

Use the commands on the File menu to manage your Schedule+ file. The commands are described in table 37.8.

Table 37.8	Schedule+ File Menu Commands
Command	**Purpose**
Export	Exports your Schedule+ data to a format compatible with one of the support file types; Schedule+ Interchange, Text, Timex Data Link Watch, or Other Systems
Import	Imports data into your Schedule+ schedule from Schedule+ Interchange, Text, or Other Systems
Archive	Creates an archive file
Backup	Backs up a schedule
Restore	Restores a schedule from a backup

Chapter 38

Using Microsoft Office on a Network

by Robert Garrison

John Donne wrote "No man is an island unto himself."

As a user of Microsoft Office, you're not a user unto yourself either. After all, would you have a computer and *never* share anything with anyone else?

When you use Microsoft Office on a network, there is potential improvement in your productivity. You gain this productivity increase by working as a team.

In this chapter, you learn to

- Use shared dictionaries in Word

- Annotate Word documents

- Use Word document revisions

- Schedule meetings with Schedule+

- Use Shared Lists in Excel

- Use Presentation Conferencing in PowerPoint

Establishing Shared Dictionaries

You learned in Chapter 3 how to use dictionaries to check the spelling in your documents. If you are on a network and working with other users, you might want to share some common dictionaries. Or maybe there is a dictionary of terms commonly used in your office or industry. You can add up to

◀ See "Checking Spelling," p. 90

eight dictionaries to make your work easier. The default custom dictionary is called *Custom*. When you add words during a spelling check, they are added to the custom dictionary. In this section you use Word to learn more about dictionaries.

To create a shared dictionary in Word, do the following:

1. Choose Tools, Options.

2. Click the Spelling tab. The Options dialog box appears, as shown in figure 38.1.

Fig. 38.1
The Spelling tab lets you customize the guidelines for how you use dictionaries.

Tip
Misspelled words are indicated by a wavy red underline (if that option is set).

As you type, words are checked for correct spelling.

Check this when you don't want suggestions from your custom dictionaries

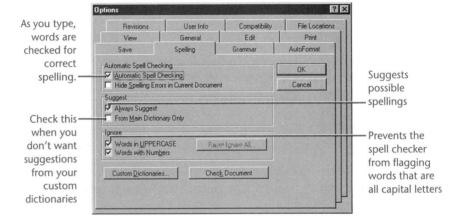

Suggests possible spellings

Prevents the spell checker from flagging words that are all capital letters

3. To add a custom dictionary, click Custom Dictionaries. The box in figure 38.2 opens.

Fig. 38.2
Working with custom dictionaries lets Office learn your special words.

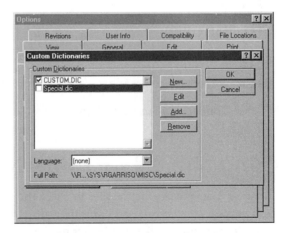

Use the Custom Dictionaries option buttons to do the following:

- ■ <u>N</u>ew allows you to create a custom dictionary.

- ■ <u>E</u>dit allows you to edit the highlighted dictionary. The dictionary is a Word document.

- ■ <u>A</u>dd allows you to make an existing dictionary, possibly from a network drive, be checked for spelling.

- ■ <u>R</u>emove takes a dictionary out of your custom dictionary list.

- ■ Full Path shows the location of the highlighted custom dictionary.

4. Click <u>N</u>ew to create a new dictionary. The Create Custom Dictionary dialog box opens (see fig. 38.3).

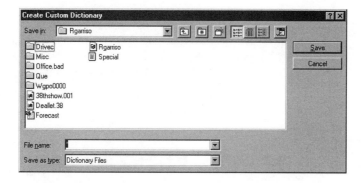

Fig. 38.3
Word can store your special words if you give it a new dictionary.

◄ See "Using File Dialog Boxes" p. 102

VIII

Using Office in a Group

5. Navigate the Save <u>I</u>n text box to place the custom dictionary in a shared network directory. Then others can use your dictionary if they add the dictionary to their custom dictionary list.

6. In the File <u>N</u>ame text box, type the name of the new dictionary. For example, type **Special** and click <u>S</u>ave. A standard Word document is created.

7. Because this is a new dictionary, there are currently no words in it. You can choose <u>E</u>dit to add words manually or add them during a spell check.

8. When finished, click OK twice to return to the document.

Tip
When typing the name of your dictionary, don't type a period or an extension. Word provides the extension DIC automatically.

Note

If you have special language or technical terms you use in your job, you can put them in a custom dictionary and use them when you need to. Removing the custom dictionaries can decrease the time to check a document if you are not using those types of words in the dictionary all the time.

Note

Why would you want to share dictionaries? If you have a large number of users on the network, each adding the same words to individual custom dictionaries, you waste a lot of room. Plus, everyone might not know the correct spelling. Using the shared dictionary helps to meet company standards through consistency.

Fig. 38.4

You can now spell check the document and add words to the special dictionary.

The word to possibly be replaced

Allows you to select your special dictionary

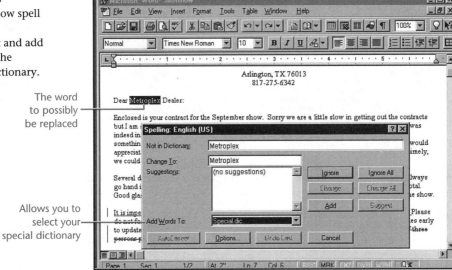

To add words to your custom dictionary during a spell check, follow these steps:

1. Choose Tools, Spelling to begin the spell check. The Spelling Dialog box appears (see fig. 38.4).

2. To add new words to your special dictionary, choose SPECIAL.DIC from the Add Words To: drop-down list.

3. Click Add to add the unrecognized word to the special dictionary.

Using Annotations

Annotations allow authors to make comments in a document without actually changing the document. One particular use of annotations is in a document that is being routed by Microsoft Exchange.

◀ See "Working with Routed Mail," p. 827

To make annotations to a document, complete the following steps:

1. Open the Word document.

2. Place your insertion point where you want to insert an annotation.

3. Choose Insert, Annotation. The Annotations window opens as in figure 38.5.

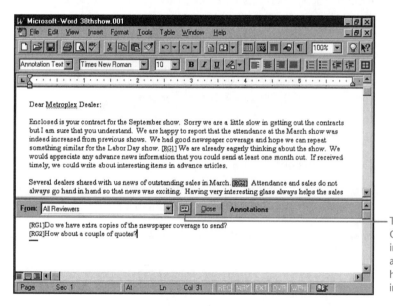

Fig. 38.5
Annotations contain comments and suggestions about a document you are reviewing.

The Insert Sound Object lets you include voice annotations if you have a sound card in your system

4. Type your comment in the annotation window. Your cursor is automatically placed there when you chose Insert, Annotation. Notice that each annotation begins with the author's initials and is sequentially numbered.

4. Click Close when you are finished with this annotation.

5. If you want to see all of your annotations, or those of other reviews, choose View, Annotations. The annotation window, shown in figure 38.5, stays open on the screen.

Tip
If the initials are incorrect, change them by editing the User Info tab after choosing Tools, Options.

Using Revision Marks

Revision marks are different from annotations. While annotations are comments that don't actually change the document, revision marks indicate changes made to the document. Revisions such as inserting text, deleting text, or changing text can show up in different colors and text fonts. Each author's revisions can be marked in a different color. Eight authors can review a document before the colors repeat. You can see how revisions will be marked in your document by choosing Tools, Options and clicking the Revisions tab.

◀ See "Changing Revision Options" p. 238

You can make revisions to your document by completing these steps:

1. Choose Tools, Revisions. The Revisions dialog box opens (see fig. 38.6).

Fig. 38.6
Use the Revisions dialog box to indicate text changes.

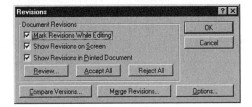

The following options are available:

■ Compare Versions compares the current document with one on disk. It will mark all changes automatically.

■ Merge Revisions makes the changes in a revised document to the original document.

■ Options allows you to set the color and style of inserted, deleted, or changed text.

2. Click the Mark Revisions While Editing check box and choose OK. Your revisions will appear on-screen as you make them.

3. Now make some changes. For example, first highlight a sentence and cut it. Then, insert that sentence at the beginning of the paragraph.

Your document will show revisions similar to those in figure 38.7.

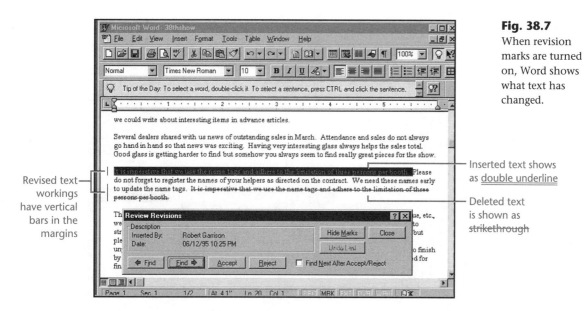

Fig. 38.7
When revision
marks are turned
on, Word shows
what text has
changed.

When you finish with revisions, you can save the file or send it to the next person if the file was routed to you. Once everyone has made all the comments and revisions necessary, someone must decide which revisions to accept to make them a part of the document. To do so, complete the following steps:

1. Choose Tools, Revisions.

2. Click Review and the Review Revisions dialog box opens (refer to fig. 38.7).

Use the Review Revisions dialog box to accept or reject the suggested revisions to your document.

Using Schedule+ for Meetings

One of the biggest challenges of the workplace today is finding time to meet to make plans and decisions. If your coworkers are all using Microsoft Office—and of course they are—you can use Schedule+ to schedule those meetings at times available to all.

▶ See "Scheduling
Your Time,"
p. 834

To schedule a meeting with coworkers, follow these steps:

1. Switch to Schedule+ and click the Planner tab. The Planner view of your Schedule appears, as in figure 38.8. Note that any previous meeting attendees will appear in the Attendees box to make it easier to schedule.

VIII

Using Office in a Group

Fig. 38.8
Making plans for
group meetings.

Monthly
Planner

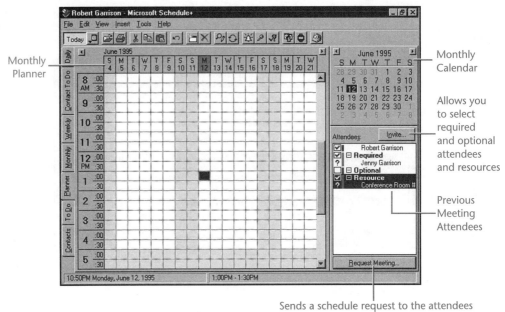

Monthly
Calendar

Allows you
to select
required
and optional
attendees
and resources

Previous
Meeting
Attendees

Sends a schedule request to the attendees

◀ See "Creating a
Message" p. 813

2. Highlight a time period for the meeting by holding the mouse down
and dragging through the required time.

3. Click Invite to select the attendees. The Select Attendees dialog box
appears, as shown in figure 38.9.

Fig. 38.9
Inviting your staff
to a meeting.

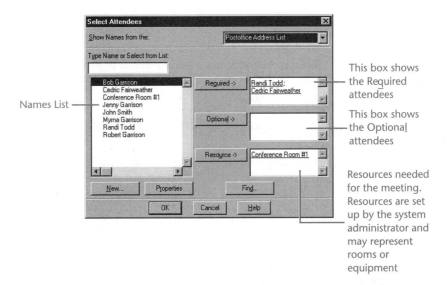

Names List

This box shows
the Required
attendees

This box shows
the Optional
attendees

Resources needed
for the meeting.
Resources are set
up by the system
administrator and
may represent
rooms or
equipment

4. Select the correct address book by using the S̲how Names from the drop-down list, usually the Postoffice Address List.

5. Highlight an individual or resource name in the name list.

6. Click Re̲quired to add the individual to the required attendance list.

7. Click Optiona̲l if the individual's attendance is not mandatory.

8. Click Reso̲urce if the name on the list is a resource.

9. Repeat steps 6–8 as needed. Click OK when finished (see fig. 38.10).

10. Click and drag on the required time of the meeting.

11. Click R̲equest Meeting and a Microsoft Exchange message window opens. Fill in the Subject Line and message text. Click Send to have Microsoft Exchange mail the schedule request.

VIII

Using Office in a Group

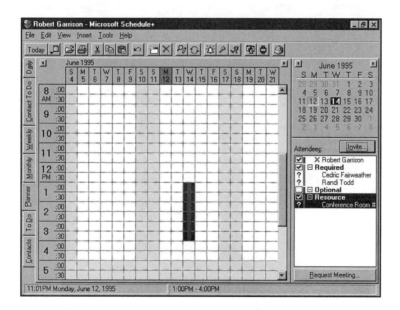

Fig. 38.10
The completed meeting schedule.

13. Click the D̲aily tab and you see your personal schedule for the day (see fig. 38.11).

14. If you want additional information about the meeting or want to change the reminder time, double-click one of the icons. The Appointment window opens (see fig. 38.12).

Fig. 38.11
A view of the scheduled meeting from the daily appointments.

Meeting icon shows it's a scheduled meeting rather than an appointment

Alarm reminder

The subject of the meeting is the subject typed in the Subject line of the meeting request message.

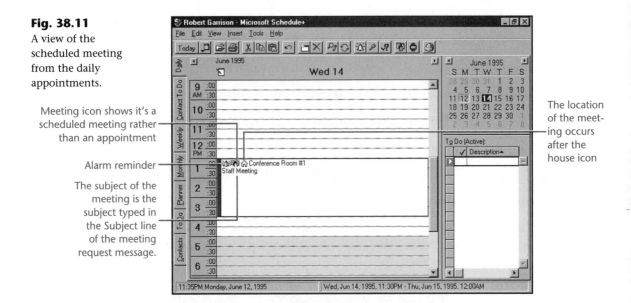

The location of the meeting occurs after the house icon

Fig. 38.12
The Appointment window shows the details of the scheduled meeting.

The General tab shows the meeting time

A description that can be edited

The reminder time, which can be adjusted

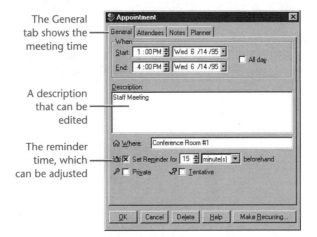

15. Click the Attendees tab to display additional information (see fig. 38.13).

You can also make notes about the meeting for your personal use. The original notes are the text of the request message. Do so by clicking the Notes tab. The Planner tab shows a mini-view of the Planner.

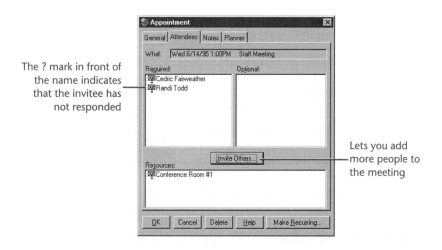

The ? mark in front of the name indicates that the invitee has not responded

Lets you add more people to the meeting

Fig. 38.13
Checking on who else is at the meeting.

Using Shared Lists in Excel

VIII

Using Office in a Group

When you work on a network with other users, you will want to use the Shared Lists feature of Excel for some of your spreadsheets. Share Lists allows multiple users to access and change a spreadsheet on a shared drive. A file saved with Shared Lists turned on can't have its cell formatting or formulas changed.

To use Shared Lists, do the following:

1. Click File, Shared Lists and then click the Editing tab. The Shared Lists dialog box appears (see fig. 38.14).

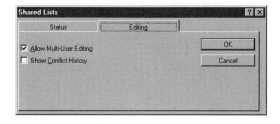

Fig. 38.14
Letting other users have access to a spreadsheet on the network simultaneously through Shared Lists.

2. Click on the Status tab of Shared Lists to see who has the file open (see fig. 38.15).

If you make a change to the spreadsheet and try to save the change while someone else is using the spreadsheet, you will be asked if you want to update the shared list. To make it easier to know what changes have been made use Show Conflict History. If Show Conflict History has been turned on for a file, a worksheet is added to the workbook that provides an audit trail of the changes made.

Fig. 38.15
Excel keeps track of who has a file open when Shared Lists is turned on for that file.

Using Presentation Conferencing

The Tools, Presentation Conference command allows you to review a PowerPoint presentation during development or to actually make the final presentation over the network. Attendees don't have to travel to the presentation—they can remain at their desk.

To conduct a conference, use the Presentations Conference Wizard to set up the presentation. As the conference moderator you can use the Meeting Minder to make notes during the presentation, add meeting minutes, and make action items. You also have available the slide navigator to preview and branch to slides as you go.

To set up the Presentation Conference you need to know the computer names of the attendees. The participants can get the name of their computer by running Network from the Control Panel and clicking on the Identification tab.❖

Part IX

Techniques from the Pros

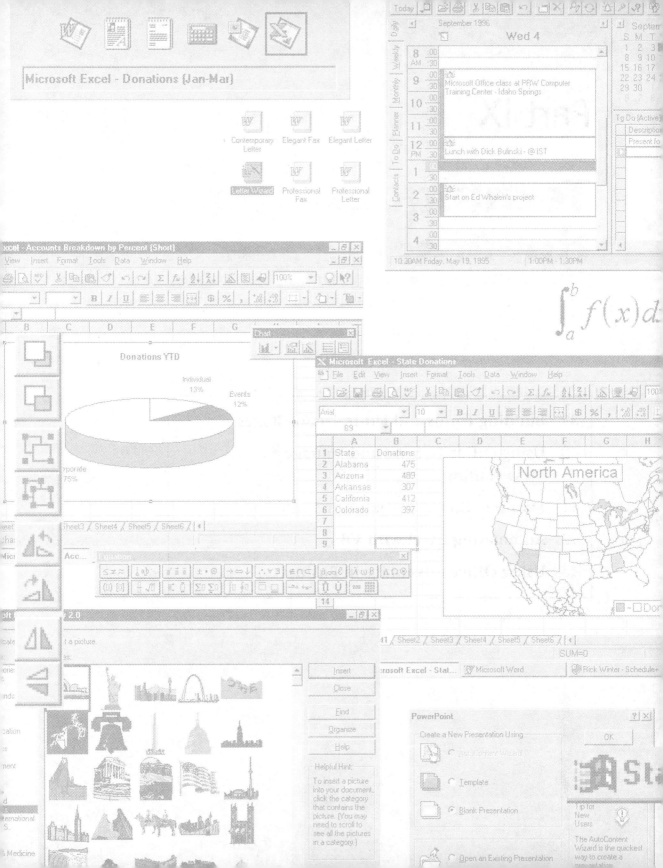

Chapter 39

Building Forms and Fill-In Dialog Boxes

Ron Person has written more than 18 books for Que Corporation, including *Using Word 6 for Windows*, Special Edition, *Using Excel for Windows 95*, Special Edition, and he was the lead author for *Using Windows 95*, Special Edition. As one of Microsoft's original consulting partners, Ron has been developing Microsoft Office solutions and training corporate developers for seven years.

In the past, one office task that word processors were not able to do well was fill in forms. Typewriters were always needed to fill in a form. Storage rooms and filing cabinets took up space just to keep months worth of inventory of forms that, in some cases, were so seldom used they were obsolete before they ever left the shelf.

Word's new forms features are a big step in the direction of being able to do away with preprinted forms. By using Word's desktop publishing features, many companies are now designing forms that they save as *templates* and print on demand. The cost savings over printing large volumes of forms can be huge.

Word now includes—in addition to its capability to produce a high-quality form on demand—features that make the task of filling in forms easy to do. By using Word's form fields, you can put edit boxes, check boxes, and pull-down lists directly into your documents. The use of {fill in} and {ask} fields enables a document to pop up dialog boxes that ask for input.

Techniques from the Pros

by Ron Person

In this chapter, you learn to

- Create a template in which you can put edit boxes, check boxes, or pull-down lists

- Lock the template to prevent users from changing unauthorized parts of a document

- Specify lists of data that show up in pull-down lists, or format the data that a user types in a data entry box

- Use a {fill in} field to display a dialog box

- Ask once for an item of data, yet use it several times throughout the document

- Create a simple macro that controls each dialog box as soon as it opens

Form Basics

A *form* is a special kind of protected document that includes fields where people can type information. Any document that includes form fields is a form. A *form field* is a location on-screen where you can do one of three things: enter text, toggle a check box on or off, or select from a drop-down list.

Tables provide the structure for many forms, because a table's cells are an ideal framework for a form's labels and information fields. You can type labels in some cells, and insert form fields in others. Tables also make adding shading and borders to forms an easy job. You can place a dark border around a selected group of cells in a table, for example, while including no border at all around other cells. With the gridlines turned off, a table doesn't have to look like a table at all, and thus makes the ideal framework for a form.

A form can be based on any type of document. A real estate contract, for example, may include several pages of descriptive paragraphs containing form fields in which you insert information. The text in the paragraphs doesn't change—you insert information in the form fields only.

You can include three types of form fields in a form: text, check box, and drop-down. You can customize each of these field types in many ways. You can format a text field, for example, to accept only dates and to print dates such as January 1, 1995, as 1/1/95, or in another format. Figures 39.1, 39.2, and 39.3 show examples of three forms that can be created using Word.

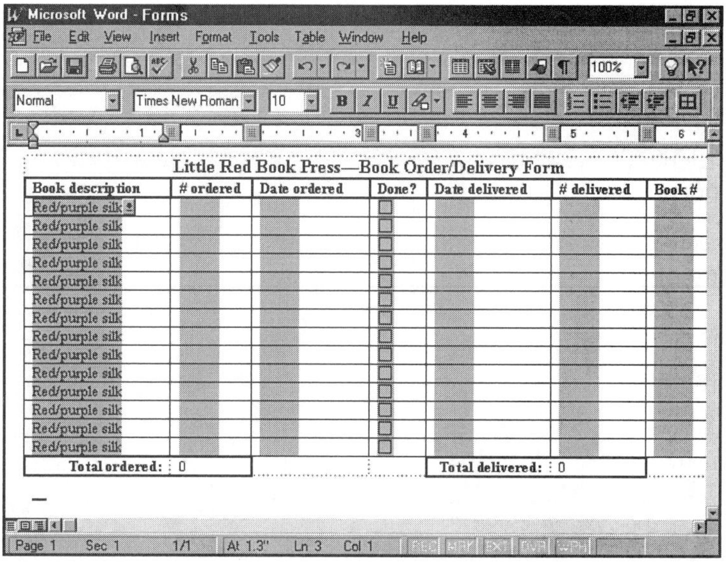

Techniques from the Pros

Fig. 39.1

An example of an order/delivery form.

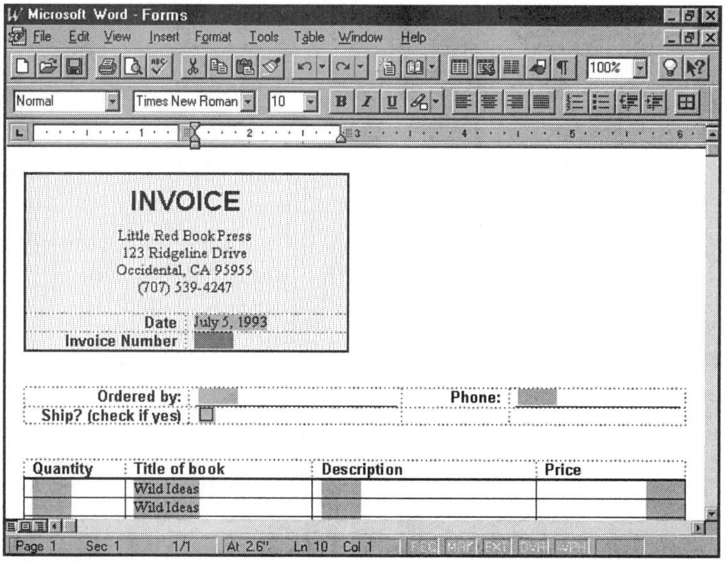

Fig. 39.2

An example of an invoice form.

You can use forms in a variety of ways to save time, effort, and money. You can create your own commonly used business forms such as sales invoices, order sheets, personnel records, calendars, and boilerplate contracts. You can print a copy of your blank form and have it reproduced in quantity, using color if you want. Then print only the information contained in your form onto your preprinted forms—the information will be positioned correctly.

Fig. 39.3

Another example of
a form.

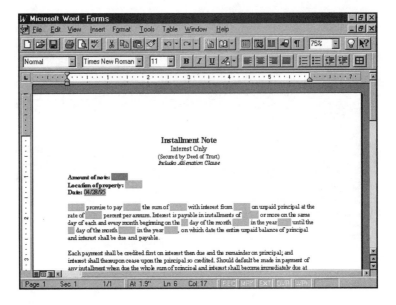

You also can automate forms that don't need to be printed at all. Distribute form templates, rather than paper forms, to people in your company. You can make forms easy to use by including helpful on-screen messages and automatic macros.

You can include calculations in forms—adding up the prices of items in a sales invoice form, for example, to show a total invoice amount. And you can add form fields to documents other than forms. When the fields are shaded, people can easily see where they should insert necessary information.

The most useful forms are based on templates, which can be used over and over again. When someone fills in such a form, he or she fills in a copy—the original does not change. (You can, of course, create a form as a document instead of a template if you plan to use the form only once.) When someone creates a new document based on your form template, they can type information only in the fields you designated when you created and protected the form.

Caution Unless you add password protection, someone using the form can unprotect it and make changes not only to the fields but also to other parts of the form. Later in this chapter, you learn how to provide maximum protection for form templates.

You can create forms by using two important tools:

■ Insert, For_m_ Field, which you use to insert and customize form fields

■ The Forms toolbar, which contains tools for building and customizing forms (see fig. 39.4).

Fig. 39.4

The Forms toolbar includes tools to help you build and customize forms.

You can display the Forms toolbar by choosing Insert, For*m* Field and choosing Show Toolbar, or by choosing View, Toolbars and selecting Forms from the Toolbars list. Alternatively, you can click with the right mouse button on the Standard toolbar, and select Forms from the drop-down list of toolbars that appears.

Building Forms

Building a simple form is a three-part process. First, you create a new template and build the *form structure*—the framework for the form—and add labels, formatting, shading and borders, and anything else that won't change when users fill in the form. Next, you insert form fields where you want to type information when you fill in the form. Finally, you protect and save the form.

Creating and Saving the Form Structure

Another way you might create a form is by using frames. By framing a table or selected text, you can position it anywhere you want on the page (see fig. 39.5). In this way, you can separate the portion of a document that contains fields in which you must insert information from other parts of the document where the text may not change.

> **Note**
>
> Before you begin designing a form on your computer, sketching it out on paper may be helpful, particularly if you're using a table as the structure for the form. By sketching out the form, you'll know how many rows and columns you need in your table, and you'll know where to type labels and where to insert form fields. Even if you change the form as you go, it's easier to start with a plan.

To create and save the form structure as a template, follow these steps:

1. Choose File, New. The New dialog box appears.

2. Select from the Template list the template you want to use as the basis for your form. In most cases, you can use the Normal template.

Fig. 39.5

Fig. 39.5

By framing selected text that includes form fields, you can create a form like this.

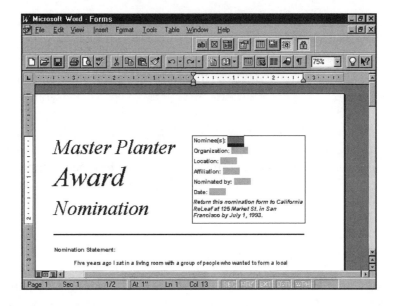

3. Select Template from the New group.

4. Choose OK.

5. Establish the form structure in one of these ways:

   Insert a table by choosing Table, Insert Table, or by clicking the Table button on the Standard toolbar. Type labels and any other text that will not change in the form. Format the table with lines, borders, and shading.

   Create a form based on paragraphs by inserting form fields where you need them as you type the text of your document. Read the next section, "Adding Form Fields," to learn how to insert form fields.

   At the top of your document, insert the table or type the text that will contain form fields. Select, frame, and position this portion of your document. Then type the remainder of the form, which includes text that will not change when you fill in the form.

6. Choose File, Save As to save the template. Type the template's name in the Save As box, then choose OK. Leave your template open so that you can add the form fields.

Tip

If you create a new form as a document, you can still save it as a template. Save it again by choosing File, Save As. Select Document Template (*.DOT) in the Save As Type drop-down list.

Templates normally are saved in the TEMPLATE folder under the folder containing Word. If Microsoft Office is installed, then templates are stored in the MSOFFICE\TEMPLATE folder.

Adding Form Fields

After you've established the structure for your form—whether it's a table, a framed block of text, or a paragraph—you can add the form fields. Form fields enable the user to enter data. As mentioned earlier, the three types of form fields are text, check box, and drop-down. You can add form fields to your template by using a menu command or by clicking buttons on the Forms toolbar.

Tip

If you're creating a form that contains many of the same form fields, save time by copying one existing form fields and pasting them into a new location.

To add form fields to your document using a menu command, follow these steps:

1. Position the insertion point where you want the form field to appear.

2. Choose Insert, Form Field. The Form Field dialog box appears (see fig. 39.6).

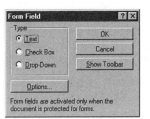

Fig. 39.6

The Form Field dialog box allows you to choose the type of field.

3. Select Text, Check Box, or Drop-Down from the Type group.

4. Choose OK. The form field appears in your document (see fig. 39.7).

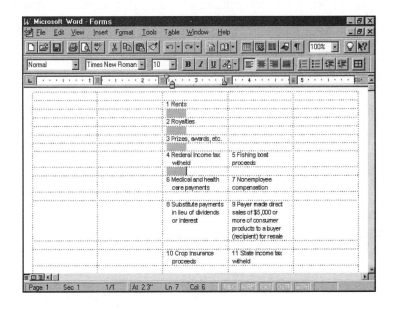

Fig. 39.7

A form field appears in your document.

◀ **See**
"Using
Toolbars in
Microsoft
Office Applica-
tions," p. 44

To add form fields to your document by using the Forms toolbar, follow these steps:

1. Display the Forms toolbar by choosing <u>I</u>nsert, For<u>m</u> Field and clicking the <u>S</u>how Toolbar button. The Forms toolbar appears (see fig. 39.8).

Alternatively, use another technique to display the Forms toolbar.

Fig. 39.8

You can use the
Forms toolbar to
simplify form
creation.

2. Position the insertion point where you want a form field.

3. Click one of the form field tools displayed at the left side of the Forms toolbar:

To insert a text field, click the Text button.

To insert a check box, click the Check Box button.

To insert a drop-down list, click the Drop-Down button. (Note that a drop-down list is empty until you customize it by adding items to the list; see the later section "Customizing Drop-Down Form Fields.")

A form field appears in your document.

4. Repeat steps 2 and 3 to add form fields to your document.

Notice that the Forms toolbar contains a Shading Options button. If you select this tool, form fields appear as shaded rectangles on your screen (see fig. 39.9). If you don't select this tool, text fields appear with no shading or border, check box fields appear with a square outline, and drop-down fields appear with a rectangular outline (see fig. 39.10).

Fig. 39.9

Form fields appear
shaded when you
click the Shading
Options button on
the Forms toolbar.

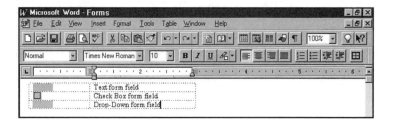

The preceding steps insert text boxes, check boxes, or lists, but you cannot use these form fields until you protect the document or template, as described in the next section.

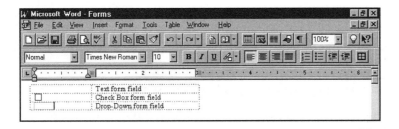

Fig. 39.10

If you don't click the Shading Options button, text form fields don't appear at all, and check box and drop-down form fields are outlined.

> **Note**
>
> Refer to the "Customizing Form Fields" section later in the chapter to learn how to customize each form field you add to your document. For example, you can customize a text field so that the current date automatically appears; you can customize a drop-down field to add items to the drop-down list.

Tip

Even if you don't want form fields shaded in your final online form, use shading while you create your form to make the fields easy to see and edit.

Protecting and Saving the Form

Until you protect a document containing form fields, you can edit any part of it, text or form fields. After the document is protected, you can fill in a form field, but you can't edit the document.

A protected form is different from an unprotected form in several ways. For example, a protected document appears in Page Layout view, and you cannot edit the document—you can only insert a response into a form field. You can't select the entire document, and you can't use most commands, including formatting commands. Tables and frames are fixed, and fields with formulas display results, rather than the formulas.

You can easily unprotect a document when you want to edit it—unless someone has protected it with a password. To learn how to use password protection, refer to the upcoming section "Protecting and Unprotecting a Form with a Password." To learn how to protect only part of a form, see the later section "Protecting Part of a Form."

As long as you designate your new document as a template, Word automatically saves it as a template (using the extension DOT) and proposes saving it in the TEMPLATE subfolder, where it *must* remain in order for Word to find it when you create a new document. To use your form as a template that appears when you choose File, New, don't change the folder or file extension. (You can, however, specify that all templates be stored in a different subfolder by choosing Tools, Options, selecting the File Locations tab, and modifying the User Templates.)

To protect and save your form, follow these steps:

1. Choose Tools, Protect Document. The Protect Document dialog box appears (see fig. 39.11).

Fig. 39.11

After you protect a document, you can't edit it.

Tip

Someone may have changed the names of your MSOFFICE folder and TEMPLATES subfolder; accept these changed names if they appear as the defaults.

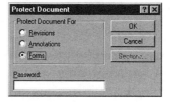

2. Select Forms, and choose OK.

3. Choose File, Save As (see fig. 39.12.) Type a name in the File Name text box, and make sure that Document Template is selected in the Save as Type list, and that the TEMPLATES subfolder in the MSOFFICE folder is selected in the folders list. The TEMPLATES folder is located under the WINWORD folder if you do not have Office 95.

4. Choose OK to save the file as a template.

Fig. 39.12

Be sure to save your form as a template.

To unprotect your form, choose <u>T</u>ools, Un<u>p</u>rotect Document.

If your form is protected with a password, you must enter the password in order to unprotect the form. See the upcoming section "Protecting and Unprotecting a Form with a Password."

To protect or unprotect your form using the Forms toolbar, click the Protect Form button on the Forms toolbar. When the button appears pressed, the form is protected; when the button appears raised, the form is unprotected.

Word has two ways of saving forms. You can save the complete form, including fields, labels, and the information you enter in the form. Or you can save just the information you entered in a form, so that you can use this data with another program. See the section "Saving an On-Screen Form," later in this chapter, for details on the second method.

Using an On-Screen Form

The great advantage to forms is that you *can't* edit them—instead, you open a blank copy of the form (thus preserving the original), and then move from field to field, filling in information as necessary.

The three types of form fields (text, check box, and drop-down) not only look different; you use a distinct approach with each type (see fig. 39.13).

Tip

When you give some-one an online form to use, be sure to give him the template. Tell him to copy the template into the TEMPLATES subfolder under the MSOFFICE folder.

Clicking this arrow displays the items in a drop-down list.

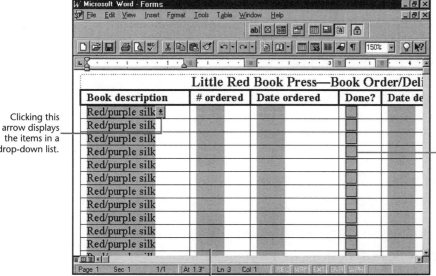

Respond to a text field by typing text or a number

Select or clear a check box by pressing the space bar

Fig. 39.13

Click the arrow or press Alt+down arrow to display the items in a drop-down list.

You can customize your form in several ways. For example, you can customize a text field to hold only dates and to format the date you enter in a certain way. Any type of field may have a help message attached so that when you enter the field or press F1, instructions for using the field appear in the status bar. In some fields, a particular response may cause some action in another part of the form; for example, a positive response to a check box field may activate another field later in the form. Be alert to what happens on-screen as you fill in your form.

To open a form, follow these steps:

1. Choose File, New. The New dialog box appears (see fig. 39.14).

Fig. 39.14

Open a form by choosing File, New.

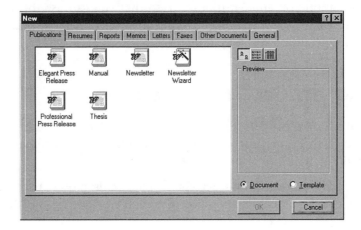

2. From the Template list, select the name of your form.

3. Choose OK. An unnamed copy of the form appears on-screen, with the first field in the form highlighted.

◀ See
"Saving, Opening, and Closing Files,"
p. 106

If your form isn't based on a template, you can still use it by opening it as a regular file. Choose File, Open, locate and select your form, and choose OK. Save it with a new name to preserve the original.

Filling In an On-Screen Form

When you open a new, protected form, the first field is selected (highlighted).

To fill in the fields in a form, follow these steps:

1. Respond to the selected field as appropriate.

   In a text field, type the requested text or number.

Check boxes toggle on and off. Press the space bar once to place a mark in an empty check box; press the space bar a second time to remove a mark from the box. (Check boxes may contain a mark by default; if so, press the space bar once to remove the mark, and press the space bar a second time to replace the mark.)

In a drop-down field, click the arrow to display a list of selections, then click the item you want to select. Or, with the keyboard, press Alt+down arrow to display the list, and press the down- or up-arrow keys to select an item from the list.

Tip
Except while a drop-down list is displayed, you can use the up- and down-arrow keys to move between fields in a form.

2. Press Tab or Enter to accept your entry. One of two things happens:

If your entry is acceptable, Word selects the next field.

If your entry is unacceptable, Word displays an error message and returns you to the current field so that you can make a correct entry. You might get an error message, for example, when you type text in a text field that's formatted to hold a number.

3. Continue filling in fields until you complete the form.

If you make a mistake and want to return to a previous field, hold down the Shift key while you press the Tab or Enter key until you reach that field. To move to the next field without making an entry, just press Tab or Enter. You can also move between fields by pressing the up- or down-arrow keys, and you can move to the beginning or end of your form by pressing Ctrl+Home or Ctrl+End.

Tip
Watch the status bar for messages that may help you fill each field in a form. You can also try pressing F1 to get help for a particular field when that field is selected.

To edit an entry in a field you've already left, use the mouse or arrow keys to position the insertion point next to the text you want to edit; press Backspace to delete characters, or type the characters you want to insert.

If you want to insert a Tab character in a field, without moving to the next field, hold down the Ctrl key as you press Tab.

Always watch the way Word interprets your response to a field. For example, if a text field is formatted to include numbers formatted with no decimal places, and you respond by spelling out a number (four, for example), Word interprets your response as 0 (zero) because it's expecting numbers, not letters. Return to the field and type the correct response.

◀ **See**
"Using Template Wizards," p. 269

If the form isn't protected, the first field isn't highlighted when you open the form, and you can't move between fields by pressing Tab or Enter. To fill in an unprotected form, use Word's normal techniques for moving the insertion point from field to field. Or better yet, protect the form by choosing Tools, Protect Document, and selecting the Forms option.

◀ **See**
"Working with Tables," p. 286

Saving an On-Screen Form

Because most on-screen forms are based on templates, they do not have names when you open them. You must save and name the forms. (If a form is not based on a template, use the following steps to save your form with a unique name. In this way, you preserve the original for future use.)

To save a form, follow these steps:

1. Choose File, Save As. The Save As dialog box appears.

2. Type a name in the File Name box, and select the folder for the form from the list of folders. You can save the form to a different drive by selecting a drive from the Save In list.

3. Choose OK.

Troubleshooting

I opened a new form and the first field isn't selected.

The form isn't protected. To fill it in, protect it by choosing Tools, Protect Document. (It may be a good idea to open the form template and protect it, so that the next time you open the form, it's protected.)

Customizing Form Fields

There are many ways you can customize form fields to make your forms more informative, more automated, and easier to use. Automatic date and time fields, for example, insert the current date or time into your form. Default entries suggest a likely response to a field. Help messages give users hints on how to fill in a particular field. Controls prevent certain types of errors. Formulas calculate results in a field. Macros run when users enter or exit a particular field. Controls prevent certain types of errors.

You can also apply most types of formatting to form fields. For example, you can make a form field boldface so that the response stands out. Or you can apply a border to a form field to add boxes in a form that isn't based on a table.

You can customize form fields while you're creating your form, by customizing fields as you insert them, or after you've created your form, by editing selected fields. To edit form fields after you've inserted them, the document must be unprotected.

To customize form fields as you insert them, follow these steps:

1. Choose <u>I</u>nsert, For<u>m</u> Field. The Form Field dialog box appears (see fig. 39.15).

2. From the Type group (<u>T</u>ext, <u>C</u>heck Box, or <u>D</u>rop-Down), select the type of form field you want to insert and customize.

3. Click the <u>O</u>ptions button. A dialog box containing options for customizing the type of form field you've selected appears (see fig. 39.16).

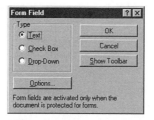

Fig. 39.15

Choose <u>I</u>nsert, For<u>m</u> Field to customize form fields as you insert them.

Fig. 39.16

If you select <u>T</u>ext from the form field Type group and then click the Options button, the Text Form Field Options dialog box appears.

To customize an existing form field, follow these steps:

1. Unprotect your document, if it's protected, by choosing <u>T</u>ools, <u>U</u>nprotect Document or by clicking the Protect Form button on the Forms toolbar.

2. Double-click the form field you want to customize, displaying the Form Field Options dialog box.

Tip
If you use a form field repeatedly in a form, duplicate it by placing it in AutoText.

Or, select the form field you want to customize by clicking it, positioning the insertion point above or below it, and pressing the up- or down-arrow key, or by positioning the insertion point next to it and holding down the Shift key as you press the right- or left-arrow key. Then do one of the following:

Click the Options button on the Forms toolbar.

Or, click the form field you want to customize with the right mouse button to display the shortcut menu. Select Form Field Options.

3. Select the options you want, and choose OK.

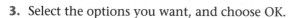

Customizing Text Form Fields

◄ See
"Using
AutoText,"
p. 213

Tip
Specifying a
field size is
particularly
important
when you
are using
preprinted
forms.

Text fields are probably the most customizable of the three form field types. You can customize them by type (regular, number, date, or calculation, for example), by default text, by the size of the field, by the maximum number of characters in the response, or by the format of the response. As with all form field types, you can also customize text fields by adding macros (see the later section "Adding Macros to a Form"), by adding Help text (see the section "Adding Help to a Form"), by renaming the bookmark (see "Naming and Finding Fields in a Form"), or by disabling the field for entry (see "Disabling Form Fields").

To specify the restrictions on a text form field, follow these steps:

1. Open the Text Form Field Options dialog box (see fig. 39.17).

Fig. 39.17

Text form fields
have numerous
customizing
options.

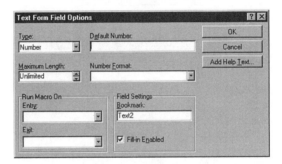

2. Select from the following types of options (see the upcoming tables for details about the Type and Format options):

OPTION	DESCRIPTION
Type (see table 39.1)	Select from six types of text entries: Regular Text, Number, Date, Current Date, Current Time, and Calculation.
Default Text	Type the text that you want to appear as the default entry in this field. Users can change the entry.
Maximum Length	Type or select "Unlimited" or the number of characters or numbers you want the field to accept (up to 255).
Text Format	Select from various types of text, numeric, and date formats, depending on what you've selected in the Type option (see table 39.2).

3. Choose OK.

You will often use two or more of these options together. For example, if you select Number as the Type, then you might choose 0.00 as the Format so that a numeric response appears in two decimal places.

TABLE 39.1   Type Options for Text Form Field Options Dialog Box

SELECT THIS OPTION:	WHEN USERS SHOULD RESPOND BY TYPING:
Regular Text	Text. Word formats the text according to your selection in the Text Format list.
Number	A number. Word formats the number according to your selection in the Number Format list, and displays an error message if user types text.
Date	A date. Word formats the date according to your selection in the Date Format list. Word displays an error message (A valid date is required) if user types text or a number not recognizable as a date, and returns user to the current field for an appropriate response. (Almost any response resembling a date will work, however.)
Current Date	No user response allowed. Word enters the current date (and updates the date when the document is opened*).
Current Time	No user response allowed. Word enters the current time (and updates the time when the document is opened*).
Calculation	Enter a formula when inserting or editing this field; no user response allowed. Word applies your formula, and prints the result of the calculation in this field. For example, you can insert a simple SUM formula to add up the numbers in a column if your form is based on a table. (Word updates the result when the document is opened.*)

You can specify that Word update the date, time, or a formula when you print your form by choosing the Tools, Options command, selecting the Print tab, and then selecting Update Fields from the Printing Options. Or you can use an exit macro to update the fields.

TABLE 39.2   Text Format Options for Text Form Field Options

TYPE OPTION	TEXT FORMAT OPTION	WHAT ENTRY LOOKS LIKE
Regular Text	Uppercase Lowercase	ALL CAPITAL LETTERS all lowercase letters
	First Capital	First letter of first word is capitalized
	Title Case	First Letter Of Each Word Is Capitalized
Number	0 0.00 #,##0 #,##0.00 $#,##0.00;($#,##0.00) 0% 0.00%	123456 123456.00 123,456 123,456.00 $123,456.00 10% 10.00%
Date	M/d/yy	1/1/95
	dddd, MMMM d, yyyy d MMMM, yyyy MMMM d, yyyy	Sunday, January 3, 1995 3 January, 1995 January 3, 1995
	d-MMM-yy MMM, yy MM/dd/yy h:mm AM/PM MM/dd/yy h:mm:ss AM/PM	3-Jan-95 Jan, 95 01/03/95 2:15 PM 01/03/95 2:15:58 PM
Time	h:mm AM/PM h:mm:ss AM/PM H:mm H:mm:ss	2:15 PM 2:15:58 PM 2:15 2:15:58
Current Date	Same as Date	Same as Date
Current Time	h:mm AM/PM h:mm:ss AM/PM H:mm H:mm:ss	3:30 PM 3:30:00 PM 15:30 15:30:00
Calculation	Same as Number	Same as Number

◀ **See**
"Working with Tables,"
p. 286

Customizing Check Box Form Fields

You can customize check box fields, which require the user to make a simple "yes or no" response, by determining size and by choosing whether they will be checked or unchecked by default. As with all form field types, you can also customize check box fields by adding macros (see the later section "Adding Macros to a Form"), by adding Help text (see the "Adding Help to a Form" section), by renaming the bookmark (see "Naming and Finding Fields in a Form"), or by disabling the field for entry (see "Disabling Form Fields").

To customize a check box field, follow these steps:

1. Open the Check Box Form Field Options dialog box (see fig. 39.18).

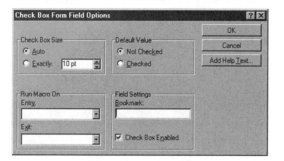

Fig. 39.18

You can make a check box exactly the size you want, and you can specify whether it's checked or unchecked by default.

2. Determine the check box size by selecting the appropriate option:

  ■ Select Auto to make the check box the same size as the text around it.

  ■ Select Exactly to make the check box a specific size. Click the up or down arrow or press the up- or down-arrow key to increase or decrease the box size. Or type the size you want; for example, type **12 pt** for a 12-point box, **.25"** for a quarter-inch box, **1 pi** for a 1-pica box, or **1 cm** for a 1-centimeter box. (When you next open the dialog box, the measurement is converted to an equivalent value in points.)

3. Determine the Default Value by selecting one of the following options:

  If you select Not Checked, the check box will be empty by default (a negative response). The user must press the space bar to check the box.

  If you select Checked, the check box will have a mark in it by default (a positive response). The user must press the space bar to deselect the box.

4. Choose OK.

Customizing Drop-Down Form Fields

A drop-down list gives users up to 25 items to choose from. It helps ensure that the user's response to a field is valid, because the list contains only valid responses. It also helps users to fill in the form, because they don't have to guess what kind of response the field requires.

You will most likely customize a drop-down form field as you insert it, because there's nothing in the list until you add items. You may want to add items to the list later, remove some items, or rearrange the items, however. You can do this by editing the drop-down field.

To add items to the list in a drop-down field, follow these steps:

1. Open the Drop-Down Form Field Options dialog box (see fig. 39.19).

Fig. 39.19

You can add items to a drop-down list, remove items from it, or rearrange the items in the list.

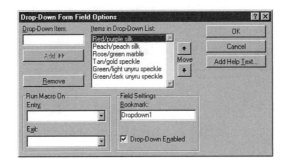

2. In the Drop-Down Item box, type the item you want to add to the list.

3. Click the Add button.

4. Repeat steps 2 and 3 to add more items to the list.

5. Choose OK.

To remove items from a drop-down list field, follow these steps:

1. Select the drop-down field and open the Drop-Down Form Field Options dialog box.

2. Select the item you want to remove from the Items in Drop-Down List list.

3. Click the Remove button.

4. Repeat steps 2 and 3 to remove more items.

5. Choose OK.

To rearrange items in a drop-down list field, follow these steps:

1. Select the drop-down field and open the Drop-Down Form Field Options dialog box.

2. Select the item you want to move in the Items in Drop-Down List list.

3. Move the item up by clicking the Move up arrow, or move it down by clicking the Move down arrow. (With the keyboard, press the up or down arrow to select the item you want to move, press Tab to select the Move up or Move down arrow, and then press the space bar to move the selected item up or down.)

4. Repeat steps 2 and 3 to move more items.

5. Choose OK.

Formatting Form Fields

Users can't format entries in a protected form when they're filling in the form. But when you're creating a form, you can apply font and paragraph formatting, as well as many other formatting options, to fields. Responses will then appear in that formatting.

You must insert a form field before you can format it. Remember, the document must be unprotected.

◀ **See**
"Working with Cells, Text Boxes, and Fields," p. 70

To format a form field, first select the form field you want to format. Then use one of the following methods to apply formatting:

- Choose the formatting command you want to use, and select the formatting options you want to apply.

- Click a formatting option on a toolbar.

- Press formatting shortcut keys.

- Click the selected field with the right mouse button to display the shortcut menu, and select Font, Paragraph, or Bullets and Numbering. Then select the formatting options you want to apply.

◀ **See**
"Formatting Text," p. 190

Disabling Form Fields

In most forms, you want users to respond to each field. But sometimes you'll want to disable a field so that users cannot respond. You may want to include a default entry in disabled fields.

To disable a form field, follow these steps:

1. Unprotect the document, if necessary.

2. Select the field you want to disable, and display the Form Field Options dialog box.

3. Clear the appropriate option: Fill-In Enabled (for text fields), Check Box Enabled (for check box fields), or Drop-Down Enabled (for drop-down fields).

4. Choose OK.

Naming and Finding Fields in a Form

Each form field you insert in a document has a name: its *bookmark*. You can use this bookmark to help you find a field quickly. By default, Word numbers the fields you insert, calling them Text1, Check7, Dropdown13, and so forth. You can name a form field whatever you want (subject to bookmark naming rules, however).

To name a form field, follow these steps:

1. Unprotect the document, if necessary.

2. Select the field and display the Form Field Options dialog box.

3. In the Field Settings group, select the Bookmark text box and type the name.

4. Choose OK.

To find a named form field, follow these steps:

1. Unprotect the document.

2. Choose Edit, Bookmark.

3. Type the name you want to find in the Bookmark Name box, or select it from the list.

4. Click the Go To button. Word displays the field, but doesn't close the dialog box. Go to another field, or choose Close to close the dialog box.

Adding Help to a Form

By adding help messages, you can make it much easier for users to respond correctly to a field in your form. When the field is selected in your form, help messages can appear in the status bar at the bottom of the screen, or as a message box displayed when the user presses the F1 key.

You can type your own text for a help message, or use an existing AutoText entry. For example, you may have an AutoText entry that reads Press F1 for Help, which you include as a status bar help message in each field for which you've included F1 help (see fig. 39.20).

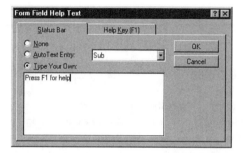

Fig. 39.20

Help can appear in the status bar if you use the Status Bar tab.

To add help to a form field, follow these steps:

1. Display the Form Field Options dialog box for the field to which you want to add help.

2. Click the Add Help Text button.

3. Select the Status Bar tab to add a line of help in the status bar, or select the Help Key (F1) tab to add help that appears as a message box when the user presses F1 (see fig. 39.21).

Tip

If you add F1 help to a field, also include a status bar message reading Press F1 for help so that users know where to find help.

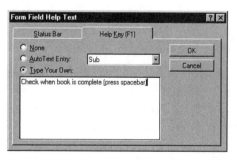

Fig. 39.21

Help can appear as a message box when the user presses F1 if you use the Help Key (F1) tab.

4. To add your own help message, select the Type Your Own option and type your message (up to 255 characters).

   Or, to use the text of an AutoText entry as help, select the AutoText Entry option, and select the AutoText entry you want to use from the list.

5. Choose OK.

6. Choose OK again to close the Form Field Options dialog box and return to your document.

If you're including status line help messages, be aware that even if your form is protected, users can turn off the status line. Also be aware that users have no way of knowing whether F1 help is attached to a field (though a message in the status line can help, if the status line is displayed). If your form is based on a template, try including a message (to alert users to the presence of F1 help) in an AutoNew macro that runs when users create a new form.

> **Note**
>
> Help users fill in your form, or give them some instructions about what to do with the form when they're finished with it, by including a helpful message as part of an AutoNew macro that runs when users open the form. (AutoNew macros are attached to templates, and run when you create a new document based on the template. This idea works best for forms that are based on a template.)

Adding Macros to a Form

Macros can automate your forms in many ways. They can activate or deactivate fields, depending on the user's response to an earlier field. They can update fields that contain calculations. They can cause Word to skip over unneeded fields.

To use a macro in a form, you must create the macro before you apply it to a particular field in the form. Macros run at one of two times: when the user enters the field or when the user leaves the field.

When you record or write macros for your form, be aware that macros use bookmarks to locate particular fields, and make sure that your form contains no duplicate bookmark names. You can find out the automatic bookmark name of any field, or give the field a new bookmark name, by selecting the field, displaying the Form Field Options dialog box, and then looking at the Bookmark text box (for details, see the "Naming and Finding Fields in a Form" section, earlier in this chapter).

To make your macros useful, attach them to the template your form is based on. You can do this most easily as you create the macro, or you can attach a macro to your template by choosing File, Templates, clicking the Organizer button, and then selecting the Macros tab.

Before you can apply macros to a field, the document must be unprotected. And remember, before you can apply a macro to a form field, you must create the macro.

To apply a macro to a form field, follow these steps:

1. Select the field to which you want to apply a macro, and display the Form Field Options dialog box.

2. If you want the macro to run when the user moves the insertion point into the field, select the Entry option in the Run Macro On group, and select the macro you want from the list.

    Or, if you want the macro to run when the user moves the insertion point out of the field, select the Exit option in the Run Macro On group, and select the macro you want from the list.

3. Choose OK.

If no macros appear in either the Entry or Exit list, no macros are available for your form's template. You must either create a macro, or attach it to your template.

Protecting and Unprotecting a Form with a Password

If you don't want users to change your form, protect it with a password. In this way, anyone who attempts to unprotect the form must supply the password (including you—don't forget your password).

To password-protect a document, follow these steps:

1. Choose Tools, Protect Document. The Protect Document dialog box appears (see fig. 39.22).

Fig. 39.22

Type your password in the Password box.

2. Select the Forms option.

3. Select the Password box, and type your password. Choose OK. The Confirm Password dialog box appears (see fig. 39.23).

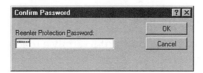

4. In the Reenter Protection Password box, retype your password. Spelling, spacing, and capitalization must match exactly. Choose OK. (If you don't retype the password exactly as you originally typed it, you get an error message. Choose OK and try again.)

5. Choose OK to return to your document.

To unprotect a password-protected document, follow these steps:

1. Choose Tools, Unprotect Document, or click the Protect Form button on the Forms toolbar. If the document is password protected, the Unprotect Document dialog box appears (see fig. 39.24).

2. Type the password exactly as you originally typed it in the Password box. Spelling, spacing, and capitalization must match exactly.

3. Choose OK. If you typed the password correctly, your document will be unprotected. If you typed the password incorrectly, Word displays a message that the password is incorrect, and you must choose OK to return to your document, which remains protected.

Protecting Part of a Form

If your form is divided into sections, you can protect parts of it, while leaving other parts unprotected. You can include password protection for the protected sections.

To protect or unprotect part of a form, follow these steps:

1. Choose Tools, Protect Document. The Protect Document dialog box appears.

2. Select the Forms option.

3. Click the Sections button to display the Section Protection dialog box (see fig. 39.25).

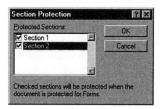

Fig. 39.25

You can protect part of a document if it's divided into sections.

4. In the Protected Sections list, select each section you want protected, so that it appears with a mark in the box. Clear each section you want unprotected.

5. Choose OK to return to the Protect Document dialog box. (If you want to protect the sections with a password, do so now. For details, see the earlier section "Protecting and Unprotecting a Form with a Password.")

6. Choose OK to return to the document.

Converting Existing Forms

The forms you want to create may already exist on paper or in another program's format. Sometimes the easiest way to convert a form is to simply retype it, but at other times you may want to use existing data.

You can use a scanner to help you retype an existing form. Scan the form as a picture, and insert it into a text box. When a picture is in a text box, you can move it to the layer behind the text in your document. In the text layer, you can trace over the scanned form to create your new form. When you're finished, select and delete the scanned form.

Although you can't import form fields from a document created by another program into a Word document, you can import text. If a form exists in another program, import the text, format it as you need it, and add the form fields. You can change text to a table by selecting the text and choosing T<u>a</u>ble, Con<u>v</u>ert Text to Table. To learn about tables, see Chapter 11, "Working with Tables and Borders."

Printing a Form

◀ **See**
"Printing
Documents,"
p. 134

There are three ways you might want to print a form. You might want to print it exactly as it appears on-screen, including the labels, any graphics, and the data in the fields. You might want to print the data onto preprinted forms only. Or you might want to print the labels and graphics only, to create a preprinted form.

Printing the Filled-In Form

To print the entire form, including everything that appears on your screen, use Word's usual printing commands. Use this method to print forms that you've already filled in.

To print the entire form, follow these steps:

1. Fill in the form, or open a filled-in form.

2. Choose <u>F</u>ile, <u>P</u>rint.

3. Select the printing options you want from the Print dialog box, and choose OK.

To learn more about printing options, refer to Chapter 8, "Proofreading and Printing Documents."

Printing Form Data Only

Print only data when you're using preprinted forms. Because you use the same form template to print the blank form as you use when you print only the data, the form data will line up correctly with the fields.

To print only data onto a preprinted form, follow these steps:

1. Insert the preprinted form into your printer.

2. Choose <u>T</u>ools, <u>O</u>ptions.

3. Select the Print tab (see fig. 39.26).

4. Select Print Data Only for Forms from the Options for Current Document Only group, and choose OK.

5. Choose File, Print, select printing options, and choose OK.

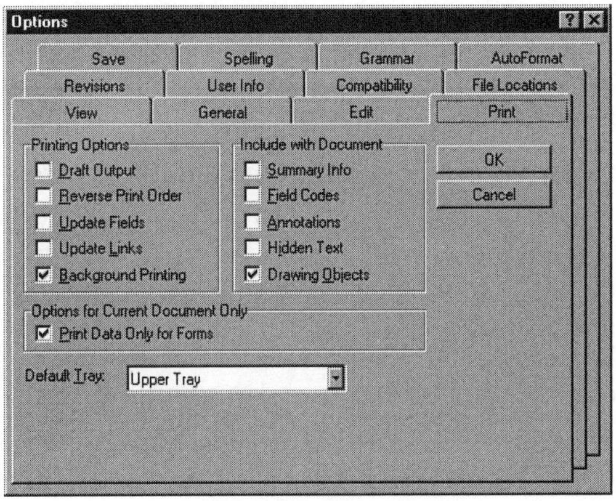

Fig. 39.26

Choose Tools, Options to print form data only.

Notice that this procedure ensures that each time you print this form, you will print data only. Repeat the procedure, deselecting the Print Data Only for Forms option in step 4, if you want to print the entire form.

Printing a Blank Form

To make your own preprinted form, print the form only, without the data.

To print a blank form, follow these steps:

1. Choose File, New, select the form you want to print from the Template list, and choose OK.

2. Without filling in the form, print it by choosing File, Print, selecting printing options, and choosing OK.

Remember that fields in a form appear shaded if the Shading Options button is selected in the Forms toolbar. This shading does not appear when you print your forms. If you want shading to appear on a printed form, use Format, Borders and Shading to shade selected areas of your form.

Troubleshooting

When I print the form data, it doesn't line up with the form fields on the preprinted form.

Be sure you're using the same form to print your data as you used to create the pre-printed form.

Saving Data Only

You may want to use the data you collect in your forms with another program, such as a database. To do that, save only the data, and import the data into the other program. Word saves a copy of the data as a Text Only document (with the extension TXT), creating a comma-delimited document containing only the responses in your fields.

Many applications can read the data stored in comma-delimited files. Microsoft Excel, for example, can open and automatically separate each piece of data into a worksheet cell if the file uses the file extension CSV (comma separated values).

To save data only from your form, follow these steps:

1. Choose Tools, Options.
2. Select the Save tab.
3. In the Save Options group, select the Save Data Only for Forms option.
4. Choose OK.
5. Choose File, Save As to save and name your data file.

Building Forms with Fill-In Dialog Boxes

With {fillin} fields, you can design a form letter so that you need to enter a data item (such as a name) only once—no matter how many times it appears in the letter. This feature is extremely useful for filling out invoices, contracts, proposals, or business forms in which the majority of the body copy remains unchanged. {fillin} fields are useful also when you need to insert personal phrases in mass mailings. Figure 39.27 shows a document you can create to demonstrate how {fillin} fields work.

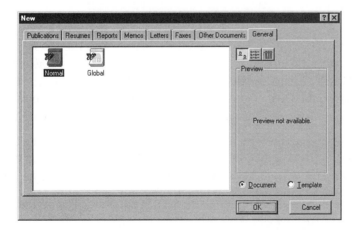

Fig. 39.27

Field codes can
enter data or
display dialog
boxes that prompt
users to enter data
that can be used
repeatedly through
the document.

First you should create a new template for form letters.

To create a new template, follow these steps:

1. Choose File, New. The New dialog box appears (see fig. 39.28).

Fig. 39.28

By using a template
to create a form,
you prevent users
from accidentally
changing the
original.

2. Select the Template option in the New box.

Normal should already be selected in the Template list.

3. Select a different template on which to base the letter, if you prefer. You may have created a template, for example, that includes a letterhead or company logo.

4. Choose OK.

5. Modify the template to include any body text, graphics, tables, and so on that you want in the form letter. Format the template's page layout to account for letterhead, if necessary.

Keep the template open and on-screen so that you can add {fillin} fields as described in the next section.

Using {fillin} Fields

To set up your template to prompt the user to enter key information, use {fillin} fields. Figure 39.29 shows a dialog box prompt generated by a {fillin} field.

Fig. 39.29

The {fillin} field is an easy way to ask users to enter data in a dialog box. You don't need to create a macro to display the dialog box.

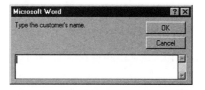

To insert the {fillin} field code in a document, move the insertion point to where you want the operator's input to appear. Choose Insert, Field. Make sure that [All] is selected in the categories list, then select Fill-in from the Insert Field Names list. In the Field Codes text box, move the insertion point past FILLIN, type the user prompt—enclosing it in quotation marks—and choose OK.

Tip

Enclose prompts of more than one word in quotation marks (" "). If you don't enclose a phrase in quotation marks, Word uses only the first word.

Alternatively, you can type the {fillin} field into the template. To do this, move the insertion point to where you want the results to appear, then press Ctrl+F9, the Insert Field key. Position the insertion point between the field characters, and type the following field type and instructions:

```
fillin "Type the customer address."
```

To display the dialog box requesting the customer's name, and to update the {fillin} field, follow these steps:

1. Select the field character at either end of the code to select the {fillin} field.

2. Press F9. The Fillin dialog box appears.

3. Type a customer address in the box. To start a new line in the box, press Enter. Choose OK to complete the box and insert your entry in the document.

The entry you typed appears in the document in the same location as the field code. Text following the inserted entry is pushed down or right, just as if you had manually typed text in the location. To switch between displaying fields and their results, press Alt+F9, or display the Options dialog box (by choosing Tools, Options) and click the Field Codes check box in the View tab.

Reusing Field Results

If you use field codes in form letters, you can request an input from the operator once, but have that information appear in multiple locations. To reuse an entry from one {fillin} box in other locations in a form letter, you must use the following three field codes:

- {set bookmark data} assigns data to a bookmark, which stores information so that it can be reused later. In the next example, because the data argument for {set} is a {fillin} field, the operator's entry in response to the [fillin] field is stored in the bookmark name Custname. If the data is explicit text that doesn't change, such as Montana, you must enclose it in quotation marks. Don't include a space in the bookmark name.

- {fillin [prompt]} displays an input box in which the operator can enter data. The brackets ([ ]) indicate that the prompt is optional.

- {ref bookmark} displays the contents of a bookmark at the field location. You enter this field to repeat a bookmark's contents in other locations within the document.

Figure 39.30 shows a field code that requests the customer's name and stores it in the Custname bookmark. The {fillin} field requests the name. The {set} field sets Custname equal to the {fillin} entry. The {ref} field displays the entry stored in Custname. You can use {ref} throughout the letter, following the {set} field, even though the data was entered only once.

In figure 39.30, the {fillin} field data was entered into a dialog box. The {set} field code then stores the entry in the bookmark Custname. The data stored in Custname can be redisplayed anywhere in the document with {ref Custname}. The {ref} field code references the data stored in that bookmark. You can reuse {ref} as many times as you want in the document. Using switches, you can format the information that {ref} returns.

Tip

To update {fillin} fields throughout an entire document, select the entire document, then press F9 (Update).

Tip

You can make up your own single words to use as bookmarks.

Fig. 39.30

The combination of {fillin}, {set}, and {ref} field codes enables the user to fill in one dialog box and have the data used throughout a document.

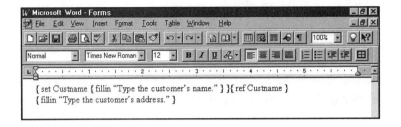

As you may recall, *nested* fields are one field code inside another field code. In the example, a {fillin} field is nested inside a {ref} field. The result of the {fillin} is used to supply one of the arguments required by the {ref} field. To build the nested field in figure 39.30 from the inside out, follow these steps:

1. Position the insertion point where you need to insert the entry.

2. Press Ctrl+F9, the Insert Field key.

3. Between the field characters, type **fillin**, a space, then a prompt to the operator (enclosed in quotation marks), such as **"Type the customer's name."**

4. Select the field you just typed. To select field characters and field contents, select a field character at one end or the other to select the entire field.

5. Press Ctrl+F9 to enclose the selection in field characters.

   This step *nests* the first field entirely inside another set of field characters. The insertion point moves to directly follow the first field character.

6. Directly after the first field character, type set, a space, and then the appropriate bookmark, such as Custname. Leave a space after the bookmark, but don't leave spaces in the name.

This new nested field requests a name and stores it in the bookmark, but the entry doesn't appear on-screen. To see the field's result, you must update the field.

To update both of these new fields and see the customer's name requested and displayed, follow these steps:

1. Select the entire line (or lines) containing both fields.

2. Press F9 (Update Fields).

   A dialog box appears, requesting the customer's name (refer to fig. 39.29).

3. Type the entry as requested.

4. Choose OK.

The {set} field stores in the bookmark the name you entered in the {fillin} field. The {ref bookmark} field displays the contents of a bookmark in the letter. You can enter a {ref bookmark} field in multiple locations in the document, wherever you need the name repeated. In figure 39.31, the Custname bookmark is repeated at the last line on the screen. The new contents of {ref bookmark} don't appear, however, until each {ref bookmark} field is updated.

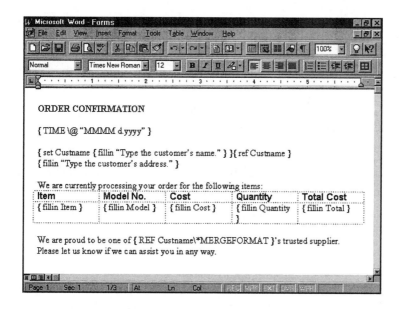

Fig. 39.31

Reuse data by repeating the {ref bookmark} combination wherever you want the data displayed. {ref} only displays the new data when it is selected and updated.

After you enter all the field codes, choose File, Save As, and choose OK to save the template.

These fields display data entered in the address block; they also request and display the type, model, and cost of the items the customer ordered. The switch * mergeformat, used in the {ref bookmark * mergeformat} field, ensures that the formatting you applied to the field name in the document doesn't change when the field is updated. The format of field results matches the format you apply to the letter r in ref.

The inclusion of the * mergeformat switch is controlled by the Preserve Formatting During Updates option in the Field dialog box.

Saving and Naming the Template

This document must be saved as a template because you opened it as one. To save your template, choose File, Save As. In the File Name text box, type an eight-letter name to describe your form. Notice that you cannot change many of the text or list boxes. Choose OK. Word saves the template and adds the extension DOT. When you save a new template, give it a name that reflects the type of document it creates.

Updating Fields in a Form

To test the fields you entered, update them. This action will display new values, or enable you to enter new ones.

To enter data in the {fillin} fields and update the {ref} fields, follow these steps:

1. Choose File, New, and select a template containing {fillin} fields. Choose OK.

2. Move the insertion point to the top of the document, then press F11 to select the next field. (Press Shift+F11 to select the preceding field, or select the entire document by choosing Edit, Select All to update all fields.)

3. Press F9 to update the selected field or, if the entire document is selected, to update each field in turn, from the beginning to the end of the document.

4. Type the data requested, and choose OK.

Tip
To preserve the previous entry, select Cancel; nothing is produced if no previous entry existed.

If an error appears at a field's location, display the field codes in the document. Check for correct spelling and spacing. Use one space between field types, instructions, and switches.

Creating a Macro to Update Fields Automatically

Because this type of fill-in form is designed for repetitive use, you can have Word automatically prompt the user for the information as soon as the document is opened. You can do this with an automatic macro that updates all fields in the document when the document opens. With the fill-in template as the active document, follow these steps:

1. Choose Tools, Macro. The Macro dialog box appears (see fig. 39.32).

2. Type **AutoNew** in the Macro Name box.

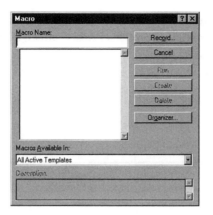

Fig. 39.32

You can record a macro that automatically updates field codes when a document or template opens.

3. In the Macros Available In list, select the Documents Based on [template] option, where [template] is the name of the template. The macro will be available only to this template or to documents that originate from this template.

4. Click the Record button.

5. Enter a description, such as **Automatically updates all fields**, in the Description box.

6. Choose OK.

The Macro Record toolbar appears, and the REC indicator is highlighted in the status bar, indicating that the recorder is on. Follow these steps to record a process that updates all fields in the document:

1. Press Ctrl+5 (use the numeric keypad) to select the entire document.

2. Press F9. A prompt generated by the first {fillin} field appears.

3. Click the Cancel button for each {fillin} prompt.

4. Press Ctrl+Home to return the insertion point to the top of the document.

5. Click the Stop button in the Macro Record toolbar.

Choose File, Save All to save the macro and close the template. To test the macro, follow these steps:

1. Choose File, New.

2. Select the template from the Use Template list.

3. Choose OK.

When you open the document, the AutoNew macro runs the update macro. Enter a response to each dialog box, or choose Cancel. If the macro doesn't run correctly, record it again. If you rerecord, using the same name (AutoNew), Word asks whether you want to replace the previous recording. Choose Yes.❖

Chapter 40

Using Office To Send and Manage a Mass Mailing

Mary Sue Brown is a trainer with broad experience in the Microsoft Office Suite. Mary has vast spreadsheet experience and has prepared business plans and presentations using a variety of word processing and graphics applications. She trains beginning, intermediate, and advanced levels of Microsoft Word, Excel, PowerPoint, and Access.

Suppose that you want to prepare customized letters to your 3,000 customers in the Western Region announcing the appointment of a new regional manager.

Or maybe you just had post cards printed announcing a new product line. Now you need to print labels, with customer account numbers, in ZIP code order, for all customers who spent over $100 with your company last year.

Sound overwhelming? Well, projects like these can be. But careful planning can eliminate the worry and make mass mailings routine. I especially like the Word Mail Merge feature because you can see sizable results. It is a great accomplishment to type one letter and a list of names, then have hundreds of letters print.

I have used Word and Excel extensively to create customized Employee Benefit statements and custom letters, with over 40 merge fields and many data sources. I am confident that you will appreciate the ease with which Word allows you to create and edit merge documents and create professional looking documents.

Techniques from the Pros

by Mary Sue Brown

In this chapter, I share my experience with simplifying mass mailings through planning and elimination of redundancy.

Specifically, you learn to

- Create a Mail Merge main document
- Create a Mail Merge data source
- Insert Merge fields
- Sort a data source
- Merge the main document and data source into customized form letters
- Use data from an Excel spreadsheet
- Use the Address Book in Microsoft Word
- Select data from the data source that meets specific criteria
- Create labels using Mail Merge
- Create envelopes using Mail Merge

Creating a Main Document

The first step in preparing a mass mailing is to create the letter you want to send. In other words, create a main document.

A *main document* includes the standard text and graphics that are part of each form letter. Word has simplified the process for you with the Mail Merge Helper. The Mail Merge Helper will take you step by step through the process of creating a main document and a data source. There is no need to memorize and repeat the steps in creating custom documents—just follow Word's lead.

Creating the Main Document File

To create a main document using Mail Merge Helper, follow these steps:

1. Choose the Tools, Mail Merge command. The Mail Merge Helper dialog box appears, as shown in figure 40.1.

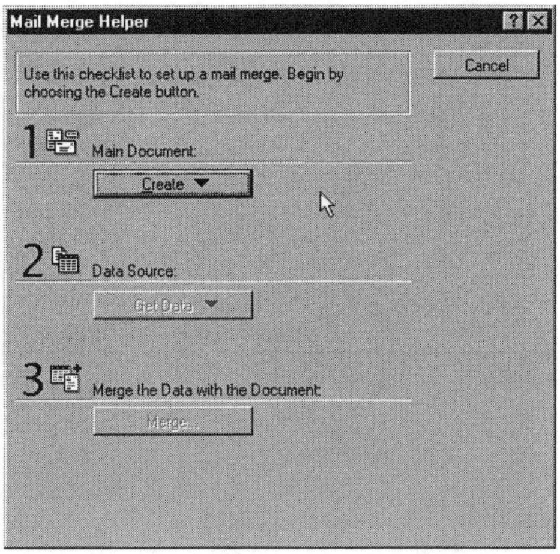

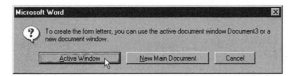

Techniques from the Pros Techniques from the Pros Techniques from the Pros

Fig. 40.1

Click the Create button to begin the process for creating a mail merge.

2. Under Step 1, choose the Create button.

3. From the drop-down list, choose Form Letters. The dialog box shown in figure 40.2 appears.

Fig. 40.2

Use this dialog box to tell Word if you want to use the Active Window or begin a New Main Document.

4. If the letter you want to use is in the active window, choose Active Window.

   Or if you want to create a new document to use as your main document, choose New Main Document.

Notice that the type of document you selected (Form Letters) and the name of your main document are now listed under Step 1, as shown in figure 40.3.

Fig. 40.3

Under Step 1 in the Mail Merge Helper dialog box, you see the type of document and the name of your main document.

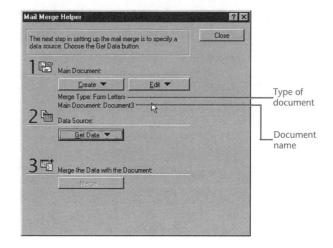

Editing the Main Document

So you took a stab at Mail Merge, but you need to make some changes to either your main document or the data source. Or maybe you created and named a document but did not yet add the body text (see fig. 40.4). This means you'll need to edit your document.

Fig. 40.4

Your letter with information from your data source gives you an example to see if you used the correct fields and if they are in the correct places.

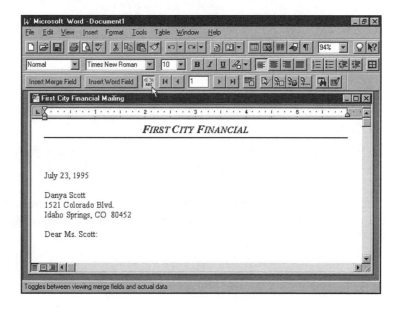

To enter or edit text in the main document, click the <u>E</u>dit button under Step 1. The name of the file appears in the dialog box. Click the name of your main document to open it.

Remember that a main document includes the standard text and graphics that will be part of each letter. If you have a letter you have used before, you need to delete the name and address of the last recipient.

If you are creating a letter from scratch, type the paragraphs that will be standard to all letters. Omit things like name, address, city, state, ZIP, etc. You will insert these items as merge fields later.

> **Note**
>
> So you don't have to type the current date each time you use the same main document, position your cursor on the line where you want the date to appear. Then choose <u>I</u>nsert, Date & <u>T</u>ime. Locate the date format you want and select the Insert as Field option, located at the bottom of the Date and Time dialog box. Now, each time you open this main document, the current date appears.

Creating a Data Source

A *data source* is a Word table that holds the variable information that you will put into your letter to customize it. The data source holds the names, addresses, phone numbers, and account numbers of your customers, for example.

Planning Your Data File

The most important step to creating a data source is plan, plan, plan. And the most important feature of the database is *flexibility*. Take the time to identify all the information about the letter recipients that you could ever need when sending a mass mailing. Then group that information into fields.

A *field* is a category of information. For example, the phone book has fields for last name, first name, suffix (MD, Sr., III, etc.), city(maybe), and phone number. Your document may include fields such as first name, last name, salutation, address, city, state, ZIP code, account number, and previous year's sales. And all of the fields related to one person or company called a *records*.

> **Note**
>
> As you begin creating your data source, having too many fields is better than having too few. Adding one field of information later to thousands of records will be time consuming and will increase the chance of data entry errors. Deleting an unnecessary field takes just a few simple keystrokes.

When designing your database, consider how you plan to arrange, or sort, your data. Do not include more than one piece of information in the same field. For example, if you want letters to print alphabetically by last name, you need two fields in your data source: first name and last name. One category, called *name*, does not allow you the flexibility to sort by last name.

Entering the Fields in Your Data Source

To create the fields in your data source, follow these steps:

1. Open your main document.

2. Choose Tools, Mail Merge to open the Mail Merge Helper dialog box.

3. Under Step 2, click the Get Data button.

4. To create a new data source, click Create Data Source. A list of common field names appears on the right side of the Create Data Source dialog box, as shown in figure 40.5.

Fig. 40.5

You can use a mixture of the commonly used field names and names you create yourself.

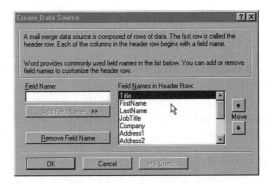

5. Remove the field names you do not want to include by selecting the field name and clicking the Remove Field Name button. Repeat until only the field names you want are listed on the right.

6. Add a field name that is not listed by typing the name in the Field Name box and clicking the Add Field Name button.

7. Rearrange fields by selecting a field name and clicking the up or down Move arrow to the right of the field names listed.

8. When all the field names are listed in the correct order, click OK.

9. When prompted to save your data source, type a file name. Because the data source is separate from the main document, be sure to give it a different name.

10. If you are ready to add data to your data source, click Edit Data Source on the Mail Merge Toolbar; if you want to return to your main document, click Edit Main Document.

Adding Information to Your Data Source

To add information to your data source, follow these steps:

1. Open your main document.

2. Click the Edit Data Source button on the Mail Merge toolbar. The Data Form dialog box appears, as shown in figure 40.6.

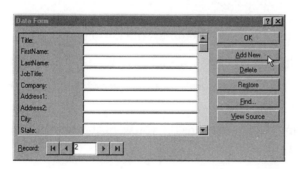

Fig. 40.6

Use the Data Form dialog box to enter variable information for your mailing.

3. Type the first field of information. Press Enter to move to the next field. Repeat until you have completed all applicable fields.

You do not need to enter information in every field. If a field does not apply, leave it blank.

4. To add another record, choose the Add New button. Repeat data entry until all records are input.

> **Note**
>
> When you get to the last field in the record, you can press Enter to move to a new record form so you don't have to click the Add New button.

5. After you have entered all records, click OK.

Editing a Data Source

After you have entered all your data into the data source document, you'll probably need to edit it. Undoubtedly, you'll need to delete records or change data periodically. Editing a data source is just like editing any Word document. One advantage, however, is that the Mail Merge Helper has a Find feature that eliminates the hassle of scrolling and searching for a specific record.

The first step in editing a data source is to locate the record you want to edit:

1. View any record in the data form by clicking the Edit Data Source button on the Mail Merge toolbar.

2. Choose the Find button on the right of the dialog box.

3. Identify a unique piece of information about the record you want, for instance account number or Social Security Number. Type that information in the Find box. Then press the tab key.

4. Select the field in which this information will be located.

5. Choose Find First to locate the first record that meets the criteria you entered.

6. Click Find Next until the record you want appears. Click the Close button on the Find dialog box.

With the record displayed, make the necessary changes. Then click OK to return to your document.

After locating a record, you may decide to delete it altogether. To delete a record, click the delete button on the right of the Data Form box.

Inserting Merge Fields

After the standard elements of the letter are complete and you have created your data source, you are ready to identify where to place the variable pieces of information in the main document. This process involves inserting merge fields.

In the example shown in figure 40.7, First City Financial is using Mail Merge to send letters to clients about refinance opportunities.

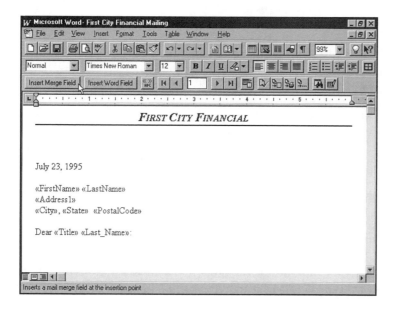

Fig. 40.7

Merge fields are the fields of information that enable you to make a form letter look like a personal letter.

Merge fields are the categories of information that you included in your data source, like first name, city, or state. You use merge fields to tell Word specifically where to put each piece of variable information in the letter.

To insert merge fields into your main document, follow these steps:

1. Open your main document.

2. Place the insertion point where the first variable piece of information should appear.

3. Click the Insert Merge Field button on the Mail Merge toolbar.

4. Select the name of the field you want. The name of the field will appear in <<brackets>> on your document.

5. Type any words, spaces, or punctuation that may be required between fields (see following Note).

6. Insert another merge field. Repeat until all fields are entered.

> **Note**
>
> When creating a letter, include punctuation in places like the "Dear" line. A standard letter contains this line when all merge fields are included:
>
> Dear <<Title>> <<LastName>>:

Sorting Records in Your Data Source

I think the hardest lesson I learned in mail merge was regarding sorting. I remember taking the time to create all the mail merge components and printing my letters. They looked great. But the letters were in alphabetical order, not ZIP code order for mailing. I had over 300 letters!

My choices were to throw away all the letters and start over or to sort the actual printed letters manually into ZIP code order. I chose the sorting option and spent hours wishing I hadn't missed this one critical step: sorting the data in my data source before performing a mail merge and printing.

To avoid my mistake, decide the order in which you want to print your letters and sort the data before creating your form letters.

Planning Your Sort

Although planning your sort is not required to perform a merge, it can save you a lot of time in the end. If you do not identify your sort fields ahead of time, you may find yourself sorting and resorting until you get the results you want.

When you are planning to sort, you can select up to three fields for sorting. You can choose only one field if that's all you need.

The first field is the largest grouping. The second field is how you want records sorted within the first group, and the third field is how you want records sorted within the second group.

Suppose that your data source has fields for First Name, Last Name, and Sales Region. If you want records sorted alphabetically in Sales Region, your first field would be Sales Region, your second field would be Last Name, and your third field would be First Name.

Sorting Data According to Certain Fields

To sort your data according to fields you specify, follow these steps:

1. Open your main document.

2. Click the Mail Merge Helper button on the Mail Merge toolbar to open the Mail Merge Helper dialog box.

3. Under Step 3 on the Mail Merge Helper dialog box, click the Query Options button to open the Query Options dialog box shown in figure 40.8.

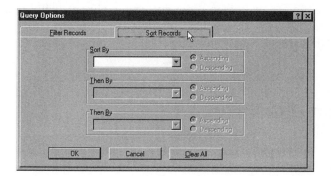

Fig. 40.8

Use the Sort Records tab to organize your data source before you merge your document.

4. On the Query Options dialog box click the Sort Records tab.

5. Select the first field in the Sort By category. Then press the Tab key.

6. Select the second field in Then By category. Then press the Tab key.

7. Select the third field in the next Then By field. Then click OK.

8. Click the Close button when you are finished with Mail Merge Helper.

Viewing the Order of the Data

To view your data source to verify that sorting produced the results you want, follow these steps:

1. Click the Edit Data Source button on the Mail Merge toolbar.

2. Choose the View Source button.

3. Scroll through the document to ensure the records are in the proper order.

4. On the Mail Merge toolbar, click the Mail Merge Main Document button.

Merging the Main Document and Data Source

Now that the major components of the project are in place, it's time to merge the two documents into one document of form letters.

You have two options when merging the files. You can merge files directly to the printer or you can merge them to a third file of form letters that appear on your screen.

If you are using a new main document that you're merging for the first time, I suggest merging to the screen. Your custom documents will not always look as you anticipate once you get all of the variable information entered. By merging data to the screen, you will save many reams of paper and trips to the printer.

Checking for Errors

Regardless of which option you choose, you should first check to make sure the merge will work properly. You may waste a great deal of time and material if you print hundreds or thousands of letters without checking them first. There are many different errors you may encounter, but Word is very helpful in taking you directly to the problem and helping you determine what the exact problem is. In other words, follow Word's lead.

To check a mail merge for errors prior to merging to the printer or to another document, use these steps:

1. Open the main document.

2. From the Mail Merge toolbar, click the Check for Errors button. If there are no errors, Word will indicate that no errors were found. If errors do exist, Word gives you the option of correcting them now or later. In either case, Word will take you directly to the field or record that has the problem.

Merging Directly to the Printer

If your job shows no errors, you can merge a main document and the data source directly to the printer:

1. Open the main document.

2. On the Mail Merge toolbar, click the Merge to Printer button.

3. Click OK to send the merge directly to your printer.

Merging to the Screen before Printing

If you don't want the letters to go to the printer yet, you can merge the two documents to a third document and view it before printing.

> **Note**
>
> If you are working with a main document for the first time, I recommend that you merge to a third document and not directly to the printer. It's not uncommon for merged form letters to look different than expected after all the custom information is included.

To merge a main document and the data source to a third document, follow these steps:

1. Open the main document.
2. On the Mail Merge toolbar, click the Merge to New Document button.
3. View the new document, called Form Letters by default. Scroll through the first several pages to ensure that merge fields went to the right place and page breaks worked.
4. If everything looks good, from the menu, choose File, Print to print to your default printer. Then click OK.

> **Note**
>
> If you merge two documents and do not get the results you expected, don't try to edit each page of the document individually. You can save a lot of time if you simply close the Form Letter document without saving it, edit the main document or data source, and perform the merge again.

Merging Data from an Excel Worksheet

Suppose that you already have data entered into an Excel worksheet. The good news is that you don't have to retype the data. In fact, if you have a lot of names to enter, I recommend that you use Excel to create a data source. For large numbers of records, Excel has much greater capability to manage, sort, and edit than a Word table does.

Creating an Excel Database

To create a database in an Excel worksheet (which holds up to 16,384 records), use these steps:

1. Open or switch to Excel.

2. Choose File, New, or click the New button on the Standard toolbar.

3. Your field names will be the column headings of your worksheet. Type the name of your first field in cell A1. Press the right arrow or tab key on your keyboard or click in cell B1.

4. Type the second field name in cell B1. Press the right arrow or tab key on your keyboard. Repeat until all field names are listed as column headings.

5. Click in cell A2. Begin typing your data. Save often.

Tip
Don't worry about the order of the data. Your goal in this first stage should be accuracy. You can sort the database later.

Using Your Excel Worksheet as a Mail Merge Data Source

Now you can use your Excel database information as your mail merge data source:

1. Return to Word.

2. Open your main document.

3. From the Mail Merge toolbar, click the Mail Merge Helper button.

4. Under Step 2, choose Get Data.

5. Choose Open Data Source.

6. In the Files of Type box, select All Files, as shown in figure 40.9.

7. Click the Excel file in which you saved your data.

8. Click the Open button.

After you have attached your Excel file as the data source, you can insert merge fields and perform the merge as you do with any other data source. See sections "Inserting Merge Fields" and "Merging the Main Document and Data Source" earlier in this chapter.

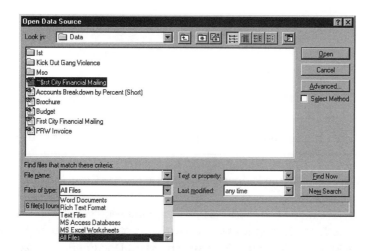

Techniques from the Pros Techniques from the Pros Techniques from the Pros

Fig. 40.9

The Open Data Source dialog box looks and works just like the Open File dialog box.

Using the Address Book for Merging

One of the new features in Microsoft Word is the Address Book. You can use your Contact List from Schedule+ or your Personal Address Book from Microsoft Exchange as your data source. Microsoft Exchange allows you to create a Personal Address Book you can use to send electronic mail (e-mail) as well as paper mail. One of the pieces of Schedule+ is the Contact List. You can create and maintain a list of names and addresses and use this list to contact business associates, friends, and family. If you have a list of names and addresses in the Contact List of Schedule+ or the Personal Address Book, you can attach this list to your merge document.

◀ See "Scheduling Your Time," p. 834

◀ See "Using Microsoft Exchange," p. 809

You first need to create your Contact List in Schedule+ or your Personal Address Book in Microsoft Exchange. Then follow these steps:

1. Open your main document.

2. From the Mail Merge toolbar, click the Mail Merge Helper button.

3. Under Step 2, choose Get Data.

4. Select Use Address Book. The Use Address Book dialog box appears, as shown in figure 40.10.

Fig. 40.10

Select the Address Book you want to use.

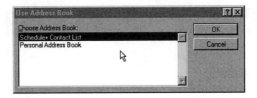

5. In the Choose Address Book list, select the list you want to use and click OK.

6. In the Mail Merge Helper dialog box, click the Close button.

After you have made your address book the data source, you can insert merge fields and perform the merge as you do with any other data source. See sections "Inserting Merge Fields" and "Merging the Main Document and Data Source" earlier in this chapter.

Specifying Data Selection Rules

If your data source is in Word, Excel, Schedule+ or the Personal Address Book you can specify the criteria that each record must meet to be included in the Mail Merge. This selection process enables you to maintain information in one location instead of having multiple databases, or worse yet, having the same name in multiple databases.

Deciding Which Fields Have Rules

Creating selection rules can be a bit tricky. When you use more than one rule, you need to connect the rules with an "And" or an "Or". If you use the wrong word or the wrong Compare To condition, you may not have any records merged. I suggest that before you explore Word's Query options, you write down which records you want and which field holds the information you will be searching. You can specify one rule (all ZIP codes beginning with 8) or multiple rules (all last names beginning with B with ZIP codes beginning with 5) up to a total of 6 rules.

If you want to use multiple rules and you want to merge records that meet *all* of the rules, use *And*. If you want to merge records that meet either rule, use *Or*. The above example would use And to meet both conditions.

The other problem you may encounter is narrowing your search too much. In the preceding example you will get all the records with the last name beginning with B *and* within those records where the ZIP codes begin with 5.

Identifying Data Criteria

So you may use a large database for multiple merge operations, you may want to determine specific rules for the records you will select. To specify rules within your data source, follow these steps:

1. Open your main document.

2. On the Mail Merge toolbar, click the Mail Merge Helper button.

3. Under Step 3 on the Mail Merge dialog box, choose Query Options. The Query Options dialog box is displayed (see fig. 40.11). You see two tabs: Filter Records and Sort Records.

4. Click the Filter Records tab.

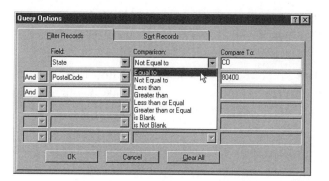

Fig. 40.11

In the Query Options dialog box, enter information to tell Word which records you want to use.

5. In the Field column, click the down arrow to display the names of your fields. Select the field name for which you want to create a rule.

6. In the Comparison column, click the comparison you want Word to make, such as Not Equal to or Equal to.

7. Click in the Compare To column. Type the value you want Word to check records against. For example, if you want Word to locate all records with a ZIP code beginning with 8, enter **80000**, as shown in figure 40.12.

8. Click OK.

9. Click the Close button on the Mail Merge Helper dialog box.

10. Click the View Merged Data button on the Mail Merge toolbar.

By using the View Merged Data button, you can toggle between merged data in your letter and the letter with the merge fields displayed.

Fig. 40.12

Enter criteria to
choose records to
merge into form
letters.

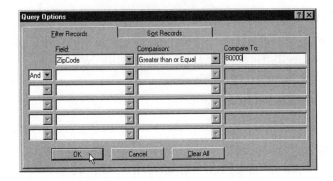

Creating Labels Using Mail Merge

After you create your letters, you may want to create labels for mailing purposes.
Or you may want to send a preprinted postcard as a follow-up to everyone who
received a specific mailing.

Creating labels isn't difficult. All you need to know is the type of label you are
using. Then you create a label document and make it your main document. You
can reuse the data source you created for your letters.

Creating the Main Document
for Mailing Labels

Commonly, once letters are printed you will want to create labels to stick on
the outside of envelopes.

To create mailing labels using Mail Merge, follow these steps:

1. Choose Tools, Mail Merge. The Mail Merge Helper dialog box appears.

2. Under Step 1, choose Create.

3. From the drop-down list, choose Mailing Labels. A message dialog box
   from Word appears.

4. Click New Main Document to create the document that will serve as your
   label template.

Setting Up the Merge

Now you can tell Word where your data is stored, what style of label you are
using, and where to place specific merge fields. Word walks you through these
steps:

1. From the Mail Merge toolbar, click the Mail Merge Helper button.

2. Under Step 2, choose the Get Data button. Then choose Open Data Source.

3. Select the name of the file that holds your data.

4. After you have selected a file, Word prompts you to set up the main document for labels. Click Set Up Main Document to specify the label size and type. The Label Options dialog box appears (see fig. 40.13).

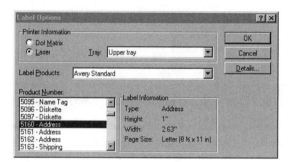

Fig. 40.13

Use this dialog box to set up your label document.

5. Under Printer Information, select the type of printer you have (Dot Matrix or Laser).

6. Next to Label Products, select the brand of labels you have.

7. Under Product Number, select the style of label you have (the style number is on the outside of the box). Then click OK. The Create Labels dialog box opens (see fig. 40.14).

> **Note**
>
> To move quickly to a specific Product number, make sure the highlight bar is in the Product Number list box, type the first number in the product number. The listed product number items scroll to the beginning of the section where those labels should be listed. To find Avery 5160 Address labels, for example, type 5 and then scroll down just a few times.

8. To add merge fields to your label, click Insert Merge Field. Locate and select the name of the first field from your data source. Repeat until all the fields you want on your label are listed.

Fig. 40.14

Use this dialog box to insert merge fields for your labels.

> **Note**
>
> When you are adding merge fields to your label, be sure to include all spaces and punctuation that you want to appear on each label.

9. Click OK.

10. Click the Close button on the Mail Merge Helper dialog box.

Editing the Format of a Label

Once you create the initial format for your label, you may want to make formatting changes. You can go back and edit the format of a label. To return to the label setup process, follow these steps:

1. Open your main document.

2. From the Mail Merge toolbar, click the Mail Merge Helper button.

3. Under Step 1, click the Edit button. Word takes you through the same steps you went through to create the document initially.

Printing the Labels

To create custom labels, follow the same steps outlined in "Merging the Main Document and Data Source" earlier in the chapter.

Creating Envelopes Using Mail Merge

Envelopes are an alternative to labels when you are deciding how to address your form letters. Creating envelopes is not difficult, but a main consideration is whether your printer tray automatically feeds envelopes. If not, you may find that sticking labels on envelopes is easier than manually feeding hundreds of envelopes.

Creating the Envelopes File

If you want to print envelopes, you will first create a main document which will identify both the size of the envelope and location of the Merge Field.

To create envelopes using Mail Merge, follow these steps:

1. Choose Tools, Mail Merge. The Mail Merge Helper dialog box appears.

2. Under Step 1, choose Create.

3. From the drop-down list, choose Envelopes. The Change Document dialog box appears.

4. Click New Main Document to create the document that will serve as your envelope template.

Setting Up the Merge

Now you can tell Word where your data is stored, what style of envelope you are using, and where to place specific merge fields:

1. From the Mail Merge toolbar, click the Mail Merge Helper button.

2. Under Step 2, choose the Get Data button. Then choose Open Data Source.

3. Select the name of the file that holds your data.

4. After you select a file, Word prompts you to format the main document for envelopes. Click Setup Main Document to specify the envelope size and type.

5. Click the Envelope Options tab in the dialog box (see fig. 40.15).

Fig. 40.15

Use this dialog box to set up your envelope options.

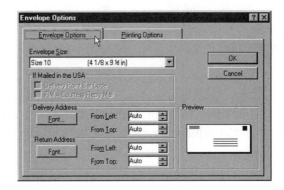

6. Under Envelope Size, select the size of envelope you are using.

7. Under Delivery Address, type specific top and left margins, if your requirements are different from a standard envelope.

8. Under Return Address, type specific top and left margins, if your requirements are different from a standard envelope.

9. Click the Printing Options tab (see fig. 40.16).

Fig. 40.16

Use this dialog box to set up your envelope print options.

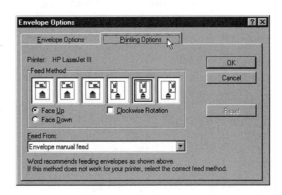

10. Under Feed Method, select the way your envelopes will feed.

11. Under Feed From, select whether your printer will feed envelopes from a print tray or will require manual feed. Then click OK.

12. To add merge fields to your label, click the Insert Merge Field button on the Mail Merge toolbar. Locate and select the name of the first field from your data source. Repeat until all the fields you want on your label are listed. Click OK after you insert all the fields for your envelope.

13. Click the Close button on the Mail Merge Helper dialog box.

> **Note**
>
> When formatting your main envelope document, be sure to include all standard spacing and punctuation in your sample envelope.

Editing the Format of an Envelope

If you want to change the envelope size or the location of merge fields on your envelope, you can edit the format of an envelope later. To return to the envelope setup process, follow these steps:

1. Open your main document.

2. From the Mail Merge toolbar, click the Mail Merge Helper button.

3. Under Step 1, click the Setup button. Word takes you through the same steps you went through to create the envelope initially.

Printing the Envelopes

To create custom envelopes, follow the same steps outlined in "Merging the Main Document and Data Source" earlier in the chapter.❖

Chapter 41

Manipulating and Analyzing Data

Robert Voss, Ph.D., is an independent consultant and trainer who has been training users on Microsoft Office applications for over six years. He has made significant contributions to many Que books, including *Using Excel 5, Special Edition* and *Special Edition Using Excel for Windows 95.*

If all Excel did was perform algebraic computations in worksheets, it would still be a powerful tool, but certain tasks need more than number-crunching. If you use Excel extensively, you will undoubtedly find situations where the result depends on different conditions. Some of these conditions may depend on specific values or a range of values in a given cell. In other situations, you may want Excel to look up an answer from a list. You may also need to summarize data in a list based on certain criteria. Excel provides a number of features to facilitate this kind of processing and analysis.

In this chapter, you learn how to

- Use formulas to manipulate text

- Write formulas that make decisions based on conditions you specify

- Test input values to make sure these values are in the correct range

- Use lookup tables to find such information as tax and commission rates

- Analyze data in lists with database functions

Techniques from the Pros

by Robert Voss

Manipulating Text

Excel enables you to manipulate text, numbers, and dates. Text manipulation is handy for combining text and numbers in printed invoices, creating titles from numeric results, and using data from a database to create a mailing list. With Excel, you can use formulas to manipulate text in the same way you use formulas to calculate numeric results.

◀ **See**
"Using Operators in Formulas" p. 374

Use the concatenation operator, the & (ampersand), to join text, numbers, or cell contents to create a text string. Enclose text in quotation marks. You don't need to enclose numbers in quotation marks. Do not enclose cell references in quotation marks. You can reference cells that contain text or numbers. For example, consider the following formula:

="This "&"and That"

This formula displays the following text:

    This and That

> **Note**
>
> Text used in a formula must always be enclosed in quotes. Excel assumes that text not in quotes is a name. This situation causes a #NAME? error if a name with this spelling is not defined.

You also can join text by referring to the cell address. If A12 contains the text, John, and B12 contains the text, McDougall, you can use the following formula to combine the first and last names:

=A12&" "&B12

The result of the formula is the following:

    John McDougall

Notice that a space between the two quotation marks in the formula separates the text contained in cells A12 and B12.

You also can use the CONCATENATE function to produce the same result. The formula =CONCATENATE(A12," ",B12) also returns John McDougall.

Excel also enables you to convert a number to text. You can refer to a number as you refer to a cell filled with text. If A12 contains 99 and B12 contains the text, Stone St., use the following formula to create the full street address:

=A12&" "&B12

The result of the formula is the address:

```
99 Stone St.
```

When you refer to a number or date in a text formula, the number or date appears in the general format, not as the number or date appears in the formatted display. Suppose that cell B23 contains the date 12/25/95, and you enter the following formula:

="Merry Christmas! Today is "&B23

The result of this formula is the following:

```
Merry Christmas! Today is 35058
```

You can change the format of the number with the FIXED( ), DOLLAR( ), and TEXT( ) functions. These functions change numbers and dates to text in the format you want. With dates, for example, you can use the TEXT( ) function to produce the following formula:

◀ **See**
"Formatting Numbers"
p. 341

="Merry Christmas! Today is "&TEXT(B23,"mmm dd, yy")

The result appears as the following:

```
Merry Christmas! Today is Dec 25, 95
```

You can use any predefined or custom numeric or date format between the quotation marks of the TEXT( ) function.

The TEXT( ) function is a handy way to trick large numbers into exceeding the width of a column without producing the #### signs that indicate a narrow column. The TEXT( ) function also is useful for numeric titles. If you want the number $5,000,000 stored in A36 to fit in a narrow column, for example, use the following formula, which displays the formatted number as text so the number can exceed the column width:

=TEXT(A36,"$#,##0")

Using Formulas To Make Decisions

Excel's IF( ) function can make decisions based on whether a test condition is true or false. Use IF( ), for example, to test whether the time has come to reorder a part, whether data was entered correctly, or which of two results or formulas to use.

The IF( ) function uses the following format:

IF(*logical_test,value_if_true,value_if_false*)

If the *logical_test* (condition) is true, the result is *value_if_true*; but if the *logical_test* is false, the result is *value_if_false*. The result values can display text with an argument such as "Hello", calculate a formula such as B12*6, or display the contents of a cell such as D35. IF( ) functions are valuable in macros for testing different conditions and acting according to the results of the test conditions.

Consider the following formula:

=IF(B34>50,B34*2,"Entry too low!")

In this example, the IF( ) function produces the answer 110 if B34 is 55. If B34 is 12, however, the cell that contains the function displays this text:

Entry too low!

Making Simple Decisions

To make comparisons, use IF( ) functions. Figure 41.1 shows an Accounts Aging Analysis worksheet in which Excel checks how long an amount has been overdue. Using IF( ) functions and the age of the account, Excel displays the amount in the correct column.

Fig. 41.1

Use IF( ) functions to test ranges, such as the ages of these accounts.

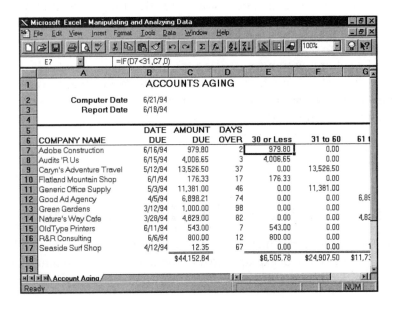

The first few times you use IF( ) statements, you might want to write an English sentence that states the *logical_test,* or the question you want to ask. The question also should state both results if true and if false. For example, each cell from E7 through E16 uses an IF( ) statement equivalent to the following sentence:

> IF the value in the DAYS OVER column is less than 31, show the adjacent value in the AMOUNT DUE column, but if this condition is not true, then show zero.

The IF( ) function equivalent of this statement for cell E7 appears in the formula bar as the following formula:

> =IF(D7<31,C7,0)

In this example, D7 contains the DAYS OVER for row 7, and C7 contains the AMOUNT DUE for row 7. To prevent displaying all zeros on the sheet, choose Tools, Options, display the View tab, and clear Zero Values.

> **Note**
>
> To display a blank cell for specific conditions, use a formula similar to the following:
>
> =IF(D7<31,C7,"")
>
> Nothing is entered between the quotation marks, so this function displays a blank cell for the false condition. Remember that Excel can hide zeros for the entire worksheet if in the Options dialog box, you deselect Zero Values in the View tab.

Making Complex Decisions

In column F of the worksheet shown in figure 41.1, the IF( ) question needs to be more complex. The IF( ) functions in column F must test for a range of values in the DAYS OVER column. The DAYS OVER columns must be more than 30 and less than 61:

◀ **See** "Entering Functions," p. 391

> If the value in the DAYS OVER column is greater than 30 and the value in the DAYS OVER column is also less than 61, then show the value in the AMOUNT DUE column; if this is not true, show zero.

The IF functions in F7 through F17 use the following formula to check for DAYS OVER in the range from 31 to 60:

> =IF(AND(D7>30,D7<61),C7,0)

◀ **See**
"Examining
Some Sample
Functions,"
p. 397

The AND() function produces a TRUE response only when all the elements within the parentheses meet the conditions: D7>30 is true *AND* D7<61 is true. When the AND() function produces TRUE, the IF() formula produces the value found in C7.

When you want to check for a number within a range of values, use an AND() function as shown here, for the AND() function to be TRUE, all the arguments must be true. An AND() function is most frequently used to test whether a number or date is within a range.

An OR() function is another type of logical test. An OR() function produces a TRUE response when any one of its arguments is TRUE. OR() functions are usually used to match one value against multiple values. For example,

=IF(OR(B12=36,B12="Susan"),"OK","")

If the value in B12 is either 36 or Susan, then the formula results in the text OK. If the value in 36 is neither of these, then the result is nothing ("").

Checking Data Entry

◀ **See**
"Entering Data,"
p. 305

Whether you enter data in a database form or make entries directly into the cells of a worksheet, you can prevent accidental errors by using formulas that automatically cross-check data as you enter it. Figure 41.2 shows an example of a data-entry form that uses formulas to cross-check entered data. The formula bar shows the formula used to check the data in cell D4. This formula produces no result, "", if the date entered in D4 is after 1/1/1995. However, if the date entered is prior to 1/1/1995, then the message appears in the formula's cell.

> **Note**
>
> Excel worksheets can contain items seen in dialog boxes, such as scrolling lists, pull-down lists, check boxes, and groups of option buttons. Two new data entry devices also are available: a spinner to quickly *spin* through a range of numbers and scroll bars to let you drag across a wide range of numbers. The result from these devices appears in a worksheet cell where you can use it just as though it had been typed.

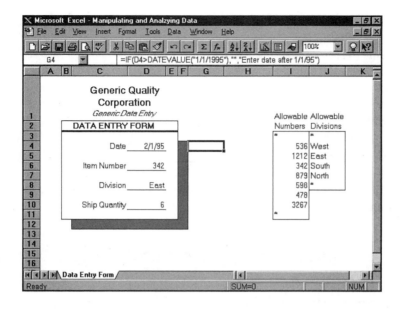

Fig. 41.2

In this data-entry
form, the data in
columns I and J
serve as tables of
valid inputs for the
Item Number and
Division entries in
cells D6 and D8.

Figure 41.3 shows the same form with incorrect data entered. Notice the
warnings that appear to the side of the data-entry cells. The formulas used in
those cells are given in the following table:

Cell	Cross-Check	Formula
G4	Date after 1/1/95	=IF(D4>DATEVALUE("1/1/1995"), "","Enter date after 1/1/95")
G6	Item number in list	=IF(ISNA(MATCH D6,13:I11,0)), ("Invalid Number","")
G8	Division name in list	=IF(ISNA(MATCH(D8,J3:J8,0)), "West, East, South, North","")
G10	Range of quantities	=IF(AND(D10>4,D10<21)," ","5 to 20 units")

In each of these formulas, an IF( ) function combined with a conditional test
decides whether the entry in column D is correct or not. The formula in cell G4
checks whether the date serial number from D4 is greater than the date in the
IF( ) function. If the serial number is greater, the blank text " " is displayed. If
the value in D4 is not greater, the function displays the prompting text.

> **Note**
>
> If the user needs to remember and type many different possible entries, an excellent data entry method is the use of a pull-down list or scrolling list placed on the worksheet.

In cell G6, the MATCH() function looks through the values in I3:I11 to find an exact match with the contents of D6. The 0 argument tells MATCH() to look for an exact match. When an exact match is not found, the function returns the error value #N/A!. The ISNA() function detects #N/A! values when a match is not found; it displays the text warning Invalid Number. When a match is found, " " (nothing) is displayed on-screen.

Fig. 41.3

In this data-entry form, formulas in column G display warnings when the user makes invalid entries.

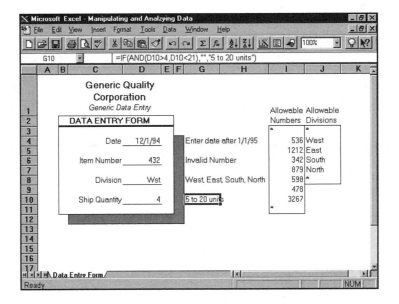

Note that when you use MATCH(), the items in the list do not need to be sorted if you use a 0 *match-type* argument as with the LOOKUP() functions. MATCH() also returns an error if an exact match is not found; whereas, a LOOKUP() function may return a near but incorrect result.

Cell G8 uses the same MATCH() method to check the division name against acceptable spellings. If you use large lists of possible entries, you might want to use the pull-down or scrolling lists that can be placed on a worksheet. Selecting from a list reduces the chance of typing an error or of forgetting an entry item.

The value of Ship Quantity must be 5 to 20 units. Therefore, the formula in G10 uses an AND( ) statement to check that the number in D10 is greater than 4 *and* less than 21. When both checks are true, nothing is displayed. If the number is out of the range, the function displays the message `5 to 20 units`.

Using Formulas To Look Up Data in Tables

You can build a table in Excel and look up the contents of various cells within the table. Lookup tables provide an efficient way of producing numbers or text that you cannot calculate with a formula. For example, you might not be able to calculate a tax table or commission table. In these cases, looking up values from a table is much easier. Tables also enable you to cross-check typed data against a list of allowable values.

Excel has two techniques for looking up information from tables. The first method uses LOOKUP( ) functions. Although easy to use, these functions have the disadvantage of giving you an answer whether or not the function finds an exact match. The list in the table also needs to be in sorted order—another disadvantage. This method is good, however, in situations such as creating volume discount tables.

The second method uses a combination of the INDEX( ) and MATCH( ) functions to find an exact match in a table, regardless of whether the list in the table is sorted. If Excel cannot find an exact match, the function returns an error so you know an exact match wasn't found. This method is good for exact matches, such as looking up the quantity on hand for a specific product. In this case, you need to find an exact part number, not the next closest item.

Using LOOKUP Functions on Tables

Excel has two functions that are useful in looking up values in tables. The VLOOKUP( ) function looks down the vertical column on the left side of the table until the appropriate comparison value is found. The HLOOKUP( ) function looks across the horizontal row at the top of the table until the appropriate comparison value is found.

◀ **See**
"Other Functions," p. 402

The VLOOKUP( ) and HLOOKUP( ) functions use the following forms:

VLOOKUP(*lookup_value,table_array,col_index_num,range_lookup*)

HLOOKUP(*lookup_value,table_array,row_index_num,range_lookup*)

The VLOOKUP( ) function tries to match the value in the left column of the table; the HLOOKUP( ) function tries to match the value in the top row. These values are the *lookup_values*. The *table_array* describes the range that contains the table and lookup values. The *col_index* for the VLOOKUP( ) function or the *row_index_num* for HLOOKUP( ) tells the function which column or row, respectively, contains the result. The first column or row in the table is always numbered 1. The fourth argument, *range_lookup,* is optional and is explained in the next section.

The list you use for comparison in the table must be in ascending order. For the lookup function to work correctly, the cells in C11:C15, in figure 41.4, must be sorted in ascending order. The function searches down the first column of a VLOOKUP( ) table or across the first row of an HLOOKUP( ) table until it meets a value larger than the *lookup_value*. If the *lookup_values* are not in ascending order, the function returns incorrect results.

Fig. 41.4

The VLOOKUP( ) function finds information in a vertical table.

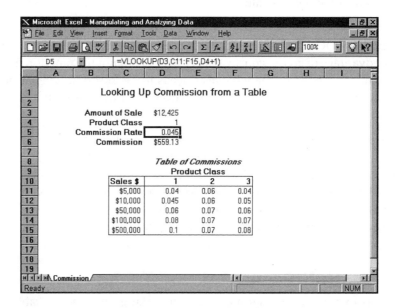

Figure 41.4 shows an example of a VLOOKUP( ) table that locates sales commissions. The VLOOKUP( ) and HLOOKUP( ) commands are helpful for looking up data in commission or tax tables because these tables contain data that can be difficult to calculate exactly. The sales on which a commission is based, for example, may fall between two numbers in the list. The formula that finds this sales commission is in cell D5. The VLOOKUP( ) function, as shown in the formula bar of the example, is used in the following formula:

=VLOOKUP(D3,C11:F15,D4+1)

The VLOOKUP( ) function looks down the left column of the table displayed in the range C11:F15 until a Sales $ amount larger than D3 ($12,425) is found. VLOOKUP( ) then backs up to the previous row and looks across the table to the column specified by D4+1. The formula D4+1 results in 2, the second column of the table. (Sales $ is column 1. The value 1 is added to D4 so the lookup starts in the Product Class portion of the table.) The VLOOKUP( ) function returns the value .045 from the table. The commission is calculated by multiplying .045 by the amount of sale, which is $12,425.

The VLOOKUP( ) function doesn't use the headings in row 10. These headings are shown for the user's benefit.

Finding Exact Matches

You can also use the VLOOKUP( ) and HLOOKUP( ) functions to look up data from a table and use an exact match to find the information. The data you are looking up can be text or numbers. If Excel doesn't find an exact match in the list, an error value warns you that the table contained no matches.

Using exact matches against a list is one way to prevent data-entry errors. Imagine a case in which an operator must enter an item number and an item description that belongs to this item number. To reduce data entry errors, you might want to have the operator enter the description using a pull-down list. An Excel LOOKUP( ) function or INDEX(MATCH( )) function combination can then use the description to lookup the item number from a list. This technique not only reduces typing but cross-checks the item number by displaying either an accurate description or an error message if the number is incorrect.

> **Note**
>
> While the combination of INDEX( ) and MATCH( ) is the most accurate way of matching and retrieving data from a table, it is slow when used with large or multiple tables.

The optional fourth argument (*range_lookup* in the Function Wizard) controls whether a VLOOKUP( ) or HLOOKUP( ) function looks for an exact match or the next largest value that matches. To find values that are an approximate match when an exact match is not available, use TRUE or omit the range_lookup argument. To specify an exact match, use FALSE as the fourth argument, as shown below:

    =VLOOKUP(D3,C11:F15,D4+1,FALSE)

If you entered the preceding formula in cell D5, it would return the #N/A error value because an exact match for the $12,425 in cell D3 cannot be found in the Sales $ column.

Using MATCH and INDEX Functions

If your source list is not sorted, the lookup functions cannot work correctly. However, in this case you can use a combination of the MATCH and INDEX functions to look up values. In figure 41.5, Excel enters the item description if the item number is entered. If the item number is nonexistent, the worksheet displays #N/A in the Description cell (C8).

Fig. 41.5

Use a combination of INDEX and MATCH to find an exact match in an unsorted table.

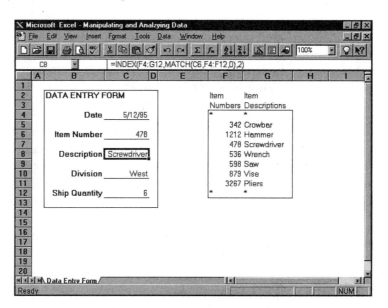

The following formula found in cell C8 looks up and enters the description:

=INDEX(F4:G12,MATCH(C6,F4:F12,0),2)

The two functions used in this formula follow this syntax:

=INDEX(*array,row_num,column_num*)

=MATCH(*lookup_value,lookup_array,match_type*)

In the INDEX() function, *array* is the entire range that contains data. (It can also be an array constant.) If you enter the INDEX() function with the Function Wizard in working through these examples, select the set of arguments that match the INDEX() arguments shown above. The *row_num* and *column_num* arguments designate the row and column that specify a value in the *array*. For example, for the range F4:G12, a *row_num* of 5 and a *column_num* of 2 causes INDEX() to return Wrench.

In the MATCH() function, the *lookup_value* is the value for which you are searching. In the example, this value is the item number found in C6. The *lookup_array* is an array in a row or column that contains the list of values that you are searching. In the example, this array is the column of item numbers F4:F12. The *match_type* specifies the kind of match required. In the example, 0 specifies an exact match.

In the example, therefore, the MATCH() function looks through the range F4:F12 until an exact match for the contents of cell C6 is found. After an exact match is found, the MATCH() function returns the position of the match: row 4 of the specified range. Notice that the MATCH() function finds the first match in the range. For an exact match, the contents of the range F4:F12 do not need to be in ascending order.

You also can omit the *match_type* or specify *1* or *-1*. If the *match_type* is omitted or is 1, then MATCH() finds the largest value in the *lookup_array* equal to or less than the *lookup_value*. If *match_type* is omitted or is 1, the *lookup-array* must be in ascending order. If the *match_type* is -1, MATCH() finds the smallest value greater than or equal to the *lookup_value*. If the *match_type* is -1, the *lookup_array* must be in descending order.

In the formula shown in figure 41.5, the INDEX() function looks in the range F4:G12. The function returns the contents of the cell located at the intersection of column 2 and row 4, as specified by the MATCH() function. The result is `Screwdriver`.

The item numbers and descriptions in the table are outlined to identify the table. The asterisks (*) at the top and bottom of the table mark the corners of the ranges. The function continues to work correctly as long as you insert all new data item codes and descriptions between the asterisks.

Calculating Tables of Answers

Because of the *what if* game made possible by electronic worksheets, worksheets are extremely useful in business. Worksheets provide immediate feedback to questions, such as: "What if we reduce costs by .5 percent?," "What if we sell 11 percent more?," and "What if we don't get that loan?"

◀ **See**
"Performing 'What-If' Analysis with Scenarios," p. 451

When you test how small changes in input affect the result of a worksheet, you are conducting a *sensitivity analysis*. You can use Excel's Data, Table command to conduct sensitivity analyses across a wide range of inputs.

Excel can create a table that shows the inputs you want to test and displays the results so you don't need to enter all the possible inputs at the keyboard. Using a combination of a data table and the *Dfunctions*, you can do quick but extensive database analysis of finance, marketing, or research information.

You can have more than one data table in a worksheet so you can analyze different variables or database statistics at one time.

You can use the <u>D</u>ata, <u>T</u>able command in the following two ways:

- Change one input to see the resulting effect on one or more formulas.

- Change two inputs to see the resulting effect on only one formula.

One Changing Variable and Many Formulas

Among the best (and most frequently used) examples of sensitivity analysis is a data table that calculates the loan payments for different interest rates. The single-input data table described in this section creates a chart of monthly payments for a series of loan interest rates.

Before you create a data table, you need to build a worksheet that solves the problem you want to test. The worksheet in figure 41.6 calculates a house or car mortgage payment. The following formula in cell D8 handles that task:

=PMT(D5/12,D6*12,D4)

Fig. 41.6

Build a worksheet with a result you want to analyze.

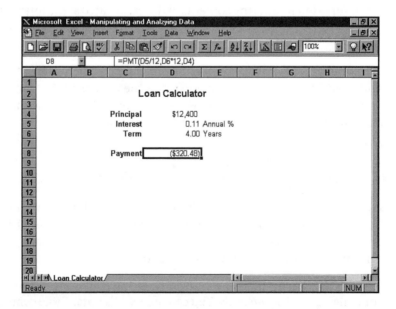

To build a data table, take the following steps:

1. Build the worksheet.

2. Enter the different values you want tested. You can enter the values in any sequence.

   Cells C11:C17 in figure 41.7 show the interest rates to be used as inputs in the sensitivity analysis.

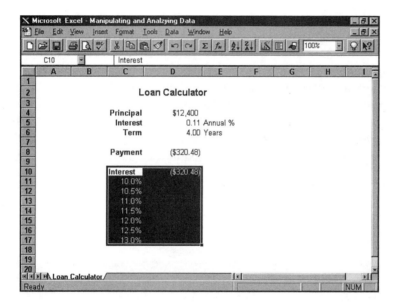

Fig. 41.7

The first step in creating this table of mortgage payments is to enter the range of interest rates to be evaluated.

3. In the top row of the table, row 10, above where the results appear, enter the address of each formula for which you want answers. In this cell, you also can enter the formula directly rather than reference a formula located elsewhere.

   In figure 41.7, cell D10 contains =D8. Therefore, the results for the payment formula in D8 are calculated for each interest rate in the table. To see the results of other formulas in the table, enter these formulas in other cells across the top of the table. For example, you can enter more formulas in E10, F10, and so on.

4. Select the cells that enclose the table. Include the input values in the left column and the row of formulas at the top, as shown in figure 41.7. In figure 41.7, you should select C10:D17. The results fill into the blank cells in D11:D17.

5. Choose Data, Table to display the Table dialog box (see fig. 41.8).

Fig. 41.8

Enter row or column input cells in the Table dialog box.

6. Enter a <u>R</u>ow Input Cell or <u>C</u>olumn Input Cell. Click or point to the cell in which you want to type the variable numbers listed in the table.

   In this example, the <u>C</u>olumn Input Cell is D5. You should enter **D5** in the <u>C</u>olumn Input Cell text box. The <u>C</u>olumn Input Cell is used rather than the <u>R</u>ow Input Cell because in this table the values being tested in the table are the interest rates that go down the left-most column. If you wanted to manually calculate payment amounts, you would type these interest rates into cell D5. By entering D5 into the <u>C</u>olumn Input Cell, you are telling Excel to test each interest rate in the left column of the table by entering that rate into cell D5. The resulting payment that is calculated for each interest rate is then placed in the adjacent cell in column D.

7. Choose OK.

The data table fills with the payment amounts that correspond to each interest rate in the table (see fig. 41.9).

Fig. 41.9

The completed table, with results in column D for each value in column C.

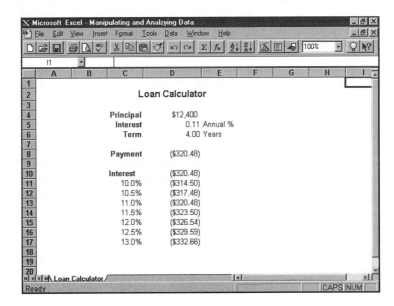

You can enter the <u>R</u>ow Input Cell or <u>C</u>olumn Input Cell by first clicking in the text box you want and then clicking on the appropriate cell in the worksheet.

If the Table dialog box covers the cells you want to select as the row or column inputs, move the dialog box.

Tip
Use the Edit, Fill, Series command or drag the fill handle across a series to fill incremental numbers for input values.

Two Changing Variables and One Formula

Figure 41.10 shows how to create a data table that changes two input values—interest and principal (the loans starting amount). The worksheet calculates the result of a formula for all combinations of those values. The top row of the table, row 10, contains different principal amounts for cell D3, the Row Input Cell. The left column of the table still contains the sequence of interest rates to use in cell D4. (If you are duplicating this example, notice that cell references in the example have changed by one row from the previous example.)

Notice that when you use two different input values, you can test the results from only one formula. The formula or a reference to the formula must be in the top-left corner of the table. In figure 41.10, cell C10 contains the reference =D7 to the payment formula to be tested.

The Table dialog box in figure 41.10 shows how the Row Input Cell is D3 because the values from the top row of the table are substituted into cell D3. The Column Input Cell is D4 because the values from the left column of the table are substituted into cell D4.

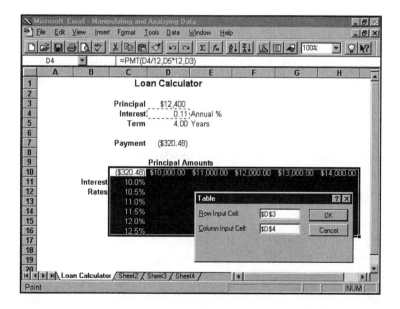

Fig. 41.10

Data tables also can change two input values used by one formula.

Figure 41.11 shows the result of a two-input data table. Each dollar value is the amount you pay on a loan with this principal amount and annual interest rate. Because each monthly payment represents a cash outflow, the results appear in parentheses to show that the amounts are negative.

Fig. 41.11

The completed data table with the results of combinations from two input values: interest and principal.

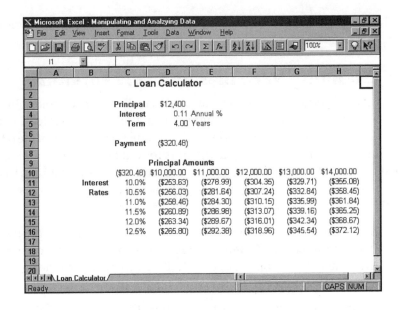

Editing Data Tables

After the data table is complete, you can change values in the worksheet on which the data table depends. Using the new values, the table recalculates. In the example in figure 41.11, typing a new Term in D5 causes new Payment amounts to appear.

You also can change the numbers or text in the rows and columns of input values and see the resulting change in the data table. In the example in figure 41.11, you can type new numbers or use the Edit, Fill, Series command to replace the numbers in C11:C15 or in D10:H10. If automatic recalculation is selected, the data table updates by default.

You cannot edit a single formula within the data table. All the formulas in this area are array formulas of the following form:

{=TABLE(*row_input,column_input*)}

To rebuild or just expand the data table, reselect the table, including new cells if you are expanding the table, and repeat the steps you used to create the original table. The new table will overwrite the old table.

> **Note**
>
> If you find data tables useful, examine the Scenario Manager, described in Chapter 18, "Managing Data," along with other more advanced methods of analysis. If you need to test a set of data inputs and find a myriad of results, then look to the Scenario Manager.

Calculating Data Tables

Large data tables or many data tables may slow down calculation. If you want the worksheet—but not the data tables—to recalculate, choose Tools, Options, select the Calculation tab and select Automatic Except Tables. Recalculate the tables by pressing F9 to calculate all worksheets or press Shift+F9 to calculate the active worksheet. If you have selected the Manual recalculation option in the Calculations tab, and you are performing a large database analysis, you might not want the worksheet and the related tables to recalculate before saving, which is the normal process. To save without recalculating, choose Tools, Options, select the Calculation tab and clear Recalculate Before Save.

◀ **See**
"Entering a Series of Text, Numbers, and Dates," p. 312

Analyzing Trends

Excel can calculate a linear regression or best-fit line that passes through a series of data. You might remember in science class recording a number of data points on a chart and then trying to draw a line through the points so that the line gave the trend of the data with the least errors. That line was a best-fit line. Points on that line are the best-fit data.

In some cases, you can use the result of these calculations to analyze trends and make short-term forecasts. Two ways of calculating the data for these trends are available. You can drag across numbers by using the fill handles, or you can use worksheet functions.

If you need to extend existing data by a few periods (cells) but don't need the corresponding best-fit data for the existing cells, you can use the method of dragging fill handles to extend the data. You can also use the Edit, Fill, Series command to create a linear regression or best-fit line. If, however, you need both original data and the corresponding best-fit data for the same periods— for example, to show original data and a best-fit line through the data—then use the worksheet function method.

Calculating Trends with Fill Handles

Figure 41.12 shows known data for regional housing starts for the years 1991 through 1994. But the future housing starts for 1995 and 1996 are unknown. If the trend from 1991 through 1994 continues, you can use a linear regression to calculate the expected starts for 1995 and 1996.

You can project this data into the empty cells to the right, 1995 and 1996, by using a linear best-fit. Select the cells as shown in figure 41.12. To fill the data in the empty cells, use the left mouse button to drag the fill handle to the right to enclose the area you want extended, and then release the mouse button. Row 4 of figure 41.13 shows the results of this procedure.

To fill a range using a growth trend, take these steps:

1. Select the cells as shown in figure 41.12.

2. Drag the fill handle to the right with the right mouse button. Excel displays a shortcut menu with Linear Trend and Growth Trend as commands.

3. Select Growth Trend.

Row 6 of figure 41.14 shows the results of this procedure.

Fig. 41.12

Using linear best-fit, extend a series by dragging the fill handle.

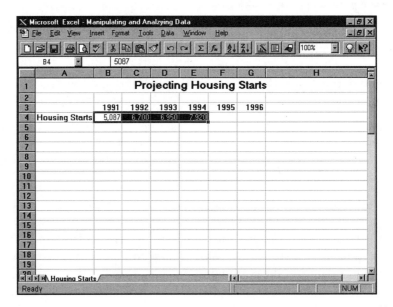

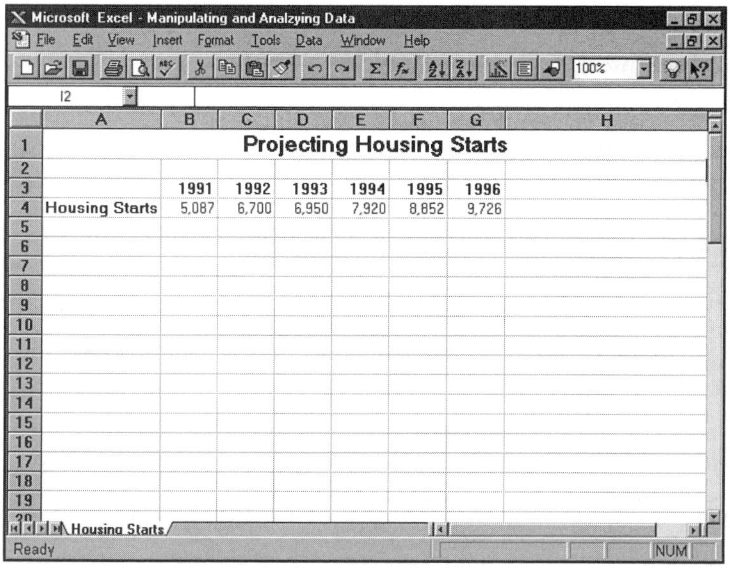

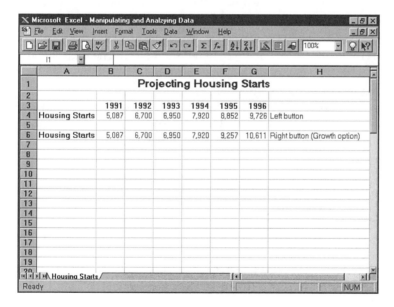

Fig. 41.13

The amounts shown for 1995 and 1996 are projections using linear best-fit.

Fig. 41.14

Create the projections for 1995 and 1996 in row 6 by dragging the fill handle with the right mouse button, then choosing the Growth Trend command.

Calculating Trends with the Data Series Command

◀ **See**
"Entering a Series of Text, Numbers, and Dates," p. 312

Using Excel's Edit, Fill, Series command, you can create best-fit data to replace or extend an original data set. You also can chart the best-fit data to create a best-fit line.

Choosing Edit, Fill, Series creates a linear (straight line) or exponential growth trend line. Using Edit, Fill, Series, you can create these two types of trend lines in two ways. Figure 41.15 illustrates the different types of trend data produced.

The original data used to produce the trends in the figure are the numbers 1, 5, and 12 shown in B4:D4. The selected range used with each command is in each of the rows from column B to column H. The different types of trend data produced use these combinations of settings in the Series dialog box:

Settings	Description of Resulting Trend
Default settings	A linear trend is produced starting with the original first data point. Calculated data replaces the original data. If charted, the trend line is forced to go through the first data point.
AutoFill	A linear trend is produced. The original data remains. Selected cells beyond the original data fill with data points for the linear trend.
Trend and Linear	A linear trend is produced and the trend is not forced to pass through the first original data point. Original data is replaced with trend data.
Trend and Growth	An exponential growth trend is produced and the trend is not forced to pass through the first original data point. Original data is replaced with trend data.

To create a trend using Edit, Fill, Series, perform the following steps:

1. Select the original data and as many additional cells as you want the trend data to extend into. In figure 41.15, for example, the cells B4:H4 may be selected.

2. Choose Edit, Fill, Series.

3. Choose one of the options described in the previous table.

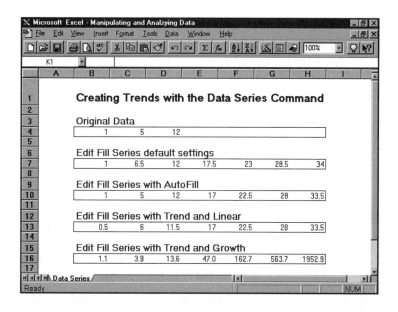

Fig. 41.15

Use the Edit, Fill, Series command to produce any of the four types of trend data shown here.

Notice that, in addition to the four trend computations shown in figure 41.15, you can produce a fifth by dragging the fill handle with the right mouse button. This produces a growth trend that does not override the original data.

Calculating Trends with Worksheet Functions

Excel's trend functions work by calculating the best-fit equation for the straight line or exponential growth line that passes through the data. The LINEST( ) and LOGEST( ) functions calculate the parameters for the straight-line and exponential growth-line equations. The TREND( ) or GROWTH( ) functions calculate the values along the straight line or exponential growth line needed to draw a curve or forecast a short-range value.

Before you use the trend analysis functions, become familiar with dependent and independent variables. The value of a *dependent variable* changes when the *independent variable* changes. Frequently, the independent variable is time, but it also can be other items, such as the price of raw materials, the temperature, or a population size. The independent variables actual data is entered as the *known-x* argument in the function, and the dependent variables actual data is entered as the functions *known-y* argument.

Imagine that you own a concrete business that depends on new residential construction. You want to plan for future growth or decline so you can best manage your firms assets and people.

After research with the help of local economic advisory boards, you assemble statistics on housing starts in the service area for the previous five years. In figure 41.12, row 4 shows the housing starts by year. After meeting with county planners, you are convinced that this area may continue to grow at the same or a slightly higher rate. You still need to estimate, however, the number of housing starts in 1995 and 1996.

In figure 41.12, the independent variables of time (*known_x*) are entered in B3:E3. The dependent variables of housing starts (*known_y*) are entered in B4:E4. If the trend from the past four years continues, you can project the estimated housing starts for the next two years with the following steps:

Tip
See "Entering Functions with the Function Wizard" in Chapter 7, "Using Functions," for detailed instructions on using the Function Wizard.

1. Select the range of cells you want the straight-line projection to fill, B6:G6, as shown in figure 41.16.

2. Enter the TREND( ) function using either the keyboard or the Function Wizard.

3. Enter the arguments for the TREND( ) function. The following line shows the correct syntax:

    TREND(*known_y's,known_x's,new_x's*)

For this example: The *known_y's* argument is B4:E4. (Housing Starts are y's because these numbers are dependent on the Year value.)

Fig. 41.16

Before entering an array formula such as TREND, select the entire range.

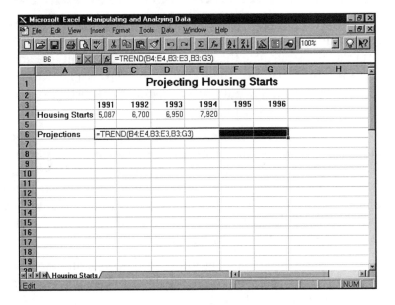

The *known_x's* argument is B3:E3. (Year is the independent variable.)

The *new_x's* argument is B3:G3, which are the years for which you want to know the values that describe a trend line.

Notice that the selected area in figure 41.16 covers the room for the resulting calculated y values.

◀ **See**
"Entering Functions,"
p. 391

◀ **See**
"Statistical,"
p. 400

4. To enter the TREND( ) function as an array function in the selected range, press Shift+Ctrl+Enter.

If the present trend continues, the result shown in figure 41.17 illustrates that years 1995 and 1996 might have housing starts of about 8,852 and 9,726.

Notice that the new *y* values in cells B6:E6 don't exactly match the known *y* values in B3:E3 because the TREND( ) function calculated the housing starts for these years according to its trend equation (a linear regression). The real number of housing starts in each year undoubtedly will be different.

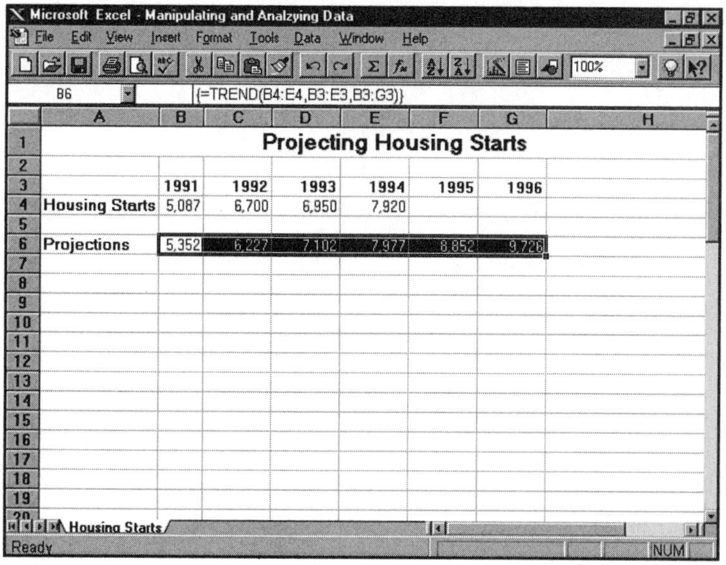

Fig. 41.17

The trend values in row 6 can help you make short-term projections. The TREND( ) function computes new values for the period of known values.

	A	B	C	D	E	F	G	H
1				Projecting Housing Starts				
2								
3		1991	1992	1993	1994	1995	1996	
4	Housing Starts	5,087	6,700	6,950	7,920			
5								
6	Projections	5,352	6,227	7,102	7,977	8,852	9,726	

B6 `{=TREND(B4:E4,B3:E3,B3:G3)}`

Chapter 42

Automating Excel with VBA

Diane Tinney is proprietor of *The Software Professional*, a business that consults the design, development, and implementation of end-user Windows-based applications. Diane specializes in building complex applications using Visual Basic for Applications (VBA). Her clients include ALCOA, EXXON, KPMG Peat Marwick, and the City of New York. Recent projects include creating a turn-key Financial Management application for mortgage consultants. She is a frequent speaker and writer on using VBA effectively and efficiently.

In Part III of this book, you learned how to use Excel to build powerful spreadsheets that automate complex or repetitive numerical tasks. In Chapter 35, "Starting Visual Basic for Applications," you learned how to record VBA macros to automate repetitive tasks. Chapter 35 also introduced you to creating basic VBA programs that automate the process of getting data input, storing the data, and then reporting the data results.

This chapter builds on your understanding of VBA by exploring specific Excel VBA solutions and by providing you with valuable programming techniques to automate more complex Excel tasks.

In this chapter, you learn to

- Manage files and folders from within VBA
- Solve common worksheet automation needs
- Respond to events
- Control and create add-ins

Techniques from the Pros

by Diane Tinney

Managing Files and Folders

Most VBA programs that you write in Excel will need to work with files and folders. VBA provides many commands that allow you to do the following:

- List files in a folder
- Change the current drive or folder
- Get and set file attribute information
- Find files
- Copy, move, and delete files

Table 42.1 lists the most commonly used file management and manipulation commands in VBA.

TABLE 42.1   VBA File Management Commands

VBA COMMAND	TYPE	DESCRIPTION
ChDir	Statement	Changes the current folder
ChDrive	Statement	Changes the current drive
CurDir	Function	Returns a string identifying the current folder path
Dir	Function	Returns a string that is the name of a folder or file that matches a file specification
FileCopy	Statement	Copies a file
FileDateTime	Function	Returns a date type value that contains the file date and time
FileLen	Function	Returns in bytes the length of a file
FindFile	Method	Displays the Excel Find File dialog box
GetAttr	Function	Returns a number representing the combined attributes of a folder or file
GetOpenFileName	Method	Displays Excel's Open File dialog box
GetSaveAsFileName	Method	Displays Excel's Save As dialog box

VBA COMMAND	TYPE	DESCRIPTION
Kill	Statement	Deletes files from the disk drive
MkDir	Statement	Creates the specified folder
Name	Statement	Renames or moves the specified file
RmDir	Statement	Deletes the specified folder
SetAttr	Statement	Sets attributes for the specified file

Working with File Paths

A VBA application often needs to determine and change the current drive and folder path. Based on user input or environmental needs, you may need to save workbooks to different disk drives or create a new folder in which to store new data.

Determining the Current Path

Use the CurDir( ) function to determine the current disk drive and folder path. CurDir( ) returns a string that contains the full DOS path for the current drive and folder. The syntax of CurDir( ) is:

```
CurDir(drive)
```

The *drive* argument is an optional string expression. If no drive argument is provided, Excel will return information about the current drive. If you supply the drive argument, Excel will return information on the specified drive.

Here are some examples you can enter into a module sheet to see the difference:

```
MsgBox "The current drive path is " & CurDir()
MsgBox "The current path on drive A is " & CurDir("A")
```

Changing the Current Path

The ChDir and ChDrive statements allow you to change the current drive or folder path under procedure control. The syntax of each is:

```
ChDrive drive
ChDir path
```

The *drive* argument for ChDrive is a string expression that represents a valid drive letter. Only letters are permitted.

The *path* argument for ChDir is a string expression that evaluates to a valid DOS folder path. The path can be a drive letter.

Here are some examples that you can type to see the difference between these two commands:

```
ChDir "C:\DOS"
ChDrive "A"
```

> **Note**
>
> Although ChDir can be used to change the current folder, it does not change the current drive. Use ChDrive to change the current drive.

Making and Removing Directories

Tip
Before creating and removing directories, be sure you have the proper rights. When removing a directory, make sure it's empty.

When you need to automate the creation of a folder from within Excel, use the VBA command MkDir(). The syntax for MkDir() takes one argument, *path*, which is a string that evaluates to a valid DOS folder path:

```
MkDir path
```

Occasionally, you will need to remove a folder from within your VBA code. The RmDir command takes one argument, *path*, which is a string that evaluates to a valid DOS directory path:

```
RmDir path
```

Here is some example code that creates a temporary folder called Temp on the current drive, and then later, perhaps after you have worked with files copied to the Temp folder, removes the folder:

```
MkDir "\Temp"
... other code statements...
RmDir "\Temp"
```

Getting and Setting File Attributes

Files have attributes associated with them that control what kind of file activities are permitted for that file. File attributes are set when the file is created. Using VBA, you can get and set file attributes from within your Excel application.

Table 42.2 lists and describes the seven DOS file attributes. The last two columns in table 42.2 provide you with the VBA constant and values for each attribute.

TABLE 42.2   File Attributes

ATTRIBUTE	DESCRIPTION	VBA CONSTANT	VALUE
Archive	Denotes whether or not a file has changed since last backed up	vbArchive	32
Directory	Denotes that the file is a disk folder or subfolder	vbDirectory	16
Hidden	Denotes that the file should be omitted from directory listings	vbHidden	2
Normal	Denotes that the file has no other attributes, other than perhaps the Archive attribute	vbNormal	0
Read-Only	Denotes that the file can only be read, not changed or deleted	vbReadOnly	1
System	Denotes that the file is part of the computer's operating system (read-only)	vbSystem	4
Volume Label	Denotes that this file is the disk's volume label filename entry	vbSystem	4

Getting File Attributes

Use the GetAttr( ) function to determine a file attribute. The syntax takes one argument, *pathname*, which is a string expression that represents a valid DOS file name, including directory and disk path. If no directory or disk drive is provided, Excel looks in the current folder or disk drive.

```
GetAttr(pathname)
```

GetAttr( ) returns an integer that is the sum of all the numeric codes for a file's attributes. To determine which attributes are set, you need to compare the value returned to the value that you want. For example, the following statement results in zero if the ReadOnly attribute has not been set, or a nonzero value if it is set:

```
Result = GetAttr("c:\msdos.sys") And vbReadOnly
```

Here is a sample VBA program module that prompts the user to enter a file path and then displays a dialog box that lists all the file attributes:

```
Sub GetFileAttr()
  Dim FileName As String
  FileName = InputBox("Enter file path")
  ListFileAttr(FileName)
End Sub
Sub ListFileAttr(FilePath)
  Dim Attr As Integer
  Dim Message As String
  Attr = GetAttr(FilePath)
  Message=FilePath & " has these attributes:" & Chr(13)
  If (Attr And vbArchive) Then _

    Message = Message & "Archive" & Chr(13)
  If (Attr And vbDirectory) Then _
    Message = Message & "Directory" & Chr(13)
  If (Attr And vbHidden) Then _
    Message = Message & "Hidden" & Chr(13)
  If (Attr And vbNormal) Then _
    Message = Message & "Normal" & Chr(13)
  If (Attr And vbSystem) Then _
    Message = Message & "System" & Chr(13)
  If (Attr And vbReadOnly) Then _
    Message = Message & "ReadOnly" & Chr(13)
  MsgBox Message
End Sub
```

Setting File Attributes

To set a file attribute, use the SetAttr() command. The syntax of SetAttr takes two arguments. The *pathname* argument is a string expression that represents the valid DOS filename folder and path. The *attributes* argument is a numeric expression that is the file attribute code number or the sum of the file attribute code numbers to be set:

```
SetAttr pathname, attributes
```

In the following example, a new workbook named BUDGET.XLS is created; the user is shown the existing file attributes and then sets the file's ReadOnly attribute.

```
Sub SetFileAttr()
  'Note: Uses ListFileAttr() function created above.
  Dim Attr As Integer
  Dim FileName As String
```

```
        FileName = "C:\Budget.xls"
        Workbooks.Add
        ActiveWorkbook.SaveAs (FileName)
        Attr = GetAttr(FileName)'Get file attributes.
        ListFileAttr (FileName) 'Show user file attributes.
        'Close file so that you can set attributes.
        ActiveWorkbook.Close
        If Not CBool(Attr And vbReadOnly) Then
          SetAttr FileName, Attr + vbReadOnly
        End If
        Attr = GetAttr(FileName) 'Get new file attr.
        ListFileAttr (FileName)  'Show user new attr.
        SetAttr FileName, Attr - vbReadOnly
        Kill FileName            'Delete the temporary file.
        MsgBox "Temporary file has been deleted."
    End Sub
```

Manipulating Files

A common file-management task in automating Excel is to find a file for a user, and then perhaps manipulate the file in some way. Common file manipulation tasks include:

- Opening files
- Saving files
- Copying files
- Moving files
- Renaming files
- Deleting files

As noted earlier, you need to check a file's attributes before performing file manipulation tasks. In addition, files such as workbooks must be closed before deleting, copying, moving, or renaming the file.

Opening and Saving Files

Invariably, your Excel application will need to find a file for a user or determine which file name the user wants to work with. Instead of using an InputBox to ask the user to enter a file name, you might prefer to use Excel's built-in File Open and File Save dialog boxes. The GetOpenFilename and GetSaveAsFilename methods allow you to control the display of these built-in dialog boxes and return the user's selection. To locate a file name, use the Dir function.

The syntax of GetOpenFilename has three optional arguments:

```
Application.GetOpenFilename(filter,index,title)
```

The *filter* argument is a string that specifies the filtering criteria. The filter list can be any of the file filters in the List Files of Type drop-down list box in the File Open dialog box. If omitted, VBA uses all files (***.***). The *index* argument is a numeric expression that specifies the index number of the default file filtering criteria. The title specifies the title of the dialog box. If omitted, the default is `File Open`.

Set up a constant that lists all the file filters you want to list in the File Type box. For example:

```
Sub FindFile()
  Const FileType = "Text Files (*.txt), *.txt," & _
        "XL 5 Templates (*.xlt), *.xlt," & _
        "Workbooks (*.xls),*xls"
  FileName = Application.GetOpenFilename(FileType, _
                  3,"Find")
End Sub
```

In the following example, the Excel File Open dialog box is displayed listing only text files. After the user selects a file, a message box displays the file name:

```
Sub OpenTextFile()
  FileToOpen = Application.GetOpenFilename _
        ("Text Files (*.txt),*.txt")
  MsgBox "The user selected " & FileToOpen
End Sub
```

The syntax of GetSaveAsFilename is the same as the GetOpenFilename method, with the addition of one argument. All four arguments are optional:

```
Application.GetSaveAsFilename(name,filter,index,title)
```

The new argument, *name*, specifies the initial file name to display in the Name text box when the Save As dialog box appears. The *filter* argument is a string that specifies the filtering criteria. The filter list can be any of the file filters in the List Files of Type drop-down list box. If omitted, VBA uses all files (***.***). The *index* argument is a numeric expression that specifies the index number of the default file filtering criteria. The *title* specifies the title of the dialog box. If omitted, the default is `File Save As`.

In the following example, the Excel File Save As dialog box displays, allowing the user to save the file as text under the suggested (default) name Temp. A message box appears to display the file name the user decided to save the file under:

```
Sub SaveTextFile()
  FileToSave = Application.GetSaveAsFilename _
        ("Temp","Text Files (*.txt),*.txt")
  MsgBox "The user selected " & FileToSave
End Sub
```

> **Note**
>
> If the user cancels the File Save As or File Open dialog boxes, Excel returns a Boolean
> value of False. Also note that GetOpenFilename and GetSaveAsFilename may change the
> current folder.

Finding a File

You can use the Dir() function to locate a file or get a list of files in a folder. The Dir() function returns the name of a file, or folder that matches the specified pattern, file attribute, or the volume label of a drive. The Dir() function syntax has the following basic syntax:

```
Dir(pathname,attribute)
```

The *pathname* argument is a string expression that specifies the filename, drive, or folder to find. The *attribute* argument is the sum of file attributes values.

Dir supports the use of the multiple character symbol (*) and the single character symbol (?) wild cards that you can use to specify files. Dir returns the first file that matches the path name. To get additional matches, call Dir again without any arguments. When no more matches can be found, Dir returns a zero length string.

Tip
Store returned file names in an array and sort the array for future use.

In the following example, a message box displays the name of the first file found in the WinWord directory that has a DOC file extension. Then, a message box displays showing the next file found. Note that in the second message box, Dir() doesn't have any arguments:

```
Sub ListFiles()
  MsgBox "The first file found is " & _
        Dir("C:\MSOffice\WinWord\*.doc")
  MsgBox "The next file found is " & Dir()
End Sub
```

Copying, Moving, Renaming, and Deleting Files

The FileCopy statement works essentially the same as the DOS copy command. The syntax is:

```
FileCopy source, destination
```

The arguments *source* and *destination* are string expressions that result in a valid DOS file name. VBA displays runtime errors if you try to copy a file to itself, to an invalid file path or name, to a disk with insufficient disk space, or if the source file is an open workbook (unless they were opened ReadOnly).

In this example, the user is prompted for a source and destination file name, and then the file is copied:

```
Sub MakeCopy()
    Dim SourceName As String, DestName As String
    With Application
        SourceName = .GetOpenFilename _
                (Title:="Copy From File")
        If SourceName = "False" Then Exit Sub
        DestName = .GetSaveAsFilename _
                (Title:="Copy File To")
        If DestName = "False" Then Exit Sub
    End With
    FileCopy SourceName, DestName
End Sub
```

The Name statement is used to rename and move files. The syntax takes two arguments, oldName and newName. Both are string expressions that evaluate to a valid DOS file name, which may include drive and folder path information. If no drive or path is specified, VBA uses the current drive and path:

```
Name oldName newName
```

Both *oldName* and *newName* must be in the same disk drive. If the directory path of *oldName* differs from the folder path in *newName*, VBA moves the file from *oldName* to *newName*.

> **Note**
>
> You can't use the Name statement to move a file from one drive to another. Instead, copy the file using FileCopy and then delete the source file by using Kill.
>
> Also, to avoid runtime errors, check attributes, file paths, disk space, and be sure that the file is closed before using Name.

To delete a file, use the Kill statement. Kill takes one argument, the file name path to be deleted. The pathName is a String expression that evaluates to a valid DOS file name and path. Kill allows you to use the DOS wild-card characters * and ? to delete multiple files with one statement:

```
Kill pathName
```

Be very cautious when using Kill. Confirm file deletion with the user before deleting the file(s). To give users an undo feature, move the file(s) to a temporary directory that is purged at the end of the day or week, rather than use Kill.

In the following example, the user is prompted for a source file to rename or move, and then for the destination file name/path. If the user wants to move a file across drives, the FileCopy and Kill statements are used instead of the Name statement:

```
Sub MoveOrRenameDemo()
    Dim oldName As String, newName As String
    oldDir = CurDir()
    With Application
        oldName = .GetOpenFilename _
                (Title:="Rename or Move From")
        If oldName = "False" Then Exit Sub
        newName = .GetSaveAsFilename _
                (Title:="Rename or Move To)"
        If newName = "False" Then Exit Sub
    End With
    If Left(oldName,1)=Left(newName,1) Then
        Name oldNameAs newName
    Else
        FileCopy oldName, newName
        Kill oldName
    End If
    ChDrive oldDir
    ChDir oldDir
End Sub
```

Solving Common Worksheet Automation Needs

In this section, you look at a variety of VBA procedures that solve a common worksheet automation need. As you explore each of these programming solutions, keep in mind that the same code structure can be adapted to automate a similar task. For example, one of the procedures toggles between fixed decimal and normal editing modes. The structure of this procedure could be easily adapted to toggle between other edit options, format options, or print options. When working with VBA, keep an open mind and experiment on a test workbook (never with the real thing!).

Toggling between Edit Modes

The edit modes in Excel provide you with many edit options meant to speed your work. A neat feature to work into your VBA application is to provide users with the ability to toggle some of these edit modes on and off as needed. To illustrate this programming technique, you will create a procedure called FixedMode( ), which toggles fixed decimal places on and off when the user presses Ctrl+Shift+F.

Generally, when programming a feature that is available interactively, you should always use the recorder. Doing so speeds your work, automatically assigns macros to menus and shortcut keys, and prevents typing errors. On the other hand, in some cases when recorder gives you so little, it may actually be faster to type the procedure in yourself.

To create the FixedMode( ) procedure, follow these steps:

1. Open the desired workbook, or create a new workbook.

2. Choose Tools, Record Macro, Record New Macro, and then click the Options button.

3. When the Record New Macro dialog box appears, type the Macro Name **FixedMode**. In the description field, type **Toggle between Fixed Decimal edit mode and normal edit mode**.

4. Select Options. Specify the shortcut key letter as a capital **F**.

5. Choose OK. This starts the recorder.

6. Choose Tools, Options, Edit.

7. Select **Fixed Decimal** and set places to **2**.

8. Stop the recorder.

9. Edit the macro so that your text matches the following:

```
' FixedMode Macro
' Toggles between fixed decimal and normal editing modes.
'
' Keyboard Shortcut: Ctrl+f
'
Sub FixedMode()
    With Application
        If .FixedDecimal = False Then
            .FixedDecimal = True
            .FixedDecimalPlaces = 2
            .MoveAfterReturn = True
        Else
            .FixedDecimal = False
            .MoveAfterReturn = False
        End If
    End With
End Sub
```

10. Save and test your work.

Finding Values in a Large Worksheet

Worksheets and workbooks are great for storing and calculating large volumes of data. But often users can't find the forest for the trees. In this section, you look at a VBA solution for finding the largest value in a table relative to the active cell's position. As you read over the techniques used in this procedure, keep in mind that this example could easily be adapted to look in a specific range or to find data that meets some other criteria:

```
'Find the largest value in a table, and move to that cell.
'
Sub FindLargestValue()
    Dim Area As Object     'The object variable identifies
                           'the area in which to search.
'
    Set Area = Selection.CurrentRegion
    Area.Find(What:=Application.Max(Area), _
    After:=ActiveCell).Activate
End Sub
```

You can attach this procedure to a button on a worksheet, add it to your menu, or assign it a shortcut key.

Using Color for Labels

Color is a powerful feature in any system. Wisely used, color can allow users to understand the meaning of data more quickly. In an income statement or budget worksheet, for example, you may want to automatically change the color of negative amounts to red so that problems can be easier to spot. The Format, Cells, Number command adjusts the font color of a cell depending on the cell's numeric value.

Performing the same trick for labels is not an interactive feature of Excel. So, a little VBA magic is required. For the following example, suppose that the current column contains labels with the text "Paid" or "Overdue". The ColorLabels() procedure changes the color of the "Overdue" items to red:

```
Sub ColorLabels()
    Dim LastCell, CellValue As String
    'Store the current cell address so we can return there when done.
    LastCell = ActiveCell.Address
    'Select the contiguous cells in the current column.
    Selection.Offset(ActiveCell.CurrentRegion.Row - _
        ActiveCell.Row, 0).Resize(RowSize:=ActiveCell. _
        CurrentRegion.Rows.Count).Select
    'Use a loop to examine the text in each cell and assign colors.
    For Each ThisCell In Selection.Cells
        'Convert to uppercase for better comparison.
```

```
            CellValue = UCase(ThisCell.Value)
            Select Case CellValue
                Case "PAID"
                    ThisCell.Font.ColorIndex = 5 'Paid items are blue.
                Case "OVERDUE"
                    ThisCell.Font.ColorIndex = 3 'Overdue items are red.
                'Note that by default, any text which is neither
                'retains the regular color.
            End Select
        Next ThisCell ' loop back and examine next cell.
        Range(LastCell).Select 'return to prior cell location.
    End Sub
```

Avoiding Flashy Screens

Lengthy macros that cause the screen to flash and the cursor to move all over the place can be a bit alarming for the unsuspecting user. In general, it is not good programming practice to show the user unnecessary tasks, display a screen the user did not ask to see (without explaining why), or leave the cursor in a different place (without explaining why).

An easy-to-implement technique is to use Excel's ScreenUpdating property to suppress screen activity. While your VBA code executes, you can display a `Please wait...` text box message.

To suppress Excel's screen activity during macro execution and display a `Please wait` message, follow these steps:

1. Open the desired workbook.

2. Select a worksheet on which to create the `Please wait` text box. Remember that it will be hidden when not in use.

3. Use the Text Box tool to create the text box. Enter the text and choose Format, Object to format it.

4. With the Text Box selected, click the Name box in the formula bar, type **WaitMsg**, and press Enter.

5. Insert or switch to a Module sheet. Enter the following code:

```
Sub PleaseWait()
    'Display the message box.
    ActiveSheet.TextBoxes("WaitMsg").Visible = True
    'Turn off screen
    Application.ScreenUpdating = False
    'Run the lengthy macro or use following macro pause code
    'so message stays on screen about 10 seconds.
    newHour = Hour(Now())
    newMinute = Minute(Now())
```

```
      newSecond = Second(Now()) + 10
      waitTime = TimeSerial(newHour, newMinute, newSecond)
      Application.Wait waitTime
      'Hide the message box.
      ActiveSheet.TextBoxes("WaitMsg").Visible = False
      'Turn on the screen
      Application.ScreenUpdating = True
  End Sub
```

6. To test your work, create a button on the worksheet that contains the text box and assign it the PleaseWait() macro.

Responding to Events

Instead of requiring the user to do something (such as pressing a shortcut key or clicking a button) to start a procedure, you can create procedures that run automatically in response to an event (such as a workbook opening).

Programming languages that allow you to write code that responds to an event are used to create *event-driven programs*. An event-driven program waits for and responds to certain events. An *event* is something that happens to an object. Opening a workbook, pressing keys, and clicking the mouse are all examples of events. Because the events occur while the program executes and directs the program's behavior, the program is called event-driven.

Event-driven programs vary in the number of events that they let you, the programmer, access. VBA allows you to attach code to the following events:

- Opening and closing workbooks
- Installing and removing add-in applications
- Activating and deactivating a worksheet or window
- Double-clicking the mouse
- Pressing a key or key combination
- Entering data in a worksheet
- Recalculating a worksheet

When one of these events occurs, VBA looks in your code for a procedure to respond to the event. These special procedures are called *event handlers*. If an event handler is found, VBA passes control to your event handler; otherwise, VBA continues with its built-in event handling.

VBA has two kinds of event handlers:

- Automatic procedure
- Event procedure

Automatic procedures have special names, such as Auto_Open, which are named for the event to which they respond. Event procedures can have any name you desire and use OnEvent properties and methods to let VBA know which event it handles.

> **Note**
>
> Opening or closing a workbook and installing or removing an add-in application are the only automatic procedures. The remaining events are handled by event procedures.

Working with Automatic Procedures

Automatic procedures are stored in a workbook or in an add-in application and execute automatically in response to specific events. Table 42.3 lists the automatic procedure events and the required procedure name.

TABLE 42.3   Automatic Procedures

EVENT	AUTOMATIC PROCEDURE NAME
Opening a workbook	Auto_Open
Closing a workbook	Auto_Close
Installing an add-in application	Auto_Open
Removing an add-in application	Auto_Close

> **Note**
>
> Make sure that you have only one Auto_Open or Auto_Close procedure in a workbook or add-in file. If Excel finds more than one, no auto-execute procedures execute.

The following example starts a VBA application running automatically when the workbook is opened:

```
Sub Auto_Open()
With Application
  .StatusBar = "Loading VBA application."
  .Calculation = xlManual
  .Caption = "My Custom VBA System"
  .DefaultFilePath = "C:\VBA_APP"
  .PromptForSummaryInfo = False
  .UserName = InputBox ("Enter your name:")
End With
With Toolbars("Auditing")
  .Visible = True
  .Position = xlFloating
  .Left = 400
  .Top = 40
End With
Application.StatusBar = False
End Sub
```

This next example automatically closes the custom VBA application, but leaves the user in Excel:

```
Sub Auto_Close()
With Application
  .StatusBar = "Closing VBA application."
  .Calculation = xlAutomatic
  .Caption = Empty
  .DefaultFilePath = "C:\Excel"
  .PromptForSummaryInfo = True
End With
Toolbars("Auditing").Visible = False
Application.StatusBar = False
End Sub
```

Tip

To exit Excel completely, issue the Application. Quit statement just before the End Sub statement.

Working with Event Procedures

An *event procedure* is a regular procedure that can have any valid procedure name. What makes the regular procedure an event handler is the use of an OnEvent method or property. OnEvent methods and properties tell VBA to execute that code whenever the specified event occurs. For example, you can create an event procedure that verifies data entry. Whenever the user enters or edits data in the specified worksheet, Excel automatically calls your event procedure.

VBA provides many OnEvent methods and properties. Using the OnEvent methods and properties, you can set or get the name of the procedure that executes in response to the event. For a complete list of OnEvent methods and properties, search the VBA help file for "Running Procedures when an Event Occurs."

Tip

To cancel an event procedure, set the object's event property to the null string " ".

The following example uses event processing to verify data entered into cells on a worksheet named "Data Entry":

```
Sub StartDataEntry()
  Application.MoveAfterReturn = False
  Worksheets("Data Entry").OnEntry = "VerifyData"
End Sub
'This proc verifies the data entered.
'Each case number represents a column.
'1=A, 2=B, 3=C
Sub VerifyData()
 With ActiveCell
    Select Case .Column
    Case 1  'this is column A
       If Not IsDate(.Value) Then
             MsgBox "Invalid date. Please re-enter."
             .ClearContents
       Else
             .NumberFormat = "mmmm d, yyyy"
       End If
    Case 2  'This is column B
       If IsNumeric(.Value) Then
             If .Value > 1 Or .Value < 0 Then
                 MsgBox "Rate must be between 0 and 1."
                 .ClearContents
             Else
                 .NumberFormat = "0.0%"
             End If
       Else
             MsgBox "Invalid discount."
             .ClearContents
       End If
    Case 3  'This is column C
       If .Value < 0 Then
             MsgBox "Amount must be positive."
             .ClearContents
       Else
             .NumberFormat = "$#,##0.00_);($#,##0.00)"
       End If
    End Select
 End With
End Sub
'This procedure turns the OnEntry event handler off.
Sub EndDataEntry()
  Application.MoveAfterReturn = True
  Worksheets("Data Entry").OnEntry = ""
End Sub
```

Working with Add-Ins

Excel's add-in applications feature is very useful. It adds functions and commands to Excel that look like they are built-in. Using VBA, you can create your own add-ins. From an application development standpoint, creating add-ins provides the following benefits:

- *Security*. Add-in code is compressed into a file format that no one else can read or edit.

- *Speed*. Add-in code executes faster than workbook procedures.

- *Streamlining*. Add-in code doesn't appear in the Macro dialog box.

Users access add-in code via menus, shortcut keys, toolbars, and event handlers. Add-ins without an Auto_Open procedure are loaded into memory in two steps. When your application first loads, Excel adds the functions to the Function Wizard and enables any menu commands, toolbars, and shortcut keys. Excel does not load the rest of the application until the user chooses an add-in function, menu choice, toolbar button, or shortcut key.

For add-ins with an Auto_Open procedure, Excel loads the entire program into memory.

Creating an Add-In

To create an add-in application, follow these steps:

1. Switch to a module in the workbook that you want to save as an add-in.

2. Choose Tools, Make Add-In.

3. In the Save File as Type drop-down list, you see `Microsoft Excel Add-In`. Type the file name that will automatically have a file extension of XLA.

4. Choose OK.

Controlling Add-Ins from VBA

To manipulate an add-in from VBA, you need to know how to refer to the add-in. VBA provides an AddIn object and an AddIns collection of all add-in applications available to Excel. To refer to an add-in, use the AddIns method:

```
AddIns(index)
```

The index argument refers to the add-ins listed in the Tools, Add-Ins dialog box. Index can be the number position of the add-in in that dialog box list. Or, index can be the name of the add-in as shown in that dialog box. For custom add-ins that you create, the name is the file name without the extension. Index can also be an array of names or numbers.

Before you can work with your own custom add-ins, you need to add them to the AddIns collection. Use the Add method of the AddIns collection object:

```
AddIns.Add(Filename, CopyFile)
```

The *filename* argument is the full path name of the add-in file. CopyFile is an optional argument that allows you to copy the file from a slower device, such as a floppy drive or CD-ROM, to the hard disk.

Once Excel knows where the add-in file is, you can install the add-in to make it available to users. This is done by setting the add-in object's Installed property to True.

The following example adds the Solver add-in and then installs it by setting the Installed property to True:

```
Sub AddInDemo()
  Set SolverAddIn = AddIns _
        .Add("C:\Excel\Library\Solver\Solver.XLA")
  SolverAddIn.Installed = True
End Sub
```

Chapter 43

Sue Plumley used her knowledge of design in desktop publishing and graphic art to manage the pre-press department of a commercial print shop before starting her own business seven years ago. She began Humble Opinions, a firm that specializes in consulting, training, and network installation, management, and maintenance. In addition, Sue has taught the use of various software applications at Beckley College in West Virginia.

Using Office Advantage in Business

In today's business world, you need to be organized, efficient, determined, and persevering. You must do all you can to stay ahead of the competition, present reasonable alternatives to your customers, keep employees happy, and yes, even make a profit.

Microsoft Office probably cannot single-handedly make your business successful—but it definitely can help. Using Microsoft Office makes my work easier than it was in the days when I used various individual applications. The program saves time, energy, and keeps my level of frustration to an absolute minimum.

I use the Office applications for many projects in my business—computer, network, and software consulting—and I would be lost without them. I complete many projects using Office:

- *Customer contact*. I keep copies of all letters as well as phone and service logs.

- *Forms*. I create expense and travel records, invoices, and purchase orders.

Techniques from the Pros

by Sue Plumley

- *Inventory.* I print out updated lists of small parts, hardware, and software in stock.

- *Sales data.* Using spreadsheets and charts, I keep a detailed record of each salesperson's progress from month to month.

- *Marketing.* I create all advertisements, fliers, newsletters, and so on in-house and often perform merged mailings.

- *Presentations.* I create various presentations to show to customers both on-screen and printed.

This chapter shows you one recent project I created to help the sales staff when quoting computer systems. Additionally, I use some of the same information in letters to customers and in a presentation for customers.

The Sales Report

In the first step of this project, I created a document in Word, with the aid of my sales staff, to help them quote computer systems and present the quotes to the customer.

> **Note**
>
> After creating the necessary documents—sales report, spreadsheets, and presentation—we copied all the documents to each salesperson's laptop for quick and easy referencing.

◀ **See**
"Adding Headers and Footers," p. 275

We divided the report into several sections: Individual, Small Business, Corporation, and Business Networking. In each section, we included an introduction, several computer system packages, and a needs sheet to fill out on-site.

Figure 43.1 shows the introductory page of the Small Business section. Included in the introduction are some sales ideas and a list of sample projects for which a small business may use a computer.

Small Business Section   24

Introduction

In today's small business, a computer is not only a great help but it may be a necessity. Consider, if you will, the many projects any business might perform on a daily, weekly, and monthly basis. Following are only a very few examples of projects a small business could expedite by using a computer:

- Payroll
- Accounts payable and receivable
- Letter-writing and tracking
- Invoicing
- Personnel reports
- Travel expenses
- Sales summaries
- Inventory
- Newsletters
- Fliers and advertising
- Form creation
- Faxing
- E-mail (internal and external)

And the list goes on and on. If a business performs any or all of the above activities, a computer would definitely be essential. Just think of the advantages to a small business that owned one or more computers; just think of the time that could be saved with a computer.

Today, any business can easily afford to purchase and use a computer system. When you think about it, no business can really afford to be without a computer. Whether you want to invest in the small system with only the basic services or the large system including printers, a modem, CD drive and so on, a computer system is a must if you want to survive in business today.

This section of the report discusses many options available for a small business. You may be interested in only one computer and one printer or in several. This section outlines available systems and describes many options to customize each deal to the customer.

Fig. 43.1

Using Word's header and footer feature helps organize the many sections of the report and adds a little flair as well.

The next several pages in the report each contain a description of a specific computer system package, the items making up the system, total price, and a spreadsheet (see fig. 43.2). I wanted to make sure the price for any item was accurate and I could change mark-up easily, so I linked the spreadsheet from Excel.

Fig. 43.2

Many pages of the report contain the cost and mark-up for hardware, so these pages are for salespersons' eyes only.

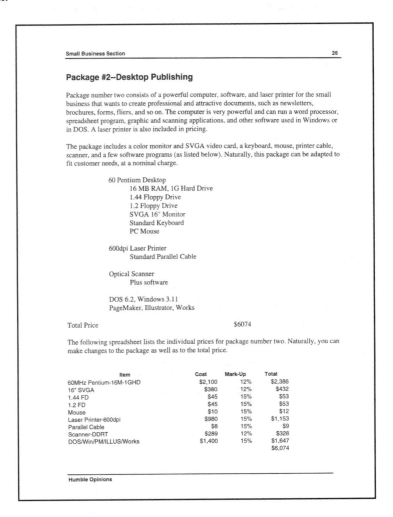

Small Business Section   26

Package #2--Desktop Publishing

Package number two consists of a powerful computer, software, and laser printer for the small business that wants to create professional and attractive documents, such as newsletters, brochures, forms, fliers, and so on. The computer is very powerful and can run a word processor, spreadsheet program, graphic and scanning applications, and other software used in Windows or in DOS. A laser printer is also included in pricing.

The package includes a color monitor and SVGA video card, a keyboard, mouse, printer cable, scanner, and a few software programs (as listed below). Naturally, this package can be adapted to fit customer needs, at a nominal charge.

    60 Pentium Desktop
        16 MB RAM, 1G Hard Drive
        1.44 Floppy Drive
        1.2 Floppy Drive
        SVGA 16" Monitor
        Standard Keyboard
        PC Mouse

    600dpi Laser Printer
        Standard Parallel Cable

    Optical Scanner
        Plus software

    DOS 6.2, Windows 3.11
    PageMaker, Illustrator, Works

Total Price $6074

The following spreadsheet lists the individual prices for package number two. Naturally, you can make changes to the package as well as to the total price.

Item	Cost	Mark-Up	Total
60MHz Pentium-16M-1GHD	$2,100	12%	$2,386
16" SVGA	$380	12%	$432
1.44 FD	$45	15%	$53
1.2 FD	$45	15%	$53
Mouse	$10	15%	$12
Laser Printer-600dpi	$980	15%	$1,153
Parallel Cable	$8	15%	$9
Scanner-DDRT	$289	12%	$328
DOS/Win/PM/ILLUS/Works	$1,400	15%	$1,647
			$6,074

Humble Opinions

Tip

Use Excel's Functions Wizard to help select a built-in function (choose Insert, Function).

The spreadsheet lists each item in the package, its cost to us, the mark-up percentage, and the total price for the customer. I can easily change costs or mark-up in the worksheet, and the formulas I created total the costs of the items. Figure 43.3 shows the spreadsheet file in Excel.

Fig. 43.3

The formula for the total price of the first item appears in the Formula bar.

```
X Microsoft Excel - Sales01                                    _ B X
File  Edit  View  Insert  Format  Tools  Data  Window  Help    _ B X

Arial          10    B I U                    $ %  ,         100%

E14              =+C14/(1-D14)
       A              B               C       D       E       F       G
 9           DOS/Win/Works          $245     15%    $288
10                                                  $2,131
11
12  PKG. #2
13                  Item            Cost    Mark-Up  Total
14          60MHz Pentium-16M-1GHD  $2,100   12%    $2,386
15          16" SVGA                $380     12%    $432
16          1.44 FD                 $45      15%    $53
17          1.2 FD                  $45      15%    $53
18          Mouse                   $10      15%    $12
19          Laser Printer-600dpi    $980     15%    $1,153
20          Parallel Cable          $8       15%    $9
21          DOS/Win/PM/ILLUS/Works  $1,400   15%    $1,647
22                                                  $5,745
23
24  PKG. #3
25                  Item            Cost    Mark-Up  Total
    Sheet1 / Sheet2 / Sheet3 / Sheet4 / Sheet5 / Sheet6 / Sheet7 /
Ready                              SUM=$2,386                  NUM
Start  X Microsoft Excel - Sal...                             2:57 PM
```

◀ **See**
"Referencing Cells in Formulas," p. 372

◀ **See**
"Using Common Steps To Link Documents," p. 689

Using a linked file means I can easily change the costs or mark-up in the original worksheet and quickly get an automatic update in the report. One reason I use Office is because of its data-sharing capabilities.

Finally, at the end of each section of the report is a Needs Assessment form (see fig. 43.4). The sales people use this form to survey each customer and fill in answers on the computer. Then, the salesperson can print the final form as a reference for compiling a quote for that customer.

◀ **See**
"Adding Text to a Table," p. 287

◀ **See**
"Formatting with Styles," p. 259

> **Note**
>
> The same headings, body text, indents, and tabs are used throughout the report to create consistency. You can use Word's styles to help format your documents, or you can use AutoFormat by choosing Format, AutoFormat or by choosing a style from the Format, Style Gallery.

Fig. 43.4

Use Word's handy table feature to create a form that's easy to read and to fill in.

Small Business Section		28

Needs Assessment

Customer:	Contact:
Address:	City/St:
Phone:	Fax:

Primary Business:

Current Hardware:

Current Software:

Software Upgrades:

Hardware Additions:

Recommendations:

Customer Comments:

Humble Opinions

Customer Letters

Many of our customers want quotes in the form of a letter. Because much of each salesperson's day is spent quoting, we decided to create a letter and envelope file to make the job easier.

The letter file contains our letterhead as well as our return address already set up in the Envelopes and Labels dialog box. Additionally, the styles and some text already are entered into the file.

When a salesperson needs to create a quote, he or she opens the file and saves it under the customer's name. The salesperson then can change and add any

Tip

A salesperson can manually link pricing data to a letter to make sure the prices are updated if the customer does not buy the system right away.

text necessary. Finally, the salesperson can copy the specific computer system package data from the sales report to the letter. Figure 43.5 illustrates a letter using linked data to present in a quote.

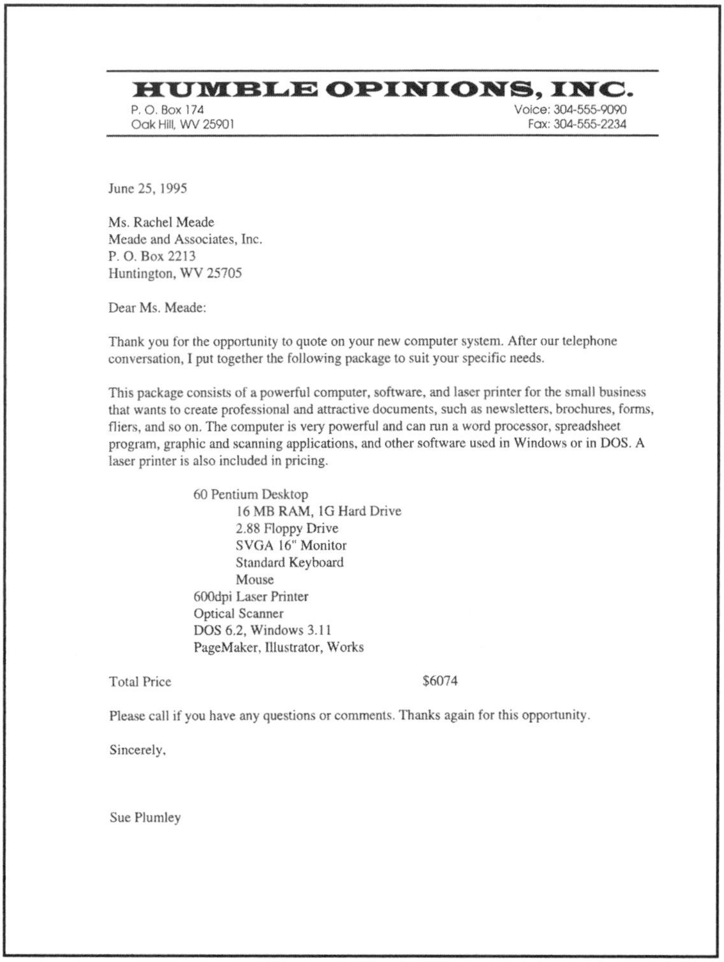

Fig. 43.5

Share data between the sales report and the letter for faster, more efficient sales.

HUMBLE OPINIONS, INC.

P. O. Box 174   Voice: 304-555-9090
Oak Hill, WV 25901   Fax: 304-555-2234

June 25, 1995

Ms. Rachel Meade
Meade and Associates, Inc.
P. O. Box 2213
Huntington, WV 25705

Dear Ms. Meade:

Thank you for the opportunity to quote on your new computer system. After our telephone conversation, I put together the following package to suit your specific needs.

This package consists of a powerful computer, software, and laser printer for the small business that wants to create professional and attractive documents, such as newsletters, brochures, forms, fliers, and so on. The computer is very powerful and can run a word processor, spreadsheet program, graphic and scanning applications, and other software used in Windows or in DOS. A laser printer is also included in pricing.

                60 Pentium Desktop
                        16 MB RAM, 1G Hard Drive
                        2.88 Floppy Drive
                        SVGA 16" Monitor
                        Standard Keyboard
                        Mouse
                600dpi Laser Printer
                Optical Scanner
                DOS 6.2, Windows 3.11
                PageMaker, Illustrator, Works

Total Price $6074

Please call if you have any questions or comments. Thanks again for this opportunity.

Sincerely,

Sue Plumley

Tip

You can use Word's Mail Merge Wizard to help you create business letters and use fields to custom-ize letters to each customer.

Note

One handy feature I often use in Word is to link two Word documents or parts of two documents together. In the letter, for example, the list of items in the package can be linked to the report so if any items change in the report, the letter is automatically up-dated. You can choose Tools, Options, Field Shading to display the linked text with a gray background so you can easily spot it in the document.

I keep the addresses of our most active customers in Word's Address Book. It's easy to quickly insert an address to the letters using the Address Book.

Creating the Presentation

◀ **See**
"Setting Up and Running a Slide Show On-Screen," p. 650

We use PowerPoint presentations to show our clients some of the computer system options available to them. We often show presentations on-screen in the office, and we print color pages for the salespeople to take with them to our customers' locations. Either way, the data within a presentation is always up-to-date.

◀ **See**
"Using a Word Outline To Create Slides," p. 720

Entering presentation data from the sales report is easy because we can link it, copy it, or embed it from Word or Excel to PowerPoint.

As an example, figure 43.6 shows the bulleted list from the introduction of the sales report as one slide in a presentation. We removed all extraneous text from the copied text so the speaker has something to say when he or she shows the presentation.

Fig. 43.6

Copied and pasted data makes the presentation quick and easy to create.

Tip

A fast and efficient method to start a presentation is by outlining the entire presentation in Word and then opening the outline in PowerPoint.

Tip

Using symbols, clip art, or pictures also helps attract and keep the customer's attention.

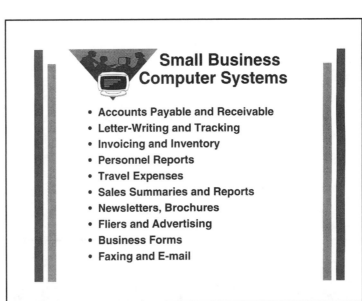

In addition to incorporating text from the introduction into the presentation, we also can add text from the package pages (see fig. 43.7). Using large, bulleted text to present the data makes it easy for the customer to see what is offered in each package.

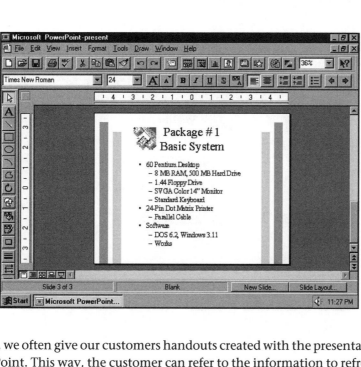

Fig. 43.7

You can create your own text, copy text, or link text to create an effective slide in the presentation.

Finally, we often give our customers handouts created with the presentation in PowerPoint. This way, the customer can refer to the information to refresh his or her memory after our salespeople leave. In addition to creating audience handouts, PowerPoint enables you to produce and print speaker's notes while you're creating the presentation.

With all of Office's capabilities, MS Graph may actually be one of the handiest. Figure 43.8 shows a 3-D column graph created for the presentation to help convince the customer of the popularity of the Pentium computer (the computer we're trying to sell them).

When creating a graph, we often use the data sheet in MS Graph to enter the data; however, we can also copy or link spreadsheet data from Excel to create a graph. This versatility means we can work more efficiently by using any data we need in the presentation.

> **Note**
>
> You can modify graph elements—such as the title, data labels, gridlines, and so on—by double-clicking the element you want to change. A related dialog box appears from which you can choose the options to modify.

Fig. 43.8

Create the graph using new data or copy data from a spreadsheet.

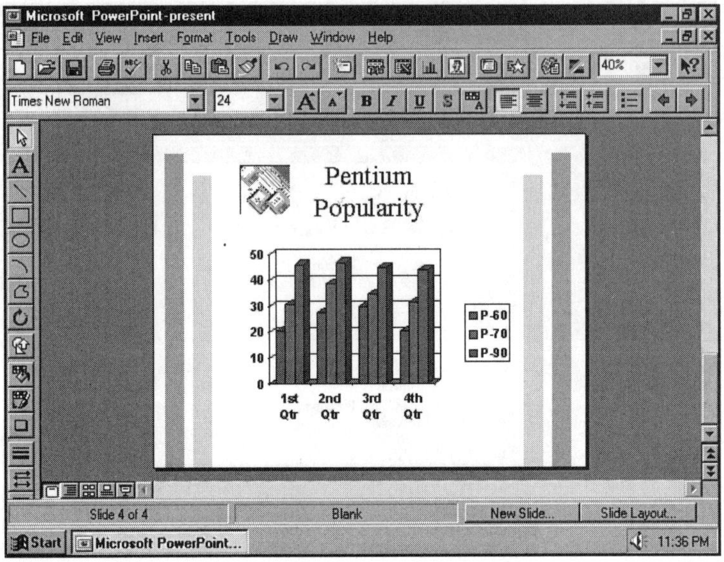

◀ **See**
"Inserting an Organization Chart," p. 602

◀ **See**
"Adding Visual Elements to a Chart," p. 475

We receive data from a variety of places to use in a presentation; one common method is to use a Word table in a slide. Also, it's easy to embed, link, or paste an Excel worksheet to a slide.

A Word about Files

When working with a project such as the one discussed in this chapter, I try to organize all related files so they are easy to find. Office and Windows 95 makes it easy for you to manage files using folders.

Tip
You can add a frequently used document to the Office menu for quick access. Choose Customize in the MS Office menu from the Microsoft Office Shortcut Bar.

Most times, I create a new folder and place all related files—Excel, Word, and Presentation—in that one folder. That way, I know where to look for my data and so do the salespeople.

Another way to store related files is to create separate folders within each application's folder. With the previous project, for example, I would create a folder called SALESREP in the Word, Excel, and PowerPoint folders. I would store all related Word files, then, in OFFICE/WORD/SALESREP, all related Excel files in OFFICE/EXCEL/SALESREP, and so on.

Figure 43.9 shows the SALESREP folder in Word and the related files saved in the folder.

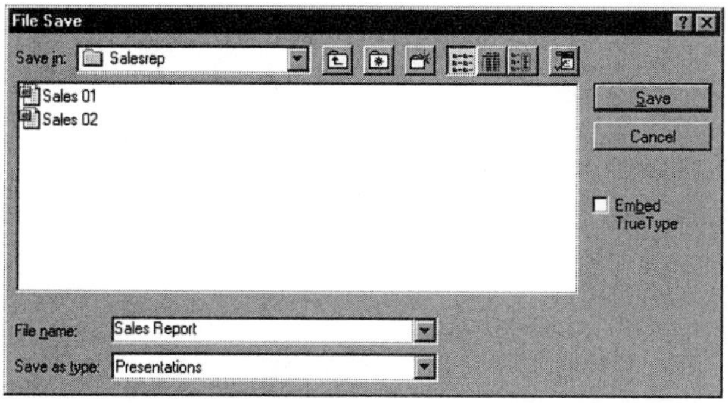

Techniques from the Pros Techniques from the Pros Techniques from the Pros

Fig. 43.9

Saving related files in their own folder makes those files easy to find and keeps the drive organized.

Finally, I name related files similarly so they are easy to recognize: SALES01.DOC, SALES02.DOC in Word, SALES01.XLS, SALES02.XLS, in Excel, and so on. This way, I have no trouble finding the right file when I need it.❖

◀ **See**
"Working with Files," p. 102

Index of Common Problems

(continues)

If you have this problem...	You'll find help here...
Interoperability: Excel worksheet is too big for my PowerPoint slide	p. 728
Interoperability: Linked documents don't appear	p. 690
Interoperability: Links in Word document don't appear highlighted	p. 691
Interoperability: Word Outline file won't go into PowerPoint presentation	p. 723
MS Graph: Datasheet window closed—how to redisplay it	p. 466
MS Graph: Datasheet window covers up the chart	p. 466
MS Graph: Graph appears on top of drawn objects or text	p. 464
Multimedia: Motion picture clips degrade image	p. 547
Multimedia: Video clip plays continuously without control buttons to stop it	p. 541
Typing and Editing: Copied text went into wrong place	p. 675
Typing and Editing: Copy and paste brought something unexpected	p. 79
Typing and Editing: Copy and paste into a dialog box	p. 666
Typing and Editing: Copy object—didn't work and original object out of place	p. 81
Typing and Editing: Drag-and-drop moves information between applications instead of copying	p. 528
Typing and Editing: Lose editing changes	p. 696
Typing and Editing: Lose information during copy	p. 675
Typing and Editing: Message—who routed to me?	p. 827
Typing and Editing: Mouse—have problems controlling it	p. 175
Typing and Editing: Paragraph mark—can't delete	p. 703
Typing and Editing: Selection doesn't stay selected	p. 309
Typing and Editing: Spelling—need to edit words in custom dictionary	p. 97
Viewing Screen and Document: Black circle with slash	p. 675
Viewing Screen and Document: Document disappeared	p. 29

(continues)

If you have this problem...	You'll find help here...
Viewing Screen and Document: Menu item lost when pressed Alt+Ctrl+minus sign (–)	p. 766
Viewing Screen and Document: Menus—customized default menus but need to get the standard menus back	p. 766
Viewing Screen and Document: Toolbar—customized default Standard toolbar but need to get Standard toolbar back	p. 763
Viewing Screen and Document: Toolbar I created contains no buttons	p. 762
Viewing Screen and Document: Colored toolbars are hard to see on black-and-white monitor	p. 763

Excel

If you have this problem...	You'll find help here...
Database: Error message with Data Form—no list was found	p. 426
Database: Error message with new record—Cannot extend list or database	p. 426
Database: Filters don't display any records	p. 431
Database: Remove data for new record	p. 423
Database: Sorts column titles along with data in list	p. 431
Files: Workspace file cannot find files	p. 320
Formatting: Center across selection doesn't work	p. 355
Formatting: Characters lost when aligning vertically	p. 355
Formatting: Characters lost when changing color	p. 361
Formatting: Columns on different worksheets need to appear the same	p. 88
Formatting: Error message after choosing AutoFormat	p. 349
Formatting: Header overflows into data when printing	p. 416
Formatting: International currency symbols in number formats	p. 348
Formatting: Page Break removal—only some page breaks removed when I want to remove all	p. 407

(continues)

Excel Continued	
If you have this problem...	**You'll find help here...**
Formatting: Page Break removal—Remove Page Break not displayed on Insert menu	p. 406
Formulas: #### appears in cell	p. 348
Formulas: #DIV/0 appears in cell	p. 378
Formulas: #N/A appears in cell	p. 378
Formulas: #NAME? appears in cell	p. 387
Formulas: #NUL! appears in cell	p. 387
Formulas: #NUM! appears in cell	p. 379
Formulas: #REF! appears in cell	p. 379
Formulas: #VALUE! appears in cell	p. 379
Formulas: Auditing features don't work (I can't see them)	p. 381
Formulas: AutoSum doesn't produce totals	p. 396
Formulas: Error message in formula with parentheses	p. 376
Formulas: Error value appears in worksheet	p. 379
Formulas: Formula appears as text in a cell instead of number or result	p. 308
Formulas: Formulas appear to calculate incorrectly	p. 376
Formulas: Range name doesn't work in formula	p. 387
Formulas: Sheet name does not work in formula	p. 374
Graphics: Chart commands on embedded chart not available	p. 486
Graphics: Data markers appear crowded	p. 494
Graphics: Formats lost on chart with AutoFormat	p. 499
Graphics: Legend—how to remove	p. 486
Graphics: Print chart instead of worksheet	p. 509
Printing: Data won't fit on page when printing	p. 416
Printing: Report page numbers all say page 1	p. 420
Printing: Print titles appear twice on first page of printout	p. 409

If you have this problem...	You'll find help here...
Programming: Procedure only works on a specific workbook	p. 770
Programming: Properties return nothing or procedure crashes	p. 773
Programming: VBA Auto execute procedure doesn't work	p. 976
Programming: VBA Name statement doesn't work to move file from one drive to another	p. 970
Typing and Editing: AutoCorrect doesn't work	p. 339
Typing and Editing: AutoFill incorrectly filled the range	p. 317
Typing and Editing: AutoFill moved data rather than AutoFilled	p. 328
Typing and Editing: Cell references change when I copy and not when I move	p. 330
Typing and Editing: Delete whole worksheet by accident	p. 320
Typing and Editing: Double-click doesn't work for editing a cell	p. 323
Typing and Editing: Drag-and-drop copied instead of moved	p. 330
Typing and Editing: Drag-and-drop copying doesn't work	p. 328
Typing and Editing: Drag-and-drop gives a warning message	p. 329
Typing and Editing: Edit, Paste gives an error message	p. 328
Typing and Editing: Edit, Paste only pasted a portion of data	p. 328
Typing and Editing: Edit, Paste only works once to copy data	p. 328
Typing and Editing: Excel converted a date to a number	p. 308
Typing and Editing: Replace feature replaces too many characters	p. 336
Typing and Editing: Replace replaces numbers in wrong places	p. 100
Typing and Editing: Spell check—I want to ignore numbers	p. 96
Typing and Editing: Spelling—I don't know exact spelling when using Find	p. 335
Typing and Editing: Undo doesn't undo problem	p. 318
Viewing Screen and Document: Note indicators don't appear in worksheet	p. 459
Viewing Screen and Document: Report Manager command doesn't appear in View menu	p. 420

If you have this problem...	You'll find help here...
Typing and Editing: Selecting text doesn't work	p. 606
Typing and Editing: Slide in wrong location	p. 583
Typing and Editing: Spell checker doesn't check some words	p. 597
Typing and Editing: Text—lost on slide	p. 625
Viewing Screen and Document: Slide show doesn't start with slide 1	p. 590
Viewing Screen and Document: Tip of the Day does not appear for PowerPoint	p. 161

Schedule+

If you have this problem...	You'll find help here...
Viewing Screen and Document: Appointment—can't see	p. 831
Viewing Screen and Document: Appointment dialog box won't open	p. 837
Viewing Screen and Document: Events not visible in schedule	p. 841
Viewing Screen and Document: Invite button not available on Attendees tab	p. 840
Viewing Screen and Document: Tasks for contacts not displayed when inviting to meeting	p. 844

Word

If you have this problem...	You'll find help here...
Files: Documents lost because of power problems	p. 244
Files: Fast save doesn't work	p. 242
Files: Password—I forgot it	p. 249
Files: Power problems cause loss of documents	p. 14
Files: Save file created in other format	p. 184
Files: Saving doesn't work in other file type	p. 184

(continues)

Word Continued	
If you have this problem...	**You'll find help here...**
Formatting: Align text left and right on same line	p. 202
Formatting: AutoFormat doesn't work	p. 269
Formatting: Bullets—don't want with every Enter	p. 203
Formatting: Column—insert to right of table	p. 287
Formatting: Columns and rows in wrong place	p. 292
Formatting: Copy formatting to other text	p. 193
Formatting: Font and alignment need to change back to normal	p. 194
Formatting: Footnote doesn't look right	p. 281
Formatting: Format—want to return to original formatting	p. 85
Formatting: Headings don't appear in table of contents	p. 279
Formatting: Hyphenation doesn't work	p. 202
Formatting: Line spacing needs to change back to normal	p. 198
Formatting: Margins are not consistent in document	p. 205
Formatting: Space—large gaps between words	p. 202
Formatting: Style applied to wrong section	p. 264
Formatting: Style—need to format words rather than whole paragraph	p. 264
Formatting: Styles inconsistent	p. 264
Formatting: Styles on template—need to know what they look like	p. 269
Formatting: Table borders don't print	p. 676
Formatting: Table of contents—don't want page numbers or dots	p. 279
Formatting: Tabs and indents—need to see settings	p. 202
Formulas: Formula does not recalculate in table	p. 298
Merge, Envelopes, and Labels: Merged letter messed up	p. 923

If you have this problem...	You'll find help here...
Merge, Envelopes, and Labels: Spacing is wrong between words in a merge	p. 930
Outlines: Copy only outline headings	p. 259
Outlines: See start of text with outline headings	p. 279
Printing: Document doesn't come out of printer	p. 225
Printing: Document prints at wrong printer	p. 225
Printing: Envelope return address margin wrong	p. 227
Printing: Margin—edges of text don't print	p. 208
Printing: Paper—can't print on long paper	p. 208
Programming: Form—first field not selected when opening document	p. 886
Programming: Form data doesn't line up on preprinted form	p. 902
Programming: Form document doesn't show programmed help	p. 895
Programming: Form fill-in prompt only displays the first word	p. 904
Programming: Form messed up by user	p. 876
Typing and Editing: Annotation initials are incorrect	p. 863
Typing and Editing: Annotation—can't get to	p. 282
Typing and Editing: Bookmark—can't delete	p. 284
Typing and Editing: Copied text to wrong location	p. 180
Typing and Editing: Deleted wrong text	p. 180
Typing and Editing: Grammar checker doesn't work	p. 218
Typing and Editing: Grammar—don't check spelling, too	p. 220
Typing and Editing: Grammar— I don't understand grammar rule	p. 247
Typing and Editing: Grammar—undo last change	p. 220
Typing and Editing: Header and footer only in part of document	p. 278
Typing and Editing: Insertion point goes to wrong place	p. 175
Typing and Editing: Reviewer's initials aren't correct	p. 282

(continues)

Index

D

J-K

L

X-Y-Z

B. oaden You. Mind And Your Business With Que

Complete and Return this Card
for a *FREE* Computer Book Catalog

Thank you for purchasing this book! You have purchased a superior computer book written expressly for your needs. To continue to provide the kind of up-to-date, pertinent coverage you've come to expect from us, we need to hear from you. Please take a minute to complete and return this self-addressed, postage-paid form. In return, we'll send you a free catalog of all our computer books on topics ranging from word processing to programming and the internet.

Mr. ☐   Mrs. ☐   Ms. ☐   Dr. ☐

Name (first) ☐☐☐☐☐☐☐☐☐☐☐   (M.I.) ☐   (last) ☐☐☐☐☐☐☐☐☐☐☐☐☐☐☐

Address ☐☐☐☐☐☐☐☐☐☐☐☐☐☐☐☐☐☐☐☐☐☐☐☐☐☐☐☐☐

☐☐☐☐☐☐☐☐☐☐☐☐☐☐☐☐☐☐☐☐☐☐☐☐☐☐☐☐☐

City ☐☐☐☐☐☐☐☐☐☐☐   State ☐☐   Zip ☐☐☐☐☐ ☐☐☐☐

Phone ☐☐☐ ☐☐☐ ☐☐☐☐   Fax ☐☐☐ ☐☐☐ ☐☐☐☐

Company Name ☐☐☐☐☐☐☐☐☐☐☐☐☐☐☐☐☐☐☐☐☐☐☐☐☐☐☐☐☐

E-mail address ☐☐☐☐☐☐☐☐☐☐☐☐☐☐☐☐☐☐☐☐☐☐☐☐☐☐☐☐☐

1. Please check at least (3) influencing factors for purchasing this book.

Front or back cover information on book .... ☐
Special approach to the content .... ☐
Completeness of content .... ☐
Author's reputation .... ☐
Publisher's reputation .... ☐
Book cover design or layout .... ☐
Index or table of contents of book .... ☐
Price of book .... ☐
Special effects, graphics, illustrations .... ☐
Other (Please specify): _____ ☐

2. How did you first learn about this book?

Saw in Macmillan Computer Publishing catalog .... ☐
Recommended by store personnel .... ☐
Saw the book on bookshelf at store .... ☐
Recommended by a friend .... ☐
Received advertisement in the mail .... ☐
Saw an advertisement in: _____ ☐
Read book review in: _____ ☐
Other (Please specify): _____ ☐

3. How many computer books have you purchased in the last six months?

This book only .... ☐   3 to 5 books .... ☐
books .... ☐   More than 5 .... ☐

4. Where did you purchase this book?

Bookstore .... ☐
Computer Store .... ☐
Consumer Electronics Store .... ☐
Department Store .... ☐
Office Club .... ☐
Warehouse Club .... ☐
Mail Order .... ☐
Direct from Publisher .... ☐
Internet site .... ☐
Other (Please specify): _____ ☐

5. How long have you been using a computer?

☐ Less than 6 months   ☐ 6 months to a year
☐ 1 to 3 years   ☐ More than 3 years

6. What is your level of experience with personal computers and with the subject of this book?

	With PCs	With subject of book
New	☐	☐
Casual	☐	☐
Accomplished	☐	☐
Expert	☐	☐

Source Code ISBN: 0-7897-0146-4

7. Which of the following best describes your job title?

Administrative Assistant .... ☐
Coordinator .... ☐
Manager/Supervisor .... ☐
Director .... ☐
Vice President .... ☐
President/CEO/COO .... ☐
Lawyer/Doctor/Medical Professional .... ☐
Teacher/Educator/Trainer .... ☐
Engineer/Technician .... ☐
Consultant .... ☐
Not employed/Student/Retired .... ☐
Other (Please specify): _____ ☐

8. Which of the following best describes the area of the company your job title falls under?

Accounting .... ☐
Engineering .... ☐
Manufacturing .... ☐
Operations .... ☐
Marketing .... ☐
Sales .... ☐
Other (Please specify): _____ ☐

9. What is your age?

Under 20 .... ☐
21-29 .... ☐
30-39 .... ☐
40-49 .... ☐
50-59 .... ☐
60-over .... ☐

10. Are you:

Male .... ☐
Female .... ☐

11. Which computer publications do you read regularly? (Please list)

_____
_____
_____
_____
_____
_____
_____
_____
_____
_____

Comments: _____
_____
_____

Fold here and scotch-tape to mail.

Windows 95 Shortcuts

Operation	Shortcut
Start Menu	
Display hidden Start	Ctrl+Esc or move pointer to screen edge
Add file/folder to Start	Drop file on Start menu
Add/Remove program	Right-click taskbar, Properties, Start Menu Programs, Add/Remove
Clear documents list	Right-click taskbar, Properties, Start Menu Programs, Clear
Taskbar	
Display hidden taskbar	Ctrl+Esc or move pointer to screen edge
Keep on top of other objects	Right-click taskbar, Properties, Taskbar Options, Always on Top
Hide taskbar	Right-click taskbar, Properties, Auto Hide
Show date	Pause pointer over time in taskbar
Change date/time	Double-click time
Change PCMCIA/Sound	Double-click PCMCIA or sound icon
Application Windows	
Maximize window	Double-click title bar
Tile windows on-screen	Right-click taskbar, Tile Horizontally/Vertically
Cascade windows on-screen	Right-click taskbar, Cascade
Minimize all to taskbar	Right-click taskbar, Minimize All Windows
Working with Files	
Open Explorer	Right-click Start, Explore
Find file/folder	Start, Find, Files or Folders, enter search data
Select adjacent files	Click first, Shift+Click last
Select non-adjacent files	Click first, Ctrl+Click others
Undelete files	Open Recycle Bin, drag file out
Copy file(s) to A:	Right-click file(s), SendTo, A:
Open document(s)	Select file(s), right-click, Open
Print file	Right-click, SendTo, printer
Moving or Copying Data	
Create scrap on desktop	Right-drag selections to desktop
Paste scrap into document	Right-drag into document, Move or Create
Copy between applications	Drag selection and drop
Copy to application on taskbar	Drag to button on taskbar, pause, drop

Microsoft Office Shortcut Keys

The Microsoft Office shortcut keys can be used in Word, Excel, and PowerPoint. An asterisk in the first column indicates that the shortcut is also available in Schedule+.

Editing	Shortcut
Undo last action*	Ctrl+Z
Redo/Repeat last action	Ctrl+Y or F4
Clear selection or character to right*	Delete
Clear selection or character to left*	Backspace
Cut selection to the Clipboard*	Ctrl+X
Copy selection to the Clipboard*	Ctrl+C
Paste from the Clipboard*	Ctrl+V
Select all	Ctrl+A
Find*	Ctrl+F
Repeat last find or Go to	Shift+F4
Find and replace	Ctrl+H

Moving	Shortcut
One character left*	Left arrow
One character right*	Right arrow
One line/row up*	Up arrow
One line/row down*	Down arrow
One word right while editing*	Ctrl+Right arrow
One word left while editing*	Ctrl+Left arrow
To beginning of line or row*	Home
To end of line or edit entry*	End
One screen up*	Page Up
One screen down*	Page Down
Beginning of document/worksheet*	Ctrl+Home
End of document/worksheet*	Ctrl+End
Next cell/column	Tab
Previous cell/column	Shift+Tab
Go to a location*	F5 or Ctrl+G

Note: Hold Shift down while you use any of the above movement keys to select that area.

Formatting	Shortcut
Bold on/off	Ctrl+B
Italic on/off	Ctrl+I
Underline on/off	Ctrl+U
Activate font button in toolbar	Ctrl+Shift+F
Activate point size button in toolbar	Ctrl+Shift+P

Other Shortcuts	Shortcut
Get on-line help or Answer Wizard*	F1
Get context-sensitive help pointer	Shift+F1
Start spell check	F7

Troubleshooting and Support Information

Que/Macmillan Computer Publishing

Order line	800-428-5331
Switchboard	317-581-3500
CompuServe	**GO MACMILLAN**
World Wide Web	**http://www.mcp.com**

Microsoft Technical Support

Customer Service (General Info/Products/Upgrades)	800-426-9400
Windows	206-637-7098
Excel	206-635-7070
Word	206-462-9673
Access	206-635-7050
PowerPoint	206-635-7145
Project	206-635-7155

Reseller Phone Numbers

Software Spectrum	800-543-4126
Softmart	800-328-1319
ASAP	800-248-ASAP

201 W. 103rd Street, Indianapolis, IN 46290 (317) 581-3500

Copyright© 1995 Que Corporation

Guide to New Features

	Feature	Description
Start	The Start button	Click the Start button to start a program, get Help, search for items on your computer, open a document, or change your system settings.
	The Windows 95 Desktop	Use drag-and-drop to place programs, shortcuts, accessories, and document icons directly on the desktop, where you can access them with a double-click of the mouse.
	My Computer	Double-click My Computer to see a listing of your system's drive and its contents.
	Explorer	Replaces File Manager with a complete listing of all drives, folders, and folder contents within your system. You can drag-and-drop to move elements.
	Folders	Hold files, applications, and other folders. Folders replace directories and Program Manager groups.
	Taskbar	At the bottom of your screen, the taskbar adds a button for every program you open during your session. Switch to any open program by clicking its button in the taskbar.
	Recycle Bin	Temporarily stores deleted files. They remain in the bin until you empty it (a safeguard against accidental deletions).
	Network Neighborhood	If your computer is connected to a network, double-click this desktop icon to see what network resources are available to you.
	File Names	Can be up to 255 characters long (as opposed to the eight-character limitation of the past).
	Shortcut menus	Right-click items to get a special, context-sensitive menu.
	Printing subsystem	The Windows 95 32-bit printing subsystem speeds the printing process and gives you more control over your printer's operation.
	Plug and Play	Insert the card for the appropriate Plug and Play hardware in your computer; when you turn on the computer, Windows 95 automatically configures your hardware for you.
	System Properties	Enable you to configure your system (accessed through the Control Panel).
	Quick View	Right-click a file to get a preview of the file's contents without opening the associated application.
	Microsoft Exchange	Reads and sends e-mail from various systems, such as Microsoft Mail, Internet Mail, or Microsoft Network. Also sends and receives faxes and other electronic messages.
	Dial-Up Networking	Access a corporate network using your modem when on the road.
	Internet Connectivity	PPP and TCP/IP are built-in, enabling you to connect to the Internet with no additional software.

201 W. 103rd Street, Indianapolis, IN 46290 (317) 581-3500

Copyright© 1995 Que Corporation